SIXTH EDITION

Becoming
a Critical Thinker

A User-Friendly Manual

Sherry Diestler

Contra Costa College

PEARSON

Boston   Columbus   Indianapolis   New York   San Francisco   Upper Saddle River
Amsterdam   Cape Town   Dubai   London   Madrid   Milan   Munich   Paris   Montreal   Toronto
Delhi   Mexico City   Sao Paulo   Sydney   Hong Kong   Seoul   Singapore   Taipei   Tokyo

In loving memory of Anne and Al Goldstein.

And for John, Zachary, Nicole, Semaje, Stuart, Jenna, Laura, and Amy,

may we continue their legacy of discernment and compassion.

Editorial Director: Craig Campanella

Editor in Chief: Dickson Musslewhite

Executive Editor: Ashley Dodge

Project Manager, Editorial: Kate Fernandes

Development Editor: Maggie Barbieri

Director of Marketing: Brandy Dawson

Senior Marketing Manager: Laura Lee Manley

Director of Production: Lisa Iarkowski

Managing Editor: Maureen Richardson

Project Manager, Production: Shelly Kupperman

Senior Operations Supervisor: Mary Fischer

Operations Specialist: Christina Amato

Art Director: Anne Bonanno Nieglos

Interior and Cover Designer: Ximena Tamvakopoulos

Cover Image: © Michael Krabs/imagebroker/Alamy

Director, Digital Media: Brian Hyland

Digital Media Editor: Rachel Comerford

Full-Service Project Management and Composition:
Douglas Bell, PreMediaGlobal

Printer/Binder: LSC Communications

Cover Printer: LSC Communications

Text Font: Sabon 10/12

Credits and acknowledgments borrowed from other sources and reproduced, with permission, in this textbook appear on pages 482–484.

Library of Congress Cataloging-in-Publication Data

Diestler, Sherry.
Becoming a critical thinker : a user friendly manual / Sherry Diestler.—6th ed.

  p. cm.

 Includes index.

 ISBN 978-0-205-06345-1

 1. Critical thinking—Textbooks. I. Title.

 B809.2.D54 2012

 370.15'2—dc23   2011021583

17

Student Edition
ISBN-10:   0-205-06345-4
ISBN-13: 978-0-205-06345-1

Instructor's Review Copy
ISBN-10:   0-205-06363-2
ISBN-13: 978-0-205-06363-5

Books à la Carte
ISBN-10:   0-205-06389-6
ISBN-13: 978-0-205-06389-5

PEARSON

Brief Contents

Contents

3 Reality Assumptions 74

It's Eleven O'Clock. Do You Know Where Your Assumptions Are?

7 The Power of Language 274

What's in a Name?

9 Fair-Mindedness 400

It's You and Me, Kid, and I'm Not So Sure About You.

10 Persuasive Speaking 442

What's Your Point? How Do You Sharpen It?

Preface

> You have the freedom to choose your actions; you don't have the freedom to choose the consequences of your actions.
>
> Steven Covey

As human beings, we face numerous daily decisions affecting our personal and collective lives. We constantly have to choose one course of action over another. It is imperative that we think critically and choose wisely because we must accept the consequences that follow the choices we make.

This text trains readers to become critical thinkers and thoughtful decision makers. After using this text, students will be able to:

- Effectively evaluate the many claims facing them as citizens, students, consumers, and human beings in relationships and make decisions based on careful consideration of both facts and values;
- Distinguish high-quality, well-supported arguments from arguments with little or no evidence to back them;
- Come to reasoned conclusions about difficult or controversial issues when both sides of a controversy seem to have reasonable arguments;
- Be alert to bias and misrepresentation in reporting and advertising;
- Discover their own "points of logical vulnerability";
- Work collaboratively with others to solve problems; and
- Become more effective advocates for their beliefs.

Becoming a Critical Thinker is designed to be interdisciplinary and to be useful in courses in critical thinking, philosophy, informal logic, rhetoric, English, speech, journalism, humanities, and the social sciences. It has also been used as either a required text or a supplement in nursing programs and in workshops on staff development and business management. There are important skills that distinguish critical thinkers across varied disciplines; the goal of this text is to present and teach these skills in a clear and comprehensive manner.

New to This Edition

As with previous editions, the sixth edition of *Becoming a Critical Thinker* has been updated with two priorities in mind. First, we wanted to retain and enhance the user-friendly format of the first five editions. Also, we wanted to update readings and concepts so that readers are able to apply critical thinking principles to current issues.

New features in the sixth edition include:

- **Stronger emphasis on decision making as the major objective of critical thinking.** This edition features new examples of individuals who have made difficult decisions and changes in their lives; for example, several individuals discuss their choices to leave secure jobs in favor of pursuing work that is less lucrative but more fulfilling.
- **New focus on the relationship between the many forms of social media and critical thinking,** featuring current research on how social media—including

Facebook, YouTube, Foursquare, Twitter, and Yelp—affect decision making and relationships.

- **Explanations of how advertisers and marketers use different strategies to influence consumers**, including eye tracking, the use of sounds and scents, product placement, and neuromarketing.

- **Updated checklist for evaluating websites and determining reliable sources.**

- **Clearer organization for enhanced comprehension,** with chapter objectives at the beginning of each chapter and marginal glossed terms that highlight important concepts throughout the chapter.

- **New articles and excerpts that cover current topics and issues** such as the effects of social media on various aspects of society; research concerning effective study habits; statistics on the increase of gangs and drugs in public schools; the effects of cell phone use on the brain; the use of applied mathematics to isolate urban crime patterns; career and workplace satisfaction; and performance-enhancing drug use in professional sports.

- **A new, four-color design** featuring engaging graphics that enhance understanding of key critical thinking concepts.

- **An updated and expanded instructor manual** with PowerPoint slides, revised tests and answer keys for each chapter, discussion of chapter exercises, and suggestions for teaching critical thinking concepts that incorporate instructional uses of social media.

MyThinkingLab

- **MyThinkingLab,** which is an interactive and instructive multimedia site that offers access to a wealth of resources geared to meet the individual teaching and learning needs of every instructor and student. Within MyThinkingLab, MyThinkingLibrary contains more than three hundred readings from classic philosophical texts to ethics-oriented case studies and critical thinking readings. Combining an ebook, video, audio, multimedia simulations, research support, and assessment, MyThinkingLab engages students and gives them the tools they need to enhance their performance in the course.

Unique Features

The process of becoming a critical thinker occurs when effective thinking concepts and skills are clearly understood and put into practice. For this reason, many aspects of the text have been chosen because of their practical application for the student:

- Each concept is explained with examples, and the examples progress from the personal to the social or political. In this way, students can see that the same skills used in understanding arguments in daily life are used in analyzing political and commercial rhetoric.

- Important concepts are illustrated through the use of graphics, photographs, and cartoons, and definitions of key words are highlighted in the margins.

- Exercises of varying difficulty are given within and at the end of each chapter to help students practice critical thinking skills.

- Emphasis is placed on understanding and analyzing the vital impact of print and electronic media on arguments. Suggestions of films that illustrate critical thinking concepts are included at the end of each chapter.

- Students are taught to construct and present arguments so that they can gain skill and confidence as advocates for their beliefs; they are also given tools for effective problem solving and decision making.

- An emphasis on understanding conflicting value systems and on ethics in argumentation and decision making is included throughout the text.
- The articles and essays selected for the text are contemporary and express a variety of social and political viewpoints and ethical concerns.
- Multicultural perspectives are presented throughout the examples and articles. Many exercises and assignments encourage students to understand the perspectives of others and to broaden their own perspectives.
- A variety of writing and speaking assignments are included at the end of each chapter as well as a "Chapter Checkup" that tests students' knowledge of the information covered and provides a guideline for reviewing important concepts.

To the Student

Making decisions about issues large and small is an integral part of daily life; we decide how to spend our time and our money, the relationships we choose to explore and keep, the college we want to attend, the work we seek to accomplish, the places we want to live, and the candidates and policies we vote for or against. Sometimes, decisions are made rashly with little forethought. It is our contention, however, that the best decisions are made by carefully considering the various—and often complex—factors that are involved in a given circumstance.

This text is intended to train you to be discerning about the messages you read or hear; to make decisions based on careful consideration of both facts and values; to be alert to bias and "spin" in reporting and advertising; and, to be able to effectively present your own viewpoints.

People who are admired for their decision making are often said to have wisdom or discernment. It is our hope that this text will empower you with the conviction and peace of mind that come from using principles of critical thinking to make wise and fulfilling decisions.

Acknowledgements

My husband, John Diestler, remains a great support. He provided expertise on the "user-friendly" format; he worked out preliminary designs for the original text and created the logos, figures, and graphics for the text; in addition, he made useful suggestions on the manuscript throughout the revision process.

I have been very blessed for this edition to once again have my original editor, Maggie Barbieri. Maggie guided me through every step of the process with her invaluable advice, expertise, and encouragement.

I am very thankful for the talented team of editors and managers at Pearson: Ashley Dodge, the executive editor, whose creative direction, problem solving, and positive support was instrumental in helping me complete this edition in a timely manner; Nancy Roberts, especially for her suggestions that added clarity and cohesion to the user-friendly format; Rachel Comerford whose innovative ideas shaped MyThinkingLab and additional digital media that accompanies the text; Shelly Kupperman for her diligence and efficiency in managing production; Anne Nieglos for her artistic vision and supervision; Ben Ferrini for facilitating the selection of images for the text; and Ximena Tamvakopoulos, who created the wonderful design for this new edition. Doug Bell and his staff, including Michelle McKenna, at PreMediaGlobal did a fantastic job of producing the text in a meticulous and timely manner.

I am grateful to students who used the text and made helpful suggestions for additions and changes; special appreciation is due to those who contributed their own writings for exercise examples—Carlota Jimenez, Kris Anne Bordalo Nuguid, Susan Bain, Warda Javed, Phil McAlpin, Sonya Shaukat, Janet Fesperman, and Carlota Morales.

Stuart Rentz, Jenna Diestler, Brian Selke, Sammy Barton, and Professors William Dorman, Helen Kalkstein, Dr. Connie Anderson, Rafaella Del Bourgo, Deborah Bauer, and Rachel Dwiggins-Beeler all gave me valuable suggestions for exercises and articles. Zach Diestler researched and reviewed numerous films to discover a variety of storylines related to critical thinking concepts.

I also wish to thank the following reviewers for their invaluable and thoughtful suggestions: Cecilia Moore-Cobb, Pitt Community College; John Kimsey, DePaul University; Michael Shroeder, Savannah State University; James Bower, Walla Walla Community College; and Charlene Tuckerson, John F. Kennedy University.

For their practical support and love that allowed me the time and energy to write the text, I thank my friends Suzanne Barton, Lori Oczkus, and Hugo and Kathleen Santucci, my husband John, and my precious children Zachary, Nicole, Semaje, Laura, and Amy Diestler, and Stuart and Jenna Rentz.

Above all, I am grateful to the Creator of the human mind.

Sherry Diestler
Contra Costa College

Becoming
a Critical Thinker

1

Foundations of Arguments

Who Is a Critical Thinker,
and When Do You Need to Be One?

A critical thinker understands the structure of an argument, whether that argument is presented by a politician, a salesperson, a talk-show host, a friend, or a child.

A critical thinker recognizes the issue under discussion and the varying conclusions about the issue.

A critical thinker examines the reasons given to support conclusions.

A critical thinker uses the structure of argument to make thoughtful decisions.

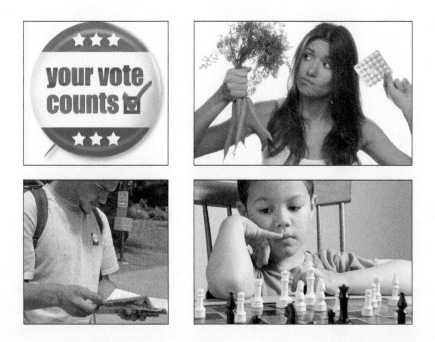

We need to use critical thinking to deal with the choices that we are constantly confronting in our lives.

- The structure of an argument
- The three parts of an argument: issues, conclusions, and reasons
- An approach to making decisions

📖 Read on **mythinkinglab.com**

🔊 Listen on **mythinkinglab.com**

We live in what has been called the Information Age because of the many messages that we receive daily from television, radio, newspapers, magazines, books, blogs, text messages, tweets, and the hundreds of millions of sites on the Internet.

Sometimes we turn to this information for its entertainment value, such as when we watch a situation comedy, listen to music, scan the sports page, or read an online movie review. But in a democratic society, in which the people are asked to vote on candidates and political propositions, we also need to use print and electronic sources to help us make decisions about our personal lives and about the direction our community, state, and nation will take.

We need to know how to understand and evaluate the information that comes our way. This book will give you tools for coming to rational conclusions and making responsible choices.

A critical thinker is someone who uses specific criteria to evaluate reasoning, form positions, and make decisions.

You can strengthen your critical thinking by becoming aware of and practicing certain skills. The skills will be covered in this text and include an understanding of

- The structure of arguments
- Value assumptions and reality assumptions that are foundational to arguments
- The quality of evidence used to support reasoning
- Common errors in reasoning
- The effect of language on perception, and
- The ways in which media frame issues

In addition, **critical thinkers** develop and exhibit personal traits, such as fair-mindedness and empathy. We will discuss how these qualities strengthen critical thinking and decision making. Finally, critical thinkers use their skills to solve problems and to advocate for causes in which they believe. This chapter covers the first skill: understanding the structure of arguments.

critical thinker
Someone who uses specific criteria to evaluate reasoning, form positions, and make decisions.

3

Stop and Think

When people hear the word *critical,* they sometimes associate it with faultfinding. The field of critical thinking, however, uses the word *critical* to mean "discerning." A film, art, dance, or music critic forms and expresses opinions on the basis of standards. The skills you will learn in this text will give you a set of standards with which to evaluate messages and make thoughtful decisions.

When you learn to communicate well in a formal situation, your skill usually transfers to informal situations as well. For example, if you learn to make an effective informative speech in the classroom, you will also feel better about introducing yourself at parties or making a spontaneous toast at your brother's wedding. This same principle applies to critical thinking skills.

When you can listen to a presidential debate and make good judgments about what each candidate has to offer, you may also be more thoughtful about less formal arguments that are presented, such as which breakfast cereal is best for you or which car you should buy. You will be better prepared to deal with sales pitches, whether written or presented in person.

The methods of discernment and decision making that you will learn apply to choosing a viewpoint on a political issue or to choosing a career, a place to live, or a mate.

In short, critical thinkers do not just drift through life subject to every message that they hear; they think through their choices and make conscious decisions. They also understand the basics of both creating and presenting credible arguments.

The Structure of Argument

The aim of argument, or of discussion, should not be victory, but progress.

Joseph Joubert, *Pensees* (1842)

When most people hear the word *argument,* they think of a disagreement between two or more people that may escalate into name calling, angry words, or even physical violence. In their book *Metaphors We Live By,* George Lakoff and Mark Johnson discuss how our metaphors for argument often affect our perception and our behavior. They claim that the metaphor *Argument Is War* "is reflected in our everyday language by a wide variety of expressions":

Argument Is War

Your claims are indefensible.

He attacked every weak point in my argument.

His criticisms were right on target.

I demolished his argument.

I've never won an argument with him.

You disagree? Okay, shoot!

If you use that strategy, he'll wipe you out.

He shot down all of my arguments.[1]

Similarly, Deborah Tannen, in her book *The Argument Culture*, notes that as a society, we frame our social issues in warlike terms:

> The war on drugs, the war on cancer, the battle of the sexes, politicians'
> turf battles—in the argument culture, war metaphors pervade our talk
> and shape our thinking. Nearly everything is framed as a battle or game
> in which winning or losing is the main concern. These all have their uses
> and their place, but they are not the only way—and often not the best
> way—to understand and approach our world.[2]

Our definition of **argument** is different. When, as critical thinkers, we speak about an argument, we are referring to a **conclusion** (often called a claim or position) that someone has about a particular **issue**. This conclusion is supported with **reasons** (often called *premises*). If an individual has a conclusion but offers no reasons supporting that conclusion, then he or she has made only a statement, not an argument.

Political slogans, often found on billboards or in television advertisements, are good examples of conclusions (opinions) that should not be relied upon because supporting reasons are not offered. If you see a billboard that proclaims, "A vote for Johnson is a vote for the right choice," or if you hear a politician proclaiming, "Education has always been a priority for me," you are encountering conclusions with no evidence; conclusions alone do not constitute an argument.

Critical thinkers withhold judgment on such claims until they have looked at evidence both for and against a particular candidate.

argument   A conclusion about an issue that is supported by reasons.

conclusion   A position taken about an issue, also called a claim or an opinion; in deductive reasoning, the inference drawn from the major and minor premises; in research, the meaning and significance of the data as interpreted by the researcher.

issue   The question or subject under discussion.

reasons   Statements of evidence given to support conclusions.

Stop and Think

Can you think of a slogan, perhaps from an advertisement or a bumper sticker, that is a statement without supporting reasons?

An argument has three parts: the *issue,* the *conclusion,* and the *reasons.*

The Issue

The *issue* is what we are arguing about; it is the question that is being addressed. It is easiest to put the issue in question form so that you know what is being discussed. When you listen to a discussion of a political or social issue, think of the question being addressed.

[1] George Lakoff and Mark Johnson, *Metaphors We Live By* (Chicago: University of Chicago Press, 1980), p. 4.
[2] Deborah Tannen, *The Argument Culture* (New York: Ballantine Publishing Group, 1999), p. 4.

Examples of Issues

- Should energy drinks be regulated?
- Should air traffic controllers be given periodic drug tests?
- Should the minimum wage be raised?
- Are the salaries paid to professional athletes too high?

The same method of "issue detection" will be useful in understanding commercial appeals (ads) and personal requests.

More Examples of Issues

- Is Alpo the best food for your dog?
- Should you marry Taylor?
- Should you subscribe to the *Wall Street Journal*?

Another way to isolate the issue is to state, "The issue is whether _____."

- The issue is whether aspirin can prevent heart disease.
- The issue is whether reproductive cloning should be banned.
- The issue is whether our community should create 200 new homes.

It is important to distinguish issues from topics. Topics are ideas or subjects. Topics become issues when a question or controversy is introduced. In the previous examples, the topics would include Alpo, Taylor, the *Wall Street Journal*, aspirin, and cloning. The issues are questions about the topics.

Issues can be about facts, values, or policies. *Factual issues,* sometimes called *descriptive issues,* concern whether something is true or false, as in the following examples:

- Does zinc prevent common colds?
- Are smog-control devices effective in preventing pollution?
- Do we have enough money to buy a new car?

Factual issues can also involve definitions, whether something or someone fits into a certain category:

- Is digital photography a fine art?
- Is drug addiction a disease?
- Is a platypus a mammal?

Issues about *values,* sometimes called *prescriptive issues,* deal with what is considered good or bad or right or wrong, as, for example:

- Is there too much violence on television?
- Is marriage better than living together?
- Are salaries of executives of major corporations too high?

Policy issues involve specific actions; often, these issues emerge from discussions of facts and values. If we find that, in fact, smog-control devices are effective in preventing pollution and if we value clean air, then we will probably continue to support policies to enforce the use of these devices. If aspirin prevents heart disease and we value a longer life, then we might ask a doctor whether we should take aspirin. If we do have enough money for a new car and we value a car more than other items at this time, then we should buy the new car.

As we have seen, all issues involve decisions about how to think about a topic or what action to take. We deliberate about issues from our earliest years. For example, children think about how to spend allowance money, what games to play, and what books to choose from the library. Teenagers consider what to wear; how much to study; what sports, musical instruments, and hobbies to pursue and/or languages to learn; and how best to spend the time and money they have. Adults make life choices concerning careers, spouses, children, friends, and homes; they also decide how to think about social and political issues and which causes, organizations, and candidates they will support.

Stop and Think

We make large and small decisions every day. List your decisions for a day, from deciding when to wake up through your evening hours. Also, look at your calendar and checkbook or credit card record and note the decisions about the use of time and money that they reveal.

Every decision that we need to make, whether it involves public or private matters, will be made easier if we can define exactly what it is that we are being asked to believe or do. Discourse often breaks down when two or more parties get into a heated discussion over different issues. This phenomenon occurs regularly on talk shows.

For example, a television talk show featured the general topic of spousal support, and the issue was "Should the salary of a second wife be used in figuring alimony for the first wife?" The lawyer who was being interviewed kept reminding the guests of this issue as they proceeded to argue instead about whether child support should be figured from the second wife's salary, whether the first wife should hold a job, and even whether one of the wives was a good person.

A general rule is that the more emotional the reactions to the issue, the more likely the issue will become lost. The real problem here is that the basic issue can become fragmented into different subissues so that people are no longer discussing the same question.

Skill

Understand the issue, make sure everyone is discussing the same issue, and bring the discussion back on target when necessary.

When you listen to televised debates or interviews, note how often a good speaker or interviewer will remind the audience of the issue. Also notice how experienced spokespersons or politicians will often respond to a direct, clearly defined issue with a preprogrammed answer that addresses a different issue, one they can discuss more easily.

If a presidential candidate is asked how he is going to balance our federal budget, he might declare passionately that he will never raise taxes. He has thus skillfully accomplished two things: He has avoided the difficult issue, and he has taken a popular, vote-enhancing stand on a separate issue. (See Exercise 1.1 on page 17.)

The Conclusion

Once an issue has been defined, we can state our *conclusion* about the issue. Using some examples previously mentioned, *we can say yes or no to the issues presented:* Yes, I believe air traffic controllers should be tested for drug usage; yes, I want to subscribe to the *Wall Street Journal;* no, I will not marry Taylor at this time; and so on. We take a stand on the issues given.

The conclusion can also be defined as the position taken about an issue. It is a claim supported by evidence statements. These evidence statements are called *reasons* or *premises*.

We often hear the cliché that "Everyone has a right to his or her opinion." This is true, in the legal sense. North Americans do not have "thought police" who decide what can and cannot be discussed. When you are a critically thinking person, however, your opinion has *substance*. That substance consists of the reasons you give to support your opinion. Conclusions with substance are more valuable and credible than are conclusions with no supporting evidence.

Critical thinkers who strive to have opinions with substance exhibit two important qualities as they try to understand the truth of a matter:

1. They realize their own personal limitations. They know that they have a lot to learn about different areas and that they may need to revise their thoughts on issues as new information comes to light. This trait is also called *intellectual humility*.
2. They make an effort to be discerning about what they read and hear. They look for good evidence and are open to hearing all sides of an issue. When they make up their minds about something, they have solid reasons for their decisions.

The term *conclusion* is used differently in different fields of study. The definition given here applies most correctly to the study of argumentation. In an argumentative essay, the thesis statement will express the conclusion of the writer. In Chapters 3 and 4, you will note a related definition of conclusion used by philosophers in the study of deductive and inductive reasoning. In addition, the term *conclusion* is used to describe the final part of an essay or speech.

How can we locate the conclusion of an argument? Try the following methods when you are having trouble finding the conclusion:

1. Find the issue and ask what position the writer or speaker is taking on the issue.
2. Look at the beginning or ending of a paragraph or an essay; the conclusion is often found in either of these places.
3. Look for conclusion indicator words: *therefore, so, thus, hence.* Also, look for indicator phrases: *My point is, What I am saying is, What I believe is.* Some indicator words and phrases are selected to imply that the conclusion drawn is the right one. These include *obviously, it is evident that, there is no doubt* (or *question*) *that, certainly,* and *of course.*
4. Ask yourself, "What is being claimed by this writer or speaker?"
5. Look at the title of an essay; sometimes the conclusion is contained within the title. For example, an essay might be titled, "Why I Believe Vitamins Are Essential to Health."

Skill

Find the conclusion or conclusions to an argument. Ask yourself what position the writer or speaker is taking on the issue.

You may hear people discussing an issue and someone says, "I don't know anything about this, but . . ." and proceeds to state an opinion about the issue. This comment is sometimes made as a means of continuing a conversation. Critical thinkers take a stand only when they know something about the issue; they give reasons why they have come to a certain conclusion. Of course, a critical thinker is open to hearing new evidence and may change his or her opinion on issues, as new information becomes available. (See Exercise 1.2 on page 17.)

Stop and Think

As humans, we have limitations in our perception and knowledge. At the same time, we have wonderful tools for discovering new truths in every area of life. What personal qualities does a person need in order to give a fair hearing to new information?

The Reasons

Everything reasonable may be supported.

Epictetus, *Discourses* (Second century)

Reasons are the statements that provide support for conclusions. Without reasons, you have no argument; you simply have an assertion, a statement of someone's opinion, as evidenced in the following classic limerick:

I do not like you, Doctor Fell
The reason why I cannot tell
But this I know, I know full well
I do not like you, Doctor Fell.

Reasons are also called *evidence, premises, support,* or *justification.* You will spend most of your time and energy as a critical thinker and responsible writer and speaker looking at the quality of the reasons used to support a conclusion.

Here are some ways to locate the reasons in an argument:

1. Find the conclusion and then apply the "because trick." The writer or speaker believes _____ (conclusion) because _____. The reasons will naturally follow the word *because.*

2. Look for other indicator words that are similar to *because: since, for, first, second, third, as evidenced by, also, furthermore, in addition.*

3. Look for evidence supporting the conclusion. This support can be in the form of examples, statistics, analogies, research studies, and expert testimony. *facts*

Stop and Think

What was your most recent "argument"? What reasons were given to you, and what reasons did you give to support your conclusion?

There is a world of difference between supporting a political candidate because his or her policies make sense to you and supporting the same candidate because he or she seems like a charismatic person. Information in the following chapters of this book will give you the skills to help you decide whether a reason supports a conclusion.

Critical thinkers focus their attention on the issue being discussed, the conclusions drawn, and the reasons given to support or justify the conclusions. (See Exercise 1.3 on pages 18–19.)

Skill

Find the reasons that support the conclusion.

As a listener: Be able to hear the issue, conclusion, and reasons given for an argument.

As a speaker: Be able to clearly articulate your own conclusion and the reasons you have come to that conclusion about an issue.

Nothing is more difficult, and therefore more precious, than to be able to decide.

Napoleon, *Maxims* (1804)

Using Reasons to Make Decisions. When people engage in formal arguments, they usually present their conclusions about issues first and then give reasons to support their conclusions. In decision making, however, people often struggle with reasons on both sides of an issue in order to reach a conclusion (decision). For example, consider the following online dialogue between two friends, jointly deciding on the issue of whether to go to a water park. Note that the conclusion (the decision to go or not to go) does not become clear until they go over the reasons on both sides.

GenPeach: Hey Claire!

ClaireDies: Hi Gen!

GenPeach: How are you?

ClaireDies: I'm okay I think. kind of tired.

ClaireDies: am I going to see you today?

GenPeach: I think so, . . . Waterworld?

ClaireDies: yeah. should I go or not?

GenPeach: If you want, IDK if I will or not. I'm so tired.

ClaireDies: Me too, and I have to pack. if you go, I will, but I don't want to go if I'm going to be the only one there

ClaireDies: my age

GenPeach: Ditto.

ClaireDies: so

GenPeach: The ? is, do we really want to go, or not?

ClaireDies: well, what's the advantage of going?

GenPeach: I was just thinking that. Um . . . water and slides and stuff, and we get to see each other

ClaireDies: and I'm leaving soon . . . but if we stay, well, I'll get to do laundry and sleep

ClaireDies: and pack and do the dishes

ClaireDies: I'm leaning towards going now

GenPeach: Negatives—small children screaming, sun, noise, more energy required than I have

ClaireDies: very true.

GenPeach: Not necessarily better than packing and cleaning

ClaireDies: we wouldn't actually have to get up. We could grab a small section of grass and sleep, sunbathe

ClaireDies: relax, read

GenPeach: Yay

ClaireDies: so . . . sounds like we should go.

ClaireDies: should we just go?

GenPeach: OK

Stop and Think

Try to list the reasons to go and the reasons not to go that the friends came up with before making their decision. Note that even routine daily decisions involve the process of weighing pros and cons (reasons) in order to come to a conclusion.

A Decision-Making Method

If you don't know where you're going, you might wind up somewhere else.

Yogi Berra

If you don't have a plan for yourself, you'll be a part of someone else's.

African American Proverb

A decision involves a dilemma between two or more alternative actions. We face these dilemmas daily in small and big ways. Virtually every aspect of our lives involves decision making, especially since we live in a "free" society in which most decisions are not made by authorities but are left to individual citizens. Decisions need to be made about a variety of matters such as whom to support in an election, which career to pursue, which school to attend, whether to marry, whether to have children, where to live, and how to budget time and money.

Many methods exist to help people make life decisions. There are different ways to evaluate reasons on both sides of a difficult decision. The question to be decided can be seen as the issue—Should I vote for Candidate A, Candidate B, or Candidate C? Should I spend money on a car or save the money for future needs? Should I go to graduate school or take a job offer now? The dilemma for the decision maker is that the future consequences of choosing one path over another are not known in the present time; the person making the decision has to choose without knowing the full implications of the choice. He or she must do what seems best with the information available in the present. (See Figure 1–1.) To come to a reasoned conclusion about a decision, it helps to weigh the reasons on both sides. Often, however, people can see many reasons to support two or more choices, and they feel paralyzed by indecision as a result.

One method that can be useful in making decisions that should also help you clarify your reasoning involves listing and giving weights to various reasons and then weighing each of your choices against those reasons.

Let's look at this decision-making method, using the example of the decision of whether to attend School X or School Y.

1. The first step in decision making is to define the dilemma in the form of an issue.

   Example

   Should I attend School X or School Y?

2. The second step in decision making involves looking at your long-term objective. It answers the question: What do I want this choice to accomplish in my life?

   Example

   I want to get a good education in my field without going into debt for more than two years.

Future
Consequences

Future
Consequences

X   You Are
Here

Preparing
to Decide

FIGURE 1–1

A decision usually involves a dilemma between two alternatives. The decision maker must
imagine the future consequences of each alternative.

Note that in this step, if either alternative does not meet your objective, the
decision is already made. If you find that School X does not have the major that
you want or that it would be too expensive to go to School X, then it no longer
is an alternative to consider.

3. In the third step, you determine which factors are most important to you concerning your desired outcome (in this case the factors in a school). You list the
factors and give an importance to each one (on a scale of 1–10, with 10 being
the highest).

Example

Strong department in my major	10 points
Affordable (low cost or scholarship)	10 points
Close to friends and family	6 points
Near a large city	5 points
Gives internship option	8 points
Campus is attractive	4 points
Good arts community nearby	7 points
Climate is mild	5 points
Feels like a good fit when I visit	9 points
Professors are accessible	8 points

Note that the criteria in this example would be different for different people.
That is why it is hard to receive advice about your decision or to give advice to
others—other people may not weigh the factors the way you do. To one person,

being in a large urban area is a major plus—to another it would be seen as a disadvantage. One person may value a close relationship with professors, while another prefers more formality and distance. One person may want to take advantage of cultural attractions nearby, while another is more interested in the sports scene on campus.

4. The fourth step gets to the heart of the reasons for and against each choice and gives you clear criteria for your decision. In this step, you take each factor and weigh it against your choices. The choice with the highest score is tentatively chosen.

Factor	Weight	School X Score	School Y Score
Example			
Strong department in my major	10 points ×	8	10
Affordable (low cost or scholarship)	10 points ×	9	5
Close to friends and family	6 points ×	8	6
Near a large city	5 points ×	5	9
Gives internship option	8 points ×	7	9
Campus is attractive	4 points ×	8	8
Good arts community nearby	7 points ×	7	10
Climate is mild	5 points ×	5	7
Feels like a good fit when I visit	9 points ×	8	10
Professors are accessible	8 points ×	9	7
Total: Weight of factor times score of choice		549	521

5. The fifth step involves tentatively choosing the highest scoring alternative. Doing this kind of decision analysis may confirm that the individual choice is the right one or that either choice would be acceptable.

   If School X is chosen, the individual has resolved his or her own issue. The "argument" for School X could be stated as follows:

   Issue: Should I choose School X or School Y?

   Conclusion: I should choose School X.

   Reasons: School X is affordable, has a good department in my major with professors that I can talk to, is fairly close to my friends and family, and might offer internship possibilities. School Y is good, too, and has an even better reputation but costs significantly more than School X.

Often, this kind of critical analysis can clarify choices for an individual. If, on the other hand, the alternative chosen does not "feel right," he or she may look at the criteria to determine why. It may be that the strength of the department and the location actually do factor higher for the individual and that the main reason for the low score for the option of School Y is the affordability. If that is the case, the individual making the decision could do more research about scholarships or about the option of getting a job to pay for School Y.

Going through this logical process and seeing which alternative "scores" higher will help you clarify your choice: If you feel satisfied with the choice, the factors listed were the important factors; if you are disappointed or uncomfortable with the choice, there may be some other, perhaps more emotionally based, factors that need to be entered into the equation.

Individual or Class Exercise: Making a Decision

Purpose: To use reasoning to make a decision.

By yourself, with a partner, or with a class group, choose a current decision that you are facing, and take it through the steps listed in the decision-making model. You can use the model for two or more alternative choices. After you have listed your criteria and the importance (weight) of each factor, rate each of your alternatives.

After weighing the alternatives, use the one with the higher score as your conclusion/decision. Then state the issue (the dilemma or choice that needed to be made), your conclusion (the alternative with the higher score), and the reasons (all of the factors that led to the high score). Whether this exercise is done individually or in groups, it would be helpful to share the results with the class as a further review of issues, conclusions, and reasons.

Ideas for the decision: A voting choice, school choice, career choice, relationship choice, or consumer choice.

Humor as Argument

Humor can also be viewed as argument—humorists often make an argument in a disarming way, using irony and exaggeration. If you listen closely to what comedians and comic writers say, you can isolate issues, conclusions, and reasons in their commentaries. Read the following excerpt from an *Onion Magazine* article about people's desires to have the latest technological device. See if you can identify issues, conclusions, and reasons.

> With the holiday shopping season officially under way, millions of consumers proceeded to their nearest commercial centers this week in hopes of acquiring the latest, and therefore most desirable, personal device.
>
> "The new device is an improvement over the old device, making it more attractive for purchase by all Americans," said Thomas Wakefield, a spokesperson for the large conglomerate that manufactures the new device. "The old device is no longer sufficient. Consumers should no longer have any use or longing for the old device."
>
> . . . "Its higher price indicates to me that it is superior, and that not everyone will be able to afford it, which only makes me want to possess it more," said Tim Sturges, owner of the old device, which he obtained 18 months ago when it was still the new device.
>
> . . . "Not only will I be able to perform tasks faster than before, but my new device will also inform those around me that I am a successful individual who is up on the latest trends," said Rebecca Hodge, whose executive job allowed her to line up for several hours in the middle of the day in order to obtain the previously unavailable item. "Its attractiveness and considerable value are, by extension, my attractiveness and considerable value."[3]

---

[3] "New Device Desirable, Old Device Undesirable," The Onion News, December 3, 2009, the onion.com.

Life Application: Tips for College and Career

When you are listening to a discussion in class or at a meeting, consider the issue being discussed, the claims being made, and the reasons given for the claims. If you have an opinion to share, frame it in terms of your position and your reasons.

When writing an essay or report, clarify your conclusion about the issue and support it with several reasons.

If you are called upon to make a speech without much time to prepare, use the same format of taking a stand on an issue and supporting it with reasons. For example, if you are asked to make a speech at your grandparent's retirement, you might say something like, "My grandmother has been wonderful to me [conclusion]. She has always encouraged my dreams, she has been there for all of my important events, and she has been a great role model [reasons]." You can then elaborate on each reason with examples.

If you are trying to get a group to come to consensus about a decision, try using the method outlined in this chapter. Help the group members define the issue that needs to be resolved and the desired outcome and have them weigh each possibility against specific criteria.

Chapter Review

Summary

1. Critical thinking about information is necessary in order for us to make clear decisions as citizens, consumers, and human beings.

2. An argument consists of issues, conclusions, and reasons.

3. The issue is the question that is raised; our decisions are made easier if we can define the issues on which we are asked to comment or act.

4. The conclusion is the position a person takes on an issue.

5. Reasons, often called premises, provide support for conclusions; reasons are acceptable or unacceptable on the basis of their relevance and quality.

6. Critical thinkers carefully consider their objectives and the reasons on all sides of an issue when they make important decisions.

Checkup

Short Answer

1. What is the difference between a topic and an issue?
2. What are some indictor words for a conclusion?
3. Cite three ways to discover the reasons used to support a conclusion.

True-False

4. Everyone's opinion about an issue has equal credibility.

5. Traits such as fair-mindedness and empathy are helpful to critical thinkers.

6. A critical thinker is someone who uses specific criteria to evaluate reasoning, form opinions, and make decisions.

Sentence Completion

7. The question that is being addressed is called the _____.

8. You will spend most of your time and energy as a critical thinker and responsible speaker looking at the quality of the _____ used to support a conclusion.

9. Since the reasons answer the question, "Why do you believe what you believe?" a good trick in isolating the reasons is to write the conclusion and then add the word _____.

10. When we say yes or no to the issues presented, we are stating our _____.

Exercises

Practice is the best of all instructors.

Publilius Syrus

EXERCISE 1.1 Purpose: To be able to identify issues.

1. Read an essay, a blog, or an editorial, study an advertisement, listen to a radio talk show, or watch a television program about a controversial issue. Decide whether the issue is primarily one of fact, value, or policy. Define the issue and see if the speakers or writers stay with the issue.

2. By yourself or as a class, come up with as many current issues as you can. Think of both light and serious issues; consider campus, community, social, national, and international concerns.

   Now, look at your list of issues and choose three that really concern you. Then, try to choose three about which you are neutral. Finally, answer these questions:

   a. What is it about the first three issues that concerns you?
   b. Why are you neutral about some issues?
   c. Do you believe there are issues on the list that should be more important to you? If so, why are they not more important to you?

EXERCISE 1.2 Purpose: To be able to isolate conclusions.

Take your list of issues from Question 2 in the previous exercise. Choose four issues and, in a simple declarative sentence, write your conclusion for each one.

Example

Issue: Should air traffic controllers be given periodic drug tests?
Conclusion: Yes, air traffic controllers should be given periodic drug tests.

Reminder

Since the reasons answer the question, "Why do you believe what you believe?" a good trick in isolating the reasons is to write the conclusion and then add the word *because*.

✳ Explore on **mythinkinglab.com**

EXERCISE 1.3 Purposes: To be able to use reasons to support a conclusion. To use knowledge gained in this chapter to both analyze and construct basic arguments.

1. Write a short rebuttal to the following example about student athletes, using reasons to support your conclusion.

   Example

   I believe student athletes should be paid (conclusion) *because*
   - They commit to certain hours and demands on their time.
   - They make money for their schools.

2. Take your conclusions from Exercise 1.2 and support each conclusion with at least three reasons. This exercise can be done alone or in classroom groups, in writing, or as a short speech. One group might present the "pro" side of an issue and another group the "con."

3. Get the editorial page of your favorite newspaper (including your campus paper) or use a favorite blog. List the issue, conclusion, and reasons given by the writer in the editorial or blog post. Use this format:

   The issue (question) is:

   The conclusion of this writer is:

   The reasons he or she gives are:

   Then evaluate the opinion piece by answering the following questions:

   a. Was the writer clear about the reasons given for the conclusion?
   b. Were there other reasons that could have been included in the argument?
   c. Did the writer express any understanding for an opposing viewpoint? If so, how? If not, can you articulate an opposing viewpoint?
   d. Were you convinced by the opinion piece? Why or why not?

4. Read the following editorials and essays. Then, isolate the issues discussed, the conclusions of the writers, and the reasons given for the conclusions. Answer the following questions:

   a. Are the reasons given adequate to support the conclusions? If not, what other reasons could have been given?
   b. Do you agree or disagree with the conclusions? If you disagree, what are your reasons for disagreeing?

5. Advertisers make arguments using both words and visual images. As with the preceding essays and editorials, see if you can identify the issue, conclusion, and

reasons given in advertisements you see online, on television, or in magazines and billboards.

Educational Ticket

Dr. Y. Huda

Some bicycle riders complain about getting tickets for running stop signs, especially when they are "just kids." Those kids who get tickets should be grateful for the important lesson to not run stop signs. If they learn from the tickets, they will live longer.

Running stop signs and red lights hurts the bicycle riders and it also hurts other people. It scares motorists, and if a motorist accidentally hit and hurt a cyclist, the motorist would feel terrible. It also hurts bicycle activists who don't want to anger motorists—if motorists are angry, they won't support measures to improve cycling, such as getting wider roads so motorists and cyclists can share the road more safely. ▇

War on Drugs Fails

We Need New Approach

Daryl A. Bergman

The war on drugs is an abysmal failure. A fresh and bold approach is needed—beginning with the legalization of marijuana and the registration of drug addicts. It's also necessary to look to other countries that have been successful. The legalization of pot would:

- Eliminate the stepping-stone to harder drugs.
- Eliminate the crime associated with large dollar street transactions.
- Provide taxes to step up law enforcement efforts (meth labs, heroin smuggling) and rehab programs.
- Free space in jails housing non-violent criminals, saving incarceration costs.

The registration of addicts would:

- Eliminate the use of dirty needles, decreasing victims of AIDS and associated health care costs.
- End warehouse rehabilitation programs.

Let's move forward to save our children. ▇

Drugged Driving

Lavelle Washington

Like alcohol, marijuana and other drugs can impair many of those skills that are imperative to good driving, such as alertness, the ability to concentrate and to read signs, coordination and reaction time. These effects can last up to 24 hours after smoking marijuana. If you combine drug use with teens' inexperience on the road and risk-taking behavior, we have a recipe for disaster. The National Highway Traffic Safety Administration (NHTSA) estimates that 10 to 22 percent of drivers involved in all vehicle crashes had recently used an illegal drug, often in combination with alcohol.

- The Department of Transportation has published two studies examining the impact of marijuana on driving performance. Marijuana—the most widely abused illegal drug—slows a driver's perception of time, space, and distance, and it leads to drowsiness and distraction.
- Research indicates that cocaine causes drivers to speed and change lanes without signaling and puts other innocent people at risk of a deadly accident.
- While it is illegal in all states to drive a motor vehicle while under the influence of alcohol, drugs other than alcohol, or a combination of alcohol and other drugs, there is no consistent method across states for identifying drug impairment. As a result, we do not know the full impact of illegal drug use on public safety.
- According to the National Commission Against Drunk Driving, impaired driving is the most frequently committed violent crime in America and every 30 minutes, someone in this country dies in an alcohol-related crash, equating to approximately 17,000 deaths per year. ■

EXERCISE 1.4 Purpose: To practice finding issues, conclusions, and reasons in humor.

Find an excerpt from a book of humor, a list of humorous quotations, or a stand-up comedy routine. You might also look at articles, blogs, or websites that feature humorous political or social commentary. Isolate the issue, conclusion, and reasons that the comedian or humor writer covers. Share your findings with the class.

You Decide

Military Draft

Although no military draft is currently in effect, males from age 18–25 who are living in the United States are still required to register. The military draft has been a contentious issue, particularly during times of war. There were Civil War draft riots, and during World War I, some three million men refused to register. The draft was protested throughout the Vietnam War, and the United States converted to an all-volunteer military in 1973. Draft registration was suspended in 1975, but was required again in 1980 under President Carter following the Soviet invasion of Afghanistan. A number of reforms have been made to the draft to make it more equitable. In the Vietnam era, students were able to defer their service until graduation. If a draft were held today, a college student would only be able to postpone induction until the end of the current semester or, for college seniors, until the end of the academic year. Those in favor of a draft argue that the new rules make the responsibilities of service equally required of all male citizens and that fulfilling the obligation of serving one's country has good effects both on the individual and on the readiness of the country. Those against the draft believe that it allows a government to infringe upon individual rights and that, if necessary, volunteers will emerge to defend the country.

For more information on the debate surrounding the military draft and additional exercises and tutorials about concepts covered in this chapter, log into MyThinkingLab at www.mythinkinglab.com and select Diestler, *Becoming a Critical Thinker*, Sixth Edition.

✳ Explore on **mythinkinglab.com**

Articles for Discussion   📖 Read the **Document** on **mythinkinglab.com**

The following article is an opinion piece on the rescue of 16-year- old Abby Sunderland who attempted to sail around the world. The French ship *Ile De La Reunion* brought Sunderland on board from her stricken craft that had been damaged in a storm.

French authorities called it a "delicate operation," and said at one point the fishing boat's captain fell into the ocean and had to be rescued. Laurence Sunderland said the crew used its dinghy in the transfer. Abby Sunderland left the French fishing boat after two days and boarded a maritime patrol boat that took her to Reunion Island, according to a statement from the office of the French Indian Ocean island's top official.

Read the article and the comments posted by readers and then consider the questions that follow.

16-Year-Old Sailor Was Already Off Course

Mitch Albom

Most parents worry if teenagers are an hour late. Just imagine if they were lost at sea.

For several tense hours Thursday, that was the case for a 16-year-old Californian named Abby Sunderland. She was in stormy waters on a yacht somewhere in the Indian Ocean, about 2,000 miles west of Australia.

And she was alone.

When I first saw the reports, my heart sank, imagining the worst. A teenager, attempting an around-the-world solo sailing trip, lost at sea forever. Her body never found. Some piece of her boat washing up years from now, reminding her grieving family of her watery grave.

I knew her journey would be criticized, and I thought it would be a long time before a kid that young would try a trip that dangerous.

How naive.

Young, Younger, Youngest

Do a Web search on "youngest person to sail around the world." It reads like a "Can You Top This?" competition.

In 1996, a 20-year-old Hawaiian named Brian Caldwell set the mark. A few months later, it was broken by an 18-year-old Australian named David Dicks. Three years later, Jesse Martin, another 18-year-old Aussie, did it with no assistance, thus upping the bar.

His mark was broken last year by a 17-year-old named Zac Sunderland. Yes, he is the older brother of Abby. You wonder what this family is feeding the kids.

Of course, Zac's mark was broken that same summer by a Brit who was—aha!—three months younger. And his record was bested last month (under some protest) by a 16-year-old Australian girl named Jessica Walton.

Abby had been alone at sea for *six months*—perhaps trying to win back the family honor—before stormy waves knocked her boat over and left her adrift.

Her rigging was broken. Her sail was in the water. The ocean, you see, doesn't really care how old you are.

Luckily, her distress beacons were detected and the storm abated enough for rescue operations to locate her. Very luckily.

Because different weather might have meant a different story. Death was a real possibility. And then her parents would be answering some pretty tough questions right now, instead of posting the headline on her blog: "Abby is fine!"

Abby is fine. Can we say the same about Mom and Dad?

Risk vs. Ridiculous

Let's face it. We're in a world of super-early achievement. A 13-year-old just climbed Mt. Everest. But no matter how much parents tell you, "We don't push," and "This is my child's dream," no kid gets to these levels without Mom and Dad encouraging, if not prodding. Where else does the money come from? The organization? Dealing with school? And something called "permission"?

The obvious question then is, why couldn't Abby's journey wait? If you want to see what sailing around the world is like, what's the matter with trying it when you're 21?

Because clearly this wasn't only about sailing. This was about beating records and grabbing fame, too. Abby's dream "since she was 13" (according to her publicity machine) was to be the *youngest* to sail around the world. She has a clothing product line called Abby16. That wouldn't sell as well if it were Abby21, would it? Of course, a year from now, if a 15-year-old broke her mark, it wouldn't mean much, either.

Which is where the parents come in. Kids have lots of dreams. A 16-year-old may want to be a stunt pilot or spend a winter alone at the North Pole. This is why the words "Not yet, kiddo" were invented.

Instead, her father, Laurence, said, "You obviously don't know Abigail," when asked by "Good Morning America" about criticism. He also said, "Let's face it, life is dangerous. How many teenagers die in cars every year?"

If he really thinks a drive to the movies and six months alone at sea are the same thing, he's hopeless. But instead of a network TV appearance, he and his wife should be on their knees right now thanking heaven they're not mourning a child in an empty coffin. Sixteen is teen-aged. A time to learn, socialize, grow up. Just being *alone* for six months at that age is a bad idea.

So is tempting death in a wintry sea.

There are normal risks. There are foolish risks. And there are risks done in the name of fame, records and clothing lines. Kids may not know the difference. Parents should.

Comment Posts

Ken Waltz

Do country's charge other sailors for their search and rescue expenses? If not, then why discriminate by age? Nations have search and rescue teams and equipment ready for many types of emergencies and the last thing we need to do in an emergency is a credit check. Not many people could afford to be rescued from even a car accident if they had to pay every expense associated with the rescue. I'm sure that the family will reward the fisherman that come to help her but most people could hardly afford to cover a private jet flying 4700 miles and circling for an hour. So what you would have is a court demanding payment for services not requested? Then you'd have people saying: Hey, you should have let me die, or just sent another boat not the plane. Sometimes rescues turn out to be false alarms, should we charge them too?

Come on all you greedy capitalists; get over the expense and be happy the girl was found alive. Thanks to the latest technology and people who care without judgment. I see this as a great test of our response abilities and feel it helps keep us prepared for the future.

Good luck on your next sailing adventure, Abby. Don't listen to these people that want to hold you down. They are only jealous that you are brave enough to try something they'd be to scared to attempt.

R. Scalzo

I hope they can cover the bill for the rescue. It should only run a few hundred thousand.

Ikie

The Aussies are paying for the rescue.

Although this young woman seems to be very good at sailing, the risk involved in this—and the risk it put her rescuers at—is too great. Certainly it is admirable to test your limits but not when you put others at risk. The pilot who went out to find her was at the limits for his plane and could have been killed because this young woman was in trouble. There has to be some thought about the consequences of a trip like this—not just to the person taking the risk—but the risk they inadvertently put others at. And, who bears the costs of the rescue? Do her parents plan to pay all the costs?

Mike V.

I'm not going to argue your position. If you feel this way fine—but if that's the case the person's age is not relevant. No one should try to go solo around the world in a sailing boat because of what you just described.

Jim

Why does everyone make it out to be about money. Do you hear any comments from these people that have a problem putting billions of dollars out every day for other people? Welfare, insurance, schooling, etc. The girl did something other than play a video game and as someone else said, which is better, a 21 year old with 2 years experience or a 16 year old with probably 10 years experience.

Fact is, her age wasn't the issue. Are we to now charge for all search and rescue services? How about when the Fire Department shows up? Should we charge for that?

Richard

Sailing solo around the world is risky business for anyone. Weather, pirates, mechanical problems, illness, giant mechanical sharks, accidents. . . . I don't think it really matters who you are or your age. The keys to surviving to talk about it are exceptional sailing skills, the ability to deal with and solve problems, an appropriate vessel and utmost preparedness.

She set sail on a robust vessel and was prepared for just about anything. Mommy and Daddy didn't send her out on an inflatable raft. It's really nobody's business to judge one way or another, but from what I can see, this young lady could sail circles around some of the best mariners in the world, and her parent's blessing was more than enough to lend testament to her abilities and game plan.

Benjamin3

As stated by the professional sailor Ian Kiernan, and by many others, she was in the Indian Ocean, known by many sailors to be the most dangerous in the world, in the middle of winter, also the most dangerous time of the year. Her parents sent her off into this knowingly in order to try to obtain a silly world record; was that worth your daughter's life? Most of you who are arguing the case that her parents were right in allowing this are completely ignoring that fact.

Don

Kids are disappearing, walking down the block. How are you going to keep THEM safe? Leave her and her parents alone.

Lisa

Don, are you really *serious* in comparing kids walking to a bus stop to kids sailing the world alone?? The level of risk cannot be compared.

BoBo the Clown

ROFL @ Don. Wow dude. Walking to the bus stop = sailing around the world solo in sailboat.

You must have grown up in Detroit. ■

Questions for Discussion

1. What are some of the many and varied issues that Mitch Albom and the commentators bring up in this article and the reader comments that were posted?

2. To what extent should parents allow children to engage in legal but risky behavior such as sailing solo around the world? Where would you draw the line as a parent?

3. What kinds of policies should be considered when individual decisions may likely impact public expenses? For example, should there be bicycle and motorcycle helmet laws and laws limiting fireworks?

The following articles give differing viewpoints on basketball player LeBron James' decision to leave the Cleveland Cavaliers and play for the Miami Heat. Read both and then consider the questions that follow.

LeBron James' Decision a Cruel Blow to His Hometown

Pat McManamon

Cleveland sports took a death blow Thursday night. A killing blow right to the gut. Through the gut, really. LeBron James eviscerated a city and an area in one all-about-me hour long show on national TV. He said he was leaving Cleveland for Miami, and he did it on a show generated by him, about him and for him. He toyed with the emotions of people who supported him, who believed because he was one of their own that he might be different. Try telling anyone in Cleveland he's different now.

It was his right, of course. He could leave if he wanted. But he hardly looked happy, hardly seemed exultant. Maybe that will come in time. Maybe he was torn over leaving his town. He did it anyway. And when he did he tore the heart out of his hometown—Akron included. Local TV in Cleveland showed all the usual shots after the announcement. The disappointed faces. The depressed sound bites. The guys in the bar holding their head in their hands. One fan called him "a coward." Another said he "ripped the hearts out of Northeast Ohio." Cleveland City Councilman Zach Reed called the entire TV production and announcement "a slap in the face." "Why would you go on national TV and tell millions of people around the world that the city you grew up in, that embraced you, is not good enough to play for," Reed said on WOIO-Channel 19. "A total slap in the face. You don't go on national television to do that." Folks felt duped, cheated, mislead, betrayed. All his words about team and area and loyalty and home . . . all seem hugely hypocritical now. James and his NBA cohorts who pulled this off did it for themselves. And James made no secret of that. He went the 'I and me' route often on his show.

He even used the third person, stating he was doing "what was best for LeBron James" and "what would make LeBron James happy." Meanwhile, kids in Cleveland who looked up to him cried. James talked his entire career about being a leader, but he wound up following. Following his friends to South Florida where they can form a self-generated superteam, in an area where it means as much to be seen at the games as it does to see the games. James had the right to choose, of course, and he chose the way that caused the most pain possible in his hometown. More power to the Heat for pulling this off, but that doesn't lessen Cleveland's pain. Cleveland now is the city that has seen a back-to-back MVP leave town, has seen consecutive American League Cy Young winners traded. Manny Ramirez left. Jim Thome. Albert Belle. And Art Modell left with his football team. Add on the dismay during the games—The Drive, The Fumble, The Elbow—and it just seems whack. Impossible to believe it all happened in one city.

James was going to be different. He grew up in Akron. He could drive 20 minutes to work, shop at Target. And he seemed to care, to understand, because he was from the area. He left. As former NFL player LeCharles Bentley said, his departure "could ruin pro sports in Cleveland" because if Cleveland can't keep one of its own, how can it attract a player from another team? "I never wanted to leave Cleveland," James said. Then why leave? A burned jersey showed up on TV, police cruisers with lights flashing parked outside the "Witness" banner. Shown the burning '23' jersey, James said he couldn't get involved in the feelings in Cleveland, that he had given his all for seven years and the seven years "we had was like no other." "I'll ultimately be happy with the decision I made and continue to be great," James said. He said his "real fans" would support him, but he didn't seem to understand that his real fans, the ones who watched him since high school, live near Akron and Lake Erie. While he continues, in his words, "to be great," Cleveland suffers. And shows more anger than any place should show over a professional sports figure. But for the fans and people in Cleveland, it feels like unrequited love. Every game James has ever played in Cleveland, going back to his high school days, was a sellout. Fans adored him, and gave him everything they could. Just like his team. The Cavs never gutted their roster to try to save money to keep him, never told him it would hold back on acquiring players until he committed. They tried to win, surrounding him with players they thought he wanted and could win with—to the point that they did all they could to try to acquire Chris Paul the past few days. Perhaps that was why Cavs owner Dan Gilbert reacted so angrily. Gilbert is a fighter, and he did not go quietly when James left, releasing a letter calling James "a former King" and his actions a "cowardly betrayal." The Cavs had done everything they humanly could to keep James happy for seven years, and he left. James seems to forget, too, that he let the people down in the Boston series. He checked out in Game 5 of Cleveland's second-round loss to the Celtics, then after said he had spoiled people in seven years. Gilbert told The Associated Press James quit and that it was "accountability time."

"He quit," Gilbert told the AP. "Not just in Game 5, but in Games 2, 4 and 6. Watch the tape. The Boston series was unlike anything in the history of sports for a superstar." Gilbert also charged James quit in the Cavs Game 6 loss against Orlando in the 2009 playoffs. "Go back and look at the tape," he said. "How many shots did he take?" Gilbert also said James never returned a phone message or text since the end of the season, and added people had "covered up for (James) for way too long. Tonight we saw who he really is." Because James didn't communicate that he wasn't coming back, the Cavs waited for him and now they're in an impossible spot in terms of trying to improve their team after all the key free agents have signed elsewhere.

He held them hostage in free agency the same way he held them hostage the last three years. It was all based on his whims, his desire to have options. He talked team, and played for the team, but had his personal end-goal in mind. The Cavs spent so much money to try to win the past three years that they now have no way to spend to win in the NBA's salary cap structure. James left the team that tried to win, and joined the team that did nothing but manipulate the roster to gain salary cap space. James left the team that tried to win and joined the team that didn't. Imagine if the Cavs had been the team gutting its roster; what would The King and his "team" have said then.

The Cavs released the obligatory statement from GM Chris Grant, and Grant did not even mention James. Grant took the stiff upper lip, saying he believed in the team's future. Gilbert was more pointed, guaranteeing the Cavs would win a championship before James did. James' entire free agent process smacks of a charade, one that was orchestrated for months to bring the threesome of James, Dwayne Wade and Chris Bosh together. The interviews, the discussions—a charade. This was their plan all along. It appears they conceived it, and now they've hatched it. Given it life. And they seemed as interested in their personal "brands" and making each other as much money as possible with their move as they did in basketball. That's the impression they gave, at least. And to make it work James created a moment on national television when the cameras could show the crushed faces in his hometown. It even became laughable when James talked about sacrificing by taking less money to sign with Miami. He told a town where unemployment is in double figures how he was "sacrificing"; when his contract will be worth, at least, $80 million. It's surprising people didn't retch right then and there. In Cleveland, a weatherman even got in on the act. Channel 5's Mark Johnson said the way James made his announcement "showed no class" and that Cleveland "saw the true character of LeBron James." "LeBron," he said. "Good riddance and Godspeed." From a weatherman. James did a lot for Cleveland. There is no question of that. He was a great player and he gave the city many great moments. But the city, too, gave him back everything it could, and he left. We are all witnesses, reads the giant banner that still hangs in downtown Cleveland. Witnesses to what, is the question. ▪

Roundup

NBA Team Owner Backs LeBron James' Decision

Mikhail Prokhorov

The players are signed, the "Decision" is made, but the passion around this year's extraordinary class of NBA free agents refuses to die down. What surprises me is the amount of negative commentary directed at the three top free agents (especially LeBron James) who decided to play on the same team and to create a great franchise together. Of course, any club owner dreams of having those players, including me, but all questions of how the announcements were made aside, I respect their choice, and no one has the right to judge them. I want to say that I support LeBron, the best athlete in the NBA. He had a truly difficult choice to make. Any move he made was sure to be viewed as wrong, and to leave many unhappy fans. Basing his decision on achieving results on the basketball court shows that the sportsman won the day, not the showman or the businessman. What is wrong with that?

We are seeing the birth of a new, dynamic team with such star players, and all of us can await the new season with great anticipation. I wish them success and give them my moral support. I will be happy for us to beat the Miami Heat in the conference finals, maybe not this season, but in the very near future. ▪

Questions for Discussion

1. Michael Jordan has been quoted as saying, "There's no way, with hindsight, I would've ever called up Larry [Bird], called up Magic [Johnson] and said, 'Hey, look, let's get together and play on one team.'" Why do you think Jordan would not have wanted to team up with the other greatest basketball players of his time?

2. Do you believe that James' decision will, as Charles Barkley commented, "change his legacy?"

3. To what extent should a player consider loyalty to his hometown when making the decision about a contract?

4. The owner of the New Jersey Nets stated, "Any move he [LeBron] made was sure to be viewed as wrong, and to leave many unhappy fans. Basing his decision on achieving results on the basketball court shows that the sportsman won the day, not the showman or the businessman. What is wrong with that?" Do you agree with his statement? Why or why not?

The following excerpt from a Broadway playbill concerns the long-term consequences of talented actress' difficult career decisions.

Onstage and Backstage

Two Jobs. One Actor. What Do You Choose?

Seth Rudetsky

Decisions, decisions. Even though much of an actor's career involves waiting for an actual role to appear, sometimes an actor has the good fortune of getting to decide between two different job offers, or, as I call it, "something that's never happened to me." Here are two career choices that actually ended with Tony Awards.

Sutton Foster got cast in the ensemble of 2002's *Thoroughly Modern Millie* and as the understudy for the title role. Before she accepted the job, she was offered the role of Eponine in *Les Miserables* on Broadway after playing it on the road. She was offered more money than she had ever earned before. Her "people" thought this was a no-brainer and that she should take the Eponine and run!

Instead, she took *Thoroughly Modern Millie* because she believed in the show and wanted to be a part of its creation. That's right . . . an actress chose being in the ensemble over having a role! Close your mouth (which just dropped open in shock) and continue reading.

The show was first staged out of town, and while Sutton was toiling in the chorus, the director asked her to play the leading role for the final dress rehearsal of the show so the star could get a break. She did it and had a wonderful time, but when the morning of opening night came around, she prepared herself to go back to the ensemble. Suddenly, she got a phone call telling her that the actress who had the lead was leaving! Sutton was offered the role, performed it out of town and on Broadway, and eventually won the Tony Award for Best Actress in a Musical. The moral: Do what feels artistically right for you. And if you have a leading role in a show, watch out for the understudy!

Another young actress-singer I know got cast in a big Broadway revival starring a bona fide Broadway star.

Naturally, she was ecstatic. But then she got offered a Broadway revival of a show that had originally run Off-Broadway. Instead of a big, brassy Broadway musical, it was a small ensemble piece and there was no guarantee of how big or small her part would be because her role was being created for the revival.

She mentioned her quandary to me one day and I told her to take the big Broadway revival. It was sure to be a hit and the other seemed too risky. Well, she ignored me and took the ensemble piece.

Who might I be referring to? Well, it's none other than Kristin Chenoweth currently starring in *Promises, Promises*. In 1999 she was offered a role in the *Annie Get Your Gun* revival starring Bernadette Peters but turned it down to play the role of Sally Brown in *You're a Good Man, Charlie Brown*.

Kristin's hilarious comedic chops plus her rendition of Andrew Lippa's (composer of the Addam's Family) "My New Philosophy" won her the Tony Award for Best Featured Actress in a Musical.

The moral of this story is to always trust your gut. And ignore any advice from me. ■

Questions for Discussion

1. Sutton Foster made the choice to be part of an ensemble rather than to play a lead role despite the disagreement of all of her "people." What were her reasons for going against what her advisers called a "no-brainer"?

2. What were the consequences of Sutton's and Kristin's risky decisions?

3. Seth Rudetsky said that the moral of these tales was to "trust your gut" when making decisions. What does that phrase mean to you?

. . . .

The following articles give differing viewpoints on the same issue. Read both and then consider the questions that follow.

Talk-Show Host Angers Disabled Community

Hand Deformity Inherited from Mom Sparks L.A. Dispute

Michael Fleeman/Associated Press

Aaron James Lampley, all 7 pounds, 14 1/2 ounces of him, was only a few hours old when a local radio station dedicated a show for the second time to the circumstances and controversy surrounding his birth.

In addressing the matter again, KFI-AM last week refueled a dispute that pitted the station against activists for the disabled and raised questions about freedom of speech and society's treatment of the disabled.

Aaron Lampley was born Wednesday morning, with ectrodactyly, which leaves the bones in the feet and hands fused. His mother, local TV anchorwoman Bree Walker Lampley, also has the condition and knew the child had a 50 percent chance of inheriting it.

Her other child, a daughter, has the condition as well.

Before the boy's birth, KFI outraged the KCBS-TV anchorwoman and advocates for people with disabilities with a July 22 call-in show in which host Jane Norris asked whether it was fair for Walker Lampley to give birth when the child had a "very good chance of having a disfiguring disease."

Critics of the show said it smacked of bigotry and illustrated societal prejudice and lack of understanding toward the disabled. KFI said the matter was handled properly and that radio talk shows are appropriate forums for controversial issues.

In KFI's second visit to the subject, this time with Norris acting as guest on Tom Leykis' afternoon show, Norris accused Walker Lampley of orchestrating a campaign to discredit her and contended she had a First Amendment right to discuss the matter.

"I was supportive of Bree's decision," Norris said on the show. "All I did, and have done, is voice my opinion of what would be right for me. I thought I handled the topic sensitively, but all [Walker Lampley has] seen fit to do is slander me."

Norris' statements did nothing to cool the situation.

"They came on the air supposedly to set the record straight. In our view, she set the record even more crooked," said Lillabeth Navarro of *American Disabled for Access Power Today.*

"This is like a bunch of thugs ganging up on the disability community. It just rained forth what caused us to be outraged to begin with."

Navarro said activists planned a protest at KFI studios.

The demonstration is part of a grassroots campaign organized in part by a media consulting firm hired by Walker Lampley and her husband, KCBS anchorman Jim Lampley.

The company, EIN SOF Communications, gives the disability rights community a public voice. The firm has sent tapes of the Norris show to disability rights groups and is helping to file a complaint with the Federal Communications Commission.

In the original show, Norris said she wasn't intending to dictate what Walker Lampley should have done. But she said she couldn't have made the same decision if she were in Walker Lampley's position.

Norris said there were "so many other options available," including adoption and surrogate parenting, and "it would be difficult to bring myself to morally cast my child forever to disfigured hands."

Throughout the show, Norris seemed to take issue with people who disagreed with her.

After a caller named Jennifer from Los Angeles said, "I don't really see why it's your business," Norris responded, "Well, I think it's everybody's business. This is life. These things happen in life. What's your problem? Do you have a problem talking about deformities?"

Norris also repeatedly referred to Walker Lampley's condition, ectrodactyly, as a disease, even though it is a genetically caused disability.

Walker Lampley and her husband, in interviews before their child was born, said Norris' first program was an attack on the handicapped and Walker Lampley personally, and was full of errors and poorly chosen remarks.

"I felt assaulted and terrorized," Walker Lampley said. "I felt like my pregnancy had been robbed of some of its joy."

She added, "I felt disappointed that someone would be so insensitive." ■

Radio Show on Rights of Disabled Defended

Crippled Woman's Pregnancy Debated

Associated Press

The chairman of the Equal Employment Opportunity Commission said a local radio station shouldn't be disciplined for a talk show that debated whether a disabled TV anchorwoman should give birth.

Chairman Evan J. Kemp, who is disabled and confined to a wheelchair, said he was "appalled and sickened" by the majority of callers to the KFI program who said KCBS anchor Bree Walker Lampley had no right to become pregnant and should abort if she did.

However, Kemp said the right of free speech should protect KFI from any Federal Communications Commission action.

Kemp's statements were published in the *Los Angeles Times*.

Lampley, who was pregnant at the time of the July, 1991, broadcast, lodged a complaint to the FCC and asked for an investigation. The newswoman, her husband, co-anchor Jim Lampley, and more than 20 organizations for the disabled asked the agency to examine whether the station and its owner, Cox Broadcasting Corp., should lose their license, be fined or reprimanded.

The couple charged the broadcast was not a thorough discussion, but rather an attack on Lampley's integrity without inviting them to appear and harassed callers who attempted to express contrary views.

Lampley gave birth five weeks after the broadcast to a boy who had the same genetic condition as his mother—ectrodactylism, in which the bones of the hands and feet are fused. There was a 50 percent chance that the baby would have the condition.

Kemp said he was not speaking out as chairman of the Washington, D.C.–based EEOC, but as a "severely disabled person" with a rare polio-like disease—Kugelberg-Welander—that may be inherited.

He said he plans to write to the FCC to defend grassroots discussions and radio talk shows such as the KFI program as necessary forums.

Questions for Discussion

1. The author of the first article states that this controversy "raised questions about freedom of speech and society's treatment of the disabled." What were the questions—that is, issues—that were raised?

2. Take one of the issues raised by the talk-show controversy, and discuss how well those mentioned in the articles defended it.

3. Comment on the following excerpt from the first article. What is your opinion of the host's response to the caller?

   After a caller named Jennifer from Los Angeles said, "I don't really see why it's your business," Norris responded, "Well, I think it's everybody's business. This is life. These things happen in life. What's your problem? Do you have a problem talking about deformities?"

4. Are there any issues discussed by radio and television talk shows that you consider inappropriate? Are certain groups targeted for criticism and others left alone, or is every topic fair game? Give examples to support your answer.

5. Each article used a different subheading to explain the controversy. The first article's subheading reads: "Hand Deformity Inherited from Mom Sparks L.A. Dispute." The second article's subheading says: "Crippled Woman's Pregnancy Debated." How do these different subheadings frame the issue? To what extent do you think they are fair and accurate statements about the controversy?

Ideas for Writing or Speaking

1. Consider the following quote from the preceding article by Michael Fleeman: "Critics of the show said it smacked of bigotry and illustrated societal prejudice and lack of understanding toward the disabled. KFI said the matter was handled properly and that radio talk shows are appropriate forums for controversial issues."

   The framers of our Bill of Rights did not anticipate the phenomenon of broadcast media. Based on your understanding of the freedom of speech, are there any issues that should not be discussed in a public forum? Does sensitivity to the feelings of a particular group make some topics less desirable for public discussion? State your conclusion and support it with reasons.

2. Take a stand on one of the issues involved in these articles. Write an essay or give a short speech expressing your viewpoint and supporting it with reasons.

3. Imagine that you are a program director for a television or radio talk show. What guidelines would you give your talk-show hosts? Give reasons for each guideline. Share your guidelines in a group, or write them in essay form.

4. Write or speak on the following: Given the power of talk-show hosts to influence large numbers of people, do you believe there should be stricter licensing requirements for this profession, as there are for doctors, lawyers, and accountants, in order to ensure a uniform code of journalistic conduct? If so, why? If not, why not?

5. Think about an issue that really interests you; it might be an issue currently being debated on your campus, or a community or national problem. The editorial pages or websites of campus, community, or national newspapers may give you more ideas to help you choose your issue.

   In the form of an essay or a brief speech, state the issue and your conclusion and give at least three reasons to support your conclusion.

   In the classroom, take a few minutes for each person to share his or her essay or speech, and see if the rest of the class understands the issue, conclusion, and reasons of the speaker. Don't use this exercise to debate issues (that will come later). At this point, strive only to make yourself clear and to understand the basic arguments of others.

6. Letter or speech of complaint: Practice using your knowledge about the structure of argument by writing a letter of complaint or doing a classroom "complaint speech," using the guidelines devised by Professor Lee Loots:

   > Constructive complaining is an important life skill. Use this letter or speech to express your dissatisfaction. Choose the most relevant aspects of the problem to discuss. A clear statement of the issue, your conclusion, and reasons distinguishes complaining from "whining." Whereas whining could be characterized as a long string of feelings expressed vehemently about random aspects of a problem, a true complaint describes the nature of the problem in an organized and concise fashion. Sincerely expressed feelings then add richness to the clear and organized content.

   To make the complaint clear, be sure to support your ideas with examples, illustrations, instances, statistics, testimony, or visual aids. To make your feelings clear, you can use vivid language, humor, and dramatic emphasis.

   Examples of topics for the complaint letter or speech: a letter or speech to a city planning commission about excessive airport noise, a letter to a supervisor about a change in salary or working conditions, a complaint to neighbors about reckless driving in the neighborhood, a complaint to housemates about sharing the workload, or a letter or speech to insurance agents about rates for college students.

7. Read the classic poem "The Road Not Taken" by Robert Frost. How does Frost use the image of two roads to illustrate the dilemma facing people who have to make a decision with unknown consequences? Write about a difficult decision you had to make or a dilemma that you are currently facing. Give

some background to the dilemma and the pros and cons of making a choice as you see them at the present time.

You might also consider a social or national decision that needs to be made, such as implementing a new policy or choosing a candidate for an election. What consequences might be the result of different policies or candidates? Given the present facts and projected short-term and long-term consequences, what choice would you advise?

The Road Not Taken

Two roads diverged in a yellow wood,

And sorry I could not travel both

And be one traveler, long I stood

And looked down one as far as I could

To where it bent in the undergrowth;

Then took the other, as just as fair,

And having perhaps the better claim,

Because it was grassy and wanted wear;

Though as for that the passing there

Had worn them really about the same,

And both that morning equally lay

In leaves no step had trodden black.

Oh, I kept the first for another day!

Yet knowing how way leads on to way,

I doubted if I should ever come back.

I shall be telling this with a sigh

Somewhere ages and ages hence:

Two roads diverged in a wood, and I—

I took the one less traveled by,

And that has made all the difference.

From *Mountain Interval* by Robert Frost. Originally published in 1920 by Henry Holt and Company, Inc.

Films for Analysis and Discussion

Films, plays, and television programs are all rich sources that illustrate the concepts in this text. For Chapter 1, you might view and write about issues, conclusions, and reasons found in fictional story lines. In addition, you can analyze how characters face personal dilemmas and struggle with decision making.

Following are some suggestions for films that illustrate some of the points in Chapter 1. Several deal with important issues and life-changing decisions that are made by the characters.

The Adjustment Bureau (2011, PG 13)

The Adjustment Bureau presents a fantasy world in which the destiny of the main characters, politician David Norris and his love interest, ballet dancer Elise Sellas, are being decided and manipulated by agents of Fate. The agents have the means to control circumstances to keep David and Elise apart so that their predetermined paths may unfold. David and Elise are forced to fight for the ability to make their own choices, and are reminded that "free will is a gift unappreciated unless fought for".

Juno (2007, PG 13)

Juno is the story of a 16 year old who becomes pregnant and then is faced with a series of decisions about her future. The film follows her thought process throughout her pregnancy as she faces numerous challenges and considers the consequences of each choice that she must make.

North Country (2005, R)

Sexual harassment might be the legal name for the struggle Charlize Theron's character, Josey, goes through in *North Country*, but her fight is about the human right to be treated with respect. After a string of low-paying jobs and abusive relationships, Josey, a single-mother of two, finds work in the male-dominated iron mines. At first, the job is seen as a golden ticket to independence and solid provision for her children, but, as time passes, the mines become a cruel and dangerous place for Josey and her female co-workers. Instead of taking the easy way out and quitting, Josey sets out for the fight of her life, turning many of her friends and family against her in the process. Much like Jonathan Demme's *Philadelphia*, this film is an uncompromising look at what can happen when one takes a stand for what is right, regardless of the personal cost and obstacles in the way.

Similar Films and Classics

Akeelah and the Bee (2006, PG)

Eleven-year-old Akeelah is just discovering her gifts and talents and deciding on the identity she wishes to portray to her middle school classmates. She needs to decide whether to take the hard road of spelling bee competition and whether to agree to the demands of her new mentor. Her mother also has to make decisions about whether to let Akeelah spend time on her spelling that takes her away from obligations at home and at school.

Pursuit of Happyness (2006, PG-13)

This film is based on the story of Chris Gardner, a salesman struggling to make a living, while his wife works double shifts and his son stays in extended day care. Chris needs to make decisions about whether to take an internship as a stockbroker, despite his time-consuming sales job. His wife has to decide whether to remain in the marriage, and both need to make decisions concerning the well-being of their son.

Good Night and Good Luck (2005, R)

In this film about the McCarthy era of the 1950s, CBS journalist Edward R. Murrow uses his talk show to make arguments against Senator McCarthy and his controversial approach to the threat of communism.

Steel Magnolias (1989, PG)

The title *Steel Magnolias* refers to a group of tough-minded Southern belles who share their lives through good times and times of struggle. The drama is centered on the wedding of a young woman named Shelby and the complications that result from her decision to have a child despite her severe diabetes.

Baby Boom (1987, PG)

In this film, a successful businesswoman has to decide whether to accept responsibility for a baby left in her care, whether to continue working and living in New York City, and eventually, whether to sell her own business for a very large profit. Each decision she makes leads to new choices and dilemmas.

2

Values and Ethics

What Price Ethics, and Can You
Afford Not to Pay?

A critical thinker understands the value assumptions underlying many arguments and recognizes that conflicts are often based on differing values.

A critical thinker is familiar with ethical standards and ethical decision making.

A critical thinker can compare and contrast ideals with actual practice.

Our values have a powerful effect on our decisions.

- Value assumptions
- Conflicts between value assumptions
- Value priorities
- Ideal values versus real values
- Ethics in argumentation
- Ethical decision making

Read on mythinkinglab.com

Listen on mythinkinglab.com

In the first chapter, we discussed the structure of argument, including issues, conclusions about issues, and reasons used to support conclusions. Understanding the structure of an argument helps us to think clearly and to make effective decisions. Chapters 4, 5, and 6 will examine the quality of evidence given to support conclusions. This chapter and Chapter 3 will cover the assumptions underlying arguments that influence all of us as we consider claims and take positions on issues.

Assumptions are ideas we take for granted; as such, they are often left out of a written or spoken argument. Just as we can look at the structure of a house without seeing the foundation, we can look at the structure of an argument without examining the underlying foundational elements. To truly understand the quality of a house or an argument, however, we need to understand the foundation upon which it is built.

Assumptions made by speakers and writers come in two forms: value assumptions and reality assumptions. *Value assumptions* are beliefs about how the world should be; they reflect an individual's viewpoint about which values are most important to consider in relation to a particular issue. *Reality assumptions* are beliefs about how the world is; they reflect what an individual takes for granted as factual information. We will look in depth at reality assumptions in Chapter 3. In this chapter, we will focus on value assumptions, which form the foundations of arguments; we will also examine ethical considerations in argumentation and decision making.

Consider the values expressed in the following newspaper column. Compare the answers given to the question, "Which fictional character do you admire most?" What are the different values represented by the choices? Do you think the careers chosen by the respondents reflect their values?

assumptions Beliefs, usually taken for granted, that are based on the experiences, observations, or desires of an individual or group.

Question Man

Fictional Character You Admire Most?

Kris Conti

Female, 23, curatorial assistant:

Howard Roark of *The Fountainhead* for never compromising his standards. His self-centeredness and arrogance [were] a problem, but I admired the fact that he had standards and lived by them. It seems that standards are fairly loose, sort of ad hoc. People go by the situation they're in rather than a set of standards that they follow. I admire someone who has ideals.

Female, 31, bank teller:

Scrooge. He was a cad but when he had a chance to turn his life around he did. I admire his ability to turn his life around, because it's hard to change. He finally found that being rich is not what makes you happy. That being a true giver and a caring person are very rich qualities, and you can be happy in spite of poverty and adversity.

Male, 28, office manager:

Bugs Bunny. I admire the way he outsmarts his rivals and talks his way out of adverse situations. He always gets the best of any situation. Of course, in the cartoon universe, it doesn't matter how, so it's not applicable in the nonanimated universe. Who's going to discuss morals once you throw the [laws] of physics and gravity out the window?

Male, 38, nuclear industry engineer:

Mr. Spock. He always has the answer. Whatever the problem is, he's always got the solution. He's witty. He's got a great sense of humor. It's just a subtle-type humor. I love that his character is very intelligent. Everything to him has a logic. It has to be logical. It has to click for him in a logical, rational way or it isn't happening.

Female, 25, Salvation Army program assistant:

Cinderella. She overcame . . . all the hardships she had to face and kept that spirit of endurance and forgiveness. She just kept plugging away and was humble. She served her stepsisters and stepmother and didn't gripe. We could all be a little more serving. Not to the point of being oppressed, but be more serving like she was. ◼

Stop and Think

Which fictional character do you admire most? What does your answer reveal about your values?

Since fictional characters are usually superhuman in some way, think also of real people you most admire—what do your choices reflect about your values?

Value Assumptions and Conflicts

Have you ever noticed how some issues are really interesting to you while others are not? Your interest in a particular question and your opinion about the question are often influenced by your **values**—those ideals, standards, and principles you believe are important and consider worthy. For example, look at the list of values below:

> Achievement, friendship, fitness, adventure, family, promise keeping, caring, compassion, privacy, public service, challenge, traditions, honesty, perseverance, change, independence, safety, community, respect, faith, cooperation, responsibility, security, creativity, justice, education, stability, integrity, meaningful work, time, freedom, peace, wisdom, loyalty, diligence, innovation, humor, love, patience, gratitude, courage, and resiliency

values Beliefs, ideals, or principles that are considered worthy and held in high regard.

We attach significance and importance to specific values that are relevant to a given issue or decision. For example, if someone values creativity, she may wish to pursue a career in the arts. Someone who values education might choose to live in poverty in order to complete a graduate degree. A person who puts a high value on public service may join the military or the Peace Corps in order to serve others.

The organization Values.com hosts a series of billboards to promote values that they consider important, and they encourage readers to submit examples of people who model a particular character trait. Each billboard contains a story of a person who exemplifies an admirable value.

Motivation

About This Billboard

When forty five year old Randy Pausch was diagnosed with pancreatic cancer he chose to focus on living rather than dying. As a computer science professor at Carnegie Mellon University, Randy was asked to deliver a 'last lecture'—a well-known tradition on campus that allowed for professors to take a break from academia and share worldly wisdom with students as if, hypothetically, they were dying and had one last lecture left to give. The only difference in Randy's case is that Randy really was dying, a fact that only motivated him more. He agreed to deliver his last lecture, 'Really Achieving Your Childhood Dreams' on September 18, 2007 to a packed McConomy Auditorium.

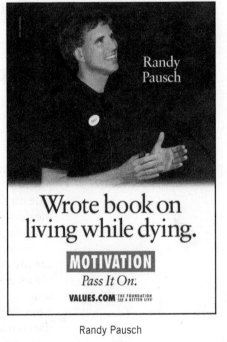

Randy Pausch

Randy began by sharing several of his boyhood dreams—some which he had achieved and others he hadn't. He describes the importance of having dreams and how you can still learn a lot by trying for your dreams even if you don't always succeed. He shares the values he has learned through his experiences that he hopes to pass on to others: integrity, honesty, character, hard work, laughter and gratitude.

Randy's last lecture received so much praise and attention that he agreed to turn it into a book by the same name. It quickly became a best seller, outlining Randy's lifelong philosophy and revealing the ultimate source of his motivation—his three young children.

Randy Pausch passed away July 25, 2008, but he continues to motivate us all, encouraging us to never give up on our childhood dreams. ■

value assumptions Beliefs about what is good and important that form the basis of an individual's opinion on issues.

value conflicts Disagreements about the priority different values should have in decision making.

Value assumptions are beliefs about what is good and important that form the basis of our opinions about issues and decisions.

These assumptions are important for the critical thinker because

1. Many arguments between individuals and groups are primarily based on strongly held values that need to be understood and, if possible, respected.
2. An issue that continues to be unresolved or bitterly contested often involves cherished values on both sides. **Value conflicts** are disagreements about the most important value to be considered concerning an issue. These conflicting value assumptions can occur *between* groups or individuals or *within* an individual.

Almost everyone in a civilized society believes that its members, especially those who are young and defenseless, should be protected. That's why we never hear a debate on the pros and cons of child abuse—most of us agree that there are no "pros" to this issue. Similarly, we don't hear people arguing about the virtues of mass murder, rape, or burglary.

Our values, however, do come into the discussion when we are asked to decide how to treat the people who engage in these criminal acts. Some issues having a value component include:

Should we have and enforce the death penalty?

Should rapists receive the same penalties as murderers?

Should we allow lighter sentences for plea bargaining?

Although most of us value order and justice, we often disagree about how justice is best administered and about what should be done to those who break the law.

Stop and Think

When you read or hear the words *should* or *ought to*, you are probably being addressed on a question of value.

You can see that the question of the death penalty centers on a conflict about the priorities of justice and mercy, two values cherished by many. Of course, a good debate on this issue will also address factual (not value-based) issues, such as whether the death penalty is a deterrent to crimes and whether the penalty is fairly administered throughout the country.

Keep in mind, however, that most people who argue passionately about this issue are motivated by their values and beliefs concerning justice and mercy. These values are often shaped by significant personal experiences. In fact, we generally hear arguments involving values from persons who are deeply concerned about an issue. Both sides of arguments involving values are likely to be persuasive because of the convictions of their advocates. For example, people who make good arguments against a new factory in their town because they value clean air and less traffic may be opposed by people making equally good arguments about the jobs and economic boost that the factory will bring.

While one person values creativity and chooses to major in the arts, a friend or family member may be concerned about the financial instability that often comes with an artistic career. An individual may wish to complete a graduate degree and live in poverty, while his spouse places a higher value on quality family time. Many people who value public service in the military or the Peace Corps contend with family members who place a higher value on personal safety.

In coming to thoughtful conclusions on value-based arguments, the critical thinker needs to decide which of two or more values is best. In other words, the thinking person must give one value or set of values a higher priority than the other. The process of choosing the most important values in an issue has been called **value prioritization**. We need to order our values when a personal, social, national, or international issue involving values is at stake.

value prioritization
The process of choosing the most important values in an issue.

Examples

We often hear arguments about the legalization of drugs, gambling, or prostitution. People may claim that legalizing these activities would lessen crime, free up prison space for more violent offenses, and direct large sums of money to the government and out of the hands of dealers, bookies, and pimps.

Those who oppose legalization of these activities may have equally impressive arguments about the problems communities would face if these activities were legalized. We need to understand the root of this argument as a disagreement about which is more important:

1. Cleaning up the crime problems caused by underground activities linked to illegal vices—that is, the value of taking care of the immediately pressing problem, or
2. Maintaining our standards of healthy living by discouraging and making it a crime to engage in activities that we as a culture deem inappropriate and harmful—that is, the value of honoring and upholding cultural standards and long-term societal goals.

If people believe that taking drugs, gambling, and prostitution are morally wrong, then no list of advantages of legalizing them would be persuasive to them. Thus, the argument starts with understanding whether the conclusion is based on values; relative societal benefits have a much lower priority for those who believe we cannot condone harmful activities.

Skill

Understand that different values form the basis of many arguments and that conflicts are often based on differing value priorities.

Think of a decision you might be facing now or in the future, such as whether you should work (or continue working) while attending school, which career you should choose, or which person you should marry. An internal conflict about a decision often involves an impasse between two or more values.

Let's say you are undecided about continuing to work. You want to devote yourself to school because in the long run you can get a better job (long-term goal). On the other hand, you'd really like the money for an upgraded lifestyle—a car or a better car, money to eat out, and nicer clothes (short-term goals).

Your career decision may involve a conflict between the value of serving others in a field such as nursing, teaching, or social work and the value of a secure and substantial salary (such as you might find in a business career) that would help you better provide for your future family.

You might think of getting serious with one person because he or she has good plans for the future and is a hard worker, but another person is more honest and has cared for you in both good and bad times. In this case, the conflict is between security (or materialism) and proven loyalty.

Whether we are considering personal issues or issues facing our community, nation, or world, we need to understand our values and decide which values are most important to us.

Class Exercise

Purpose: To isolate value conflicts and to understand how different conclusions can be based on conflicting values.

Try to isolate the various value conflicts in these personal and social issues. Some of the issues may involve more than one set of conflicting values.

Note especially how both values can be important, and we as individuals or as citizens need to make tough decisions. Creating policies for difficult problems means giving one value a higher priority than another.

The first one is done for you as an example.

1. Should teenagers be required to obtain the approval of their parents before they receive birth control pills or other forms of contraception?

   The conflict in this issue is between the value of individual freedom and privacy on one side and parental responsibility and guidance on the other.

2. Should birth parents be allowed to take their child back from adoptive parents after they have signed a paper relinquishing rights?

3. Should you give a substantial part of your paycheck to a charity that feeds famine-stricken families or use it for some new jeans you need?

4. Should undocumented residents receive amnesty?

5. Should persons be hired for jobs without regard to maintaining an ethnic mix?

6. Should you tell your professor that students in the back of the class were cheating on the last test?

7. Should superior athletes receive admission to colleges over other applicants who have higher grades or SAT scores?

8. Should criminals be allowed to accept royalties on books they've written about the crimes they committed?

9. Should you donate a kidney to a sick relative?

10. Should children of alumni donors be allowed an advantage in admissions to private universities?

Decision Making: Choosing a Job That Reflects Your Values and Enhances Your Life

The following article from *USA Today* highlights the decisions of several people who took the risk to make a change in their jobs. They each wanted to have a more fulfilling life by choosing to spend time and energy in a way that was meaningful to them; their choices reflect their most important values.

Changing Jobs Takes Guts, Yields Good Life

Lauren Ashburn

Amy Lewis dons her trademark white lab coat in her office, a stone's throw from the White House. This native of Ithaca, N.Y., is the acupuncturist to Washington's power elite. For her, it's a dream come true.

Nine years ago, Lewis, a single mother, had an epiphany and knew she had to change her life. She walked away from a six-figure salary as the youngest member of Howard University's executive team. Her career didn't bring her "joy," and she craved more time with her 5-year-old son. She fired her son's nanny and worked part-time jobs to make ends meet while attending acupuncture school.

"My mentors told me I was committing career suicide," she says with a grin. For her and others who have chosen to leave corporate America to pursue something more satisfying, making a big change can be fraught with identity crises, financial stresses and impatience to return to a "normal" life.

Listening to That Inner Voice

Ariane de Bonvoisin, founder of first30days.com and author of the companion book, *The First 30 Days: Your Guide to Making Any Change Easier,* praises anyone who can take a leap of faith and abandon a sure thing in order to do what she truly loves to do. In her experience, women are more open to making drastic changes than men. "They are searching more spiritually—for a different type of life," she says.

Like Lewis, de Bonvoisin had climbed to a lucrative corporate perch. She sometimes worked 80 to 100 hours a week as a managing director for Time Warner in New York and controlled a $500 million digital media venture capital fund. "I had climbed this big ladder, but it was the wrong ladder leaning up against the wrong wall."

De Bonvoisin started at 19 as a business consultant. She received a degree from London School of Economics and an MBA from Stanford University; she worked for Sony and Bertelsmann Music Group before being lured away by Time Warner. But it wasn't enough.

"I had my 'inner microphone' go on every morning telling me I wasn't in the right job. It took me two years to finally listen," de Bonvoisin says.

She wrote her book after traveling to India and Italy, spending time with her parents and learning how to windsurf. The No. 1 lesson she learned was to change her view of change. De Bonvoisin urges readers to believe that change is a good thing, that it's part of life and happens to everyone. She writes about recognizing negative influences and surrounding yourself with positive influences.

"Change is always easier and quicker when you reach out to others," she says. And it's especially helpful if your team includes people who have lived through similar changes.

A Friendly Push

Nicole Indelicato recently left KPMG as a senior tax associate to pursue her dream of founding a handbag company. She turned to Michele Woodward (lifeframeworks. com), former Reagan White House staffer turned executive coach, to help her make the transition. Woodward coached her for a year before Indelicato quit her corporate job.

"It's a big risk," Indelicato says. "For me, following your purpose and passion totally outweighs the safety net."

Lauren Gibbs, a public policy analyst in Washington, D.C., found her support when she walked into Lewis' acupuncture office. She was hoping Lewis would cure her migraines—which she did—but Lewis also supported Gibbs when she decided to quit her high-stress job on Capitol Hill and fulfill her dream of enrolling in graduate school.

Lewis is living proof that taking risks to follow your passions can pay off. She makes more money, sees hundreds of patients ranging from football players to high-powered litigators, creates her own schedule and doesn't miss a single one of her son's football games. "It taught my son and me about what was important."

Lewis has one piece of advice for those who are teetering on the edge of making a life-altering change: "Don't worry about what the economy says. Don't worry about what other people say. You will succeed if you believe you will." ▪

Ethics—An Important Dimension of Values

Without civic morality, communities perish; without personal morality, their survival has no value.

Bertrand Russell, "Individual and Social Ethics," *Authority and the Individual* (1949)

What is wrong is wrong, even if everyone is doing it. Right is still right, even if no one else is doing it.

William Penn

As we have discussed, values are principles and beliefs that we hold dear. Values differ from person to person, especially when they concern lifestyle choices, such as how we value spending our time.

morals Principles that distinguish right from wrong behavior; *see also* ethics.

When values concern right and wrong behavior, we call them **morals.** If we consider someone to have integrity, we may call her a moral person; conversely, we may refer to certain behavior as immoral. "Morals have a greater social element to values and tend to have a very broad acceptance. Morals are far more about good and bad than other values. We thus judge others more strongly on morals than values. A person can be described as immoral, yet there is no word for them not following values."[1]

ethics Standards of conduct reflecting what is considered to be right or wrong behavior.

When morals are codified into a system, we call them **ethics.** For our purposes, we will examine ethics as a more formal dimension of values that defines standards of right and wrong conduct. Many conflicts about values involve an ethical dimension; that is, we are asked to choose whether one action or policy is more ethical—just or principled—than another.

Look at the difference in the following value conflicts:

Should you take a job that pays more but has evening hours, which you value for studying, or should you take a job that pays less but gives you the hours that you want?

If you arrive home and notice that a cashier at a store gave you too much change, should you go back to the store and return the money?

Note that in the first example, you need to decide what you value more—the extra money or the working hours you want. There is no ethical (good-bad) dimension to this decision; you can still study even if you take the job with the less desirable hours.

---

[1] "Values, Morals, and Ethics," ChangingMinds.org, http://changingminds.org/explanations/values/values_morals_ethics.htm.

The second dilemma is about your personal standards of right and wrong, or good and evil. Do you inconvenience yourself by making a trip to the store or sending the money back because you believe it is wrong to take what does not belong to you? Or do you believe that if you didn't intend to take the money, you are not responsible? What are your standards of right and wrong, especially regarding relationships with others? Your answer to this kind of moral dilemma will reflect your ethical principles.

Philosophers and theologians have grappled with theories of ethical behavior for centuries. Several schools of thought about ethics have emerged. Some of the more common ones guiding Western thinkers are listed here. Note the value assumptions of each.

Libertarianism:	the highest ethical value is to promote individual liberty
Utilitarianism:	the highest ethical value is that which promotes the greatest general happiness and minimizes unhappiness
Egalitarianism:	the highest ethical value is equality, which means justice and opportunities distributed equally
Religious values:	the highest ethical values are based on faith and spiritual truth, such as loving God and one's neighbor
Prima facie values:	the highest ethical values are universal ethical principles, such as honesty and respect for others; these principles are considered to be self-evident and obvious to rational individuals of every culture

Sometimes, these ethical value assumptions are placed together to support a claim, as in Thomas Jefferson's Declaration of Independence, the document that argued for separation of the 13 original colonies of the United States from the rule of the King of England. Read the following excerpt from the Declaration noting how all of the value assumptions just listed are included (emphasis added).

The Declaration of Independence of the Thirteen Colonies

In Congress, July 4, 1776

The unanimous Declaration of the thirteen united States of America,

When in the Course of human events, it becomes necessary for one people to dissolve the political bands which have connected them with another, and to assume among the powers of the earth, the separate and equal station to which the Laws of Nature and of Nature's God entitle them, a decent respect to the opinions of mankind requires that they should declare the causes which impel them to the separation.

We hold these *truths to be self-evident, that all men are created equal, that they are endowed by their Creator with certain unalienable Rights, that among these are Life, Liberty and the pursuit of Happiness.*—That to secure these rights, Governments are instituted among Men, deriving their just powers from the consent of the governed,—That whenever any Form of Government becomes destructive of these ends, it is the Right of the People to alter or to abolish it, and to institute new Government, laying its foundation on such principles and organizing its powers in such form, as to them shall seem most likely to effect their Safety and Happiness.

---

libertarianism   A belief system in which behavior is considered ethical when it allows for one's individual freedom and does not restrict the freedom of others.

utilitarianism   A belief system in which behavior is considered ethical when it promotes the greatest general happiness and minimizes unhappiness.

egalitarianism   A belief system in which behavior is considered to be ethical when equal opportunities and consequences apply to all people.

religious values   An ethical system based on spiritual truth and the principles of loving God and loving one's neighbor.

prima facie values   A system of universal ethical principles, such as honesty and respect for others, that are considered to be self-evident and obvious to rational individuals of every culture.

Note that the Declaration contains references to all of the values we listed—liberty, happiness, equality, an acknowledgment of divine endowments, and self-evident truths. While all of the ethical values are given emphasis in the Declaration, different individuals give priority to one guiding principle over another. This document provides a good example of how members of a culture may espouse common values yet continue to dialogue about the relative importance of those values when considering societal issues. (See Exercise 2.1 on pages 56–57.)

Stop and Think

Most people hold values that reflect several of the ethical schools of thought, and they express these values differently, depending on the issue. An individual may be in favor of free trade (libertarian), equal educational opportunity (egalitarian), creation of national parks (utilitarian), working for faith-based charities (religious values), and a business policy of treating every customer with respect (prima facie values). It is hard to categorize most people as followers of one system exclusively over another because of complex individual differences.

Is there one particular school of thought that you embrace on most issues?

In any society, conflicting positions on issues are often based on differences in ethical value assumptions. For example, libertarians might argue that when someone has created a business on private property, that person has the right to regulate activities that take place on that property, such as smoking. People concerned about the effects of smoke on nonsmokers may give the utilitarian argument that even private restaurants and bars should ban smoking for the greater good of those who want to go to or work in those establishments.

While there are clear differences between the ethical schools of thought, there are also individual differences even within a particular ethical perspective. Issues involving conflicting values usually generate conclusions that answer the question "Where do we draw the line?" For example, one doctor who fought successfully to ban smoking in workplaces to protect the health of nonsmokers (a stand that could be seen as supporting the utilitarian value of the highest good for the most people) argued for a more libertarian view when it came to banning smoking outside. Dr. Michael Siegel "wrote dozens of scientific articles on the dangers of secondhand smoke. His testimony in court and at countless city council meetings helped push public policy toward tighter restrictions on smoking."[2] However, Siegel and others who fought hard to get rid of smoking in the workplace objected to similar attempts to ban smoking outdoors. As scientists, they did not believe that the claim that smoking outdoors causes the same secondhand smoke problems that justified the indoor smoking ban was convincing. In speaking of the zeal and success of the antismoking campaigns, Siegel stated, "It's getting to the point where we're trying to protect people from something that's not a public

---

[2] Randy Myers and Suzanne Bohan, "Outdoor Smoking Bans Rile Anti-Tobacco Leader," *Contra Costa Times*, January 5, 2007.

health hazard." At risk, he and other like-minded tobacco control advocates assert, is not only the credibility of public health officials, but also the undermining of a freedom prized in democracies—do as you wish as long as you don't harm others.[3]

Siegel was a strong and effective advocate for creating smoke-free indoor workplaces on utilitarian grounds; he drew the line—on libertarian grounds—when antismoking groups tried to ban smoking outside. In taking his stand, he showed that people with different priorities can solve problems by drawing lines in which conflicting values can be reconciled with a workable compromise. In this case, Siegel argued that the desires of both smokers and nonsmokers could be met without a severe impact on public health.

Many laws also reflect an attempt to "draw the line" in a way that incorporates several value assumptions. One such law was enacted in 1997 in Texas to help state universities reconcile the conflicting goals of admitting high-achieving students from excellent high schools and also honoring and encouraging hardworking, bright students with disadvantaged backgrounds. The value conflicts and priorities represented by the decision to admit the top 10 percent of students from every high school in the state are detailed in an article at the end of this chapter. 👓

Skill

A critical thinker is aware of his or her value priorities and how they affect dialogue and decision making. (See Exercise 2.2 on page 57.)

Ideal Values versus Real Values

> Men acquire a particular quality by constantly acting in a particular way.
>
> Aristotle

> Character is not reflected by what we say, or even by what we intend; it is a reflection of what we do.
>
> Anonymous

Ethical behavior is easier to discuss than it is to carry out. We have complex needs and emotions, and situations are also complicated. Even with good intentions, we sometimes find it difficult to make ethical choices.

Because of the effort involved in living up to our standards, most of us can make a distinction between our ideal values and our real values. An **ideal value** is *a value that you believe to be right and good.* A **real value** is *a value that you believe to be right and good and that you consistently act upon in your life.* As critical thinkers, it is important for us to understand and be honest about our own behavior and to distinguish our words from our actions.

ideal value A value considered to be right and good.

real value A value considered to be right and good that is acted upon in one's life.

[3] Ibid.

People may say they value good citizenship; they believe people should be informed about candidates and issues and express their viewpoints by voting, but they may continue to vote without studying issues and candidates. In some cases, the value of citizenship is only an ideal. For the value to be real, it must be carried out in the life of the individual claiming it as a value.

The more that our values become an integral part of our identity, the easier they are to act upon when we face tough decisions. For example, people in positions of leadership have to make decisions that impact others, sometimes for decades to come, and the way they view themselves guides their choices. Abraham Lincoln was on an extensive 12-day train journey to Washington, DC, to take his place as the sixteenth president of the United States, and he arrived 10 days before his inauguration. He was offered wonderful private accommodations from several prominent leaders but instead chose to stay at the Willard Hotel, close to the White House, stating, "The truth is, I suppose I am now public property; and a public inn is the place where people can have access to me."[4] Lincoln's view of himself as belonging to and representing the best interests of the public helped him make decisions that were consistent with his ideal values.

Lincoln had had strong and capable opponents in the campaign that led to his securing the Republican presidential nomination. His opponents had been as negative in their rhetoric about Lincoln as today's rivals are when they compete for political nominations. However, when he chose a cabinet, Lincoln did not seek "yes-men" who supported his own beliefs and who were happy that he had won the election. Instead, he chose his strongest enemies to become leaders in his cabinet.

In fact, as John Nicolay later wrote, Lincoln's "first decision was one of great courage and self-reliance." Each of his rivals was "sure to feel that the wrong man had been nominated." A less confident man might have surrounded himself with personal supporters who would never question his authority; James Buchanan, for example, had deliberately chosen men who thought as he did.

Later, Joseph Medill of the *Chicago Tribune* asked Lincoln why he had chosen a cabinet composed of enemies and opponents. He particularly questioned the president's selection of the three men who had been his chief rivals for the Republican nomination, each of whom was still smarting from the loss.

Lincoln's answer was simple, straightforward, and shrewd: "We needed the strongest men of the party in the Cabinet. We needed to hold our own people together. I had looked the party over and concluded that these were the very strongest men. Then I had no right to deprive the country of their services."[5]

In our public and professional lives, we are seen as having integrity when we act upon our ideal values. In our personal lives, we also encounter choices that challenge us to act upon our ideal values, to make them consistent with our choices. Consider the following dialogue:

> Stephanie, 21, is a virgin and had planned to stay that way until she's married. But now she finds herself very attracted to somebody... did I say "very"? She'd hoped that her values, the rules, would protect her from temptation. Now she is set adrift without a paddle because she discovered that values don't function like an automatic, invisible protective shield.
>
> "Just in case I start dating him, do you have any advice on how to stay a virgin?"

[4] Doris Kearns Goodwin, *Team of Rivals* (New York: Simon & Schuster, 2005), p. 312.
[5] Ibid., pp. 318–319.

"You mean you have values until temptations ride into town; then the values sneak out during the night? The town ain't big enough for both values and temptations. Values keep us steady through times of deep temptation. They are our road map through the minefields of challenge. It is easy to say you have values and easier still to live up to them when you're by yourself in the middle of the ocean."

"That's true."

"Values are truly only shown to exist when they are tested. If it is meaningful for you to reserve sexual intimacy for marital vows, if you feel that doing so elevates sex and you, that is admirable."

"Yeah, but how do you make the values do their thing to keep you from doing something else?"

"Values only have the power you infuse into them with your respect for them and yourself, and your will. Values without temptations are merely lofty ideas. Expediting them is what makes you, and them, special. That requires grit, will, sacrifice, courage, and discomfort. But it is in the difficulty that both the values and you gain importance. The measure of you as a human being is how you honor the values."

"When you begin dating him, clarify your position of intercourse only within marriage. If he tries to push you away from that position, you know he values you only as a means of sexual gratification. If he gets seductive and you're lubricating from your eyeballs to your ankles, this is the moment when you choose between momentary pleasure and long-term self-respect."

"That is the real choice I'm making at that point, isn't it?"

There is no fast lane to self-esteem. It's won on these battlegrounds where immediate gratification goes up against character. When character triumphs, self-esteem heightens.

One caller asked, "What if I'm too weak?" I answered that the road to unhappiness and low self-esteem is paved with the victories of immediate gratification.[6]

Skill

A critical thinker can compare and contrast ideals with actual practices. (See Exercise 2.3 on page 58.)

Ethics in Argumentation

It is terrible to speak well and be wrong.

Sophocles, *Electra* (c. 418–414 B.C.)

Ethical concerns are central to any argument. Those who seek to influence votes, sales, or the personal decisions of others need to

- Be honest about their conclusions and reasons
- Not leave out or distort important information

[6] Dr. Laura Schlessinger, *How Could You Do That?* (New York: HarperCollins Publishers, Inc., 1996), pp. 151–152.

- Thoroughly research any claims they make
- Listen with respect, if not agreement, to opposing viewpoints
- Be willing to revise a position when better information becomes available
- Give credit to secondary sources of information (See Exercise 2.4 on page 58.)

Ethical Decision Making

> Every man takes care that his neighbor shall not cheat him. But a day comes
> when he begins to care that he does not cheat his neighbor. Then all goes well.
>
> Ralph Waldo Emerson, "Worship," *The Conduct of Life* (1860)

The first step in clearheaded decision making is knowing your principles and standards. In considering difficult decisions, several "tests" can be useful to apply to your known principles. These tests can help you assess how well your decision adheres to your ethical standards.

role exchange test A test for ethical decision making that involves empathizing with the people affected by an action that is being considered.

1. The Role Exchange Test. The **role exchange test** asks you to empathize with the people who will be affected by the action you take. You try to see the situation from their point of view. You ask yourself how the others affected by your decision would feel and what consequences they would face.

You also ask whether it would be right for the other person to take the action if you were going to be the one experiencing the consequences of the decision. Using your imagination, you change places with the person or persons who would receive the effects of your decision. In short, you decide to treat the other person as you would want to be treated in his or her place.

For example, you see your brother's girlfriend out with other men. You hesitate to tell him because of the hurt it would cause and because you feel it's not really your business to interfere. However, when you do the role exchange test, you decide to tell him because you realize you would want to know if you were in his situation.

universal consequences test A test for ethical decision making that focuses on the general consequences of an action under consideration.

2. The Universal Consequences Test. The **universal consequences test** focuses on the general results (consequences) of an action you might take. You imagine what would happen if everyone in a situation similar to yours took this action. Would the results be acceptable?

Under the universal consequences test, if you would find it unacceptable for everyone in a similar situation to take this action, then you would reject the action.

For example, imagine that you are asked to join a community program for recycling cans, bottles, and paper. You enjoy the freedom of just throwing everything together in the trash, but you stop and assess the consequences if everyone refused to recycle. Your assessment may cause you to join the program.

new cases test A test for ethical decision making that asks whether a decision is consistent with decisions that would be made in similar, harder cases.

3. The New Cases Test. The **new cases test** asks you to consider whether your action is consistent with other actions that are in the same category. You choose the hardest case you can and see if you would act the same way in that case as you plan to act in this one. If you would, then your decision is consistent with your principles.

For example, you are deciding whether to vote to continue experiments that may be successful in finding a cure for AIDS but involve injecting animals with the HIV virus. Your principle is that cruelty to animals is not justified in any circumstance. To formulate a new, harder case, you might ask yourself if you would allow the research to be conducted if it would save your life or the life of your child. If you would, then you might reconsider your voting decision and reassess your principles.

Another example involves the issue of whether a photographer should turn over negatives to the police if it would help detectives identify and prosecute murder suspects (see the article at the end of this chapter about this dilemma). You may believe that freedom of the press cannot be compromised and, therefore, the photographer should be able to keep the negatives out of the investigation. Using the new cases test, imagine that someone you love dearly was the murder victim and that these photographs are the link to catching the murderer. Would that knowledge change your value priorities and your conclusion in this case?

4. The Higher Principles Test. The **higher principles test** asks you to determine if the principle on which you are basing your action is consistent with a higher or more general principle you accept.

For example, let's say your roommates are not doing their share of the housework so you are considering not doing your own share. However, because you value promise keeping and integrity, you realize that it is important to keep your part of the bargain regardless of whether they are doing their part. You decide to keep doing your share and to talk with them about keeping their part of the agreement. (See Exercise 2.5 on pages 58–59.)

higher principles test
An ethical test by which one determines if the principle on which one is acting is consistent with a higher or more general principle that one accepts.

Skill

A critical thinker uses ethical standards in argumentation and decision making.

When we make ethical decisions, the actions we take are congruent with our values. When our actions go against what we believe is right, we are prone to rationalize our behavior, rather than to admit we are not always ethical. Consider the following list of common rationalizations used to justify unethical conduct.

Common Rationalizations

Ethics in Action

Michael Josephson

I. **"If It's Necessary, It's Ethical."** Based on the false assumption that necessity breeds propriety. Necessity is an interpretation not a fact. But even actual necessity does not justify unethical conduct. Leads to ends-justify-the-means reasoning and treating assigned tasks or desired goals as moral imperatives.

II. **"If It's Legal and Permissible, It's Proper."** Substitutes legal requirements (which establish minimal standards of behavior) for personal moral judgment. Does not embrace full range of ethical obligations, especially for those involved in upholding the public trust. Ethical people often choose to do less than they are allowed to do and more than they are required to do.

III. **"I Was Just Doing It for You."** Primary justification of "white lies" or withholding important information in personal or professional relationships, especially performance reviews. Dilemma: honesty and respect vs. caring. Dangers: Violates principle of respect for others (implies a moral right to make decisions about one's own life based on true information), ignores underlying self-interest of liar, and underestimates uncertainty about other person's desires to be "protected" (most people would rather have unpleasant information than be deluded into believing something that isn't so). Consider perspective of persons lied to: If they discovered the lie, would they thank you for being considerate or feel betrayed, patronized or manipulated?

IV. **"I'm Just Fighting Fire with Fire."** Based on false assumption that deceit, lying, promise-breaking, etc., are justified if they are the same sort engaged in by those you are dealing with.

V. **"It Doesn't Hurt Anyone."** Rationalization used to excuse misconduct based on the false assumption that one can violate ethical principles so long as there is no clear and immediate harm to others. It treats ethical obligations simply as factors to be considered in decision making rather than ground rules. Problem areas: Asking for or giving special favors to family, friends or politicians, disclosing nonpublic information to benefit others, using one's position for personal advantages (e.g., use of official title/letterhead to get special treatment).

VI. **"It Can't Be Wrong, Everyone's Doing It."** A false "safety in numbers" rationale fed by the tendency to uncritically adopt cultural, organizational, or occupational behavior systems as if they were ethical.

VII. **"It's OK if I Don't Gain Personally."** Justifies improper conduct done for others or for institutional purposes on the false assumption that personal gain is the only test of impropriety. A related more narrow excuse is that only behavior resulting in improper *financial gain* warrants ethical criticism.

VIII. **"I've Got It Coming."** Persons who feel they are overworked or underpaid rationalize that minor "perks" or acceptance of favors, discounts, or gratuities are nothing more than fair compensation for services rendered. Also used to excuse all manner of personnel policy abuses (re: sick days, insurance claims, overtime, personal phone calls or photocopying, theft of supplies, etc.).

IX. **"I Can Still Be Objective."** Ignores the fact that a loss of objectivity always prevents perception of the loss of objectivity. Also underestimates the subtle ways in which gratitude, friendship, anticipation of future favors and the like affect judgment. Does the person providing you with the benefit believe that it will in no way affect your judgment? Would the benefit still be provided if you were in no position to help the provider in any way? ■

Stop and Think

Are there situations you can think of in which something may be legal but is not ethical? What about situations in which something is not legal but is ethical?

Examples of the Common Rationalizations

I. If it's necessary, it's ethical. "I need to have three years experience to get this job, so I'll put that on my resume, even though I only have two years."

II. If it's legal and permissible, it's proper. "Since my parents are divorced, my mom claims me on her income tax. Even though my dad makes a huge salary and also supports me, the state only counts my mom's salary in figuring out my college funding, so the state pays for my entire tuition, room, and board. It's probably not fair to take the money that other students need, but that's the law."

III. I was just doing it for you. "I didn't tell you that your boyfriend/girlfriend was cheating on you because I didn't want you to feel bad."

IV. I'm just fighting fire with fire. "My roommate took my jacket without asking, so I'm taking his camera."

V. It doesn't hurt anyone. "My sister wrote my essay for the online class, but that doesn't hurt anyone else."

VI. It can't be wrong, everyone's doing it. "Lots of people are leaving work early, so why shouldn't I?"

VII. It's OK if I don't gain personally. "When my shift was over, I took some pizzas from the restaurant to give to some kids who were playing on the street."

VIII. I've got it coming. "I don't get paid what I think I'm worth, so I spend time at work catching up on my e-mail."

IX. I can still be objective. "It's okay for me to receive expensive gifts from people in my district. That won't affect how I vote on their concerns."
(See Exercise 2.6 on page 59.)

Toulmin's Model: A Method for Discovering Assumptions

This chapter has focused on understanding our value assumptions and how they impact our decisions about issues. Chapter 3 will examine reality assumptions, another foundational element of argument. British philosopher Stephen Toulmin has developed a method of analyzing arguments that helps us isolate our assumptions. His method identifies **claims,** statements of an individual's belief or stand upon an issue (which are the same as conclusions); **reasons,** direct statements that provide evidence to support a claim; and **warrants,** those unstated but necessary links between reasons and claims, the glue that attaches the reasons to the claims. Warrants are the assumptions made by the speaker or writer that connect claims and reasons.

claim A statement or conclusion about an issue. The advocate for a claim will seek to prove the truth of the claim through evidence.

reasons Statements given to support conclusions.

warrants Unstated but necessary links between reasons and claims; the assumptions made by the speaker or writer that connect claims and reasons.

Example

We'll have to leave at 5 a.m. to make our flight because we'll be driving in rush-hour traffic.

Claim (conclusion): We'll have to leave by 5 a.m. to make our flight.

Reason: We'll be driving in rush-hour traffic.

Warrant: Rush-hour traffic moves more slowly than other traffic.

In the preceding example, the reason and claim of the speaker are clear, but the warrant (in this case, an assumption about reality) that shows the movement from the reason to the conclusion—why the reason is relevant support for the conclusion—is unstated. These assumptions are usually unstated because they are unnecessary in a particular context; for example, most people in a culture that deals with traffic understand the demands of rush-hour traffic.

Similarly, value assumptions often remain as unstated warrants for an argument if most people hearing the argument accept these assumptions without question. For example, if someone cuts in line in front of others who have been waiting, he or she will be told "You need to move back, because the line starts back there."

> *Claim* (conclusion): You need to move back.
>
> *Reason:* The line starts back there.
>
> *Warrant* (this is the unstated value assumption): The acceptable action is to take your turn in line, which reflects the value of fairness to everyone.

Sometimes, warrants contain both reality and value assumptions in the same argument. For example, someone might say "Be careful on that floor—it was just washed."

The argument in this case could be analyzed as

> *Claim:* Be careful walking on that floor.
>
> *Reason:* It was just washed.
>
> *Warrant:* Floors that have been newly washed are slippery (reality assumption).
>
> *Warrant:* I don't want you to slip and fall because I value your health and safety (value assumption).

Understanding reality assumptions and value assumptions as foundational, but unstated, parts of an argument becomes important when we discover that other people may hold very different assumptions and thus do not believe that our conclusions are warranted. Let's say that someone argues as follows: "There should be no restrictions on public library access to the Internet for children because children need to be able to do research on library computers." The claim (conclusion) is that there should be no restrictions on library access to the Internet for children. The reason given is that children need to be able to do research on the computers. The warrant, in this case a value assumption, is that equal access to information is important for young students.

Someone with a different take on this issue may argue that there should be restrictions on public library access to the Internet because the policy would allow minors to easily access pornographic material. The warrant in this case would reflect a different value assumption—that protection of minor children from inappropriate material is more important than unlimited access to the Internet.

When you argue that your value assumption is the *best* one for the situation, you often have to persuade others. Your warrant will require what Toulmin calls **backing,** evidence used to support a warrant. You will need to explain why your value assumption is the most important one. In the case of library access, you might state the following as backing for the warrant: "Protection of minor children from inappropriate material is important."

backing Evidence used to support a warrant.

Backing (Support for the Warrant)

- Parents trust children's sections of public libraries to be free from adult content.
- Libraries create special children's sections, in part, to isolate children from accessing and borrowing inappropriate material.
- If children need to access research material from the Internet, a librarian is available to help them.

When people *agree* about underlying assumptions, they do not need to be made explicit. However, when assumptions are controversial, they need to be acknowledged and defended. Assumptions (warrants) that are controversial need support (backing). We will look more closely at backing, the evidence for warrants, in Chapters 3, 4, and 5. As illustrated in the previous examples, when individuals have differing assumptions (warrants) about an issue, they often reflect a difference in the priority that is given to one value over another. When forming opinions and making decisions, critical thinkers need to understand and examine their own value priorities. People may agree that the values of others are also valid but believe that their own values are the most important determining factors for a particular issue, that their values "trump" the values of opposing viewpoints.

Life Application: Tips For College and Career

When you find yourself involved in a heated discussion or debate, notice if different value assumptions are held on both sides of the issue. If possible, point these out and show the importance of clarifying the different values in order to increase understanding.

When expressing your own views, be aware of the value assumptions held by others that may differ from your own. If you are trying to persuade people who have different value assumptions than you do, acknowledge and show respect (if possible) for the values they may have and explain why you give a higher priority to different values. If they see that you understand their viewpoints, they are more likely to give a fair hearing to yours.

Chapter Review

Summary

1. Value assumptions are beliefs about what is good and important or bad and unimportant; because these beliefs are taken for granted, they are part of the foundation of a person's argument.

2. Conflicts between value assumptions need to be addressed before fruitful discussions over value-saturated issues can take place.

3. Although people may agree on the importance of various values, they may disagree on which value should prevail in a given controversy. The process of choosing one value over another is called value prioritization.

4. Ethics are standards of conduct that reflect values.

5. There are several schools of thought about ethics, including libertarianism, utilitarianism, egalitarianism, religious principles, and prima facie values.

6. Ideal values are held by an individual in theory; real values are held in theory and also carried out in practice.

7. Our personal ethics are revealed by our behavior as we advocate for ideas and make decisions.

8. Several tests have been developed to help people make ethical decisions. These include the role exchange test, the universal consequences test, the new cases test, and the higher principles test.

9. Ethical decision making is undermined when common rationalizations are used to support unethical practices.

10. Toulmin's model is a method that helps us discover and detect value assumptions and reality assumptions in an argument.

Checkup

Short Answer

1. Using an example, explain value conflicts.

2. Why is it important to examine value assumptions before discussing issues in which values are involved?

3. What are some ethical principles to be used in argumentation?

4. What is the difference between an ideal value and a real value?

Matching

a. libertarianism
b. utilitarianism
c. egalitarianism

d. role exchange test
e. new cases test
f. universal consequences test

5. A test that asks you to empathize with the people who will be affected by any action you take.

6. A belief system in which behavior is considered most ethical when it allows for individual freedom.

7. A belief system that claims behavior to be ethical when the same opportunities and consequences apply to all people.

8. A test that asks you to consider whether your action is consistent with other actions in the same category.

9. A belief system that claims the highest value is that which promotes the greatest general happiness and minimizes unhappiness.

10. Under this test, if you find it unacceptable for everyone in a similar situation to take this action, then you would reject the action.

Exercises

Exercise 2.1 Purpose: To examine various value systems and how they affect decision making.

1. Examine a value system such as one of those given in the section on ethics. You might study the principles of a specific religion or a political philosophy, such as Christianity, Buddhism, or socialism. Try to list the value assumptions and principles for that system and include examples of how belief in the system affects decision making.

2. Note any similarities or differences between the system you have studied and the other value systems listed on page 45. Share your findings with the class.

EXERCISE 2.2 Purposes: To discover how policy debates are influenced by ethical standards. To discover personal standards and principles that determine how your ethical dilemmas are resolved.

1. Consider the systems of ethics discussed in this chapter. Individually, or in groups, come up with examples of situations in which the principles of one of these systems clash with the principles of another. You may want to bring in recent local or campus controversies, such as the one detailed on page 63 of the Articles for Discussion section.

   Discuss the conflicting value priorities represented by your examples.

2. Consider your own definition of ethical behavior; it may fit into one of the ethical schools of thought outlined in this chapter, or it may be a combination of several approaches. Then, using your own principles, try to be completely "ethical" for one week. As often as possible, ask yourself, "What is the best way to respond to this situation?" Keep a daily record of your ethical challenges. Then, report your successes and failures in dealing with these situations.

   Here are some examples of common ethical dilemmas: Should you defend a friend who is being criticized by another friend? Should you give money to a homeless person who approaches you? Should you tell the truth to someone even if it hurts his or her feelings? Should you tell your instructor that several students cheated on a test while she answered a knock at the classroom door? Should you tell callers your roommate isn't home if she asks you to? Should you complain about rude treatment in a store? Should you copy a friend's CD of your favorite music rather than buying your own copy?

   Your own situations will be unique. If time permits, share some ethical dilemmas that you have encountered with the rest of the class.

3. Consider the following situations alone or with a group, especially in light of the tests for ethical decision making listed on pages 50–51. What decision would you make and why?

   a. You and your friend are taking the same required history class; you are taking it on Mondays and Wednesdays, and your friend is taking it Tuesday evening. You have given up much of your social life to study for this class because the tests are hard. One Monday after the midterm, your friend calls you and wants to know what was on the test since he partied too hard over the weekend and didn't study. You have a good memory and could tell him many of the questions. Do you tell him what was on the test?

   b. You go to a garage sale and notice a diamond ring that is being sold for $10. You know that the ring is worth far more than that. What do you do?

   c. The manager of the fast-food restaurant where you work is selling food that is not fresh or prepared according to the standards of the company. You have complained to her, but she has done nothing despite your complaints. You need this job, and the location, hours, and pay are perfect for you; in fact, this boss has tailored your working hours to your class schedule. Nevertheless, you are concerned about public safety. What do you do?

   d. Your friend tells you that her boyfriend is home studying, but you see him out with another girl. What do you do?

EXERCISE 2.3 Purpose: To understand the difference between ideal and real values.

List five of your ideal values and five of your real values.

1. Describe what it would take for these ideal values to become real values for you. Think about why you have not made these ideal values real in your life.

2. Explain what changes in your habits and your priorities would be involved in order for these values to become real for you.

Example

"One of my ideal values is physical fitness. I believe it is important for everyone to keep his or her body strong through exercise and good eating habits.

"As a student, I don't take the time to exercise every day or even every other day. Since I quit the swim team, I hardly exercise at all. When I do have spare time, I sleep or go out with my girlfriend. Also, I eat a lot of fast foods or canned foods because I don't cook.

"For this ideal value to become real for me, I would have to graduate and have more time. Or, I would have to make the time to exercise. The best way would be to combine going out with my girlfriend with exercising. She likes to skate and play basketball, so we could do that together. Getting more exercise is a real possibility. Eating right is probably not going to happen soon. I would have to learn to cook or to marry someone who would cook for me. At this point in my life, I can't see how I could have a healthier diet, even though it is an ideal for me. But it's just not important enough for me to change at this time."

EXERCISE 2.4 Purpose: To examine the ethical dimensions of an argument.

Listen to a political speech or a sales pitch, or read a blog, editorial, or opinion piece. Then evaluate the message, stating whether the writer or speaker met the criteria given for ethical argumentation discussed on pages 49–50.

You might also use one of your own essays or speeches for this exercise; analyze it to see whether you were as honest as you could have been and whether you credited secondary sources of information.

EXERCISE 2.5 Purpose: To be able to utilize tests for ethical decision making.

Option one: Think about an ethical dilemma you have faced or are facing. If you did the exercise on acting ethically for a week from Exercise 2.2 # 2 on page 57, you may have a recent example. You may also use the examples listed in that exercise. In addition, you might consider a difficult ethical dilemma from your past. Then follow the directions given below.

Option two: Think about an ethical dilemma your community or nation is facing; you might also consider an international ethical dilemma. Some examples include the use of scientific information gained by Nazi experimentation on Holocaust victims, the apportionment of funds to poverty-stricken nations, the exporting of cigarettes to other nations, and the rationing of health care. Then follow the directions.

1. On your own or in class groups, take the dilemma through each of the four tests. Write about what each test tells you about the course your decision should take.

2. Come to a conclusion about the decision. Justify your conclusion by referring to the cumulative results of the tests for ethical decision making.

Example

My friend helped me get a job at his company and, after only a few months, I was told that he and I were both being considered for a promotion to management. He worked at the job for a year and he's getting married soon, so he really needs this job. I wouldn't even have known about the possibility of working there if he hadn't told me about it and arranged an interview for me. The dilemma: Should I take the promotion if it's offered to me or refuse it, knowing that it will then go to him?

The role exchange test asks me to look at the situation from his point of view. It would hurt him in two ways if I took this promotion: Mainly, he would lose the income and the chance for advancement that go with this position. Also, he would be hurt because he helped me get this job, and then I took a promotion he might have had. There's nothing wrong with my looking out for my own future, but in this case, it would be at his expense.

The universal consequences test asks me to look at general consequences of my decision and determine if it would be acceptable for everyone in this situation to take a similar action. A positive general consequence might be that all of the best people would be given promotions regardless of who needs the promotion most. The negative general consequence would be that people would routinely put their own desires ahead of what might be more fair and what might be best for other people, a "me-first" mentality.

The new cases test asks me to pick the hardest case I can and see if I would act the same way in that case, to determine whether I am consistent. To me, the hardest case would be if my parent would be given the promotion if I didn't take it. I don't live with my parents anymore, but I would step down if it meant that either of them could have the promotion.

The higher principles test asks me to look at my own ethical standards to see if my actions fit into those standards. This test is hard to use, because I value both my own advancement and my friend's welfare. But I can find the higher principle of fairness; I don't feel that it would be fair for me to take a job that he would have had since he is the person responsible for my being in the position to take it.

In conclusion, I won't take this job if it is offered to me. It would be hurtful to my friend who cared enough about me to help me get a job. Also, I wouldn't want to live in a world where people always climbed over one another to achieve success. If it were my parents, I wouldn't take a job that they wanted, even if it would benefit me personally. Finally, I believe in the principle of fairness, and I don't think it would be just or fair to take a promotion from a friend who gave me the opportunity to work for his company.

EXERCISE 2.6 Purposes: To understand common rationalizations used to excuse unethical behavior and to see how these apply to specific cases.

1. Give examples for several of the rationalizations presented earlier. For example, for "I. If it's necessary, it's ethical," you might cite unethical behavior on the part of campaign managers carried out to ensure the election of their candidate.

   Consider whether you rationalize any of your behavior in the ways mentioned on Josephson's list of common rationalizations.

2. Try to come up with a variety of situations—personal, social, and political—in which the common rationalizations are used. If the class is doing this exercise in groups, share the examples with the entire class.

3. Look for examples of people and groups facing ethical dilemmas that stick to their ethical positions, even at great cost, as in the following example.

Salvation Army Turns Down $100,000 Donation

Salvation Army spurns $100K donation as gambling money. Marco Island, Florida—The Salvation Army will not accept a $100,000 donation from a Florida Lotto winner because its local leader didn't want to take money associated with gambling.

David Rush, 71, announced the gift last week. He held one of four winning tickets in the $100 million Florida Lotto jackpot drawing of December 14 and took a $14.3 million lump-sum payment.

Major Cleo Damon, head of the Salvation Army office in Naples, told Rush that he could not take his money and returned the check, which another official had accepted.

"There are times where Major Damon is counseling families who are about to become homeless because of gambling," said spokeswoman Maribeth Shanahan. "He really believes that if he had accepted the money, he would be talking out of both sides of his mouth." ■

You Decide

Animal Rights

The use of the term "animal rights" is attributed to Australian philosopher Peter Singer. A broad spectrum of issues relating to animal rights has been debated since the time of Singer's writing in the 1970s, including whether animals have the right to not be used for food and clothing and to not be subjected to experimental research. Animal rights activists point to the pain inflicted on animals for the testing of cosmetics, oven cleaners, and other nonessential items; they also reason that animals are biologically related to human beings. Scientists argue that the biological similarity of animals to human beings makes animal experimentation vital for advances in finding cures for fatal diseases. People on both sides of this issue contend that the ability to use language and develop technology gives humans both rights and responsibilities. Those in favor of using animals for food and research give a value priority to human life over animal life. Those who are against using animals for food and research value animal life and freedom over human choices and discoveries that might enhance and prolong human life.

For more information about the debate surrounding animal rights and additional exercises and tutorials about concepts covered in this chapter, log into MyThinkingLab at www.mythinkinglab.com and select Diestler, *Becoming a Critical Thinker,* Sixth Edition.

✷ Explore on **mythinkinglab.com**

Articles for Discussion   📖 Read the **Document** on **mythinkinglab.com**

In this first article, Rick Reilly, who writes a column for *Sports Illustrated,* asks his readers to think about how they would have coached a particular game; as it turns out, the coaches' decisions set off a firestorm in a local community. Your answer will reveal your own value priorities and could lead to some interesting class discussions. For a fascinating exploration of this topic, go to this article on the *Sports Illustrated* website, and see what other readers would have done.

You Make the Call

Is It Good Baseball Strategy or a Weak Attempt to Win?

Rick Reilly

This actually happened. Your job is to decide whether it should have.

In a nine- and 10-year-old Pony league championship game in Bountiful, Utah, the Yankees lead the Red Sox by one run. The Sox are up in the bottom of the last inning, two outs, a runner on third. At the plate is the Sox' best hitter, a kid named Jordan. On deck is the Sox' worst hitter, a kid named Romney. He's a scrawny cancer survivor who has to take human growth hormone and has a shunt in his brain.

So, you're the coach: Do you intentionally walk the star hitter so you can face the kid who can barely swing?

Wait! Before you answer. . . . This is a league where everybody gets to bat, there's a four-runs-per-inning max, and no stealing until the ball crosses the plate. On the other hand, the stands are packed and it is the title game.

So . . . do you pitch to the star or do you lay it all on the kid who's been through hell already?

Yanks coach Bob Farley decided to walk the star.

Parents booed. The umpire, Mike Wright, thought to himself, Low-ball move. In the stands, Romney's eight-year-old sister cried. "They're picking on Romney!" she said. Romney struck out. The Yanks celebrated. The Sox moaned. The two coaching staffs nearly brawled.

And Romney? He sobbed himself to sleep that night.

"It made me sick," says Romney's dad, Marlo Oaks. "It's going after the weakest chick in the flock."

Farley and his assistant coach, Shaun Farr, who recommended the walk, say they didn't know Romney was a cancer survivor. "And even if I had," insists Farr, "I'd have done the same thing. It's just good baseball strategy."

Romney's mom, Elaine, thinks Farr knew. "Romney's cancer was in the paper when he met with President Bush," she says. That was thanks to the Make-A-Wish people. "And [Farr] coached Romney in basketball. I tell all his coaches about his condition."

She has to. Because of his radiation treatments, Romney's body may not produce enough of a stress-responding hormone if he is seriously injured, so he has to quickly get a cortisone shot or it could be life threatening. That's why he wears a helmet even in centerfield. Farr didn't notice?

The sports editor for the local Davis Clipper, Ben De Voe, ripped the Yankees' decision. "Hopefully these coaches enjoy the trophy on their mantle," De Voe wrote, "right next to their dunce caps."

Well, that turned Bountiful into Rancorful. The town was split—with some people calling for De Voe's firing and describing Farr and Farley as "great men," while others called the coaches "pathetic human beings." They "should be tarred and feathered," one man wrote to De Voe. Blogs and letters pages howled. A state house candidate called it "shameful."

What the Yankees' coaches did was within the rules. But is it right to put winning over compassion? For that matter, does a kid who yearns to be treated like everybody else want compassion?

"What about the boy who is dyslexic—should he get special treatment?" Blaine and Kris Smith wrote to the Clipper. "The boy who wears glasses—should he never be struck out? . . . NO! They should all play by the rules of the game."

The Yankees' coaches insisted that the Sox coach would've done the same thing. "Not only wouldn't I have," says Sox coach Keith Gulbransen, "I didn't. When their best hitter came up, I pitched to him. I especially wouldn't have done it to Romney."

Farr thinks the Sox coach is a hypocrite. He points out that all coaches put their worst fielder in right field and try to steal on the weakest catchers. "Isn't that strategy?" he asks. "Isn't that trying to win? Do we let the kid feel like he's a winner by having the whole league play easy on him? This isn't the Special Olympics. He's not retarded."

Me? I think what the Yanks did stinks. Strategy is fine against major leaguers, but not against a little kid with a tube in his head. Just good baseball strategy? This isn't the pros. This is: Everybody bats, one-hour games. That means it's about fun. Period.

What the Yankees' coaches did was make it about them, not the kids. It became their medal to pin on their pecs and show off at their barbecues. And if a fragile kid got stomped on the way, well, that's baseball. We see it all over the country—the over-caffeinated coach who watches too much Sports Center and needs to win far more than the kids, who will forget about it two Dove bars later.

By the way, the next morning, Romney woke up and decided to do something about what happened to him.

"I'm going to work on my batting," he told his dad. "Then maybe someday I'll be the one they walk." ▪

Questions for Discussion

1. What is the value conflict illustrated by the decision the coaches had to make in this case?

2. What are the various arguments given for and against the decision by the coaches, the opposing team coaches, the parents, the local journalists, and Rick Reilly?

3. What do you think the best call would be in a case like this? What does your decision say about your value priorities?

· ·

The following article illustrates a strong ethical dilemma that faces both campus newspapers and other forms of media. In this case, a murder was committed on campus and a newspaper photographer took pictures of the scene. The police wanted these pictures to help them identify the suspects; the photographer did not want to turn his work over to the police because he believed that would compromise the freedom of the press. This issue provides a good example of a conflict between libertarianism (freedom of the press) and utilitarianism (the police concern about promoting the general welfare by identifying and prosecuting criminals).

Staffer Gets Subpoenaed

Steve Logan

Police services Lt. Paul Lee delivered a subpoena to *Advocate* photographer Soren Hemmila Thursday morning to appear in Superior Court in Martinez at 1:30 P.M. Tuesday.

Lee delivered the subpoena through District Attorney William Clark and the San Pablo Police Department in connection with photographs taken of the scene after Christopher Robinson's murder on campus September 25.

Hemmila and the *Advocate* have refused to turn over unpublished photos, taken shortly after the murder, to the San Pablo Police Department.

California's shield law is designed to help news organizations protect sources and information from outside forces, including law enforcement agencies. The law also states a journalist cannot be held in contempt of court for refusing to turn over unpublished work.

Hemmila believes the photographs are protected by the shield law.

The *West County Times* reported Thursday that San Pablo police believe the photos could give them important information in prosecuting the case of the three suspects who have already been taken into custody and charged with Robinson's murder.

Hemmila said he arrived on the crime scene just as the police were putting up yellow tape. Among the photographs taken, but not published, [were] shots of the crowd in the background.

Hemmila said San Pablo Det. Mark Harrison first came to ask for the negatives "nicely," on Monday.

"I don't like being part of the investigation in this case," Hemmila said Thursday after receiving the subpoena. "I'm willing to do what it takes to protect our rights."

The subpoena said the photographs will be helpful to the police in three ways. Section one said the credibility of an eyewitness who commented in last Friday's story which ran in the *Advocate* needs to be evaluated.

Section two said the photographs will show the crime scene closer to the time of the shooting, which will allow the prosecution to evaluate the weight of the physical evidence which included expended casings at the scene.

Section three said the photographs may show whether the attack was "planned, a surprise attack, or a chance encounter that turned violent."

Hemmila said it would set a bad precedent if the *Advocate* turned over the photos.

"If we make it a [practice] to turn over the negatives to police agencies, they'll expect it in the future and they'll expect it from other publications.

"I don't want the public to think that journalists are part of law enforcement or acting in their behalf." ▪

Questions for Discussion

1. The subpoena argued that the photographs were necessary to the investigation because they may show whether the attack was "planned, a surprise attack, or a chance encounter that turned violent." If the knowledge gained from the photographs would show that the crime had been planned, would it justify turning them over?

2. Hemmila was concerned about setting a bad precedent if the *Advocate* turned over the photos. What would that precedent be and would you consider it a bad precedent?

3. Forty states and the District of Columbia have shield laws that protect journalists from releasing information and sources. In recent years, journalists have asked the U.S. Congress to create a national shield law to protect photographs, notes, and anonymous sources. Supporters of such a law are concerned that the ability to gather sensitive information would be weakened without this protection. Those opposed to such legislation are concerned about the need to find out about issues affecting national security, such as imminent terrorist threats; they are also concerned, in an age of bloggers, that almost anyone could call himself or herself a journalist and thus receive special protection.

Some news agencies frown upon the use of anonymous sources because almost any claim can be made by quoting them. The Associated Press policy allows the use of anonymous sources only when the material is information—not someone's opinion—that is essential to the report and when the source will give the information only if he or she is protected. In addition, the source must be reliable.

What do you think about national shield laws; what legislation, if any, is appropriate concerning this issue?

. . . .

The following is an interview from National Public Radio's *Weekend Edition*. The interviewees were Dr. Michael Wilkes and medical ethics specialist Dr. Miriam Shuchman. The interviewer is identified as Liane. They are discussing whether it is ethical to prescribe a placebo and pretend it is a healing drug if it actually makes the patient feel better.

National Public Radio

Liane: Michael, have you ever been tempted to be less than perfectly honest with a patient?

Michael: Absolutely. There's always that temptation, Liane. Telling the truth in medicine is one of the most difficult things to do. There is an issue that came up recently when another physician suggested that I prescribe a placebo, or sugar pill that had no biologic effects, for a patient. A 70-year-old man had just moved to town, and he came to see me to get a refill of a prescription for a sleeping pill that he'd been given for a long time. In fact, it turned out he's been taking the pill every night since his wife died several years ago. As I spoke with him, it became clear to me that he recognized that he was addicted to the sleeping medicine. In fact, he said he wanted to stop, but every time he tried to stop taking the medicine, he couldn't sleep and ended up taking a sleeping pill. Now, a doctor at the hospital suggested that I use a placebo. He said that he'd had great luck using this kind of placebo for exactly these types of addictions. The problem was that there was no way that I could use the placebo without deceiving the patient. So the issue here for me was whether doctors are justified in telling these little white lies in order to benefit the patient.

Liane: Miriam, as an ethics specialist, what do you say? What does medical ethics tell us is right in this situation?

Miriam: Well, I think the conflict for the doctor here is that he's really seeing two duties. One is not to lie to a patient, and the other is to always do what's beneficial for the patient, not to do harm. So, in this case, the doctor who suggested the placebo may think that it's most beneficial to prescribe the placebo, it won't have any side effects, and the little white lie he thinks is not as important.

Liane: So, should people be concerned that when they go to their doctor that the doctor might be prescribing a placebo?

Miriam: Absolutely not. First of all, the use of placebos in clinical practice is very rare. They're mostly used in research where people are told they're going to be receiving a placebo. And second, there are doctrines and policies around this. It's called informed consent, and what it means is that before a patient can agree to a given treatment or procedure, the doctor is obliged to inform them about the risks and benefits of that treatment, and most doctors are aware of that.

Michael: You know, it's probably worth mentioning here that experts feel that about 30 percent of the medicines that we currently prescribe really have no biologic activity. They work through the power of suggestion. Cough medicines are a great example of this sort of drug. Now that doesn't mean that cough medicines don't work. What I'm trying to suggest is that they work through an effect on the mind rather than on the body, say, on the diaphragm or in the lung tissue or muscles themselves. Anyway, I feel there are too many times when doctors aren't being truthful with patients because they feel they know what's best for the patient.

Liane: We talked about placebos, but what about lying? How often do doctors lie to their patients?

Miriam: Liane, I can't give you a statistic on that, but I don't think it happens very often. Doctors don't intentionally mislead their patients. But what does happen is that patients aren't given the information they really need to make decisions. Doctors don't give them the chance to ask the questions that would get them that information.

Liane: Michael, what happened to the man who was hooked on the sleeping pill?

Michael: Liane, we talked about it for a long time at the hospital. The bottom line was I chose not to use a placebo. The downside of that decision is that the man is still addicted to the medicine although I'm slowly weaning him off by using some behavior modification techniques.

Liane: Weekend Edition medical commentators Drs. Michael Wilkes and Miriam Shuchman. ∎

Questions for Discussion

1. What is the value conflict discussed by the doctors in this excerpt?

2. Do you believe there are times when a doctor should withhold the truth from a patient? Why or why not?

3. Dr. Miriam Shuchman said that doctors don't give patients the chance to ask the questions that would inform them more fully about their conditions. To what extent do you believe doctors should ensure that patients understand the seriousness of the illnesses they have?

In recent years, peanut allergies have been increasing and can have deadly consequences for those who are affected by them. As a result, school districts have been grappling with how to keep allergic children safe without imposing massive restrictions on nonallergic peanut butter lovers. The controversy has sparked debate in communities across the United States and Canada. The following article details how the problem is seen in one Connecticut school.

Schools' Peanut Bans Spark Backlash

Associated Press

When Terri Mauro posed the question, "What's so bad about peanut-butter bans?" on her Web site, she never expected the volume of cold and angry comments she received. "The responses are still coming in a year later," said Mauro, who considers blanket bans on peanut butter an acceptable measure to protect children with life-threatening allergies.

Peanut bans in schools often lead to a flurry of angry phone calls and letters to local newspapers. Some communities even circulate petitions asking school officials to change their minds.

"People are a little unhinged about this," said Mauro, who edits a Web site for parents with special needs children.

More schools than ever are banning peanuts and peanut products as the number of kids diagnosed with the potentially life-threatening allergy has climbed dramatically in recent years. While doctors try to figure out the reasons for the rise, the situation pits parents against each other and puts school districts in the middle.

Lisa Searles was shocked at how mad parents got in April 2007, when she asked the board of education in Seymour, Conn., to ban peanut butter at her son's elementary school.

"People were extremely rude," she said. "They just thought it was a ridiculous request."

People left nasty posts on local message boards. One online writer suggested ending the issue by putting all the allergic children in a room together and feeding them peanuts, Searles said.

When officials at Rock Creek Elementary School in O'Fallon, Mo., banned peanut butter, Jennifer Kaiser took a more reasoned approach. She attended a meeting and suggested the school find a compromise that would allow students to continue to pack peanut butter sandwiches and keep students with allergies safe.

"I thought there were better ways to handle it," the mother of two said. "As a community our job is to teach our kids to live in the world."

Banning peanuts, she said, "is not teaching children how to grow up in the real world."

Alternative to Food Bans

Parents opposed to the bans have an unlikely ally—an advocacy group for people with food allergies. The Food Allergy & Anaphylaxis Network in Fairfax, Va., recommends schools treat each student's allergy individually and adopt plans that emphasize continued vigilance rather than food bans.

More schools than ever are banning peanuts and peanut products as the number of kids diagnosed with the potentially life-threatening allergy has climbed dramatically in recent years.

"What we want is everyone always thinking there could be a possibility (of an allergic reaction) and be on guard for it," said the group's founder, Anne Munoz-Furlong.

Regardless of the group's position, a growing number of schools have implemented bans.

A recent survey of 1,174 districts by the Virginia-based School Nutrition Association found that 18 percent of schools had peanut bans in 2007, a 50 percent increase from two years earlier.

The increase in peanut bans corresponds to an increase in students diagnosed with peanut allergies. Between 1997 and 2002, the rates of peanut allergies in children under age five doubled, said Dr. Hugh A. Sampson, president of the American Academy of Allergy, Asthma & Immunology. Today, there are 400,000 school-age children with peanut allergies. Peanuts and some other foods can cause the body to go into anaphylactic shock, a life- threatening condition where a person's blood pressure drops and his or her airways narrow. The condition can normally be relieved with a dose of adrenaline, also called epinephrine. Children and adults with severe food allergies carry shots of epinephrine.

After the Seymour Board of Education shot down her request for a peanut ban, Searles has focused on other ways to keep 7-year-old Matthew safe at school, including trying to teach him to inject himself with adrenaline.

"I feel pretty confident," she said. "He's a smart kid."

The main worry for Searles, like many parents, is that her son would have a reaction without actually eating a peanut product. It's possible for Matthew to have a reaction from touching a table or utensil with peanut butter on it and then putting his hand into his mouth or rubbing his eyes, Searles said.

It's a legitimate concern, Sampson said. That's why he supports peanut bans in preschools and kindergarten classes, where students are prone to putting their hands in their mouths. As children grow older, he favors carefully cleaned peanut-free tables in the cafeteria, hand washing and other common sense precautions.

"As children get older and more responsible, you don't have to have anything like a ban," he said. "You want them to learn to deal with the situation."

Few children are at risk just by being in the same room with peanut butter, he said. No one has ever asked Janet Mitchell to ban peanuts from any of the schools in the Glynn County School District in Brunswick, Ga.

It's a move the district's culinary services coordinator would oppose even though her own son is allergic to peanuts.

"We don't ban peanut butter because we feel it is a staple among young children," said Mitchell, who works with families and school personnel to develop individualized plans for children with food allergies.

"You just can't monitor what's in every person's lunch pail," she said.

One District's Compromise

At the Mt. Diablo Unified School District outside of San Francisco, school officials have tried to reduce the risk of an allergic reaction by removing peanut products from the lunch menu, said Anna Fisher, a food services supervisor. The district still allows children to bring in peanut butter sandwiches and other peanut products.

The compromise reduces the amount of peanut butter in the lunchroom and allows children with allergies to buy lunch, Fisher said.

"I think it's been pretty successful," she said. "When people understand there's a life at risk, everyone starts to feel a little sympathy."

Sharon Terzian in Warwick, R.I., has a daughter with a life-threatening allergy to latex. She understands the concerns about peanut butter but disagrees with food bans.

"We know we can't put her in a bubble and send her to school," she said. "There's a personal responsibility for any kid." ■

Questions for Discussion

1. What is the basic value conflict represented by this article? What are the arguments of people on both sides of the conflict?

2. How could the values on both sides of this issue reflect one or more of the ethical systems discussed in this chapter?

3. What is your own viewpoint about the controversy represented by this article? What reasons do you have for your position?

4. If you were a PTA president at a school, how would you advise the administration and the parents to handle the situation?

· ·

A classic problem in higher education involves college admissions; in state universities, particularly, lawmakers and educators both struggle to create policies that balance admissions and include excellent students from traditionally high-achieving high schools while also rewarding excellent students from disadvantaged schools. In Texas, a law was created that gave anyone in the top 10 percent of his or her high school class automatic admission to any state university. The law was created when federal legislation prohibiting racial preferences was enacted.

Jay Brody, on his website collegeapps.about.com, articulates the conflict concerning the Texas statute: "While the law does provide opportunities to the disadvantaged, some believe that it works against applicants who attend strong high schools, take tough courses, but aren't in the top 10 percent of their classes. Others think that the law doesn't do enough, and that there are better ways to help disadvantaged applicants." The value priorities on both sides of this issue are discussed in the following article.

Texas College Admissions Law Under Fire

Kids in Top 10% Get in Automatically

Holly K. Hacker

DALLAS—It's been praised for keeping public universities in Texas racially diverse. It's been criticized for hurting talented students with less-than-stellar grades.

Now almost 10 years old, the Top 10% Law on college admissions still kindles emotion and debate. Three bills seeking to limit or kill the law have been filed for the January legislative session.

The law is simple: Texas students in the top 10% of their high school class are automatically admitted to any public university in the state. Legislators passed it in 1997 after a federal court effectively banned racial preferences in college admissions.

It ensures that every high school can send students to the state's premier campuses. Otherwise, some lawmakers worried, minority students at high schools lacking strong college prep programs could be shut out.

But critics say the law is too simple and that it's wrong to admit students based solely on class rank, especially those from highly competitive high schools where tough course loads and lots of extracurricular activities are the norm.

With black and Hispanic students still underrepresented at the University of Texas and Texas A&M, critics question whether the law has worked as intended. And they note that a 2003 Supreme Court ruling again allowed universities to consider race in admissions, making the Top 10% Law moot.

What the Two Sides Say

Attempts to restrict or repeal the law have failed. Supporters of the new bills hope to prevail this time.

"If at first you don't succeed, try and try again," said Rep. Beverly Woolley, a Houston Republican who has filed a bill to throw out the Top 10% Law.

"A lot of kids in my district, they go to really tough schools . . . yet the competition is so strong," Woolley said. "They're really bright students, but they're not in the top 10%."

Others say the law needs to remain.

"I haven't seen a change I'd support yet," said Sen. Royce West, a Dallas Democrat who authored the law and has defended it over the years.

West said the law rewards students with a strong work ethic and that it has helped achieve racial and geographic diversity. The University of Texas and Texas A&M University draw students from more high schools across Texas since the law took effect.

"It's an opportunity for urban Texans and rural Texans—for all Texans—to make sure they have the ability to attend the flagships in the state," West said.

Problems for School

The University of Texas at Austin is Exhibit A for those seeking changes. In 1998, 37% of University of Texas freshmen were admitted under the law. This year, it's 66%. Count only in-state students, and the number edges up to 71%.

Campus leaders say those students have done well, and they don't want the law thrown out. But they do seek some kind of cap.

"It's a capacity problem for us," University of Texas President William Powers said. "We're admitting over 70% of our Texas students on one criterion. . . . We just need more flexibility."

The law has overwhelmed a few University of Texas programs, such as the College of Business. The program is so popular that it can't admit every Top 10% student who applies. And to leave room for others, there's a 75% cap on the number of business spaces for Top 10% students.

Because students still have to apply to individual colleges, admissions officers keep busy.

"We still have to read 17,000 applications," said Gary Lavergne, who heads admissions research at the University of Texas at Austin. And with the law, he said, "We are very sensitive to the competition for the spaces that are left. We have to be very careful, and we are."

Texas A&M also gets lots of Top 10% students, though less than the University of Texas. This year, 44% of freshmen were admitted to Texas A&M under the law.

The Other Students

University of Texas officials say that, contrary to what some people think, Top 10% students do as well academically as other students. Also, many parents believe that if their child doesn't get into University of Texas under the law, they're shut out. Not true.

"If a Texas resident has a completed application on time, we don't say no. We offer other options," said Bruce Walker, admissions director. For instance, students can start at another University of Texas System school and, with high enough grades, transfer to the University of Texas at Austin. At Texas A&M, students who don't make the top 10% still get in automatically if they finish in the top quarter of their high school class with high SAT or ACT scores. ▪

Questions for Discussion

1. What values are the Texas legislators attempting to reconcile with their state college admissions policies?

2. How would you define the value conflict between those who support the Texas law and those who oppose it?

3. What do you believe are the most important factors for college admissions officers to consider when they put together a freshman class?

4. Should the college admissions factors be the same for private and public institutions, or should public colleges have different considerations? What are your reasons for your conclusions on this issue?

. . . .

Ideas for Writing or Speaking

1. See if your college has a code of ethics about cheating and plagiarizing. If so, write about this code; take a position on the principles given (agree or disagree with them) and give support for your conclusions. If your college does not have a code of ethics, write one and justify (give reasons for) each of the principles you include.

2. "The Legacy I'd Like to Leave"

   Imagine that you are 80 years old. Your son, daughter, niece, nephew, husband, wife, friend, or coworker is making a speech about you at a party held in your honor. In this speech, he or she mentions your fine qualities and the things you have accomplished in your life. He or she talks about the special traits you have that are treasured by those who know and love you.

   Write the speech, using this format:

   a. List the personal qualities you'd want to have and how they have been specifically evidenced in your life.

   b. List the accomplishments you will have achieved. Again, be specific in your descriptions.

   c. Then analyze what you would need to do (either internally or externally, or both) to merit that kind of tribute in your old age. What ideal values would have to become real for you? What choices would you have to make about your career, your personal life, and your priorities?

3. Write an essay in which you take a position (agree or disagree) on one of the following quotes. Support your conclusion about the quote with specific reasons.

   a. "To educate a person in mind and not in morals is to educate a menace to society." President Theodore Roosevelt

   b. "In looking for people to hire, you look for three qualities: integrity, intelligence, and energy. And if they don't have the first, the other two will kill you." Warren Buffet

   c. "The great secret of morals is love." Percy Bysshe Shelley, *A Defence of Poetry* (1821)

   d. "We must never delude ourselves into thinking that physical power is a substitute for moral power, which is the true sign of national greatness." Adlai Stevenson, speech, Hartford, Connecticut, September 18, 1952

   e. "Can ethics be taught? At some point in life, ethics must be taught. People are not born with innate desires to be ethical or to be concerned with the welfare of others." Dr. Katherine Smith and Dr. L. Murray Smith

   f. "I believe we are the sum total of all that we do, i.e., what we 'do' is who we 'are.' This is true because as adults we make deliberate choices in our actions. Therefore, our actions describe our inner selves, what sacrifices we're willing to make, what evil we're willing to perpetrate. It is with awareness that we persist in negative, ugly, and destructive deeds in one or more areas. Our actions are the blueprint of our character." Dr. Laura Schlessinger

   g. "When the Nazis came to power, I looked to the universities that prided themselves upon their intellectual freedom, and they failed me. I looked to the German press, which prided itself on the freedom of the press, and it failed me. Until at last the churches stood alone, and that for which I once had little regard earned my respect." Albert Einstein, after World War II

   h. "To sin by silence when they should protest makes cowards of men." Abraham Lincoln

   i. "The purpose of ethics in business is to direct business men and women to abide by a code of conduct that facilitates, if not encourages, public confidence in their products and services." Dr. Katherine Smith and Dr. L. Murray Smith

   j. "To know what is right and not to do it is the worst cowardice." Confucius

4. *Part A:* List some values you hold. These can be character traits such as honesty, fairness, and compassion. You can also list concerns such as peace, freedom of speech, family ties, ethnic identity, health, wealth, competition, or cooperation.

   To isolate some of your values, consider the professions that interest you. If you want to be a high school coach, you may value sports, young people, and/or education. If you want to be an artist, you may value beauty and creativity.

   Also, consider how you spend your free time. Different values may be expressed by those who spend time reading science fiction, shopping, volunteering at a nursing home, socializing, or working on a political campaign.

   Try to list at least three values reflected in your life.

   Part B: Next choose a controversial issue and take a position on this issue; your position should reflect a value you hold. Examples of controversial topics with a value dimension include capital punishment, surrogate parenting, homelessness, nuclear power, active and passive euthanasia, socialized medicine, welfare, immigration, and environmental policies. You might look up issues that are currently being considered by the Supreme Court; many of the court's rulings establish the precedence of one value over another.

After you have chosen an issue and taken a position reflecting your value, arrange your ideas in the following manner:

a. Give several reasons to support your position. Give both moral and fact-based reasons. Use examples and evidence to strengthen your reasons.

b. State some good reasons why you think a person might believe the opposite of what you believe. For example, if you are against compulsory drug testing for athletes, state why someone might argue in favor of it.

c. Conclude by indicating if and how your initial belief was changed by considering the opposite viewpoint. Or, conclude by stating why your initial belief was not changed, despite your fair consideration of the arguments against your belief.

Films for Analysis and Discussion

Many film, theatrical, and television plots involve different value assumptions, priorities, and conflicts. When you go to a movie or theater, or watch a television program, notice the value conflicts that are shown through the plot and expressed by the various characters. Here are a few examples.

The Fighter (2010, R)

The Fighter is based on the true story of boxer Micky Ward and his half-brother, a former boxing star turned crack addict. As Micky's career takes off, he must make a series of value-based decisions concerning his girlfriend, his family members, and his career; the consequences of each decision weigh heavily on him when he has a chance to compete for the world welterweight championship.

The Dark Knight (2008, PG 13)

The Dark Knight involves the agonizing decision of Batman (Bruce Wayne) to save either the woman he loves or the man who can save Gotham City. The decision and the consequences that follow provide a dramatic example of personal ethical dilemmas.

Million Dollar Baby (2004, PG-13)

This film follows the dreams of Maggie (Hilary Swank) to become a boxing contender under the tutelage of Frank (Clint Eastwood), the only man she thinks can help her realize her dream. Through pure determination and negotiation, Maggie breaks the hardened Frank and convinces him not only to train her but also to manage her career as a female boxing champion. The film is full of inner conflicts, involving both values and ethics, for each character we encounter. Initially, Frank is conflicted by the prospect of training a "girl boxer," afraid she is too old and will not only lose every fight she's in, but also get seriously hurt in the process. As the film progresses, Frank faces an unsettling ethical dilemma that will change the course of both Maggie's and Frank's lives forever.

Similar Films and Classics

Sister Act (1993, PG)

In this film, Whoopie Goldberg plays Deloris Van Cartier, a lounge singer trying to make it big. She has many decisions to make that involve value conflicts, including whether to stay with her mobster boyfriend, who is still married, whether to enter a witness protection program after she witnesses a murder, whether to become involved in a convent choir, and whether to leave the choir before an important performance.

The Mighty Ducks (1992, PG)

This film reveals, in the opening segment, a painful event that shaped the life of Gordon Bombay, who has since become a successful lawyer. After a charge of drunk driving, Gordon is assigned to work with young players, and the experience forces him to examine the values he learned at a young age. Note especially how he is given an opportunity to display the congruence between his real values and ideal values toward the end of the film.

Do the Right Thing (1989, R)

In this acclaimed Spike Lee film, which takes place primarily on one hot day in Brooklyn, many different characters represent specific beliefs and values. Note how their various beliefs affect their behavior in relationships and the decisions they make.

Chariots of Fire (1981, PG)

This film about British sprinters competing in the 1924 Olympics is filled with value conflicts. Eric Little has to decide whether to compete or devote himself completely to his missionary goals; he also has to decide whether to compete on a Sunday, a day that he holds sacred. The Olympic committee has to decide whether or not to change the time of the race to accommodate Eric, the top contender for the 100-meter race. In addition, a teammate has to decide whether to let Eric compete in his place in the 400-meter slot.

The Fountainhead (1949)

This classic film, based on the book by Ayn Rand, concerns an idealistic architect who must decide between his artistic vision and the compromises necessary to sustain work in his field.

3

Reality Assumptions

It's Eleven O'Clock. Do You Know
Where Your Assumptions Are?

A critical thinker understands that people have different assumptions about
the world that form the basis of opinions; he or she also examines these assumptions.

A critical thinker understands basic patterns of deductive reasoning.

A critical thinker uses deductive reasoning to test logic, discover truth,
make decisions, combat prejudice, and argue constructively.

Our viewpoints are based on our assumptions about reality.

THIS CHAPTER WILL COVER

- Reality assumptions
- Patterns of deductive reasoning
- The use of deductive reasoning to test logic, discover truth, make decisions, combat prejudice, and argue constructively

Read on **mythinkinglab.com**

Listen on **mythinkinglab.com**

We learned in the last chapter that when an issue involves a conflict of values, we need to examine the value assumptions and priorities that are foundational to the argument under consideration; in other words, there is no point in bringing in evidence to support a point of view until we address the clashing values.

If someone believes that legalizing drugs is morally wrong, that person will probably not be moved by a lot of statistics that show that we could save money and cut down on crime by legalizing drugs. Someone with a strong value assumption on an issue is not usually swayed by a discussion of the practical benefits of a policy or an action that contradicts his or her values. When a discussion neglects to consider conflicting value assumptions on both sides of an issue, stalemates occur, and new and improved evidence does little to help these stalemates.

The critical thinker who wants to argue on a value-saturated issue needs to clearly and directly address the conflict in values and try to persuade those who believe differently to rethink their value assumptions on that issue.

Reality Assumptions

As we discussed in Chapter 2, another foundational aspect to any argument is the underlying assumptions about reality that the various advocates for an issue hold. **Reality assumptions** are beliefs about what is true and factual about the world, and so they are sometimes called *factual assumptions* or *descriptive assumptions*. They are based on the unique experiences and education of each individual. Reality assumptions are sometimes directly stated by a writer or speaker, but they are usually implied.

The fascinating element of assumptions is that they are often hidden to the people arguing for different conclusions. Finding hidden assumptions in arguments is like reading or watching mysteries; you accumulate clues from what people say and then make guesses about the important things they believe but aren't directly *stating*. For example, consider the different reality assumptions in the following

reality assumptions Assumptions about what is true and factual that are sometimes stated and sometimes implied; these assumptions are often taken for granted.

excerpt from an article about the usefulness of standardized tests for predicting college success:

> George Mason University professor and radio commentator Walter Williams has stated that high school students should not apply to colleges where average SAT scores are at least 200 points higher than theirs.[1] While Williams does not assume that the SAT and ACT tests are necessarily reflective of a student's intelligence, he does assume that they signify less preparation for the literary and mathematical demands of college. Other educators hold very different assumptions. Muhlenberg College does not require SAT or ACT scores and [its] dean of admissions and financial aid Christopher Hooker-Haring believes that the SAT may merely predict the degree of struggle for first-year college students. He lists other qualities that the SAT does not measure that will help a student survive the adjustment of the first year, including "work ethic, determination, motivation, love of learning, and grit."

Let's look at Walter Williams' argument, using the Toulmin model that was introduced in Chapter 2. His *claim* is that high school students should not apply to colleges at which average SAT scores are 200 points higher than theirs. His *reason* is that the students will not likely succeed based on the *warrant* (the unstated reality assumption) that the SAT and ACT scores are accurate predictions of how well students are prepared for the literary and mathematical demands of such colleges.

Christopher Hooker-Haring, on the other hand, would offer the *claim* that students should not use standardized test scores as a measure of future success. His *reason* is that the tests may predict only the degree of struggle for first-year students. His *warrant* (reality assumption) is that what will get students through the challenges of the freshman year are their character qualities that are not measured by the tests.

Note that both educators share similar values—the value of education and the value of students surviving the first year successfully. Their differences are about what actually will help students succeed. They have different beliefs about what is true and factual for freshman students; these beliefs are their reality assumptions.

Reminder

An *assumption* can be defined as a belief, usually taken for granted, that is based on the experience, observations, or desires of an individual or group. Conflicts in value assumptions address the questions "What is right?" and "What should we do or be?"; conflicts in reality assumptions address the questions "What is true and factual?" and "What do we take for granted or as a given fact?" Critical thinkers need to be aware of the assumptions that are basic to arguments they are hearing or making.

❋ Explore on **mythinkinglab.com**

The College Board, creator of the SAT test, aims to assure students and admissions officers that their tests are useful predictors of college success. In 2005, the Board added a writing component, assuming that the additional test would give students and colleges better expectations of student ability to do college work. To test their reality assumption, the Board did a study of the effect of the additional test

---

[1] Jay Matthews, *Washington Post*, Tuesday, April 2, 2002, p. A07.

and found that scores from the new writing section are somewhat better at predicting grades in the first year of college than the two other SAT sections.[2]

When two people or two groups hold different assumptions, they need to stop and examine the assumptions that frame their arguments rather than continuing to build arguments on those assumptions. As hidden assumptions are brought to the surface, light is shed on the different positions taken on an issue. Then "all the cards are on the table," and people have the opportunity to test and modify assumptions or to see more clearly why they have a strong conviction about an assumption.

Skill

A critical thinker examines the reality assumptions of self and others that form the foundations of arguments.

Detecting Reality Assumptions

> In times of rapid change, a strategic failure is often caused by an incorrect or false assumption.
>
> Dr. Mike Teng

One reason that some assumptions are hidden from us is that they are so deeply ingrained; they may surface only when we come across a person or a group that holds different assumptions. We may be confronted with a different set of assumptions than our own when we are involved in a classroom debate. Because assumptions are often based on what we have experienced in our own environments, they may surface when we are in unfamiliar situations, such as when we travel to a new place and are exposed to a different culture.

Most North Americans assume that if an interview or meeting is set for 1:00, then the arrival time should be slightly before 1:00, but people from other cultures may view time differently. The expected arrival time could be anywhere between 1:00 and 3:00 for members of some cultures. Because of the differing assumptions across cultures, North Americans who are sent abroad by their organizations are often given training about the assumptions commonly made in the country they will be visiting.

When traveling to another country, we can be sensitive to what is expected of us as visitors and act accordingly. In defending our conclusions on an issue, however, we need to bring the differing assumptions to light so that the discussion is clear and rational.

Examples of Differing Reality Assumptions

- Some people assume that anyone can change and therefore any prisoner can be rehabilitated. Other people assume that there are individuals who are "career criminals" with little hope of being rehabilitated.
- Some people assume that the way to increase employment is to lower taxes. Other people assume that the way to increase employment is to establish more government programs that would provide jobs for the unemployed.

---

[2] "Study: SAT Scores Predict Academic Success," *The Seattle Times,* http://seattletimes.nwsource.com/html/nationworld/2008003426_sat18.html.

- Some people assume that our lives are shaped by circumstances. Others believe that our lives are primarily shaped by our attitudes and decisions.
- Some people assume that men and women are essentially alike. Other people assume that men and women have significant psychological differences.
- Some people assume that early academic pre-school education prepares children for elementary school. Other people assume that play is the best preparation for elementary school.
- Some people assume that alcoholism is a condition largely created by genetic factors. Other people assume that alcoholism is a result of lifestyle choices.

Other assumptions involve differing definitions of words:

- One person assumes that *love* is an emotion that may or may not be permanent. Another person assumes that *love* is a commitment that is not based on emotional changes.
- One person assumes that *censorship* is any restriction on speech or writing; another assumes *censorship* to mean a complete banning of ideas or publications.

In an article on the dispute among obesity experts over the definition of fat entitled "Millions Suddenly Became Fat Without Gaining Any Weight," Steve Rubenstein writes:

> The United States defines a fat person as anyone with a "body mass index," or BMI, of 27.6 or higher. The World Health Organization defines a fat person as anyone with a BMI of 25 or higher. As a result of these different definitional assumptions, Americans don't actually weigh any more, according to the latest numbers. But, in keeping with the leaner international threshold for fatness, more of them are fat.[3]

Reminder

Individuals continually make assumptions about reality. We need to examine the assumptions we make and try to detect the assumptions that others make. When we have a foundational disagreement about reality assumptions, we should discuss those assumptions before we discuss any arguments built upon them. For example, if we believe that people can be rehabilitated, we must understand why we believe that and be able to defend our basic belief. We also need to understand why someone else would believe that people cannot be rehabilitated.

✳ Explore on **mythinkinglab.com**

When we realize that an argument involves differing reality assumptions, we need to search for evidence that will prove or disprove the assumptions. For example, the body mass index (BMI) index discussed earlier was long considered the best measure for predicting problems caused by obesity. A more recent long-term study, conducted in part by the University of Georgia, disputes that assumption. In this study, researchers found a more reliable indicator for medical problems in adulthood.

[3] Steve Rubenstein, "Millions Suddenly Became Fat Without Gaining Any Weight," *San Francisco Chronicle*, October 11, 1996, p. A6.

"We wanted to identify which clinical measure of childhood body composition best predicts long-term cardio-metabolic health risks," said study lead author Michael Schmidt, an assistant professor in the UGA department of kinesiology, part of the College of Education. "We were able to compare a wide range of body composition measures and found that waist circumference seems to be the best measure to predict subsequent risk."

Schmidt said that the findings should help clinicians measuring body composition identify children most at risk for future health problems in a simple and cost effective manner.

The study used data collected as part of a 20-year follow up of 2,188 Australians who participated in a national childhood health and fitness survey in 1985, when aged 7 to 15 years. As adults, they then attended one of 34 study clinics held across Australia between 2004 and 2006, where they underwent a range of health and fitness assessments. Most prior studies of the long-term consequences of childhood obesity have used the body mass index (BMI), a ratio of weight to height, as the primary measure of childhood obesity, Schmidt explained. While useful, BMI doesn't distinguish between fat and non-fat weight or indicate where the fat is located. In contrast, waist circumference measurements capture the amount of fat located centrally in the body, a location that prior studies have shown to be particularly detrimental to cardio-metabolic health. "This likely explains the stronger associations we observed between waist circumference and adult metabolic syndrome," added Schmidt.[4]

Much research is conducted to determine whether commonly held assumptions are true or are simply persistent myths. For example, many people assume that going outside with wet hair may help cause a cold, even though most medical experts have long maintained that colds are caused by a virus and not by wet or cold conditions. According to Dr. Kristie Leong,

There's no proof that going outside with wet hair—even in the winter— brings on a cold. For that matter, getting your feet or body chilled won't sentence you to the common cold either—at least according to most research.

The idea that wet hair causes a cold when the temperatures drop was tested in several studies, including one published in the esteemed *New England Journal of Medicine*. The results soundly dispelled the idea that having wet hair, wearing wet clothes, or getting chilled increases the risk of a cold. Still, not even all experts agree—despite the research.

Colds are caused by the common cold virus, usually a rhinovirus or a coronavirus. The common cold is highly contagious and easily transmitted when people work and play in close quarters. Since people spend more time indoors when the temperatures drop, colds are more common in the winter. Thus, it may seem that going outside with wet hair in cold weather was what brought on a cold, when, in actuality, the cold victim was already carrying the virus and would have developed symptoms anyway.[5]

[4] Michael Schmidt, "Study: Waist Circumference, Not BMI, Is Best Predictor of Future Cardiovascular Risk in Children," http://www.eurekalert.org/pub_releases/2010-10/uog-swc101410.php.

[5] Kristie Leong, "Does Wet Hair Cause a Cold?" http://healthmad.com/conditions-and-diseases/does-wet-hair-cause-a-cold/#ixzz12NvAP2WU.

Extinct Fox Not Extinct, Found in California

Zachary Shahan

The assumption that the Sierra Nevada red fox is extinct was recently discovered to be false.

Fox Thought to Be Extinct Found in California

Three weeks ago, U.S. Forest Service biologists thought they found a fox in the mountains of central California that is supposed to be extinct.

The biologists looked to experts at the University of California, Davis to confirm this finding. Sure enough, the fox they stumbled across was this thought-to-be-extinct fox, a Sierra Nevada red fox (*Vulpes vulpes necator*).

How the Sierra Nevada Red Fox Was Found and Identified

Photographs of the fox were taken by a Forest Service trail camera near Sonora Pass and showed the fox biting a bait bag of chicken scraps. The bait bag was shipped to two expert wildlife genetics researchers working in the UC Davis Veterinary Genetics Laboratory, Ben Sacks and Mark Statham. Regarding these researchers, UC Davis writes: "Since 2006, they have radically altered our understanding of red foxes in California, supplying information crucial to conservation efforts."

Analyzing DNA from saliva they scraped off the tooth punctures on the bag, Sacks and Statham confirmed that the spotted fox was definitely a Sierra Nevada red fox.

"This is the most exciting animal discovery we have had in California since the wolverine in the Sierra two years ago—only this time, the unexpected critter turned out to be home-grown, which is truly big news," Sacks said. (The wolverine found in the Sierra Nevada "was an immigrant from Wyoming," UC Davis reported.)

California Red Fox Research and Findings

Sacks and his colleagues are leaders in California red fox research. Some of their key research and findings are as follows:

Four years ago, Sacks began analyzing California red fox DNA collected from scat, hair and saliva from live animals, and skin and bones from museum specimens. Until then, the expert consensus was that any red fox in the Central Valley and coastal regions of the state was a descendant of Eastern red foxes (*V.v. fulva*) brought here in the 1860s for hunting and fur farms.

Sacks and his colleagues have confirmed that red fox populations in coastal lowlands, the San Joaquin Valley and Southern California were indeed introduced from the eastern United States (and Alaska). But they have also shown that:

- There are native California red foxes still living in the Sierra Nevada.
- The native red foxes in the Sacramento Valley (*V.v. patwin*) are a subspecies genetically distinct from those in the Sierra.
- The two native California subspecies, along with Rocky Mountain and Cascade red foxes (*V.v. macroura* and *V.v. cascadensis*), formed a single large western population until the end of the last ice age, when the three mountain subspecies followed receding glaciers up to mountaintops, leaving the Sacramento Valley red fox isolated at low elevation.

With so many species going extinct these days, it is great to see one "coming back to life." ■

Here are some other examples of new information used to challenge common assumptions:

- It has often been assumed that older students who commute and work off campus might be at a disadvantage. However, a recent study by Carol A. Lundberg, professor of education and organizational leadership at Azusa Pacific University challenges that assumption. Her study found that older students are not negatively affected by spending less time on their campuses. They are as academically successful as traditional-age students, and their social needs are met through the workplace and through other social connections. Also, they tend to have better relationships with faculty and administrators.[6]

- People who buy gift cards may be unpleasantly surprised when their reality assumptions about the value of the cards prove false. For years, retailers were able to charge monthly fees for the cards, much to the surprise of consumers:

> Last Christmas, Norman Vinson bought his wife Arlene several $50 gift cards at the Brea Mall. The cards seemed easy enough to use, but when she tried to pay for $109 worth of lingerie at a mall department store with two of the cards and $9 in cash, her cards were declined because they weren't worth enough. The couple called the toll-free number on the back of the cards to check the balances. They learned they were being charged a $2.50 monthly service fee for not using the entire value of the cards within six months. And the phone calls, it turned out, cut the cards' value further by 50 cents each. "Here's the whole thing about the whole shootin' match: You go in and buy a $50 gift card, and you assume you're buying someone a certificate that they can use for $50," said Vinson. That's not necessarily true, he has learned. . . . Gift cards can come with many strings attached.[7]

Recently, the Federal government, under the Credit Card Accountability Responsibility and Disclosure Act of 2009, enacted laws removing many hidden fees, but consumers still need to check out the information about a gift card rather than assuming that the value of the card will be the same as the purchase value:

> "This is definitely a step in the right direction," said Michelle Jun, a staff attorney at Consumers Union, a consumer advocacy group. "We still urge consumers who receive gift cards to use them fast and use them all."
>
> Consumers should use gift cards quickly to avoid inactivity fees and to ensure that the card is not forgotten, she said. There is also the possibility that a retailer could go bankrupt, she added, in which case its gift cards become worthless.
>
> Jun said consumer advocates had urged the Fed to include a cap on the monthly fees issuers are allowed to charge after a year of inactivity.
>
> At present, the amount varies widely from state to state. In California, for example, issuers can charge up to $2 a month, while Connecticut laws prohibit the monthly fee altogether, Jun said.[8]

[6] Carol A. Lundberg, "The Influence of Time—Limitations, Faculty, and Peer Relationships on Adult Student Learning: A Causal Model," *The Journal of Higher Education*, volume 74, November/December, pp. 665–688, 2003.

[7] Lisa Munoz, "Gift Cards May Bite Recipient," *Orange County Register*, September 22, 2003.

[8] Ben Rooney, "Gift Card Fees: Fed Cracks Down," http://money.cnn.com/2010/03/23/news/economy/gift_card_regulations/index.htm.

- Psychologists often disagree about the major influences shaping human behavior. One columnist refutes the assumptions of some modern schools of thought as follows:

> Post-Freudian psychology posits that every human behavior has an antecedent, and that it was acquired (learned) by way of some social interaction. If this is true, it follows that a child's behavior is shaped largely by how he/she is "parented." This is fiction. Nonetheless, it has had a powerful effect on today's parents, and especially mothers, many of whom live on the razor's edge of a gnawing fear that every bad thing their children do reflects upon them, that it "tells" of some dreadful parental (most likely maternal) sin of omission or commission.
>
> The flip side of this is that today's parents—again, especially moms—are convinced that their children's accomplishments are evidence they are doing many constant good works in their children's lives. . . . Don't get me wrong. The way a child is raised, the quality of discipline and love he receives from those who care about him, makes a difference, but it is not the whole story. The fact that every child has a mind of his own means not only that right and proper parenting does not produce a child who will not misbehave, but also that right and proper discipline may not cure misbehavior. In other words, sometimes the best discipline does not "work," even when parents work diligently at it. This is evidence not of some biological dysfunction, but of a dysfunction that is even more fundamental to being human—the will to rebel, to prove that no one is qualified to tell you what to do. . . . There's nature, and there's nurture, and then there's free will, and the most powerful of the three is definitely the latter.[9]

- Sometimes politicians make assumptions that are insulting to their constituents. In one election, candidates offended an audience of female researchers by continually referring to what they would do about breast cancer if they were elected to office: "Scientists are repelled by what they see as the condescending assumption in these campaigns; that mentioning breast cancer is a sure way to win the female vote."[10]

We frequently revisit and question assumptions about the past when they turn out to have been harmful. In a remarkable interview given by Fidel Castro, the long-time communist ruler of Cuba, he stated that his policies did not serve his country well:

> The revolutionary leader told a visiting American journalist and a U.S.-Cuba policy expert that the island's state-dominated system is in need of change, a rare comment on domestic affairs from a man who has taken pains to steer clear of local issues since illness forced him to step down as president four years ago.
>
> The fact that things are not working efficiently on this cash-strapped Caribbean island is hardly news. Fidel's brother Raul, the country's president, has said the same thing repeatedly. But the blunt assessment by the father of Cuba's 1959 revolution is sure to raise eyebrows.

[9] John Rosemond, "Living with Children," *All About Kids Parenting Magazine,* June 18, 2003.
[10] Gina Kolata, "Vying for the Breast Vote," *New York Times,* November 3, 1996.

Jeffrey Goldberg, a national correspondent for *The Atlantic* magazine, asked Castro if Cuba's economic system was still worth exporting to other countries, and Castro replied: "The Cuban model doesn't even work for us anymore."[11]

The Importance of Examining Assumptions

In our age of accelerated research in many fields, a number of ideas that were once generally accepted have come into question. Researchers frequently discover that what was assumed to be factual might not be true; it may have been true at one time, or it may never have been true at all. When we build arguments on assumptions that are not grounded in truth, our arguments are faulty, and the actions we recommend will not achieve our desired ends. We may sound logical and reasonable, but we lead others and ourselves astray. Conversely, when we keep current with research from reliable sources, we are able to make the most effective decisions.

For example, a number of years ago, officials in King County in the state of Washington found that, contrary to their assumptions, they had almost twice as many suicides as homicides in their county:

> The Seattle–King County Department of Public Health reported that suicide is a major public health problem, the second most common cause of death among adults ages 20–24. In recent years, the suicide rate has continued to climb in that county. . . . The Seattle-King County medical examiner stated that most people assume homicide is a bigger problem than suicide because suicides are rarely reported by the media.[12]

A common assumption has been made that the often rainy weather in the Pacific Northwest contributed to the suicides, but a public health study found that, instead, the highest number of suicides were committed in July. The real causes of suicide were determined to be, first and foremost, terminal or chronic illness. Other factors included a decline in the quality of life, unemployment, marital and financial problems, and relationship problems.

Researchers and investigative reporters often uncover questionable assumptions such as the ones discovered in King County. When we examine assumptions with the goal of discerning what is true, we can take more useful action. Some of the reality assumptions that were discovered to be *false* about King County include:

1. Homicide is more common than suicide.
2. The area's gloomy weather contributes to high suicide rates.

In this case, supervisors considering the research from the Seattle–King County Department of Public Health may decide to put more funding into preventing suicides instead of concentrating their efforts mainly on homicides. In so doing, they can focus on fighting the most common causes of suicide. Rather than looking for antidotes to gloomy weather, they can support efforts to control pain for those who suffer from terminal or chronic illness; also, county officials can offer more services to people who are unemployed or struggling with financial and relationship problems.

[11] Three Sonorans, "Fidel Castro Says Communism Doesn't Work in Cuba," http://tucsoncitizen.com/three-sonorans/2010/09/09/fidel-castro-says-communism-doesnt-work-in-cuba.

[12] Jennifer Bjorhus and Peyton Whitely, "New Report Debunks Myths on Suicide," *Seattle Times*, February 15, 1996.

> # Reminder
> Assumptions should be examined in the light of the best information available; then decisions can be optimally helpful and productive.
>
> ✳ Explore on **mythinkinglab.com**

Myths and Facts About Suicide

Myth: People who talk about suicide don't kill themselves.

Fact: Eight out of ten suicides have spoken about their intent before killing themselves.

Myth: People who kill themselves really want to die.

Fact: Most people who commit suicide are confused about whether or not they want to live or die. Suicide is often a cry for help that ends in tragedy.

Myth: Once the depression seems to be lifting, would-be suicides are out of danger.

Fact: At such a time, they are most vulnerable to a reversal: something can go wrong to make the person even worse than before. The person's apparent calm may be due to having already decided on suicide.

Myth: When people talk about suicide, you should get their minds off it, and change the subject.

Fact: Take them seriously; listen with care; give them the chance to express themselves; offer whatever help you can. ∎

Another example of the need to examine assumptions relates to the use of prescription medicine. Because of the availability of numerous new medications and treatments, doctors and pharmacists have to consider more factors in treating patients than they may have in the past. Because harmful, and even fatal, side effects can occur when two different drugs are prescribed to the same patient, pharmacists have to make judgment calls about whether to assume that doctors know about interactions between the drugs they have prescribed.

One investigative report warns consumers not to assume that pharmacy computer systems that check for drug interactions are always accurate. Dr. David Kessler, past commissioner of the U.S. Food and Drug Administration (FDA), is quoted as saying, "It is simply untenable. . . to walk into a pharmacy and receive a bottle of pills and no other information. It is not good patient care."[13]

To prevent patients from making harmful assumptions, pharmacists now ask patients to wait for consultations about the medications they are receiving.

The FDA advocates increased communication between consumers and health care providers to avoid harmful assumptions concerning prescriptions:

> The large number of drugs on the market, combined with the common use of multiple medications, makes the risk for drug interactions significant. "Consumers need to tell doctors what they're taking and ask questions, and health professionals could do a better job at trying to get the information they want," says Timothy Tracy, Ph.D., a professor in the school of

[13] Susan Headden, "Danger at the Drugstore," *U.S. News and World Report,* August 26, 1996.

pharmacy at the University of Minnesota, Twin Cities campus. He says there is a pervasive attitude that the term "medications" only refers to prescription drugs. "So rather than asking patients what medications they take, doctors should make the questions specific: 'Are you taking any over-the-counter medication? Are you taking any herbal treatments or vitamins?'"[14]

The FDA also advises consumers to be wary of common reality assumptions concerning dietary supplements, including common vitamins. On the FDA website, the following checklist is given:

Check your assumptions about the following:

- #1 Questionable Assumption—

"Even if a product may not help me, it at least won't hurt me." It's best not to assume that this will always be true. When consumed in high enough amounts, for a long enough time, or in combination with certain other substances, all chemicals can be toxic, including nutrients, plant components, and other biologically active ingredients.

- #2 Questionable Assumption—

"When I see the term 'natural,' it means that a product is healthful and safe." Consumers can be misled if they assume this term assures wholesomeness, or that these foodlike substances necessarily have milder effects, which makes them safer to use than drugs. The term "natural" on labels is not well defined and is sometimes used ambiguously to imply unsubstantiated benefits or safety. For example, many weight-loss products claim to be "natural" or "herbal" but this doesn't necessarily make them safe. Their ingredients may interact with drugs or may be dangerous for people with certain medical conditions.

- #3 Questionable Assumption—

"A product is safe when there is no cautionary information on the product label." Dietary supplement manufacturers may not necessarily include warnings about potential adverse effects on the labels of their products. If consumers want to know about the safety of a specific dietary supplement, they should contact the manufacturer of that brand directly. It is the manufacturer's responsibility to determine that the supplement it produces or distributes is safe and that there is substantiated evidence that the label claims are truthful and not misleading.

- #4 Questionable Assumption—

"A recall of a harmful product guarantees that all such harmful products will be immediately and completely removed from the marketplace." A product recall of a dietary supplement is voluntary and while many manufacturers do their best, a recall does not necessarily remove all harmful products from the marketplace.[15]

---

[14] "Tips for the Savvy Supplement User: Making Informed Decisions and Evaluating Information," January, 2002, www.cfsan.fda.gov/-dms/qa-sup19.html. Updated: 05/07/2009.

[15] Ibid.

Sometimes, faulty assumptions are caused by erroneous research with dire implications. Note the simple, but alarming, mistake in the following excerpt on the flawed report about Himalayan glaciers melting at an startling rate. Ten authors worked on the report, and none of them noticed the glaring error in their documentation.

Himalayan Glaciers Melting Deadline 'a Mistake'

Pallava Bagla

The Himalayas hold the planet's largest body of ice outside the polar caps.

The UN panel on climate change warning that Himalayan glaciers could melt to a fifth of current levels by 2035 is wildly inaccurate, an academic says.

J Graham Cogley, a professor at Ontario Trent University, says he believes the UN authors got the date from an earlier report wrong by more than 300 years.

He is astonished they "misread 2350 as 2035." The authors deny the claims.

Leading glaciologists say the report has caused confusion and "a catalogue of errors in Himalayan glaciology."

The Himalayas hold the planet's largest body of ice outside the polar caps—an estimated 12,000 cubic kilometres of water.

They feed many of the world's great rivers—the Ganges, the Indus, the Brahmaputra—on which hundreds of millions of people depend.

'Catastrophic Rate'

In its 2007 report, the Nobel Prize-winning Inter-governmental Panel on Climate Change (IPCC) said: "Glaciers in the Himalayas are receding faster than in any other part of the world and, if the present rate continues, the likelihood of them disappearing by the year 2035 and perhaps sooner is very high if the Earth keeps warming at the current rate."

"Its total area will likely shrink from the present 500,000 to 100,000 square kilometres by the year 2035," the report said.

It suggested three quarters of a billion people who depend on glacier melt for water supplies in Asia could be affected.

But Professor Cogley has found a 1996 document by a leading hydrologist, VM Kotlyakov, that mentions 2350 as the year by which there will be massive and precipitate melting of glaciers.

"The extrapolar glaciation of the Earth will be decaying at rapid, catastrophic rates — its total area will shrink from 500,000 to 100,000 square kilometres by the year 2350," Mr Kotlyakov's report said.

Mr Cogley says it is astonishing that none of the 10 authors of the 2007 IPCC report could spot the error and "misread 2350 as 2035."

"I do suggest that the glaciological community might consider advising the IPCC about ways to avoid such egregious errors as the 2035 versus 2350 confusion in the future," says Mr Cogley. ▪

As critical thinkers, we need to actively discover and then question the assumptions underlying arguments so we are not building arguments on a false foundation. Conversely, when we critically examine what it is we take for granted, we have the advantage of gaining a strong and solid conviction for those ideas and principles we believe to be true. Knowing why we believe what we believe helps us be more credible and effective when we present an argument. Examining the reality assumptions of others helps us understand and assess their arguments more clearly.

Class Exercise

What Are the Assumptions?

Purpose: To detect unstated reality assumptions.

One way to detect reality assumptions is to create a brief outline of an argument you hear. Use the elements of the Toulmin method (see an explanation of this method in Chapter 2) as illustrated in the following examples:

> *Trials and executions should be televised—the public has the right to know what's going on in our courts. Information about the judicial system needs to be more widely disseminated.*

Using the skills we've discussed so far, we could outline the argument as follows:

Conclusion/claim: Trials and executions should be televised.

Reason: The public has the right to have more information about the courts and the judicial system.

Value assumption/warrant: Freedom of information is an important value.

Reality assumption/warrant: Televising trials and executions would inform the public about our judicial system.

Someone with different value and reality assumptions might reply as follows:

> *Trials and executions should not be televised—it would turn our criminal justice system into a form of entertainment.*

Conclusion/claim: Trials and executions should not be televised.

Reason: Televising trials and executions turns our criminal justice system into a form of entertainment.

Value assumption/warrant: Citizens should not be entertained by criminal behavior.

Reality assumption/warrant: People would watch trials and executions primarily for entertainment.

Let's look at another brief argument, outlining the conclusion, reasons, value assumption, and reality assumptions.

> *All teenagers should have the hepatitis B vaccination starting at 12 years old. Hepatitis B is a sexually transmitted disease that can be fatal. It can also be transmitted through intravenous drug use.*

Conclusion/claim: All teenagers should have the hepatitis B vaccination.

Reasons: Hepatitis B is a sexually transmitted disease that can be fatal. It can also be transmitted through intravenous drug use.

Value assumption/warrant: Health and prolonged life are important.

Reality assumptions/warrants: All teenagers are at risk of being sexually active or using drugs. Children are at risk for these activities starting at age 12. A vaccination will protect teenagers from the effects of this disease.

Using the previous example, can you create a different argument based on different assumptions about reality?

For more practice on "assumption detection," read the following statements and find assumptions that are being made by the speaker. Often, you can find more than one possible reality assumption.

After you have completed this exercise, discuss whether you agree with the assumptions you discovered.

1. He should try out for the NFL right after high school. If he makes it, he won't need a college degree.

2. You can't go to the party in that outfit. No one will want to talk to you.

3. The death penalty is proof that we value revenge more than we value people. We should save and rehabilitate people rather than giving up on them.

4. Charlene is really successful—she's only 28 and she's making $120,000 a year!

5. There is good news in that rape is on the decline in this county—there are 20 percent fewer police reports this year than last year at this time.

6. Bolger's coffee is the best—it's mountain grown. That gives it great taste.

7. The people in that city don't care about the homeless—their city council voted against contributing $80,000 to a county fund to help the homeless.

8. They won't trade their lunches if you give them Twinkle cupcakes, and Twinkle will give them the energy they need to do well in school.

9. You're going to love this blind date—I've known him since fourth grade and he's a great friend of mine.

10. Let's put the county dump in Smallville—it hasn't had a turn as a dumpsite yet.

11. Let's just live together—why do we need a piece of paper to prove our love?

12. The newspaper didn't print my editorial—I guess the editors don't really believe in free speech.

For more practice, see Exercise 3.1 on page 106.

Deductive Reasoning

> If we lose a sense of the value of truth, we will certainly lose something, and we may very well lose everything.
>
> Bernard Williams, philosopher

In the first part of this chapter, we examined reality assumptions. We saw that sometimes our assumptions about reality, about what is true and what is false, contrast with those of others. How can we discover whether our assumptions are true and whether they are able to provide good evidence for our conclusions?

Philosophers, theologians, scholars, and critically thinking people are all concerned with truth, and many have tried to define truth over the centuries. Vincent Ryan Ruggiero, author of *Beyond Feelings,* gives this definition:

> The truth about something is what is so about it, the facts about it in their exact arrangement and proportions. . . to look for the truth is to look for the

correct answer, the answer that completely expresses reality in the matter. Whatever difficulty we may find in discerning or stating the truth is beside the point.[16]

Being a critical thinker means having a curious and questioning attitude about reality and examining the reality assumptions you hold and that others present to you in arguments. Critical thinkers realize that their knowledge and perceptions are limited, and they look for solid evidence before accepting or advocating a viewpoint. When new information becomes available, they revisit and reexamine their reality assumptions about an issue, always striving to discern the truth.

In many of our routine daily decisions, we don't spend a lot of time questioning our thinking. However, as we face the important decisions of our life as people in relationships, and as students, professionals, citizens, and consumers, we do need to question why we believe what we believe, and whether our beliefs are true.

How can we examine how we think and question our own reasoning or the reasoning of others? How can we overcome our own subjective perceptions? What tools are available to help us look critically at information, make reasonable decisions, and know that we are being "logical" in our thinking?

Those who study reasoning have come up with two general frameworks for testing the logic of our reasoning and for discovering truth; these frameworks are inductive and deductive reasoning. **Inductive reasoning** involves finding truth by making observations. The observations might be made through statistical polling, controlled experiments, or relevant examples and analogies. Our observations, when made carefully, can lead us closer to the truth of a matter. Good inductive reasoning tells us what will *probably* occur in a given situation based on what observation tells us *usually* occurs. We will look at inductive reasoning in Chapters 4 and 5.

> **inductive reasoning**
> The process of finding truth by making observations; these observations may be from statistical polling, controlled experiments, or relevant examples and analogies.

While inductive reasoning gives us *probabilities* of what is true in a given situation, **deductive reasoning** is structured in such a way as to give us *certainty* about what is true in a given situation. The conclusion's certainty is established when deductive arguments contain true premises (reasons) stated in the correct form.

> **deductive reasoning**
> The process of inferring a conclusion by putting forth true premises in a valid format.

Validity in Deductive Arguments

> Fallacious and misleading arguments are most easily detected if set out in correct syllogistic form.
>
> Immanuel Kant

> The syllogism is one of the most valuable tools we have in trying to determine the truth.
>
> Robert J. Gula

In a **deductive argument**, formal patterns are used to reveal the logic of our reasoning. These patterns give us a tool for "quality control"; when the correct deductive form is followed, the reasoning is logical and the argument is called **valid**. The basic patterns of deductive reasoning, which will be discussed in this section, help us test whether our thinking is valid and therefore logical. The pattern of a deductive argument can be considered its form; the statements placed in the pattern can be

> **deductive argument**
> An argument that follows formal patterns of reasoning and is aimed at establishing the certainty of a conclusion through presenting true premises in valid form.

> **valid argument** An argument structured in a correct deductive format; an argument structured in such a way that if its premises are true, then its conclusion must be true.

[16] Vincent Ryan Ruggiero, *Beyond Feelings: A Guide to Critical Thinking* (Mountain View, CA: Mayfield Publishing, 1990), p. 25.

considered its content. Correct form makes an argument valid, which is a formal term for "logical"; accurate content makes it true. When the form is valid and the content is true, the argument is called **sound.**

The formal patterns that create the framework for deductive reasoning are called syllogisms. A **syllogism** is a deductive argument (usually written in three steps) that moves logically from a major and a minor premise to a conclusion. The conclusion is inferred or derived from the premises. Let's look at the classic example of a syllogism given by Aristotle more than 2,000 years ago:

> All men are mortal. (This categorical statement is called the **major premise.**)
>
> Socrates is a man. (The **minor premise** expresses an instance of the principle set out in the major premise.)
>
> Therefore, Socrates is mortal. (Conclusion—the **conclusion** is inferred—follows from—the major and minor premises.)

This pattern of deductive reasoning can be coded in letters as follows:

> All As are Bs.
>
> m is A.
>
> Therefore, m is B.

In this deductive argument, the first premise (all As are Bs) is a universal or **categorical statement,** a statement in which members of one class are said to be included in another class.

This categorical statement is the major premise. The second statement, called the minor premise, gives a particular instance of the principle set out in the major premise. The final statement is the conclusion that is logically inferred from the major and minor premises.

Let's look at some other common examples of deductive reasoning, noting their specific patterns. A **conditional syllogism** contains at least one hypothetical (if–then) premise. In a conditional (hypothetical) premise, we are asserting that if the first part of the statement is true, then the second part is also true. We call the first part (represented by A) the antecedent, and the second part (represented by B) the consequent. Here are some common forms of conditional/hypothetical syllogisms.

1. Modus ponens. The term **modus ponens** means "the way of affirmation" or affirming the antecedent.

> If A, then B. (major premise; we are stating that the antecedent (A) leads to the consequent(B)
>
> A (minor premise; we are affirming that the antecedent is true)
>
> Therefore, B. (conclusion; if the antecedent is true, the consequent is also true)

Examples

> If our team wins the playoff game, it will be in the championship game.
>
> Our team did win the playoff game.
>
> Therefore, our team will be in the championship game.

---

sound argument A valid deductive argument whose premises are true.

syllogism A deductive argument usually consisting of two premises and a conclusion.

major premise The statement in a syllogism that sets forth a general principle. (The major premise contains the term that is the predicate of the conclusion.)

minor premise The statement in a syllogism that expresses an instance of the principle set out in the major premise. (The minor premise contains the term that is the subject of the conclusion.)

conclusion In deductive reasoning, the inference drawn from the major and minor premises of a syllogism.

categorical statement A statement in which members of one class are said to be included in another class. This statement may be used as the major premise of a syllogism.

conditional syllogism In deductive reasoning, a syllogism whose major premise asserts that if the condition cited in the first part of a statement is true, then the claim cited in the second part of the statement will follow.

modus ponens A valid conditional/hypothetical syllogism in which the antecedent is affirmed.

If the weather report says that it will rain today, I will need my raincoat.

The weather report says that it will rain today.

Therefore, I will need my raincoat.

Keep in mind the difference between a statement or assertion and an argument. Remember that in a deductive argument, the conclusion is inferred (drawn or understood) from the premises that are given. A common error is to take one premise alone as constituting an argument. The first premise given earlier, "If our team wins the playoff game, it will be in the championship game" is only a statement. This statement, called a **hypothetical statement**, sets up a condition. The condition needs to be fulfilled (or not fulfilled) for the argument to be complete. Conditional (or hypothetical) statements are used commonly in our lives in the form of warranties, contracts, threats, or predictions.

Your instructor may have given you a contract at the beginning of the semester that states the following:

1. If you get 80 percent of the points required, you will receive a B.

    This is a conditional or hypothetical statement. It doesn't assert that you have 80 percent of the points in the class or that you have a B. But if you add another statement:

2. You have 80 percent of the points required (and that is true), then we arrive at the conclusion that:

3. You will receive a B in the class.

Note that if the first two statements in this format are true, then the conclusion must be true. When the conclusion must be true, we have deductive certainty.

hypothetical syllogism
See conditional syllogism. A syllogism in which the major premise presents a condition ("if A, then B") or a possibility ("either A or B") that is resolved in the minor premise so that a valid conclusion can follow. The condition or possibility is resolved in the minor premise in the form of affirmation or denial. Conditional and disjunctive syllogisms (defined on page 92) are forms of hypothetical syllogisms.

Stop and Think

What are some examples of hypothetical statements you have heard?

Here is another valid conditional/hypothetical syllogism:

2. Modus tollens. The term **modus tollens** means denying the consequent.

> If A, then B.
>
> Not B. (Here the consequent is denied.)
>
> Therefore, not A. (Since the consequent is denied, the antecedent must also be denied in the conclusion.)

modus tollens   A valid conditional/hypothetical syllogism in which the consequent is denied.

Examples

If I have strep throat, then the culture will be positive.

But the culture is not positive.

So, I don't have strep throat.

If I have to get up now, my alarm will go off again.

But my alarm hasn't gone off again.

Therefore, I don't have to get up now.

chain argument   A form of argument that builds and depends on a series of conditions being met.

3. Chain argument. A third form of the conditional argument is often called a **chain argument:**

> If A, then B.
> If B, then C.
> Therefore, if A, then C.

Examples

If you lower the fat in your diet, you will lower your cholesterol.

If you lower your cholesterol, you will reduce the risk of heart disease.

Therefore, if you lower the fat in your diet, you will reduce your risk of heart disease.

If evidence of the suspect's DNA is found at the crime scene, then we can connect him with the crime.

If we can connect him with the crime, then we can have him stand trial.

Therefore, if the suspect's DNA is found at the crime scene, then we can have him stand trial.

If I want to get a good grade in this class, I need high quiz points.

If I need high quiz points, I need to study for the quizzes.

Therefore, if I want to get a good grade in this class, I need to study for the quizzes.

Reminder

Deductive arguments must follow the correct pattern in order to be considered valid. If our reasoning follows the steps outlined in these forms, our arguments are considered valid. If they do not follow the correct form, we have not provided adequate support for the conclusion, even if the conclusion happens to be true.

✳ Explore on **mythinkinglab.com**

disjunctive syllogism
A hypothetical syllogism in which two possibilities are given in the major premise and one is assumed to be necessarily true. In the minor premise, one of the possible alternatives is negated, and the remaining alternative is then affirmed in the conclusion.

4. Disjunctive syllogism. Another common pattern of deduction is found in the **disjunctive syllogism:** A disjunction is an "or" statement. In a disjunctive syllogism, it is claimed that only one of two possibilities (disjuncts) is true; if one possibility is true, then the other possibility is not true. The two alternative possibilities are presented in the major premise; one of them is denied in the minor premise and the other is affirmed in the conclusion. The pattern for this syllogism is structured as follows:

> Either A or B.
> Not B.
> Therefore, A.
> or
> Either A or B.
> Not A.
> Therefore, B.

Either Ramon took the car to work or he took the bus.

But Ramon didn't take the bus to work.

Therefore, Ramon took the car.

My phone is either at Brianna's house or at work.

It's not at Brianna's house.

Therefore, it's at work.

Closely related to the disjunctive syllogism is an argument by elimination. An **argument by elimination** seeks to logically rule out various possibilities until only a single possibility remains. The following valid patterns are arguments by elimination:

> **argument by elimination** A valid syllogism that seeks to logically rule out various possibilities until only a single possibility remains.

Either A, or B, or C.

Not B or C.

Therefore, A.

The car's problem is the alternator, the generator, or the battery.

It's not the alternator or the generator.

Therefore, it's the battery.

Either A, or B, or C.

If B or C, then D.

Not D.

Therefore, A.

Either Rachel bought dinner, Roy bought dinner, or Sammy bought dinner.

If Roy or Sammy bought dinner, then they skipped baseball practice.

But Roy and Sammy did not skip baseball practice.

Therefore, Rachel bought dinner.

Using Toulmin's Method to Understand Deduction

We don't speak in syllogisms, but we can test the logic of our reasoning by placing it into a syllogism. In fact, many of our assertions are what philosophers call enthymemes; an **enthymeme** is a syllogism with a premise implied rather than directly stated. The missing parts—the assumptions of the speaker or writer—are expected to be supplied by the listener or reader. When we discover the missing part, the implied premise, we can place the argument in one of the standard deductive patterns.

> **Enthymeme** A syllogism with a key part or parts implied rather than directly stated.

As we discussed in previous sections, British philosopher Stephen Toulmin has developed a method of dissecting arguments that helps us isolate the implied premises. His method identifies claims (which are the same as conclusions), reasons, those supports for the claims that are directly stated, and warrants, those connections between reasons and claims that are taken for granted (the reality assumptions). The warrants are the implied premises; they are the "glue" that attaches the reasons to the claims.

When the warrant is clarified, the reasoning of the speaker or writer is more fully revealed, and we are able to see if the reasoning is valid.

For example, you may say, "You shouldn't take that class—the teacher gives too much homework." (This preceding statement is the enthymeme.)

Claim/conclusion: You should not take that class.

Reason: The teacher gives too much homework.

Warrant/reality assumption: If too much homework is given, a class should not be taken.

Written as a conditional syllogism, the reasoning would be revealed:

If a teacher gives too much homework, a class should not be taken.

That teacher gives to much homework.

Therefore, that class should not be taken.

Someone might respond to this argument by saying, "I like having a lot of homework—it helps me learn the material." This response challenges the warrant that if too much homework is given, a class should not be taken; the objection is not about the logic of the reasoning but about the assumption that too much homework is a negative factor.

For another example, let's say that you and a friend are planning to drive to a movie. You may say, "We're almost out of gas—we need to stop on the way to the movie." This enthymeme could be dissected as follows:

Claim/conclusion: We need to stop for gas on the way to the movie.

Reason: We're almost out of gas.

Warrant/reality assumption: If we're out of gas, we need to stop and get some more or we won't make it to the movie.

We can also see the reasoning pattern by putting the enthymeme into a conditional syllogism, as follows:

If we're almost out of gas, we need to stop and get some more.

We're almost out of gas.

Therefore, we need to stop and get some more.

Let's say, though, that your friend responds to your comment, "We need to stop at a gas station on the way to the movie" by stating, "No, we don't need to stop; we're fine." Using Toulmin's model, your friend's argument is as follows:

Claim/conclusion: We don't need to stop.

Reason: We're fine. (We have enough gas to get to the movie.)

Reality assumption/warrant: If we have enough gas to get to the movie, we don't need to stop.

The enthymeme "No, we don't need to stop; we're fine," could be expressed in a conditional syllogism as follows:

If we already have enough gas to get to the movie, we don't need to stop for more.

We already have enough gas to get to the movie.

Therefore, we don't need to stop for more.

This sample disagreement points out an important element of deductive reasoning; a deductive argument may be valid (i.e., follow the correct pattern), as are both of the preceding arguments, without being true. The untrue premise can be seen as a faulty reality assumption. The conclusion may follow from the premises, but one or both of the premises may not be true, and the truth is what we are seeking.

Toulmin's method emphasizes the need to pursue truth in argumentation. The claims and reasons of each person need evidence, or what Toulmin calls **grounds.** In this case, both you and your friend would have to provide evidence that you do or do not have enough gas to make it to the movie. He might give examples of how the gauge was close to empty before, but he was still able to travel the distance it would take to get to the movie. You may have kept track of how many miles you have gone since the last time the tank was filled and do the math to determine if you have enough gas left to get to the movie. Or you could take your chances and find out if you have enough gas by not filling up and seeing if you make it to the movie.

Both of you have reasoned logically, and the syllogisms outlining your reasoning are both valid. But only one of you has a sound argument in which both the major and the minor premises are true. When the premises of a valid syllogism are true, the truth of the conclusion is certain.

When we know that an argument is sound, we can accept the conclusion of that argument with confidence. We can make good decisions based on the information given in a sound argument because the argument is both logical and true, as conveyed by the following chart.

grounds Evidence offered to prove a claim. Grounds can consist of statistics, examples, research, physical evidence, logical reasoning, and expert opinion.

	True	False
Valid	Sound Argument: Correct Form True Premises	Unsound Argument: Correct Form, Untrue Premises
Invalid	Unsound Argument: Incorrect Form, True Premises	Unsound Argument: Incorrect Form, Untrue Premises

Reminder

1. Understanding the process of deductive reasoning helps you realize what you are assuming to be true when you state your position on issues.
2. When an argument is valid and the premises are true, the conclusion must be true, and the argument is called sound.

✳ Explore on **mythinkinglab.com**

The Uses of Deductive Reasoning

Why is it useful to learn the patterns of deductive reasoning? Using deductive reasoning can

1. Illuminate and clarify our beliefs (reality assumptions) and help us consider whether those beliefs are rational. If we find that our beliefs are rational and logical, we may act on them. If they are irrational, we can challenge and revise them.

2. Help us discover truth, particularly in situations in which there is a right and wrong answer.
3. Help us make decisions, particularly when there are established rules, laws, and guidelines to follow.
4. Help us recognize and challenge stereotypes and prejudicial statements.
5. Help us understand argument.

Deductive Reasoning Helps Us Discover Reality Assumptions and Test Our Logic

As we discussed in the previous section, deductive reasoning can help us examine everyday reality assumptions. Sometimes, when we examine our assumptions, we see that they are logical and true, and we feel more confident about our reasoning. At other times, we uncover assumptions that are not based in truth but on unquestioned beliefs. In his book *The Psychology of Persuasion,* Robert Cialdini gives an example of an unquestioned, faulty assumption. Cialdini tells about a friend who was having trouble selling some turquoise jewelry. She had priced the jewelry reasonably, put it in a central location in her store, and told her sales staff to push it.

> Finally, the night before leaving on an out-of-town buying trip, she scribbled an exasperated note to her head saleswoman, "Everything in this display case, price × 1/2," hoping to just be rid of the offending pieces, even at a loss. When she returned a few days later, she was not surprised to find that every article had been sold. She was shocked, though, to discover that, because the employee had read the "1/2" in her scrawled message as a "2," the entire allotment had sold out at twice the original price.[17]

Cialdini explains what happened in a way that reveals how we need to examine our reality assumptions in order to be more critical thinkers:

> The customers, mostly well-to-do vacationers with little knowledge of turquoise, were using a standard principle—a stereotype—to guide their buying: "expensive = good." Thus the vacationers, who wanted "good" jewelry, saw the turquoise pieces as decidedly more valuable and desirable when nothing about them was enhanced but the price.
> . . . It is easy to fault the tourist[s] for their foolish purchase decisions. But a close look offers a kinder view. These were people who had been brought up on the rule "You get what you pay for" and who had seen that rule borne out over and over in their lives. Before long, they had translated the rule to mean "expensive = good." The "expensive = good" stereotype had worked quite well for them in the past, since normally the price of an item increases along with its worth; a higher price typically reflects higher quality. So when they found themselves in the position of wanting good turquoise jewelry without much knowledge of turquoise, they understandably relied on the old standby feature of cost to determine the jewelry's merits.[18]

[17] Robert B. Cialdini, *The Psychology of Persuasion* (New York: William Morrow, 1993).
[18] Ibid.

In this situation, the customers relied on a reality assumption, which can be expressed in the major premise of the following syllogism:

If an item is expensive, it must be good.

This jewelry is expensive.

Therefore, this jewelry must be good.

They literally paid a price for not questioning the truth of this assumption.

Clarifying and questioning our reality assumptions can also help us grow beyond self-imposed limitations. Our assumptions about reality may keep us from trying new things that we really are capable of accomplishing; by uncovering faulty reality assumptions, we can make necessary changes in our lives.

For example, someone we'll call Linda might say, "I can't take that speech class." Her friend LeVar asks why, and Linda responds, "I can't take the class because I'd have to give speeches." Linda's confident friend says, "So what?" to which Linda says with great emotion, "If I have to take a speech class, I'll just fall apart and die!" LeVar, knowing the principles of deductive reasoning, helps Linda look at her logic through the pattern of chain argument.

If I take a speech class, I'll have to give speeches.

If I have to give speeches, I'll get nervous.

If I get nervous, I'll fall apart and die.

Therefore, if I take a speech class, I'll fall apart and die.

Considered in this light, Linda is able to see that, although her reasoning is valid (i.e., logical in its pattern), it is not true. She is "catastrophizing" her situation, making it much more serious than it is. Certainly, it may be uncomfortable for her to give a speech, but it is not a life-threatening situation. She can see that discomfort need not be catastrophic. The way we speak sometimes both reveals and creates our thoughts about situations. Using the tools of deductive reasoning to objectify her thoughts, Linda may be able to adjust her thinking to reality, rather than continuing to function with exaggerated fears. (See Exercise 3.2 on pages 106–107.)

Using Deductive Reasoning to Discover Truth and to Make Decisions

What eludes logic is the most precious element in us, and one can draw
nothing from a syllogism that the mind has not put there in advance.

Andre Gide, *Journals*, June 1927

Deductive reasoning is most useful when the major premise is known to be true, to be a "given." Then we can test the truth of individual cases that may fall under the category or condition of the major premise.

For example, using a categorical syllogism, we can assert that some As do fit into an all-encompassing category (B) and give us valuable certainties. Let's consider some biological truths in this light. All women with an HCG (human chorionic gonadotropin) level above 5 are pregnant. Any cold-blooded vertebrate of the class *Reptilia* including tortoises, turtles, snakes, lizards, alligators, crocodiles and extinct forms are considered reptiles, and all persons with a blood alcohol level of .08 in the state of Illinois are legally drunk. Because of these known "alls," solid conclusions can be drawn: Doctors can tell individual women if they are pregnant; veterinarians, scientists, and pet store owners can identify reptiles; and police officers in Illinois can ascertain whether individual drivers are legally drunk. You might discover that you and several members of your immediate family have type A blood. Because this is a known truth, if you need a blood transfusion, type A family members can be approached to volunteer.

Hundreds of conditions and illnesses have been studied inductively (through observation), and the results of the studies have given us truth that can be used deductively in diagnosis. When the symptoms of a particular condition or disease are known, doctors and patients use these given truths to diagnose individual cases.

For example, in Figure 3–1, readers can use a medical guide to see whether they have a serious condition. The chart is based on the truth about insect bites and stings. The individual reading the chart tries to confirm or deny the symptoms that apply to his or her specific case.

Note that this chart reveals major premises (what is known to be true about insect bites in descending order of danger) and also the conclusion for each case. The chart allows patients to reason deductively by fitting in their own symptoms as the minor premise. Then patients can know how serious their condition may be and what conclusion is justified (i.e., what action to take).

A reader of this chart can easily use a chain argument to discover if a given condition might be serious and he or she can then make a good decision about treatment.

Insect Bites or Stings

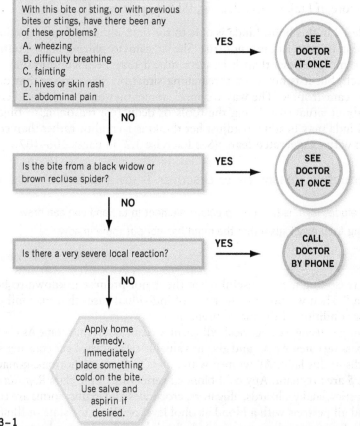

FIGURE 3–1

A medical chart helps patients reason deductively about the seriousness of their symptoms.

Example

Let's say a spider has bitten your friend. If she is wheezing and having difficulty breathing, you can reason deductively as follows:

If wheezing and breathing difficulties follow an insect bite, the bitten person is experiencing a serious allergic reaction.
Marites is wheezing and having breathing difficulties.
Therefore, Marites is experiencing a serious allergic reaction, and
If someone is experiencing a serious allergic reaction, he or she should see a doctor at once.
Marites is experiencing a serious allergic reaction.
Therefore, Marites should see a doctor at once.

Stop and Think

Can you create syllogisms that would fit other symptoms described in this chart?

Deductive reasoning is also used to establish whether an individual case fits into a specific legal category.

The application of most laws can be clarified through deductive reasoning. For example:

If you went through a red light and caused an accident, you are liable for the damages.

You went through a red light and caused an accident.

Therefore, you are liable for the damages.

There are also specific rights and responsibilities in most business transactions. For example, hotel guests and hotel owners each have specific rights, and each may be liable for violating those rights. Lawyers in disputes between business owners and customers refer to the legal regulations when determining whether or not they have a case or a defense.

Deductive reasoning is also used to discover the truth about criminal cases and what the law requires a jury to conclude about the innocence or guilt of a defendant.

Consider a prosecutor and a defense attorney presenting arguments to a jury. One famous criminal case involved two young men who shot and killed their parents. There was no question that the boys committed the crime. The argument in their trial centered on their motivation: Was the killing a premeditated act by two children hoping to receive an inheritance, or was it an act motivated by years of abuse and a desperate sense of helplessness and rage? Reconstructing the positions of both the prosecution and the defense in simple terms, we might note the following argument. The prosecutor's basic argument could be outlined as follows:

If children murder their parents in cold blood, they deserve to be punished to the full extent of the law.

These children murdered their parents in cold blood.

Therefore, they deserve to be punished to the full extent of the law.

The defense attorney admitted that the children murdered their parents, but she added information that brought her to a different conclusion about sentencing:

> If children murder parents because they fear abuse, there are mitigating circumstances to the murder.

> If there are mitigating circumstances, then the children deserve a lighter sentence.

> Therefore, if children murder parents because they fear abuse, they deserve a lighter sentence.

When jurors can follow the logic of the arguments presented, they can examine the evidence for both the prosecution and the defense in order to make their determinations.

On a lighter note, deductive reasoning can also reveal truth in various instances of daily living, especially those involving cultural rules and traditions. Numerous examples of this usage include the rules for sports and games; traditions for births, weddings, and funerals; codes of conduct; and general agreements about sportsmanship and fairness. When people make comments regarding various activities and situations, they are often made as enthymemes, those statements that imply, but do not directly state, a complete syllogism.

Note the statements that follow and how they can be "decoded" as conclusions of valid deductive arguments.

Conversation between two golfers:
"Why isn't Fred finishing the round?"
"He was disqualified because of his clubface." (Enthymeme)

Decoding

The rules of golf state that no foreign material shall be applied to the clubface for the purpose of influencing the movement of the ball.

If foreign material is applied to the clubface for the purpose of influencing the movement of the ball, the player shall be disqualified. (Major Premise = the rule)

Foreign material was applied to the clubface used by Fred. (Minor Premise = the specific violation of the rule)

Therefore, Fred is disqualified. (Conclusion)

As stated earlier, Fred can argue whether the minor premise is true or even whether someone may have tried to disqualify him by applying material to his club; however, the *logic* of the rule still applies, and Fred would have to argue that the minor premise is not true in his case.

"My son and his fiancée have finalized their wedding date, so we can reserve the restaurant for the rehearsal dinner."(Enthymeme)

Decoding

In our wedding tradition, if a son is getting married, his parents arrange and pay for the rehearsal dinner. (Major Premise)

Our son is getting married. (Minor Premise)

Therefore, we arrange and pay for the rehearsal dinner. (Conclusion)

Again, these statements highlight how reasoning is used logically. This syllogism is valid and makes sense within the context given. However, the truth factor may change the reality. If the son and his fiancée decide to elope, or to have a small, family wedding at a courthouse, traditional rules would not apply.

Class Exercise

Purpose: To discover the logical reasoning behind the following enthymemes.

A. Decode the following statements (enthymemes) as syllogisms. Then discuss whether there are instances in which they may not be true.

Example

One player to another in a Scrabble game: "You have to take those letters off— you can't use Maine as a word."(Enthymeme)

Decoding

Proper names are prohibited in Scrabble. (Major Premise)

Maine is a proper name. (Minor Premise)

Therefore, Maine is prohibited as a Scrabble word. (Conclusion)

1. Usher to guest at wedding: "If you're with the bride, you need to sit on this side."
2. Teacher to student: "You got marked down a grade because you were one day late turning this paper in."
3. Former Red Sox Manager Don Zimmer was fined $5,000 for running across the infield and lunging at Pedro Martinez.
4. After Martinez grabbed Zimmer by the head and tossed him to the ground at Fenway Park, he was fined $50,000.
5. During a game of blackjack: "With 22 points, you're out of this round."
6. Teacher to young students: "You must use your 'inside' voices because we're back in the classroom."
7. Concession worker in theatre lobby: "Intermission is over, so you need to finish your coffee."
8. Steward to airplane passengers: "It is time to shut off cell phones and other electronic devices because we are taking off now."
9. Garden shop employee to customer: "If you have a shady yard, you don't want to buy these flowers."
10. Financial planner: "We always advise our customers to diversify their assets—have some stocks, some bonds, a variety of investments, to cover the fluctuations in markets."

B. Watch a television program that features a civil trial, such as *People's Court* or *Judge Joe Brown*. Write the plaintiff's argument, the defendant's argument, and the judge's verdict as a syllogism. Comment on the validity and truth of the judge's ruling.

Reminder

Deductive arguments follow formal patterns of reasoning and are aimed at establishing the certainty of a conclusion. The conclusion's certainty is established when deductive arguments contain true premises (reasons) that are stated in the correct form.

✳ Explore on **mythinkinglab.com**

Using Deductive Reasoning to Combat Prejudice and Stereotyping

Much of Aristotle's early work on syllogisms involved categorization of elements of the natural world. These categories help us understand our world by noting distinguishing features of different species, as exemplified by the following categorical syllogism:

All animals that nurse their young and have hair are mammals.

Brown bears nurse their young and have hair.

Therefore, brown bears are mammals.

Deductive reasoning works well in biology, medicine, engineering, electronics, and law because the categories are well established and agreed upon by experts in each field. Because we are applying individual cases to previously determined "truths," we can know for certain that our conclusions are true within these contexts.

A critical thinker needs to distinguish between major premises that fit into these limited truth categories and major premises that have not been and often *cannot* be proven. Although we can say what all mammals have in common, we cannot generalize about groups of people based on ethnicity, religion, gender, political affiliation, profession, or economic status because we cannot study every member of these groups. When we try to fit all Democrats, Cubans, teenagers, or musicians into an all-encompassing mold, we suffer from what general semanticists call a "hardening of the categories," a belief in rigidly held but untrue reality assumptions.

Prejudicial statements involve deductive reasoning that is untrue and unproved, but often logically valid. Let's say that you hear someone comment: "Of course Lisa's a terrible driver—she's a woman!" This enthymeme could be placed into a syllogistic format as follows:

All women are terrible drivers.

Lisa is a woman.

Therefore, Lisa is a terrible driver.

You can see that if the premises of this syllogism were true, then the conclusion would be true. But the major premise given here could never be proven true; we cannot know *all* about any group of individuals.

Stereotyping is a form of classifying people, places, or things according to common traits. Stereotyping works for identical inanimate objects. For example, all computers of a certain model should perform exactly the same functions. If you have a computer that does not perform to specifications, you have a defective model. The manufacturer will likely repair your model or replace it so you have the model you expected. You can easily fashion a sound deductive argument about a computer:

All ZX model computers are 2.5-GHz machines.

My computer is a ZX model.

Therefore, my computer is a 2.5-GHz machine.

Manufacturers often print logos and numbers on machines to highlight the stereotypical mold into which they fit, so that buyers know exactly what they can expect from the particular model chosen.

When we stereotype people, however, we are classifying them in ways that do not meet the truth criteria in deductive reasoning. Even if Lisa has been in a number of accidents and has difficulty driving, it's not because she is a woman. The term *woman* refers only to the trait of being female. Every female and every male have numerous individual characteristics that distinguish them from others and make it impossible to fit them into a convenient mold. Because it is impossible to know and study all mem-

stereotyping Classifying people, places, or things solely on common traits while ignoring individual differences that make these comparisons invalid.

bers of any human ethnic, religious, gender, political, economic, or interest group, a stereotype about groups of people can always be challenged as untrue, and arguments based on stereotypes are therefore unsound. (See Exercise 3.3 on page 107.)

Skill

A critical thinker uses reasoning to recognize and challenge stereotyping and prejudice.

Using Deduction to Understand Argument and to Argue Constructively

Deductive reasoning is an important tool for constructive argumentation. As we noted in the first chapter, an issue involves controversy, that is, more than one plausible side of an argument. Understanding the process of deduction helps us outline our own reasoning and the reasoning of others, so that we can see, first, if it is logical (valid; following correct form) and, second, if it is grounded in truth.

Consider this syllogism:

All drivers who speed are subject to a fine.

You are speeding.

Therefore, you are subject to a fine.

In this example, you might agree with the major premise but question the minor premise.

For our purposes, we will call the questionable premise the **premise of contention** or **contentious premise**. Critical thinkers will argue about the premise of contention rather than about the conclusion. That is to say, critical thinkers will argue about reality assumptions, the premises that lead to conclusions.

When people argue about conclusions, stalemates are inevitable. Adults end up sounding like children arguing over who left the door open:

"You did it."

"No, I didn't."

"Yes, you did."

"No, I didn't.". . .

Parents who weren't at the scene of the crime have little basis for a rational judgment on an issue like this. Only real evidence (fingerprints, videotapes, or witnesses) would help them get to the truth.

The same frustrating process occurs in some sexual harassment cases, often called "he said, she said" issues. If there are no witnesses, tapes, letters, or other forms of evidence, then the accuser has no proof of being a victim and the accused has no proof of being innocent. Focusing on conclusions without accompanying evidence statements creates no-win arguments.

So what can we reasonably do in arguments that seem to lead to stalemates? Let's take the highly charged issue of abortion. At demonstrations, we may witness a scene that is hardly more sophisticated than the one between children noted previously, as the advocates for both sides focus on conclusions:

"Unborn children are worthy of protection."

"No, they're not."

premise of contention
The premise of a deductive argument that is under dispute. This is also often called the contentious premise.

"Yes, they are."

"No, they're not.". . .

If we can use deductive reasoning to uncover the beliefs of both sides, we can then focus our efforts on fruitful areas of inquiry. For example, we might outline the "pro-life" argument as follows:

All human life is valuable and worthy of protection.

An unborn child is a human life.

Therefore, an unborn child deserves protection.

Those who are "pro-choice" would find the minor premise to be the premise of contention; the contentious factor is whether or not an unborn child is a human life. In a similar manner, we might outline the pro-choice reasoning as follows:

Tissue masses have no civil rights.

A fetus is a tissue mass.

Therefore, a fetus has no civil rights.

Which is the premise of contention in this syllogism?

Both syllogisms are valid since the conclusions follow logically from the premises. But the premise of contention in both cases is the minor one. So, each side needs to focus efforts on proving that its minor premise is true.

Note here that the arguments sound different depending on the terminology used—*unborn child, fetus, tissue mass, human life*. Chapter 7 will focus on the power of words to shape our perceptions of an issue.

Reminder

In deductive arguments, a critical thinker will (1) outline his or her argument and the argument of the other person, (2) determine if the arguments are valid, (3) find the premise(s) of contention, and then (4) argue that his or her premises are true and therefore his or her argument is sound.

✳ Explore on mythinkinglab.com

Life Application: Tips for College and Career

When you are listening to a discussion in class or at a meeting, try to find and understand the reality assumptions that are held by various speakers. Also look for reality assumptions that form the basis of policies at work and at school (for example, note the assumptions behind a policy that requires uniforms for certain jobs) and that form the rules for games and sports.

   If you are arguing for a change in policy, try to present the old policy in the form of a logical syllogism and then show why the new policy would be more useful.

Chapter Review

Summary

1. Reality assumptions are beliefs about what is true and false; these beliefs are often taken for granted, and they are part of the foundation of a person's argument.

2. Reality assumptions need to be brought to light and examined so that those who make them do not build arguments on faulty foundations.

3. Reality assumptions can be discovered and examined through deductive reasoning and through the Toulmin model of argumentation.

4. In deductive reasoning, the conclusion is inferred from the premises. When the premises follow correct syllogistic patterns, the argument is considered valid.

5. A conclusion derived from true premises that are expressed in a valid form creates a sound argument.

6. Deductive reasoning helps us discover and examine our underlying reality assumptions, find both logic and truth in an argument, make clear decisions, combat prejudice and stereotyping, understand argument, and argue constructively.

Checkup

Short Answer

1. How can deductive reasoning be used in daily life?

2. What is the difference between a value assumption and a reality assumption?

Sentence Completion

3. When the premises of a deductive argument follow the correct form, we call the argument _____.

4. When the premises of a deductive argument follow the correct form and are also true, we call the argument _____.

5. A deductive argument containing two premises and a conclusion is called a _____.

6. Beliefs about what is true or false that are often taken for granted are called
_____ _____.

7. While inductive reasoning looks at probability, deductive reasoning aims to establish
_____.

True-False

8. General semanticists call stereotyping a "hardening of the categories."

9. When we build an argument on assumptions that are not grounded in truth, our arguments are faulty and the actions we recommend will not be likely to achieve our desired ends.

10. The premise of contention is the area of agreement in an argument.

Exercises

EXERCISE 3.1 Purpose: To find assumptions made by professionals in various fields. Consider your major area of study. What are some assumptions made by people in that field? If you study dance therapy, then you must assume that dance can be psychologically helpful to people. If you study ecology, then you must believe living organisms have a vital relationship to each other and their surroundings.

Example

"I am studying early childhood education because I assume children need some structured experiences before they get to kindergarten. I also assume they learn best if they have lots of time to be creative and explore. And I assume they need lots of interaction with other kids to learn to share and relate.

"I have argued with some of my teachers who assume children should learn to read before kindergarten. We know that children can learn to read early and they can learn some math, but my assumption is they'll burn out if they have to study so young. And I also assume they'll catch up and be happier than kids who had to read so early in life."

EXERCISE 3.2 Purpose: To examine how reality assumptions affect decisions.

Think of several decisions you have made recently (voting, consumer, relational) and try to find the reality assumption behind the decision. Express the reality assumption as a major premise in a deductive argument.

Example

"My boyfriend was invited to my family reunion, which lasted over a weekend. We went out to breakfast and lunch with my parents each day, and I noticed that he never offered to pay for anything; he let my parents pick up the tab in every case. I was really upset and decided that he wasn't marriage material. My reality assumption fits into a chain argument: If a man is serious about a relationship, he will want to impress a woman's family. If he wants to impress a woman's family, he will offer to pay for meals when they go out. Therefore, if a man is serious about a relationship, he will offer to pay for meals when they go out.

"I was really angry on our way back to school, and I told him I thought he was really selfish for not offering to pay for our meals when we went out. He was surprised and hurt and said that he would have been glad to pay, but he thought it would be rude to offer, since he was a guest. He was actually raised to believe that it is insulting to hosts to offer to pay for meals. Then I realized that he always pays when we go out and doesn't even ask me to pitch in. Acting on my reality assumption would have broken us up."

EXERCISE 3.3 Purpose: To construct syllogisms from prejudicial statements.

Most prejudicial statements can be unraveled as valid arguments with false premises. Think of a prejudicial statement that has been directed at you (or a friend) in the past. Reconstruct that statement into a syllogistic form.

Example

"My friend is on welfare because her husband left her and her two children. She can't find a job that would make enough money for her to afford childcare. When people find out she is on welfare, they tell her she should be working and not sponging off of society. Their reasoning is that

    All people on welfare are lazy.

    You are on welfare.

    Therefore, you are lazy.

"There might be some people who fit into this description, but it's unfair to put all people who need welfare into this category. I think if people understood my friend's situation, they would be less judgmental and more sympathetic."

You Decide

Illegal Drugs

The debate over whether marijuana and other drugs should be legalized involves a number of different reality assumptions. Those in favor of legalization assume that taking drugs is part of individual freedom; that there are more harmful drugs, such as alcohol and nicotine, that are legal; and that legalization would provide needed revenues through sales taxes. They also assume that legalization would eliminate or lessen crime involving gangs who sell drugs. Those against legalization assume that adverse health consequences would be costly and that the implicit approval of drug usage would harm the creativity, academic performance, and safety of children. They also assume that general work productivity would decrease and that crime and gang violence involving drugs would continue to be a problem.

For more information on the debate surrounding illegal drugs and additional exercises and tutorials about concepts covered in this chapter, log into MyThinkingLab at www.mythinkinglab.com and select Diestler, *Becoming a Critical Thinker*, Sixth Edition.

✳ Explore on **mythinkinglab.com**

Articles for Discussion

⬚●⬚ Read the Document on mythinkinglab.com

As we have discussed, reality assumptions form the basis of our opinions and our decisions. New research may reveal that our long-held assumptions about an issue should be questioned or changed. In the following article, the author cites a number of current studies that refute common reality assumptions about studying and learning. He points out that new evidence can give students and parents information to make studying and test taking more effective than it is when they follow popular misconceptions.

Forget What You Know About Good Study Habits

Benedict Carey

Every September, millions of parents try a kind of psychological witchcraft, to transform their summer-glazed campers into fall students, their video-bugs into bookworms. Advice is cheap and all too familiar: Clear a quiet work space. Stick to a homework schedule. Set goals. Set boundaries. Do not bribe (except in emergencies).

And check out the classroom. Does Junior's learning style match the new teacher's approach? Or the school's philosophy? Maybe the child isn't "a good fit" for the school.

Such theories have developed in part because of sketchy education research that doesn't offer clear guidance. Student traits and teaching styles surely interact; so do personalities and at-home rules. The trouble is, no one can predict how.

Yet there are effective approaches to learning, at least for those who are motivated. In recent years, cognitive scientists have shown that a few simple techniques can reliably improve what matters most: how much a student learns from studying.

The findings can help anyone, from a fourth grader doing long division to a retiree taking on a new language. But they directly contradict much of the common wisdom about good study habits, and they have not caught on.

For instance, instead of sticking to one study location, simply alternating the room where a person studies improves retention. So does studying distinct but related skills or concepts in one sitting, rather than focusing intensely on a single thing.

"We have known these principles for some time, and it's intriguing that schools don't pick them up, or that people don't learn them by trial and error," said Robert A. Bjork, a psychologist at the University of California, Los Angeles. "Instead, we walk around with all sorts of unexamined beliefs about what works that are mistaken."

Take the notion that children have specific learning styles, that some are "visual learners" and others are auditory; some are "left-brain" students, others "right-brain." In a recent review of the relevant research, published in the journal *Psychological Science in the Public Interest*, a team of psychologists found almost zero support for such ideas. "The contrast between the enormous popularity of the learning-styles approach within education and the lack of credible evidence for its utility is, in our opinion, striking and disturbing," the researchers concluded.

Ditto for teaching styles, researchers say. Some excellent instructors caper in front of the blackboard like summer-theater Falstaffs; others are reserved to the point of shyness. "We have yet to identify the common threads between teachers who create a constructive learning atmosphere," said Daniel T. Willingham, a psychologist at the University of Virginia and author of the book "Why Don't Students Like School?"

But individual learning is another matter, and psychologists have discovered that some of the most hallowed advice on study habits is flat wrong. For instance, many study skills courses insist that students find a specific place, a study room or a quiet corner of the library, to take their work. The research finds just the opposite. In one classic 1978 experiment, psychologists found that college students who studied a list of 40 vocabulary words in two different rooms—one windowless and cluttered, the other modern, with a view on a courtyard—did far better on a test than students who studied the words twice, in the same room. Later studies have confirmed the finding, for a variety of topics.

The brain makes subtle associations between what it is studying and the background sensations it has at the time, the authors say, regardless of whether those perceptions are conscious. It colors the terms of the Versailles Treaty with the wasted fluorescent glow of the dorm study room, say; or the elements of the Marshall Plan with the jade-curtain shade of the willow tree in the backyard. Forcing the brain to make multiple associations with the same material may, in effect, give that information more neural scaffolding.

"What we think is happening here is that, when the outside context is varied, the information is enriched, and this slows down forgetting," said Dr. Bjork, the senior author of the two-room experiment.

Varying the type of material studied in a single sitting—alternating, for example, among vocabulary, reading and speaking in a new language—seems to leave a deeper impression on the brain than does concentrating on just one skill at a time. Musicians have known this for years, and their practice sessions often include a mix of scales, musical pieces and rhythmic work. Many athletes, too, routinely mix their workouts with strength, speed and skill drills.

The advantages of this approach to studying can be striking, in some topic areas. In a study recently posted online by the journal *Applied Cognitive Psychology*, Doug Rohrer and Kelli Taylor of the University of South Florida taught a group of fourth graders four equations, each to calculate a different dimension of a prism. Half of the children learned by studying repeated examples of one equation, say, calculating the number of prism faces when given the number of sides at the base, then moving on to the next type of calculation, studying repeated examples of that. The other half studied mixed problem sets, which included examples of all four types of calculations grouped together. Both groups solved sample problems along the way, as they studied.

A day later, the researchers gave all of the students a test on the material, presenting new problems of the same type. The children who had studied mixed sets did twice as well as the others, outscoring them 77 percent to 38 percent. The researchers have found the same in experiments involving adults and younger children.

"When students see a list of problems, all of the same kind, they know the strategy to use before they even read the problem," said Dr. Rohrer. "That's like riding a bike with training wheels." With mixed practice, he added, "each problem is different from the last one, which means kids must learn how to choose the appropriate procedure—just like they had to do on the test."

These findings extend well beyond math, even to aesthetic intuitive learning. In an experiment published last month in the journal *Psychology and Aging,* researchers found that college students and adults of retirement age were better able to distinguish the painting styles of 12 unfamiliar artists after viewing mixed collections (assortments, including works from all 12) than after viewing a dozen works from one artist, all together, then moving on to the next painter.

The finding undermines the common assumption that intensive immersion is the best way to really master a particular genre, or type of creative work, said Nate Kornell, a psychologist at Williams College and the lead author of the study. "What seems to be happening in this case is that the brain is picking up deeper patterns when seeing assortments of paintings; it's picking up what's similar and what's different about them," often subconsciously.

Cognitive scientists do not deny that honest-to-goodness cramming can lead to a better grade on a given exam. But hurriedly jam-packing a brain is akin to speed-packing a cheap suitcase, as most students quickly learn—it holds its new load for a while, then most everything falls out.

"With many students, it's not like they can't remember the material" when they move to a more advanced class, said Henry L. Roediger III, a psychologist at Washington University in St. Louis. "It's like they've never seen it before."

When the neural suitcase is packed carefully and gradually, it holds its contents for far, far longer. An hour of study tonight, an hour on the weekend, another session a week from now: such so-called spacing improves later recall, without requiring students to put in more overall study effort or pay more attention, dozens of studies have found.

No one knows for sure why. It may be that the brain, when it revisits material at a later time, has to relearn some of what it has absorbed before adding new stuff— and that that process is itself self-reinforcing.

"The idea is that forgetting is the friend of learning," said Dr. Kornell. "When you forget something, it allows you to relearn, and do so effectively, the next time you see it."

That's one reason cognitive scientists see testing itself—or practice tests and quizzes—as a powerful tool of learning, rather than merely assessment. The process of retrieving an idea is not like pulling a book from a shelf; it seems to fundamentally alter the way the information is subsequently stored, making it far more accessible in the future.

Dr. Roediger uses the analogy of the Heisenberg uncertainty principle in physics, which holds that the act of measuring a property of a particle (position, for example) reduces the accuracy with which you can know another property (momentum, for example): "Testing not only measures knowledge but changes it," he says—and, happily, in the direction of more certainty, not less.

In one of his own experiments, Dr. Roediger and Jeffrey Karpicke, who is now at Purdue University, had college students study science passages from a reading comprehension test, in short study periods. When students studied the same material twice, in back-to-back sessions, they did very well on a test given immediately afterward, then began to forget the material.

But if they studied the passage just once and did a practice test in the second session, they did very well on one test two days later, and another given a week later.

"Testing has such bad connotation; people think of standardized testing or teaching to the test," Dr. Roediger said. "Maybe we need to call it something else, but this is one of the most powerful learning tools we have."

Of course, one reason the thought of testing tightens people's stomachs is that tests are so often hard. Paradoxically, it is just this difficulty that makes them such effective study tools, research suggests. The harder it is to remember something, the harder it is to later forget. This effect, which researchers call "desirable difficulty," is evident in daily life. The name of the actor who played Linc in "The Mod Squad"? Francie's brother in "A Tree Grows in Brooklyn"? The name of the co-discoverer, with Newton, of calculus?

The more mental sweat it takes to dig it out, the more securely it will be subsequently anchored.

None of which is to suggest that these techniques—alternating study environments, mixing content, spacing study sessions, self-testing or all the above—will turn a grade-A slacker into a grade-A student. Motivation matters. So do impressing friends, making the hockey team and finding the nerve to text the cute student in social studies.

"In lab experiments, you're able to control for all factors except the one you're studying," said Dr. Willingham. "Not true in the classroom, in real life. All of these things are interacting at the same time."

But at the very least, the cognitive techniques give parents and students, young and old, something many did not have before: a study plan based on evidence, not schoolyard folk wisdom, or empty theorizing. ▪

Questions for Discussion

1. In this article, UCLA professor Robert A. Bjork states, "We walk around with all sorts of unexamined beliefs about what works that are mistaken." What are some of the unexamined beliefs about teaching styles and learning styles that are discussed in the article?

2. What are some of the research findings cited in the article that may help students get more out of their studying?

3. What do the researchers quoted in this article say about the process of testing and self-testing?

4. How is motivation cited as an important factor in the outcome of studying? How does your own motivation affect your study habits?

In the following article, columnist Leonard Pitts Jr. discusses and challenges current assumptions about racism held by many in the academic community. As you read it, notice the logical bases of his arguments. Try to put them in the form of categorical or conditional syllogisms.

Can Blacks Be Racist?

Leonard Pitts Jr.

"Black people cannot be racist."

It's been maybe 20 years since the first time I heard some member of the black intelligentsia say that on an afternoon talk show. Naturally, all hell broke loose.

Years later, all hell still awaits repair.

I base that assessment on the response to something I did in a recent column. Namely, I defined racism as "this practice of demeaning and denying based on the darkness of skin."

Man, what'd I want to go and say that for? The flood of letters has been unrelenting, dozens of aggrieved Caucasians wanting your poor, benighted correspondent to know that racism, thank you very much, is also felt by those whose skin is not dark at all. Several folks figured I must be one'a them black folk who considers black folk incapable of racism. One individual went so far as to contend that yours truly, like most blacks, hasn't a clue what racism really is.

Well, golly, where to begin?

First, my take on the "blacks can't be racist" argument: Unassailable logic, unfortunate rhetoric.

People who make that argument reason as follows: Yes, blacks can be prejudiced or bigoted, but not "racist" because racism involves systemic oppression—the wielding of power. As blacks neither wield power nor control the system, the reasoning goes, it's beyond their ability to be racist.

I get impatient with people who make the argument in those terms, terms that seem, frankly, calibrated to produce more confrontation than insight. Most people who hear the point framed in that way are, understandably, unable to get past those first inflammatory words: "Blacks can't be racist."

So let's frame it another way. Let's allow that black folks can, indeed, be racist. Or prejudiced, intolerant, biased, bigoted or any other word that floats your boat. Black people are, after all, members of the human race and, as such, are heir to all the idiocy by which human beings are beset.

But with that established, let's also say this: It's an affront to common sense to suggest there is equivalence between black-on-white bigotry and its opposite. This is the point the black intelligentsia's rhetoric has obscured and people like my correspondents have denied, avoided and ignored. As an aggregate, bigoted blacks have much less power to injure whites than vice versa. They also have less history of doing so. These are incontrovertible facts that render hollow the yowling demands that the racism of blacks be accorded a place in the national consciousness commensurate with that of white people.

Hey, when you find a black bigot, feel free to censure and ostracize him or her as the circumstance warrants. I don't care. Just don't pretend the transgression is what it is not. Don't claim it represents a significant threat to the quality of life of white Americans at large.

Because if it represents such a threat, then where are the statistics demonstrating how black bias against whites translates to the mass denial of housing, bank loans, education, employment opportunities, voting rights, medical care or justice? And please, spare me the anecdote about Jane, who couldn't get into school, or Joe, who lost his job, because of affirmative action.

Not the same. Not even close. There are, in fact, reams of statistics documenting that racism has fostered generation after generation of Joes and Janes—not to mention Jamillas, Rasheeds and Keshias—in the African American community. And those numbers come not from the NAACP, the Nation of Islam, the Congressional Black Caucus or any other group with an ax to grind but, rather, from the federal government and from university think tanks. Yet even with those bona fides, some people find evidence of white racism's power dishearteningly easy to ignore.

They have to, I suppose. Otherwise, they wouldn't be able to continue pretending an equivalency that does not exist. And somewhere inside, even THEY must recognize that fact.

Put it like this: If given the option of going through life as a white man suffering the effects of black racism or the reverse, I know which one I'd choose. ▪

Questions for Discussion

1. Pitts makes the following comment:

   > My take on the 'blacks can't be racist' argument: Unassailable logic, unfortunate rhetoric.

   > People who make that argument reason as follows: Yes, blacks can be prejudiced or bigoted, but not 'racist' because racism involves systemic oppression—the wielding of power. As blacks neither wield power nor control the system, the reasoning goes, it's beyond their ability to be racist.

   Can you phrase his commentary as a deductive argument? Why does he call the argument unassailably logical but unfortunate in its rhetoric?

2. What point is Pitts making in this column about the difference between black and white bigotry?

3. What are some of the negative effects of racism towards African Americans that Pitts cites in the article? Do you believe that racism has lessened since this article was first published?

. . . .

Andrew Lam is a writer and commentator on cultural issues. In the following article, he discusses how he realized that his definition of "garbage" changed when his cousin came to visit him from their native Vietnam. Notice as you read that Lam also is made aware of how his reality assumptions and value assumptions changed when he became assimilated to his new country.

Wasted Food, Discovered Souls

Andrew Lam

Last week, I took a cousin newly arrived from Vietnam for a tour of downtown San Francisco, hoping to impress him with America's architectural grandeur. But the tall and shiny high-rises were all too overwhelming for him, and my cousin became very quiet.

Then, as we walked past a large garbage bin filled with papers and boxes, he suddenly stopped and stared, "Brother," he said. "In Vietnam this stuff is all money."

This relative of mine is not an environmentalist. His comment simply reflects his own frugal, third world background. Everything is useful; nothing ever goes to waste.

Back home, he told me, a family could live for a week recycling these papers. "I can't believe they throw all this stuff away," he said, shaking his head. And I felt a slight tug of guilt. My garbage, too, is often full of papers and cans and discarded food.

Yet I am not unfamiliar with his feelings of indignation. I, too, came from that agrarian-based ethos in which land is sacred and everything yielded from the good earth must be treasured. Indeed, what I throw away today would have astounded me years ago.

When my family and I first came to America two decades ago as refugees, my job was to spy on the supermarket across the street from our apartment. When they threw away expired food, my brother and I would spring into action. One night, as we dragged a carton full of outdated frozen pizzas, TV dinners, and cookie dough across the parking lot, we were stopped by a policeman.

Red-faced and stuttering, we offered to return the food to the garbage bin, but the policeman shrugged. "Help yourself, boys," he said, and walked away. But my brother and I never went back. If we were once shocked by America's opulence, we have long since learned to take it for granted that, well, there's plenty more where that came from.

But my cousin got me thinking: Perhaps a sure sign of successful assimilation into an over-developed society is when an immigrant tosses away his sense of frugality and his deep appreciation for what once sustained him.

At home after our excursion, my cousin helped me prepare dinner. A few pieces of apple and pears accidentally fell from my chopping block onto the floor. Immediately, he stooped to pick them up. "You don't have to do that," I wanted to say, but something in his meticulous gesture stopped me.

Instead, as I watched him, a distant and long-cherished memory emerged. I am five years old standing at the edge of a golden rice field at harvest time in the Mekong Delta where my family came from, and watching farmers stoop to gather rice.

I had wanted to show my cousin America's grandeur, but it was he who showed me something else far lovelier. There, on the shiny tile floor of my kitchen, my cousin, too, was busy gathering bits of our old identities—scattered pieces of our soul. ▪

Questions for Discussion

1. What are the differing assumptions of Andrew Lam and his cousin about both the high-rise buildings and the contents of the garbage bins in San Francisco?

2. Lam states, "I, too, came from that agrarian-based ethos in which land is sacred and everything yielded from the good earth must be treasured. Indeed, what I throw away today would have astounded me years ago." How do you think Lam's assumptions about garbage were changed?

3. America is referred to as an "over-developed" society in this article. Do you believe that a society can be overdeveloped? To what extent can development and appreciation of the land harmoniously coexist?

The following humorous article, created by *The Onion,* provides a good example of how deductive truth is subject to change when new information is discovered or when definitions are changed.

Background: Pluto was considered the 9th planet from 1930 until 2006. This smallest and most distant planet had always been somewhat different from the other planets because it was tiny, solid, and moved in a less circular, more elongated orbit than the other eight. While the other planets moved within the boundaries of the constellations of the zodiac, Pluto's path was above and below that band.

Classification is critical to any field of study, and in August 2006, the International Astronomical Union redefined the term "planet" and then reclassified Pluto as a "dwarf planet" based on their decision that a planet should be large enough that its gravity would clear out its region in space. That demoted Pluto to the status of "dwarf planet," a category that it shares with the former asteroids Eris, Ceres, and other objects yet to be discovered.

Bearer of Bad News

NASA Launches Probe to Inform Pluto of Demotion

In August, the International Astronomical Union downgraded Pluto to a dwarf planet. The panel of experts met to officially redefine the characteristics of a planet. To deliver the news to the distant orb about its newly lowered status, scientists at NASA's Kennedy Space Center launched a special messenger probe in September.

"It's tough, but we thought giving it to Pluto straight was the right thing to do," NASA Chief Engineer James Wood said. "After all, it put in 76 years as our ninth planet—it just didn't seem fair to break the news with an impersonal radio transmission beamed from Earth."

The Consoler probe is scheduled to reach Pluto in 2016. Upon landing on the planetoid's surface, the probe will relay to Pluto the news of its demotion, then orbit the tiny celestial body and radio messages of gratitude for its eons of planetary service to convince Pluto that it is still a highly valued part of the solar system's configuration.

"Pluto is more than 3.5 billion miles from the sun," Wood said. "Launching that probe felt like the best way to avoid alienating it any further."

Wood said Consoler will "take pains" to explain to Pluto that the reasons for the demotion "had nothing to do with anything it did personally."

"It was a great planet, and it will be a great dwarf planet," Wood said of Pluto's tenure. "No one is questioning its orbit around the sun, and of course Pluto's gravity and pressure gradient force is plenty sufficient to maintain hydrostatic equilibrium. Pluto still has three moons: Charon, Hydra and Nix. No one's going to take that away from it."

Scientists at NASA have taken precautions that word of the demotion will not reach Pluto before Consoler does. The New Horizons probe, which will pass by Pluto in July 2015, has been instructed to maintain radio silence. It is, however, programmed to congratulate nearby Eris and Ceres for their promotion from asteroids to dwarf planets.

"The Consoler probe will reach Pluto on a Friday, if our calculations are correct," Wood said. "It's always better to do this kind of thing right before the weekend." ▪

Questions for Discussion

1. Consider this major premise of a categorical syllogism:
   A planet is a large spherical object that orbits a star and does not emit light. What needs to be added to this premise to exclude Pluto from being classified as a planet (i.e., how did the experts officially redefine Pluto)?

2. The first official AIU list of the Sun's planets includes Mercury, Venus, Mars, Jupiter, Saturn, Uranus, and Neptune. For 76 years before the official list came out, students were taught that there were nine planets. How does this new categorization exemplify the tentative nature of our knowledge?

3. What changes in curriculum need to be made when a new discovery makes our former assumptions outdated?

4. Read more about it: Trace the reasons why Pluto was considered a planet for so long and the factors creating the change. Also, look for areas of new discovery set in motion by the changed definition of planets and dwarf planets.

Ideas for Writing or Speaking

1. Explain three or four assumptions made by your culture, subculture, or family. These assumptions can be about use of time and/or resources; holiday traditions; the roles of men, women, and/or children; or the place of work, family, and citizenship.

Examples

"One assumption of my family is that everyone will go to college. My parents were expected to go to college by their parents, even though their parents didn't have the money to go themselves.

"It was never directly stated that we had to go to college; it was just taken for granted that we would. My parents would start sentences by saying, 'When you go to college . . .' or 'After you finish college. . . .'

"When my little brother decided to get a job right after high school, everyone was in shock. It never occurred to us that we wouldn't all go straight to college. After he worked two years in a warehouse, my brother did decide to attend college. Maybe he was living up to the family's expectations, but I think he was hoping for an easier life! (from a student).

"My parents were a little more than displeased with my practice SAT test score. I scored in the low 2100s, and let's be blunt here, if it weren't for my Asian parents, I'd probably be out celebrating right now. But they were thoroughly unhappy with me, and my mother began her typical rant of 'I think we need to focus on the other two kids now that our hopes and dreams are going to be wasted in this one' soon after she saw the score sheet. . . . My Dad just shook his head at me and glared at the paper in his hand; my mother paced around the house wondering what she had done wrong. . . . I'm pretty sure people think that

I'm being arrogant when I say that I can't get anything lower than a 2300 (and that's pushing it) on my SATs, but it's just so hard to understand unless you're actually sitting at the dining table and your mother says, 'Cynthia, I'm expecting no less than a 2350 from you, Look at Jeffrey, he got a perfect score.'"[20]

2. Choose a social, political, or religious movement or group and write about three assumptions that guide this group. Take a position, agreeing or disagreeing with the assumptions of this group. Begin with an introductory paragraph that contains your conclusion (thesis statement). Then write a paragraph for each assumption you discuss. End with a paragraph that summarizes your beliefs about the underlying assumptions of this group.

   Some possible organizations and belief systems to research for this assignment: Greenpeace, the Young Republicans, the Democratic Party, the Libertarian Party, Christianity, Hinduism, Judaism, Islam, Buddhism, Action for Children's Television, The National Rifle Association, Mothers Against Drunk Drivers, the Society for the Prevention of Cruelty to Animals, and Amnesty International.

3. Using the same organizational format as Idea 2, explore the assumptions made by both sides of a controversial issue. For example, you might explore the assumptions of people who support and people who are against tuition for community colleges. One assumption of those who support tuition might be that people work harder when they have to pay for education; an assumption of those against tuition might be that fees are an unnecessary and prohibitive burden on the poor and that they are therefore "classist."

   Find several assumptions on both sides of your issue. Then explain which assumptions you believe to be the most reasonable and why.

Films for Analysis and Discussion

He's Just Not That Into You (2009, PG-13)

This film involves many examples of people misreading clues about the behavior of others. It centers on a young woman, Gigi (Ginnifer Goodwin) who is seeking to find a lasting romance and who makes faulty reality assumptions about why her dates don't return her calls and her interest. She meets a man named Alex (Justin Long) who helps her to stop "jumping to conclusions" and to interpret the behavior of other men more accurately. The film is based on a book whose authors wanted women to understand that they often make faulty assumptions about the behavior of men because of their own wishful thinking.

Taken (2008, PG 13)

Taken is a thriller that highlights the varying assumptions the characters make that affect their safety as well as their relationships. It is the story of Bryan (Liam Neeson), a former government agent and his daughter Kim (Maggie Grace) who lives with her mother and wealthy stepfather. Kim, a 17 year old, is planning a trip to Europe with a girlfriend, and her parents make different assumptions about her ability to handle this trip without adult supervision. When Kim arrives in Paris, she and her friend make assumptions that get them into deadly danger, and Bryan must

[20] Cynthia Meng, *Outstanding: Growing up Asian*, 2e (Shidai Zhuanji Chinese Literary Collections, Inc.: 2010), pp. 130–131.

use all of his skills to try to rescue them. Note the numerous reality assumptions throughout this film, from assumptions about the value of different birthday presents to assumptions about who can and cannot be trusted.

The Departed (2006, R)

This film keeps the audience making assumptions and guesses about what is really true even though much information seems to be provided at an early stage. Within the first few minutes of the film, we find out that there is a police informant within the Boston mafia (Leonardo DiCaprio) and someone working for the mafia in the Massachusetts' State Police Department (Matt Damon). Although the men have not met, their actions determine the fate of both their lives. What is assumed to be the truth almost never is in this film, and even when the credits roll, the answers aren't delivered in a nicely wrapped package.

Similar Films and Classics

Crash (2005, R)

This film involves a number of characters of different racial, ethnic, professional, and socioeconomic backgrounds. Note the many assumptions and stereotypes made by the characters and how they all turn out to be wrong.

The Verdict (1981, R)

The Verdict is a fascinating story in which a lawyer realizes that the willingness of all parties to settle out of court will hurt his client and hide the truth of the medical malpractice that brought the lawsuit. Note the self-protective assumptions made by most of the defendants.

To Kill a Mockingbird (1962)

This story, told from the point of view of a woman remembering the events of her childhood, makes many statements about stereotyping and harmful reality assumptions. The main character's father, a lawyer who defends an unjustly accused black man in 1932 Alabama, is the voice of reason about the trial and other life lessons. The father Atticus tells his daughter, "You never know someone until you step inside their skin and walk around a little."

Twelve Angry Men (1957)

This classic story, which has since been made into a TV movie, tells of the struggles of a jury to reach a unanimous verdict in a murder trial. Each juror makes different reality assumptions and sticks to them until a second look at the evidence creates a breakthrough. This is an excellent example of the various perspectives that emerge when a group decision needs to be made.

Television Shows for Analysis and Discussion

Crimes are often solved using a process of deductive reasoning. There are numerous television programs that deal with the unraveling of crimes. Some of these are reality programs, such as *The Forensic Files,* and *The First 48.* Newsmagazine shows such as *Dateline NBC* and ABC's *20/20* often contain stories of crimes that were or still are difficult to solve. The many programs on civil court proceedings present examples of how judges use deductive reasoning to render a decision on a case. In addition, fictional shows about crime, which often base their stories on real cases, will provide examples of the use of deductive reasoning. Some of these programs include *CSI*, *Bones*, and *Law and Order*. *House* provides excellent illustrations of how assumptions about medical diagnoses are tested and proven or disproven.

Reality shows that focus on diverse lifestyles, such as *Trading Spouses*, *Wife Swap*, or *What Not to Wear* provide very clear examples of different reality assumptions about various aspects of daily living.

4

Inductive Arguments

Statistical and Causal Generalizations

Prove It to Me—What Are the Statistics?

A critical thinker understands the basics of polling and the legitimate uses of statistical research in supporting conclusions.

A critical thinker understands the structure and uses of inductive reasoning, including statistical and causal generalizations.

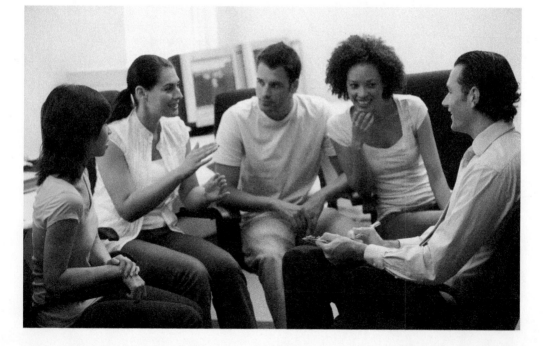

Much of the information we use to support our claims comes from statistical research and polling data.

THIS CHAPTER WILL COVER

- The use of statistical evidence in arguments
- The reporting of statistical data
- The use of causal generalizations

📖—⎡Read on **mythinkinglab.com**

((•—⎡Listen on **mythinkinglab.com**

I n the last three chapters, we focused on the foundations of arguments, including issues, reasons, conclusions, value assumptions, and reality assumptions. We looked at deduction as a tool to help us discern the logic and the truth of the statements we make and to help us base our decisions on sound reasoning.

As we discussed in the first chapter, anyone can have an opinion (i.e., form a conclusion) and give reasons for that opinion. But a critical thinker evaluates the quality and credibility of the reasons before offering or accepting a conclusion. Inductive arguments aim at establishing strong, if not absolutely certain, conclusions. Inductive strength is based on good evidence from which we can draw useful generalizations.

In this chapter, we will consider the kinds of evidence and the quality of the evidence used to support inductive generalizations; we will learn principles for evaluating both statistical generalizations and causal generalizations.

Inductive Reasoning

> Do not confuse opinion, attitude, personal bias, speculation, personal assurance, or unsupported generalization with hard, factual evidence.
>
> Robert J. Gula, author of *Nonsense*

Thus far, we have looked at the concept of deductive certainty and the criteria for developing a sound deductive argument. Ideally, all of the issues that we face could be resolved with certainty by following correct reasoning. In our human state, however, very few conclusions can be proven beyond a shadow of a doubt. Even our criminal court system asks only that a conclusion be proven "beyond a *reasonable* doubt." That means the evidence does offer strong and compelling support for the conclusion with the reservation that there may be an *unusual* exception. When we offer evidence that gives weight (but not complete certainty) to a conclusion, we are reasoning inductively.

Inductive arguments are evaluated on the basis of their strength. A strong inductive argument does not guarantee the truth of the conclusion, but it does provide solid support for the conclusion.

If we can present evidence to prove that a premise (assertion, statement) is very *likely* to be true, we have valuable information on which to base our decisions. In addition, if we know there may be exceptions, we can understand them when they are encountered.

The process of **induction** or inductive reasoning occurs when we use facts or research findings to make generalizations. Stated in coded form, we offer proof that *most* As are Bs. Therefore, if I encounter an A, it is probably a B. However, I realize that there are exceptions. Robert Pirsig explains the difference between induction and deduction in his book *Zen and the Art of Motorcycle Maintenance*:

> Two kinds of logic are used, inductive and deductive. . . . If the cycle goes over a bump and the engine misfires, and then goes over another bump and the engine misfires, and then goes over a long smooth stretch of road and there is no misfiring, and then goes over a [third] bump and the engine misfires again, one can logically conclude that the misfiring is caused by the bumps. That is induction. . . .
>
> If, from reading the hierarchy of facts about the machine, the mechanic knows the horn of the cycle is powered exclusively by electricity from the battery, then he can logically infer that if the battery is dead the horn will not work. That is deduction.[1]

Most of the issues we face on a daily basis involve inductive reasoning. We gather facts from our background experiences and our reading and research—experiential and empirical data—to come to conclusions that make sense to us because of their strength. We then use these conclusions to guide our decisions and actions. For example, let's say a woman receives a call from her sister who tells her that she has developed breast cancer. The woman does some research and talks to her own doctor. Her inductive reasoning goes like this:

> Researchers claim that most women who have a family history of breast cancer (P) have an increased risk for developing breast cancer (Q). (Most Ps are Qs).
>
> My mother (m1) developed breast cancer (Q).
>
> My sister (m2) developed breast cancer (Q).
>
> My two aunts (m3 and m4) had breast cancer (Q).
>
> Since m1, m2, m3, and m4 constitute family members, I have a family history (P); I (m5) am P.
>
> Therefore, it is likely that I (m5) also have an increased risk for developing breast cancer (Q). (Conclusion—m5 will probably be Q, because most Ps are Qs.)

Can you see that the conclusion "It is likely that I also have an increased risk for developing breast cancer" is not a certainty, but a strong possibility? The woman who reasons in this way can now examine her choices in a logical manner. She can do a reasonable risk assessment about her chances of developing cancer and also her

induction (often called inductive reasoning) The process of drawing generalizations from known facts or research to give strength and support to conclusions.

[1] Robert M. Pirsig, *Zen and the Art of Motorcycle Maintenance: An Inquiry into Values* (New York: William Morrow, 1974), p. 99.

chances of recovery if she were to develop this form of cancer. She may choose to be tested more frequently than someone without a similar family history. Some women faced with this family history have had healthy breasts removed before cancer could develop. These women will never know if they might have "dodged the bullet" and avoided the disease without having taken these measures. But they reasoned that, in their individual cases, the probability was high enough and the consequences grave enough to justify their actions.

When you use **inductive reasoning,** you look at evidence and draw conclusions that are not certain, but likely. These conclusions are called *inductive generalizations*. All inductive generalizations are *possible,* but within the range of possibility, some are much more *probable* than others because they are based on good, convincing evidence (see Figure 4–1).

inductive reasoning (often called induction) The process of finding truth by making observations; inferring general laws and truths from specific instances.

Reminder

Critical thinkers use the process of induction to draw reasonable conclusions and to make thoughtful decisions.

✳ Explore on **mythinkinglab.com**

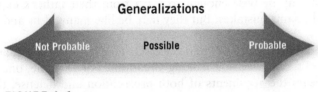

Generalizations

Not Probable   **Possible**   Probable

FIGURE 4–1

Strong evidence makes conclusions more probable.

Many deductive premises are derived from previous inductive arguments with strong evidence. For example, a parent may present the following major premise of a deductive argument to a son or daughter heading off to college:

If you charge more on your credit card than you can afford, you will get yourself into debt.

The student—let's call him David—leaves for school and is suddenly faced with the responsibility of handling finances above the tuition and housing that his parents have paid and a small scholarship that gives him the money for books. David gets a part-time job to cover the expenses of clothing, entertainment, gas, insurance and repairs for his car, and any other goodies he may wish to buy.

David has been careful not to use the credit card that was sent to him, but he does keep it in his wallet, just in case. As the school year goes by, some unexpected expenses use up most of his salary, and David starts using the credit card: He has to have a brake job on his car, he wants new clothes for a dance, and he meets someone that he'd like to take out for dinner and a movie once a week.

When some of David's friends ask him to join them on a vacation during the winter break, he knows he can't afford to go but decides to charge the trip anyway. When he returns from his vacation, a bill from his credit card company reveals that his monthly payment has gone up for the third time.

If he took the time, David might reason:

> The first time I overcharged, I owed more to the credit card company every month.
>
> The second time I overcharged, I owed so much that I had to extend my working hours to pay the credit card bill.
>
> The third time I overcharged, I realized that my monthly payment would be used just to pay the finance charge, and it would take several years to pay off what I owe.
>
> Because of all of these incidents, I'm in debt.
>
> Therefore, if I overcharge on credit cards, I will be in debt.

David has come to this conclusion *inductively*, through a series of experiences. He has learned from his mistakes that it is harmful to overcharge on his credit cards. Probably, David will pass his wisdom on to his own future children, in the form of a *deductive* argument:

> If people overcharge on their credit cards, they will be in debt.
>
> I overcharged on my credit card.
>
> Therefore, I was in debt.

His children may be wise enough to learn from their father's experience and avoid making the same mistakes. But they may be like many of us and come to the truth inductively, through personal trials and errors.

Inductive generalizations, such as those discovered in David's case, are also foundational to more formal decision-making situations. For example, once a jury in a criminal trial hears the arguments of both prosecution and defense, the members of the jury begin to use inductive reasoning to examine the evidence. They receive some information that is definitely true; for example, they may know that a murder has been committed. They may also receive undeniably factual information about the DNA of the victim and of the defendant and about the legal issues involved in the case.

However, the jury will hear different interpretations about what may be concluded from the given factual information. Both sides will try to convince the jury of the strength of their arguments by presenting the statements of experts and of witnesses; by citing research, statistics, and forensic evidence; by using examples of similar cases; and by searching for a pattern or sequence of events that would explain that the defendant did (or did not) commit the crime. Their interpretations of the various types of evidence will be expressed as inductive generalizations.

In this chapter and the next, we will focus on methods of examining and assessing the strength of evidence used to support conclusions in inductive arguments, whether the issue is the guilt or innocence of a defendant, the probable diagnosis of an illness, the qualifications of a political candidate, the usefulness of a product or service, or the importance of a social cause.

When you understand various forms of inductive reasoning, you are better equipped to evaluate the quality of the evidence people give for their conclusions. You can then defend convincing arguments and refute poorly supported arguments. You will be ready to strengthen your own reasoning and to make good decisions based on that reasoning.

Statistical Evidence

Statistical evidence, which leads to the form of inductive reasoning known as **statistical generalizations,** refers to data collected by polling and research studies. Pollsters and researchers use systematic methods to get results with great predictive value; that is, they can tell us what probably will happen in a given situation. For example, a Gallup poll or a Harris poll generally reflects how people will vote and who will be elected to political office.

Why do we carry out research aimed at generating accurate statistics? One motivation for doing research is to have a sense of control over our individual and collective futures; as critically thinking people, we want to act clearly, deliberately, and responsibly. We want to be prepared for future events. We can anticipate the future, which is unknown, by reasoning from known facts and observations; that is the process of reasoning inductively.

On a daily basis, we use statistics to make predictions and decisions in our personal lives. For example, if you've been on three blind dates arranged by your cousin and they have all been terrible, you will probably predict that a fourth date arranged by this person will turn out the same way. If you have noticed that a particular route home from school is usually congested during commuting hours, you might choose to take another route or schedule your classes for less busy times. Or, you might watch a baseball game and predict that because the batter has a .350 average and has been doing well the last few games, he will make at least a base hit right now. You're surprised if he strikes out. On the other hand, a batter with a .220 average who has just recovered from an injury would not be likely to get a good hit. If he does, you are again surprised.

As individuals, we reason inductively by generalizing from observations we make about our own circumstances and experiences. As a society, we use more formal research methods to get accurate information about social issues such as rates of disease and drug and alcohol usage; patterns of criminal activity; likely election results; and public opinion about government policies. We use this information to make decisions about our future direction; statistical research helps us decide which programs should be funded or denied funding, which should be modified, and which goals we are likely to achieve.

statistical evidence
Data collected by polling and research studies that can be used to make statistical generalizations.

statistical generalizations
Inferences drawn from statistical evidence that are used to give strength to inductive arguments.

The Many Uses of Statistics

Numerous professions rely on statistics. Lending companies use statistics on interest rates to support their arguments that people should get car and home loans or refinance existing loans. Real estate agents show statistics on public school test scores to clients to convince them to buy a home in a particular neighborhood. Weather forecasters use statistics to help them make predictions, and seismologists use statistics about past earthquakes to predict the progression of future earthquakes. Political advisers use statistics to decide the popularity of candidates and policies. Advertisers collect evidence on the size and nature of magazine, newspaper, and website audiences to decide where to place their advertisements. The Nielsen ratings give commercial advertisers a good idea of which television channels are being watched in a given time slot.

New ways to gather statistics are often discovered. One method, called a "Q" (Quality) score, has become the industry standard for measuring how audiences feel about politicians, products, celebrities, broadcast and cable programs, brand names, and even performers of the past. Q scores actually summarize the various perceptions and feelings that consumers have into a single, but revealing, "likeability" measurement. This research looks beyond the numbers of viewers of programs and assesses the connection people feel with a program or product.[2]

The categories of performers who are assessed by Q scores include a wide range of public figures such as actors and actresses, reality show contestants, musicians, consumer reporters, athletes, authors, chefs, comedians, models, directors, and business executives.

Q score companies promise to deliver information that goes beyond the Nielson ratings and to let producers and advertising executives know how viewers feel about individual celebrities as well as cartoons, brands, and specific programs. The assumption is that people will be attentive to advertisements or programs that are connected to their favorite candidates, actors, athletes, and other famous figures. Producers and advertisers pay thousands of dollars to receive Q score information that identifies which celebrity would be a good spokesperson for their products, an attractive, recognizable model for a commercial, or a desirable star for a television show.

One columnist notes the impact of the Q score as follows:

> The research into who watches television, when and why, has produced an entire sub-industry of pollsters and numbers-crunchers. One of the best-kept secrets, and at the same time one of the most valued tools of network executives, is the so-called "Q" score.
>
> That's short for TvQ, the periodic report's title, with the "Q" standing for qualitative. Essentially, average viewers are asked which stars and shows they recognize, then asked to rate them in terms of best-liked personalities and programs. The results are invariably hush-hush, but they are prized by network execs as a measurement of what shows create audience favorites, even if they're low-rated.[3]

When a celebrity is involved in a controversy or an important, career-changing decision, advertisers are interested in the public's reaction, and they seek out Q-score statistics. For example, consider the following article that followed LeBron James' decision to move to the Miami Heat in 2010. Note that his decision not only affected his Q score but also took a toll on the Q scores of some of his teammates.

LeBron's Q Score Takes Huge Hit

Darren Rovell

Miami Heat guard LeBron James has a lot of work to do on his reputation. That's at least according to the latest Q Score, released exclusively to CNBC, on Tuesday morning.

---

[2] Jennie L. Phipps, "TVQ and Cable Q Measure Series' Popularity with Targeted Viewers," *Television Week*, April 21, 2003.
[3] Jonathan Burlingame, "Television," *Contra Costa Times*, January 12, 1990, p. 10 C.

Following James' move from the Cleveland Cavaliers to the Miami Heat, and the way he announced it in the ESPN hour-show dubbed "The Decision," the general population has changed its opinion of the man nicknamed King.

In January 2010, The Q Scores Company took a poll of the general population and found that 24 percent of people thought of James in a positive light, compared to a 22 percent negative opinion.

Henry Schafer, executive vice president of the company, told CNBC that the average sports personality has a 15 percent positive score and a 24 percent negative score.

"LeBron's positive score at that time was the highest we had ever seen it," Schafer said.

But since "The Decision" show on July 8, things have gone seriously downhill for the NBA star.

LeBron's Q Score Today?

Schafer says that now only 14 percent of the general population see him as a positive figure, a 41.6 percent drop, while 39 percent view him in a negative light, a 77 percent decline.

In fact, LeBron is now the sixth most disliked sports personality, according to The Q Score Company, behind Michael Vick, Tiger Woods, Terrell Owens, Chad Ochocinco and Kobe Bryant.

"Instead of his change to the Heat being seen as the best way he can win a championship, many have looked at it and how he chose to announce it as a selfish move," Schafer said.

Perhaps equally as interesting is the fact that James has apparently dragged down the general population's opinion of his new teammates.

Dwyane Wade's positive Q score went from 21 in January to 15 today.

His negative Q score rose from 18 in January to 25 today. Chris Bosh—whose move to Miami was part of what sealed the deal for LeBron—saw even a worse drop. His positive Q score only fell from a 13 in January to a 12 today, but his negative Q Score rose from 21 percent in January to 35 percent today.

Schafer says that LeBron's "Decision" was one of the most detrimental acts—not related to any anti-social behavior—by a sports personality since the Q Scores were first developed more than 45 years ago.

Stop and Think

How might advertisers or television and film producers use some of the information gathered from Q scores?

Just as Q score researchers and the Nielson Company help television executives decide which programs and personalities are worth keeping, other companies track statistics concerning target populations for products and services. For decades, businesses have catered to the baby-boomer market, those 76.1 million individuals born between 1946 and 1964. Advertisers continue to use music, celebrities, and ideas that appeal to them to sell cars, vacations, and "age-defying" products. Since the 1960s, baby boomers have been considered the major target audience influencing the economy.

Now, as the baby boomers are aging, business leaders and marketers are turning their attention to a new group, the tween market. Generally defined as children between the ages of 8 and 14, statistics show that tweens have lots of disposable income. Research by the Canadian Television network YTV cited purchasing power in that country alone totaling $1.8 billion, with projected increases of 10 percent each year, and the research firm NPD Funworld (a marketing organization) credits tween spending with bringing $3 billion of new money to the marketplace.[4] And *Business Week* reports that there are nearly 21 million tweens (ages 6–12) and young teens in the United States who control more than $50 billion in purchasing power.[5] As a result of their spending power, tweens are rapidly becoming a primary focus of advertisers and programmers. In addition, retailers use statistics to follow and capitalize on trends in the financially powerful teen market. During recent recessionary times, marketers noted that fashion spending was down by 14 percent for teens in the United States. But a survey by the investment banking and asset management firm, Piper Jaffray noted that more "value-oriented" clothing spending and technology purchases were both strong. Piper Jaffray's "Taking Stock With Teens" survey is a research project focused on gathering input from approximately 4,500 students with an average age of 16.5 years. Teen spending patterns, fashion trends, and brand and media preferences are periodically assessed through visits to geographically diverse high schools in nine states, and through an online survey of a wider group of teens from 37 states.

> Among the 2011 survey's results are the findings that teen buying trends in portable devices show the rising popularity of Apple's iPhone and iPod. The market share of iPhone rose to 17 percent, and, in the next six months, 37 percent of surveyed teens intend to purchase an iPhone (up from 31 percent one year ago). iTunes has remained the dominant music provider with 95 percent market share among online music services. Netflix appears well-positioned for increased DVD-by-mail usage and movie streaming, which collectively represents 63 percent of movie rental activity among teens, up from 42 percent two years ago.[6]

Business leaders also use statistics when they research "best practices" for the workplace. The American Psychological Association gives awards to companies who create exemplary working environments for their employees. Note how their research is used in the following excerpt from Northwestern University.

Healthy Work Environments Give Companies a Competitive Edge

Kelly C. Doherty

Two Chicago-area companies recently won Psychologically Healthy Workplace Awards from the American Psychological Association.

[4] Paul A. Peterson, "Tweens Take Over: Y Generation Is the Wunderkind of Brand Marketing," *TDMonthly*, June, 2003.

[5] *Business Week Weekend,* "Tween Power Purchasing Strength of Kids," December 12, 2006. businessweek.com, http://www.businessweek.com/mediacenter/video/bwweekend/2422f1b1427994.

[6] "Piper Jaffray Concludes 21st Semi-Annual Spring 2011 Taking Stock with Teens Survey," April 11, 2011. http://green.tmcnet.com/news/2011/04/11/5435552.htm.

The awards are based on five criteria: employee involvement, work-life balance, employee growth and development, health and safety and employee recognition, along with an over-arching theme of communication, said Alan Graham of the APA. Psychological health and business can be mutually beneficial, to both companies and employees, said David Ballard, assistant executive director for marketing and business development at the APA.

Leaders Bank, headquartered in Oak Brook, won one of the five main awards. Sara Mikuta, chief financial officer, said the bank had employee health and wellness in mind from the beginning. When Leaders Bank opened 10 years ago, "we hired a social worker," to come in and help with team building and strategies in order to provide a psychologically healthy environment for employees, Mikuta said.

ATI Physical Therapy, based in Bolingbrook with locations in five states, received a Best Practices Honor for its Get Fit employee-led wellness program. The Get Fit program helps to create a "team spirit" among employees as the different offices hold friendly competitions to meet their health goals, said Lisa Gutierrez, vice president of human resources. This program, along with open communication, company-supplied healthy snacks, and schedule flexibility help ATI to live by their motto of "our work, our life, our balance," Gutierrez said.

Mental health in the workplace can affect customer service and client interaction. Brian McKenna, director of counseling at OMNI Youth Services, a former award winner in the northwest suburbs, said health and wellness at his company means counselors and other staff can better serve the youth they work with.

"Taking care of employees takes care of the bottom line," said Jennifer Thompson, associate professor of the business psychology department at the Chicago School of Professional Psychology.

In addition to keeping employees satisfied, motivated and able to manage stress, a psychologically healthy workplace can result in higher productivity, lower health costs and turnover rates, and an increase in morale, Ballard said.

Facts and Figures

Five criteria that applicants are evaluated on for the Psychologically Healthy Workplace Awards

- Employee involvement
- Work-life balance
- Employee growth and development
- Health and safety
- Employee recognition

By the numbers:

- 74 percent of employees say work is a significant source of stress and one in five has missed work as a result of stress
- 55 percent of employees say they were less productive at work as a result of stress
- 52 percent of employees report they have considered or made a decision about their career, such as looking for a new job, declining a promotion or leaving a job, based on workplace stress
- 52 percent of employees say job demands interfere with family or home responsibilities, while 43 percent say home and family responsibilities interfere with job performance

- 31 percent of adults experience stress as a result of managing work and family responsibilities and 35 percent cite jobs interfering with their family or personal time as a significant source of stress ∎

When the baseball commission did statistical research on steroid use and found that between 5 percent and 7 percent of players tested positive, that discovery prompted them to create a drug policy that imposes fines and suspensions. "In my view of the world, it's hard to say use is rampant based on these results," said Robert Manfred, baseball's vice president for labor relations. "But 5 percent is not an acceptable number to us. From our perspective, it's still a problem that we'll continue to work on until we reach zero."[7] Unfortunately, there are new challenges to the goal of zero drug use for baseball players, as drugs become more sophisticated and testing methods have not caught up to them.

> The major problem of the league now is on how to cope up with chemists who are creating new performance-enhancing drugs. Since there are already reliable tests for anabolic steroids, many of the professional athletes including baseball players are shifting to the use of human growth hormone because the current tests can't effectively detect this substance. HGH can only be detected using blood tests but the major league is still using urine tests to determine if the player is doping. Another problem is the creation of several designer steroids for which most manufacturers alter the chemical composition to make it undetectable during laboratory tests.
>
> The commissioner is also skeptical on the actual number of baseball players who are using steroids and other performance enhancing drugs. "I've had a player tell me that a drug test is an intelligence test. There is no test for HGH. There are a number of athletes taking steroids with a doctor's prescription. So I'm skeptical about how much drug use is still going on," Vincent said. He wrote an article last month for the Wall Street Journal, which details his views on the use of steroids in sport. It was titled "Doping Has No Place In Sports: A good left-handed pitcher should be worth more than a good blood chemist."[8]

Government agencies also conduct statistical studies to determine the best use of taxpayer dollars. If the statistics tell us that the rate of teenage pregnancy is down but the rate of teenage drug use is up, then government and community efforts can be focused on current drug problems. If student scores in math and science are declining but scores in English and history are high, then more attention can be usefully directed to improving education in math and science.

Sometimes the results of statistical research offer evidence that local, national, or international spending priorities need to be changed. Several states, for example, have created more stringent rules for young drivers based on statistical findings. In Illinois, research on auto accidents showed that, even though only 6 percent of drivers were 16 years old, they accounted for 16 percent of crash fatalities. As a result, the state strengthened its graduated license program by requiring young drivers

[7] Jim Salisbury, "Baseball Fails Goal on Steroid Test Results" *Contra Costa Times,* November 14, 2003.
[8] "Baseballs Steroid Era Isn't Over Says Commissioner," http://www.steroidsources.com/Steroid-Information/2010/06/baseballs-steroid-era-isnt-over-says-commissioner/.

to increase their training to 50 hours, including 10 hours of night driving, in order to qualify for an initial license. Parents or legal guardians must sign a letter verifying that young drivers applying for a license have completed the requirements. Drivers must be 18 years old to have a full license, and restrictions on the license still apply until they reach the age of 21.

As we've discussed, statistics are used to create relevant policies that address real societal problems. Individuals also use statistical research to make decisions about personal choices; for example, statistics are used to advise students about issues that take a toll on success in college and on their health and well-being. The following data on college drinking are offered by a peer counseling website for Cal Poly University:

> Here are a few sobering statistics on how drinking too much, too often can put a serious damper on your dreams of achieving academic glory—or even your dreams of just graduating:
>
> According to the Core Institute, an organization that surveys college drinking practices, 300,000 of today's college students will eventually die of alcohol-related causes such as drunk driving accidents, cirrhosis of the liver, various cancers and heart disease.
>
> 159,000 of today's first-year college students will drop out of school next year for alcohol- or other drug-related reasons. The average student spends about $900 on alcohol each year. Do you want to know how much cash the average student drops on his or her books? About $450.
>
> Almost one-third of college students admit to having missed at least one class because of their alcohol or drug use, and nearly one-quarter of students report bombing a test or project because of the aftereffects of drinking or doing drugs.
>
> One night of heavy drinking can impair your ability to think abstractly for up to 30 days, limiting your ability to relate textbook reading to what your professor says, or to think through a football play.
>
> 90% of all campus rapes occur when alcohol has been used by either the assailant or the victim.
>
> At least one out of five college students abandons safe sex practices when they're drunk, even if they do protect themselves when they're sober.
>
> 55% of female students and 75% of male students involved in acquaintance rape admit to having been drinking or using drugs when the incident occurred.
>
> 60% of college women who are infected with STDs, including genital herpes and AIDS, report that they were under the influence of alcohol at the time they had intercourse with the infected person.
>
> According to the Centers for Disease Control, 1 in 1,500 college students is HIV positive, and the fastest-growing populations of American people infected with HIV are teenagers and young adults.[9]

[9] Cal Poly peer counseling website. www.hcs.calpoly.edu/peerhealth/alcohol/info_students_stats.html. Update: 8/25/2009.

How the Research Is Done

As we have seen, in this age of the proliferation of statistical information, most people and professions are influenced by the findings of research studies, and these studies are frequently used as a basis for making significant decisions. Check your local or national newspaper or news-oriented websites on any given day, and you will probably notice several reports concerning recent research studies. How do we determine the quality of the statistical evidence we hear or read? To answer this question, we need to have a basic understanding of how the research is carried out.

When someone creates a research study, he or she needs to consider three questions:

1. What do I want to find out?
   This is called the **characteristic of interest.**

2. Whom do I want to know about?
   This is called the **target population.**

3. Whom can I study to get accurate answers about my entire target population?
   This is called the **sample.** We usually can't study everyone in a given target population, so we have to observe some representative members of the population. For polling, the minimum sample size is usually 1,000.

characteristic of interest
The specific question that a researcher seeks to answer concerning a given population.

target population
The group about which a researcher wishes to generalize.

sample   Members of the target population who are studied by a researcher.

Skill

Understand the basic structure of statistical research.

Examples

Characteristic of interest: What are the most popular television programs in the United States?

Target population: Residents of the United States who watch television.

Sample: At least 1,000 randomly selected Americans who watch television.

Characteristic of interest: Who will win the next U.S. presidential election?

Target population: Americans who are eligible to vote.

Sample: At least 1,000 randomly selected Americans who are eligible to vote.

Characteristic of interest: Whether Canadian parents want screens on all Internet sites that advise of violent or sexual content.

Target population: Canadians who are parents.

Sample: 1,000 randomly selected Canadian parents.

The characteristic of interest and target population are fairly easy to identify. The quality of statistical research depends largely on the sample drawn from the target population. For a study to be accurate and reliable, several things must be true about this sample.

The Sample Must Be Large Enough

Any sample studied must be sufficiently large to justify the generalizations drawn from the research. Otherwise, we are dealing in poor experimental design or even stereotyping. If someone says, "Men are terrible cooks—both my brother and my boyfriend have burned dinners this year," she is generalizing from a couple of cases. Her outline would look like this:

Characteristic of interest: Whether men can cook well.

Target population: One-half of the human race.

Sample: My brother and my boyfriend.

Sometimes when we stand back and look at what someone is claiming and the evidence she uses, we can see how inadequate the argument is. Yet how often do we talk like this or agree when others talk like this?

A real problem in both statistical and experimental research is having the resources to study a sufficient sample. Researcher Frank Sulloway discusses this problem:

Small studies are less reliable than large studies. The typical behavioral study involves about 70 subjects. Owing to statistical error, studies routinely fail to confirm relationships that are known to be true for larger populations. . . . Everyone knows that girls at age eighteen are taller than they are at age fourteen. In samples of only 70 subjects, this lawful relationship will be validated statistically less than half the time! Common sense dictates that findings should count more if they are based on 10,000 subjects than if they are based on 100.[10]

Sulloway suggests that when only small samples can be studied, researchers combine the results of several studies in order to draw more reliable generalizations.

Stop and Think

Assess the adequacy of sample size relative to a target population by outlining the following claims that are based on inadequate samples. State the target population, the characteristic of interest, and the sample.

"Asians are so good at math; there are four of them in my algebra class, and they have the top scores."

"People who live in that part of town are so weird—I saw two women with green hair there last week."

"Men have such a hard time showing their feelings—my dad has never cried in front of us."

There are many theories about why we so easily jump to hasty conclusions about a whole group of people (target population) based on a small sample of people. One theory is that we feel more secure in this complex world when we can place everyone in a narrowly defined category.

[10] Frank Sulloway, *Born to Rebel* (New York: Pantheon Books, Random House, Inc., 1996).

Another theory is that we are not trained or motivated enough to be careful about our generalizations. Many of us enjoy giving our opinions, but we're not willing to expend the time and energy to find the data that are required to prove them. So we give opinions about topics we really are just guessing about; other people do the same thing and we call it "conversing" and "socializing" and everybody's happy. If we happen to hear reliable evidence about a topic of interest to us, we add that to our conversation too.

Most of us get defensive about our pet stereotypes and indefensible positions and don't like people to shake us up. However, as we become critical thinkers, our positions will be taken more carefully and backed up with the kind of evidence that gives us real confidence about the opinions we share with others.

Reminder

The sample must be large enough—that is, enough people must be studied—to justify the generalizations made by the researchers.

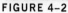 Explore on **mythinkinglab.com**

The Sample Must Represent the Target Audience

representative A quality of a research sample in which the sample has the same significant characteristics in the same proportion as the target population.

When a sample is **representative,** the people studied are like the people about whom you wish to generalize. For example, if you want to study the effects of fluoride on children in the United States, it would not be enough to study only children who live in the Northeast. If you draw a conclusion from your research, it must reflect the entire target group.

For a sample to be representative, it must have the same significant characteristics in the same proportions as the target group; this principle is illustrated in Figure 4–2. If the sample does not have these characteristics, then it is not

FIGURE 4–2

A representative sample has the same significant characteristics in the same proportion as the target population.

representative and is called **biased.** A biased sample does not provide adequate evidence to support a conclusion.

A common problem with modern social science research is that many researchers are college professors who use their students as "volunteers" for their studies. While some extrapolations from student samples to the general population are reasonable, other findings may relate more specifically to college students on a particular campus rather than to larger segments of the population. Student populations generally reflect a limited age grouping, and students on a given campus may be more politically liberal or conservative than the general population. Their ideas about an upcoming election can't be generalized to (be said to represent) the larger public. And if the sample studied comes from only one class—say, political science—it may not even be representative of the college as a whole.

biased A sample that does not reflect a random, representative population. A biased sample does not provide adequate evidence to support a conclusion.

The Sample Must Be Random

Randomness is closely linked to the representativeness of a sample. It has been found that you can draw solid conclusions about a large target population by using a much smaller, but representative and randomly selected, segment of that population. **Randomness** means that every member of the target population has an equal chance of being chosen as part of the sample. For example, pollsters might choose a random method of interviewing residents of a particular city by calling every tenth name in the local directory. Statisticians have discovered that a truly random sample is generally representative of the target population.

randomness A condition that allows every member of a target population to have an equal chance of being chosen as part of the sample.

Using random samples of the target population makes the results of a study accurate with a small percentage of possible error. Polls could show that a certain candidate will get approximately 25 percent of a vote with a "margin of error" of 5 percent, which means he or she will probably get 20 percent to 30 percent of the vote. The margin of error decreases as the random, representative sample increases in size.

Checklist for Polls and Statistical Studies

A well-designed poll can provide a reasonably accurate snapshot of thoughts and opinions of a population. When fundamentals are not followed, however, polls can quickly become both misleading and unreliable.

Stone Analytics, Inc. www.secondmoment.org

You might think, at this point, that the requirements of a good statistical study are hard to meet; yet, despite the difficulties involved with the need to find random, representative, and sufficiently large samples of a target population, it can be and is done frequently. For example, you can review polling predictions about election results and find them to be quite accurate. In addition, research organizations, like Marketing Evaluations, the originators of the Q score, provide useful information about candidates and other well-known individuals. Note how the company explains the size and representativeness of their research on target audiences.

Performer Q measures the familiarity and appeal of personalities in a variety of categories to determine targeted audience attraction. Performer Q data enable our clients to make informed decisions about a specific personality's demographic appeal and/or examine the field of possible alternatives.

Performer Q studies are conducted as follows:

- Studies are fielded every six months in January & July.
- Each study measures over 1,700 personalities, whose names and descriptions are submitted by full-study subscribing clients. Individual orders are also accepted.
- Each personality is rated by a nationally representative sample of 1,800 children, teens, and adults.[11]

Skill

Analyze the quality of statistical evidence by noting the size, representation, and randomness of the sample.

Questions to Ask About Statistical Reports

When you need to critically evaluate reports of statistical studies, consider the following questions:

1. **What is the sample size?** For national public opinion polls, it is a general principle that at least 1,000 randomly selected individuals who are representative of the target population will give reliable results.

   When a research study involves carefully supervised testing and training of subjects or expensive material (like the studies discussed in Chapter 5), a much smaller sample might be optimal. For example, it is unreasonable and undesirable to have hundreds of subjects test an experimental drug that may be helpful in treating a particular disease but may also have significant side effects.

2. **Is the sample representative in all significant characteristics and in the proportion of those characteristics?** For example, if 10 percent of a state's voters are age 65 or older, are 10 percent of the sample voters in this age range? If the sample is not representative, then the study is considered biased.

3. **Have all significant characteristics been considered?** Sometimes it is hard to know exactly which factors about the target population are significant. Does the sex and age of the target matter? What about ethnicity or educational level?

4. **If the study is a poll, are the questions biased?** In other words, are they slanted to bring about a particular response? For example, consider the following "loaded" questions:

   a. Do you believe that the government has a right to invade private lives by taking a census?

   b. Do you approve of preventing thousands of senior citizens from enjoying a safe, affordable, and lovely retirement home in order to protect a moth?

   Because these questions are biased toward the obviously "correct" answer, the information gathered from them is unreliable.

---

[11] Marketing Evaluations, Inc. The Q Scores Company. http://www.qscores.com/performer.asp.

Reminder

The answers that pollsters receive (and media report) greatly depend on precisely what the pollsters ask and how they ask it. . . . The answers are sometimes determined (and always influenced) by the questions—the exact wording of the questions posed by the interviewers, the order in which the questions are asked, and in some cases even the way in which they are asked (in person or via the telephone or by a male or a female). For this reason, the answers are seldom very meaningful unless you also know about the questions that elicited them.[12]

✳ Explore on **mythinkinglab.com**

5. **What is the credibility of the polling organization or research institute?** In most cases, we read about a study on a website or in a magazine, newspaper, or textbook. Since we get an abridged version of research from these sources, it is helpful to note whether polls were conducted by credible organizations such as Gallup, Harris, Roper, Pew, and Rasmussen and whether research studies were done under the auspices of universities or reliable "think tanks."

6. **Is the survey biased because of the vested interest of the company that paid for it?** If a company is paying for a survey to promote a product or service, there may be bias involved in the design and the results. Journalist Patricia Rodriguez notes the findings and sponsors of several surveys conducted by polling organizations:

- Americans believe the best learning and information source today is the Internet. (Sponsored by Internet provider Prodigy)
- The majority of Americans polled plan to travel during the holidays. (Sponsored by online travel service Expedia.com)
- Movies, CDs, and video games are tops on teens' holiday wish lists. (Sponsored by Sam Goody, which sells movies, CDs, and video games)

---

[12] David Murray, Joel Schwartz, and S. Robert Lichter, *It Ain't Necessarily So* (Lanham, MD: Rowman & Littlefield Publishers, 2001), p. 98.

- Two out of three doctors who offer nutritional advice to their patients recommend that said patients eat more yogurt. (Sponsored by Dannon, which makes, you guessed it, yogurt)[13]

You can use the preceding checklist to help you feel more confident about using statistical evidence to support conclusions. The checklist can also help you refute inadequate and unreliable evidence.

Using Surveys as Evidence

Sometimes, surveys can yield helpful, accurate information. Consider the survey from the office of the Inspector General on identity theft investigations that is cited in the following excerpt:

> Question: *I'm a student; why do I need to be concerned about identity theft? I don't have a lot of money or assets; why would I be a target for identity theft?*
>
> Answer: Being a student does not safeguard you against identity theft, one of the fastest-growing consumer crimes in the nation. Identity thieves don't steal your money; they steal your name and reputation and use them for their own financial gain. They attempt to steal your future! Identity theft literally steals who you are, and it can seriously jeopardize your financial future.
>
> Imagine having thousands of dollars of unauthorized debt and a wrecked credit rating because of identity theft. Also, the unfortunate reality of identity theft is that it is you, the victim, who is responsible for cleaning up the mess and reestablishing your good name and credit. The experience of thousands of identity theft victims is that this frustrating experience often requires months and even years.
>
> In fact as a student, you may even be more vulnerable to identity theft because of the availability of your personal data and the way many students handle this data. A recent national survey of college students found that:
>
> - Almost half of all college students receive credit card applications on a daily or weekly basis. Many of these students throw out card applications without destroying them.
> - Nearly a third of students rarely, if ever, reconcile their credit card and checking account balances.
> - Almost 50 percent of students have had grades posted by Social Security number.
>
> All of these factors make students potential identity theft victims.[14]

In contrast to the useful warnings taken from the Inspector General surveys, one method of research that may lead to interesting speculations, but is not generally considered accurate or reliable, is the mail-in, call-in, or text-in survey. Let's imagine that a magazine asks its readers to respond to questions about how they spend their

---

[13] Patricia Rodriguez, "Be on Guard for Ridiculous Survey Results," *Knight Ridder Newspapers,* December 18, 2001.

[14] "Don't Let Identity Thieves Steal Your Future," www.ed.gov/about/offices/list/org/missedidtheft.

money. If the magazine has a circulation of 10,000 and it receives only 2,000 replies, which would be a high response rate, it can't really draw any information from those 2,000 answers because the sample is no longer random. Those who answered are a select group—they have something in common, which is that they are readers of this particular magazine who had the time and inclination to answer the questions and send them in. You can't use this survey to generalize about how most people spend money. Another problem is that survey questions often do not reflect what people would really do in a given situation; they reflect only what people would like to think they would do. If you ask someone if he or she uses money for necessities before luxuries, the person might answer yes, but his or her checkbook could reveal a completely different reality.

In addition, it's possible for someone to send in several surveys to skew the results or just as a prank. Survey results can be more controlled than these examples indicate, but you are safe to conclude that most mail-in or text-in surveys you read about on websites or in magazines and newspapers are not representative and therefore don't provide reliable support for your conclusions. The same principle holds for television surveys. Sometimes the host of a cable or network program will ask people to text or e-mail a vote on a particular question related to a current event or a celebrity. The responsible programs usually post the warning, "This is not a scientific poll."

Reminder

Good statistical evidence requires an adequate sample that is randomly selected from a representative group in the target population. When you find evidence like this, you can accept it as accurate and use it for your personal decision making and argumentation.

✴ Explore on **mythinkinglab.com**

Statistical Generalizations

> Statistical thinking will one day be as necessary for efficient citizenship as the ability to read and write.
>
> H.G. Wells

Keep in mind that although you may get information from a well-conducted study, the conclusion will not be true in every case. Statistical evidence reflects only what can *generally* be expected; conclusions about such evidence are called statistical generalizations. They add *strength,* not certainty, to your conclusions. For example, it might be discovered that most hyperactive children in a study responded well to dietary changes; this finding does not mean that every child will respond in the same way. We might read about a study showing that most sports magazine readers are men, but that does not mean every reader is male. Knowing that most of the readers are men helps the magazine recruit the most appropriate advertisers.

Remember that inductive strength is based on good evidence from which we can draw useful generalizations (see Figure 4–3). In short, we can get important information from statistical research that helps us make decisions or gain knowledge in a

FIGURE 4-3

A good inductive argument provides strong support for the conclusion.

general way. Still, we need to allow room for the complexities of individual people and not expect that what is generally true will be true for everyone.

Class Exercise

Purpose: To analyze the quality of one reported study.

Read the following report of a statistical study, keeping the following questions in mind:

1. What is the conclusion of the researcher?

2. How representative of the target population was his sample? Was the sample size adequate?

3. Which methods did he use to gather his data? Are these methods reliable?

4. In the second paragraph, the reporter implies that these research results would be duplicated in other classrooms. Do you agree or disagree and why?

5. To what extent is the headline given to this article a responsible one?

At a Lecture—Only 12 Percent Listen

Bright-eyed college students in lecture halls aren't necessarily listening to the professor, the American Psychological Association was told yesterday.

If you shot off a gun at sporadic intervals and asked the students to encode their thoughts and moods at that moment, you would discover that:

- About 20 percent of the students, men and women, are pursuing erotic thoughts.
- Another 20 percent are reminiscing about something.
- Only 20 percent are actually paying attention to the lecture; 12 percent are actively listening.
- The others are worrying, daydreaming, thinking about lunch or—surprise—religion (8 percent).

This confirmation of the lecturer's worst fears was reported by Paul Cameron, 28, an assistant professor at Wayne State University in Detroit. The annual convention, which ends Tuesday, includes about 2,000 such reports to 10,000 psychologists in a variety of meetings.

Cameron's results were based on a nine-week course in introductory psychology for 85 college sophomores. A gun was fired 21 times at random intervals, usually when Cameron was in the middle of a sentence. ■

The Reporting of Statistical Studies: Truths, Half-Truths, and Distortions

> Newspapers like to stress the importance of the news they report, not to qualify or minimize its possible significance.[15]

As we have noted, studies are not usually reported in the popular media in their complete context. Instead, excerpts from a study are given, and sometimes the reader or listener gets an incomplete or distorted picture of what was really discovered by the research. Reporters are pressured to give us dramatic news that compels us to read, and they don't want to stress the uncertainty about results of a study that may exist in the scientific community.

One of the most important responsibilities of those reporting studies is to give us a true picture of what was discovered so that we can draw reasonable generalizations. Both raw numbers and percentages should be used so that we can assess the significance of any findings; for example, a report might claim that a new study shows a 50 percent drop in the rate of teenage pregnancies. But on closer examination, we might discover that the sample was taken from only one high school in which the number of pregnant girls went from 4 to 2. Obviously, the sample size is too small to make any relevant claim about teenage pregnancy rates. Conversely, a study involving an entire state may find 200 more teenage pregnancies for a given year across the state, yet the researcher could claim a seemingly small 5 percent increase in pregnancies if 4,000 had occurred in the previous year.

Advertisers may also "lie with statistics." For example, a bicycle store could place an ad thanking the public for "doubling" the volume of sales this year. That ad could mean, in reality, that sales of the bicycles went from 5,000 to 10,000 for the year or that sales went from 1 to 2.

Statistics can also be distorted by the terms a journalist uses to characterize their significance. For example, if a governor receives a 40 percent disapproval rating on how he is handling education reform and a 36 percent approval rating with the rest of the respondents undecided, a reporter could say, "*Many* voters disapprove of the governor's handling of education, and *only* 36 percent of those polled approve." Conversely, a reporter could "spin" the statistics in the other direction by saying that "*only* 40 percent of voters disapprove of the governor's policies on education, while 60 percent either approve or are undecided."

Reporters may also choose to discuss poll results without giving the actual numbers to readers. Using the previous example, a reporter could leave out the specific data and just state that "polls indicate that there is increasing disapproval and uncertainty among voters concerning the governor's policies on education."

Another problem with reports of statistical studies is that headlines may distort the actual findings of the study. An article summarizing a study of the effect of video games on college life presented a balanced look at the positives and negative findings of the researchers. Unfortunately, the headline "Study Surprise: Video Games Enhance College Social Life" slants the information and could be misleading to readers who scan the headline or who read only the first part of the article. The headline "spins" the report as essentially good news about video games as a social and interactive activity; it takes a discerning reader to note some of the problems

[15] Murray, Schwartz, and Lichter, *It Ain't Necessarily So* (Lanham, MD: Bowman & Littlefield Publishers, 2001).

associated with students who spend a large amount of their time playing video games, including lower grades and test scores for younger game players, that are given in the latter part of the article. (See Exercise 4.1 on page 156.)

Causal Generalizations

> Scientific research may at first glance sound specialized or even forbidding as a topic, but in fact it is research results—of a remarkable variety, from health news to environmental alarms to the latest findings on child-rearing practices—that increasingly construct the public agenda.[16]

Statistics and controlled studies (which will be discussed in the next chapter) are often used to draw inductive generalizations about the causes of conditions or events. We attempt to determine causal connections for several reasons: First, we seek to eliminate current difficulties and resolve general problems that affect individuals and society as a whole; second, we want to prevent future problems; and finally, much great investigation is motivated by sheer human curiosity.

On an individual level, we look for causes in order to eliminate problems that arise in daily life. We might seek to understand why our car is making a certain sound, why our checkbook doesn't balance, why our dog seems lethargic, or why we lost a job or an important relationship. If we find a cause, then we hope we will find a cure for our present difficulties as exemplified in the following column by the late Ann Landers.

Ann Landers

Dear Ann Landers:

If it weren't for one of your recent columns, I might be either dead or paralyzed. I owe you a large debt of gratitude.

For about a week, I had been experiencing temporary numbness in my left arm and hand. The numbness was sometimes accompanied by periodic paralysis of my left hand. My first thoughts were that I either hit my crazy bone or had perhaps been using my computer too much.

As I read your column describing the symptoms of a stroke, I immediately recognized that my numbness matched the early warning signs you had mentioned. I dropped the newspaper and went directly to the emergency room. The CAT scan revealed a large mass of blood in the crevice between my brain and my skull.

Fortunately, the operation to drain the fluid was a complete success, and the doctors say there should be no lasting effects. For this, I am extremely thankful. Please know I am enormously grateful to you, Ann, for the perfect timing of that column. ■

We also look for causes of societal problems in order to resolve them and to ensure that these problems do not occur again. This search for causes occurs when we have car, train, and plane accidents; outbreaks of food poisoning; oil spills; a trend of lower test scores; or a disease that is becoming an epidemic.

[16] Ibid., p. 1

In addition, we seek causes in order to eliminate potential problems that affect the general public: Seat belts and air bags were created and altered as a result of understanding the causes of the kinds of human injury that can occur after the impact of a collision; baby furniture and toys are modified or recalled based on our understanding of their possible harmfulness to children; the government may look at inflationary trends caused by the infusion of more money into the country before it takes action to stimulate a failing economy; and premarital counselors can advise engaged couples about the major causes of divorce and help them address important issues before they get married.

Consider the following examples of research that was done to enhance our decision making on a variety of topics.

On the decision to require and support helmet laws for bicycle riders:

> Less than two percent of motor vehicle crash deaths are bicyclists. The most serious injuries among a majority of those killed are to the head, highlighting the importance of wearing a bicycle helmet. Helmet use has been estimated to reduce head injury risk by 85 percent. Twenty-one states and the District of Columbia have helmet laws applying to young bicyclists; none of these laws applies to all riders. Local ordinances in a few states require some or all bicyclists to wear helmets. A nationwide telephone survey estimated that state helmet use laws increase by 18 percent the probability that a rider will wear a helmet. Helmets are important for riders of all ages, especially because 86 percent of bicycle deaths are persons 16 and older.
>
> The following facts are based on analysis of data from the U.S. Department of Transportation's Fatality Analysis Reporting System (FARS).
>
> A total of 714 bicyclists were killed in crashes with motor vehicles in 2008. Bicyclist deaths were down 29 percent since 1975 but were up 14 percent since 2003. The decline since 1975 among female bicyclists (50 percent) was larger than the decline among male bicyclists (24 percent).
>
> Ninety-one percent of bicyclists killed in 2008 reportedly weren't wearing helmets.[17]

On the causes of homelessness in Seattle:

> According to stats available from the King County Committee to End Homelessness, 8349 individuals were counted as homeless in Seattle on a single night in January. Almost 6000 had scored beds in shelters or in transitional housing for that night, and the rest—over 3000—bedded down on the streets, in doorways, or under highway overpasses. . . . 36% of the homeless population consisted of single adult men; 13% were single adult women; 1% were unaccompanied youth; and 50% were families with children. *Half of all the individuals in King County's shelters are children aged 0–17*—an especially dire statistic for anyone who cares about the future.

[17] From the Insurance Institute for Highway Safety, http://www.iihs.org/research/fatality_facts_2008/bicycles.html.

What are the chief causes of homelessness in our region?

Shortages of affordable housing. Less than 1% of King County's apartments are affordable to families with incomes lower than 30% of median income ($23,350 for a family of 4). Even if both parents work full time, two minimum-wage jobs can't cover housing as well as food, transportation, etc. It takes an income of $17–$21/hour to pay for a 2-bedroom apartment at our County's average rental rate of $985/month.

Poverty due to low wages or unemployment. People who can't afford all the necessities—housing, utilities, transportation, children's needs, health care, food—must make triage decisions. Homelessness is one possible result.

Domestic violence. Of the more than 7000 homeless individuals counted in January 2007, 1000 young people and women (some with young children) said that violence in their homes was a major reason why they were homeless.

Psychiatric disorders, chemical addictions, and other illnesses. 20–25% of homeless Americans have a severe mental illness that has gone untreated. Statistics on homeless people are less certain, but many are addicted to drugs or alcohol and remain untreated. The rates of other chronic and acute health problems in this population are high.

The institutional revolving door. People are discharged from hospitals, prisons, and jails right back to the streets again, even if they have no viable options for shelter.

Legal barriers. People who lack proper documentation are denied access to subsidized housing programs, and so are people who were convicted of felonies in the past, even if they've rehabilitated their lives and are employed. The development of affordable housing can be blocked by land use and zoning regulations.

Particular challenges for people of color. In Seattle, median household income and home-ownership are significantly lower for people of color than for whites. More than half the children in King County foster care are children of color, and statistics show that people who spent time in foster care as children are more likely than others to experience homelessness.

Absence of family or community support. For people lacking a stable network of family and friends, a single crisis (car breakdown, child's illness, downsized job) can spiral down into homelessness, and without such a network the chances of making it back into housing are low.[18]

On reasons for the consumer trend of accessing Netflix online:

Netflix subscribers are continuing to consume more and more of their video content online, with 61% of them watching at least 15 minutes of streaming video during the company's second quarter.

That's nearly double the number of subscribers doing so last year (37%) and a decent bump from the company's first quarter, where 55% watched at least 15 minutes using the Watch Instantly service.

Of course, you'd expect this kind of growth given the moves Netflix is making to add Watch Instantly to consumer electronics, ranging from

[18] Judy Lightfoot, "Homeless in Seattle," http://blog.seattlepi.com/judylightfoot/archives/174831.asp.

Xbox 360 to Playstation 3 to Roku. Just a couple weeks ago, stats revealed that the company's website traffic jumped 46% year-over-year thanks in no small part to its shifting strategy.

We expect this trend of video consumption moving to the Internet to only continue over the next few years and for Netflix to be a major player as it migrates from the DVDs-by-mail model to an online service that competes with the likes of Hulu Plus.

On the whole, Netflix continues to grow at an impressive clip. The company also revealed today that it has hit 15 million subscribers, with revenue growing 27% year-over-year to $519.8 million during the second quarter.[19]

On the causes of deterioration of the coral reef:

Causes of deterioration, and degradation, of coral reefs can be numerous, and many are propagated by man. Let's look at both natural causes and man-made.

It surprises many people to learn that there are natural causes for the destruction of coral reefs, but it should not. Coral atolls are basically dead coral reefs from coral that died by being pushed above the water. The earth may seem solid, but it moves over time and as the coral gets shoved up, it deteriorates and forms islands. Even white sand beaches around volcanic islands in the Caribbean are from degraded coral reefs. The volcanoes can have an up-welling or spew out lava that destroys and deteriorates the reefs. All things living have a beginning and an end, and nature has been deteriorating coral reefs for thousands of years! There is also silting and such from rivers that can degrade a reef and break it up quickly.

Man has been destroying the reefs for much less time, but is making up for that by going much quicker and using a variety of ways. They can increase the silting by plowing fields along the coast or rivers that empty into the sea, or by building there and having the lots drain dirt into the ocean.

Plowed fields will also be using pesticides to kill both weeds and insects, as well as worms. The herbicides can kill the algae that are symbiotic and essential for the coral, and the insecticides kill the polyps of the coral. The same applies to the houses and buildings built near the shore. All this results in coral deterioration, and all could be easily controlled or stopped.

There is also pollution from boats and beach goers. They dump rubbish, spill oil and destroy the oceans, causing massive deterioration of coral reefs.

Then there is global warming; is it natural or caused by humans? Whatever the reason, it causes massive deterioration of the coral reefs. The warmer waters causes the coral to die and then the bacteria start to work and grow much faster; this deteriorates the coral reefs. There are also stronger storms being spawned, which physically break up the coral reefs.

Between nature and man, the deterioration of the coral reefs is proceeding at the fastest pace ever. We cannot really alter nature, but we can slow down the harm from humans![20]

[19] Adam Ostrow, "Netflix Users Watching More Movies and TV Shows Online," http://mashable.com/2010/07/21/netflix-online-stats/.

[20] James Johnson, "Causes of Deterioration of Coral Reefs," www.helium.com/items/1748137-destruction-of-coral-reefs.

On Coca-Cola's decision to expand investments in the Philippines:

> The Coca-Cola Company has renewed its strong commitment to the Philippines with a pledge to increase investments in this country by $1 billion over five years.
>
> "Our new commitment to invest $1 billion in our business over five years will strengthen production and distribution and help development of new products to refresh Filipino consumers," said Coca-Cola Pacific Group president Glenn Jordan.
>
> "This investment is a proof point of our strong commitment to the Philippines, our confidence in the prospects of the Filipino economy and the continued growth of a broader and more affluent middle class in the Philippines."
>
> Jordan revealed the positive developments of Coca-Cola's operations in the Philippines, including the ongoing construction of a mega bottling facility in Misamis Oriental. The plant, scheduled to begin operations next year, will be one of the largest plants in the region and is expected to generate significant employment opportunities in the area.
>
> Coca-Cola Philippines recorded double-digit growth in the first half of 2010, led by its flagship brand Coca-Cola. The company has also expanded its portfolio of beverages. In the last six months it has launched "Samurai" energy drink and the ready-to-drink tea "Real Leaf"—brewed from 100 percent whole green tea leaves. In addition, the company will expand its "Minute Maid" brand, which features real pulp and juice.
>
> The Coca-Cola Company—which operates 23 plants and 42 sales offices with over 7,800 direct employees across the Philippines—will focus its new investment on strengthening marketing execution and enhancing system logistics and delivery capabilities in order to better serve the company's expanding customer and consumer base.[21]

On causes for South Korea's having the world's highest traffic accident rate of 10,300 people killed and 426,000 injured in crashes every year in a country of 46 million people and also on causes of other social problems that South Koreans face:

> South Koreans call it ppalli ppalli ("hurry hurry")—doing everything quickly, from leaving planes to eating, walking and driving. . . . "Ppalli ppalli was the main driving engine behind the nation's rapid industrialization," said Yoo Suk-choon, a sociologist at Seoul's Yonsei University. South Korea was reduced to ashes during the 1950–53 Korean War, but has built itself into the world's 11th-largest economy.
>
> However, government officials and social critics blame ppalli ppalli for many ills: traffic jams, corruption, slipshod construction and the reckless expansion by corporations on borrowed money, which proved a disaster during Asia's 1997–98 financial crisis. Today, after decades of rushing, there are calls for a more leisurely lifestyle.
>
> The government, supported by labour groups, is pushing legislation to introduce a five-day work week. Most Koreans still work a half-day on Saturdays. "Korean workers need to live more humanely," said

---

[21] "Coca-Cola to Invest US$1 Billion More in RP," http://goodnewspilipinas.com/?p=12928.

Park Kwang-woo, a policy coordinator at the Korean Confederation of Trade Unions, the country's largest labour group.[22]

On the connection between drugs, alcohol, and strokes:

Years of research now show that drugs are significant risk factors for stroke. Some drugs can cause stroke by directly affecting blood vessels in the brain while others do it indirectly by affecting other organs in the body such as the heart or the liver. Common substances known to increase the risk of strokes include:

Alcohol: Although alcohol in moderate amounts can protect you from having a stroke, excessive intake can increase your risk of having one. Specifically, chronic excessive alcohol intake can precipitate hemorrhagic stroke. This is in many cases the result of harmful effects of alcohol on the liver, as this organ makes proteins which are necessary to prevent spontaneous bleeding. However, most of the risk of stroke with excess alcohol intake appears to be due to a combination of high blood pressure and impaired blood clotting mechanisms.

Cocaine: There is a clear association between cocaine use and stroke. The most important ways by which cocaine use increases the risk of stroke include:

- By increasing blood pressure and causing bleeding in the brain
- By causing narrowing of blood vessels in the brain
- If used in its intravenous form known as crack cocaine, it increases the risk of infections in the heart valves, or endocarditis, a condition that can lead to embolic stroke

Heroin: Heroin is a commonly abused drug in the United States. Similar to intravenous cocaine, intravenous heroin also increases the risk of endocarditis, a condition in which bacteria enter the blood and grow over the valves of the heart. Small pellets of these bacteria, known as septic emboli, may leave the heart, head towards the brain and cause a stroke. Because heroin is injected, its use also increases the risk of diseases transmittable by the sharing of needles such as HIV and hepatitis C.

Amphetamines: There have been many reports of amphetamine use in the hours before suffering a major stroke. Amphetamines appear have a powerful ability to cause high blood pressure. As high blood pressure is the number one risk factor for stroke, it is not surprising that amphetamine use can increase a person's risk for stroke.[23]

As we can see from these excerpts, we are constantly using research findings to determine causal connections that inform our personal and policy decisions on a variety of topics.

Over the past few centuries, philosophers and scientists have developed specific theories of cause and effect. These theories help us make **causal generalizations,** which can then be used as evidence to support a conclusion. Keep in mind, however, that what is believed and accepted as causal today may change as new information

causal generalizations
Generalizations based on causal factors; that is, they state that a particular factor is responsible for a specific effect. These generalizations are used to strengthen inductive arguments.

[22] Sang-Hun Choe, Associated Press.
[23] Jose Vega, "Recreational Drugs, Alcohol, and Stroke," http://stroke.about.com/od/strokeprevention/a/drugs_stroke.htm.

becomes available. The following section will review the most common theories of causation.

Hume's Conditions for Cause and Effect

The British philosopher David Hume (1711–1776) created one of the earliest theories of cause and effect. He reasoned that we are justified in saying that one thing is the cause (x) of an effect (y) if the following three conditions are met:

1. *X*, the cause, *preceded y*, the effect, in time.
2. *X* and *y* are *contiguous* (in contact with one another) in time and place.
3. There is a *history* of (1) and (2); that is, there is a history of x preceding y and of x and y being related in time and place.

The first condition is clear; if one thing causes another, the cause must come before the effect. But we should also note that sometimes the cause and effect appear to occur at the same time; for example, as soon as I pull the plug on my lamp, the light goes out.

The second condition specifies the need for a relationship in time and space between a cause and an effect. For example, in outbreaks of diseases caused by "sick buildings," a connection is made between workers (often on particular floors) who experience the onset of the same illness. The reminder that causes and effects must be connected guards against superstition and unlikely causes.

The third condition helps us justify a causal effect by pointing to a regular tendency. A florist can reason that every year, on certain holidays, the demand for flowers goes up. A public school teacher can chart a tendency for a consistent reduction in math skills over summer vacation. A doctor can anticipate that a patient will be nauseated as a side effect of many types of chemotherapy. A driver can note which roads are regularly jammed during the week because of rush hour. Conversely, if there is no history of regularity between a particular cause and a particular effect, then a critical thinker should wait for such a trend to surface before accepting an alleged causal connection.

Even when all of Hume's criteria are met, it is hard to distinguish between a correlation (two events occurring together in a regular pattern) and a specific causation. We can, for example, look at studies that show a connection (correlation) between violent criminals and their abusive parents. But it is difficult to explain fully why some of these violent criminals from abusive homes have siblings who are nonviolent, productive, and functioning members of society. In other words, it is easier to see the connections and associations in time and space between two conditions than it is to prove that one of the conditions caused the other.

However, when we come across a strong correlation between two conditions or activities, we should consider whether there is a possible area of causation to be explored. Consider these statements by MIT research scholar and author Frank Sulloway:

> There is an old maxim that "correlation is not causation." Although this is certainly true, it is also true that, under some circumstances, correlations provide a reasonably reliable guide to causation. For example, the correlation between winning a million dollars in the lottery and having more money to spend is very high, and these two outcomes are obviously related in a causal manner. We must employ common sense in deciding whether, and to what extent, correlations suggest a causal relationship. Even when correlations do

not warrant the assumption of causality, they generally suggest that *some other variable, itself associated with the two correlated variables,* is causally involved in the observed relationship. As we introduce additional variables into a statistical analysis, we can often pinpoint the most likely source of "causation."[24]

Theories of technical causation, which we turn to now, can help us better understand causal connections between conditions.

Technical Causation

Another format for determining causation specifies two different types of conditions between causes and effects.

A **necessary condition** is a condition (state of affairs, thing, process) that must be present if the effect is present. Equivalently, if the necessary condition is absent, then the effect cannot occur.

One of the necessary conditions of life as we know it is oxygen. Some of the necessary conditions of a fire are oxygen, a flammable material, and a form of ignition. If we know the necessary conditions of an event, then we can prevent it from happening. Remove any of the necessary conditions and the effect does not take place. A necessary condition is a prerequisite for the effect. Thus we can speak of a necessary condition as a cause, or one of the causes, of an event.[25]

A **sufficient condition** is a condition (state of affairs, thing, process) that automatically leads to the production of another event. If the condition is present, then the effect will definitely occur. The sufficient condition creates the effect.

Swallowing cyanide is a sufficient condition for death. The difference between a necessary and a sufficient condition is that although a necessary condition must be present, it will not produce the effect by itself. The sufficient condition is able to produce the effect by itself. Usually the sufficient condition is really a set of necessary conditions, all of which must be present at the same time and place. For instance, a combustible material, oxygen, and the combustion point are all necessary conditions for a fire. Together all three constitute the sufficient condition for a fire. If we know the sufficient condition of an event, then we can produce it at will. Thus we can speak of a sufficient condition as a cause of an event.[26]

> **necessary condition**
> A condition (state of affairs, thing, process) that must be present if a particular effect is present. Equivalently, if the necessary condition is absent, then the effect cannot occur.

> **sufficient condition**
> A condition (state of affairs, thing, process) that automatically leads to the production of another event. If the condition is present, then the effect will definitely occur. The sufficient condition creates or causes the effect.

Stop and Think

It has been said that holding elections is a necessary but not a sufficient condition for establishing a democracy. What do you believe would be other necessary factors that would become sufficient for establishing a democratic government?

Multiple Causes

Finding the exact cause of an event or an effect can be very difficult, even in technical matters. We often must look at **multiple causes,** a combination of causes leading to a

> **multiple causes**
> A combination of causes that are presumed to lead to a specific effect.

[24] Salloway, *Born to Rebel*, pp. 72–74.

[25] Nicholas Capaldi, *The Art of Deception* (Buffalo, NY: Prometheus Books, 1987), p. 158.

[26] Ibid.

specific effect. A particular business might be successful because of a combination of the needs of the community, the location of the store, and the advertising campaign. A person may die because of a combination of a weak heart, a diet with a large proportion of fat, and an overexertion in exercise. The weak heart could be further traced back to a family history of heart disease. Taken in combination, these factors may be sufficient to cause death.

There are multiple causes to social problems. For example, a number of researchers have found that teen alcohol and drug use occurs at higher levels in affluent areas.

> It's not just a matter of children having more money to spend, though that is a factor. Disconnected families and pressures to succeed push youths to destructive behaviors, say researchers, sociologists and others trying to help these children. Adults in many wealthy areas are often loathe to acknowledge that such problems exist in their world. "The amount of denial on this issue is phenomenal," said Madeline Levine, psychologist and author of *The Price of Privilege*.[27]

Other researchers agree that the pressures to succeed, the glamorous appeal of drugs to students who don't see the social problems they create, the absenteeism and denial of parents, and the numerous extracurricular obligations of students all are factors in the higher incidence of alcohol and drug use. "The association of wealth and teen substance abuse holds true internationally," said Shirley Beckett Mikeel, deputy director for the Association of Addiction Professionals. She has worked with groups from France, England, Egypt and New Zealand."[28]

The phenomenon of multiple causes makes it difficult to provide evidence beyond a reasonable doubt in many legal cases. For example, over the years people have sued tobacco companies because, they claim, the tobacco caused them to develop lung cancer. However, despite convincing evidence about the harmfulness of tobacco, people have difficulty proving that tobacco is the only cause, sufficient by itself, for the development of lung cancer. Until recently, lawyers for the tobacco companies argued successfully that there are, in any given case, other possible causes for a person's susceptibility to lung cancer and that other people who smoke a similar amount of tobacco have not contracted the disease.

The difficulty of establishing causal connections and then proving them in court is chronicled by Jonathan Harr in his book *A Civil Action*, which he spent eight years researching and writing. The book deals with the case of eight children in Woburn, Massachusetts, who contracted leukemia as the result, their families claim, of toxic pollution from industrial plants near their homes. The lawyer, Jan Schlictmann, who took on the polluting corporations in court, believed in the truth of his clients' case but also knew that the case would be difficult to prove.

> The children's illnesses and the contamination of two water wells that served their homes had been documented. What was missing was proof that the two industrial plants, owned by Beatrice Foods Co. and W.R. Grace and Co. were responsible for the contamination and that the chemicals had caused the children's illnesses. . . .
> He hired geologists to prove that Beatrice and Grace had contaminated the wells. And he hired medical experts to establish a link

---

[27] Eric Louis, "Lap of Luxury Breeds Higher Rates of Teen Substance Abuse," *Contra Costa Times*, February 19, 2007.
[28] Ibid.

between leukemia, the cause of which was unknown, and the contaminated water.

The millions spent in preparing for trial virtually bankrupted Schlictmann and his firm. . . . [In court] he had to confront an unsympathetic judge and high-paid corporate attorneys who used every motion and procedural sleight of hand to block his way.

A split decision that absolved Beatrice of responsibility and held little promise of final victory over Grace forced Schlictmann to settle the case for $8 million. The settlement gave a measure of satisfaction and compensation to the Woburn families, but it wasn't enough to pay Schlictmann's bills.[29]

The Woburn case, which generated 159 volumes of depositions and trial testimony, is a good example of the difficulty in proving a causal connection against the doubts generated by good defense attorneys. In gathering the necessary expertise to make a case, Schlictmann spent so much money that his car and furniture were repossessed, and the bank foreclosed on his home. Most lawyers have to believe that they can prove their cases with a "preponderance of the evidence" before they will take such risks.

The practice of allowing juries to assign a portion of blame for an injury to the plaintiff and a portion to the defendant is a response to the difficulty jurors have determining the precise cause of a problem. In one case, a male psychologist was accused of causing pain, suffering, and suicidal tendencies in a female patient with whom he had had sexual relations. The psychologist admitted to having had sex with his patient, but he produced explicit love letters she had sent to him. In addition, his attorneys presented information about the patient's previous sexual history; the psychologist, as defendant, was not required to reveal details of his own sexual history. As a result of the evidence presented by the defense, the jury softened the verdict by assigning 18 percent of the blame to the patient and 82 percent of the blame to the psychologist. They reasoned that although he had broken his professional ethics, she had contributed to that breakdown. (See Exercise 4.2 on pages 156–158.)

Immediate Causes

In searching for causes, we should also consider the **immediate cause** of a problem. We can ask, "What factor makes the difference between an event happening or not happening?" (In folk wisdom, this might be expressed as "the straw that broke the camel's back.")

The immediate cause is preceded by other factors that led up to the effect; these less immediate causal factors are called **remote causes.**

If someone causes an accident because of driving drunk after a party, we have the immediate cause of the collision. Remote causes of the accident would be the lack of a designated driver for drinkers at the party and the decision of the driver to have alcohol rather than soda; had there been a designated driver or a sober driver, the accident probably would not have happened.

In a discussion of the human costs that result when a community does not have affordable housing, Theresa Keegan refers to remote causes of a young man's death: "To this day, I can still recall the regrets uttered during an interview almost a decade ago by a caring, loving mom whose 16-year-old son had been stabbed to death. She had been working, not for personal fulfillment, but simply to keep a roof over their heads. And her working meant he was left on his own. Regret didn't even begin to describe her grief.

immediate causes A causal factor that immediately precedes the effect.

remote causes Factors or conditions that led up to but did not immediately precede the effect.

[29] Willy Morris, "Civil Author Nearly Beaten by Case," *Contra Costa Times*, October 10, 1996.

A lack of affordable housing wasn't cited as a cause on his death certificate, but that's what can happen when the struggle for basic shelter dictates our actions."[30]

In many cases, critical thinkers have to ask the question, "Where do we draw the line in our search for causes?" (See Exercise 4.3 on pages 158–159.)

Mill's Analysis of Cause and Effect

British philosopher John Stuart Mill (1806–1873) formulated several specific methods (which he called canons) to help us systematically discover causes; Mill's canons are foundational to what we now called controlled studies (which will be covered in Chapter 5). Let's look at two of these methods, the method of agreement (or similarity) and the method of difference.

Method of Agreement

method of agreement
A theory of causation postulating that the cause of an effect is found by noting that X is the only factor always present when Y (the problem or the good effect) occurs; therefore, X causes Y.

Using the **method of agreement,** a cause is found by noting that X is the only factor always present when Y (the problem or the good effect) occurs; therefore, X causes Y.

Let's say a family of four is on vacation and goes to Chicken King for lunch. Dad orders nuggets, fried chicken, fries, and a root beer. Sister has the same thing except she isn't thirsty so she doesn't order the root beer. Mom used to be a vegetarian, so she can't handle the fried chicken, but the nuggets don't look like chicken, so she has them with the fries and the root beer. Brother orders the same as Dad, but hates potatoes, so he doesn't order the fries. That night, they all wake up with painful cramps and stay up most of the night dealing with upset stomachs. The chart of this particular scenario could look something like Figure 4–4.

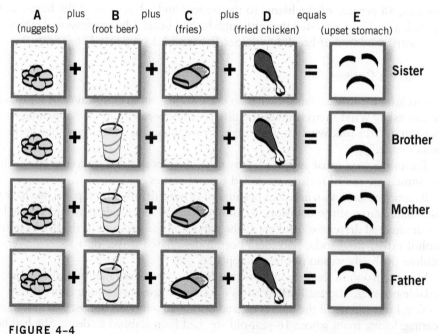

FIGURE 4–4
The Method of Agreement

---

[30] Theresa Keegan, "Lack of Affordable Housing Is Costly," *Contra Costa Times,* June 1, 2003.

Using the method of agreement, it can be easily seen that the one thing that is present in every individual's meal is the order of nuggets. The evidence leads to the inductive generalization that the nuggets (X) caused the family members to have upset stomachs (Y).

Method of Difference

Using the **method of difference,** the cause is found by noting that the only difference between the event or effect (called Y) happening or not happening is whether one element—X—is present.

Using our previous example, let's look at one particular member of the family again. Dad recovered from the illness but the next day decides to eat at Chicken King again. He might have decided never to set foot again in that, or any other, Chicken King, but instead he experimented, using the method of difference. He ordered the same meal as the day before, but he decided not to have the nuggets. The chart of the scenario could look like Figure 4–5.

method of difference
A theory of causation postulating that the cause of an effect is found by noting that the only difference between the event or effect (called Y) happening or not happening is whether one element—X—is present.

FIGURE 4–5

The Method of Difference

That night the father had no symptoms, and the next day notified the Chicken King manager that by using the method of difference following the method of agreement, he believes the nuggets caused his family's stomach aches.

In this example, the sample is of course too small and the surrounding conditions too uncertain for a valid generalization. However, it does serve to highlight the contrast between the method of agreement and the method of difference. These methods are used, separately and together, to conduct valid research experiments.

Scientists and other professionals use the method of difference to make useful discoveries. For example, if a patient reports to a psychologist that he is depressed, he might be asked to keep a journal, detailing the times of most and least depression. If the psychologist discovers the most depression (Y) occurring on Sunday night and Monday morning, then she might conclude that the depression is related to a return to work (X) after the weekend. Although the return to work may not turn out to be the cause, it provides a useful avenue of inquiry.

A famous example of the use of the method of difference occurred when Edward Jenner, a nineteenth-century British physician, was investigating a cure for smallpox. He discovered that a certain group of people—dairymaids—rarely got the disease. What was the difference between the dairymaids and the larger population?

On further investigation, Jenner discovered that most of the dairymaids had had cowpox, which is similar to smallpox but not usually deadly to human beings. Because they had had cowpox, they were immune to the smallpox; the cowpox had "vaccinated" them against smallpox. So cowpox (X) caused the positive effect (Y) of immunization from the illness. From this discovery, Jenner came upon the notion of vaccinating people against smallpox.

Using Difference and Similarity Together to Determine Cause

Often the method of agreement (similarity) and the method of difference go together. Both methods are evident in Robert Cialdini's discussion of fixed-action patterns in animal behavior:

> When a male animal acts to defend his territory, for instance, it is the intrusion of another male of the same species that cues the territorial-defense tape of rigid vigilance, threat, and if need be, combat behaviors. But there is a quirk in the system. It is not the rival male as a whole that is the trigger; it is some specific feature of him, the trigger feature. Often the trigger feature will be just one tiny aspect of the totality that is the approaching intruder. Sometimes a shade of color is the trigger feature. The experiments of ethologists have shown, for instance, that a male robin, acting as if a rival robin had entered its territory, will vigorously attack nothing more than a clump of robin-redbreast feathers placed there. At the same time, it will virtually ignore a perfect stuffed replica of a male robin without red breast feathers.[31]

In the case of these male birds, X (the presence of red-color feathers) makes the difference between the territorial response Y happening or not happening. And whenever the red feathers are present, whether or not there is a real threat to the robin, he will react in the same way.

If a patient is having allergic reactions, a doctor may begin a systematic search for the causes of the ailment. The patient might be told to stop eating food typically involved in allergies (for example, wheat, sugar, and dairy products). Then, after a period of time, the suspected allergens are introduced one at a time; if the allergic reactions reoccur, the patient is advised to eliminate the food that triggered the reactions. If the patient continues to eliminate this food and finds that the allergic reactions are gone, then the process of reasoning from evidence to a cause has been successful in this case. X is the only food that caused the reaction Y; and in every case in which X is eaten, the reaction occurs.

Mill's basic concepts are foundational to the scientific method in which experiments are conducted in order to discover or eliminate strong support for causal connections. The data from these studies can help us make reliable causal generalizations, as we will see in the next chapter.*

---

[31] Robert B. Cialdini, *The Psychology of Persuasion* (New York: William Morrow, 1993), p. 3.

* Two of Mill's methods that we did not cover here—the method of residue and the method of concomitant variation—are also useful in discovering causal links. You may wish to read about these methods to further your understanding of theories of causation.

Life Application: Tips for College and Career

Be aware that any personal, professional, national, or international problem has multiple causes, and avoid placing blame simplistically on only one factor. Make it a habit to look for both remote and immediate causes of problems, especially when you are in a position to come up with or vote on possible solutions.

Use strong statistics to make rational decisions concerning risks. As *Time* magazine writer Jeffrey Kluger suggests, focus on probable outcomes of your daily actions rather than worrying about remote possibilities:

> Shadowed by peril as we are, you would think we'd get pretty good at distinguishing the risks likeliest to do us in from the ones that are statistical long shots. But you would be wrong. We agonize over avian flu, which to date has killed precisely no one in the U.S., but have to be cajoled into getting vaccinated for the common flu, which contributes to the deaths of 36,000 Americans each year. We wring our hands over the mad cow pathogen that might be (but almost certainly isn't) in our hamburger and worry far less about the cholesterol that contributes to the heart disease that kills 700,000 of us annually.[32]

Chapter Review

Summary

1. The strength of a conclusion is based on the quality of evidence used to support the conclusion.

2. Statistical evidence can be gathered from polling a sample of a target population about a given topic, which is called the characteristic of interest.

3. Samples used to collect data must be sufficiently large, randomly chosen, and representative of the target population. When a sample is not representative, the study is biased.

4. Surveys can yield useful information when they are based on statistical research; however, mail-in, call-in, or text-in surveys usually yield inadequate statistical evidence because they do not reflect a random and representative sample.

5. Studies reported in both print and electronic media are abridged; critical thinkers will read them carefully and do further investigation of the findings before using them to support conclusions or decisions.

6. Philosophers and scientists have developed several theories of causation; among these are Hume's conditions for cause and effect, theories of technical causation, and Mill's canons of cause and effect.

[32]Jeffrey Kinger, "How Americans Are Living Dangerously," November 26, 2006, Time.com

Checkup

Short Answer

1. What are some uses of statistical generalizations?
2. What problems can occur with the reporting of statistical evidence?
3. Why is it helpful to look at multiple causes of a problem?
4. Why are mail-in, call-in, or text-in surveys unreliable sources of evidence?

Sentence Completion

5. A _____ sample is random and adequate in size.
6. Finding a cause by noting the factor that is always present when the effect occurs is called the method of _____.
7. A condition that must be present if the effect is present is called a _____ condition.

Matching

    a. Characteristic of interest
    b. Sample
    c. Target audience

8. The group about which a researcher wishes to generalize.
9. Members of a target population who are studied by a researcher.
10. The specific question that a researcher wants to answer.

Exercises

EXERCISE 4.1 Purpose: To become aware of how reporting of scientific research may distort information.

1. Look at articles about research online or in your local or national newspaper. See if the headlines accurately summarize the research. Then note whether the reporter is making claims that are not clearly supported by the research.

2. Compare and contrast two or three articles on the same research study to see how the information is presented and therefore is likely to be received differently by the readers. Note the headlines given to the different articles and whether they 'spin' the results of the research towards a specific conclusion.

EXERCISE 4.2 Purpose: To understand the need to consider multiple causes when addressing social problems.

Read the following excerpts from articles on various issues. For each one, identify the multiple causes of the problem as given in the article; discuss what policies are currently addressing these causes. If no policies are mentioned, come up with your own suggestions for dealing with the various causative factors.

What Are the Risk Factors for Breast Cancer?

A risk factor is anything that affects your chance of getting a disease, such as cancer. Different cancers have different risk factors. For example, exposing skin to strong sunlight is a risk factor for skin cancer. Smoking is a risk factor for cancers of the lung, mouth, larynx (voice box), bladder, kidney, and several other organs.

But risk factors don't tell us everything. Having a risk factor, or even several, does not mean that you will get the disease. Most women who have one or more breast cancer risk factors never develop the disease, while many women with breast cancer have no apparent risk factors (other than being a woman and growing older). Even when a woman with risk factors develops breast cancer, it is hard to know just how much these factors may have contributed to her cancer.

There are different kinds of risk factors. Some factors, like a person's age or race, can't be changed. Others are linked to cancer-causing factors in the environment. Still others are related personal behaviors, such as smoking, drinking, and diet. Some factors influence risk more than others, and your risk for breast cancer can change over time, due to factors such as aging or lifestyle. ■

Multiple Causes of Suicide

Although the nature-versus-nurture debate still rages in some psychiatric circles, most researchers who study suicide fall somewhere in the middle. "You need several things to go wrong at once," explains Victoria Arango of the New York State Psychiatric Institute, which is affiliated with Columbia-Presbyterian Medical Center. "I'm not saying that suicide is purely biological, but it starts with having an underlying biological risk." Life experience, acute stress and psychological factors each play a part, she asserts. At the root of the mystery of suicide, however, lies a nervous system whose lines of communication have become tangled into unbearably painful knots. ■

Self-Segregation

Students Stick with Same-Race Groups

Gina Pera

Why do most teens hang out with friends of the same race? It's just "more comfortable" to be with people who share your background, say thousands of teens in essays submitted to *USA Weekend*. In fact, we got more mail on this topic than any other in the survey. Most also agree that adolescents possess a strong need to belong, and race provides the most obvious visual identity. At the same time, seven in 10 say they have a close friend of another race.

Here are the other reasons survey respondents cite most often:

Peer Pressure. At some schools, making friends of another race creates problems with same-race friends. "If I talk to a person of another race, some black friends will say, 'You're stuck up,'" says Chavonda Pighet, 15, a black student at South

Robeson High School in Rowland, N.C. Her friends tell Chavonda that she should pick one group or the other. "But that's not right. I try to spend time with both."

Fear of Rejection. Venturing beyond the comfort of a familiar group is a risk. For some, it comes at too high a price. "People of other races ask too many questions about my culture, which is Mexican-Indian and Native American," says Swift Sanchez, 14, of Forks (Wash.) High School. "They try to watch what they say, but they slip and say racial things." Twin sister Fawn agrees. "If I make a mistake around some white people, they say 'Look at that stupid Indian.'"

Safety in Numbers. Some kids fear for their safety, says Anthony Harris, 14, of Chicago's Luther High School South. "They think all black people sell drugs, all Mexicans carry knives, all white people listen to heavy metal," says Harris, who is black. As a result, teens seek the protection of the group "just in case something happens, like a fight."

Ignorance. Teens, who face big changes as they grow up, want to feel secure, says Luke Kozikowski, 13, of St. Stanislaus School in Chicopee, Mass. So the races separate to avoid conflict. "But then they feed on each other's fears." The only way to really feel comfortable with different kinds of people, says Kozikowski: "Take a chance and get to know them one at a time." ▪

Why Do People Start to Smoke?

There are not many smokers around who started smoking after the age of eighteen. In fact, the majority of smokers took up the habit in their early or mid teens.

At such a young age, you don't really think about the health risks of smoking, and you certainly do not realize how addictive smoking can be. As a teenager you probably think that you can try smoking a few times and then take it or leave it.

However, the reality is that it doesn't take long to become addicted to nicotine and smoking. Within a short period of time, children can experience the same cravings and withdrawal symptoms as an adult, as well as smoke as many cigarettes or more.

There are several reasons as to why children or teenagers start smoking.

Peer pressure plays an important part. Many children start smoking because their friends have tried it or smoke themselves.

Those children may have started as they have grown up in an environment where their parents, grandparents and older siblings smoke, and so they smoke in order to look and act like them.

Other children start smoking as an act of rebellion or defiance against their parents or people of authority. ▪

EXERCISE 4.3 Purpose: To distinguish immediate from remote causes of an event or effect.

1. Do some research on a social or national event and try to isolate the causes, both immediate and remote, of this event. For example, if you researched the U.S. entry into World War II, you would go beyond the attack on Pearl Harbor,

as far back as World War I, to see all the influences that both compelled and restrained U.S. involvement. Other examples would be immediate and remote causes of homelessness, an outbreak of wildfires, sexually transmitted diseases, the high school drop-out rate, the state of a political party, the rise of corporate conglomerates, the war in Afghanistan, an oil spill, or the challenges of the foster care system. How far back can problems related to these topics be traced?

2. Study the arguments used by the prosecution or by defense attorneys in a trial that attempts to prove a cause-effect relationship between events. Examples would be trials against manufacturers of faulty products, such as silicone implants or dangerous toys, or trials in which one person claims that damage was done to them by another person or by a company, such as complaints about the effects of secondhand cigarette smoke or video display terminals. Investigative news programs, such as *Frontline, 60 Minutes,* and *20/20* often feature stories about such trials, and they make transcripts of their programs available to the public. Look at the statements made by the attorneys for both the prosecution and the defense, and find examples of arguments claiming or denying a cause-effect relationship. Summarize these arguments and comment on their persuasiveness both to the jury and to you as a critical thinker.

You **Decide**

Performance-Enhancing Drugs

Every year, thousands of athletes are tested in an effort to detect and discourage the use of performance-enhancing drugs, and statistical research suggests that the majority of professional athletes pass the tests. However, a number of athletes, both amateur and professional, have been punished for using the drugs in highly competitive sports. Both athletic communities and sports fans have generally supported a ban on performance-enhancing drugs because of the advantage that they are presumed to give to the athletes who use them and the harmful long-term health consequences associated with them. Those who oppose a ban on performance-enhancing drugs argue that athletes should have the freedom to choose whatever helps them succeed; they cite the use of megavitamins, special clothing, and sports psychologists as examples of legal means of gaining an advantage. They also contend that some of the newer drugs are not easily detectable. Those in favor of a continued ban argue that if drug enhancement becomes common in a sport, then persons who prefer not to use the drugs will be forced out of the highest level of competition. They contend that if athletes will have to take drugs in order to be competitive, then their freedom of choice will be limited.

For more information on the debate surrounding performance-enhancing drugs and additional exercises and tutorials about concepts covered in this chapter, log into MyThinkingLab at www.mythinkinglab.com and select Diestler, *Becoming a Critical Thinker,* Sixth Edition.

❋ Explore on **mythinkinglab.com**

Articles for Discussion   📖 Read the Document on mythinkinglab.com

In the United States, there is an increasing community concern about the epidemic of methamphetamine use. According to statistics cited by one source, "Few local governments, especially in rural areas, have the resources to deal with the devastating effects. Robberies and burglaries have increased because of meth, as have domestic violence, assaults, and identify theft. Child welfare officials report an increase in out-of-home placements because of meth. Meth-lab burn victims end up in hospitals at a tremendous cost to hospitals and state Medicaid programs. Hallucinations, weight loss, skin sores, disfigured or destroyed teeth, and brain damage are among the physical results of meth use."[33]

One group that has been sharing information on the national methamphetamine problem is the National Association of Counties. This association did a study of 45 states that is summarized in the following excerpt from a County Coroner's office.

The Meth Epidemic

The swift rise of the use and distribution of methamphetamine . . . has overwhelmed our communities and government services. The increasing widespread production, sales, and use of methamphetamine (also sometimes known as "speed"), is now affecting urban, suburban and rural communities nationwide. County governments across the nation are on the front lines in responding to the methamphetamine crisis. This insidious drug causes a whole host of problems including legal, medical, environmental, and social ones. County and city services (and the taxpayers) must pay for investigating meth labs and distribution cases, making arrests of offenders, holding these suspects in jails, prosecuting them, providing treatment services, probation services, and cleaning up toxic lab sites along with social services costs.

In an alarming number of methamphetamine arrests, there is a child in the home. Social workers and law enforcement officers find that the children are frequently suffering from neglect and abuse. The National Association of Counties (NACo) recently conducted surveys of law enforcement and county child welfare officials in order to determine the impact of meth on government services and their communities. The results were from 500 counties from 45 states. Here is a summary of their results:

- Meth is a growing problem that is now national in scope. Of the 500 responding law enforcement agencies, 87% report increases in meth-related arrests starting three years ago. A number of states, including California, reported 100 percent increases. Seventy percent found robberies or burglaries have increased because of meth use. . . . The Sheriff's Office has experienced a growing number of theft and burglary cases committed by meth addicts especially involving thefts from cars, commercial burglaries, mail theft, and identity theft. Some counties have also experienced a 62 percent increase in domestic violence because of meth use.

- Meth is the leading drug-related local law enforcement problem in the country. Fifty-eight (58%) percent of the counties surveyed stated meth was their largest drug problem.

[33] "Meth Epidemic Moves From Rural Places to Cities," http://www.ruralschools.org/news/survey.html (Organizations concerned about Rural Education, accessed August 11, 2007.)

- Meth related arrests represent a high proportion of crimes requiring incarceration. Fifty percent (50%) of the counties estimated that 1 in 5 of their current jail inmates were housed because of meth related crimes. The problem was even worse in the other half of counties surveyed. . . . Jails are also experiencing a rise in inmate populations, especially in female inmates. One Sheriff from a northern California county stated his female inmate population has risen 30% in the last couple of years due to methamphetamine.

- Other crimes are increasing as a result of meth. Seventy percent of the responding counties stated that along with burglaries, robberies, and domestic violence, assaults and identity thefts have also increased.

In addition to the resulting crime, the production of methamphetamine produces a number of environmental issues as well. The makeshift labs vary in sophistication and can be located in barns, garages, back rooms of businesses, apartments, hotel rooms, storage facilities, vacant buildings, residences, and vehicles, including RVs. This drug, which is smoked, injected, or ingested, is synthetic, cheap, and relatively easy to make in these labs. They frequently will use pseudoephedrine, the ingredient in cold medicines, and common fertilizers and solvents. The materials are dangerous and highly explosive. During my law enforcement career, I have been to a number of meth lab sites where explosions from the manufacturing process had set the residence aflame. In addition, the chemical waste products from this manufacturing process are frequently dumped into the ground, sewer systems, or alongside roads. Even more disturbing is the impact that meth is having on children. The NACo study also found that meth is a major cause of child abuse and neglect.

- Forty percent of all the child welfare officials in the survey reported increases in out-of-home placements of children due to meth in the last year.

- During the past 5 years, 71% of the counties in California alone reported an increase in out-of-home placements due to meth, as did Colorado.

In addition, 59% of county officials stated that the particular nature of the meth user parent has increased the difficulty of family reunification.

The rising number of foster children due to meth use is greatly impacting county welfare systems and the need for more foster parents. As these children are moved around in an overburdened social service system, their parents may be in jail, awaiting treatment, or not seeking treatment. One study found that these children often stay in out-of-home placement three times as long as other children. In addition, many of these children have special needs.

Law enforcement and social service providers in Santa Cruz County are already studying this drastic burden on county services to devise some solutions. However, this widespread problem will take a commitment from all of us, including the public, to solve it with the appropriate resources that will be required. ▩

Questions for Discussion

1. What statistics cited in the article show that methamphetamine addiction is a serious and growing problem?

2. What are the many costs of addiction to society as a whole?

3. The article mentioned specific increases in difficulties associated with methamphetamine use in a community—what were some of these new or newly aggravated problems?

4. What should be done on a national and local level to combat methamphetamine use and its effects?

· ·

A fascinating PBS *Frontline* program covered the efforts of one reporter to investigate the causes of the methamphetamine epidemic that had been plaguing his Oregon community for years and is rapidly spreading across the United States. Reporter Steve Suo compared statistics in addiction rates and saw that they went up and down in a consistent pattern across the country; he then searched for the causes of the consistent ups and downs of these rates. He also persisted in tracing the reasons why it took so long for the problem to be addressed seriously by federal levels of government.

You can download a transcript of the program and watch it on www.pbs.org/wgbh/pages/frontline/meth/view/. If you choose to read the transcript or watch the program, consider the following additional questions:

5. What factors in the *Frontline* program indicate that meth addiction is an international issue?

6. Why was the U.S. Congress slow to understand and enact legislation to curb the meth problem?

7. How did the interests of pharmaceutical companies affect the proposed solutions to the meth problem?

8. *Frontline* added several personal stories to their coverage of the methamphetamine problem. Why is it important to connect statistics with examples of how an issue impacts individuals? How does the combination of data and narrative strengthen the argument that meth is a serious problem?

· ·

When new technologies are embraced by millions of people, the unintended consequences of their use eventually emerge and capture the interest of researchers. The following article by British journalist Joe Elvin focuses on multiple causes of the addictive nature of social networking on Facebook.

Understanding Facebook Addiction

Why Is Social Networking So Addictive? How Did We Get Addicted?

Joe Elvin

A few explanations as to why Facebook addicts spend so many hours browsing photos, trying new applications and Facebook stalking.

More than 350 million people have signed up to social networking website Facebook since its creation by Harvard University student Mark Zuckerberg in 2004. Recent stats revealed by the website revealed that over half of them log into their account every day and more than 3.5 billion pieces of content are shared every week.

Facebook is arguably the biggest phenomenon of the Internet and has made Zuckerberg the world's youngest self-made billionaire. The average user spends 55 minutes every day on the website but what is it that makes Facebook so addictive?

Facebook Gives a Sense of Self-Worth

Humanistic psychologist Abraham Maslow developed a theory that humans have three basic needs. One of these was the need for love, affection and belongingness. Humans need a sense of self-worth and a Facebook profile has become the perfect tool for people to let the world know all about their interests, their thoughts and their life.

Facebook allows users to talk and share as much as they like about themselves without fear of being labeled as self-obsessed. After all, self-explanation is the purpose of the website and updates aren't being directed at anyone in particular.

Nobody feels obliged to acknowledge what they read so each message received by a friend makes users feel important, interesting and appreciated. Every notification is a small buzz of self-esteem.

Facebook Stalking

Another human instinct is the need to know what is going on around us, and Facebook lets users become very aware of friends' activities. Many like to know a little too much and Facebook allows users to pry into the lives of others without the fear of being branded a nosey parker.

The ability to view photos and spy on others' conversations without them ever knowing is what makes Facebook such a thrill for so many of its users. The term for such behaviour has been defined as 'Facebook stalking.'

Furthermore, many people are either too busy or too shy and conserved to phone up old friends just to see how they are getting on. The same can be said for developing new friendships which can prove awkward and time-consuming. Facebook allows us to do both with greater ease.

The Facebook Community

Facebook has developed to the point where most 18–30s from developed countries would struggle to find a peer who hasn't signed up. Because of its sheer popularity it is now possible to arrange parties, meetings or get-togethers solely through the website. Many Facebook addicts feel that that could be missing out if they don't check their profiles as often as they do.

Facebook on Mobile Phones

Facebook is an instant cure for loneliness and with the recent introduction of a mobile version of the website, it is easier than ever to instantly network with others.

Almost one fifth of users are now accessing the site through their mobile phones and official statistics suggest that users become on average 50% more active once they do so. As a new decade begins, it seems that the world's Facebook addiction isn't going to stop growing any time soon.

Questions for Discussion

1. What are the multiple causes of "Facebook addiction" that are given in this article?

2. To what extent do the addictive habits described in this article fit you or your friends?

3. Do you agree that Facebook addiction is a real and growing problem? Why or why not?

The following article reviews research on another current trend, that of 'hooking up.' The researchers concluded that the college students they studied were not aware of the negative physical and psychological costs of this behavior.

ISU Researcher Studies Consequences of 'Hooking Up'

Study Focuses on Risk Behavior

AMES, Iowa—Iowa State University researchers said their studies on hooking up found that students often underestimate the consequences of their risky behavior.

Hooking up is the process of meeting friends and strangers to engage in intimate behaviors ranging from kissing and fondling to sexual intercourse. Recent national studies show that more than 70 percent of college students are now hooking up.

Iowa State University sociologist Teresa Downing-Matibag is studying the trend of more students hooking up. The research focuses on the physical and emotional consequences to sexual intimacy without investing in relationships.

"In the study we found that students grossly underestimate their susceptibility to getting sexually transmitted infections due to hooking up," said Downing-Matibag.

Downing-Matibag said she is actively promoting healthier intimate relationships among young people at Iowa State University.

"Once we can have that honest conversation with them, we can meet them where we are. Then we can talk to them about taking that next step to protect themselves," said Downing-Matibag.

A study published last year tracked 71 college students' hookup behaviors. The study found that students often underestimate their vulnerability to sexually transmitted diseases (STDs) during hookups, placing too much trust in their partners, not discussing use of prophylactics, and/or not understanding the STD-related risks of certain sexual practices.

"I got an e-mail from a young man who said, 'thank you for doing your research and publicizing this—three years ago I made a bad decision and now I'm living with HIV AIDS," said Downing-Matibag.

Downing-Matibag said students need to become better aware that they're engaging in risky behavior that could have serious life consequences.

"I want to promote a movement on campus that encourages students to be more reflective about the decisions they're making and the longer term implications of those decisions for their well-being," she said. "And I'm not just talking about their sexual well-being, I'm talking about well-being in their future families and longer-term relationships."

Downing-Matibag said a University of Washington study shows that rates of infidelity are rising among both young married men and women. She said she sees a possible connection with the hookup college culture.

"I think it's been within the last decade that students developed the language to talk about casual sex and we decided to call it 'hooking up,'" Downing-Matibag said. "And I think having that language and talking openly about it has made us more aware of the fact that it's happening. But it's also, in some ways, made it appear more normative. Even so, we haven't done a good enough job of educating students about the risks. The United States has the highest rates of sexually transmissible diseases in the developed world."

Downing-Matibag said her research also shows that men and women cited similar reasons for hooking up. Although the women subjects were more likely than men to indicate an interest in dating their recent hookup partners, the majority of women in the study, similar to the men, were not seeking committed relationships, said Downing-Matibag.

Iowa State University crime statistics show that the number of sexual assaults reported on campus doubled in a year from 11 in 2008 to 20 in 2009.

"You never know if more people are being assaulted or if more people are just reporting. We really don't have enough information to make a conclusion; however, I think students have become more aware of the resources on campus," said Steffani Simbric, with the Iowa State University Public Safety Department.

Campus outreach groups educate on sexual safety and support those who have been assaulted.

Downing-Matibag said it all comes down not to lecturing students, but meeting them halfway.

"In order to talk with students about safer sex and relationships, we need to meet them where they are," said Downing-Matibag.

You can learn more about the research on the Iowa State University website. ■

Questions for Discussion

1. The Iowa State researchers said that their studies on hooking up found that students often underestimate the consequences of their risky behavior. What examples did they give from their studies?

2. Were the findings of the researchers similar to what you have observed about dating practices on college campuses? If not, what differences have you noticed?

3. Have you seen changes in dating and mating rituals during your own lifetime? If so, what are the changes, and why do you think they occurred? If not, do you know someone of an older generation who has observed such changes?

4. Given the research findings, to what extent do you agree with Teresa Downing-Matibag that students need to be more reflective about the long-term consequences of their decisions?

. . . .

The following article reports on research about the rise of drug usage and the increasingly aggressive presence of gangs in schools. Educators, parents, community leaders, and government agencies use this research to make decisions on ways to prevent and deal with the negative effects of these growing trends.

Drugs, Gangs on the Rise in Schools

Survey Shows Increase in Gang Activity and Drug Use in Nation's Schools

Salynn Boyles

Aug. 20, 2010—The nation's public schools earn a failing grade when it comes to protecting teens from drugs and gang activity, a nationwide survey suggests.

About one in four surveyed teens attending public schools reported the presence of both gangs and drugs at their schools, and 32% of 12- and 13-year-old middle school children said drugs were used, kept, or sold on school grounds—a 39% increase in just one year.

The findings suggest that as many as 5.7 million public school children in the U.S. attend schools with both drugs and gangs.

Former U.S. secretary of Health, Education and Welfare Joseph Califano Jr. calls drugs and gang activity a cancer on the nation's public schools.

"It is just outrageous," he tells WebMD. "It is nothing less than state-sanctioned child abuse to require parents to send their kids to schools where drugs and gangs are present."

Califano directs the National Center on Addiction and Substance Abuse (CASA), which conducts the annual back-to-school survey of teen and parent attitudes on drug and alcohol abuse.

Survey: Gangs Are Everywhere

For the first time this year, the 12- to 17-year-olds who participated in the survey were asked about the presence of gangs at their school. Among the findings:

- 46% of public school students, but just 2% of private and religious school students, said there were gangs at their school.
- Compared to teens in schools without gangs, those in schools with gangs were nearly twice as likely to report that drugs were available and used at school (30% vs. 58%).
- Compared to teens attending schools without gangs and drugs, teens attending schools with drugs and gangs were 12 times more likely to have tried cigarettes, five times as likely to have used marijuana, and three times more likely to have used alcohol.

Califano says gangs have spread far beyond their traditional urban settings of New York, Chicago, and Los Angeles. They are now found in much smaller cities and suburbs and even rural areas.

Gang expert Carter Smith agrees that gangs are a growing problem in places where they have not been recognized before.

In 2002, Smith moved to the historic town of Franklin, Tenn., near Nashville—a popular destination for tourists and one of the last places one would expect to find gangs.

On his first visit to a local park with his then young sons, Smith spotted gang graffiti.

The 2008 gang-related shooting death of a student from a Franklin high school shocked the sleepy community.

A member of a gang, the student was returning home from a party when he was shot by rival gang members who pulled up beside his SUV and opened fire.

"Parents who live in wealthy communities shouldn't think their schools are immune to gang activity," Smith tells WebMD. "Schools are only immune when the parents and school administrators refuse to accept the presence of gangs."

Public Schools vs. Private Schools

The survey highlights a widening gap between public and private schools with regard to drug and alcohol use.

In CASA's 2001 survey, 62% of public school students and 79% of private and religious school students said they attended drug-free schools. In the latest survey, less than half of public school students (43%) and 78% of private school students said their school was free of drugs.

Teens in public schools were 23 times more likely to report gang activity in their schools than teens in private schools.

Califano says parental involvement may be as important as economic advantage in explaining the gap. He points to New York City parochial schools where parents who can't afford tuition work to pay for their children to attend.

"These schools are in really poor neighborhoods, right next to failing public schools," he says. "Yet they are graduating almost all of their kids."

This year's survey found that parental involvement and strong family ties were among the strongest influences in whether teens smoked, drank alcohol, or used recreational drugs.

Compared to teens with strong family ties, those with weak ties were four times as likely to try tobacco or marijuana and three times as likely to drink alcohol.

CASA Director of Marketing Kathleen Ferrigno says simple things like knowing your teen's friends and eating family meals together can have a big impact.

And parents should never accept drinking and drug use as a normal part of growing up, she tells WebMD.

"We know that kids who smoke, drink, or use drugs at an early age have a high risk for addiction as they get older," she says. "Drinking, smoking, and drug use should never be viewed as a rite of passage."

Questions for Discussion

1. What were the survey's general conclusions about drug use and gang presence in schools? What statistics did the authors use to support their conclusions?

2. What differences were noted between public and private schools concerning drugs and gangs?

3. What suggestions were offered to prevent drug use and gang involvement? To what extent do you believe that these suggestions could be effective? What would you propose to address the problems of drugs and gangs in public schools?

Ideas for Writing or Speaking

Using the following format, create a persuasive speech or essay on an issue of your choice. Use statistical research to support your conclusion.

1. Find an issue that interests you. The more interest you have in the issue, the more conviction you will have in your writing or speaking.

2. Write out your conclusion about the issue. Your position on the issue should be clearly articulated and will form your thesis statement.

3. Begin your essay or speech with an introduction that provides a context for your issue and your position. You may also use important statistics to gain the attention of your readers or listeners. Put your thesis statement at the end of your introduction, and follow the thesis statement with a brief 'preview' of the key reasons you will use to support your conclusion.

4. Identify and expand upon the reasons that support your conclusion in the body of the essay or speech. Concentrate on statistical evidence. You may also include examples and expert testimony to complete your support.

5. Use the conclusion of your essay or speech to restate your major points and to reemphasize the importance of your conclusion. Remind your readers or listeners of the points you brought out in your introduction, bringing these points full circle in your closing thoughts.

Longer-Term Writing Assignment

The purpose of this assignment is to give you an in-depth understanding of a social, national, or international problem and the many factors that enter into changes in policy. This may be done as a long-term project for an individual or a group.

Begin by asking yourself, "What is a continuing community, campus, national, or international problem that concerns me?" Or, take the advice of English professor Bruce Reeves, and fill in the blank on the following question: "If we can send a man to the moon, why can't we _____?" For example, you might think, "If we can send a man to the moon, why can't we solve world hunger?" Or, "Why can't we stop the drug cartels?" "Why can't we provide jobs for everyone?" "Why can't we have peace in the Middle East [or somewhere else]?" "Why can't we rid our town of pollution from the local factory?"

Then, begin researching the problem. You will learn more about research in the next chapter, but begin with the knowledge you have gained in this chapter. Look up statistics that relate to your problem, being careful to note how the research has been carried out.

After you read Chapter 5, begin the rest of your research using a minimum of six sources of information, including studies done about this problem and the opinions of experts who have written or spoken about it. If the problem you are studying is local, try to interview officials who are in a position to address the problem or who have worked on the problem.

Take notes on the background of the problem, including the history of the problem, the scope of the problem, and the impact or effect of the problem. Try to list multiple causes that contribute to the problem.

As you research this problem, consider past efforts to solve it. To what extent were those efforts successful? Where there have been failed policies, explain why they have failed.

Note also any current or recent proposals about this problem. For example, if you are writing on the difficulty of ending homelessness, consider why past proposals have not been approved or successfully implemented. Also, consider the chances of success for any current proposals.

When you have finished studying this problem, create a proposal for a solution to this problem. Support your proposal, showing how it will resolve the difficulties that previous proposals have come up against. Also, explain how it will not create more problems than it solves.

If you find that you can't come up with a solution to the problem, then explain what variables make it too difficult to solve. State what would have to change for a resolution to be possible.

In sum, your paper or speech should include a complete explanation of the background and scope of the problem, the harm it creates, the policies that have not worked against this problem, and your proposed solution to the problem or analysis of why it can't currently be solved. Also, include a bibliography of all sources you used in researching this problem.

Films for Analysis and Discussion

Moneyball (2011)

Moneyball is based on the book with the same title. It tells the story of Oakland A's General Manager Billy Beane (played by Brad Pitt) and his successful use of computer-generated statistical analysis to draft players for his team. Beane was on a tight budget and had fewer resources than many other managers, but he believed in using the laws of probability to predict a player's potential. His inductive reasoning about choosing specific players leads him to create a superior roster.

The Constant Gardener (2005, R)

This film stars Ralph Fiennes as a widower searching for the truth about the death of his beloved wife, played by Rachel Weisz. As it turns out, the truth involves corrupt corporations covering up deaths all over Africa, and he might be their next target. The film combines flashbacks of Weisz discovering the corruption with present scenes of Fiennes researching the cover-up of both his wife's death and much more. This film provides a good illustration of discovering truth through the researching of causes and effects.

Similar Films and Classics

Erin Brockovich (2000, R)

This true story is about an unemployed single mother who gets involved in one of the biggest class action lawsuits in American history. Note the search for causes of poisonings afflicting community residents and the series of events that lead Erin to be a focal point of the investigation.

A Civil Action (1998, PG-13)

Actor John Travolta plays Jan Schlictmann, a lawyer who agrees to represent eight families whose children died from leukemia; he attempts to link the deaths to two large corporations that leaked toxic chemicals into the water supply of Woburn, Massachusetts. Note the personal cost to Schlittman that is discussed earlier in this chapter in our section on *Multiple Causes.*

The China Syndrome (1979, PG)

This film explores a young reporter's discovery of an accident at a nuclear power plant and how the incident is covered up by those who wish to keep it a secret. Note how difficult it is to seek the truth about an incident when those with vested interests do not want full disclosure.

CHAPTER

5

Inductive Generalizations
Controlled Studies
and Analogies

Who Said So, and Who Are They Anyway?

A critical thinker understands the credible use of controlled studies, expert testimony, and generalizations from analogies to support arguments.

Critical thinkers carefully evaluate research and expert opinion in order to make good decisions.

THIS CHAPTER WILL COVER

- The use of controlled studies in arguments
- The criteria for credibility of controlled studies
- The use and misuse of expert testimony in supporting conclusions
- The use of analogies in inductive reasoning

Read on mythinkinglab.com

Listen on mythinkinglab.com

I n the previous chapter, we considered the use of statistical studies and causal generalizations as evidence (reasons) to support conclusions. In this chapter, we will focus on the inductive generalizations that come from *controlled studies;* we will also look at the importance of *expert testimony.* We will then examine another commonly used form of inductive reasoning, that of generalizing from *analogies.*

Researchers use controlled studies to make observations and draw conclusions about many subjects, including human and animal behavior and solutions to medical problems. These studies are called *controlled* because they use specific methods for comparing groups of subjects. Other researchers can duplicate these methods so that the accuracy of the findings can be verified.

The conclusions drawn in carefully controlled scientific studies are inductive generalizations; a good study shows us what will *probably* or *usually* occur in a given circumstance.

Some of the elements of controlled studies are the same as those used by polling organizations. A researcher still focuses on the three questions discussed in Chapter 4:

1. What do I want to find out? (the characteristic of interest)
2. Whom do I want to know about? (the target population)
3. Whom can I study to get accurate answers about my target population?
   (the sample)

As with polling, researchers usually can't study everyone in a given target population, so they have to observe *some* members of the population. The number of subjects depends on how precise an answer the researcher needs. Preliminary results leading to *additional* studies can be gathered from a very small sample. For example, if a researcher discovers that 20 women with kidney problems have a negative reaction to the drug ibuprofen, these findings can be used to justify the funds for a larger study.

In medical research, the design of a study is called the **protocol.** Two groups of **subjects** (people or animals) who are alike in all *significant* (relevant) aspects need to be studied in order for the research to have the element of **control.** Control involves weeding out extraneous factors that could affect the outcome of a study.

protocol
The design of a controlled research study.

subjects People or animals studied to get information about a target population.

control The process of weeding out extraneous factors that could affect the outcome of a study between two groups of subjects, in which one group is exposed to a variable and the other is not.

Research Design

A good research design includes the following:

1. A **question** to answer: This is the characteristic of interest concerning a targeted population. A researcher begins with a question, such as, "What is the effect of the new drug Z on migraine headaches?"

2. A **hypothesis:** This is a speculation about what will be discovered from the research: "The drug Z will shorten migraine headaches caused by restricted blood vessels."

3. A **sample** of individuals to study: The sample should be randomly selected and representative of the target population. The sample is divided into two groups (see Figure 5–1).

   a. A **control group:** A group of subjects from the sample who get either no treatment or a **placebo** (a sugar pill or harmless substance that has no effect).

   b. An **experimental group:** A group of subjects from the sample who are exposed to a special treatment called an independent *variable;* for example, this group would be given the drug to assess its effects in comparison with similar people who are not given the drug or who are given a placebo. Significant results may be discovered when the only difference between the control group and the experimental group is that the experimental group is exposed to the **independent variable.**

4. **Data:** The observations made by the researcher as he or she completes the study.

5. **Conclusions:** After the study is carried out, the researcher compiles the data and draws conclusions; the researcher interprets the meaning and significance of the data. The researcher is particularly interested in the effect of the independent variable on the experimental group.

In addition, researchers carefully consider the *implications* of the findings, which means that they will speculate about further research that can be done to answer questions related to the study.

Researchers can draw accurate conclusions and eliminate alternate explanations for the results of their research if the studies are carefully designed to fit the criteria described in the next section. The generalizations they draw may be used as evidence in inductive arguments.

question The characteristic of interest concerning a targeted population.

hypothesis A speculation about what will be discovered from a research study.

sample Members of the target population who are studied by a researcher.

control group A group of subjects from the sample who get no treatment or a placebo and are thus a test benchmark.

placebo A pill or other treatment that has no medical value or effect (sometimes called a 'sugar pill') that is given to the control group in a research study.

experimental group A group of subjects from the sample who are exposed to a special treatment called the independent variable.

data The observations made and information collected by the researcher as he or she completes a study.

conclusions The researcher's summary and interpretation of the meaning and significance of the study results.

independent variable The special treatment given to the experimental group in a research study. Exposure to the independent variable should be the only difference between the control group and the experimental group.

Control Group   Experimental Group

FIGURE 5–1

The experimental group receives the special treatment called the independent variable.

Stop and **Think**

How is a controlled study based on Mill's method of difference?

Criteria for Evaluating Research Findings

Science is always simple and always profound. It is only the half-truths that are dangerous.

George Bernard Shaw, *The Doctor's Dilemma* (1913)

Junk science makes junk law.

Dr. James Dobson

Interesting findings from research studies are often reported in newspapers and magazines or on websites and television programs. Most of these reports don't give complete information about the research design. In addition, writers and speakers often make claims using general phrases like "studies have shown," "research tells us," or "experts believe" without discussing any specific evidence. Before accepting the results of research as reliable, the following questions should be asked:

1. How large was the sample? As we discussed previously, a small sample can suggest areas for further research; for example, one study on the prevention of heart disease involved only 47 subjects but was the cause of considerable hope in the scientific community. *L.A. Times* reporter Thomas H. Maugh III notes the following:

> A small clinical trial has shown for the first time that it is possible to use drugs to remove plaque from clogged arteries, a finding that could lead to radically new ways to treat heart disease, the No. 1 killer in the United States.
>
> Infusions of a genetically engineered mutant form of high-density lipo-protein, the so-called good cholesterol, over a five-week period were shown to reduce plaque volume in patients suffering from chest pain.
>
> "This is an extraordinary and unprecedented finding," said Dr. Steven Nissen of the Cleveland Clinic Foundation, who led the study reported in the *Journal of the American Medical Association*.[1]

[1] Thomas H. Maugh III, "Drug for Heart Disease Called Breakthrough," *L.A. Times*, November 5, 2003.

Preliminary studies that show great promise should receive our attention and the funding and resources of our universities and hospitals. One reporter asked Dr. Nissen if he would proceed to conduct more research after the initial small studies proved hopeful. Nissen replied:

> "Absolutely. And I think it is important for everyone to understand that this is not an available therapy. It's investigational. But we are so encouraged by these results that now we have a good reason to do studies in thousands of patients. And I'm really very confident that when we go ahead and study this in a larger group, we're going to find that targeting the HDL, the good cholesterol, can actually turn around this disease, and it can do it much faster than we ever believed."[2]

Scientists can be enthusiastic and hopeful about promising studies. As critical thinkers, however, we need to remember that more complete studies need to be conducted before we can use the research findings as factual support for our conclusions.

Studies with an inadequate sample are sometimes reported in the news media because of their fascinating results. If you read about a remarkable study, be especially careful to pay attention to information about the sample used by the researcher. Consider the following research reported under the heading "FYI, True Love Is the Best Drug." Was the sample large enough to justify the conclusion expressed by the headline?

> While the verdict may still be out on whether love is stronger than hate, new research suggests it is at least healthier. In a study of older, happily married couples, Ohio State University researchers found that abrasive arguments weakened the couples' immune systems, making them more vulnerable to illnesses and infectious diseases. Scientists had asked 31 couples ages 55 to 75 to discuss the issues that caused problems in their marriage. Blood samples were taken at regular intervals and monitored for changes in hormone levels and immune function. The more negativity the couples expressed toward each other, the more their immune systems weakened.[3]

Remember that websites, newspapers, magazines, and television programs want to present interesting information to readers and viewers. Most reporters are not trained in research design, so they are not usually skilled at examining methodology; their primary job is to create a good story. The "story" they create can be found in the headline used to summarize the article, which often claims far more than is merited by a limited study.

2. Is the study reliable? As we discussed in Chapter 4, if a sample is not representative of the target group, then the study is biased and not reliable; the results cannot be generalized to a larger population. In the previous example about married couples, the reporter generalized about all couples from a small group of couples, ages 55 to 75. Remember that representativeness means having the same characteristics in the same proportion as the target population. Consider the following claim made in

[2] Ibid.
[3] Staff and wire reports, "FYI, True Love Is the Best Drug," *Contra Costa Times*, September 10, 1996, p. E1.

an article entitled "Marijuana-like Substance in Brain Could Help Treat Parkinson's, Researchers Say":

> Neuroscientists have found that a substance similar to the active ingredient in marijuana but produced naturally in the brain helps to control mobility— and may offer a novel target for treating Parkinson's disease. Stanford University researchers reported today in the journal *Nature* that marijuana-like "endocannabinoids"—one of the many chemicals used in the brain to transmit signals from one neuron to another—form part of the neural machinery that directs normal movement.[4]

The article later notes that this experiment was done only on mice, that it would take years of research to reach the human testing stage, and that

> THC, the active ingredient in marijuana, activities the same class of receptors as the natural chemicals but has effects throughout the brain, and no demonstrated benefits in terms of improved mobility . . . one thing the findings don't suggest is that smoking marijuana might help alleviate Parkinson's.[5]

3. Are there alternative explanations for the findings? Have all of the important factors of the data been considered? There might be explanations for findings in research other than the ones given by the researchers. For example, if the members of the experimental group know they are receiving the treatment, they may report positive changes based solely on their expectations (that is, if Joanne knows she received the new drug that cures headaches, she may expect to feel better and then actually feel better—she may experience a self-fulfilling prophecy). To control for this kind of error, researchers generally try to conduct **blind studies** in which the participants are not told whether they belong to the experimental group or the control group.

Also, researchers may unconsciously exaggerate the improvement they see in the experimental group, especially if the study results are very important to them. For this reason, **double-blind studies** are often conducted; in these studies, neither the experimenter nor the participants know which is the control and which is the experimental group.

One study conducted in three Illinois cities compared the accuracy of eyewitness identifications of suspects between the traditional and the "reform" method of identification. In the traditional method, several individuals—including the suspect—are lined up and viewed simultaneously by the witnesses. In this method, the police are aware of the suspect's identity. The traditional method is blind; the witnesses don't know who the police suspect. The reform method is double blind—in the reform method, witnesses look at people or pictures one by one, and the officer or officers present do not know the identity of the suspects and aren't working on the case.

Of the 319 simultaneous lineups conducted using the traditional method, the suspect identified by police was chosen 59.9 percent of the time. Of

blind studies Studies in which subjects are not told whether they belong to the control group or the experimental group.

double-blind studies Studies in which neither the experimenter nor the subjects know which is the control group and which is the experimental group.

---

[4] Carl T. Hall, "Marijuana-like Substance in Brain Could Help Treat Parkinson's, Researchers Say," *Chronicle Science Writer,* Wednesday, February 7, 2007, sfgate.com.
[5] Ibid.

229 sequential lineups using the reform method, the suspect was chosen only 45 percent of the time.

> Sheri Mecklenberg, general counsel to the Chicago Police and director of the study, said she found the results surprising and hoped they would generate further study. "This is important for everyone. What police, defense attorneys and prosecutors want is better witness identification," she said.
>
> But the study was criticized by Gary Wells, a professor of psychology at Iowa State who has published more than 100 articles on the topic. Wells' chief concern was that the simultaneous lineups were conducted by investigators working the cases. That makes the results hard to compare, Wells said.
>
> "The reason that we so vehemently push the double-blind is because of a concern that the lineup administrator unintentionally influences the person's choice, leads them to pick the suspect," he said.[6]

In addition to the problems associated with bias, it is also difficult to design research studies that help us discover the causes of problems. For example, we wouldn't want researchers to take identical twins and encourage one to become a smoker to see if her lungs deteriorated over time while her nonsmoking sister's lungs remained clear. As a result, we often are hampered by limited information, evidence we can collect from past *occurrences,* as we seek to discover reasonable causal generalizations.

Some sample groups are difficult to study, as discussed by columnist Linda Seebach in the following excerpt:

> American education suffers from an excess of experiment and a shortage of research. The difference is that research studies are carefully designed to test an educational theory by comparing one group of students who have tried a new method with a similar group who have not.
>
> The difficulty is that such research is expensive and complicated. New medicines are tested for safety and efficacy by "double-blind" tests in which neither doctors nor patients know who is getting the experimental drug. But education can't be conducted blind; children, and their parents, know perfectly well what is going on in their classrooms.
>
> Recruiting children for a research study can lead to errors, if the parents who consent are unlike those who don't in some way the researchers don't know about.
>
> So the staple fare of education journals is success stories told by enthusiastic teachers reporting on their own classroom experiments. The stories are true, they may even be inspiring, but they don't prove any general principles.[7]

Similarly, studies of the effects of various medical treatments and procedures don't always lend themselves to double-blind studies. Controlled studies on the effects of vaccines would be invaluable for doctors, parents, and pharmaceutical

---

[6] Annie Sweeney, "Traditional Police Lineup Works Better: Study," *Chicago Sun Times,* March 29, 2001. Copyright Chicago Sun Times, 2006.

[7] Linda Seebach, "Education Lacks Enough Research," *Contra Costa Times,* September 1, 1996.

companies, but researchers find them difficult to do, particularly because children in a control group would have to go without vaccinations.

> Dr. Donald W. Miller, Jr. (who teaches cardiac surgery at the University of Washington medical school) notes that health officials consider a vaccine to be safe if no bad reactions—like seizures, intestinal obstruction, or anaphylaxis—occur acutely. The Center for Disease Control has not done any studies to assess the long-term effects of its immunization schedule. To do that they would have to conduct a randomized controlled trial, where one group of children is vaccinated on the CDC's schedule and a control group is not vaccinated. Investigators would then have to follow the two groups for a number of years, not just three to four weeks, as has been done in the existing vaccine safety studies.[8]

4. Are the results statistically significant? When a finding is labeled **statistically significant**, it is probable that the reported effect will occur again in similar circumstances. For example, let's say there are 100 persons in an experimental group and 100 persons in a control group, and 13 more in the experimental group react to the treatment (the independent variable). With that proportion of difference in reaction, researchers can conclude that there is a 95 percent probability that the treatment (and not a chance occurrence) caused the effect, and they can call their study statistically significant.

statistically significant
The result of an experiment that will occur again in similar circumstances.

5. Have other researchers been able to duplicate the results? There is always a first discovery of a link between a treatment and an effect on people. However, if a study reveals an important finding, then other researchers may try similar experiments to verify the results of the research and to look for applications of the discovery. When others have tried to do the same experiment and failed, the results are considered unreliable.

Duplicate studies are often conducted on products that make incredible claims, and these studies often refute the claims of the original researchers; for example, many companies declare, often through infomercials, that their research has discovered the "fountain of youth." One such youth-restoring product was discussed as follows on a medical talk show:

> *Jill:* I'm calling to find out about human growth hormone, HGH. I have friends on it that say wonderful things about it and that it is a fountain of youth. Then I read an article about HGH and a lawsuit. I am wondering what the lawsuit is about and if HGH is dangerous?
>
> *Dr. Dean:* Be very careful. I would think most of what they're experiencing and telling you about is probably a placebo effect.
>
> A few years ago, there was a study that claimed all kinds of benefits from HGH. Then they repeated the study carefully in a double-blind fashion—it turns out that it is not a good thing. It will give you sore and aching muscles that will grow tumors. This is not the fountain of youth, nor does it increase strength. It is one of those things that got out of hand.
>
> The lawsuit you have heard about is where the company who makes HGH agreed to pay a criminal fine and restitution, like $50 million, because

---

[8] "Vaccination Consideration," stewardshipdiaries.wordpress.com/2010/07/27/.

they promoted growth hormone for a medical use that was not approved by the FDA.

As part of their fine, they have to educate physicians about the approved indications, which are for growth hormone deficient people, usually kids, and people with kidney disease. There are some other syndromes that it has been approved for as well.[9]

The original study that caused companies to sell "growth hormone therapy" to stop or reverse aging was conducted on only 21 men, 12 of whom were given growth hormone and experienced significant side effects. Because so many people spent money on the magical aging cures promised by companies, actions were taken against those making such claims and promises based on inadequate research.

In April 2003, *Nature's Youth*, LLC, of Centerville, Massachusetts, voluntarily destroyed approximately 5,700 boxes of "Nature's Youth HGH" with a market value of about $515,000. The destruction took place after the FDA notified the company that claims made for the product were unsubstantiated and therefore illegal. The company had claimed that the product, which it described as a growth hormone releaser, would enhance the body's natural production of human growth factors and insulin-like growth factor-1; improve physical performance; speed recovery from training; increase cardiac output; and increase immune functions; and was "your body's best defense against aging."

In 2005, Edmund Chein, M.D., who operates the Palm Springs Life Extension Institute (PSLEI) in Palm Springs, California, was placed on five years' probation during which he must (a) pay $10,000 to the State of California for costs, (b) take courses in ethics, prescribing practices, and recordkeeping, (c) refrain from making unsubstantiated advertising claims, and (d) either have his practice monitored or participate in an intensive professional enhancement program. The clinic's website states that PSLEI specializes in "optimized total hormone balancing by returning hormone levels to values consistent with a younger person." The grounds for discipline included inappropriately and negligently prescribing HGH plus insulin to a patient who was neither deficient nor diabetic.

In 2009, Sean Shafer and *The Compounding Center, Inc.,* of Phoenix, Arizona were charged with illegally distributing HGH. The indictment alleged that the company's website touted impermissible uses of HGH for "anti-aging" purposes and that from 2001 through 2006, nine doctors made more than 400 purchases totaling more than $1.1 million. The indictment also states that Shafer, in his capacity as the manager of the wholesale department of the Compounding Center, also sold a number of HGH kits to two undercover operatives who specifically told him that the purchases were for bodybuilders and athletes.

Although growth hormone levels decline with age, it has not been proven that trying to maintain the levels that exist in young persons is beneficial. Considering the high cost, significant side effects, and lack of proven

---

[9] Dr. Dean Edell, "Growth Hormone Is Not the Fountain of Youth," www.healthcentral.com (accessed April 15, 1999).

effectiveness, HGH shots appear to be a very poor investment. So called "growth-hormone releasers," oral "growth hormone," and "homeopathic HGH" products are fakes.[10]

Some areas of concern require studies that take years to complete, and subsequent research is done to verify the results of the original studies. For example, a large international study of the risk of brain cancer from cell phone use has yielded inconclusive results (see pages 182–183 on contradictory studies for more on this issue). "Although the study provides no definitive evidence of increased risk of brain cancer from mobile phones, observations at the highest level of cumulative call time and the changing patterns of mobile phone use, particularly among young people, warrant further investigation, researchers said."[11]

6. Does the researcher claim that the study proves more than it was designed to prove? Some researchers may be too hopeful or excited about the implications of a study they conducted; for example, if a small sample of cancer patients has been helped by an experimental drug, the researcher needs to limit the reporting of results to the findings of this particular study. News media often report the results of a study in such a way as to magnify its significance. For example, a headline on the research site *Science Daily* reads "Love Takes Up Where Pain Leaves Off, Brain Study Shows" In the opening paragraph, the results are summarized as follows:

> Intense, passionate feelings of love can provide amazingly effective pain re-lief, similar to painkillers or such illicit drugs as cocaine, according to a new Stanford University School of Medicine study.[12]

The article goes on to discuss the fact that the areas of the brain activated by intense love are the same areas activated by pain killers. The reader is not told that this research was done on a very small sample of young subjects, using only a mild administration of pain, until the twelfth paragraph:

> Researchers recruited 15 undergraduates (eight women and seven men) for the study. Each was asked to bring in photos of their beloved and photos of an equally attractive acquaintance. The researchers then successively flashed the pictures before the subjects, while heating up a computer-controlled thermal stimulator placed in the palm of their hand to cause mild pain. At the same time, their brains were scanned in a functional magnetic resonance imaging machine.
>
> The undergraduates were also tested for levels of pain relief while being distracted with word-association tasks such as: "Think of sports that don't involve balls." Scientific evidence has shown in the past that distraction causes pain relief, and researchers wanted to make sure that love was not just working as a distraction from pain.
>
> Results showed that both love and distraction did equally reduce pain, and at much higher levels than the levels noted by concentration on the

---

[10] Stephen Barrett, "Growth Hormone Schemes and Scams," http://www.quackwatch.org.

[11] Science Daily, "Mobile Phone Use and Brain Cancer Risk," http://www.sciencedaily.com/releases/2010/05/100517085204.htm.

[12] "Love Takes Up Where Pain Leaves Off, Brain Study Shows," *Science News, Science Daily,* http://www.sciencedaily.com/releases/2010/10/101013173843.htm, October 14, 2010.

photo of the attractive acquaintance; however, the two methods of pain reduction used very different brain pathways.

"With the distraction test, the brain pathways leading to pain relief were mostly cognitive," Younger said. "The reduction of pain was associated with higher, cortical parts of the brain. Love-induced analgesia is much more associated with the reward centers. It appears to involve more primitive aspects of the brain, activating deep structures that may block pain at a spinal level—similar to how opioid analgesics work.[13]

AOL reported this same study with a similarly exciting headline and some of the same promising opening paragraphs.

Study: Love Is Like Cocaine, Codeine

Over the centuries, countless poets and songwriters have compared the power of romantic love to the transformative effects of any number of therapeutic or recreational drugs. According to a new study, such writerly claims are not the stuff of fiction.

In fact, love is akin to a pain killer, like codeine, researchers at Stanford University and the State University of New York at Stony Brook found.

"Intense, passionate feelings of love can provide amazingly effective pain relief, similar to painkillers or such illicit drugs as cocaine," said a press release for the study, which was published in the journal *PloS One*.[14]

The writer of the AOL report discusses the bad news about the limits of the research findings at the end of his article:

Like with all drugs, however, once the initial throes of passion die down, it can be a rocky road ahead, as Stanford's Scope blog noted:

The problem is, this phase of love rarely lasts longer than a year or two and often gets replaced by bone-crushing pain—which the scientist didn't measure in this study.[15]

When a study is promising, the researcher can suggest further studies that would be needed to make solid discoveries about the effectiveness of a treatment. As critical thinkers, we need to carefully consider the evidence presented in an article that pulls us in with promises of a greater research breakthrough than has actually occurred.

7. Has the research been done by a respected institution? Research from a well-established institution such as the National Institutes of Health or Johns Hopkins University is generally considered credible. Be careful in your judgments, however, if research from one reliable source contradicts research from another reliable source; it is best to withhold judgment or to accept conclusions tentatively in these cases.

8. Are the researchers biased? Even if the research organization is well respected, the company that commissioned the research may have a vested interest in the outcome of the study.

---

[13] Ibid.

[14] David Knowles, "Study: Love Is Like Cocaine, Codeine," http://www.aolnews.com/2010/10/13/study-love-is-like-cocaine-codeine/.

[15] Ibid.

In a study on the effects of prostate medicines, note how one of the pharmaceutical companies that funded the research found fault with it. Do you think the criticism of the study it funded reflects bias?

> The first head-to-head comparison of the nation's two most popular medicines for prostate trouble found that one gives significant relief while the other is virtually worthless.
>
> The two medicines, Hytrin and Proscar, are taken by millions of older men to relieve the symptoms of an enlarged prostate gland.
>
> The study found that Hytrin eases men's discomfort by about one-third, while Proscar works no better than dummy sugar pills.
>
> . . . The study was financed by Merck & Co., which makes Proscar, and Abbott Laboratories Inc., the maker of Hytrin.
>
> Although both companies approved the study's design, Merck discounted its significance as publication approached in today's issue of the *New England Journal of Medicine*.
>
> Dr. Glenn Gormley, a Merck research official, said that in hindsight, the study was not set up properly to answer the question of which drug is better.[16] (See Exercises 5.1 and 5.2 on pages 205–206.)

Reminder

Inductive reasoning is the process of making generalizations from specific observations.

✳ Explore on **mythinkinglab.com**

Controversy in Research Findings

If you read the previous section, you probably have an appreciation of how difficult it is to do research that yields accurate results. Good studies require time and money to complete. Even studies that use the scientific method and produce clear results are sometimes criticized by scientists or others who find flaws in the researcher's methods or conclusions. You may be familiar with studies of the effects of a substance on rats that show that the substance causes cancer. Studies like these may be criticized on the basis that researchers were comparing human and rodent metabolism when they drew their conclusions; findings of such studies are also routinely criticized because the proportionate doses given to the rats are often much higher than human subjects would ingest.

The effects of various social influences, such as video games, are frequent subjects of research studies and often yield contradictory results. The headline of the following excerpt makes bold claims concerning the detrimental effects of violent video games. In the article, a critic of the research refutes these claims, and even the researcher himself seems to be uncertain of the implications of his analysis of video game studies.

[16] Daniel Q. Haney, "The Battle of Prostate Medicines," *Contra Costa Times*, August 22, 1996, p. B1.

New Analysis Reasserts Video Games' Link to Violence

Sharon Jayson

A new review of 130 studies "strongly suggests" playing violent video games increases aggressive thoughts and behavior and decreases empathy.

The results hold "regardless of research design, gender, age or culture," says lead researcher Craig Anderson, who directs the Center for the Study of Violence at Iowa State University in Ames. His team did a statistical analysis of studies on more than 130,000 gamers from elementary school age to college in the USA, Europe and Japan. It is published today in *Psychological Bulletin*, a journal of the American Psychological Association.

But Christopher Ferguson, an associate professor at Texas A&M International University in Laredo, says in a critique accompanying the study that the effects found "are generally very low." He adds that the analysis "contains numerous flaws," which he says result in "overestimating the influence" of violent games on aggression.

Ferguson says his own study of 603 predominantly Hispanic young people, published last year in *The Journal of Pediatrics,* found "delinquent peer influences, antisocial personality traits, depression, and parents/guardians who use psychological abuse" were consistent risk factors for youth violence and aggression. But he also found that neighborhood quality, parents' domestic violence and exposure to violent TV or video games "were not predictive of youth violence and aggression."

Anderson says his team "never said it's a huge effect. But if you look at known risk factors for the development of aggression and violence, some are bigger than media violence and some are smaller."If you have a child with no other risk factors for aggression and violence and if you allow them to suddenly start playing video games five hours to 10 hours a week, they're not going to become a school shooter. One risk factor doesn't do it by itself."

But he notes that video game violence is "the only causal risk factor that is relatively easy for parents to do something about." ▪

When people read research studies, they are often seeking information in order to make good decisions. Adults who guide children want to know whether certain activities are harmful, and almost everyone seeks to reduce pain and prolong life. Advances in medicine and technology provide great benefits, but their long-term effects are unknown and therefore, often controversial.

The following excerpt on cell phone safety highlights the problems created when both sides of a hotly debated subject can be supported by research.

Study Says Cell Phones Cause Brain Tumors—Are You Safe?

Several years ago a caller to "The Larry King Show" claimed he got a brain tumor from using his cell phone. It set off a nationwide frenzy about the safety of cell phones. Things died down after the claim was discredited. But a new study that says cell phones may be more dangerous than we think could whip up those fears again.

A group called the International EMF Collaborative issued a report titled "*Cellphones and Brain Tumors: 15 Reasons for Concern.*" The lead author of the report did not mince words with the *Los Angeles Times:* "Cell phones are causing brain tumors."

Lloyd Morgan, a retired electronics engineer, went on to say, "Industry-backed studies try to hide that fact. But if you read them carefully, you can see there are risks."

The study, which calls the risk of brain tumors from regular use of cellphones "significant," says kids are at greater risk than adults because their still-developing brain cells are more vulnerable to electromagnetic radiation that comes from holding a cell phone to your ear.

More than 40 scientists and officials from 14 countries have publicly endorsed the findings of Morgan's report.

Morgan said he doesn't expect cell phones to be banned. But what he would like to see is speakers removed from phones, so people would have to listen through earplugs, thus keeping the phone, and potential radiation, away from their heads.

He would also like to see cigarette-style warnings on cell phones, telling users that talking on the phone can be hazardous to their health. "Not everyone who smokes three packs a day gets lung cancer," he said. "Not everyone who uses a cell phone will get brain cancer. But everyone who does is at higher risk."

While the merits of this research are debated, the world waits for results of a decade-long study on cell phone safety. Dubbed "Interphone," its release has been delayed for years, as researchers argue over how to interpret the data. Some say the findings show a clear link between long-term cellphone use and brain tumors. Others are not so sure.

The $24-million Interphone study was funded in part by the wireless industry, which some say has been pressuring researchers to soft-pedal some of the report's more troublesome findings, such as indications that using a cellphone for more than 10 years may increase your cancer risk.

So far, reputable health groups such as The World Health Organization and the National Cancer Institute say there is no conclusive link between cell phones and brain tumors. The Cancer Institute, in fact, says rates for brain cancer have held relatively steady for the last decade, as cell phone use has exploded.

But according to the Illinois-based Central Brain Tumor Registry of the United States, the leading database of brain cancer cases, there has been an increase in some types of tumors. Carol Kruchko, president of the registry, said scientists are still trying to determine the reason for the increase.

CTIA—the Wireless Assn., a U.S. industry group, insists that cellphones pose no danger to users. "The peer-reviewed scientific evidence has overwhelmingly indicated that wireless devices do not pose a public health risk," said John Walls, a spokesman for the association. "In addition, there is no known mechanism for microwave energy within the limits established by the FCC to cause any adverse health effects." ■

The problem of divided opinion about the validity of a study is a difficult one, but as consumers of information, we can either withhold judgment until more conclusive evidence is presented or give credence to a study with evidence we believe is strong enough to influence our current decisions. For example, if we read that one study showed that a low-fat diet contributed to reduced cholesterol rates and another study showed no significant relationship, we might still choose to believe that there is a good chance of reducing cholesterol with the low-fat diet. The critical thinker realizes that researchers are not in agreement about the ultimate prevention and cure of elevated cholesterol levels, but he or she chooses to make some dietary changes based on limited research because "It can't hurt and it might actually help my heart."

A more difficult problem with research is avoiding errors that could affect the results of a study. Consider the following commentary concerning research studies conducted by young scientists:

> Errors may occur through improper laboratory practices, faulty equipment, accidental mix-ups, poorly designed experiments, inadequate replication of research results, or any number of other reasons, some involving negligence and others occurring through no fault of the scientist.
>
> . . . Error is, in fact, inherent in any endeavor carried out by fallible human beings. The great possibility of error is one of the reasons why judgment is so important in science and why a scientist, who has avoided error, designed good experiments, exercised good judgment, and discovered something new about the nature of things in the universe can experience such a thrill of achievement.[17]

John Ioannidis, an epidemiologist at the University of Ioannina School of Medicine in Greece, says that small sample sizes, poor study design, researcher bias, selective reporting, and other problems combine to make most research findings false. But even large, well-designed studies are not always right, meaning that scientists and the public have to be wary of reported findings.[18]

Given the possibility of error in experimentation, the question arises: "Whom should I believe?"

> "We should accept that most research findings will be refuted. Some will be replicated and validated. The replication process is more important than the first discovery," Ioannidis says.
>
> But Solomon Snyder, senior editor at the Proceedings of the National Academy of Sciences, and a neuroscientist at Johns Hopkins Medical School in Baltimore, . . . says most working scientists understand the limitations of published research.
>
> "When I read the literature, I'm not reading it to find proof like a textbook. I'm reading to get ideas. So even if something is wrong with the paper, if they have the kernel of a novel idea, that's something to think about," he says.[19]

As critical thinkers, we must live between two extremes. One is an attitude of cynicism and anti-intellectualism that says, "Scientific research studies can never be trusted because there are too many possibilities for error." The other extreme is an attitude of passive reverence for the scientific method that says, "Scientists are the geniuses who are trained to carry out the studies that have brought us so many great advances, so I am not intelligent or educated enough to question any research I read." Both of these attitudes are inappropriate for the critically thinking individual. Research can be credible if it is carried out in the correct manner, and you are quite

---

[17] Francisco J. Ayala, "Point of View: For Young Scientists, Questions of Protocol and Propriety Can Be Bewildering," *The Chronicle of Higher Education*, November 22, 1989, p. A36.

[18] Kurt Kleiner, "Most Scientific Papers Are Probably Wrong," August 30, 2005, NewScientist.com news service.

[19] Ibid.

capable of understanding the basic elements of research and evaluating specific studies you read or hear about. Use the factors we have discussed in this chapter to consider the quality of research studies and the implications for important decisions you need to make.

Remember that when we evaluate new or controversial findings, we also need to consider the credibility of the publication, website, or broadcaster reporting the study. Do the reporters have a reputation for being thorough and careful before they report on a study? Is there a science editor for the media source who knows which studies deserve to be reported and how they can be accurately summarized? We also need to consider the credibility of the institution that did the study: Was it carried out by a questionable sexuality researcher who spends a lot of time on the talk-show circuit? Was there possible bias in the research as, for example, a study commissioned by a tobacco company claiming that cigarettes are not harmful to the lungs? Or was it done by a reputable research institution with no known biases?

A general rule of thumb is, if you are going to use information or report information to others, you need to verify your sources, just as a good journalist would. Then you can present the information to others with confidence and credibility.

Skill

Read and consider original studies before making decisions based on controversial research findings.

We can't always keep up with advances in any given field of research. As critical thinkers, we can look at the reliability of the reports we hear or read, do more intensive study of those reports in which we are interested, and note the most recent findings on any interesting topic of research. (See Exercise 5.3 on pages 206–207.)

Read the following article about a study on seasickness as a humorous review of some basic elements of controlled studies.

Sickening Experiment on Human Subjects

Steve Rubenstein

Scientists were paying people $200 to throw up in San Francisco this week. It was too good a deal to miss.

They do these sorts of things at the University of California at San Francisco. Researchers are always looking for guinea pigs willing to try experimental drugs. In this case, the drug was a new anti-seasickness pill. The ad said you could make $200 for popping the pill and taking an eight-hour boat ride.

There was only one condition. You had to be the nauseous type. Somehow I qualified.

Dozens of people, many with holes in their pants, signed up for the voyage. It was encouraging to see so many selfless people pitching in for science.

"People will do anything for $200," explained one researcher. "Even this."

Before sailing away, we had to take a physical. It was a snap. The main thing the doc seemed interested in was whether I was the throw-up type. It's no good testing seasickness pills on people who don't get seasick.

"How do you feel on boats?" the doc asked, in that concerned demeanor of his calling.

"Terrible," I said. "Lousy. I head straight for the rail."

It was the right answer. The doc's face lit up like the penlight in his breast pocket. He put my chart in the active file. I was in.

On the appointed day, we men and women of science assembled at the hospital to take our pills. Since it was a scientific study, only half of us would be getting capsules containing the actual drug. The other half would receive capsules containing sugar, a placebo. A researcher handed out the pills randomly.

We weren't supposed to know which capsule was which, of course. That wouldn't be scientific. But the capsules, made of clear plastic, were easy to tell apart. The drug looked like tiny time pills, and the placebo looked like sugar. Someone sure screwed up, the doc said, especially because many people believe seasickness is a state of mind.

"What did you get?" we guinea pigs asked each other.

"Placebo," said one sad-eyed soul. "Darn. I'm a goner."

We were to swallow the pill precisely at 8 a.m. The researcher took out her digital watch.

"Place the pill in your right hand," she said. "Prepare to swallow."

We three dozen strangers stood abreast, pills in hand, united in time and place.

"Five, four, three, two, one. Swallow."

Gulp.

Into the buses we marched, and off to Fisherman's Wharf. We had a job to do.

The seas looked calm, which did not sit well with one of the passengers on the boat. His name was Kirt, and he turned out to be the president of the company that was trying to market the new drug. He had paid $80,000 to UCSF to conduct the impartial study—which he cheerily denied would be any less impartial because of his busybody presence on the boat—and said the last thing he wanted to see was calm seas. Sick people is what he wanted.

"I don't want everyone to throw up," he said. "I just want the right people to throw up. The placebo people."

And then we shoved off on our mission. Eight nauseating hours on the high seas.

"Don't worry," the skipper told Kirt. "I'm going to get these people sick for you." ▪

Questions for Discussion

1. What controls did the researchers use for this study?

2. Since this article is humorous, and probably exaggerated, we can't claim it as serious evidence of faulty research. Given that disclaimer, what areas of potential error in the study design did the author point out?

3. If you were to set up a study to test a new anti-seasickness pill, how would you design your research? (See Exercise 5.4 on page 207.)

Checklist for Making, Evaluating, Repairing, and Refuting Arguments

Make things as simple as possible—but no simpler.

Albert Einstein

So far, we have looked at the structure of argument. We've noted that an argument contains a conclusion or claim about an issue. The conclusion/claim is supported by reasons, sometimes called premises. We have seen that in both deductive and inductive arguments, the quality of the evidence is what distinguishes a strong argument from a weak one.

When making an argument, you want to be prepared to defend each part of it. You should anticipate the objections others may make to your argument and "repair" any weak aspects.

Following is a checklist that you can use to make, evaluate, and repair your own arguments; you can also use it to refute the arguments of others.

For a deductive argument:

1. Check that the argument is valid; put your reasoning into a syllogism, using the correct structure.

    If a proper syllogistic form has not been used, repair the argument by using a correct form.

    Let's say Marina's friend Sam told her that he wanted a job at the college bookstore, but he didn't get it.

Example of Invalid Argument

If he didn't show up for the interview, he didn't get the job.
He didn't get the job.
Therefore, he didn't show up for the interview.

This is invalid because the form the speaker used is not correct, i.e., logical:

If A, then B.
B
Therefore, A

Her friend may have shown up and still not received the job.
A valid syllogistic form is:

If A, then B.
A.
Therefore B.

The argument is repaired by using the correct form:

If he didn't show up for the interview, then he didn't get the job.
He didn't show up for the interview.
Therefore, he didn't get the job.

2. Check that your premises are true and accurate.

Ask yourself, "Does the major or minor premise assume any facts that have not been proven?"

If so, repair the argument by backing up any assumptions with evidence.

Example: When Marina gives Sam her logical assessment of the situation, he replies: "You're wrong. I did show up for the interview, but they needed someone who had experience as a cashier and that's why I didn't get that job."

Even though Marina's form was correct, and therefore her syllogism was valid, her major and minor premise were untrue. Now the corrected reasoning would be:

> If someone doesn't have cashier experience, they won't get the job at the bookstore.
>
> Sam doesn't have cashier experience.
>
> Therefore, Sam didn't get the job at the bookstore.

3. If your conclusion follows from true premises that are stated in the correct form, your argument is *sound*. Now that Marina has repaired her reasoning with the correct form and true premises, her argument is sound.

Refuting a deductive argument:

1. Point out any reasoning that is not valid, i.e., that does not follow proper syllogistic forms.

2. Point out any premises that aren't true.

3. Point out cases in which the premises may seem true and the argument may be valid, but the conclusion can still be false; in other words, point out any other possible facts that make the argument questionable, particularly by using more accurate information.

Example

If Rachel got the part of Antigone, then Rebecca didn't get the part.
Rachel got the part of Antigone.
Therefore, Rebecca didn't get the part.

This appears to be a sound argument, but it can be "trumped" by more current and reliable information. If the director decided to change his original plan and double-cast the part of Antigone, then both Rachel and Rebecca could have gotten the part.

More up-to-date or more accurate information often trumps information that was considered true at one time but is no longer true. Laws change, cures for diseases are found, and new technology emerges, making it possible to refute many claims with new evidence.

For an inductive argument:

cogent argument
An inductive argument based on strong, credible evidence.

When an inductive argument is based on strong evidence, it is called a **cogent argument**. To create a cogent inductive argument, use the following guidelines.

1. Check that the evidence you are using to support your claims—statistics, examples, controlled studies, expert testimony, and analogies—is reliable and accurate.

Use the checklists on pages 135–138 to evaluate statistical and causal generalizations and on pages 173–181 to evaluate controlled studies.

2. Check that the conclusions you draw are based on a preponderance of the evidence.

3. Determine whether you are using the most current research from credible sources; be willing to adjust and therefore repair your argument when more accurate or reliable information becomes available.

Research as many sources as possible before coming to a final conclusion or making a decision.

To refute an inductive argument, use the same criteria listed above (1, 2, and 3) to find weaknesses in reasoning and evidence.

For both deductive and inductive arguments, imagine how people with different assumptions or beliefs might respond to your reasons and conclusions. Then be prepared to answer their objections. If necessary, strengthen your argument by repairing areas that are weak. Continue to look for and use the most credible and current support for your argument.

Class Exercise

Defending and Refuting Arguments

Purpose: To practice examining and strengthening arguments.

As a group, create an argument, using the simple format given below. In your own small group, come up with as many objections to the argument as possible. Be prepared to defend your group's argument from the objections that will be raised by other groups. You may do this as an impromptu class exercise or as a prepared debate.

Defenders:

We believe _____ based on the following evidence _____.

Refuters:

We have noted the following errors in your reasoning and evidence _____.

When each group has created an argument and checked it, groups can present to the class. The other groups should then offer objections and allow the defenders to repair (or continue to defend) them.

Consider doing some classroom parliamentary debates. This dynamic form of debating provides great practice in making, repairing, and refuting arguments.

Use of Authority: Expert Testimony

In addition to drawing generalizations from controlled studies, writers and speakers frequently find strong support for their conclusions from the testimony of experts. An **expert** is an individual who has education, significant experience, or both in a given area; experts are usually recognized and respected by their peers in their specific fields of endeavor. An expert stays up-to-date on current research in his or her field. We turn to experts in many areas of our daily lives: We personally consult doctors, dentists, lawyers, mechanics, counselors, and salespersons. As a society, we

expert An individual who has education, significant experience, or both in a given area. The testimony of experts is used to support conclusions in arguments.

rely on scientists, engineers, judges and numerous other experts, all of whom are supposed to have more knowledge and experience in their fields than we do.

We also rely on friends and acquaintances who have become knowledgeable about various subjects because they spend time on and keep up with these subjects; for example, we might consult a friend we respect who has read all about the candidates for an upcoming election. We listen to what she says because she has credibility as an informed voter. When we buy a car or a camera, we might consult a friend who works on his car or who has studied photography because we see him as having more expertise than we do. Even for small purchases, like clothing, we may ask a friend for advice if we believe this person has a significant knowledge of fashion trends.

The phenomenon of consulting acquaintances before we make decisions has been labeled the **two-step flow** of information (see Figure 5–2). Our expert friends, who are called **opinion leaders,** first (step 1) get their information from the media (television, the Internet, Twitter, Facebook, magazines, newspapers, and books), and then (step 2) pass this information on to us. In our information-saturated age, this method makes sense; we can't be informed about everything, so we become experts in the areas on which we spend our time, and others become experts in other areas, and we share information. We learn from one another's experiences, mistakes, and successes and save time (and sometimes money) in the process.

Advertisers and campaign managers are well aware of this two-step phenomenon as they carefully choose media to best reach their target audiences. If they can get the opinion leaders to vote for their candidates or to use their products, the rest of

two-step flow
The phenomenon of consulting friends or acquaintances who have expertise in a given area before making decisions. The friends, called opinion leaders, first (step 1) get their information from the media and then (step 2) pass this information on to others.

opinion leaders   People who are well informed, often through the media, about specific information and issues.

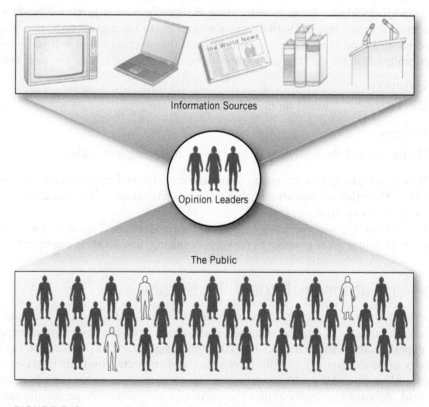

FIGURE 5–2

Two-Step Flow of Information.

us will follow. News of the person or product will travel by word of mouth or social media to the secondary audiences. (See Exercise 5.5 on pages 207–208.)

Use of a network of friends may work well for personal decision making, but it won't work to quote these friends in papers or speeches. You can't say "Vote for candidate X for senator; my friend Mark, who reads all the major political blogs and newsmagazines, thinks he has the best foreign policy" and expect your audience to be convinced.

Nor can you say "I know a woman who works for a pharmacy, and she thinks that 80 percent of the people who get prescriptions for Valium are drug addicts" as evidence that Valium users are addicted to drugs. It may be true that this drug is carelessly prescribed, and it may be true that candidate X is the best person for senator; however, the writer or speaker needs to use support that is generally recognized as valid in order to present a strong argument.

An expert who can be used to add strength to arguments has relevant academic credentials and/or significant experience in the area in question. Individuals who are seen as experts in a field are recognized by their colleagues or by the general public, or both. This recognition often comes as a result of publishing articles or books, earning advanced degrees or positions, coming up with valuable discoveries, or attaining success or acclaim in their areas of expertise.

People who fit these categories have credibility in their fields, and their opinions are generally considered reliable sources of evidence for a particular argument.

The author of the following passage is a professional tracker. Trackers are experts in deciphering markings such as human and animal footprints; often, they are called upon to study crime scenes. They can draw inductive generalizations about an event by looking for predictable "signs." After years of intense observation, an expert tracker is able to ascertain whether a person who left footprints is right- or left-handed; he can also determine the person's approximate weight, among other factors. Tom Brown has trained himself to discern accurate information from a crime scene even after rain has covered the area.

An Opinion with Substance

Tom Brown Jr.

I took the class into the woods and stopped by a drainage ditch. The bottom was covered with soft sandy soil. It was also covered with animal prints. I asked the class to notice all the prints that were visible. They named two animals and guessed at two more. There were eleven, not counting the dog.

When I ask for prints, I'm not just looking for clear sharp markings of large well-known animals. I'm searching for an explanation of every mark on the ground. . . . As I study the markings a picture begins to form in my mind of what passed the spot I am checking before I arrived. My mind begins to place animals in space and time.

Something began to take shape as I noticed the age of the different tracks. . . .

"Wow!" I yelled. "Look at that." It had all come together, and I began to explain the scene to the class as I pointed to the markings that were the tracks of a dog and a rabbit, which had been on this spot at the same time.

"Dog came down, saw the rabbit before it smelled him. Maybe a cross wind. He jumped after the rabbit. Here is his first set of four running prints." I pointed. "Here, here, here, and here. Here is the rabbit moving up the side of the ditch to that sweet new grass." Again I pointed to markings that looked almost as if someone had scraped the dirt with a branch. "The rabbit sees the dog, does a boogie here, and races down the hill. He made two gigantic leaps. See where he jumped? See where the dog leaped for him and missed? Skidded here, regained his balance, and followed up the other side, there." . . .

"How did you do that?" Kay asked.

"I sat for days on the edge of a field and watched rabbits feed, breed, bear young, and avoid danger. After each happening, I would study the marks that had been left in the earth. I can tell when a rabbit is sitting or standing, agitated or calm. Whenever a dog came through the field and happened on a chase, I would follow its every marking, remembering what my eyes had seen just moments before. After a great amount of time, I began to recognize those signs as I happened onto them."

Experts in various fields enable many areas of society to function in a more effective way. For example, mathematicians and scientists have come up with models of human interaction to help police departments solve crimes. The following excerpt concerns a University of California, Los Angeles (UCLA) professor who uses his academic expertise to help the Los Angeles Police Department.

Can Math and Science Help Solve Crimes?

Researchers Try to Predict and Prevent Crime Using Sophisticated Mathematical Models

Stuart Wolpert

UCLA's Jeffrey Brantingham works with the Los Angeles Police Department to analyze crime patterns. He also studies hunter-gatherers in Northern Tibet. If you tell him his research interests sound completely unrelated, he will quickly correct you.

"Criminal offenders are essentially hunter-gatherers; they forage for opportunities to commit crimes," said Brantingham, UCLA associate professor of anthropology. "The behaviors that a hunter-gatherer uses to choose a wildebeest versus a gazelle are the same calculations a criminal uses to choose a Honda versus a Lexus."

Brantingham has been working for years with Andrea Bertozzi, UCLA professor of mathematics and director of applied mathematics, to apply sophisticated mathematics to urban crime patterns. They and their colleagues have built a mathematical model that allows them to analyze different types of criminal "hotspots," where many crimes occur, at least for a time.

They believe their findings apply not only to Los Angeles but to cities worldwide. Crime hotspots come in at least two different types. There are hotspots generated by small spikes in crime that grow (which the researchers call a "super-critical hotspot"), and a second type of hotspot that looks the same from the surface, but is not, in which a large spike in crime pulls offenders into a central location (which they call a "subcritical hotspot"). Policing actions directed at one type will have a very different effect from policing actions directed at the second type.

"This finding is important because if you want the police to suppress the hotspot, you want to be able to later take them out and have the suppression remain—and you can do that with only one of the two, in the subcritical case," Bertozzi said.

"Unless you are really looking for them, and our model says you should, you would not suspect these two types of hotspots," Brantingham said. "Policing actions directed at one type will have a very different effect from policing actions directed at the second type. Just by mapping crime and looking at hotspots, you will not be able to know whether that is generated by a small variation in crime or by a big spike in crime.

"If you were to send police into a hotspot without knowing which kind it is, you would not be able to predict whether you will just cause displacement of crime—moving it somewhere else, which is what our model predicts if it's a hotspot generated by small fluctuations in crime—or whether you will actually reduce crime," he said. "Many people have argued that adding police to hotspots will just push crime somewhere else, but that seems not to be true, at least in certain cases. You get displacement in some cases, but not nearly as much as many people thought."

…Researcher Brantingham said. "Good science is done in small, incremental steps that can lead to big benefits in the long term. We are trying to understand the dynamics of crime and to make small but significant steps in helping our police partners come up with policing strategies that will help to reduce crime.

"We have to do what biologists and engineers have been doing for years, which is to try to understand the fundamental mechanics and dynamics of how a system works," he said. "Before you can make predictions about how the system will behave, you have to understand the fundamental dynamics. That's true with weather forecasting, where you run a climate simulation, and true with crime patterns."

The LAPD is at the world's forefront of knowing where crime is occurring and responding very quickly, Brantingham said. ▪

Skill

Recognize legitimate and illegitimate uses of expert testimony.

Problems with Expert Testimony

When listening to an argument, a critical thinker should consider some common problems associated with expert testimony:

1. Use of experts in the wrong field of expertise
2. Use of experts who are not recognized as experts
3. Use of experts who are paid for their testimony
4. Use of experts who are biased
5. Experts who do not realistically limit their own expertise
6. Expert testimony that is contradicted by equally expert testimony

1. Use of experts in the wrong field of expertise. The most visible form of this problem occurs in advertisements in which a person who is respected in one field is used to endorse a product out of his or her area of expertise. It is a legitimate use of authority for an athlete to promote sports equipment, but some ads capitalize on good-looking or popular celebrities by using them to promote cars, shampoos, or cereals.

In a famous ad campaign, an actor in a white coat and stethoscope announced, "I'm not a doctor, but I play one on TV." Ads frequently feature people in doctors' uniforms and hospital settings giving advice on medications. The words *doctor dramatization* may be written on the screen as a disclaimer. However, consumers might easily overlook these vague words or take them to mean that a real doctor is dramatizing his recommendation of the product.

Be careful of slick 'expert' advertisements by nonexperts, which are generally accompanied by impressive costumes and backgrounds. If real expertise isn't mentioned in an endorsement, don't assume there are credentials lurking somewhere in the person's background.

Sometimes a celebrity endorsing a product has professional credentials, but those credentials don't directly relate to the product being promoted. For example, Dr. Phil McGraw, who has a degree in psychology, has written a book entitled *The Ultimate Weight Solution: The 7 Keys to Weight Loss Freedom*. His book is a major bestseller and was promoted on his own popular television talk show as well as on NBC's *Today* show. While it can be argued that there is a psychological component to weight loss that Dr. Phil legitimately discusses in his book, he has come under criticism for using his name and image to endorse a line of nutritional supplements, including vitamins, power bars, and meal-replacement drinks. *New York Times* writer Sherri Day notes the following:

> Of course, celebrity licensing and endorsement deals have long been a mainstay of consumer marketing, but few talk-show hosts have so closely associated the products they endorse with the content of their television programs. McGraw's licensing deal with *Shape Up* crosses another barrier, one that has been regarded as sacred: Unlike books or videos, the products can directly affect viewers' health. And because McGraw carries the honorific "doctor"—though he is a clinical psychologist and not a physician—his critics say that consumers are more likely to trust his recommendations.
>
> "As soon as we heard the prospect of him going into the nutritional food category, it was kind of like 'What?'" said Sid Good, the president of Good Marketing, a consumer products consultant in Cleveland. "It's always different when you step into the medical field. There are a different set of assumptions that we make as consumers in terms of what our expectations are and the appropriateness of who's giving us the advice."[20]

2. Use of experts who are not recognized as experts. Most areas of expertise today are in the midst of increasingly new discoveries. If someone is considered an expert based on experience or education completed years ago and if the person has not kept up with his field, then he or she is questionable as an expert. When a finding by an expert is quoted, a date should accompany the quotation so we know when the discovery was made.

The importance of current information accounts for the advice to look up recent research when you want to support a position. Books are good sources of support; however, in some fields, a book that is even a few years old becomes obsolete due to new information. Some of your textbooks are in the tenth or eleventh edition because of the need for updating information. Social science books need to be constantly updated because of changing political, economic, and cultural realities; for example, a history book that is just a year old will not have included a newly elected president or new borderlines between countries. Although foundational theories are essential, current ideas and events in any field are also important.

Sometimes a person's credentials are distorted. Having "doctor" in front of one's name can mean that one is a physician, a dentist, a recipient of a doctoral degree in an academic field, a chiropractor, or a psychologist. Critical thinkers seek to understand

[20] Sherri Day, "Dr. Phil Risks Credibility Selling Diet Supplements," *New York Times,* November 4, 2003.

what a title means, the reputation of the institution that conferred the title, and, if possible, the credibility the titled person has with his or her colleagues. The claims made by this person can then be considered in light of a reasonable assessment of his or her position as an expert.

3. Use of experts who are paid for their testimony. One fairly obvious consideration in listening to evidence based on expertise is to find out whether the authority is paid for the testimony or endorsement. Some people are paid to promote products. A salesperson may genuinely believe that a brand new truck will meet your needs, but he is not the only person to ask about it because of the conflict of interest built into his role. Similarly, an expert witness, such as a physician who is called to testify on behalf of a defendant in a trial, may fully believe in the defendant's case but lose credibility if she is paid for her testimony. One study from the University of North Carolina Medical School showed that radiologists who were not involved as paid experts in a case came to very different conclusions from those who were paid for their testimony:

> A study by University of North Carolina at Chapel Hill researchers found that 31 radiologists who reviewed the CT scans used in a medical malpractice lawsuit did not agree with the conclusions reached by four paid medical expert witnesses in the case.
>
> This suggests that the use of radiologists who are blinded to both the medical outcome and the litigation in such cases may be a more objective way of determining whether or not the standard of care has been met, said Richard C. Semelka, MD, lead author of the study and professor of radiology in the UNC School of Medicine.[21]

We may be misled by experts who stand to make a profit from our lack of knowledge of their profession. If you suspect that an expert may be advising you based on "what's in it for him," get a second opinion, as did columnist Thomas Sowell in the following excerpt:

> The other day, the lights suddenly went out in the bathroom. After our amateur attempts to find out what was wrong got us nowhere, my wife found an electrician in the *Yellow Pages* and had him come over.
>
> He did all kinds of investigating in all kinds of places and came up with the bad news: None of the usual things was wrong. What was wrong was probably that a wire had gone bad somewhere in the walls.
>
> He conjured up a picture of a broken live wire dangling somewhere in those walls, ready to ignite something, so that we could wake up in the middle of the night with the place engulfed in flames. My wife was upset and I didn't find the prospect all that great myself. What could we do?
>
> The electrician said that he would have to open up the walls and just track down the place where this dangerous wire was. His estimate of how much it would cost was not cheap.
>
> I thanked him and paid him for his time, but said that obviously we would have to get a second opinion before undertaking something that drastic. He said he understood, but urged that we get that opinion very soon— today—because of the danger involved.

[21] "UNC Study Questions Use of Paid Medical Expert Witnesses in Malpractice Cases," Friday, July 23, 2010, http://news.unchealthcare.org/news/2010.

This time I decided that the *Yellow Pages* were not the way to go. I phoned a very reputable contractor I know who had done some work for us a couple of years earlier and asked for his recommendation of an electrician.

Enter electrician number two—and exit electrician number two less than five minutes later. The lights were back on and not a wall had been touched. What was wrong was so simple that the first electrician undoubtedly realized immediately that we must not know anything about electrical systems if we had not fixed it ourselves.[22]

4. Use of experts who are biased. Many people feel so strongly about an issue that they join with others who have similar beliefs, forming clubs, unions, and associations. They often are or become experts in their areas of interest, but their expertise is sometimes accompanied by a strong bias.

For example, those who lobby together for gun control may become highly knowledgeable about laws and regulations across the various states; similarly, members of the National Rifle Association gain expertise on the various statutes affecting gun ownership. Neither of these groups can be considered impartial and unbiased in a discussion of gun control. This does not mean a critical thinker should not listen to them; in fact, most websites, editorials and televised debates on this issue and on other controversial issues involve individuals with strong biases, and many of these individuals try to present a balanced viewpoint. However, critical thinkers keep in mind that they are hearing the facts from particular points of view, and they listen for possible exaggeration of the benefits of, or problems with, proposed policies.

Another form of bias may be inherent in a particular approach to an area of expertise. Various methods of psychology are practiced by different counselors, and various approaches to medical treatment are taken by different physicians. One doctor may treat hyperactivity with medication, while another may favor eliminating foods to which the hyperactive child may be allergic. Because of the different viewpoints espoused by experts in the same discipline, critical thinkers try to learn as much as possible and to get a number of professional opinions before making an important decision. (See Exercise 5.6 on pages 208–209.)

5. Experts who do not realistically limit their own expertise. Contemporary societies value and rely upon expertise; we have made great progress in many areas of learning, and we have experienced impressive technological advances. It is important to recognize however, that even experts cannot know *everything* about a given field. That is why doctors, lawyers, engineers, educators, and almost all other professionals specialize in limited areas within their fields. Even then, conferences are continually held to discuss and share new findings and sometimes to refute commonly held assumptions about a particular body of knowledge. An expert who serves the larger community well will limit his or her pronouncements to what is known to be true and will withhold judgment or give a variety of possibilities for the areas that are still unknown or controversial. When experts in a field go beyond what they know for certain to be true, people's lives can be severely impacted, as illustrated in the following excerpt from Thomas Sowell, syndicated columnist and author of the book *Late-Talking Children*:

> Phone calls and e-mails from parents began coming to me immediately after *Dateline NBC* broadcast a feature on very bright children who are years late in beginning to talk. . . .

[22] Thomas Sowell, "Who Do Poor Turn to in a Pinch," *Contra Costa Times*, July 29, 1996, p. A–10.

What ignited all this interest was the story of Carol Gage's son Collin, a bright but late-talking little boy on whom "experts" had hung a variety of dire labels. Now 7 years old, Collin is talking and his intellectual abilities and social development are beginning to belie the labels.

All too many parents of similar children have encountered similarly hasty and dogmatic "experts"—in the school system especially. One of the mothers who contacted me told of her son's being put into classes for retarded children, even though his IQ later turned out to be 149. Tragically, false diagnoses like these are all too common.

A man in the group I studied had an IQ of 180 but, when he was a child, his mother was warned that someday he might have to be "put away." Nuclear physicists Albert Einstein and Edward Teller were both suspected of being mentally retarded as small children, because they both talked late. So was famed 19th century pianist Clara Schumann.

No one really understands why some children who are very bright are also very late to begin speaking. But the worst problem is not ignorance. It is arrogance and dogmatism on the part of too many professionals to whom desperate and trusting parents turn for help. Some children have been declared "retarded" or "autistic" on the basis of less than 10 minutes' observation.

There is no disgrace that our knowledge is not what we would like it to be. The disgrace is the pretense that it is, at the expense of vulnerable children and their distressed parents.[23]

6. Expert testimony that is contradicted by equally expert testimony. One characteristic of the Information Age is the proliferation of research carried out by individuals, corporations, universities, and think tanks. The outcome of one study may be diametrically or partially opposed to the findings of another study done by an equally prestigious person or group. In addition, we are seeing that today's discovery can sometimes be tomorrow's mistake; that is, current research often makes research of a few years ago obsolete, and even dangerous. Such was the case for the pregnant women of the 1950s who were routinely given the drug DES to prevent miscarriages; this drug was later found to have done significant damage to their daughters and grandchildren. Conversely, dire predictions about the permanent and devastating effects of children born to crack-addicted mothers have proven to be largely unfounded; when these babies have been placed in healthy homes, they grow up with few discernable differences and "the long-term effects of such exposure on children's brain development and behavior appear relatively small."[24]

When we consider the problems of varied expert testimony, we can understand why some people have become cynical about all medical pronouncements; they may fear catching hepatitis from drinking fountains because "next year, they'll find out that hepatitis is transmitted through water." This attitude is not reasonable, but there is wisdom in choosing a *healthy* skepticism.

A healthy skepticism looks at pronouncements from authorities and considers their credentials, whether they have support from their colleagues, and whether their ideas make sense.

---

[23] Thomas Sowell, "Experts Who Aren't," *Contra Costa Times*, April 5, 1999.
[24] Susan Okie, "The Epidemic That Wasn't," http://www.nytimes.com/2009/01/27/health/27coca.html.

Researcher Frank Sulloway explains a useful way to interpret contradictory research findings. In his book on birth order and personality, he discusses why we can trust his findings about the personalities of firstborn children, despite some studies whose results contradict these findings:

> The question we need to ask about any topic of research is whether significant results exceed "chance" expectations, especially in well-designed studies. *Meta-analysis* allows us to answer this question.
>
> . . . [Seventy-two] of the 196 studies on birth order display significant results that are consistent with my psychodynamic hypotheses. Fourteen studies yield contrary results. The remaining 110 studies are not statistically significant in either direction. What does this mean? In any group of 196 studies, chance will produce about 10 spurious confirmations, give or take a random fluctuation in the error rate. We can be 99 percent confident that chance will produce no more than 21 spurious confirmations. The likelihood of obtaining 72 spurious findings is less than 1 in a billion billion! In spite of occasional negative findings, the literature on birth order exhibits consistent trends that overwhelmingly exceed chance expectations.[25]

Sulloway's statistical analysis, summarized in Table 5–1, shows us that when many studies are combined, we can draw good generalizations about the meaning of the research, keeping in mind that a generalization shows what is likely—not certain—to be true in any given individual case.

By contrast, when two respectable experts or institutions disagree and there is no clear-cut weight of evidence, critical thinkers have two options: They can remain neutral until more confirming studies are completed, or they can do more personal research. Personal research includes finding relevant journal articles in the library or on the Internet, interviewing people in the field, and calling the institutions that have done the studies to request copies of their findings (because, as previously discussed, they are usually summarized only briefly by the standard media sources).

Personal research becomes crucial when we need to make decisions about our own lives and encounter contradictory opinions about what we should do. Such was the case for reporter Daniel Borenstein, who was being treated for cancer of the head and neck. He started by seeking treatment from his friend, a medical oncologist:

> At first, I didn't appreciate that there are different types of oncologists. Randy is a "medical" oncologist, the sort of doctor who administers chemotherapy to treat cancer. As I learned, one must not confuse him with a radiation oncologist.
>
> Although choosing Randy as my doctor for my chemotherapy was easy because he was a good friend, I realized soon after I started my treatment that I would need to pick a radiation oncologist—and make key decisions about where to radiate. I had no idea that I would travel across the country searching for the answers.
>
> . . . After two rounds of chemotherapy, I had my second body scan, the first one since starting treatment. The results: The visible cancerous node

[25] Frank Sulloway, *Born to Rebel* (New York: Random House, 1996).

TABLE 5–1 Summary of 196 Controlled Birth-Order Studies, Classified According to the Big Five Personality Dimensions

Behavioral Domain (by Degree of Confirmation)	Outcome[a]	Likelihood of Outcome by Chance[b]
Openness to Experience		
Firstborns are more conforming, traditional, and closely identified with parents.	21 confirming (2.2 expected) 2 negating 20 no difference	*Less than 1 in a billion*
Conscientiousness		
Firstborns are more responsible, achievement oriented, organized, and planful.	20 confirming (2.3 expected) 0 negating 25 no difference	*Less than 1 in a billion*
Agreebleness/Antagonism		
Laterborns are more easygoing, cooperative, and popular.	12 confirming (1.6 expected) 1 negating 18 no difference	*Less than 1 in a billion*
Neuroticism (or Emotional Instability)		
Firstborns are more jealous, anxious, neurotic, fearful, and likely to affiliate under stress.	14 confirming (2.4 expected) 5 negating 29 no difference	*Less than 1 in a billion*
Extroversion		
Firstborns are more extroverted, assertive, and likely to exhibit leadership.	5 confirming (1.5 expected) 6 negating 18 no difference	*Less than 1 in a million (but studies conflict)[c]*
All Results Pooled	72 confirming (9.8 expected) 14 negating 110 no difference	*Less than 1 in a billion billion*

Note: Data are tabulated from Ernst and Angst (1983:93–189), using only those studies controlled for social class or sibship size. Each reported finding constitutes a "study."

[a]Based on a "chance" confirmation rate of 5 percent.

[b]Based on the meta-analytic procedure of counting confirming studies versus all other outcomes (Rosenthal 1987:213); one-tailed tests. With the expected number of confirming studies set to a minimum of 5, all statistical comparisons are significant at $p < .005$ For Openness, $z = 13.19$; for Conscientiousness, $z = 12.14$; for Agreeableness, $z = 8.44$; for Neuroticism, $z = 7.68$ for Extroversion, $z = 5.01$; for all results pooled, $z = 20.39$.

[c]In this one instance I have compared positive and negative studies together, versus those showing no difference, and employ a two-tailed test.

Source: Frank Sulloway, *Born to Rebel.* Copyright © Springer-Verlag New York, Inc. Reprinted with permission.

had shrunk to 30 percent of its original size. And its "brightness" on the scan, the measure of the intensity of the cancer, was similarly about one-third the pretreatment level.

"It's a huge, huge success for the chemotherapy," Randy told me when I saw him the next day.

Randy had been reviewing the latest studies on treatment for head-and-neck cancer like mine. As he put it, "I want to hit you with the kitchen sink once" to minimize the chances of the cancer returning. The original plan was three rounds of chemotherapy, which would take nine weeks, followed by six to seven weeks of daily radiation treatment. But Randy was adjusting my therapy, making it more intense than originally planned.

First, he explained, studies showed that the radiation would be more effective if given concurrently with additional chemotherapy. So—and here was the big surprise—when I underwent the radiation phase, I would also receive more chemo. The radiation therapy would be daily Monday through Friday for six to seven weeks. The concurrent chemo would be administered weekly. . . .

Randy was not a radiation expert. So we agreed that, before I started my radiation at Alta Bates' Herrick campus in Berkeley, I would go to the UC San Francisco medical center for a consultation.

Imagine my surprise when Jeanne Quivey, a leading radiation oncologist at UCSF, told me that the preradiation chemotherapy I had endured was a waste of time.

Since then, I've come to fully appreciate that medicine can be as much an art as a science; that some doctors want to be on the cutting edge and others want to use the most-proven treatment.

To Quivey, there was no doubt about the best tool for fixing my cancer. "We think the curative treatment is the radiation," she said. At her institution, patients like me were treated primarily with radiation, sometimes with simultaneous chemotherapy.

She was quite clear: Chemo in advance of radiation does not add to the cure rate for cancers like mine. Actually, she added, one study found it was harmful. Until there was a change in the survival rate, UCSF would not use chemotherapy before radiation.

Searching to make sense of this surprise, I noted that there seemed to be a split in the medical community on the treatment. Quivey was unyielding. "There might be a split in the community," she said, "but the data is on my side."

This wasn't just a theoretical dispute. This was a core disagreement about the underlying rationale of my therapy that also extended to other key questions, such as how much of my head and neck to irradiate, what chemotherapy to give me at the same time, and what drugs, if any, I should receive during the treatment to protect my salivary glands from the radiation.

What if Quivey were right? What if Randy were wrong? There was no compromise position between them. How could I receive treatment from a medical oncologist and a radiation oncologist if they weren't working from the same playbook?

Randy was surprised to hear my account of the appointment with Quivey. To be sure, he had warned me that he was using new therapies. He had told me the data were still evolving. And if we waited for conclusive studies on survival rates that would be years down the line—way too late to help me.

Moreover, Randy wasn't just making up the three-drug preradiation chemo regimen as he went along. It was being studied and used at one of the leading hospitals in the nation—the Dana-Farber Cancer Institute, affiliated with Harvard University, in Boston. I had seen some of the research, and Randy had been following it carefully. We decided I should see Roy Tishler, the radiation oncologist on that research team. . . . Meanwhile, I started reading medical studies, including the one Quivey cited as showing advance chemo could be harmful. That research, it turned out, looked at patients who were treated from 1965 to 1993. Those patients didn't receive the three-drug treatment I was given. One of those drugs, Taxotere, wasn't available back then.

As the doctors debated my future, there was good news about the effects of the chemotherapy I had received. My third body scan showed no cancer activity. It didn't mean I was cancer-free, only that the levels were below what the scan could detect.

The one thing the doctors all agreed on was that I still needed the radiation—and the sooner, the better. But the devil was in the details.[26] (Note: Daniel Borenstein had several other issues to decide after receiving contradictory advice from seven doctors he consulted. Fortunately, he chose treatment that has left him alive and in remission.)

There is often controversy in study results and approaches to medical treatment; there is also controversy in expert witness testimony at congressional hearings, public forums, and criminal trials. When government officials and juries have to rely on circumstantial evidence that is interpreted by experts, they may not know whom to believe. They need to rely on their best assessment of the credentials of the experts and the soundness and strength of the evidence they present. (See Exercise 5.7 on page 209.)

Reasoning by Analogy

Another interesting and common form of inductive generalization involves reasoning from analogies. When someone uses analogies to support an argument, he or she is drawing a comparison, saying in essence: I have evidence that this idea, event or policy works well (or does not work well) in one or more cases; therefore, I infer that it will work well (or not work well) in other, similar situations.

Have you ever taken a test with questions like those in Figure 5–3?

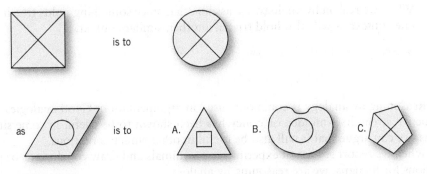

FIGURE 5–3

Reasoning by analogy is useful when the items are comparable in significant ways.

[26] Daniel Borenstein, "Learning to Decipher Language of Treatment," *Contra Costa Times*, February 11, 2007.

reasoning by analogy
Comparing one idea or plan to another for the purpose of supporting a conclusion. When we reason by analogy, we assume that since an idea, process, policy or event is similar in one way to another idea, process, policy or event that it is also similar in another significant way.

This test measures the ability to **reason by analogy.** If you answered B, you correctly identified the analogous drawing; both drawings contain two figures (X and 0) that have the same relationship to the figure that encloses them.

When speakers or writers use analogies, they describe something (an object, event, idea, or process) and compare it to something else. The *claim* is that the two things are alike in important ways. Reasoning by analogy can be coded as follows:

A is to B as C is to D.

Reasoning by analogy, comparing one idea or plan to another, is one of the major forms of evidence used by speakers and writers. For example, schoolteachers, police officers, firefighters, city planners, and other professionals often share ideas with others who do similar work, because they know that what worked in one community might work in another. Conferences and conventions for people in the same profession are all about sharing what is useful in one context, under the assumption that it will also be useful in another, similar context.

We will consider effective reasoning by analogy for the remainder of this chapter. In the next chapter, we will focus on faulty analogies and other errors in reasoning.

The human mind's ability to reason by analogy begins at an early age and continues throughout life. A child may reason, "Camp is just like school—I have to get up early and do what the counselors tell me." A friend may help parents understand a child's jealousy of a new baby brother or sister by comparing the arrival of the new baby to a spouse bringing home a new mate. An elderly person may complain, "This nursing home is like prison—the food is lousy, I have to follow too many rules, and no one comes to visit me."

Reasoning by analogy is useful in two ways:

1. We are able to explain a new or difficult idea, situation, phenomenon, or process by comparing it to a similar idea or process that is more familiar.
2. We are able to give reasons for a conclusion by showing that our idea or program has worked at another time or in another place. We are also able to show that an idea or policy we don't favor has not worked well in another context.

Reminder

When we reason by analogy, we assume that since something holds true in one context, it will also hold true in another, similar context.

✳ Explore on **mythinkinglab.com**

Reasoning by analogy is commonly used in argumentation. Good analogies add inductive strength; if an idea or policy has been shown to be useful in some situations, we can argue that it will also be useful in other similar situations.

When we report studies of experiments on animals and draw conclusions or predictions for humans, we are reasoning by analogy.

Example

A researcher may report that when rats are confined to an overcrowded cage, they exhibit antisocial behavior; a conclusion is then drawn about humans, comparing crowded rats to city dwellers. The researcher may suggest that overcrowded conditions are a factor in increased criminal activity.

When we look at a specific past event to justify a conclusion about a current policy, we are reasoning by analogy.

Example

Someone may argue that Prohibition didn't work in the 1920s—people still found a way to make alcohol and an underground criminal network was supported. In the same way, it is argued, making drugs illegal today simply means that people will get them from dealers at a high price.

When we compare a system in one place to a system in another, we are reasoning by analogy.

Example

Politicians may cite the prescription drug affordability in Canada as a way to argue for better prescription drug access in the United States.

In a commentary on teen curfews, law professor Dan M. Kahan challenges criminologists "who ridicule curfews as empty gestures that do little to address the root causes of juvenile delinquency." Kahan believes that curfews are effective because they free juveniles from the pressure to appear tough by hanging out at night and breaking the law to impress their peer group. Using inductive reasoning by analogy, Kahan states:

> Many cities that have adopted curfews, including New Orleans, San Antonio and Dallas, have reported dramatic drops in both juvenile criminal activity and juvenile criminal victimization.[27]

When you notice someone supporting a position by comparing one idea, situation, or plan to another, stop and evaluate whether the comparison is valid. If it is, you have a good analogy, which may be used to add inductive strength to your conclusions. (See Exercise 5.8 on page 209.)

Life Application: Tips for College and Career

Use studies to help you make important life decisions. If you or a loved one has been recommended to take a course of action in relation to a particular condition or disease, check out the most recent studies concerning the suggested treatment. Prepare questions to ask the doctors based on your research.

Use current research to make other decisions. Whether you are deciding to take a job in a particular industry, to buy a certain product, or to pursue a program of graduate study, gathering the information that is easily available from online journals, magazines, and experts in a field helps you choose beneficial courses of action.

---

[27] Dan M. Kahan, Comentary for *The Washington Post*, reprinted in the *Contra Costa Times*, November 17, 1996, p. A17.

Chapter Review

Summary

1. Scientific discoveries are often made through controlled studies; a well-designed study can be repeated by other researchers and thus can lead us closer to the truth about an issue.

2. A good research design includes a characteristic of interest, a hypothesis, and a sample of the target population, which is divided randomly into a control group and an experimental group.

3. The only significant difference between a control group and an experimental group is the treatment received by the experimental group.

4. The data gathered from a study are used to draw conclusions and to suggest areas for further study.

5. A critical thinker will review a study according to specific criteria to determine the extent to which the study is valid or biased.

6. The findings of many studies are considered controversial by experts in the field. When studies are controversial, critical thinkers withhold judgment or accept findings provisionally.

7. When using authoritative testimony as a support for conclusions, critical thinkers should consider whether the expert is educated and/or experienced in a field that is relevant to the issue under discussion.

8. Problems with using expert testimony include the use of experts in the wrong field of expertise, the use of experts who are not recognized as experts, the use of experts who are paid or biased, the use of experts who don't realistically limit their expertise, and the use of expert testimony that is contradicted by equally expert testimony.

9. Reasoning by analogy, comparing one idea or plan to another, is a form of inductive evidence used both to explain and to persuade.

Checkup

Short Answer

1. What are some questions to ask about a study to determine whether it is valid or biased?

2. How should critical thinkers respond when a study is controversial?

3. What distinguishes someone as a genuine expert in a given field?

4. How are generalizations from analogies useful in supporting conclusions?

Sentence Completion

5. A speculation about what will be discovered from a research study is called the _____.

6. A group of subjects who are given no treatment is the _____ _____.

7. The researcher's interpretation of the meaning and significance of the findings is called the _____.

8. A group of subjects who are exposed to a special treatment is called the

   _____ _____.

9. A randomly selected and representative part of the target population is the

   _____.

10. A sugar pill or other treatment that is meant to have no real effect on the subjects of the study is called a _____.

Exercises

EXERCISE 5.1 Purpose: To understand and use criteria for evaluating research.

Analyze the following examples in light of the criteria given for evaluating research findings. Then answer the following questions:

1. To what extent did each study meet the criteria for evaluating research? What are the strengths and weaknesses of each design?
2. Are there factors the researchers overlooked in designing their studies? If so, what is needed to improve the design?
3. Does one study have a better design than the other? If so, how?

Examples

A researcher is interested in a new treatment for controlling the effects of the AIDS virus. He designs a study, called the protocol, which involves two groups of patients who have recently (within the past six months) tested positive for the virus. One group receives the new drug, and the other group receives a placebo. There are no special dietary changes, and no other treatments are given to the two groups. The only difference between the groups is that one is taking the drug and the other is not. The subjects in the experiment don't know whether they have the real drug or the placebo; that way the alternate explanation that they felt better because they expected to feel better (the placebo effect) is eliminated. As progress with the two groups is monitored, the researchers should be able to determine if the new drug has any positive effect.

A researcher wants to find out if test performance in college is improved when students eat a breakfast that is high in carbohydrates. She chooses two randomly selected groups of students and asks them to follow a breakfast plan for a semester. Because she does not want them to know that she is trying to discover the effect of diet on test scores, she tells them the test is for cholesterol ratings.

The control group is given a skimpy breakfast of a low-carbohydrate drink. The experimental group is told to eat a breakfast loaded with carbohydrates that include toast and cereal. Each subject keeps a diary of what he or she had for breakfast. Teachers are asked to report on the morning test scores of the groups of students. At the conclusion of the semester, the test scores are compared to see if the experimental group did better than its peers in the control group.

EXERCISE 5.2 Purpose: To experience what goes into the design of research studies.

Design a study of your own. Pretend you have unlimited money and people and decide what you want to find out. Then create a study with a control group and an experimental group. You can be serious or humorous—the research topic is not important. The only important thing is your understanding of the scientific method.

This is a good exercise to do with a partner because you can get more ideas on how to control against alternative explanations for your results.

You might also try to carry out your study with a small sample and to report your findings to the class, including your design, your results, and your conclusions. Remember that a small sample can point to an interesting study to be carried out with a larger, more representative group.

Examples of Questions to Study

- Does garlic cure the common cold?
- Does listening to quiet music lower students' heart rate before a test?
- Do people get more or less work done when they are sitting in an attractive room versus an unattractive room?
- Do young children learn math better if they work with real items (coins or beads) or with worksheets?
- Do people who have no seasickness when sailing also have no seasickness when on a motorboat?
- Do people who have not eaten for a few hours buy more food at a supermarket than those who have just eaten?
- Do athletes perform better after watching comedians?

As you can see, the possibilities of what inquiring minds would like to know are endless. Once you decide on your question and determine your hypothesis, state how you would find a control group and an experimental group, how you would guard for error, and how you would analyze your results.

EXERCISE 5.3 Purpose: To explore the effect of reported research on decision making.

For a few days, consider how decisions you have made are based on information you've read about or heard about. Did you choose to have or not to have a surgical procedure because of research findings you read? Have you invested in a particular stock or mutual fund based on reports of a successful track record? Do you read safety and performance studies in consumer magazines before buying a car? Do you text more than talk because of concerns about the effects of cell phones on the human brain?

Are any of your decisions about the food you eat (fat content, cholesterol content, sugar or salt content, balance of food groups) based on research? If so, do you remember what the research said and where you read or heard about it? If you take vitamins, ask yourself why you take them and what research led you to make vitamin supplementation a daily habit.

What about exercise options? Do you regularly exercise, and if so, have your decisions about what kind to do and what equipment or clothes and shoes to wear been based on research studies?

To complete this exercise, answer the following:

1. What is the habit you have acquired, the action you have taken, or the item you have purchased?

2. What factors led you to make the decision to acquire the habit, take the action, or buy the item?

3. What have been the effects (if any) of your decision? To what extent has your life been enhanced by your decision? How might your life be different if you had not made the decision?

EXERCISE 5.4 Purpose: To gather data from personal research.

Choose one of the following options for a personal experiment.

1. Chart your study habits for a week or two. Note if you have a regular time and place for studying. Is the equipment you need readily available (computer, pens, paper)? Do you review notes shortly after class? Do you study alone or with others? What distractions intrude upon your study time (texting, e-mail, music, television, radio, phone, snack breaks, visitors)? After you have charted your habits, look at your record and draw conclusions about where time is well used, where it is wasted, and how it could be put to better use.

2. Chart your eating and exercise habits for a week or two. Then look at your record and draw some conclusions about your lifestyle. Does your record reflect healthy nutritional choices; a rushed, erratic schedule; or a combination of both? Do you exercise regularly? Try to predict what will happen to your health if you continue to eat and exercise in this way.

3. Try a lifestyle experiment on yourself. Change an aspect of your daily life: Set and stick to consistent study habits; limit the time that you use your cell phone or personal computer; do a certain aerobic or bodybuilding exercise; reduce your intake of fat or sugar; or eliminate caffeine, tobacco, or a food you crave (some nutritionists believe that people are allergic to foods that they crave). Keep a record of how you feel after adhering to your new program for two weeks or a month, and report the results to your instructor. (It can also be interesting for several people to work together on this, forming an experimental group.)

EXERCISE 5.5 Purpose: To gain a practical understanding of how the two-step flow influences decision making.

Consider some voting or buying decisions or some decisions about medical treatment you've made lately. Did you consult an expert or a knowledgeable friend before making your choices? If not, on what basis did you make your decisions?

Try to list your three most recent decisions and trace any outside influences on those decisions.

Examples

"I used to read a popular weekly newsmagazine in order to be informed. A friend of mine who is a professor told me about another magazine he likes better because it gives more in-depth coverage of issues. I switched to this other magazine and I really like it. I enjoy getting a broader report on current events." (from a retired businessman)

"I developed a breast infection—very common for nursing mothers—and didn't want to make a trip to the doctor for antibiotics. The doctor wouldn't prescribe the drugs without seeing me, so I called a friend of mine who is an expert in herbs. She suggested home remedies, which I took for several days; they did keep me from getting worse. But I wanted to get better faster, so I gave in and made the appointment." (from a mother of an infant)

"My friend is a photographer, and so I consulted him about what to look for in a digital camera. I thought I knew which one I wanted to buy until he pointed out some features that were lacking in my choice. When I told him everything I needed and the price I could afford, he came up with two good choices for me to consider." (from a college student)

EXERCISE 5.6 Purposes: To discover examples of bias on websites, and in books, magazines, or televised programs. To consider biased viewpoints.

1. Try to isolate an incident of possible bias in your reading or viewing. You might go through your textbooks and note any examples that seem to support a particular viewpoint or political stand. When you watch a television interview show, note whether the host gives equal time and courtesy to all points of view, or whether he or she seems to favor one side over the other. If you watch a debate, note the slant or "spin" given to both sides of the issue. Many cable news programs, websites, and news magazines are considered to have a bias, either conservative or liberal or radically left or right; find an issue that is covered by two sources with different biases and contrast the presentation of the issue.

Example

I recently received a "questionnaire" about whether I thought a large superstore should be allowed to locate in our county. I tend to favor allowing the superstore to be here, but I also understand the concern our county supervisors have about megastores hurting our smaller grocery stores and grocery chains. I saw my favorite local coffee shop lose a lot of business when a big coffee chain came to our town.

The questionnaire I received didn't mention this other side of the issue—the welfare of small stores hurt by the power of large superstores to take most of their business. Instead, these were a couple of the questions they asked:

- Which do you think is the most important problem facing our county? Education, Crime, Property Taxes, Affordable Housing, Jobs, Growth, or Big Box Stores? (Obviously all of the other issues are going to come out higher than big box stores.)

- Should the decision to have large-scale retailers be made by consumers or by the Board of Supervisors? (This question doesn't take into account the responsibility the board has been given by the people for issues such as growth, small business concerns, traffic, and the desire of some towns in the county to keep a small-town look.)

- Could our county use more than $500,000 in new sales tax revenue and 500 new jobs from a superstore?

  Yes, No, or Don't Know (Clearly the obvious "yes" vote here can be used to say that people favor the store.)

Whoever came up with this survey seems to want to use it to argue that the will of the people is being ignored by the "power-hungry" board of supervisors. Otherwise, the questions would be more neutral and would reflect both sides of the issue.

2. Take an issue and create viewpoints for several characters. For example, you could imagine the responses of a police officer, an addict, a drug dealer, a parent, and a politician to the idea of legalizing drugs. What natural biases might influence their responses? Working alone or in groups, write out each of

their possible responses and note the similarities and differences. This exercise works well as a role-play followed by a class discussion.

EXERCISE 5.7 Purpose: To recognize controversial expert testimony.

Find an example of expert testimony contradicted by equally expert testimony; editorial pages sometimes contain pro-con arguments of this nature, or you can find them in *USA Today* on the debate page, on numerous network and cable programs such as public broadcasting's *Newshour,* CNN's *360 with Anderson Cooper,* Fox's *On the Record,* or ABC's *Nightline,* or online at network and cable television websites. State the basic areas of disagreement and the reasons given for each side's conclusions. Then decide which of the arguments you would support and explain why.

Also, you might focus on controversial criminal investigations revisited by programs such as NBC's *Dateline* or ABC's *20/20* that show how evidence has been found that allows for a new trial; for example, DNA evidence is used frequently to reexamine the guilt or innocence of people convicted of crimes.

EXERCISE 5.8 Purposes: To understand the usefulness of analogies as learning tools and to increase familiarity with the common use of analogies.

Although we are considering analogies as they relate to persuasion, analogies are also useful in conveying information. Ask a teacher you respect how he or she has used analogies to explain a difficult process to students. Find two or three examples of these kinds of analogies and share them with the class.

EXERCISE 5.9 Purpose: To gain experience in evaluating the credibility of websites.

One of the biggest challenges for critical thinkers is to evaluate websites and decide which are credible and which are not.

Use the following tool to evaluate websites so that you base your arguments and decisions on reliable information.

Website Checklist

Look at the website you are using as a resource. How many of the following points can you answer yes to in relation to this site? The more times you answer Yes, the more likely the page is of high quality.

Title of Web site: _____

URL: _____

Date evaluated: _____

Authority

Authority means that the person, institution or agency responsible for a site has trustworthy qualifications and knowledge.

- Is it clear who developed the site?
- Does the person, institution or agency responsible for a site have the qualifications and knowledge to do so?
- Has the author clearly provided contact information including: e-mail address, snail mail address, phone number, and fax number?
- Has the author clearly stated his or her qualifications or credentials, or provided some personal background information?
- Is the site supported by an organization or a commercial body?

Purpose

The author should be clear about the purpose of the information presented in the site. What is the purpose of the site and does the content support it?

- Does the domain name of the site indicate its purpose?
- Is the site well organized and focused?
- Are the links appropriate for the topic of the site?
- Are the links evaluated in any way?
- Is the information geared to a specific audience?

Coverage

One author may claim to present comprehensive coverage of a topic while another may cover just one aspect of a topic.

- Does the site claim to be comprehensive?
- Are the topics explored in depth?
- Is the website valuable compared to others on the same topic?
- Does the site provide its own information or depend on outside links?
- Does the site have relevant outside links?

Currency

It is important to know when a site was created, when it was last updated, and if all of the links are current.

- Is the date the information was first written given?
- Is the date the information was placed on the Web given?
- Is the date the information was last revised given?
- Are the links up-to-date and reliable?
- Is the site fully developed? (ie. no construction signs)

Objectivity

Objective sites will present information with a minimum of bias, without the intention to persuade.

- Is the information presented without a particular bias?
- Does the information avoid trying to sway the audience?
- Does the site avoid advertising that may be a conflict of interest with the content?
- Does the site avoid trying to persuade or sell something?

Accuracy

It is the responsibility of the reader to evaluate the information presented.

- Is the information reliable? If the author is affiliated with a known institution, this could be an important clue.
- If statistics and other factual information are presented, are proper references given for the origin of the information?
- From the reading you have already done on the subject, does the information on the site seem accurate?
- Is the information provided comparable to other sites on the same topic?
- Does the text follow basic rules of grammar, spelling and composition?
- Is a bibliography or reference list included?

You **Decide**

Cloning

Reproductive cloning is a technology used to create an animal that is an exact genetic duplicate (i.e., that has the same nuclear DNA as another currently or previously existing animal). Human cloning became a controversial issue when the first sheep, named Dolly, was successfully cloned by a group of Scottish scientists; other scientists have since used the technology to clone cattle and livestock.

The debate on human reproductive cloning provides a great example of an issue that involves a variety of perspectives about "where we draw the line" in scientific experimentation. The primary questions surrounding the issue of human cloning are whether it is safe and whether it is ethical. Those in favor of human cloning include people who believe it could help infertile couples. Those against human cloning believe that it undermines individualism and could create problems with social equality --either because the cloned humans would be considered inferior or because the cloned humans would be designed to be superior. Some questions that arise from this debate include: Should parents have a right to clone? Would clones be subhuman or superhuman? Is there a danger that clones would be subjected to experimentation or produced in order to be used as organ donors?

For more information on the debate surrounding cloning and additional exercises and tutorials about concepts covered in this chapter, log into MyThinkingLab at www. mythinkinglab.com and select Diestler, *Becoming a Critical Thinker*, Sixth Edition.

✳─Explore on **mythinkinglab.com**

Articles for Discussion   📖─Read the **Document** on **mythinkinglab.com**

The following article gives a humorous look at the frustrations of a writer who is constantly exposed to contradictory reports about research studies, and who sets out to determine what he can believe. The bulleted section at the end of the article is an excellent checklist for critically examining the research we read.

Food News Blues

Anthony Schmitz

Not long ago I set a coffee cup on the table and opened the newspaper to a piece of good news. "New Study Finds Coffee Unlikely to Cause Heart Ills," read the headline. One thing less to worry about, I thought, until I remembered a story from a few weeks before. That morning the headline warned, "Study: Heart Risk Rises on 4, More Cups Coffee Daily." My paper does this all the time. Concerning the latest dietary findings, it flips and flops like a fish thrown to shore.

"Medical research," it declared one Wednesday, "repeatedly has linked the soluble fiber in oats with reductions in serum cholesterol." By Thursday of the next week all that had changed. "Studies Cast Doubt on Benefits from Oat Bran," the headline cried. Once again the paper offered its readers a familiar choice. Which story to believe? This week's, or last week's, or none at all?

The paper in question is the *St. Paul Pioneer Press*. It's a respectable provincial daily, not unlike the papers in Houston, Detroit and dozens of other cities. One day, recently, the news editor, Mike Peluso, said he'd take a crack at explaining his paper's flip-flops.

Peluso is compact, graying, more grave than jocular. He met me at the newsroom door. "You want a cup of coffee?" he asked, pointing at a vending machine. No, I said, trying to recall whether this week coffee was good or bad. Peluso shrugged and headed for his cluttered cubicle. Beyond its flimsy walls reporters jabbered into phones.

I arranged the coffee and oat bran clippings on a paper-strewn table. Peluso examined them one by one. He grimaced. He sighed. He swallowed black coffee from a paper cup.

"How do you reconcile the conflicting claims?" he asked himself. "One month coffee can't hurt you, the next month quit coffee and your heart will tick forever."

Exactly.

Peluso shook his head. "I don't know, I don't have any answers for that. You've got to talk about the real world here."

For Peluso, the real world looks something like this: News of a hot nutrition study gets beamed into the newsroom from wire services such as Associated Press, the *New York Times* or the *Baltimore Sun*. Peluso and his staff poke at the story, trying to find flaws that argue against putting it in the paper. By and large it's a hamstrung effort. Never mind that the reporter who wrote the piece is thousands of miles away. She'd defend the story anyway. The paper's own health reporter is scant help; he's been on the beat two months.

Meanwhile, Peluso knows that his competitors—another daily paper, plus radio and television news—won't spend a week analyzing the study. They'll run it today. Which is to say Peluso will, too. But the story the reader sees won't be as detailed as the piece that came over the wire. Compared with the *New York Times* or the *Washington Post*, the *Pioneer Press* is something of a dwarf. Stories get trimmed to fit. Subtleties and equivocations—the messy business of research—don't always make the cut.

"Look," said Peluso, "we're not medical authorities. We're just your normal skeptics. And it's not like we're inventing the research. We're simply reporting on it. We present what's there and let people draw their own conclusions."

"So what should readers make of all the contradictory advice you offer them?"

Peluso sighed again. "I don't know," he said. "You've got to take everything with a grain of salt until the last word comes in. I hate to tell people I don't believe everything I read, but the fact is anybody who believes everything they read is nuts."

Researchers whose work makes news soon learn that the match between science and journalism wasn't made in heaven. Richard Greenberg, a microbiologist who directs the office of scientific and public affairs at the Institute of Food Technologists, has watched what happens when the scientific method collides with journalistic technique.

"The first thing you've got to remember," says Greenberg, "is that science is not fact. It is not truth. It is not Holy Scripture. It's a compendium of information. You try to put all the research together and come to a consensus. Just because somebody runs a study that comes to a particular conclusion doesn't change everything that's gone before."

Scientists don't generally reach consensus in time for the next deadline. After 30 years of study, coffee's link to heart disease remains an open question. Four plus cups a day may slightly increase the risk, though some research suggests only decaf is linked to heart problems. Similarly, a decade's worth of oat bran experiments have served only to get a good argument going. Some studies suggest oat bran isn't any better at lowering cholesterol than white bread. If you eat enough of either, the message goes, you won't have room for fatty food. Others say oat bran has innate—though so far inexplicable—cholesterol-lowering properties.

While on their way to answering the big questions about fat or cholesterol or fiber, researchers often pause and dicker merrily about the design flaws in one study or the dicey statistical analysis in another. "Among ourselves," says one epidemiologist, "we're more interested in the detail of how things are done than in saying right now whether oat bran's good for you."

For journalists it's exactly the opposite. The arcana of statistical analysis and research design are boring at best, baffling at worst. The big question is whether oat bran will keep your heart ticking.

"The reporter and headline writer are trying to distill the meaning of the latest piece of research," says Greenberg. "They're trying to grab the eye of the reader. They're searching for absolutes where there are no absolutes. And this is what happens. One day you read caffeine is bad. Then you read that if you take the caffeine out, coffee is OK. Then you hear that the solvent that takes out the caffeine is dangerous. Then you find out the caffeine isn't dangerous after all. It so confuses the public they don't know whom to believe. And the truth is, there wasn't really any news in any of these studies. Each of them was just another micromillimeter step toward scientific consensus."

For Greenberg, news exists in those rare moments when scientists weigh the evidence and agree to agree—when the American Heart Association, the National Cancer Institute or the National Academy of Sciences pronounces that you ought to eat less fat, or more vegetables.

But by the terms of journalism, scientific consensus is a dead-letter file. If everybody agrees, there's no conflict, there's no news. In comparison, debates such as those about coffee or oat bran are a newsroom gold mine. Contradictions and conflict abound. Better still, almost everyone has oatmeal or coffee in the cupboard.

"You can't convince an editor not to run this stuff," says Howard Lewis, editor of the newsletter *Science Writers*. "My advice is that they do it for the same reason they run the comic strips and the astrological columns. But I feel it's all a hoax. Usually they're not accomplishing anything except sowing panic or crying wolf."

A Purdue communications professor raised a stir few years back when he suggested that research news might be more harmful than helpful. Writing in the journal *Science, Technology and Human Values,* Leon Trachtman observed that 90 percent of the new drugs touted in newspaper reports never reached the market or were driven from it because they were ineffective, too toxic or both. Readers relying on this information would have made wrong choices nine times out of 10.

So who's served, Trachtman asked, by publicizing these drugs before there's a scientific consensus on them? "When there's no consensus, why broadcast contradictory reports?" Ultimately, he said, readers are paralyzed by the pros and cons. He asked whether the result will be contempt for research, followed by demands to stop wasting money on it.

Not surprisingly, Leon Trachtman got blasted for implying that a scholastic elite ought to be making decisions for us. Among the critics was David Perlman, a science editor who writes regularly about health and nutrition. Often, Perlman says, research leads to public debates. Will avoiding fatty foods really lengthen your life? Should government experts try persuading people to change their eating habits? It's debatable. But citizens can hardly take part if they're capable of nothing more than numbly accepting expert advice. "To abdicate an interest in science," says Perlman, citing mathematician Jacob Bronowsky, "is to walk with open eyes toward slavery." Perlman trusts people's ability to sort through well-written news.

"It's not just the masses who are confused," says Trachtman. "It's the same for well-trained scientists once they're out of their field. I think people ought to establish a sensible, moderate course of action, and then not be deflected from it every morning by what they read in the paper."

But let's face facts. Do you have the resolve to ignore a headline that declares, "Sugar, Alzheimer's Linked"? If you can't help but play the game, you can at least try to defend yourself from nonsense by following these rules:

- *Count the legs.* First, ask if the group studied bears any relation to you. Don't let research done only on four-legged subjects worry you. Pregnant rats, for instance, are more likely to bear offspring with missing toes after getting extremely high jolts of caffeine. What's this mean for humans? Probably nothing. There's no evidence that drinking moderate amounts of caffeine causes human birth defects.

  If research subjects have two legs, read closely to see if they're anything like you. Early research that helped launch the oat bran fad involved only men, most of whom were middle-aged. All had dangerously high blood cholesterol, which reportedly fell after they ate a daily cup-plus of oat bran—enough for a half-dozen muffins. Fine, unless you're female, have low cholesterol already, or can't stand the thought of eating half a dozen bran muffins every day.

- *Check for perspective.* Even if you're a match for the group being studied, don't assume the results are significant. "Check if the journalist gets the perspective of other people in the field," says Harvard epidemiologist Walter Willett. "People who have watched the overall flow of information are in a good position to say, 'Well, this really nails it down,' or 'That's interesting, but it needs confirmation.'"

- *Ask how many guinea pigs.* Quaker Oats research manager Steven Ink, who's written a guide to nutrition studies, says the best research uses at least 50 subjects. By this standard, we should look askance at the recent study showing that eating 17 tiny meals a day lowers cholesterol. Only seven people took part. But rules of thumb don't always work. A small number can be meaningful if the effect observed is large and consistent. You don't need to feed 50 people cyanide to figure out that it's going to be bad for everyone.

  What's more, Ink advises, subjects shouldn't be fed quantities of food that no one in his right mind would eat. One example is the recent study showing that trans fatty acids such as those in margarine may be bad for your heart. Subjects ate three times more trans fatty acids than the average American.

  Finally, any group tested should be compared to a similar group. Early studies that linked coffee to heart disease were skewed because coffee drinkers differed greatly from the control group. The coffee drinkers were more likely to smoke and eat a high-fat, high-cholesterol diet. Both habits carry bigger heart risks than does drinking coffee.

- *Wait for confirmation.* "Don't let one study change your life," says Jane Brody, the *New York Times* health writer. She waits for three types of food research to agree before changing her eating habits.

  First, she looks for studies of large groups that show a link between a food and good or bad health—Italy's big appetite for olive oil and its low rate of heart disease for instance. Then she watches for lab evidence in test animals that suggests how the food causes its effect in people. Finally, she considers human experiments in which two groups are compared—one eating the food, the other not eating it, with neither group knowing which is which.

  Applying this rule to her own meals, Brody skimps on butter and favors olive oil. She eats plenty of fruits and vegetables, lots of potatoes, rice, beans and pasta, and modest amounts of lean meat. "This plan won't make you sick, has a good chance of keeping you well, and is immune to these fads that are here today and gone tomorrow," Brody says.

- *Hunt for holes.* No matter how carefully you read, you'll have to rely on the information your newspaper chooses to supply. If the big mattress ad on an inside page gets dropped at the last minute, the editors may suddenly have room for an exhaustive treatment of the latest coffee study. But if a candidate for national office gets caught with his pants down, the space required for a thorough exposé may mean the coffee piece gets gutted.

When editors at the *St. Paul Pioneer Press* got hold of a wire service report debunking oat bran, they found room for the first two-thirds. The third that didn't fit held a stern critique by other experts. They charged that the study contained too few people (20 female dietitians), didn't control the rest of what they ate, and started with subjects who had unusually low cholesterol.

"The reader really has to be skeptical," says Frank Sacks, the Harvard researcher whose oat bran study was under attack. "Take my case, for instance. The reporter really ought to say that this is a new finding, that it needs to be replicated. This is a warning sign that you have to wait a while. Reporters hate that when you say it. They call it waffling. But the truth is your hot new finding might not be confirmed down the line. You hate it when that happens, but it happens time and again.

"The real conservative advice is not to take any of this stuff in the newspaper with a whole lot of credence," says Sacks. "You could just wait for the conservative health organizations like the American Heart Association to make their recommendations and then follow their advice."

I called the American Heart Association to get its line on oat bran and coffee. "We don't have an opinion," said John Weeks somewhat plaintively.

"We get calls every day from the media," said Weeks. "They want to know what we think about every new study that comes out. And we don't have an opinion. We don't try to assimilate every new study. Our dietary guidelines would be bouncing all over the place if we did. Once the evidence is there, we move on it. Until then, we don't."

The Heart Association is sticking with the same dietary advice it's dispensed since 1988, when it last revised its model diet. Eat less fat. Eat more grains, vegetables and fruit. The evidence that oat bran lowers cholesterol is so limited that the association makes no specific recommendations about it. Concerning coffee, the group has nothing to say.

Weeks' advice for whipsawed newspaper readers has a familiar ring. "What people need to keep in mind," he said, "is that one study does not a finding make."

"You mean," I asked, quoting Mike Peluso's newsroom wisdom, "I'm nuts to believe everything I read?"

Said Weeks, "That's exactly correct." ■

Questions for Discussion

1. Consider the following paragraph from the article:

   "But by the terms of journalism, scientific consensus is a dead-letter file. If everybody agrees, there's no conflict, there's no news. In comparison, debates such as those about coffee or oat bran are a newsroom gold mine. Contradictions and conflict abound. Better still, almost everyone has oatmeal or coffee in the cupboard."

   Should newspapers and magazines report controversial studies or wait until there is scientific consensus for the findings of the studies? What are your reasons for your answer?

2. What habits, if any, have you changed because of research that was reported by the popular media? (Consider dietary and exercise habits as well as advice on car safety, product safety, durability of consumer goods, and so on.) To what extent has the advice been helpful?

3. What is the best approach to the reading of research in popular media? Should you believe nothing, everything, or some things? Do you agree with the guidelines for reading research that are given in this article?

. . . .

One of the most important effects of research is its role in shaping public policy. In 2010, the Federal Highway Administration decided to change the all-capital street signs in communities across the United States from upper case to mixed upper- and lower-case signs. Residents of some cities, including New York, objected to the new policy. Federal officials countered with the need for public safety reflected in the research on the improved visibility of the mixed-case signs.

Read the following article and the research on which the policy was based.

$27 Million to Change NYC Signs from All-Caps

Jeremy Olshan

The Capital of the World is going lower-case.

Federal copy editors are demanding the city change its 250,900 street signs—such as those for Perry Avenue in The Bronx—from the all-caps style used for more than a century to ones that capitalize only the first letters.

Changing BROADWAY to Broadway will save lives, the Federal Highway Administration contends in its updated Manual on Uniform Traffic Control Devices, citing improved readability.

At $110 per sign, it will also cost the state $27.6 million, city officials said.

"We have already started replacing the signs in The Bronx," city Transportation Commissioner Janette Sadik-Khan told The Post. "We will have 11,000 done by the end of this fiscal year, and the rest finished by 2018."

It appears e.e. cummings was right to eschew capital letters, federal officials explain.

Studies have shown that it is harder to read all-caps signs, and those extra milliseconds spent staring away from the road have been shown to increase the likelihood of accidents, particularly among older drivers, federal documents say.

The new regulations also require a change in font from the standard highway typeface to Clearview, which was specially developed for this purpose.

As a result, even numbered street signs will have to be replaced.

"Safety is this department's top priority," Transportation Secretary Ray LaHood said last year, in support of the new guidelines. "These new and updated standards will help make our nation's roads and bridges safer for drivers, construction workers and pedestrians alike."

The Highway Administration acknowledged that New York and other states "opposed the change, and suggested that the use of all upper-case letters remain an option," noting that "while the mixed-case words might be easier to read, the amount of improvement in legibility did not justify the cost."

To compensate for those concerns, in 2003, the administration allowed for a 15-year phase-in period ending in 2018.

Although the city did not begin replacing the signs until earlier this year, Sadik-Khan said they will have no trouble meeting the deadline, as some 8,000 signs a year are replaced annually simply due to wear and tear.

The new diminutive signs, which will also feature new reflective sheeting, may also reflect a kinder, gentler New York, she said.

"On the Internet, writing in all caps means you are shouting," she said. "Our new signs can quiet down, as well."

As we discussed in the previous article, when media report on policy decisions that are based on research, they don't have the space to include all of the background information. The government recommendations on using mixed-case lettering in a clearer font were based on extensive computer-simulated, lab-based font legibility studies on subjects ranging in age from 22–45. Previous studies had also indicated that improving sign legibility for older drivers would also improve it for younger drivers, so the road studies (field testing) were done using older subjects.

A summary of the research upon which the policy of changing street signs is based states:

> The research objective was to improve highway guide sign legibility by replacing the 40-year-old guide sign font with a new font called Clearview. It was believed that the current guide sign font's thick stroke design, made with high-brightness materials and displayed to older vehicle operators, exhibited a phenomenon known as irradiation or halation. Irradiation becomes a problem if a stroke is so bright that it visually bleeds into the character's open spaces, creating a blobbing effect that reduces legibility. The Clearview font's wider open spaces allow irradiation without decreasing the distance at which the alphabet is legible. Results are presented of two daytime and two nighttime controlled field experiments that exposed 48 older drivers to high-brightness guide signs displaying either the current or the Clearview font. The Clearview font allowed nighttime recognition distances 16 percent greater than those allowed by the Standard Highway Series E(M) font, without increasing overall sign dimensions.[28]

[28] Philip M. Garvey, Martin T. Pietrucha, and Donald Meeker, "Effects of Font and Capitalization on Legibility of Guide Signs," *Transportation Research Record*, No. 1605, 1997. pp. 73–79.

Questions for Discussion

1. According to the article, the Transportation Commissioner for the Bronx said that "some 8,000 signs a year are replaced annually simply due to wear and tear."[29] Do you believe that the reporter should have revised the headlined estimate of $27 million to reflect the normal replacement costs of the signs over a 15 year period? Do you believe that the headline was 'sensationalized' to create discussion and controversy over this issue?

2. According to the article, "The Highway Administration acknowledged that New York and other states 'opposed the change, and suggested that the use of all upper-case letters remain an option,' noting that 'while the mixed-case words might be easier to read, the amount of improvement in legibility did not justify the cost.'" Because of the concerns expressed by several cities, the Highway Administration extended the completion dates of sign changes to 15 years. How can the financial priorities of a city or state be balanced against the safety decisions of the federal government?

3. The Transportation Commissioner for the Bronx stated, "'On the Internet, writing in all caps means you are shouting,' she said. 'Our new signs can quiet down, as well.'" How is this analogy used to help explain the potential effects of the new signage?

In the following article, we read about a controversial new treatment for post-traumatic stress disorders. The treatment, if given shortly after a traumatic event, limits the negative memories that some victims suffer for years. Some professionals and victims are very excited about the positive potential of this treatment, while others fear it may create a dangerous outcome.

Could a Pill Help Fade Traumatic Memories?

Suppose you could erase bad memories from your mind. Suppose, as in a recent movie, your brain could be wiped clean of sad and traumatic thoughts.

That is science fiction. But real-world scientists are working on the next best thing. They have been testing a pill that, when given after a traumatic event like rape, may make the resulting memories less painful and intense.

Will it work? It is too soon to say. Still, it is not far-fetched to think that this drug someday might be passed out along with blankets and food at emergency shelters after disasters like the tsunami or Hurricane Katrina.

Psychiatrist Hilary Klein could have offered it to the man she treated at a St. Louis shelter over the Labor Day weekend. He had fled New Orleans and was so distraught over not knowing where his sisters were that others had to tell Klein his story.

"This man could not even give his name, he was in such distress. All he could do was cry," she said.

Such people often develop post-traumatic stress disorder, or PTSD, a problem first recognized in Vietnam War veterans. Only 14 percent to 24 percent of trauma victims

[29] Jeremy Olshan, "$27 Million to Change NYC Signs from All-Caps," *New York Post,* September 30, 2010. http://www.nypost.com/p/news/local/bronx/million_kuj8X4Z2VolVhXnCymfkvM.

experience long-term PTSD, but sufferers have flashbacks and physical symptoms that make them feel as if they are reliving the trauma years after it occurred.

Scientists think it happens because the brain goes haywire during and right after a strongly emotional event, pouring out stress hormones that help store these memories in a different way than normal ones are preserved.

Taking a drug to tamp down these chemicals might blunt memory formation and prevent PTSD, they theorize.

Some doctors have an even more ambitious goal: trying to cure PTSD. They are deliberately triggering very old bad memories and then giving the pill to deep-six them.

The first study to test this approach on 19 longtime PTSD sufferers has provided early encouraging results, Canadian and Harvard University researchers report.

"We figure we need to test about 10 more people until we've got solid evidence." said Alain Brunet, a psychologist at McGill University in Montreal who is leading the study.

It can't come too soon.

The need for better treatment grows daily as American troops return from Iraq and Afghanistan with wounded minds as well as bodies. One government survey found almost 1 in 6 showing symptoms of mental stress, including many with post-traumatic stress disorder. Disability payments related to the illness cost the government more than $4 billion a year.

The need is even greater in countries ravaged by many years of violence.

"I don't think there's yet in our country a sense of urgency about post-traumatic stress disorder" but there should be, said James McGaugh, director of the Center for the Neurobiology of Learning and Memory at the University of California at Irvine.

He and a colleague, Larry Cahill, did experiments that changed how scientists view memory formation and suggested new ways to modify it.

Memories, painful or sweet, don't form instantly after an event but congeal over time. Like slowly hardening cement, there is a window of opportunity when they are shapeable.

During stress, the body pours out adrenaline and other "fight or flight" hormones that help write memories into the "hard drive" of the brain, McGaugh and Cahill showed.

Propranolol can blunt this. It is in a class of drugs called beta blockers and is the one most able to cross the blood-brain barrier and get to where stress hormones are wreaking havoc. It already is widely used to treat high blood pressure and is being tested for stage fright.

Dr. Roger Pitman, a Harvard University psychiatrist, did a pilot study to see whether it could prevent symptoms of PTSD. He gave 10 days of either the drug or the dummy pills to accident and rape victims who came to the Massachusetts General Hospital emergency room.

In follow-up visits three months later, the patients listened to tapes describing their traumatic events as researchers measured their heart rates, palm sweating and forehead muscle tension.

The eight who had taken propranolol had fewer stress symptoms than the 14 who received dummy pills, but the differences in the frequency of symptoms were so small they might have occurred by chance—a problem with such tiny experiments.

Still, "this was the first study to show that PTSD could be prevented," McGaugh said, and enough to convince the federal government to fund a larger one that Pitman is doing now.

Meanwhile, another study on assault and accident victims in France confirmed that propranolol might prevent PTSD symptoms.

One of those researchers, Brunet, now has teamed with Pitman on the boldest experiment yet—trying to cure longtime PTSD sufferers.

"We are trying to reopen the window of opportunity to modulate the traumatic memory," Pitman said.

The experiments are being done in Montreal and involve people traumatized as long as 20 or 30 years ago by child abuse, sexual assault or a serious accident.

"It's amazing how a traumatic memory can remain very much alive. It doesn't behave like a regular memory. The memory doesn't decay," Brunet said.

To try to make it decay, researchers ask people to describe the trauma as vividly as they can, bringing on physical symptoms like racing hearts, then give them propranolol to blunt "restorage" of the memory. As much as three months later, the single dose appears to be preventing PTSD symptoms, Brunet said.

Joseph LeDoux, a neuroscience professor at New York University, is enrolling 20 to 30 people in a similar experiment and believes in the approach.

"Each time you retrieve a memory it must be restored," he said. "When you activate a memory in the presence of a drug that prevents the restorage of the memory, the next day the memory is not as accessible."

Not all share his enthusiasm, as McGaugh found when he was asked to brief the President's Council on Bioethics a few years ago.

"They didn't say anything at the time but later they went ballistic on it," he said.

Chairman Leon Kass contended that painful memories serve a purpose and are part of the human experience.

McGaugh says that's preposterous when it comes to trauma like war. If a soldier is physically injured, "you do everything you can to make him whole," but if he says he is upset "they say, 'suck it up—that's the normal thing,'" he complained.

Propranolol couldn't be given to soldiers in battle because it would curb survival instincts.

"They need to be able to run and to fight," Pitman said. "But if you could take them behind the lines for a couple of days, then you could give it to them after a traumatic event," or before they're sent home, he said.

Some critics suggest that rape victims would be less able to testify against attackers if their memories were blunted, or at least that defense attorneys would argue that.

"Medical concerns trump legal concerns. I wouldn't withhold an effective treatment from somebody because of the possibility they may have to go to court a year later and their testimony be challenged. We wouldn't do that in any other area of medicine," Pitman said. "The important thing to know about this drug is it doesn't put a hole in their memory. It doesn't create amnesia."

Practical matters may limit propranolol's usefulness. It must be given within a day or two of trauma to prevent PTSD.

How long any benefits from the drug will last is another issue. McGaugh said some animal research suggests that memory eventually recovers after being squelched for a while by the drug.

Overtreatment also is a concern. Because more than three-quarters of trauma victims don't have long-term problems, most don't need medication.

But LeDoux sees little risk in propranolol.

"It's a pretty harmless drug," he said. "If you could give them one or two pills that could prevent PTSD, that would be a pretty good thing."

Klein, the Saint Louis University psychiatrist, said it would be great to have something besides sleep aids, antidepressants and counseling to offer traumatized people, but she remains skeptical about how much long-term good propranolol can do.

"If there were a pill to reduce the intensity of symptoms, that would be a relief," she said. "But that's a far step from being able to prevent the development of PTSD." Only more study will tell whether that is truly possible. ■

Questions for Discussion

1. Dr. Roger Pitman used the drug propranolol in his pilot studies. What was he trying to discover, and how did he conduct his research? What limits did Dr. Pitman acknowledge in his research?

2. While Pitman was concerned about using propranolol to prevent post-traumatic stress, other researchers are hoping to be able to cure PTSD through the drug. What is the design of their research, according to this article?

3. What are the main areas of controversy and concern over the research and treatment possibilities for PTSD discussed in the article? Do you share those concerns?

4. If you were involved in a traumatic incident, would you want the option to be treated with propranolol? Why or why not?

Ideas for Writing or Speaking

1. *Research paper or speech*. The purpose of this assignment is to help you become familiar with using research to support your conclusions. Many intelligent people will give good reasons for their conclusions; however, they may not take the time to study current research findings to support their reasons.

   Your objective for this paper or speech is to find out how well you can substantiate the reasons for your conclusion.

   Since the issue you choose will be controversial, there will be opinions on both sides. You need to show, with your research, that your reasons are stronger than the reasons given by the opposition.

   The steps to take to prepare this essay or speech are as follows:

   a. Choose a controversial issue that you can research. It is important that the issue is one that has been studied by researchers and discussed by experts.
   b. Take a stand on the issue, or formulate a tentative hypothesis. A hypothesis states what you believe your conclusion will be after you conduct your research.
   c. Find at least four sources of research to support your conclusion. These sources include reports of studies done on the issue and articles and comments by experts that can be culled from professional journals, newsmagazines, or broadcast interviews. If you know an expert, you can arrange for an interview and record the comments as authoritative testimony.

   Also, find some experts arguing for the opposing side of the issue, so that you can address their reasoning in your essay or speech.

   d. Complete a rough draft of your essay or speech, which should include your issue, conclusion, reasons, and evidence to support your reasons. Also, in the body of the essay or speech, address and acknowledge the strongest reasons given by those who draw the opposite conclusion, and say why these reasons are not strong enough to justify that conclusion.

e. Write the final form of your speech or essay, adding an introduction and conclusion. The introduction should highlight the importance of your issue; you can use quotes, statistics, analogies, or anecdotes to gain the attention of your audience and also include a 'preview' of your key supporting points. The conclusion should include a summary of your reasons and reemphasize the importance of your issue and the validity of your position.

2. *Pro-con paper or speech.* The purpose of this assignment is to explore the reality that issues are controversial because there is usually valid reasoning on both sides. In addition, when you complete this assignment, you will be a more experienced researcher and a more discerning thinker about the quality of reasons given to support conclusions. To complete this assignment, do the following:

a. Choose a controversial issue. For this assignment, it is best if you do not feel strongly about the issue because you need to be objective about the good reasons on both sides. However, do choose an issue that is interesting to you, so you are motivated to read about it.

b. Write your issue in question form, so you can clearly see the pro and con sides of the issue by answering yes or no to the question. For example, you might write: "Does secondhand smoke cause cancer?" Those who answer yes are on the "pro" side of this issue; those who say no are on the "con" side.

c. Find eight sources of research on your issue. Four should be pro and four should be con. The sources may be online articles; newspaper, journal, or magazine articles; books; transcripts of radio or television broadcasts in which experts testify; or personal interviews you conduct with an expert on the issue. (Some experts will give you their time, so don't hesitate to call for an interview.) A bibliography of these sources should be handed in with your finished product; use standard bibliographical form.

d. Study the research that you compile and choose three reasons for supporting the pro side of the issue and three reasons for supporting the con side. These reasons should be the best you can find for each side. Write out the reasons for each side, using evidence to support each reason.

e. Finally, take a position on the issue and state why you found the reasons for that position to be more credible. (You can see now why you should start off being as neutral as possible on this issue.) Acknowledge the strengths of the other side while explaining why you found your chosen side's position to be stronger. Conclude your essay or speech by commenting on what you learned in the process of studying both sides of an issue.

Films for Analysis and Discussion

It's hard to look at McDonald's the same way after seeing Morgan Spurlock's *Super Size Me* (2004, PG), a film that documents Spurlock's month-long journey of eating only what is on the McDonald's menu in order to explore the consequences on his health and to draw some generalizations about the connection between fast food and obesity. Note especially how Spurlock does research on himself; listen also for the expert opinions he hears. This film provides a good review of causal and statistical generalizations.

Similar Films and Classics

Waiting for Superman (2010, PG)

This controversial film looks at problems with the American educational system by contrasting a successful charter school with the surrounding public schools. Educational experts and policy makers are quoted to support the film's premises. Both supporters and critics of the film agree that the educational system is broken in many ways, but they see the major causes of the breakdown differently. To understand the controversy, read the commentaries from those who agree with its premise and those who disagree either before or after you watch the film.

Who Killed the Electric Car? (2006, PG)

This documentary looks at the forces pushing for and against the consumer adoption of the electric car. Note especially how the use of electric cars versus SUVs affects the environment, the dependence on foreign oil, consumers, and the automobile industry.

Thank You for Smoking (2005, R)

This film looks at how a lobbyist, Nick Naylor, tries to make the argument for the tobacco industry despite all of the evidence about the harmfulness of cigarette smoking. Note especially how Nick argues for his points against the preponderance of research and reason.

6

Reasoning Errors

*I Know What I Think—
Don't Confuse Me with Facts.*

A critical thinker recognizes errors in reasoning.

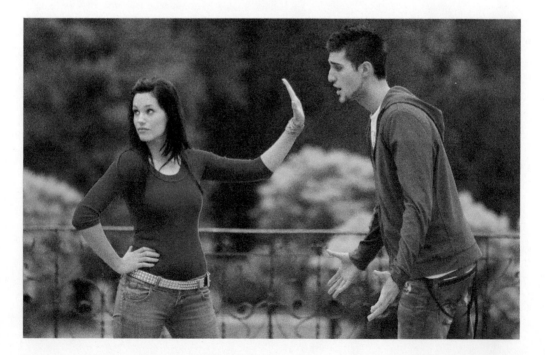

A critical thinker avoids errors in reasoning that are harmful to discussion and decision making.

THIS CHAPTER WILL COVER

- Fallacies (errors in reasoning) in the form of reasons that do not provide adequate support for conclusions
- Fallacies in the form of statements that lead listeners away from the real issue
- Useful approaches for handling fallacies

📖—[Read on **mythinkinglab.com**

((•—[Listen on **mythinkinglab.com**

U nderstanding an argument is a complex process, as we have seen. We need to know what someone is concluding (claiming) about a particular issue or problem and the reasons for his or her position. And we need to assess the strength of an argument by considering the quality of evidence used to support a conclusion.

When we look at an individual's support for his or her beliefs, we may perceive that something doesn't make sense, but we may not have words for whatever seems faulty in the reasoning. This chapter will cover some terms that are used to characterize typical errors in reasoning. These errors occur so often that they have acquired a name of their own: **fallacies.**

Keep in mind, as you read this chapter, that the fallacies discussed are simply labels given to faulty reasoning. Don't be concerned about labeling every faulty reason perfectly. Instead, use this discussion of fallacies as a general tool to help you analyze the quality of reasons given for a conclusion. Knowing common fallacies can help you to avoid using them in your own arguments and to refute faulty reasoning in the arguments of others.

Fallacies can be categorized as (1) reasons that seem logical but don't adequately support the conclusion or (2) statements that distract listeners from the real issue.

fallacies Errors in reasoning. Fallacies can be seen as (1) reasons that seem logical but don't necessarily support the conclusion or (2) statements that distract listeners from the real issue.

Inadequate Reasons as Fallacies

Reasons that sound good and logical but do not provide adequate support for the conclusion are the first fallacies to consider. These are tricky because they use the form of good reasoning, but they don't have real substance. Whether used unconsciously or deliberately, inadequate reasons cannot be used as evidence to prove conclusions.

The major categories for insufficient reasons are faulty analogies, false cause, slippery slope, straw man, hasty conclusion, false dilemma, and begging the question.

Faulty Analogies

As we discussed in Chapter 5, analogies can be legitimately used to create inductive strength for an argument. If we can show that an idea or policy has been useful in some instances, we can generalize that it will be useful in another, similar situation.

Because analogies are used commonly, we must be careful not to accept them uncritically. The key to an accurate analogy is that *the two things being compared are similar in all significant aspects*. If there are significant differences between the items being compared, then we have a **faulty analogy.**

faulty analogy   Comparison of one situation or idea to another that disregards significant differences that make the comparison invalid.

Sometimes the faulty comparison is easy for a critical thinker to see. Let's look at a typical use of analogy in advertising, that of comparing a product to an experience:

> *Springsoft fabric softener smells great. It's like hanging your clothes out in the fresh air.*

Similarities between a fabric softener and hanging clothing in the fresh air are that both are used while getting clothes dry and both presumably smell good.

Differences can be noted as follows:

Springsoft	Fresh Air
Smell induced by chemicals	Smell from fresh air
Recurrent cost involved	One-time clothesline cost
Quick when used with dryer	Time consuming

You can see that comparing *Springsoft* with fresh air is not accurate in all of the dimensions that are significant to a consumer. It would be more accurate to ask consumers to buy *Springsoft* because it has a nice fragrance and makes clothes feel softer. So why don't advertisers just state the facts?

Advertisers, politicians, salespeople, lawyers, teachers, and other advocates usually realize that a powerful picture is worth more than a detailed argument. A swim instructor may know that asking children to put their arms out straight is more effective when she adds, "like Superman does." Campaign managers realize that a powerful negative image leveled against an opposing candidate may have greater impact than a reasoned case against him. Advertisers reason that parents who want to believe that they are doing the best for their children may respond to the idea of infusing fresh air and sunshine into their clothes, especially when the fresh air and sunshine come in an easy-to-use product.

Faulty analogies occur when we compare one situation or idea to another and disregard significant differences that make the comparison invalid. For example, to compare plans for overcoming racism in the United States to plans that work for the Finnish people would be fallacious: Finland does not have racial diversity similar to the United States. Similarly, someone might suggest that we look at the low rate of theft in some countries and adopt a comparable prevention plan. The problem is that some countries have punishments that are not likely to be adopted by North American voters and legislators, such as the removal of a hand for stealing.

People may use faulty analogies to excuse their actions. One example occurred when 78 students at Dartmouth College were charged with cheating. While discussing the upcoming homework, their professor had clicked on a website that contained the answers. The professor had promised that he would secure the site, but he forgot to do so, and these students presumably got their answers directly off the

Web. In an article in the *Boston Globe,* writer David Abel comments on how the students used faulty analogies to justify their actions:

> Some of the students compared their predicament to a professor leaving the answers to an exam on a classroom blackboard. Others likened it to a professor leaving the answers in an unlocked desk drawer. Either way, the two analogies reflect an increasing concern among educators ranging from elementary teachers to Ivy League professors: Cheating is getting a lot easier.
>
> . . . For Scot Drysdale, the chairman of Dartmouth's Computer Science department, the past few weeks have been tense, with a groundswell of students countering the cheating charges, claiming the professor set them up.
>
> But Drysdale never bought into the copying-off-the-blackboard analogy. In his view, despite the ease of clicking onto a Web site, some effort, how-ever minimal, was necessary to find the answers, kind of like opening a desk drawer.
>
> "Sure it was easy," he said. "But they still had to go looking for it. That's the point."[1]

Faulty analogies are used frequently when social issues are discussed. You might hear someone claim there is no problem with violence on television or in movies. The person taking this position might say, "I watched television shows all my life and I turned out just fine." The problem with this reasoning is that the quantity of programs and the standards for violent content are different from the programming of 20 or 30 years ago. The speaker may or may not be right about the effect of televised violence, but this comparison does nothing to prove his or her point.

Faulty analogies are often accompanied by a limited understanding of significant changes that make our current world different from the world of previous generations.

We also encounter faulty analogies in personal relationships when one person gives advice to another. For example, if a grandparent tells you that he or she used to walk five miles in the snow to get to school, suggesting that you or your children should do the same, you would have to consider the difficulty of implementing this plan in a culture where parents are afraid to let their children even play in the front yard without supervision.

Or let's say a friend of yours is advising you about how to prepare for a speech you have to give for a class. He or she might say, "Just relax and don't prepare too many notes. That's what I did, and I got an A." That method may work for your friend but may be totally inappropriate for you; you may be the kind of person (like most of us) who needs to have good notes and to practice a speech before giving it to a class.

A common problem with people who give advice is their assumption that what worked for them will work for you—a classic case of faulty analogy.

When you see someone supporting a position by comparing one idea, situation, or plan to another, stop and evaluate whether the comparison is valid. If it is, you have a good analogy and a good reason to listen to the speaker. If it is not a valid comparison in some important way, then you have a faulty analogy. (See Exercise 6.2, pages 257–258.)

---

[1] David Abel, "Peek Performance: Does the Internet Create More Cheaters, or More Skillful Ones?" *Boston Globe,* March 19, 2000, p. C-1.

> # Reminder
>
> A faulty analogy follows this format:
>
> 1. A is being compared to B. There are some points of similarity between A and B.
> 2. However, the differences between A and B are strong enough to make the comparison invalid. In everyday language, a faulty analogy is "like comparing apples to oranges."
>
> **Critical thinking response:** Point out the significant differences that make the comparison between A and B too weak to use as support for the argument.
>
> ✳ Explore on **mythinkinglab.com**

False Cause: Post Hoc Ergo Propter Hoc

false cause (post hoc ergo propter hoc) A fallacy that occurs when there is no real proof that one event caused another event; there is only evidence that one event came after another event.

False cause, also called **post hoc ergo propter hoc** (post hoc for short), is an interesting fallacy that is committed frequently in reasoning about personal, social, and political issues. The Latin translates to "after this, therefore because of this" and refers to the practice of stating that because one event followed another, the first event caused the second event. As we discussed in Chapter 4, cause-effect reasoning is sometimes relevant and valid; it is used extensively in psychology (a person may have a fear of abandonment because he or she was abandoned as a child), in history (Jewish people became merchants in parts of Europe because they were not allowed to purchase land), in business (sales increased after a new advertising campaign), in medicine (you are tired and run down because of low blood sugar), in politics (she had 78 percent of the votes and lost 50 percent after the last-minute smear campaign by her opponent), and in economics (the economy began to recover when interest rates were lowered).

In all these cases, research and reasoning could prove one event came after another and that, in all probability, the first event was a cause of the second event. The fallacy of post hoc occurs when there is no real proof that one event *caused* another event; there is only evidence that one event came *after* another event. **Correlation,** a close connection between two events, is not the same as **causation.** With no evidence of causation, we may be prone to superstition.

correlation A relationship or connection between two objects or events. Noting a correlation is sometimes the first step in exploring causation, but it does not equal causation.

Stevie Wonder's classic song "Superstition" refers to the superstitious beliefs that bad luck is caused by people walking under ladders or breaking mirrors. Through his lyrics, Stevie warns his listeners that superstitions reflect wrong thinking and create needless suffering. The same can be said for positive superstitions that keep people bonded to unproven beliefs, such as the notion that a lucky penny or rabbit's foot brings good fortune or success. Superstitions are common to many cultures and professions. Actors use the phrase "break a leg" because of the superstition that saying "good luck" will bring bad luck. Superstitions are also connected to sports teams; after the Boston Red Sox, an outstanding team with many national titles, sold Babe Ruth to the New York Yankees in 1919, they experienced a losing streak that lasted until 2004. The inability to win a World Series championship was attributed to the "Curse of the Bambino."

causation A connection between two events in which it is established that one event caused the other.

Superstition is the clearest example of false cause. Superstitious thinking is uncritical thinking. A superstitious person may reason fallaciously, "I got fired because I walked under that ladder yesterday" or "The reason I failed the test is that I didn't forward the 'good luck' email that was sent to me last week." What's especially dangerous about superstitious thinking is that if a person really *believes* he is somehow "cursed," he may *act* as if he is cursed and make the curse come true because of his expectations.

However, the post hoc fallacy is often more subtle than mere superstition; it consists of reasons that are not supported by adequate evidence. For example, politicians are fond of blaming budget deficits and unemployment rates on their predecessors ("I didn't get us into this mess—the previous administration did"). The problem is that this reasoning ignores the more complicated factors that need to be understood in order to change the current situation for the better. The blaming process is often at the root of a post hoc fallacy, and it short circuits constructive action that could alleviate a problem.

Here are some examples of post hoc fallacies based on shifting the blame and therefore not taking responsibility:

> "The reason our team lost is because we weren't playing at home."

> "I failed the class because the teacher hated me."

> "I saw how you put your television set in the car. The reason it doesn't work is that it was poorly placed in your car after you left our repair shop."

> "I ate three pieces of pie at Joanne's house because I didn't want to hurt her mother's feelings."

> "I can't find my soccer ball because a large green and brown monster came and ate it while I was sleeping." (Small children also use fallacies.)

Although many post hoc fallacies are based on blame and rationalization, some are based on a lack of information to substantiate a valid reason—in other words, sometimes we just don't know the real cause of a particular problem.

In our frustrated attempts to find reasons and therefore solutions or explanations for situations, we may rush to assign blame without fair and careful analysis. Then our investigations are weakened because we may be tempted to address surface and not deeper causes for problems, and we may look for singular rather than multiple causes.

For example, if we say that homelessness is usually the result of lack of confidence in the ability to find work and successfully manage work (false cause in many cases), then we look for a solution to fit the false cause. So homeless people are given motivational lectures and training. Some individuals may be helped by this approach, but we still have the basic problem of homelessness. Some of the homeless may be mentally unfit for employment or seminars; some may be displaced homemakers who would rather be in the parks with their children than shuffled off to training; some may be fully equipped to work, but lack a mailing address and phone number that would help employers contact them; some may be perfectly happy in a homeless condition; and some may welcome job training but find it difficult to get hired. Problems are complex, and a single cause doesn't address them accurately. We would do better to get at the root and diverse causes of social problems, rather than try to find quick fixes to what may not be the complete problem. (See Exercise 6.3, page 258.)

Reminder

False cause follows this format:

1. A occurs before B or B occurs after A.
2. With no other evidence than the fact that A occurred before B or B occurred after A, it is concluded that A caused B.

Critical thinking response: Point out that the correlation between A and B does not confirm a causal link between them. Give examples of other factors that could have caused B.

✳ Explore on **mythinkinglab.com**

The Slippery Slope

slippery slope A fallacy that occurs when serious consequences of a potential action or policy are predicted and not substantiated by evidence.

Slippery slope refers to the domino effect. If you push one domino in a pattern, then all the others will fall. A slippery slope argument states that if one event occurs, then others will follow, usually in an inevitable and uncontrollable way. Any domino effect argument involves a prediction about the future and is therefore based on speculation. Still, this form of reasoning can be valid, even when opponents call it a slippery slope, if the interpretations are soundly based on existing facts and reasonable probabilities. For example, in the 1970s, people used to discuss the possibility of a domino effect in Southeast Asia; they believed that when the United States left Vietnam, then not only Vietnam but also Cambodia would fall to the communists. This concern proved to be valid.

When school-based health clinics were introduced, some parents complained that this was the first step in birth control devices being distributed by schools. This argument, which was dismissed as a slippery slope argument, did prove to be valid. Many school-based health clinics now offer birth control and reproductive counseling.

There are also cases in which an individual is refused a reasonable privilege because it would probably call for the privilege to be extended to too many others. For example, let's say you are a day late paying your auto registration. The clerk would probably still have to charge you a penalty because "If I make an exception for you, I would need to make an exception for everyone."

The slippery slope fallacy occurs when undesirable consequences of a single act are predicted and not substantiated by evidence. For example, many people fight the idea of making tobacco advertisements illegal despite overwhelming evidence concerning the harmfulness of this substance. The slippery slope argument given is that if cigarette advertising is made illegal because tobacco harms people, then pretty soon advertising for eggs and milk would be curtailed because of the cholesterol content of these products.

The problem with this argument is that eggs and milk are not analogous to cigarettes; although there is a high cholesterol content in these products, they are also extremely nutritious in other ways, whereas no nutritional or health value has been found for cigarettes. Therefore, it's not likely that advertisements for eggs or other healthy products would be disallowed just because tobacco ads would be.

Another example of the use of the slippery slope fallacy concerns Gregory K., a severely abused child in Florida who successfully sued to "divorce" his parents so that he could live with his foster family, who wanted to adopt him. The boy's parents were divorced, the father was an abusive alcoholic, and the mother was so neglectful of the child that he had been placed in foster homes for several years. Lawyers for the boy feared for his life should he return to this environment. Lawyers for the state social workers, however, claimed that allowing a boy in this circumstance to sue his parents could lead to other children suing to leave their parents because they were denied the latest style of shoes or video games. As one writer stated, revealing the fallacious slippery slope nature of this argument:

> If the lawyers really believe that, it doesn't say much for their own profession. Are there attorneys who would handle some brat's Ninja Turtle—deprivation case? Not likely, especially if the kid didn't have a fat retainer fee in his piggy bank. And are the lawyers saying there are judges who would take a frivolous suit seriously, and not toss it out as nonsense?
>
> No, if the Florida boy wins his case what we'll probably see are other suits filed by kids who will be saying that they have had it with parents who are dope heads, drunks, sadists; parents who don't know how to take care of children and are unwilling or incapable of learning. And that they've had it with social service agencies that don't provide real social services."[2]

In an interview about cloning, Margaret McLean, director of Biotechnology and Health Care Ethics at the Markkula Center for Applied Ethics at Santa Clara University, talked about how the public fears a slippery slope in the potential applications of cloning technology:

> People reacted when nuclear transfer technology produced [the cloned sheep] Dolly. This birth announcement was quite unexpected. There were fears that we'd do such things as clone babies to harvest their organs. But we don't do these kinds of things now. Things like this—where we think of life merely as a means to an end—would be leaps off the slippery slope and into the abyss.[3]

There are also examples in personal communication in which the slippery slope fallacy occurs. If you ask for a day off work to take your sick dog to the vet and your employer says, "I can't give you the day off because then everyone would want the day off," you have probably encountered this fallacy. Not everyone is going to want the day off, and most people would not take advantage of your situation to ask for similar time off. Your need for time off is not based on negligence (as is the case with people who pay bills late and are penalized); your need is based on an emergency.

[2] Mike Royko, "When Mother and Father Don't Know Best," *This World,* May 3, 1992, p. 4.
[3] Charan Sue Wollard, "Margaret McLean," *San Jose Mercury News,* March 5, 2000, p. 7.

Reminder

The slippery slope follows this format:

1. Someone proposes an idea or plan of action.
2. Someone else predicts that implementation of the idea or action would create a series of undesirable, and even catastrophic, consequences. No solid evidence is given to support this prediction.

Critical thinking response: Remind the speaker or audience that predictions about the future are always speculative and that there is no compelling evidence that the predicted dire consequences would take place if the idea or plan were implemented.

✳ Explore on **mythinkinglab.com**

Straw Man

straw man A fallacy in which an opponent's argument is distorted or exaggerated and then more easily attacked.

Straw man is a clever and subtle, but quite common, way of distorting and then attacking an opponent's argument. Someone using the straw man technique will take his or her opponent's claims and exaggerate or distort them. He or she then proceeds to destroy this newly created, false, more easily attacked argument (the weaker, easily defeated "straw" man). It is as if a boxer is in the ring with a real, living opponent and an opponent made of straw. The boxer knocks out the straw opponent and declares victory, while the real opponent still remains untouched.

For example, in advocating for gun control of semiautomatic weapons, a debater might claim, "I believe that AK47s should be outlawed—no one needs that level of firepower to be protected." A fair response would be to address whether or not AK47s have a legitimate use and then to discuss that legitimate use. A speaker who uses the straw man argument might instead respond as follows: "As we can see, my opponent is against the use of firearms for self-protection—and so she would allow criminals to possess firearms and deny their use by law-abiding citizens." The argument has been extended to a discussion of whether *any* firearms can be owned by citizens. If the speaker can convince his audience that his opponent would like to ban all firearms from private citizens, he has a much stronger rebuttal. The problem is that the issue is confined to AK47s, and so his extended straw man argument only confuses the debate.

Philosopher Gary N. Curtis writes about a common straw man called "extreme man":

> Extreme positions are more difficult to defend because they make fewer allowances for exceptions, or counter-examples. Consider the statement forms:
>
> • All P are Q.
> • Most P are Q.
> • Many P are Q.
> • Some P are Q.
> • Some P are not Q.
> • Many P are not Q.
> • Most P are not Q.
> • No P are Q.

The extremes are "All P are Q" and "No P are Q." These are easiest to refute, since all it takes is a single counter-example to refute a universal proposition.[4]

In other words, when we take a reasonable, moderate, arguable position of another person and make it sound like an extreme position, we can more easily refute the extreme position. In most social and political issues, there are moderate and extreme positions. Few people are at the extreme end of the spectrum, with no exceptions to their positions. For example, on the question of immigration, the extreme positions would be the complete ending of new immigration on one end and allowing immigration with no restrictions at all on the other end. Consider the following exchange that starts out as a reasonable discussion:

Paul: We can't keep allowing illegal aliens to settle here without going through the process that other immigrants have gone through. The increase in population is draining our state's resources.

Rochelle: But the immigrants take the jobs that citizens won't take—they pay sales tax and they strengthen the economy.

Paul: So you're saying just open the borders completely and let everyone have free health care and free education.

Rochelle: I didn't say that. But it sounds like you don't want to let any new people come to this country. How selfish can you get?

Can you see that Paul and Rochelle started off with moderate positions but then characterized each other's position at the extremes, the "all" or "none" positions. This happens frequently in communication on an issue about which people are passionate. Curtis states that using this fallacy creates not only a "straw man," but also a "straw demon" out of the other person's argument.

Let's look at some other examples of straw man. Notice how the second speaker changes the issue into one that is easier to refute than the real issue under discussion.

Angela: I think we should wait until we've graduated and have jobs before we get married.

Giorgio: So having tons of money is more important to you than our being together. How can you be so materialistic?

Choral director: I'd like to introduce some contemporary music into our concerts.

Member of choir: So you want to throw out hundreds of years of classical music just to appease a new audience! That's a terrible idea.

Often a straw man is used to argue against a restriction deemed important to a particular group. For example, if a bookstore decides to sell only "family-friendly" books, it may be accused of censorship or of banning books rather than making a free market choice to restrict what it sells. Similarly, a radio station may decide against playing certain music that does not appeal to its intended audience; the station manager may be accused of censoring that music, when, in fact, she has not prevented people from buying the music or listening to it on another station.

The effect of a straw man can be to confuse the issue and the audience. A critical thinker combats this fallacy by pointing to the limits of the original issue and showing how they have been extended to an entirely different issue.

[4] Gary N. Curtis, "Logical Fallacies: The Fallacy Files," www.fallacyfiles.org.

Hasty Conclusions

Labels are devices for saving talkative persons the trouble of thinking.

John Morley, "Carlyle," *Critical Miscellanies*
(1871–1908)

hasty conclusion   A fallacy in which a generalization is drawn from a small and thus inadequate sample of information.

When we want to know the answer to a serious problem or event, we may be tempted to draw a **hasty conclusion,** or hasty generalization—that is, to make a claim based on insufficient information. In Chapters 4 and 5, we looked at polls and controlled studies that did not provide good evidence because conclusions were based on a sample of evidence that was too small or that was not representative of a target population. When a pollster does not study a sufficient number of voters, she cannot draw a valid conclusion about election results. Similarly, when a researcher makes claims about how a drug will affect *all* people based on a small study of college students, he is drawing a hasty conclusion.

Hasty conclusions are encountered when people take a stand or make a claim based on limited evidence. When someone defends a position without adequate support for that position, faulty reasoning has occurred; we may say that the person is "jumping to conclusions." Professionals usually strive to be careful about their judgments—reporters make sure that their sources are reliable, doctors perform tests before they diagnose a serious condition, and police officers gather sufficient evidence before making an arrest. Sometimes, however, there is a "rush to judgment," as was the case when a high school student was arrested and accused of stabbing another youth; the arrest was based on his having a black sweatshirt (witnesses attested the perpetrator wore a black sweatshirt with a hood) in his car. Before the young man was cleared by four alibi witnesses who testified that he was at a classmate's home working on a school project, his name was released to the media, and he was confined to jail and reported to be the prime suspect.

One citizen who was disturbed by the rush to judgment in this incident posted an editorial with the title "Forever Changed":

> An innocent family has been forever changed due to what Pleasant Hill police Lt. Enea has referred to as "unfortunate." How can those sworn to serve and protect Anthony Freitas and our entire community call jailing an innocent high school student, without even checking out his alibis, "unfortunate"?

Was it his "misfortune" to own a black sweatshirt (which had no hood or pockets)? Was it his "misfortune" to have a job that required the use of a box-cutting tool?

Have the police reports been made public record? We have to wonder what process was used in identifying Anthony as a suspect (while the true perpetrator was roaming free).

Why did it take Pleasant Hill investigators six days to speak with the fourth adult alibi? How do we prevent this "misfortune" from happening to our children? The Freitas family has incurred considerable financial, as well as mental, "misfortune." Will there be restitution?

The entire Pleasant Hill community should seek answers or throw out their black sweatshirts.[5]

We may also jump to conclusions in our personal lives when we hear a few facts or make a few observations and then make a sweeping generalization. For example, someone may be treated poorly by a few people in an organization and jump to the conclusion that all people in that organization are rude. Or someone may have spoken to a Republican who has no sympathy for the unemployed and jump to the conclusion that all Republicans are cold and heartless.

Drawing generalizations on a small sample of information is the basis of prejudice. When we are prejudiced, we stereotype and prejudge people and situations instead of taking the responsibility for considering the realities of each circumstance. The antidote to prejudice is more information and experience, but we sometimes fail to get more information; we draw hasty conclusions because it is the simplest route to take. It's easier to just take someone's word for it when he or she says "you can't trust that company" or "this candidate doesn't care about the environment" than it is to do our own research. Other times, we are more comfortable living with our uncritical assumptions because they have become a part of our thinking patterns: If we stereotype people and situations, then we assume we know what to expect from them.

If we believe that only Republicans or Democrats or Independents can govern best, then we know whom to vote for without having to think about individual qualifications. A teacher may classify students as good, mediocre, or poor based on a few assignments, rather than giving them the chance to succeed over time. You can see how uncritical interpretations can have lasting negative effects for both individuals and society.

One significant type of hasty conclusion is called the **self-fulfilling prophecy.** When someone makes a self-fulfilling prophecy, he or she starts with an unproven conclusion, such as, "I'm no good in math," and then acts as if this conclusion is a fact (he or she doesn't bother to study math and fails the tests), proving the assertion that he or she is poor in math.

self-fulfilling prophecy
A process whereby an expectation becomes a reality.

There are two types of self-fulfilling prophecies—those that other people make about us and those we make about others or ourselves. If you think back to labels given to you by teachers, peers, or parents in early years, you may find that they have become fulfilled in your life.

For example, if you were told that you were going to do well in sports, you probably assumed that was true and had the confidence to succeed; on the other hand, if an art teacher told you that you were a terrible artist, you probably

[5] Hector Merino, "Forever Changed," *Contra Costa Times,* January 5, 2007.

accepted this evaluation and gave up on art. You assumed that the conclusion was true and then acted as if it were true. Finally it *became* true.

Examples

"You'll never be able to learn geometry."

"I always strike out."

"He's a really selfish guy."

"I'll never learn to swim."

"You can't talk to those punks."

"That textbook is too hard to understand."

"People from that neighborhood are so rude."

The self-fulfilling prophecy has been operative on a societal level in forms such as bank runs and escalating tensions between ethnic and political groups. On personal levels, self-fulfilling prophecies are responsible for limitations we place on ourselves and our abilities.

As critical thinkers, we are responsible for knowing if personal or group limitations are the results of careless predictions. Then we are empowered to change our attitudes and our actions. (See Exercises 6.4 and 6.5 on pages 258–259.)

Reminder

A hasty conclusion follows this format:

A generalization is made on a sample that is too small or not broad enough to be representative of all of the elements of the target population, *or*

1. A limited number of observations are made about A (A may represent a group or an individual).

2. A sweeping generalization about A is drawn from these limited observations.

Critical thinking response: Check the amount and quality of evidence before making or accepting a conclusion.

✳ Explore on **mythinkinglab.com**

The False Dilemma

false dilemma (either-or fallacy)
An error in reasoning that occurs when one polarizes a situation by presenting only two alternatives, at two extremes of the spectrum of possibilities.

Human cloning: Will it be a lifesaving scientific advance, like penicillin? Or will it prove to be a horrible mistake that unleashes untold devastation upon humanity, like the accordion?[6]

Another error in reasoning, common in both personal and political communication, is the **false dilemma** or the **either-or fallacy**. When someone makes this error, he or she polarizes a situation by presenting only two alternatives, at extreme ends

---

[6] Dave Barry, "No Clowning, Here's Your Personal Cloning Manual; Copies Available," *Miami Herald*, December 30, 2001.

of the spectrum of possibilities. Any other reasonable possibilities besides these two extremes are left out of the statement, and the careless listener may believe that the issue is limited to the two choices given.

Examples

"Do you want four more years of overspending and poor priorities or do you want four years of prosperity and sensible spending?" (*Note:* You may be able to prove that the incumbent candidate can be fairly criticized on his or her spending priorities, but does that mean that the only alternative is your new candidate or that the new candidate will be as flawless as is implied?)

"Do you want to give your family the same, boring potatoes for dinner tonight, or do you want to give them the exciting taste of Instant Stuffing?"

"Sure, you can go ahead and date Jesse and end up with a broken heart and bad memories; but wouldn't it be better to go out with me, since I know how to treat you right and show you a good time?"

"If you don't go to college and make something of yourself, you'll end up as an unhappy street person."

Polarization leads a listener away from a reasonable consideration of the complex problems involved in most decision-making situations and presents one conclusion as perfect while the other is seen as disastrous.

Example

My boyfriend used false dilemma when it was time to decide what to do during the weekends. I am a dance lover and I always tried to convince him to go dancing, but he always polarized the situation. He used to say to me: "Do you prefer to go to a crowded place where there is too much noise, people cannot talk because of the loud music, and we would sweat a lot, or would you prefer to go to a nicer place where we can relax, enjoy a delicious meal, and talk without shouting?"

The false dilemma can be a dangerous fallacy because it leads us to simplistic solutions and encourages us to give our allegiance to a person or idea without considering a solution that would more fully address complex problems.

In an interview in the *Atlantic Monthly,* Barbara Dafoe Whitehead points out the false dilemma that her interviewer proposes when he asks her about the cause of increasing problems in children:

> Journalists Caryl Rivers and Judith Stacey contend that it's poverty, not family structure, that is at the root of many children's problems. How do you respond?
>
> "Poverty is terrible for children, and it causes tremendous hardship. I share with Rivers and Stacey the view that when twenty-two percent of American children are in poverty, there is a serious problem that must be addressed. I don't dispute their contention that poverty is hard on kids and at the root of many children's problems. But it is not an either-or proposition. There is a well-worn debate that pits family structure changes against economic changes and says that one is the reason for children's problems. There's evidence that points in both directions.

Family structure causes poverty in some cases and poverty causes families to break down. To me it's an unnecessarily polarized debate and one that I'm not going to enter."[7]

Sociologist Deborah Tannen also confronts the tendency to reduce social problems to a false dilemma. She writes the following in her book *The Argument Culture:*

> I suggest that finding a solution to any major question or issue is virtually impossible when everything is defined in extremes. Our blind devotion to this approach will always get us into trouble, because most people are usually in the middle, and most issues have many sides.[8]

Tannen suggests that in argumentation we would benefit by

> experimenting . . . with formats other than debate for framing the exchange of ideas. The change might be as simple as introducing a plural form. Instead of asking, "What's the other side?" we might ask instead, "What are the other sides?" Instead of insisting on hearing "both sides," we might insist on hearing "all sides."[9]

The error of false dilemma is easy to make for two reasons:

- We like to think solutions are clear-cut and simple; a simple solution saves us time and effort in understanding all the complexities of a situation.
- Our language encourages polarized thinking by including few words to describe a middle ground between extremes. Look at this list:

Beautiful . . . . Ugly
Strong . . . . Weak
Extroverted . . . . Introverted
Brave . . . . Cowardly
Happy . . . . Sad

Although we have words that describe the extremes (poles) of a state of being, we have few words describing a middle ground. To put yourself in the middle of these adjectives, you have to say "sort of happy," "somewhat happy," "average," or "medium."

Since our language is polarized, our thinking tends to be polarized if we don't make the effort to be more accurate. In our statistically oriented culture, we tend to use numbers to let us know where things stand on a polarized continuum. We might say "On a scale of 1 to 10, how happy are you with our plan?" or "On a scale of 1 to 10, how close are we to closing this deal?" We use numbers to fill in where words are lacking in order to express ourselves more accurately.

As a critical thinker, you can tell someone who is creating a false dilemma that you believe the situation to be more complex than it is being described. You can then draw attention back to the issues, by asking questions such as "What specific changes does your candidate propose to make if she is elected?" or "What is so good about Instant Stuffing?"

[7] Barbara Defoe Whitehead, "What We Owe," *The Atlantic Monthly,* February 1997.
[8] Deborah Tannen, *The Argument Culture* (New York: Ballantine, Random House, 1999), p. 352
[9] Ibid., p. 26.

Reminder

A false dilemma follows this format:

1. Someone claims that there are only two polarized explanations of a problem, two polarized solutions to a problem, or two polarized choices to be made.

2. Other reasons for a problem or possible solutions or choices are dismissed, often with a warning of dire consequences "unless the best alternative is chosen."

Critical thinking response: Point out the polarization of the issue and ask the speaker for other choices in between two extremes. Focus on the complexity of the issue; also point out the fact that no single candidate or plan is without flaws.

✴ Explore on **mythinkinglab.com**

Begging the Question

The fallacy of **begging the question** is one of the more subtle ways a speaker or writer attempts to argue for his or her position. Begging the question takes place in two ways:

1. The speaker makes a claim and then asks you to prove that his or her claim is not correct. Instead of giving reasons for a conclusion, the speaker places the burden of proof on the listener or on the person being debated. For example:

   "How do you know I can't do psychic surgery?"

   "Show me that space aliens don't exist!"

   "Why do you think they call it Up Close?"

   "Why wouldn't you call 1–800-Dentist to get the best professional care?"

   "Isn't it worth $16 a month to protect your family with $250,000 worth of life insurance?"

   Don't be trapped into proving someone else's conclusion. It's hard enough to prove your own!

2. The second way a person can beg the question is by building on an unproven assumption in his or her argument as if it were a given fact. The classic example is "Have you stopped beating your wife?" This question assumes the husband has beaten his wife. Notice how there is no way to answer this question with a "yes" or "no" without confirming that the speaker's assumption is correct. This form of begging the question has also been called a *loaded question* because the question is "loaded" with at least one—and sometimes several—questionable assumptions.

Other Examples

"Why are you always so defensive?"

"How can you vote for a dump site that is going to destroy the environment?"

"Why are you supporting a team that is going to lose the Super Bowl?"

begging the question
A fallacy that occurs when a speaker or writer assumes what needs to be proven.

Loaded questions are used in surveys to get a desired response, and they are also used to "close" sales, as in the following examples:

Survey question: "Do you want to continue supporting a candidate who only cares about pleasing special interest groups?"

Sales question: "Do you want to charge that now or put it on layaway?" (This question presumes that the customer is planning to buy the item.)

Begging the question does not always mean that a question is asked. People can beg the question when they give reasons to support their conclusions without giving evidence for these reasons. For example, a speaker might say:

Since legalizing drugs would reduce the crime rate, we have to consider where our legislative priorities are.

Can you see that the speaker here has made the assumption (interpretation, inference, guess) that the crime rate would be reduced if drugs are legalized and then used that assumption to support his conclusion? It could be that the legalization of drugs would reduce crime, but that possibility has to be supported with evidence before it can be used as a reason.

Begging the question is also called circular reasoning, as in the following example:

If it's on television, it has to be a good show, because only good shows get on television.

The speaker in this example is using the assumption that only good shows get on television as proof that a particular show is good. No evidence has been offered to support the assumption that only good shows get on television.

Reminder

Begging the question follows this format:

1. A conclusion is claimed to be true.
2. The reasons (premises) given for the conclusion have not been proven by the speaker or writer; instead, the truth of the reasons is assumed by the speaker or writer.
3. Sometimes, the listener is challenged to prove that the conclusion is not true.

Critical thinking response: Instead of accepting an unproven assertion or trying to answer a question that is based on an unproven assumption, ask the speaker for the evidence that supports his or her claim.

✳ Explore on **mythinkinglab.com**

Skill

Recognize when reasons given to justify a conclusion are not sufficient.

Fallacies That Mislead

To this point, we have examined errors that occur when the reasons given for a particular conclusion do not adequately support the conclusion. The second category of fallacies is characterized by reasons that lead the listener away from the real or primary issue. Common examples of this type of fallacy are red herrings, ad hominem, two wrongs make a right, ad populum, appeal to tradition, appeal to pity, and equivocation.

The Red Herring

The **red herring** fallacy gets its name from an old practice of drawing a herring—a smoked fish—across a trail to distract hunting dogs from following a scent. In this manner, the hounds were led away from their prey; this technique was used by criminals who didn't want to be found and had access to smoked fish. Similarly, when someone can distract your attention by getting you on the defensive about a different issue than the one under discussion, that person has taken you off track of the real, or original, issue.

Children are particularly skillful at using red herrings; it's one of their best defense mechanisms against parental demands.

red herring A fallacy in which reasons offered to support conclusions lead the listener away from the issue under consideration.

Examples

Mother: Get that sharp stick out of here!
Child: That's not a stick. It's a laser beam. I need it to perform surgery on some space aliens.

Father: Joey, it's time to brush your teeth and get in bed.
Joey: You didn't tell that to Suzy.
Father: (getting off track) Suzy's older than you.
Joey: But I'm taller than she is.

If this child is successful, he will have gained extra time, and he might even be able to stall long enough for his parent to forget what time it is.

What a child does purely in the pursuit of having his or her way, he or she may learn to do as an adult in defense of a larger cause.

Example

When Reform Party founder H. Ross Perot was running for president of the United States, he was questioned at a conference of newspaper editors. *Philadelphia Inquirer* columnist Acel Moore wanted specific answers about Perot's proposals concerning the drug problem in the United States.

Acel Moore: Let this audience know. I haven't heard it.
Mr. Perot: Do we have to be rude and adversarial? Can't we just talk?
Mr. Moore: If you're going to be a candidate for the President of the United States, I think you should have to go through that process. And part of the process is being asked questions of a very specific nature, and coming forth with some responses.[10]

---

[10] Ted Koppel, "The Unknown Ross Perot," *Nightline*, April 23, 1992.

Red herrings are used often in politics because there are many topics politicians may not wish to discuss. They may not have knowledge of the topic, or they may be unprepared to answer difficult questions about it because by taking a stand, they are sure to alienate or anger some part of their electorate. You can often encounter red herrings in political interviews and press conferences.

Examples

Interviewer: Your position on immigration has been confusing to some people. Can you clarify your position on giving driver's licenses to undocumented immigrants?

Politician: Immigrants are valuable members of our society. We're a country founded on immigrants. As a matter of fact, my family immigrated here only a few years before I was born.

Reporter: Mr. Secretary, why won't the president admit that he wrote those memos with his signature on them?

Secretary: Why are you reporters always attacking this president and defending his opponents?

Reporter: Senator, are you planning to run for president again?

Senator: I am very happy working as a senator and accomplishing many valuable goals for our nation. This has been a very productive session of Congress.

If the politician can get the interviewer to turn the discussion to his own experience as an immigrant, he will have avoided answering a question that he doesn't want to answer. If the secretary can get the reporters to defend themselves, they will have been led away from the issue of whether the president wrote the memos. If the senator can change the subject and focus on her current accomplishments, she has sidestepped the reporter's question while increasing her own current credibility at the same time. People use red herrings to move the dialogue away from an issue that is uncomfortable for them to a different issue that can be more easily discussed.

People also use red herrings to defend against a reasonable criticism:

Brielle: I was upset when you didn't come to my game Friday.

Manu: I guess that makes me the worst friend ever and that's just one more reason why you don't like me.

Carlos: I can't believe you "forgot" to tell me that you put a dent in my car yesterday.

Kevin: You care more about that car than about your friends. You're always so concerned about that car.

When reasonable statements or claims are "extended" by the other person, confusion and fighting are likely. It's important for speakers to stay with the original subject and not be pulled into a defensive exchange on an irrelevant or tangential subject.

Reminder

A red herring follows this format:

1. One person brings up topic A.
2. The other person brings up topic B under the guise of being relevant to topic A (when topic B is actually not relevant to topic A).
3. If the second person is successful, topic A is abandoned. The subject has been changed to topic B.

Critical thinking response: Remind the speaker of the original topic. You may also offer to discuss topic B at another time.

✴ Explore on **mythinkinglab.com**

Ad Hominem: Attacking the Person

Ad hominem is a Latin term meaning "to the man" or **attacking the person.** Ad hominem occurs when a person is attacked on a personal quality that is irrelevant to the issue under discussion. For example, someone might say that a woman is not qualified for a position on a city council because she's a homemaker, or someone might say that an actor has no right to take a position about environmental issues.

In these cases, the people should not be judged because of their professional affiliations: A homemaker could do as well as anyone else in city government, and an actor is also a citizen who has the right to speak out (even if he or she does have the advantage of a larger audience than the average person).

The use of ad hominem arguments has been a staple of political rhetoric for a long time. Consider the following accusations that were used in the presidential campaign of 1800, which is said to have been characterized by "ugly insults coming from both sides":

> President John Adams was accused of being "a fool, a gross hypocrite and an unprincipled oppressor." His opponent, Thomas Jefferson was called "an uncivilized atheist, anti-American, a tool for the godless French."[11]

People may resort to an ad hominem argument when they can't think of strong reasons to counter someone else's arguments; they may also use ad hominem in a desperate attempt to discredit someone whose motives they distrust. Such was the case for trial lawyer and founder of the Trial Lawyers College, Gerry Spence, who writes about his own unfortunate use of an ad hominem argument in the courtroom:

> As a young lawyer, I stared at the ceiling numberless nights fretting about how to meet the power of an opposing lawyer in a case for a terribly injured client. My client had been brain-damaged by a defectively designed crane and was left without a sense of who or where he was. He deserved justice. But the insurance company refused to pay a penny. As they often do, they brought in their famous lawyer to defend the manufacturer. To get justice for my client, I had to win against this man.

ad hominem (attacking the person)   A Latin term meaning "to the man" or attacking the person. Ad hominem occurs when a person is attacked on a personal quality that is irrelevant to the issue under discussion.

---

[11] Abby Collins-Sears, "Shortcomings of Founding Fathers Studied," *Contra Costa Times,* February 20, 1996, p. A-3.

. . . I found myself completely obsessed with my fear of this handsome charmer, who was the epitome of wrong to me. I talked to every lawyer who would talk to me about him. The more I listened, the more I discovered that he had no apparent Achilles' heel. Moreover, everyone seemed to like him, even those whom he had beaten. I lay awake at night devising scores of arguments to the jury. At last I came up with this one:

"Ladies and gentlemen,

"Mr. Randolph Hightower is a mighty nice man. But when this case is over he will suffer neither loss nor gain from anything you do. His fee from his client will be the same, win or lose. No matter what your verdict, when this case is over he will simply pull out another file and try another case for the same client he represents here today. And when Mr. Hightower walks into court tomorrow, despite what the facts may be in that case, he will have the same nimble smile for the next guy, the same perfect demeanor, the same kindly exterior. It frightens me. No matter what the facts, no matter where justice lies, no matter how evil his client or his cause, he will always remain the same—kindly appearing, marvelously poised, unpretentiously compelling—in short, wonderful.

"I am afraid you will like him more than you like me, for, in truth, he is more likeable than I. I am afraid you will feel closer to him than you do to me, for indeed, he seems like the kind of man you would like to have as a friend, while I am sometimes abrasive and difficult to approach.

"I am afraid that you will therefore decide the case in his favor, because you like him, when justice demands that you decide for my client. That is my fear. I have thought about it a lot."

Later, I actually made this argument to the jury. To my bitter shock, the jurors found against my client. Afterward, one of the jurors was kind enough to speak to me about my argument.

"Mr. Spence, didn't you trust us?"

"Why, of course," I quickly replied. "Why do you ask?"

"Because you took great pains in telling us that you were afraid we would approach this case as a personality contest. This case was not a personality contest, Mr. Spence. We decided this case on the facts, not on who the nicest lawyer was."

Suddenly I realized I had proven beyond doubt that I was not nice. Too late, I realized that I had spent my time defending against the lawyer, rather than presenting the justice of my case to the jurors…. I realized I didn't have the first idea who my opponent was. As the years have passed, I now know him as a genuinely nice man who saw himself as merely representing his client's interests to the best of his ability.[12]

Some logicians believe that discussing an opponent's personal qualities is always a diversionary tactic. However, there are times when attacking the person is valid, because the area of attack is pertinent to the issue under consideration. For example, it is relevant to say that you won't vote for someone for class treasurer (or Congress) because you know she can't balance her checkbook and has overspent her credit cards. It is relevant to refuse to vote for a certain person to be a deacon in a church if he is continually gossiping about other church members. It is relevant to question an environmentalist who travels to speaking engagements about global warming on private

---

[12] Gerry Spence, *How to Argue and Win Every Time* (New York: St. Martin's Griffin, 1996), pp. 35–36.

jets. It is relevant to refuse to vote for a candidate who promises to care about the elderly but lacks a record of supporting legislation aimed at helping senior citizens. In these cases, personal character and conduct are relevant to the position being sought.

It is hard to determine the relevance of some aspects of personal character. A frequent point of discussion in presidential elections is whether the personal integrity of a candidate is an important factor for voters to consider. Elections generate interesting speculations about what traits and behaviors constitute the character of a leader.

For example, during former President Clinton's impeachment trial, public opinion was divided over the effect of his actions on his ability to govern. A national debate focused on questions such as "Is the president's personal life, even if conducted in the Oval Office, any business of the citizens?" "Is there a correlation between being dishonest with a spouse and being untrustworthy as a public servant?" "Is lying to the public an impeachable offense when the lying is about personal conduct?" Most of these questions boiled down to the general question, "Does character count?" If so, then a leader's personal character and moral authority are relevant to citizens. If not, then questions of personal character can be seen as ad hominem attacks.

Many citizens contended that a president's personal life is irrelevant and that he should be judged on the basis of job performance. The Senate's finding that the president's behavior did not "rise to the level of impeachment" seemed to be a support for this position.

However, in the subsequent 2000 election year, most writers and political analysts believed that Vice President Al Gore, recognizing that character was a relevant criterion to much of the electorate, chose Senator Joe Lieberman as his running mate to add ethical credibility to the ticket. *Boston Globe* columnist Thomas Oliphant wrote that Gore used Lieberman's "recognized morality to buck the Clinton monkey on his back."[13] Before Gore's announcement of his choice of running mate, he was behind in the polls by 17 points. After the announcement, he was only 2 points behind—a very dramatic difference.

In the 2007 race for the Democratic presidential nomination, there were some heated exchanges early on between the camps of candidates Hillary Rodham Clinton and Barack Obama, particularly after Hollywood producer David Geffen held a huge fundraiser for Obama and referred to the Clintons as liars. However, as the campaign got underway, it seemed that both senators wanted to project integrity and move away from the ad hominem attacks. Glenn Thrush made these observations from Selma, Alabama:

> Sens. Hillary Rodham Clinton and Barack Obama nearly trampled each other yesterday trying to seize the high road in their first joint appearance as 2008 rivals.
>
> After an ugly spat earlier this month—and a bitter behind-the-scenes tussle for black support—both Democrats viewed a ceremony commemorating the 1965 civil rights march here as a chance to prove they aren't at each other's throats....
>
> "It's excellent that we have a candidate like Barack Obama, who embodies what all of you fought for here 42 years ago," said Clinton referring to the landmark "Bloody Sunday" march across the Edmund Pettus Bridge that led to the Voting Rights Act.
>
> Obama, for his part, said Clinton was "doing an excellent job for this country and we're going to be marching arm-in-arm."[14]

---

[13]Thomas Oliphant, "Breaking Barrier of Bigotry," *Boston Globe*, August 8, 2000.

[14]Glenn Thrush, "Hillary, Obama March Together," Newsday.com, March 5, 2007.

If someone attacks the character, appearance, personality, or behavior of another person, ask yourself, "Is this aspect of the person a relevant part of the issue?" If it is relevant to the issue under discussion, it may be used as evidence. If it is not relevant to the issue, then you have discovered an ad hominem fallacy. (See Exercise 6.6, page 259.)

Reminder

Ad hominem follows this format:

1. Person A makes a claim or asks for your vote or your support on a specific issue.
2. Person B attacks person A on an irrelevant personal trait rather than on the claims that person A makes.

Critical thinking response: Discuss how the personal traits of person A are not relevant to the claims, proposals, work, or candidacy of person A.

✳ Explore on **mythinkinglab.com**

Two Wrongs Make a Right

Two wrongs make a right
A fallacy that is used to excuse bad behavior on the grounds of other bad behavior; the fallacy occurs when someone rationalizes that one person's or one group's action is justified because some other person's or group's action is just as bad or worse.

Closely related to the ad hominem fallacy is the fallacy called **two wrongs make a right**. This fallacy occurs when someone rationalizes that one person's or one group's action is justified because some other person's or group's action is just as bad or worse. This fallacy is often used to excuse bad behavior on the grounds of other bad behavior.

Examples

"You can't blame me for going out with someone else when you're so moody all the time."

"It's not fair to give me a ticket—at least three people were going even faster than I was."

"Yes, I hit my sister, but only after she stuck her tongue out at me."

"Of course I cheated on the test—everyone else was cheating too."

"Why should I pay my taxes when the money is misused by our governor?"

"I downloaded only 20 copyrighted songs—other people have taken many more than that."

Making excuses for our own wrongful actions by pointing out the wrongful actions of others does not justify them. Sometimes, people justify their actions on the assumption that a similar unjust action would be taken against them. For example, someone may be undercharged at a store and not give the money back because "If they overcharged me, they wouldn't try to find me to give me my money back."

There are times, however, when a wrongful action can be justified by the wrongful or threatening action of another. In these cases, we can provide relevant and legitimate reasons for taking an otherwise wrong action, as the following examples show:

Parent to child:	Why did you grab your brother—you really scared him!
Child to parent:	I'm sorry he got scared, but I had to grab him because a car was coming right at him.
Storeowner to manager:	Why did you open the safe for that criminal?
Manager:	Because he had a gun and might have hurt everyone in the store if I didn't.

In these cases, the wrongful action is justified by the circumstances.

A subcategory of the two wrongs make a right fallacy (and related to the ad hominem fallacy) is called the **look who's talking** fallacy. This fallacy is committed when someone denies a claim because he or she believes that the speaker who is making the claim is hypocritical.

look who's talking
A fallacy that is committed when someone denies a claim because they believe the speaker who is making the claim is hypocritical.

Examples

Judy:	I wish I could lose some weight.
Erik:	I know that exercising is supposed to help.
Judy:	Why should I listen to you? I don't see you moving off the couch!
Parent:	Taking drugs is really harmful and is not a way to solve your problems.
Child:	How can you say anything to me about that? Didn't you do drugs when you were in high school?

The fact that a speaker may not now or in the past have "practiced what he or she preaches" does not mean that what he or she has to say is without merit. In fact, someone who has made mistakes in the past may have the most credibility in advising others to avoid his or her own mistakes. For example, many effective substance abuse counselors were once users themselves, and their personal experiences often give them valuable insight into their clients' thinking and behavior. However, even if someone doesn't follow his or her own advice, the advice may still be good.

It is valid to point out hypocritical *behavior* without denying the sound arguments of others, as in the following examples:

Janelle:	I'm irritated that my lab teacher is so concerned about our being there on time. Half the time, she shows up late herself.
Norma:	That is unfair. But there's no point in being late if it will affect your grade.
Sean:	Steve keeps telling me I need new tires, so he won't go anywhere in my car!
Jose:	He's right about the tires, but he should be just as concerned about the brakes in his car.

In these cases, no one is denying the validity of the teacher's rules or Steve's comments; they are just pointing out the hypocrisy of their behavior.

> # Reminder
>
> Two wrongs make a right (plus look who's talking) follows this format:
>
> Person A acknowledges a wrong or unfair action but rationalizes the action by pointing out someone else's equally wrong or unfair action, *or*
>
> 1. Person A points out Person B's mistake or bad behavior.
> 2. Person B responds by pointing out another action that is equally bad or worse, arguing that it cancels out his or her own bad behavior. In the case of look who's talking, the equally bad behavior involves hypocrisy.
>
> **Critical thinking response**: Acknowledge the equally bad or worse behavior, but remind the person that it does not justify his or her own actions.
>
> ✴ Explore on **mythinkinglab.com**

Ad Populum: Jumping on the Bandwagon

ad populum   A fallacy that consists of a false appeal to the authority of "everyone." This fallacy is based on the assumption that a course of action should be taken or an idea should be supported because "everyone" is doing it or believes it.

The **ad populum** fallacy is another one we seem to learn from early childhood. This fallacy consists of a false appeal to the authority of "everyone." We are told that a course of action should be taken, or an idea should be supported, because "everyone" is doing it or "everyone" believes it.

American society has been said to produce individuals who are *other-directed,* which means that the opinions and approval of others are important motivating factors. The other-directed person is contrasted with the individual who is *inner-directed* and derives his or her motivation and approval mostly from internalized sources.[15] Some of our societal clichés that reveal the tendency toward other-directedness include "keeping up with the Joneses," "the in-crowd," or simply "everybody's doing it."

Advertisers capitalize on our tendency to jump on the bandwagon and follow the crowd by using slogans such as "Who's in Your Network?" and "The Pepsi Generation." Or, assertions are made without any proof, such as "This is the way America cleans," or "This is where America goes for dinner." The number of people attending the first weekend of a new movie is offered as proof that the movie must be great. Infomercials feature representatives of every possible audience member in order to convince viewers that "people like you" are using and benefiting greatly from a product. Sometimes advertisers don't even use words; they just show large numbers of people who are happily consuming their products. If you stop and think about these "reasons" for buying products, they seem silly. So why do advertisers continue to use them? Because they work; many people want to identify with the right products, to be cool and accepted.

Examples

"Join the millions of satisfied customers who have purchased a Crocodile pickup. What are you waiting for?"

"That's not fair. All the other kids get to go to the Dismembered Druggies concert!"

"Hey, America: Introducing your new turkey stuffing mix!"

"Everyone is using our wireless service! Sign up today!"

[15] David Riesman, *The Lonely Crowd* (New Haven, CT: Yale University Press, 1950), pp. 19–26.

Reminder

Ad populum follows this format:

1. An assertion is made that most people approve of, purchase, or take part in X.
2. Therefore, it is claimed that X is desirable and should be bought or supported.

Critical thinking response: State directly that the numbers of people voting for a candidate, supporting a proposition, or buying a product are not your criteria for decision making. Ask for specific reasons to support a candidate or policy or to buy a product.

✳━Explore on **mythinkinglab.com**

Appeal to Tradition: "We've Always Done It This Way"

Closely related in its format to the ad populum fallacy is the **appeal to tradition**, which occurs when a belief or action is supported simply because it conforms to traditional ideas or practices. In both ad populum and appeal to tradition arguments, the conclusions of the speakers or writers may be fine, but the reasons are not relevant to the conclusions. You should drink Pepsi or Coke if you like the taste but not because "everyone" is drinking it. Similarly, you may not want to change the way you are doing something because it works well for you, not because it has always been done that way; the folk wisdom on that is "if it ain't broke, don't fix it."

appeal to tradition
A fallacy that occurs when a belief or action is supported on the ground that it conforms to traditional ideas or practices.

Traditions held by families, organizations, and nations are wonderful in their ability to bind us together and give us a sense of belonging. These traditions are not what we are suggesting when we discuss "appeal to tradition" as a fallacy. In fact, in our "new and improved" society, we might note the fallacy of "appeal to change" or "appeal to the novel." Just because a product or approach to a problem is new does not mean that it is an improvement on the old product or policy.

Sometimes a newly elected candidate or manager in an organization may make changes without considering the reasons why a particular system is in place. Often, nonincumbents campaign on the idea that we need change, but they don't tell us what that change will involve or how the change will be an improvement over the current situation; in fact, there are times when changes solve one problem but then create a host of new problems that leaves us in a worse position than we were before the changes. Novelty alone is not an adequate reason to vote for a candidate, to support legislation, or to buy a product.

There are times, however, for a reasonable discussion about whether something should be done a different way or with a different person. In such cases, it is not useful to say, "We need to do it this way because we've always done it this way." That statement is an appeal to tradition that short-circuits useful dialogue or needed change.

Examples

"Vote for Smith. We've always had a member of the Smith family in our state legislature."

"All the men in our family are lawyers; you will be too."

"Our workers have always been happy working 9 to 5; there's no need to change that schedule."

As noted by these examples, the fallacious appeal to tradition gives an irrelevant and distracting reason for an opinion. It may very well be that the company mentioned in the last example should not change its working hours or create flextime for its employees; it may find it needs all the workers available at the same time. However, to offer "we've always done it this way" as a reason does nothing to engender a meaningful discussion of the possibilities of useful change and, in fact, obscures the issue.

Reminder

An appeal to tradition follows this format:

1. X has been traditional in that it has been done for some time.
2. Therefore, X is claimed to be the only way or the best way to do things.

Critical thinking response: Ask for reasons against a proposed change other than that it is not how things have been done in the past. Point out advantages of a new approach or a change from the status quo. Show that the proposed changes will not cause bigger problems.

✳ Explore on **mythinkinglab.com**

Appeal to Pity

We all go through hard times and face different challenges in life. Sometimes our difficulties are completely out of our control, such as the death of a loved one, an accident or medical condition that leaves us disabled, or the loss of income due to a company going out of business. However, sometimes our problems are brought on by our own lack of planning or foresight. We may take on too much—a job, family obligations, school, volunteer work, and fun activities—and then appeal to others to bail us out of the natural consequences and conflicts that our schedules bring. Or we may neglect our responsibilities and then want others to fix the problems we have brought on through this neglect.

appeal to pity A logical fallacy that occurs when someone argues that others should follow a course of action or hold a certain belief for no other reason than that they should feel compassion for the irrelevant claims or irresponsibility of the speaker.

An **appeal to pity** occurs when someone argues that others should follow a course of action or hold a certain belief for no other reason than that they should feel compassion for the irrelevant claims or irresponsibility of the speaker. For example, a student may miss many classes during a semester without good reason but may realize too late that a poor grade will affect his athletic scholarship. An argument is then given to the instructor as follows: "I really need a better grade in last semester's class or I won't be eligible to play and that will affect my whole future." Although the student's claim is true, it is irrelevant to the conclusion that a better grade should be given, since compassion about the poor grade earned is not a justification for raising the grade.

Other appeals to pity may sound like this:

"You really should go out with me because I'll be very upset if you don't."

"I know you're on a diet, but I slaved all day on this feast, so you should indulge just this once."

"You may have a lot to do, but it won't be any fun for me if you don't come to the party."

Not all appeals to compassion or emotion are fallacious. There are many times when the appeal is directly relevant and thus provides a good reason for the conclusion of the speaker, as noted in the following examples.

Examples of Relevant Appeals to Compassion

A televised scenario is presented to show starvation in another country and to appeal to those with means to help out: "Look at these children who have no running water and whose mothers have to watch them go hungry. Your contribution of just 50 cents per day would relieve this starvation and perhaps save a life." This is a genuine appeal to compassion for those who are victims of their unfortunate circumstances. (Note that reputable charities are happy to provide financial statements and other information that verifies their credibility.)

Parent to child: I know you want to go to the ocean for winter break, but Grandma is getting much worse, and this may be our last time to be together as a family. You could bring a lot of joy to her by coming home that week.

Child to parent: It's really out of the way to take Keisha home, but she got out of class too late for the bus. Since it's so cold out, could we give her a ride?

We all have emotions and feelings, and sometimes they are relevant to a speaker's conclusion. When they are irrelevant and are used to circumvent rational thought and individual responsibility, they are fallacious appeals to pity. (See Exercise 6.7, page 260.)

Reminder

An appeal to pity follows this format:

Person A wants Person B to take a course of action simply on the basis of empathy for Person A's dilemma. Person A has no legitimate reasons as to why Person B should take this action.

Critical thinking response: Ask for reasons, besides misplaced compassion, why the course of action should be taken. Show sympathy for Person A's problem, and then explain why you cannot agree with his or her position or comply with his or her request.

✳ Explore on **mythinkinglab.com**

Equivocation

Change is inevitable, except from vending machines.

If you think nobody cares, try missing a couple of payments.

When everything is coming your way, you're in the wrong lane.[16]

---

[16] T. Edward Damer, *Attacking Faulty Reasoning: A Practical Grade to Fallacy-Free Arguments* (Beverly, MA: Wadsworth, 1995, 3rd ed.), pp. 157–159.

equivocation A logical fallacy in which the same word is used with two different meanings.

When we look at language in Chapter 7, we will see that words can be misleading because they often have more than one meaning. **Equivocation** occurs when someone uses a different meaning of a word already discussed in order to win a point. You can discover equivocation by noting that a word that is used to mean one thing in a statement is then twisted to mean another thing in a second statement.

Lewis Carroll showed the frustrating experience of talking with an equivocator in his novel *Through the Looking Glass*:

> "We can never have jam today," the Queen insisted.
>
> "But it must come to jam some day," Alice protested. "After all, the rule is, 'jam every other day.'"
>
> "Precisely," said the Queen. "'Jam every other day.' But today is not any other day, you know."[17]

The basic form of the fallacy of equivocation is

a. A statement is made using term X with one meaning.

b. A rebuttal is made using term X with a second meaning.

c. A conclusion is then drawn using term X with the second meaning.

The term *equivocation* comes from the Latin terms *equi* (equal) and *vox* (voice)—and means "with equal voice." When a term is used *univocally* in an argument, it always has the same meaning, but when it is used *equivocally*, more than one meaning is given an equal voice. Here are some examples of arguments that contain this fallacy:

Carla: It is well known that the average family has 2.5 children (premise #1).

Ray: Well, Linda's family is very average (premise #2), so they must have 2.5 children (conclusion).

The problem here is that the key term *average* is used in more than one sense. With the first premise, the term is used in the sense of statistical averages. But the second premise switches to another sense of average, this time meaning "not unusual." By equating the two, the crazy conclusion of a family having a fraction of children is reached. Often the speaker or writer who is equivocating makes an argument that sounds logical; however, the argument can only be reliable if key words maintain the same meaning throughout the argument. The problem with equivocation is that a second meaning of an ambiguous word is taken, as in the following examples:

"You are against murder, so you must be against capital punishment."

Written as a deductive argument, this would be the speaker's case:

All killing is murder.

Capital punishment is killing.

Therefore, capital punishment is murder.

To those who believe that all killing is equivalent, this would be a valid argument. To those who distinguish murder as criminal action from capital punishment, the argument involves equivocation.

"I don't know what the fuss is about natural foods—everything I eat comes from some part of the earth, so there isn't any difference."

[17] Lewis Carroll, *Through the Looking Glass*, 1862, online library through Project Gutenberg.

This argument changes the accepted definition of natural foods:

> Everything that originates with natural materials can be considered natural food.

> Fast food originates with natural materials.

> Therefore, fast food is natural food.

Sister to brother: Maybe I did hurt your arm. But you hurt me just as much by telling Dad.

In this case, the sister is changing the meaning of *hurt*, saying that telling a parent about being hurt is the same thing as inflicting a physical injury.

Political candidate 1:   Our country should be focused on children.

Political candidate 2:   If your party gets elected, we *will* have children running the country.

Political candidate 2 has used equivocation to change candidate 1's definition of children to an insult to candidate 1's political party.

Reminder

Equivocation follows this format:

1. Person A makes a statement or takes a position on an issue.
2. Person B takes a term from Person A's statement and attributes a second meaning to that term.
3. Person B then draws a conclusion based on the second meaning of the term. The original issue is then lost in the verbal confusion.

Critical thinking response: Point out that Person B has changed the meaning of the term as Person A was using it. Define the term as Person A meant it. Offer to discuss Person B's new issue after Person A's issue is discussed.

✳ Explore on **mythinkinglab.com**

Stop and Think

In the late sixteenth century, Catholics were forbidden to practice their religion in England, and priests were forbidden to enter the country. The Jesuits managed to smuggle priests into England, and they wrote a manual called *A Treatise of Equivocation,* which instructed priests and their flocks on techniques to answer government interrogators without committing the sin of lying. One example of these equivocation techniques suggested using ambiguity by saying "A priest lyeth not in my house" (meaning, to the interrogator, that they were not harboring an illegal priest, but meaning, to the Catholic, that the priest did not tell lies). The Jesuits believed that equivocating to avoid unfair punishment (which sometimes included death by public torture) was justifiable. To what extent do you agree with their assessment?[18]

---

[18] Lady Antonia Fraser, *Faith and the Story of the Gunpowder Plot* (New York: Double-day, 1997).

Skill

Recognize reasons that are irrelevant and lead listeners away from the real issue.

Stop and Think

You may find it hard to categorize errors in reasoning under one label or another; some speakers manage to use a whole group of fallacies at once.

Example

"Everyone knows the governor is unreliable; if we keep trusting him not to raise taxes, we could all be in debt by next year."

The statement in the previous Stop and Think box could be an example of begging the question, since the speaker reasons from an unproven assumption that the governor is unreliable. It could also be ad populum, since the speaker uses the phrase *everyone knows* to support his claim. It could be seen as ad hominem, an attack on the character of a person that is unconnected to an issue. Finally, it could be called a slippery slope argument, because the speaker predicts catastrophic results from the action of trusting the governor.

The bad news is that writers and speakers who are not careful in their reasoning may lump several errors together and leave you to wade through the verbal mess. The good news is that you don't need to be obsessed with finding the exact title of a fallacy and attacking your opponent with it. You only need to see that certain reasons people give to justify their conclusions are insufficient or irrelevant. The labels we give to the reasoning errors are useful to help us define and avoid inadequate and faulty support for our conclusions. These labels also provide guideposts for evaluating and refuting the reasons others give.

Life Application: Tips for College and Career

In your academic, professional, and personal life, make it a practice to "stop and think" about arguments that you are hearing, particularly from charismatic, articulate individuals who seem to have a great way with words. Try to discern if their reasons genuinely support their conclusions, or if the reasons are actually inadequate or irrelevant to the issue at hand, despite the convincing manner of the speaker. Use the approaches given in the chapter to question their reasoning in a respectful but firm manner.

Address the negative self-fulfilling prophecies in your own life. Move beyond limitations that are imposed by others or by past thoughts and experiences. If you weren't good in a subject in high school, that doesn't mean that you won't become strong in that subject in college—keep pursuing good instruction in areas of study and skill that you enjoy. As you continue to learn, you will gain new insights and abilities and grow as a person and a professional.

Chapter Review

Summary

1. Errors in reasoning are called fallacies.

2. One type of fallacy involves reasons that sound logical but provide inadequate support for conclusions. These include faulty analogy, false cause, slippery slope, straw man, hasty conclusion, false dilemma, and begging the question.

3. A second type of fallacy is found in reasons that lead listeners away from the real issue. These include red herring, ad hominem, ad populum, appeal to tradition, appeal to pity, two wrongs make a right, and equivocation.

4. An error in reasoning may be hard to classify. The important point for the critical thinker is that the recognition of fallacies helps us analyze the quality of reasons given to support conclusions.

Checkup

Short Answer

1. What is the difference between fallacies that mislead and fallacies that do not provide adequate support for conclusions?

2. Analogies are a major form of inductive reasoning. What makes an analogy faulty?

3. How does a hasty conclusion relate to the size of a sample?

True-False

4. The post hoc fallacy is concerned with future events.

5. The slippery slope fallacy has also been called the domino effect.

6. An example of the ad hominem fallacy would involve being urged to buy a product because "everyone else is buying it."

Matching

a. Begging the question
c. Appeal to tradition
b. Red herring
d. Ad populum

7. Using various means to change the issue under discussion.

8. Taking a course of action because of the number of other people who appear to be taking this course of action.

9. Putting the burden of proof for your conclusions on the listener.

10. Suggesting that because a certain action has been taken in the past, it should continue to be taken.

Exercises

EXERCISE 6.1 Purposes: To practice isolating errors in reasoning. To notice overlap in categories of fallacies.

1. Find errors in reasoning on websites, magazine, newspaper, or television advertisements or in blog posts or letters to the editor. You may discover that a

particular inadequate reason may fit the description of several fallacies. Share the errors you find with your class.

2. There are other common fallacies in reasoning. Find examples of other types of fallacies that are not listed in this chapter (from other instructors or textbooks). Explain these to your class.

3. In a class group, come up with two examples of each of the fallacies. Then, as a class, play the game "What's My Fallacy?"

What's My Fallacy?

Fallacies Involved

faulty analogy	red herring
post hoc (false cause)	appeal to tradition
slippery slope	begging the question
hasty conclusion	ad populum
ad hominem (attacking the person)	either-or (false dilemma)
straw man	equivocation
two wrongs make a right	appeal to pity

Game Rules

Object of the game: To accumulate points by correctly guessing the fallacies of the other teams.

Form class teams of three to six persons each—give your team a name.

Each team should put between 14 and 28 fallacies (1 or 2 for each category) in random order on paper or cards; this step may be done in groups during class, or the team may assign several fallacies to each member to do at home. These fallacies should be no more than a few sentences. For example, a team might say, "How can you vote for him for student body president—he's a vegetarian!" This would obviously be an instance of ad hominem, attacking the person rather than his policies.

Each team needs: one reader, one scorekeeper, one to two referees

Scoring

Each team must have at least 18 errors in reasoning to read to the other teams.

The lead team (each team is the lead team when its members stand in front of the class to read their list of fallacies) earns one point for each appropriate example and loses one point for each inappropriate example.

Guessing teams win two points for each correct answer and lose one point for each wrong answer. You may wish to have one guessing team have a chance to guess the fallacy before moving on to the next team (for example, moving from team 1 to team 2 to team 3), or you may have all of the teams try to guess at one time.

In order to get two points for a right answer, the guessing team must be recognized by the referee of the lead team and say *why* the fallacy was chosen. The answer must satisfy the lead team and the instructor. The instructor may award one point for a close answer.

Your instructor may decide to award points toward a grade for this exercise or may just use the game to help you practice recognizing fallacies.

In most classes, an interesting discussion of what distinguishes one fallacy from another will occur; this discussion will help you recognize fallacious reasoning more easily.

EXERCISE 6.2 Purpose: To utilize criteria for evaluating reasoning by analogy.

Consider the following analogies and evaluate their validity. Note similarities that make the analogy useful and persuasive and/or significant differences that make the analogy misleading.

1. While discussing the issue of whether schools should ban peanut butter, one mother expressed the desire for the school community to become aware of the problem and involved in efforts to prevent tragedies associated with the allergy:

   > To San Ramon parent Leslie Mague, the issue is terrifyingly simple. Bringing a peanut butter sandwich to school is like bringing "a loaded gun or a land mine: You don't know when it will go off," she said. Her son Braden was 33 months old when an Asian peanut noodle dish sent him into anaphylactic shock. "Within seconds, he swelled up like a balloon," she said.[19]

2. This excerpt is from an introduction given by Ted Koppel of ABC's *Nightline*, when he did a program on the founder of the Reform Party, Ross Perot. Perot ran a very successful third-party campaign for president of the United States in 1992, gaining 19 percent of the popular vote.

   > *Koppel:* How do you figure the phenomenon of Ross Perot? Why do so many people who know next to nothing about the man seem so enchanted by him? A few years ago, I mulled over the same question with regard to the enormous popularity of Vanna White. She of *Wheel of Fortune*, you ask? The very one. She is, after all, a lovely woman with an engaging manner and a charming smile, and no one, but no one, lights up letters on a board better than she. But that still doesn't explain the depth and breadth of Vanna's popularity. The world is full, after all, of thousands of equally lovely, engaging, and charming women. What is it, then, about Vanna?

   > And then it struck me. Of all the people on television whose names we know who are not playing somebody else, we probably know less about Vanna, that is, what she thinks and believes, than almost anyone else, and so we can project onto her what we would like her to believe.

   > So, too, with Ross Perot. He is enjoying the support of conservatives, liberals, and moderates precisely because, like Vanna, Ross doesn't go into much detail.[20]

3. Homosexual men and women had been traditionally excluded from the armed forces, and the recently repealed "don't ask, don't tell" policy did not necessarily foster an atmosphere of acceptance.

   > When this topic was first debated in Congress, one argument for completely lifting an exclusionary policy is that gay men and women are a minority group just like Hispanic Americans and African Americans and that no other minority group is banned from the military.

   > In an argument given for keeping gays out of the military, the assertion was made that separate living quarters would have to be provided to keep straight and gay personnel apart, just as similar policies provide separate living quarters for heterosexual men and women in the military.

---

[19] Jackie Burrell, "Peanut Allergy Problems Mitigated at Area Schools," *Contra Costa Times*, September 10, 2003, p. a01.

[20] Ted Koppel, "The Unknown Ross Perot," *Nightline*, April 23, 1992.

4. A couple sued a landlord for refusing to rent to them because of their sloppy appearance; they claimed discrimination in the form of "lookism" (prejudice against someone because of how they look). In defending himself, the landlord stated, "You wouldn't hire someone who was out of shape as an employee in a health spa, and you wouldn't want a receptionist for an investment firm who had purple hair. So why should you have to rent an apartment to people who look sloppy?"

EXERCISE 6.3 Purpose: To discover diverse causes for a given phenomenon.

1. Look at the problem of substance abuse in our culture and answer the following questions: What are some of the simplistic or false (post hoc) reasons given for the problem? What might be some of the deeper causes of this problem, and what solutions are implied by these causes?

2. Do a short paper or speech on the causes of a social, national, or international problem. Take a position on which causes were immediate, which remote, which sufficient, and which necessary for the problem to develop. If some analysts of your problem commit the fallacy of assigning a false cause, say how. Support your position with evidence.

EXERCISE 6.4 Purpose: To analyze the effect of hasty conclusions and self-fulfilling prophecies.

Think of some personal and some cultural hasty conclusions and self-fulfilling prophecies. How did they come about and how did they become "fulfilled"? What could be done to change attitudes and/or actions now?

Example

"During a Winter Olympics skating competition, one of the medal contenders for pairs figure skating fell during a crucial performance. The commentator for CBS said that a reporter had once written that this skater seemed to be having trouble with jumps. The commentator explained that after the skater read this article, she continually had trouble with her jumps.

"I noticed that this skater seemed hesitant about her jumps during the Olympics. I wondered if a sports psychologist could help her get over what seemed to be a self-fulfilling prophecy. Her coach and her psychologist could help her to form a positive attitude. She could come to believe she's good at jumping by practicing and watching her jumps. The evidence of many successful jumps completed in practice sessions would change her negative expectation and she would perform better in competition."

EXERCISE 6.5 Purposes: To think of ways to respond to situations more critically. To consider how to avoid hasty conclusions.

Read each situation, noting what an uncritical thinking response would be. Then give an example of what a critical thinking response might be.

Example

A candidate for your state assembly is campaigning door-to-door and asks for your vote. You tell her that your major concern is funding for local schools.

She tells you that she is very concerned about this problem also and has given it much consideration.

Uncritical thinking response: Vote for the candidate without further information.

Critical thinking response: Ask the candidate about her specific concerns and the solutions she proposes; follow up with questions about the details of the candidate's proposal. Ask about the sources of funding for any programs she proposes. Also ask her to comment on the proposals of other candidates. Check out the plans of other candidates and weigh them carefully before voting. Also consider the general platform of other candidates to assess the overall consequences of voting for a given candidate.

1. Your friend from your 10:00 class tells you to meet her at the cafeteria early.

   Uncritical thinking response: Arrive at the cafeteria at 9:45, assuming your friend wants to tell you something or to walk to class together.

   Critical thinking response: _____

2. You are depressed because you seem to be gaining weight. While switching channels on your television set one night, you catch a promotional show on a weight-loss supplement that claims you can lose weight just by taking it twice a day. The commentator for the program says that significant research has been done on this product, showing that it is a real breakthrough. There are several testimonies from the audience about how well this supplement has worked for them to promote rapid weight loss. Also, a famous actor is endorsing the product.

   Uncritical thinking response: Dial the 800 number on the screen and charge the product.

   Critical thinking response: _____

3. You are invited to a birthday party at your friend's house. She is a good friend, but each time you have attended a party at her house you have had a bad time. Once, you got food poisoning from the fried chicken; another time, it seemed as though everyone had a date except you. You've started to predict that you'll have a terrible time at her parties. What do you do?

   Uncritical thinking response: Stay at home.

   Critical thinking response: _____

   Add other situations to which you have responded uncritically. What could you have done differently?

EXERCISE 6.6 Purpose: To determine if there are cases in which personal qualities are relevant reasons for rejecting political candidates.

List the elements of personal character that are important for a president or elected representative. What in a candidate's background, if anything, would prevent you from voting for him or her? Are there things about a person that would bother you if they had occurred recently, but you would overlook if they had occurred in his or her past? How far back into someone's background would you look when making your voting decision?

EXERCISE 6.7 Purpose: To distinguish between legitimate and fallacious appeals to emotion.

Expand your awareness of appeals to pity in two ways:

1. Take the examples given in the Appeal to Pity section (page 250) and state the conclusion and reasons given for the mini-arguments they represent. Note the differences between legitimate and fallacious appeals to compassion.

2. In a small group or by yourself, list some of your own examples of legitimate and fallacious appeals to pity. Share these with the class and see if you all agree on which are good reasons to support a conclusion and which involve an irrelevant and thus fallacious reason.

You Decide

Responding to Terrorism

Rational individuals can agree that terrorism, the killing of innocent people to achieve political and social ends, is unethical and unjustifiable. Disagreement and debates on this topic generally involve the treatment of terrorists. Should terrorists be tried in criminal or military courts? Is "enhanced interrogation" justifiable? Should terrorist leaders be assassinated? When Osama Bin Laden was killed by American Navy Seals in 2011, several controversies emerged, such as whether Bin Laden should have been given a religious funeral service, whether he should have been buried at sea, and whether photos of his body should have been released to the press. President Obama decided not to release the photos, and supporters of his decision agreed that the release could endanger our troops and our allies in the war on terror by inciting violence. They also argued that "two wrongs don't make a right" and that keeping the photos private was a form of "taking the higher moral ground" by not gloating over an enemy and by providing a regard for human life not shown by terrorist activity. Those in favor of releasing the photos argued that they would serve as necessary proof that Bin Laden had been killed and put a stop to hasty conclusions in the form of conspiracy theories. They also argued that the photos would provide some reliable closure for the families of victims of the 9/11 attacks.

For more information on the debate surrounding responding to terrorism and additional exercises and tutorials about concepts covered in this chapter, log into MyThinkingLab at www.mythinkinglab.com and select Diestler, *Becoming a Critical Thinker,* Sixth Edition.

✳ Explore on **mythinkinglab.com**

Articles for Discussion   Read the Document on **mythinkinglab.com**

Discovering fallacies is sometimes a complicated process. If you think you've detected a fallacy, first stop and ask yourself, "What is the issue and conclusion of the writer?" Then see if the statement in question fits one of the two criteria for fallacies. Is it an assertion that gives insufficient evidence for the conclusion (and thus does not adequately support the conclusion), or is it a statement that leads the listener away from the real issue under discussion? If the statement fits one or both of these criteria, then you can identify the particular fallacy with confidence.

Consider the following examples, all from editorial pages. When you read two sides of an issue, try to distinguish which points genuinely support the writer's conclusion and which are fallacious. If you discover fallacious reasoning, think about whether the author could have made his or her point with better support.

Here is some background information for the first two letters to the editor: Kerri Strug is a gymnast who performed despite a serious injury to her ankle, thus supporting her team's Olympic victory. To some viewers, it was an act of courage; others believed that the act sent the wrong message. Following are two opinions.

Ashamed of Strug's Sacrifice

Sylvia Lacayo

I'd never been more ashamed to be American after I watched in horror the women's gymnastics competition in which Kerri Strug "sacrificed herself" for the team by vaulting on an injured ankle.

Then I saw the next morning's headline on the *Times*, which summarized the event as "Magnificent." To sacrifice children for the greediness of coach Bela Karolyi isn't magnificent. It's not magnificent to expect kids to peak at the age of 18.

Columnist Sam McManis, who reported the "magnificent" story, says they're adults and make their own choices. Strug's 18 years mean nothing, knowing that practically her entire life has been manipulated to please her coaches' desires. To please Karolyi is her only choice.

She may be an adult legally, but her squeaky, Mickey Mouse voice over the reporter's microphone proved she's no adult and her limited life proves she's never been a kid.

Gymnasts are neither kids nor adults. They're pawns in Karolyi's and NBC's ratings supervisors' game of greed and power. It's a game those adults choose to play, but don't say Strug chooses to play it. I'm 19 years old, and I know that leaving the Georgia Dome in a stretcher, crying in pain, could never be my dream. ■

Kerri Strug Made Reader Cheer

Joshua C. Logan

While Sylvia Lacayo "watched in horror" as Kerri Strug "sacrificed herself" and won the gold for the USA women's gymnastics team, I cheered once Kerri finished her vault. She showed strength and courage. If Lacayo had her way, Strug would have quit. But Strug showed that she wasn't going to give up.

Lacayo's attack in saying that Bela Karolyi's "greediness" pushed Strug into the vault is simply ignorant. Why would Karolyi need another gold medal? He was the coach of the greatest gymnast ever. Bela Karolyi did his job and encouraged her to give it her all.

According to Lacayo, Strug's "Mickey Mouse" voice is proof of immaturity. Not only is it mean to make fun, but the assumption is false again. Strug pushed herself and fulfilled her dream as an athlete. Sounds like maturity to me.

I and most Americans, rejoice over Strug and her teammates' victory in Atlanta. Those are the people I want to represent me and my great nation. ▪

The following letter to the editor was written in response to a question put to readers: "What needs to be done to reduce the number of sex crimes and cases of sexual harassment of women in the military?" What do you make of the writer's response to the stated issue? Do you detect any logical fallacies in his reasoning?

Keep Women Off the Streets

Larry Bunker

End the front line involvement of women in the police and fire-fighting departments. It has been a horrible experiment, and there is really only one solution. They can stay behind the desks and push all the papers they want, but get them off street duty.

Placing female officers as partners in squad cars has not only endangered the lives of veteran police officers but also increased the cases of sexual harassment. Don't kid yourself, we, the taxpayers are paying huge sums of awards resulting from integrating the sexes. If women don't want to be harassed, then keep them away from male occupations.

Another thing, if a policeman is only allowed to use his weapon when in imminent danger, who do you think will draw and shoot first? A six-foot-six ex-football player or a five-foot-two ex-dancer? If you have more mass than the arresting officer, you are more in danger of being shot. Watch out, guys.

What examples do we have in history where women were shown to have the courage, strength, and stamina to fight crime or fight fires? Isn't this just another sad and dangerous way to get more votes?

To those who comment that women have been successful in these areas, I would say that you haven't faced facts. We the public are more than ever responsible for our own safety. I say, stock up on guns and fire extinguishers—you're going to need them. ▪

In the following editorial, written for the University of Pittsburgh's paper, *Pitt News,* author Shannon Black points out the fallacies of hasty conclusions and the slippery slope that are common to chain e-mails.

E-Mail Chain Letters Deceive

Shannon Black

Every morning, I check my e-mail in the event that something of dire importance has been sent to me over the course of the night. Instead, I usually find myself sorting through junk mail and chain letters.

The spam doesn't annoy me; I find it more hilarious than believable that a prince from Nigeria needs money to save his family. The e-mails that do bother me are particular kinds of chain letters that are sent to me in bulk.

I have no problem with chain e-mails that threaten me with tragedy or bad luck if I dare to delete them rather than passing them on to 68 people in 10 seconds. I happen to like toying with fate, and oftentimes I find myself waiting a few moments for the promised catastrophe to occur after I press the delete key. Fortunately, despite the massive amounts of chain e-mails I've refused to forward, I've never once been the victim of any of their ominous threats.

The particular chain e-mails that drive me crazy are the ones that can easily be mistaken for propaganda. Such letters attempt to argue a point or state an opinion. I find nothing wrong with spreading e-mails about important news or beliefs; I'm guilty of occasionally sending my friends e-mails about issues that are important to me. Some of the chain e-mails that get passed around, however, are filled with fallacies and bizarre exaggerations.

I have reached a point where I simply cannot stand reading another chain e-mail that tries to prove a point with false information. Perhaps I expect too much from the Internet, but I always hope that people will begin to catch on and stop forwarding glaringly false e-mails. Upon the realization that trying to stop such e-mails is futile, I've decided to fight back by refusing to pass on any e-mail found to be false. In doing this, I've discovered the chain e-mails that are the most popular and that need to be discontinued.

If an e-mail suggests that sending it to a hundred people will save the life of a small child, it's not real. Millionaires and businesses cannot track how many people a letter is sent to. It's highly improbable that the "generator" of the e-mail would ever be able to spend enough time and energy figuring out just how many e-mail addresses a single letter has spread to. E-mails like this can be safely deleted without any guilty feelings.

. . . The story of a brave, young student in a classroom standing up for what he believes, against the tyranny of a biased teacher is a very popular e-mail. If there is a surprise twist at the end with the speaker being a famous, historical person it is probably fabricated. While I'm sure Mark Twain and Albert Einstein stood up for what they believed in, it is not very practical to think that someone took down their speech verbatim before spreading it around the Internet. These can also be tossed.

. . . Not all chain letters are bad. Chain e-mails can be a lot of fun when they are used to send out jokes or update people on current events. They can also, however, be filled with lies and cruel or exaggerated statements. Rather than blindly forwarding them in their original form, take the time to make sure their facts are correct. A quick stop at Snopes.com—a website that specializes in debunking Internet myths—can clear away any misunderstandings. If going to Snopes takes up too much time, hitting the delete key doesn't take much effort. I highly suggest it. ■

The following two readings—an excerpt by Luke Warner and an article by Australian writer Andrew Fenton discuss whether it is important for celebrities to "practice what they preach" when they urge others to show concern for the environment and for people living in poverty. In your opinion, are the articles voicing legitimate concerns, ad hominem attacks, or both?

Sunday Times Reveals Some Eco-Celeb Shame

Luke Warner

November 29, 2009

The UK's Sunday Times Online posted an article this weekend on some of the raging eco-hypocrisy rampant in Hollywood these days. While the Euro-critics love to take down US celebrities there is something to be said for keeping it real.

Sheryl Crow, John Travolta, Trudie Styler, Chris Martin, Harrison Ford and others are taken to task for not walking their talk. Among the egregious offenses are Crow's 30 person entourage which followed behind *her* biodiesel tour bus in 13 gas-powered vehicles as well as Al Gore's bill for heating his indoor swimming pool. Several celebs were also outed for flying a variety of hairstylists and chefs halfway across the world for single events.

Perhaps my favorite quote was from Chris Martin about his daughter: "As she gets older, hopefully she'll come and see us when she wants. I always thought it'd be cool to be in school and say, 'I'm not coming in today—I'm off to Costa Rica to see my dad play.' I do think that wins you a few points." According to the Times, Martin did point out that he paid for the planting of mango trees to offset the carbon emissions of his tours and flights home. I'm guessing that's A LOT of mangoes . . . on someone else's land.

Promoting extravagant air travel AND skipping school? Yikes.

Check out the full article for some more revelations as well as a thumbs up for the lifestyles of Ed Begley Jr. and Woody Harrelson.

All of these folks have done great things for a variety of causes and it's great when public figures bring attention to important issues. But it's even better when their lives can truly reflect their intentions. ▪

Rwanda Is So Hot Right Now

Andrew Fenton

How can we believe celebrities flying around in private jets preaching about the big issues, asks Andrew Fenton.

It's really easy to take cheap shots at celebrity hypocrites who support trendy causes. It's fun too.

After all, isn't there a fundamental contradiction in having movie stars living in 32 bedroom mansions in Beverly Hills telling the rest of us to consume less? Or being preached to about anti-consumerism by rock stars whose luxurious, pampered lifestyles depend on the funds generated by ticket, CD and merchandising sales? Is it right that Paris Hilton, the poster girl for decadent, meaningless overconsumption plans to go to Rwanda next month to draw attention to childhood poverty?

This week Leonardo DiCaprio's new film *The 11th Hour* opens in cinemas. It's a grab bag of gloomy scenarios about the impending end of the world overlaid with footage of hurricane Katrina and other natural disasters. Leo solemnly intones a call for our society to radically rethink our over-consumption of natural resources and to start to live more sustainably. The message itself is laudable—it's just Leo undermines his own call for action by constantly jetting around the world, leaving the film wide open to accusations of hypocrisy from right-wing attack dogs like Fox News' Sean Hannity.

"You are lecturing Americans about a planetary emergency, a crisis of global proportions," Hannity told filmmakers Nadia and Leila Conners.

"Yet your co-producer (DiCaprio) is putting a bigger carbon footprint in one hour in his private jet than an average American will put driving an SUV for a year. I am sure there are people at home who are saying, 'when you change your lifestyle, I will consider changing mine.'"

It's a similar story with Jennifer Lopez, George Clooney, Brad Pitt and Julia Roberts, all of whom have enthusiastically and publicly embraced hybrid cars. Problem is, they'd have to drive them around the world a few times to save the same amount of carbon they burn up in just one trip on a private jet.

"We're all trying the best we can, truly we are," an exasperated DiCaprio said recently.

Barbara Streisand—who famously declared a 'Global Warming Emergency' two years ago—is another good example of the perils of preaching one thing and doing another. She's consistently called on the public to start conserving energy and water yet spends $22,000 a year watering her lawns and gardens, and her enormous mansion reportedly has an air-conditioned room solely devoted to her fur coats.

The token nature of trendy celebrity causes reached a zenith in April this year when the *Pimp My Ride* crew made an Earth Day special. As American comedian Lewis Black pointed out at the time, the last people who should be giving environmental lessons are a bunch of guys who spend each episode hotting up cars to the point where they're as fuel inefficient as possible.

That same day Oprah handed out energy efficient light globes to her entire audience—which probably won't go too far towards undoing the damage caused by the day she gave everyone in her audience free cars.

Daily Telegraph Opinion Editor Tim Blair takes a certain malicious glee in exposing the hypocrisy of celebrities on his blog. He cites the Live Earth worldwide series of concerts in July as a particularly egregious example.

"The concept of getting rock stars to tell people to rein in their lifestyles I think was a masterstroke," he says. "I mean, you've got people who are bywords for excess and consumption and destruction and gigantic wasteful lifestyles telling people to reduce their carbon footprints! It's amazing anyone turned up—because it's hard to walk when you're doubled over laughing."

Like many conservatives, Blair reserves particular venom for Al Gore, the former U.S. vice-president and maker of *An Inconvenient Truth*.

"How can you be Al Gore and do this when you're flying around in private jets, charging $150,000 to $250,000 to give a speech telling people to live a more simple lifestyle? It's hysterical."

Blair points out that Gore owns a massive property in Tennessee that consumes a phenomenal amount of power. But, in Gore's defense, it must be said he has realized his 930 sqm house with its 20 bedrooms and eight bathrooms does generate some negative publicity and has since installed some solar panels.

As enjoyable as it is to beat up on celebrity hypocrites, there is always the sneaking suspicion that some critics are simply playing the man and not the ball. That is to say, their excessive focus on the hypocrisy of stars is a way of discrediting the message and to excuse inaction by the rest of us on the environment.

"Pointing out eco-celeb's lifestyle contradictions is one of the many strategies that the frightened, confused and lazy use to delay action on the environment," argued environmentalist Erin Courtenay on the *TreeHugger* website last month.

"Too often the criticisms imply that a green-celeb's errors render their environmental message moot and their actions meaningless."

Courtenay makes a fair point in that we need to separate the debate about the need to act on the environment from our discussion of the hypocrisy of celebrities.

But as Blair points out, the only reason we even listen to their environmental message is because of who they are—not because they actually have any real knowledge of the subject.

How can we engage with the underlying scientific debate when the discourse is reduced to trendy slogans uttered by the rich and famous?

Does Leonardo DiCaprio really understand the intricacies of scientific debate about the release of methane from clathrate compounds that are hypothesised as a cause for other warming events in the distant past, including the Permian-Triassic extinction event and the Paleocene-Eocene Thermal Maximum?

Or is DiCaprio just an actor?

"We've totally devalued expertise," says Dr Jackie Cook, from the School of Communications at University of South Australia. "We don't understand knowledge or research any more, we only understand opinion and image. What we have to do is shift from the surface into the depths (of an issue) but image floats faster through the (media's) system than anything else." ■

Questions for Discussion

1. Famous people have the potential to raise concerns about important issues. Writer Jeff Bercovici credits celebrities for increasing public awareness of important global issues. In his article for the Canada Free Press, "Green Fakers: Why Eco-Hypocrisy Matters," he also points out that it "is surprising the way celebrities react to such charges" (of not practicing a "green" lifestyle), "sometimes by ignoring them outright, sometimes by spouting lame self justifications, but rarely, if ever, by acknowledging the disconnect and vowing to lead a humbler, cleaner, more sustainable existence." Do you agree with his assessment and the need for celebrities to "practice what they preach"?

2. A quote from the article states: "'Pointing out eco-celeb's lifestyle contradictions is one of the many strategies that the frightened, confused and lazy use to delay action on the environment,' argued environmentalist Erin Courtenay on the *TreeHugger* website last month." To what extent, if any, do you believe that Courtenay is herself using an ad hominem argument against those who complain about celebrities? Could her point be made in a more effective way?

3. The author of the article calls Sean Hannity a "right-wing attack dog." Do you consider that characterization an ad hominem attack? Why or why not?

4. Is it an ad hominem argument or a legitimate concern that those at the forefront of global issues are not academic experts concerning the policies that they support?

. . . .

The issue of global warming has become a primary international concern. It was the subject of former Vice President Al Gore's Oscar-winning documentary *An*

Inconvenient Truth and is a key topic in scientific conferences. The National Academy of Sciences, the UN's Intergovernmental Panel on Climate Change (IPCC), and other noted scientists and organizations have reached consensus that global warming is a reality and that measures must be taken to prevent catastrophic international consequences. There are also credible scientists, who have been labeled "deniers," who agree that global warming is a reality but raise questions concerning the subissues of the extent of humans' role in causing global warming, the consequences that will or will not come from the warming, the extent of the warming to come, and the ability of humans to affect changes.

In the following article, writer and radio host Dennis Prager discusses his objection to the analogy made by writer Ellen Goodman concerning those who raise questions about this issue.

On Comparing Global Warming Denial to Holocaust Denial

Dennis Prager

In her last column, *Boston Globe* columnist Ellen Goodman wrote: "Let's just say that global warming deniers are now on a par with Holocaust deniers."

This is worthy of some analysis.

First, it reflects a major difference between the way in which the Left and Right tend to view each other. With a few exceptions, those on the Left tend to view their ideological adversaries as bad people, i.e., people with bad intentions, while those on the Right tend to view their adversaries as wrong, perhaps even dangerous, but not usually as bad.

Those who deny the Holocaust are among the evil of the world. Their concern is not history but hurting Jews, and their attempt to rob nearly six million people of their experience of unspeakable suffering gives new meaning to the word "cruel." To equate those who question or deny global warming with those who question or deny the Holocaust is to ascribe equally nefarious motives to them. It may be inconceivable to Al Gore, Ellen Goodman and their many millions of supporters that a person can disagree with them on global warming and not have evil motives: Such an individual must be paid by oil companies to lie, or lie—as do Holocaust deniers—for some other vile reason.

The belief that opponents of the Left are morally similar to Nazis was expressed recently by another prominent person of the Left, George Soros, the billionaire who bankrolls many leftist projects. At the World Economic Forum in Davos last month, Soros called on America to "de-Nazify" just as Germany did after the Holocaust and World War II. For Soros, America in Iraq is like the Nazis in Poland.

A second lesson to be drawn from the Goodman statement is that it helps us to understand better one of the defining mottos of contemporary liberalism: "Question Authority." In reality, this admonition applies to questioning the moral authority of Judeo-Christian religions or of any secular conservative authority, but not of any other authority. UN and other experts tell us that there is global warming; such authority is not to be questioned.

Third, the equation of global warming denial to Holocaust denial trivializes Holocaust denial. If questioning global warming is on "a par" with questioning the Holocaust, how bad can questioning the Holocaust really be? The same holds true with regard to Nazism and the George Soros statement. Claiming that America in the Iraq War is morally equivalent to Nazi Germany in World War II trivializes the unparalleled evil of the Nazis.

Fourth, the lack of response (thus far) of any liberal or left individual or organization—except to defend Ellen Goodman—or from the Anti-Defamation League, the organization whose primary purpose has been to defend Jews, is telling. Just imagine if, for example, an equally prominent Christian figure had written that denying America is a Christian country is on a par with denying the Holocaust. It would have been front-page news in the mainstream media, the individual would have been excoriated by just about every major liberal individual and group, and the ADL would have cited this as an example of burgeoning Christian anti-Semitism and Holocaust trivialization. But not a word at the ADL on Soros's comments about de-Nazifying America or Goodman's Holocaust-denial comment.

Fifth, and finally, the Ellen Goodman quote is only the beginning of what is already becoming one of the largest campaigns of vilification of decent people in history—the global condemnation of (a) anyone who questions global warming; or (b) anyone who agrees that there is global warming but who argues that human behavior is not its primary cause; or (c) anyone who agrees that there is global warming, and even agrees that human behavior is its primary cause, but does not believe that the consequences will be nearly as catastrophic as Al Gore does.

If you don't believe all three propositions, you will be lumped with Holocaust deniers, and it would not be surprising that soon, in Europe, global warming deniers will be treated as Holocaust deniers and prosecuted. Just watch. That is far more likely than the oceans rising by 20 feet. Or even 10. Or even three. ■

Questions for Discussion

1. Prager makes the point that those who question issues surrounding global warming are seen as having evil motives. To what extent do you believe that bad motives are attributed to "deniers"?

2. What problems does Prager have with the analogy made by writer Ellen Goodman in which she compares global warming denial to Holocaust denial?

3. Prager further objects to an analogy implied by George Soros. What is that analogy and do you believe it is valid or faulty?

4. To what extent do you agree or disagree with Prager's comments on the use of the admonition to "Question Authority"? What criteria should we use to distinguish a credible questioning of research from one based in hateful or selfish motives?

· ·

The following article reports on a study on possible causal links between Facebook use and grade point averages. As you read the article, see if you believe that the study cited justifies such a causal connection or whether the *Daily News* writer has drawn a hasty conclusion from the research. Note the researcher's own comments on her study found in the *Questions for Discussion*.

Does Facebook Make You Dumber?

Study Shows Users of Social Networking Site Get Lower Grades

Rosemary Black

Facebook time might be cutting into homework time, according to a new study that examined the grades of college-age users.

Does Facebook make you dumb and dumber?

College students who use the social networking site spend less time studying and get poorer grades than non-users, according to a new study.

The 219 students surveyed by Ohio State University doctoral candidate Aryn Karpinski had GPAs that ranged from 3.0 to 3.5, while Facebook abstainers had GPAs between 3.5 and 4.0. Not surprisingly, the Facebook students averaged 1 to 5 hours of studying per week while non-users hit the books for 11 to 15 hours a week.

"I am not saying that Facebook causes poor academic performance," says Karpinski, who co-authored the study with Adam Duberstein of Ohio Dominican University. "I am saying that the research shows that there is a relationship between Facebook use and academic performance."

The students who participated in her research didn't see Facebook as a problem, Karpinski notes. In fact, 79% of the students surveyed said that they didn't think Facebook impacted their academic performance, she says.

Educators have mixed opinions on whether or not Facebook causes flunking. And it seems unlikely that college students would be willing to trade Facebook time for higher grades, says Scott Testa, a St. Joseph's University marketing professor.

College students who use the social networking site Facebook spend less time studying and get poorer grades than nonusers, according to one study.

"These students were raised with computers from day one and they are the generation that has embraced electronic communication from the start," he says. "It is the social media for 18 to 23 year olds. It's very rare for an undergraduate to not have a Facebook page."

Pace University professor Cathy Dwyer, Ph.D., says that even if students weren't on Facebook, they'd find something else to spend their time on. And, she says, Facebook certainly has a positive side, especially in this economy. "Facebook offers students a way to reconnect with their professors and classmates if they get laid off," she says. "It can help with the job search."

But Los Angeles psychotherapist Dr. Leslie Seppinni says Facebook is to blame for college kids socially isolating themselves.

"Whereas before they might join a study group or go [to] a study hall with other students to study, now they keep their computer next to them and continue to look at Facebook while trying to read a book," she says. "We are raising a society of young adults in whom face to face communication and being able to read a face is lacking. You just don't learn social skills when you're sitting in front of a computer on Facebook for five hours."

So does the author of the study think students should wean themselves from Facebook?

"I think they should engage in more self-monitoring," Karpinski says. "There are individual differences, meaning that some students may be able to be on Facebook for long periods of time and their GPAs will still be high. Also, I'm sure that if it wasn't Facebook, it would be another distraction."

Like getting together with friends face to face once in awhile, maybe? ■

Questions for Discussion

1. Do you believe that the headline for this article implies that Facebook is a causal factor in low grades?

2. One of the researchers suggests that social networking may not be the reason for lower GPAs by Facebook users. What are other explanations given for the disparity in grades? Can you think of other explanations for the research findings?

3. Here are other headlines concerning the same study. How does each of the headlines suggest a causal link between Facebook and lower grades despite the researchers' acknowledgement of the study's limitations?

   a. Study Says Facebook Can Impact Studies—UPI.com
   b. Facebook Fans Do Worse in Exams—Times Online
   c. Study: Facebook Users Get Lower Grades in College—Computerworld
   d. What Facebook Users Share: Lower Grades—TIME.com
   e. College Facebook Fans Get Lower Grades—InformationWeek
   f. Facebook Use Linked to Less Textbook Time—USATODAY.com
   g. Does Facebook Make You Dumber? Study Shows Users of Social Networking Site Get Lower Grades—New York Daily News

4. The researcher herself did not say that Facebook use caused lower grades but only that there is a relationship between Facebook use and academic performance. She responded to an Ohio State University site that criticized the reporting of her study in the following excerpt from an e-mail she sent to the critic. Does this excerpt change your viewpoint on the research as summarized

in the article? Based on your understanding of research, what can actually be concluded from what Karpinski calls her pilot study?

My name is Aryn Karpinski and I just wanted to write to you about my study that you posted on your website. I wanted to thank you for noting that some media outlets had sensationalized the information presented in the study. I appreciate your efforts to help represent research findings accurately.

I also agree with you completely regarding your comments about other "distractions" (e.g., It is pretty obvious that Facebook is a distraction but then again so is partying, TV, beer pong, playing sports, and anything else that college students do in their free time.). Conceivably, anything that takes away from study time could be correlated with GPA. So your assessment of other potential distractions that consume free time or not-so-free-time is spot on. Also, I'm sure that if I conducted this study at any other institution (e.g., Michigan, as you noted), the results would be different.

To explain my reasoning behind the study, I have included a little more information that may help shed light on some things.

As you know, this is a REALLY basic study. I just planned to do this for the conference to get some ideas and network with more experienced and qualified researchers in this area. I really wanted to have a dialogue with others who are looking into similar phenomena. The media completely sensationalized it, as you know. I have never dealt with the media, and did not anticipate this. I obviously know better now.

In a nutshell, the main purpose of my study was to EXPLORE (pilot study!) the demographic composition of a Facebook user at the college level. I also wanted to investigate academic achievement in relation to Facebook use. The demographic details were not the focus of the media's attention, as you know.

This research is correlational, which the media does not seem to understand. I have pushed the correlation versus causation aspect in all my interviews, and most media sources seem to get that in the article somewhere (at least lately). I am not saying that Facebook CAUSES poor academic performance. I am saying that the research shows that there is a RELATIONSHIP between Facebook use and academic performance. There are a host of third variables that need to be examined that are potentially influencing this relationship such as personality, work, extracurricular involvement, other activities, etc. Also, I'm sure that if it was not Facebook, it would be another activity (as you noted in your post).

I am fully aware of the limitations of my study, and merely want people, personnel at universities, researchers, parents, students, and tech-saavy [sic] people like yourselves to think about this intricate relationship (and start a dialogue).

. . . This is a very difficult area to research (i.e., social networking sites), and I can see how researchers and professors may dedicate their lives to examining phenomena like this.

My study is easy to criticize statistically and methodologically, obviously. But know that I am fully aware of what the problems are. I acknowledge the limitations of doing this research (especially survey research). Please know that I know there are many other people more qualified to speak on this topic (including you), who have dedicated their lives to this topic or the general field of technology research. I know this. I am learning along with everyone else.[21]

Ideas for Writing or Speaking

1. Write an argumentative essay or speech about a current issue in which you include several examples of fallacious reasoning. At the end of the essay or speech, identify the fallacies you have committed. Share your papers or speeches with the class and see if your errors in reasoning can be isolated.

2. Write a critique of an editorial or essay from a blog, newspaper, or magazine. Point out the fallacies made by the writer of the editorial or essay. Also, discuss valid reasoning on the part of the writer.

3. Choose an issue about which you have strong opinions. Read some viewpoints by people who oppose your opinion on this issue; errors in their reasoning will usually be obvious! List and explain several errors made by your opponents or one major error that weakens their arguments.

   Next, look critically at your own viewpoint. What errors are committed by those who favor your position on this issue? List and explain these errors.

Films for Analysis and Discussion

Because logical fallacies appear regularly in our daily lives, they are also prominent in film and on television. You may encounter many of our errors in reasoning on cable talk shows and on television dramas. Situation comedies, such as *The Office, Modern Family,* and *30 Rock* create characters that are often unreasonable and illogical in their interactions with one another. Here are some examples of films that illustrate logical fallacies.

I Can Do Bad All By Myself (2009, PG-13)

This Tyler Perry movie concerns a number of individuals with troubled pasts and present issues. It is full of examples of hasty conclusions and stereotyping and also shows the difficult but possible journey toward healing and acceptance in relationships.

Little Miss Sunshine (2006, R)

This hilarious and heartbreaking comedy is a master class in resiliency and overcoming self-fulfilling prophecies in our personal lives. The film's focus is the Hoover family, a dysfunctional but loving group of misfits who travel from New Mexico to California on their way to the "Little Miss Sunshine" beauty pageant. Along the

---

[21] "Ohio State Researcher Aryn Karpinski Conducts Study Concluding Facebook Causes Lower Grades," updated at http://pulse2.com/2009/04/14/ohio-state-researcher-arynkarpinski-conducts-study-concluding-facebook-causes-lower-grades/.

way, they encounter a plethora of obstacles, both physical and emotional, that send them on a slippery slope of bad judgments and crazy thinking.

Bulworth (1998, R)

This film tells the story of a politician who has put out a contract on his own life in order to collect on an insurance policy for the sake of his family. Note especially the ad hominem attacks he makes, as well as the use of two wrongs make a right and straw man.

Fargo (1996, R)

Fargo follows a murder investigation carried out by Marge Gunderson. Marge is a logical and systematic investigator, and her rationality is offset by the fallacious reasoning of most of the other characters in the film. Note especially the following fallacies: two wrongs make a right, ad hominem, post hoc, red herring, and begging the question.

Bringing Up Baby (1938)

This classic film is an entertaining look at hasty conclusions and red herrings. The comedy follows a serious paleontologist and an heiress with a pet leopard as they search for a priceless bone.

7

The Power of Language

What's in a Name?

A critical thinker understands the power of language and
how it can be used or misused in an argument.

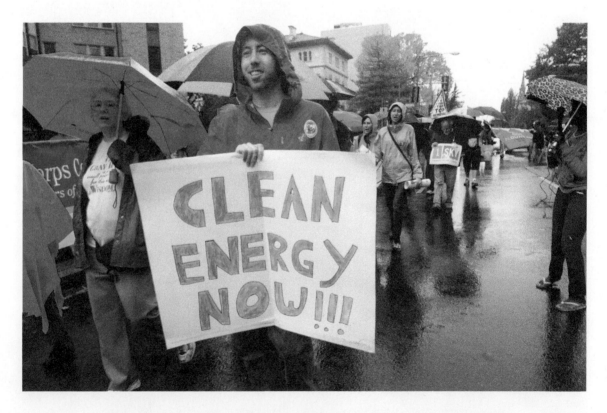

The words and symbols we choose reflect our viewpoints and express our identities.

THIS CHAPTER WILL COVER

- The power of words to frame arguments
- How words influence perception
- Vagueness, ambiguity, doublespeak, and weasel words

Read on **mythinkinglab.com**

Listen on **mythinkinglab.com**

> If language be not in accordance with the truth of things, affairs cannot be carried on to success.
>
> Confucius, *Analects* (6th c.b.c.)

In his definition of man, Kenneth Burke said, "Man is the symbol-using animal."[1] Language is the powerful system of symbols that enables us to communicate in ways no other creatures can. Speechwriters for politicians or businesspersons can be paid thousands of dollars for a short speech. Those who are willing to pay these enormous fees know that the words that are used and the way they are organized can make or break a campaign, a statement, or a crucial proposal.

On a smaller scale, many professionals attend workshops that focus on how to present ideas—how to sell cameras, clothing, or food by using the correct phrasing. For example, some large supermarket chains train their checkout clerks to ask, "Is plastic okay?" They assume that if people are asked if they want paper or plastic bags, they will opt for the more expensive paper bags. By asking in a way that narrows the customers' responses to a polite yes or a less polite no, they hope to cut down on the expenses of using paper. Other salespeople are trained to show some items to a customer and ask, "Will you be using cash or credit today?" before the potential buyer has even decided whether to make a purchase.

Employees who work in front office or public service positions are often taught to handle the public by speaking in ways that reflect courtesy and diffuse anger. You may have noticed that in a well-managed office or store, you can complain and receive sympathetic words from a receptionist or clerk (even if you don't get what you want from them). For example, a receptionist may say, "I'm so sorry that you've had to wait so long for the doctor; we've had a number of emergencies today." Websites that encounter problems loading content will often display apologetic words to solicit sympathy and patience from their users.

[1] Kenneth Burke, *Language as Symbolic Action: Essays on Life, Literature, and Method* (Berkeley: University of California Press, 1966), p. 3.

In our personal lives, we think about phrasing things to get the desired results. Teenagers and adults may rehearse their opening words carefully before calling a potential date. Children think about and practice how to ask their parents for treats or money. You may have experienced a time when you sat in your room or car rehearsing what you were going to say to someone; we usually engage in that kind of preparatory behavior when we are dealing with a stressful situation—an important job interview, a confrontation of a loved one, a proposal of marriage, or a request for a change in salary or working hours. We believe, consciously or unconsciously, that our choice of words and the way we say those words will affect our interactions with others.

This chapter will explore the influence that words have on people, especially as citizens and consumers. We will look at the way words can help us clarify issues and, conversely, how words are sometimes used to make issues more obscure and difficult to understand.

Denotation and Connotation

What's in a name? A rose by any other name would smell as sweet.

Shakespeare, *Romeo and Juliet*, 1595–1597

The first principle to understand is that words, as symbols, are extremely powerful. To comprehend this idea, consider two terms, *denotation* and *connotation*.

The **denotation** of a word is the specific object or act that a word points to or refers to. Words such as *dog, van, walk,* and *swim* and proper nouns such as *Marisa* all point to objects, actions, or persons; the words denote these objects, actions, or persons. In some academic fields, the term *denotation* is used to mean the word's dictionary definition.

Connotation refers to all the images—positive, negative, or neutral—that are associated with any given denotation. The connotations of words include their emotional meanings, which may be different for different individuals.[2]

If you think about these definitions, you can see that although denotations are the same for everyone, connotations vary from person to person. For example, for citizens of the United States, Thanksgiving denotes a national holiday that takes place on the fourth Thursday in November. According to this excerpt from an editorial writer, the holiday has diverse connotations:

> Thanksgiving has different and sometimes multiple images for each of us. The Pilgrims and Indians dining at Plymouth. A joyous (or stressful) gathering of family and friends. Travel. A day off work. Time away from school. The beginning of the end for the American Indians. The official start of the shopping season. Soup kitchens and food banks.[3]

denotation   The specific object or action that a word points to, refers to, or indicates.

connotation   All the images—positive, negative, or neutral—that are associated with any given denotation by an individual or a group. The connotations of words include their emotional meanings. Both concrete and abstract words have connotations that are different for different individuals.

---

[2] For our purposes, we are using the definition of *connotation* used by general semanticists who study the effects of words on thinking and behavior. Some scholars employ different meanings of this term; you may wish to consult a formal logic text for definitions of this term that are used in that context.

[3] Pat Craig, "Let's Not Forget the Little Things," *Contra Costa Times*, November 28, 1996, p. A-27.

Stop and Think

Think of the name of a holiday that you celebrate. What images are associated with that day for you? How might the name of that holiday evoke different images for other people?

Connotations are so powerful that various organizations have been asked to change their names when they are perceived to be offensive to a particular group. A council of local governments in the Washington, D.C. area passed a resolution requesting that the Washington Redskins football team change its name because of the connotations that were perceived to be insulting to Native Americans. Carol Schwartz, one of the authors of the resolution, said that she is a football fan and loves the team but has been bothered by the name, which she claims dates back to a time when bounties were placed on American Indians and bloody scalps, or "red skins," were proof of a kill. "The use of this degrading and dehumanizing term for a team name is offensive and hurtful to Native Americans and to many people who reject racial stereotypes, racial slurs and bigotry as socially and morally unacceptable," her resolution reads.[4]

Karl Swanson, the spokesman for the Redskins, made it clear that the resolution would not influence the team to change its name. He said he had expressed the team's positions clearly in a letter sent to Ms. Schwartz, accusing her of spreading "misinformation" about the origin of the team name. Mr. Swanson says the name *Redskins* refers to the American Indian practice of painting the faces and bodies of warriors with red clay prior to battle. He said the Redskins have always depicted Indians in an honorable fashion and that the team has repeatedly found a "striking amount" of support from fans and the general population.[5]

In a recent poll conducted by Vanity Fair, most respondents favored keeping Native American mascot names.

Poll: Native American Team Names Here to Stay

Should Native American References Be Kept in Sports?

The name of a sports franchise is a brand with few peers in business and 78 percent of Americans wish to keep even the controversial ones, while only 12 percent want them retired.

It is interesting to note the history of the sports teams known as the Braves and the Redskins. Both were originally named for Boston teams, one baseball and one football, in 1912 and 1933, respectively. The Braves' name derived from an affectionate nickname of a club that the team owner belonged to. The Redskins were renamed in 1933 (they were also formerly known as the Braves) in honor of the team's Native American coach, Lone Star Dietz.[6]

The issue concerning the use of Native American names and mascots is still controversial. See more about a ban on these names in the article entitled "Race-Based Team Names Not Tolerated in Wisconsin" at the end of this chapter.

---

[4] Matthew Cella, "Council Votes for Redskins to Change Name," *The Washington Times*, January 10, 2002.
[5] Ibid.
[6] http://www.cbsnews.com/stories/2010/06/01/60minutes/main6537729.shtml.

Another group that has requested name changes is PETA, People for the Ethical Treatment of Animals. Leaders of this group believe the names of some cities and towns promote negative connotations of animals:

> People for the Ethical Treatment of Animals on Tuesday asked Contra Costa supervisors to consider changing the unincorporated town's name to "Unity," in tribute to the Union Oil Company, which employed many East Bay residents through much of the 20th century. The name Rodeo, PETA says, conjures images of a brutal anachronistic sport that glorifies animal cruelty.
>
> ... One town leader found "Unity" far less desirable than "Rodeo." The town's name (pronounced ro-*day*-o) is Spanish for "roundup." It acknowledges the annual cattle event that took place every March, after the grazing season, early in the town's history, said Diane Leite, an advisory committee chairwoman.
>
> The *Californio* lore certainly carries a more positive connotation than renaming Rodeo after an oil refinery, she said. After 100 years of heavy industry, the town's land is difficult to develop because of toxic exposure. "We were a cattle town, and it's something to be proud of," she said. "I don't think we should name our town after the oil industry."
>
> PETA's campaign coordinator Lisa Franzetta acknowledged the irony of an animal rights group pushing to commemorate a refining facility. But, she said, the town is certainly free to come up with an alternative. PETA has sought politically correct titles before. The group recently asked officials in Hamburg, Germany, to consider the name "Veggieburg," Franzetta said. And, to no avail, they suggested Fishkill, N.Y. try on "Fishsave" for size.[7]

More recently, PETA has asked the popular British duo Pet Shop Boys to change their name to one that they believe would have more positive connotations.

Pet Shop Boys Reject PETA Name Change Request

Abi Silvester

Much as they may protest at the accolate, the Pet Shop Boys have become a British institution. But PETA recently got in touch with the duo to ask them to do away with over 20 years of pop history, and change their name to something more animal-friendly.

What snappy new band name did PETA suggest? Read on after the jump to find out. . . .

PETA wanted Neil Tennant and Chris Lowe to change their band's name to "The Rescue Shelter Boys," in a bid to draw attention to the plight of millions of unwanted animals up for adoption all over the world.

Although the Boys themselves declined the request, they did so with typical gentility, commenting on their official website that the request "raises an issue worth

[7] Peter Felsenfeld, "PETA Thinks Rodeo Not PC, Asks Town to Change Its Name," *Contra Costa Times*, October 22, 2003.

thinking about." PETA's letter requests the name change due to the cruelty which they allege takes place in the pet trade. If the band were to agree to the name change, it continues, it would "encourage your millions of fans to consider giving a home to an abandoned or unwanted animal from an animal shelter."[8]

People may write to advice columnists to get help in responding when they feel insulted by a label, as the following excerpt from a "Miss Manners" column illustrates:

> *Question:* A group of women was giving testimony before a congressional committee regarding an issue of serious concern to them. When it came his turn to question them, a certain Southern senator said, "Mr. Chairman, we've got a lovely group of ladies here. We thank you for your presence. I have no questions."
>
> The senator surely thought he was being gentlemanly, but the women felt they were being patronized and did not hide their displeasure at being referred to as "lovely ladies."
>
> Is it ever correct for a government official, or anyone for that matter, to make such remarks? If not, what would be the proper response to discourage such offenses from being recommitted? This sort of thing seems to occur frequently.
>
> Was the senator rude, or were the women overly sensitive?
>
> *Answer:* The senator was rude, but not in the purposeful sense of delivering an insult. The manners he used were once considered gracious in any setting, although they are now widely recognized to suggest, when employed in a clearly nonsocial situation, that the chief contribution of ladies is to be decorative.
>
> There is, however, a grandfather clause, by which elderly people who are obviously unaware of changes are not taxed for mild offenses that are well meant. Miss Manners is thinking of closing this down soon, because there has now been ample time for gentlemen to understand changes that began a quarter of a century ago. In any case, politicians usually do not wish to avail themselves of the excuse that they are unaware of what is going on in the modern world.
>
> You did not tell Miss Manners which senator it was, so she will kindly presume that he was not being wily and purposely trivializing their appearance—and in such a way that they probably looked petty and ill-tempered in bristling. It would have been better to reply graciously, "How kind of you, Senator; we gather this means that you fully support what we are saying."[9]

In addition to having emotional reactions about how we are labeled as members of a group, we also have strong feelings about individual names. The name *Terry,* for example, simply refers to a given person (denotation); still, I may have a positive connotation for the name while you may dislike the name because of a negative experience you had with someone named Terry in your life. *Washington Post Magazine* writer Gene Weingarten says that it is possible to track the historical roots and the popularity of names back to 1900 on a federal

---

[8] http://www.hippyshopper.com/2009/04/pet_shop_boys_reject_peta_name_change_request.html.

[9] Judith Martin, "Time to Say Goodbye to Patronizing Phrases," *Contra Costa Times*, August 14, 1995, p. A-2.

database. He writes the following about his concerns that current names are too trendy:

> Increasingly, people are no longer naming children for their ancestors or heroes or even favorite actors or athletes—names with some sense of history or reverence or accomplishment—and are choosing trendy names that to them seem hip or creative.... When you do this, your victim is your own child. I know of a kid, born in the mid-1960's, who used to introduce himself thus: "Hi, my name is Caribou, but you can call me Mike."... For as long as humans have been responsible for naming their offspring, there have been bad names. The 1910 list of names shows many Clarabellas. Ova was somewhat popular, as was Fanny. And a bunch of boys regularly got saddled with Elmer and Thurston. But these are mostly names that have slid into disfavor over the years.... Adolph, for example, was a reasonably popular name that plummeted in popularity after about 1930.[10]

The tendency to name children after pop culture figures seemed to have resurfaced in 2010, according to writer Victoria Leigh Miller:

> Child actor Jaden Smith (son of Will and Jada) starred in a remake of the 1984 movie, "The Karate Kid." His name – albeit spelled "Jayden" – is at a whopping #5 on the boys list. (Mom Jada makes the list on the girl's side at #95.)
>
> ... It's time to step into the "Twilight Zone." Yep, Jacob and Isabella rank at #2 for boys and girls names for 2010. And I'm sure the "Twilight" series had nothing to do with it at all, right? The "Twilight" movie, "Eclipse," came out in the summer of 2010, and it featured the ultra-popular characters Jacob and Bella.[11]

Names and labels help us clearly understand the difference between denotation and connotation. For example, names connected to heritage are often filled with meaning for individuals and cultures. At the end of this chapter, one writer talks about the significance of the names given to him and his friends by their Vietnamese parents and how much is lost when these names become "Americanized." Try Exercise 7.1 (pages 304–305) to see if you and another person have a disagreement about the connotations of names.

The Power of Connotation

As we have discussed, we have personal connotations for words based on our unique past experiences as individuals; we also have cultural connotations associated with names and words. When the famous child star and cultural icon Shirley Temple was at the height of her career, thousands of parents named their daughters Shirley after her, but in the succeeding generations, very few did.

Lawyers, generally aware of the power of connotations, will be careful about the words they use to make their cases to a jury. For example, the lawyer for defendant Alex Kelly, who was accused of raping a 16-year-old girl "skillfully managed the information that was presented to the jurors. He often referred to Kelly's father, who

---

[10] Gene Weingarten, "Madisonness," *Washington Post Magazine,* September 21, 2003.
[11] Victoria Leigh Miller, "2010's Baby Names," http://news.yahoo.com/s/ac/7409738_2010s_baby_names__with_a_pop_culture_bent.

owned a plumbing business, had substantial real estate investments, and posted a $1 million bond for his son, as 'a plumber.'"[12]

Semanticists, who study the meaning of words, use a tool that allows them to assess the cultural connotations of a word. This tool is called a **semantic differential**. Researchers give a list like the following to groups of people in order to assess the connotative meaning of a word. The word is rated on a scale from one extreme to the other.

semantic differential
A tool that allows semanticists to assess the connotations of a word for a particular group.

Fast	...	...	...	...	...	Slow
Strong	...	...	...	...	...	Weak
Beautiful	...	...	...	...	...	Ugly
Active	...	...	...	...	...	Passive
Brave	...	...	...	...	...	Cowardly
Good	...	...	...	...	...	Bad
Powerful	...	...	...	...	...	Powerless

Meaning is based on three dimensions: Is the word good or bad? Is it active or passive? Is it powerful or weak? Note that all of the polar dimensions given in the semantic differential fit into one of these three categories.

In several classroom studies of the words *lady* versus *woman,* it was discovered that most students see the term *lady* as good, passive, and weak, while the word *woman* is seen as neither good nor bad, but as active and strong. The term *rock star* is seen as powerful, active, and bad. Advertisers commission studies of words to discover if the name they will give to a car, cola, or laundry detergent has positive connotations for their target audiences.

Stop and Think

Look at names given to products and businesses. What images do you believe the companies want to have associated with their goods or services? Which brand names do you consider successful, and which names don't work?

We can say that a name or word is just a label and has no effect on us, but consider the following examples:

- When you go into a gift or novelty store, you are likely to see a section of "over the hill" paraphernalia for people who are turning 30, 40, 50, or 60. You know that, logically, when you have a birthday, you are essentially the same biochemical and emotional being you were the day before. Yet when the label *30* or *40* is attached to you, you may suddenly experience a sense of anxiety or mild depression because of the connotations (images) associated with that age. Conversely, ask young children how old they are and they will usually be quite conscious of whether they are 5 or $5\frac{1}{2}$ or $5\frac{3}{4}$ and will use these minute distinctions as status symbols among their peers. People who reach the age of 21 in the United States (the age of full adult privileges) will sometimes say with surprise, "I don't *feel* 21," or "I don't feel different." The main difference is in the label.

[12] William Glabberson, "For Juries, the Truth vs. the Whole Truth," *New York Times,* November 16, 1996.

- If you believe that abortion is wrong, do you want to be described as *anti-abortion, anti-choice,* or *pro-life?* Do you want to use the word(s) *fetus, products of conception, unborn, preborn,* or *baby?*

- If you believe that abortion is a right, do you want to be described as *pro-abortion, anti-life,* or *pro-choice?* Do you want to use the word(s) *fetus, products of conception, unborn, preborn,* or *baby?*

- Food libel laws, also known as "food disparagement laws," "veggie libel laws," or "veggie hate laws," are laws passed in 13 U.S. states that make it easier for food industry interests to sue their critics for libel. These 13 states are Alabama, Arizona, Colorado, Florida, Georgia, Idaho, Louisiana, Mississippi, North Dakota, Ohio, Oklahoma, South Dakota, and Texas. Many of the food-disparagement laws punish First Amendment–protected expression, establish a lower standard for civil liability, and allow for punitive damages and attorneys' fees for plaintiffs alone, regardless of the case's outcome. This means that even if a defendant is found innocent of libel, he or she may still have to pay the legal fees for his or her prosecution.[13] The produce police have also struck in Louisiana, where a new law prohibits "disparagement of any perishable agricultural or aquacultural food product."[14] Could this lead to a Crawfish Anti-Defamation League?

- Leonore Hauck, a managing editor for the *Random House* dictionary division, discussed how definitions change to reflect current sensibilities. "One of the definitions of 'girl' in 1947 was 'a young, unmarried woman.' Today we say, 'a young, immature woman, esp. formerly, an unmarried one.' The word 'formerly' shows you how the meaning has changed, and a note warns the reader, 'Many women today resent being called girls.'"[15]

  However, even more recently, the term *girl*—when used by women in a casual conversation—has become acceptable again. "We've taken back the word and are using it the way we want—girl power, girl talk," said Jane Pratt, the 34-year-old editor of her eponymous new magazine, *Jane.* "It's about girls supporting each other and reveling in what's fun about being a girl.... Girl power means something different from feminism." Now *girl* crops up throughout pop culture. "Girls rule" emblazons T-shirts. A college women's crew scrawls, "You row, girl" on the side of the team van.[16]

- The Food and Drug Administration (FDA) "ordered milk labels changed to give Americans a better idea of how much fat is in that glass. Those jugs of 2 percent milk that were labeled 'low-fat' were to be renamed 'reduced fat.' Only 1 percent milk can be called 'low-fat,' while skim milk, the healthiest choice, can be advertised as 'fat-free' or 'nonfat' milk. The change came after consumer advocates complained that Americans were misled into believing milk with 2 percent fat was healthier than it actually is."[17]

  In addition, the U.S. Food and Drug Administration warns milk and ice cream manufacturers not to use the terms *no hormones* or *hormone free* on their

---

[13] Jim Sincock, "Food Libel Laws," http://www.localsustainability.net/2009/08/food-libel-laws/, August 2, 2009.

[14] Amy Bernstein, "Eye on the '90s," *U.S. News and World Report,* December 23, 1991, p. 17.

[15] Patricia Holt, "The Woman Who Decides What Goes in Webster's," *San Francisco Chronicle,* October 24, 1991, p. E-5.

[16] Carla Hall, "It's a 'Girl' Thing for Women," *Los Angeles Times,* November 19, 1997, p. A1.

[17] "Milk Cartons to Reflect Clarification of Fat Context," 2002, MooMilk.com (no author).

products. Warning letters from the FDA explain that these are false claims because all milk contains naturally occurring hormones, and milk cannot be processed in a manner that renders it free of hormones.[18]

- Studies investigating the way in which authority status affects perceptions of size have found that prestigious titles lead to height distortions. In one experiment conducted on five classes of Australian college students, a man was introduced as a visitor from Cambridge University in England. However, his status at Cambridge was represented differently in each of the classes. To one class, he was presented as a student; to a second class, a demonstrator; to another, a lecturer; to yet another, a senior lecturer; to a fifth, a professor. After he left the room, each class was asked to estimate his height. It was found that with each increase in status, the same man grew in perceived height by an average of a half-inch, so that as the "professor," he was seen as two and a half inches taller than as the "student."[19]

- Dennis Baron, professor of English and linguistics at the University of Illinois at Urbana-Champaign, notes the following: "McDonald's wants Merriam-Webster to take its McJob and shove it. McDonald's CEO Jim Cantalupo is steamed that the latest edition of *Merriam-Webster's Collegiate Dictionary* defines 'McJob' as low-paying, requiring little skill, and providing little opportunity for advancement. Three years ago, the *American Heritage Dictionary of the English Language* ran a similar definition, and the *Oxford English Dictionary* includes 'unstimulating' in the mix of descriptors branding McJobs as dead-end. Cantalupo calls such negative definitions 'a slap in the face' to American restaurant workers.... Merriam-Webster announced that it was sticking by its definition, which reflects the way McJob has been used for at least 17 years. Dictionary editors regularly include words far more controversial and offensive because their job is to record how the rest of us use our language, and we don't always use it politely."[20]

- Recently, there have been lawsuits involving what some call "file sharing" and others call stealing or "piracy":

> These aren't just academic arguments. They're ammunition in a battle that's raging online to shape the way the public thinks about copyrights. The first salvo was fired by the original Napster, which defined itself as a file-sharing network. That won the semantic high ground by defining unauthorized downloading as "sharing," not "copying" or "duplicating." The implication was that users of these networks were merely being generous with something they possessed, not usurping the rights of copyright holders.
>
> Record labels, music publishers and movie studios contend that copyrights are indeed property, entitled to the same protection as a home or a car. To counter the notion of "sharing," they've advanced an equal powerful metaphor: downloading as theft. "When you go online and download songs without permission, you are stealing," the Recording Industry Assn. of America says on its website. "Piracy is theft, and pirates are thieves, plain and simple. Downloading a movie off of the Internet is the

---

[18] "FDA Warns Milk Producers to Remove 'Hormone Free' Claims From the Labeling of Dairy Products," U.S. Food and Drug Administration, www.fda.gov, September 12, 2003.

[19] Robert B. Cialdini, *The Psychology of Persuasion* (New York: William Morrow, 1993), p. 223.

[20] Dennis Baron, "McLanguage Meets the Dictionary," *Chronicle of Higher Education*, 50 (17): B-14.

same as taking a DVD off a store shelf without paying for it," adds the Motion Picture Assn. of America. The imagery has been echoed by the news media, lawmakers and college administrators. It's even found its way into the online term-paper site FratFiles.com, which offers a model essay, "Illegal downloading 'is' stealing" (yes, there are shortcuts even for ethics assignments).[21]

- In the continuing debate over immigration, people of varying points of view choose different terms to describe the people involved in the issue. Note the difference in connotation in the following common terms: *guest workers, undocumented workers, migrant workers, undocumented folks, undocumented immigrants, illegal immigrants, illegal aliens.* The term chosen by a speaker or writer is a strong indicator of the viewpoint he or she takes on the issues surrounding immigration.

Reification: When Words Take on More Power Than Reality

Imagine yourself subject to a classroom experiment. You are sitting in class, about to see a film. To make the session more festive, your instructor gives you crackers and a homemade paté to munch as you view the movie. You enjoy the hearty taste of this snack, and when the film is over and the lights go back on, you ask for the recipe. Your teacher then informs you that you have been eating dog biscuits with canned cat food on top.

If you are like many people, you may experience a sense of nausea and disgust, though some cat food and dog food is perfectly edible for humans and is more nutritionally balanced than most fast food. But the labels put on this food, the words themselves, not the actual products, might make you sick.

In the same way, some people feel special when they are served expensive caviar or sweetbreads. The fact that they are eating fish eggs or cow organs has no jarring effect on them because there are such powerful, positive connotations associated with the names of these foods.

reification A process by which words become more powerful and real than objective reality.

Reification occurs when words themselves become more powerful and influential than objective reality. It involves treating words—which are abstract symbols—as if they were concrete realities. It leads to human foibles such as those found in the following examples and readings:

- Paying more money for "name brands" that may have the same ingredients as generic brands of products.
- Feeling confident when wearing designer label jeans or unworthy when wearing possibly higher quality jeans that don't carry the popular label.
- Feeling like you can't succeed in a math or writing course because a teacher in fourth grade said you were "poor in math" or because of one previous grade.
- Feeling overweight even when you are at or below your ideal weight because you were called fat years ago. (Karen Carpenter, a singer who died of complications of anorexia nervosa, was reportedly very upset about a critic who referred to her as overweight, and that label may have contributed to her obsession with her weight.)

---

[21] Jon Healey, "File 'Sharing' or 'Stealing'? The Semantic Debate Over Whether Copyright Infringement Is Theft," latimes.com, February 18, 2008.

- Two people having a good conversation at a party until one person mentions that he or she works as a therapist, professor, doctor, minister, or judge, which then makes the other person uncomfortable.
- In "primitive" cultures, being subject to stomach cramps because you know that someone is sticking needles in a doll with your name on it. Or in "sophisticated" cultures, creating hotel elevators that go from floor 12 to floor 14, leaving out the (presumably unlucky) thirteenth floor. (Note that this arrangement is especially true in hotels that house gambling casinos, presumably filled with people concerned about maximizing their "luck.")

The following article highlights the power of reification by showing how brand names and images affect our thinking and decision making about products.

Brand-Ate to Innovate: The Pepsi/Coke Challenge

Marty Baker

The Pepsi Challenge was a marketing tour de force. It proved that in a blind taste test, most consumers prefer Pepsi. So why hasn't that analytical proof pushed the needle in Pepsi's favor? Read Montague, Director of the Human Neuroimaging Lab at Baylor College of Medicine, has shown the true power of branding on the brain.

Montague decided to repeat the Pepsi Challenge, but added a twist of technology. Using a non-invasive technique called Functional Magnetic Resonance Imaging (FMRI) he was able to reveal which parts of the brain are active in real time.

When Montague and his team gave a taste of an unnamed soda to his volunteers he found that more people preferred Pepsi. On the scan, images of the ventral putamen, one of the brain's key reward centers, had a response that was five times stronger than for people who preferred Coke.

The surprise came when Read repeated the experiment. This time, telling volunteers which brand they were tasting. Nearly all the subjects then said they preferred the Coke. Moreover, different parts of the brain fired as well, especially the medial prefrontal cortex, an area associated with thinking and judging. The subject's brains were proving that their experience of the Coke brand influenced their preferences.

The work of Montague and other studies proves that branding goes beyond images and memory recall. The medial prefrontal cortex is a part of the brain known to be involved in our sense of self. It fires in response to a stimulus—an image, name or concept—that resonates with who we are. Something clicks, and we are more likely to buy.

The science of neuro-marketing is now in its infancy. But what it has proved is that branding isn't the latest marketing ploy, but a glimpse into how our brains are affected by smart messaging and marketing.

The "magical" power of words is also discussed by social psychologist Robert Cialdini as he explains why businesses create contests in which participants are asked to write short essays praising their products, as in this online example from winfreestuff.com:

> *Girlfriend* has one Sony Ericsson Jalou worth $179 to give away!
>
> Simply tell them in 25 words or less what is your favorite feature of the Sony Ericsson Jalou and why?

> A common way for businesses to cash in on the "magic" of written declarations occurs through the use of an innocent looking promotional device. Before I began to study weapons of social influence, I used to wonder why big companies such as Procter & Gamble and General Foods are always running those "25-, 50-, 100 words or less" testimonial contests. They all seem to be alike. The contestant is to compose a short personal statement that begins with the words, "Why I like... " and goes on to laud the features of whatever cake mix or floor wax happens to be at issue. The company judges the entries and awards some stunningly large prizes to the winners. What had puzzled me was what the companies got out of the deal. Often the contest requires no purchase; anyone submitting an entry is eligible. Yet, the companies appear to be strangely willing to incur the huge costs of contest after contest. The type of product doesn't matter; the process is the same. Participants voluntarily write essays for attractive prizes that they have only a small chance to win. But they know that for an essay to have any chance of winning at all, it must include praise for the product. So they find praiseworthy features of the product and describe them in their essays. The result is... hundreds of thousands of people in America who testify in writing to the product's appeal and who, consequently, experience that "magical" pull to believe what they have written.[22]

Sometimes reification can cause life-or-death consequences; superstitious and confused thinking can get people into deep trouble. Consider the story of a 25-year-old Frenchman, Lucien Schlitz, and his 19-year-old first mate, Catherine Plessz, who set out on a long cruise for the tropics aboard a 26-foot steel cutter called the *Njord*. They started in the Mediterranean Sea, which was so rough that it put the boat on its side. The boat righted itself, but later a freak wave swept over the boat, and both Lucien and Catherine found themselves in the water. Through desperate efforts, both managed to get back on board, but they no longer had a rudder (steering mechanism), so they were adrift.

The boat was still whole even though it had been knocked around by the storm. It would seem, to our clear, dry heads, that the logical thing would be to remain on board with the comforts of food, water, and blankets and to wait for help. But Lucien's mind was stressed and fatigued and he began to think obsessively about the life raft. He was terribly concerned that it wouldn't inflate, so he pulled it open, nearly losing it to the wind in the process. Since it measured six feet across, he couldn't fit it in the cockpit, so he moored it to the back of his steel boat.

[22] Robert B. Cialdini, *The Psychology of Persuasion* (New York: William Morrow, 1993), p. 80.

Soon after that, by mental processes that would surely be a feast for any psychologist, the only solution that seemed left to Lucien and Catherine was to take refuge in the *life* raft which represented safety (emphasis added)—still, as we see it, in a pattern of psychological aberration which explains the inevitability of everything they did.... Lucien and Catherine had now sought safety in their life raft after throwing into it some tinned food, some distress flares, two 20-litre jerricans of water, a compass and the leather sack with their money and their papers. Then the line linking them to the *Njord* parted.[23]

Over the next days, Lucien and Catherine needlessly suffered great thirst, hunger, sleep deprivation, and cold from being frequently tossed into the water by the waves upsetting the raft. On the twelfth day,

just as they had decided that survival was too difficult and they would make a quick end to it by drinking all the rest of their water at once for a last sensation of well-being, they were spotted at fifty yards, despite 8 foot troughs, and rescued by a cargo ship.[24]

This extended example reveals that we can give a word or phrase (in this case, *life raft*) power of its own and make faulty decisions based on that word or phrase.

Skill

Recognize the power we can attach to words. Pause and consider the facts, knowing how labels can be deceiving.

Meanings Are in People

General semanticists, who study the effects of words on people, have articulated some key principles to guide our responsible use of words.

Their main principle is the following: *The word is not the thing.* They use the analogy of a map (the words) showing a particular territory (reality). The map can give us information about the territory, but it is only a visual representation of the territory, and it can never show all the details of the territory. Our responsibility as thinkers is to realize that words are limited and to check out the territory before we draw hasty conclusions. If Lucien and Catherine, the sailors just discussed, had had the strength and wisdom to think over their options, they would have realized that, though their inflatable raft was *called* a life raft, their lives were more secure if they remained on board their cutter and sent up flares from there, saving the raft for use as a second vessel. In fact, the sailboat *Njord* was found adrift, but sound and dry, many days before Lucien and Catherine were rescued from their ordeal.

The meaning of words lies in people and not, magically, in the words themselves. Misunderstandings of words and phrases can be clearly seen when people speak different languages, as illustrated in the following news feature.

[23] Bernard Robin, *Survival at Sea* (Camden, ME: International Marine Publishing Company, 1981), p. 112.
[24] Ibid., p. 114.

Case Closed: Bladder Threat, Not Bomb

Drunken German Served 9 Months

Warren Richey

A drunk German tourist who triggered a bomb scare as he tried to tell a frightened flight attendant that he really, really, really had to go to the bathroom was a free man on Wednesday after more than nine months in prison.

Johann Peter Grzeganek, 23, told a judge in federal court in Fort Lauderdale that it was all a misunderstanding.

He said when he warned a flight attendant that it was "going to explode," he was referring to his bladder, not the plane.

The pilot wasn't taking any chances. He turned the plane around, dumped his fuel, and returned to Fort Lauderdale airport.

The plane was searched. No bomb.

Grzeganek was charged with knowingly making a false bomb threat on an aircraft in flight, a crime that carries a 20-year minimum mandatory sentence with no parole.

Faced with the prospect of growing old in prison, Grzeganek agreed to plead guilty to four lesser charges.

Unable to make his bond, he remained in prison waiting for his day in court, which arrived Wednesday.

Prosecutors came to the sentence hearing prepared to ask Chief U.S. District Judge Norman Roettger to keep Grzeganek behind bars for two to three years.

Roettger had a different idea. The chief judge, who understands German, read in court a letter Grzeganek wrote from his cell.

Grzeganek, who speaks little English, admitted to having been drunk the night of the flight. He said he drank heavily in part because he fears flying.

He also said he needed to use a bathroom. When the need became an emergency, he sought relief. The plane was in a steep climb at the time. An English-speaking flight attendant stopped him. He told her in German, according to his letter, "I have to go to the bathroom, my bladder is full and going to explode."

The attendant, Beate Westerhouse, testified it appeared Grzeganek was drunk and preparing to urinate in the aisle.

Westerhouse told him to get back in his seat.

"He said, 'No, no, no, the roof would go'" Westerhouse said.

"I took this to mean that something would make the roof explode," she said.

Roettger asked if she had ever heard the German phrase: "Then the roof flies." It is a colloquialism, Roettger said, that means a person needs to use a bathroom.

Roettger sentenced Grzeganek to time served. ▪

Cross-cultural confusions are not unusual. Some linguistic theorists and scholars believe that our language profoundly shapes our perception. Edwin Sapir and Benjamin Whorf created the Sapir-Whorf hypothesis, which states that language both reflects and affects our view of reality. To some extent, we are trained to see the world based on the language we learn. For example, most languages have words that represent and create a unique awareness of the world. Georgina Pattinson wrote for BBC News about Adam Jacot de Boinod's book *The Meaning of Tingo,* in which the author gives many examples of words and phrases with no English equivalent.

The Japanese have the term *katahara itai,* which indicates the action of laughing so much that one side of your abdomen hurts; the German's say *Kummerspeck*—literally, "grief bacon"—to describe the excess weight gained from emotion-related overeating, and the Dutch have the word *Ultwaaien* for "walking in windy weather for fun." Albanians have 27 separate expressions for a moustache. For Hawaiians, a *kualanapuhi* is an officer who keeps the flies away from the sleeping king by waving a brush made of feathers. *Tingo* comes from the Easter Island language of Pascuense and means "to borrow objects from a friend's house, one by one, until there's nothing left."[25]

Jacot de Boinod used over 280 dictionaries and 140 websites to compile his list of words and phrases, and he is convinced that a country's dictionary says more about culture and national character than a guide book. Hawaiians, for instance, have 108 words for sweet potato, 65 for fishing nets, and 47 for banana.[26]

We can see that phrases and words do frame experience for individuals and cultures. If someone perceives subtle differences in moustaches and sweet potatoes, he or she is seeing a different reality from someone who doesn't. Most professions also involve learning a complex vocabulary. While many laypersons may know the words *cells* and *carcinoma* (cancer of the epithelial cells), doctors, researchers, and other medical professionals learn to distinguish squamous cell carcinomas from adenocarcinoma of glandular cells and from carcinoma of transitional cells. Their training teaches them to recognize and identify abnormalities so that they can prescribe the best courses of treatment for their patients. They have been taught the terminology that allows them to "see" the world differently. In a similar way, musicians, athletes, lawyers, stockbrokers, dancers, and a host of other specialists expand their perceptions of reality through technical vocabularies.

Our frames of reference, our unique windows on the world, are influenced by our culture, expectations, personalities, values, experiences, ages, genders, and educational levels. Even when people speak the same language, misunderstandings frequently occur because of what words mean to different individuals. Dictionary definitions are useful for providing knowledge, but they often fall short in creating understanding among people. For example, *Webster's New International Dictionary* may define *love* as "a deep and tender feeling of affection for, or attachment or devotion to, a person or persons," but we can't rely on that definition when a significant other says, "I love you."

We need instead to find out what the word *love* means to an individual. Does it mean, "I want to marry you," "I enjoy your company," "I love every person and you're a person," "I will always be with you no matter what happens," or something else?

Skill

Realize that meanings are in people. Ask, "What do you mean?" whenever a word or phrase is unclear or is a potential source of misunderstanding.

The skill of clarifying what a word or phrase means to someone else may seem so simple as to be insulting to your intelligence, and yet it is one of the most valuable

[25] Georgina Pattinson, "Tingo, Nakkele, and Other Wonders," *BBC News Magazine,* September 26, 2005.
[26] Ibid.

and underused skills we have. We are inclined to make assumptions when we hear a phrase, a political speech, or a commercial message; we tend to believe that what the other person means is what we would mean if we had used those words.

Uncritical assumptions are common with the use of relative terms, such as *cold, hot, probable, generous, inexpensive,* or *beautiful;* there are also relative phrases, such as *a short distance, light housekeeping,* or *an easy test.* Although these words have a general definition, they often mean different things to different people. For example, if your friend wants you to meet her at class "early" and gives you no further explanation, it's possible that one of you may arrive a few minutes before class starts and the other may be waiting there for an hour.

Our tendency to project our own meaning onto the words of others explains why we are so often disappointed with blind dates ("This person is wonderful"), political candidates ("I care about the 'little people' in America"), or products ("Great energy all day long"). We want to believe that there is the perfect date, political solution, or energy drink. Sometimes we don't take time to question what the people who say these words really mean, as illustrated in the following article.

Sure I'm Committed... Oops... Bye-Bye

Dr. Laura Schlessinger

Simply saying words such as *committed* or *love* does not mean there actually is commitment or love. Then why say the words? Because of the instant gratification brought upon by such declarations; gratifications like sex or enhanced (temporary, of course) sense of self. Listen to Cliff.

Cliff, thirty-nine, is in a difficult situation right now. He's been dating a twenty-seven-year-old woman for two and a half months. That's ten weeks of weekends they spent together, amounting to about twenty days of actual contact time.

"We had a committed relationship and it seemed like our relationship was made in heaven. Then she was diagnosed with lupus and I went over to talk with her and tried to explain my feelings."

"What feelings are those, Cliff?"

"That I can't marry her because of her health condition."

"I guess you only enjoy relationships when they look like they're made in heaven, and don't come burdened with the realities of earth."

"Well, I suppose. Maybe 'made in heaven' was a poor choice of words."

"No, I imagine it accurately expresses that you like your relationship pretty and neat."

"Well, yeah."

"Cliff, I don't know if you're ever going to find a perfect situation with nothing unpleasant or challenging to deal with, but I guess you could just move on and keep trying."

"If we were already married, it would be a life-long commitment and that would be different."

"You already used the word *committed* before. You said you were committed already."

"I didn't mean that really."

"I guess you really meant the sex was good and she was fun."

"Is there a way to explain my feelings to her?"

... "Realistically, there isn't much between you. Your predicament shows why infatuation and recreational sex should not be used as criteria for the notion of commitment. You are at the point of committed to good sex, good times, good fun, good feelings."

... Cliff had sex, which I think ought to be serious business, and told his lady he was committed; when there was an opportunity to show that the commitment meant something, he showed it meant nothing. ■

Often, the cause of projecting our personal meanings onto words spoken by others may lie in our emotional need to believe that something is true; other times, we are just untrained or too busy or lazy to pursue the reality of what is being said to us. And sometimes speakers or writers make things so confusing that it takes a grand effort to understand them. Consider a report that reads: "We have confirmed that the overturning of the presidential veto to create an amendment protecting the flag has been enforced."

In states where voters are given choices about public policies through propositions, there is often confusion in the wording of these propositions. For example, a number of years ago, in California, if you voted *yes* on a particular proposition, that meant you were saying *no* to nuclear power plant expansion; if you voted *no,* that meant you were saying *yes* to this expansion. More recently a *yes* vote on a proposition meant that you were voting *no* to big box stores, and a *no* vote meant that you were voting *yes* to big box stores. When ballot measures are confusing, voters may end up casting votes they don't really mean.

To help us defend against words that don't clearly represent reality, we will examine four common problems with language: vagueness, ambiguity, doublespeak, and weasel words. We will focus especially on the deliberate exploitation of these problems by advertisers, salespersons, politicians, and others.

The Problem of Vagueness

A word or phrase is *vague* when its meaning is unclear. **Vagueness** is a common problem in public discourse. Some politicians will use only vague, abstract terms that have generally positive connotations and not define what they mean, hoping that each listener will like the sound of the promises being made. When asked for specific details about their plans, they may commit the fallacy of "ignoring the question" (see the first example). Conversely, sincere politicians will say they have a plan for "increased aid to the needy" and then define what they mean by *aid,* what they mean by *the needy* and then what, precisely, they have in mind.

vagueness A problem that arises with the use of nonspecific or abstract words. A word or phrase is vague when its meaning is unclear.

Good reporters will notice vague language and press politicians and other policy makers to explain themselves. If they explain using only more vague, abstract terms, be careful about supporting them (because you don't know what you're supporting).

Example

Reporter: Mr. Candidate, you mentioned you have a comprehensive plan to deal with our terrible traffic problems. Can you tell us what is involved in this plan?

Candidate: Gladly. I plan to use all available resources to create a wide-range solution to this problem that has plagued us for years.

| Reporter: | Can you be more specific? Are you planning expansions, and would these cause greater tolls or taxes for the citizens? |
| Candidate: | As I've said, the program will be quite comprehensive and each citizen will be considered and served. If I'm elected, you're going to see some incredibly positive changes. |

This candidate appears bright enough to describe his program in glowing terms, but he is unwilling or unable to detail what he is actually proposing. Perhaps the candidate hasn't formulated a plan, or perhaps he avoids giving details about his plans for fear of alienating special-interest groups.

Vagueness is a problem in many common interchanges, as noted by the examples below.

Family:	Can you tell us if this operation on our mother's hip is dangerous and also, will she have use of her leg afterward?
Surgeon:	All surgery has risks and these things are always hard to predict.
Family:	Well, can you give us typical recovery rates and times?
Surgeon:	Each person is different, but you can rest assured we are doing everything in our power to help.

In this example, everything the surgeon said may be true, but she has not provided any statistics or details to help the family feel at ease. Health care professionals are busy people, and they can't afford to make promises they may not be able to keep; still, you need to press for information so you can make the best decisions for your health and the well-being of your loved ones.

Darlene:	Paul, I really love you, and I think it would be good for our relationship if we started seeing other people.
Paul:	What are you saying? Do you want to break our engagement?
Darlene:	No, nothing like that. I just think it would be healthy for us to date other people.
Paul:	Are you interested in seeing someone else?
Darlene:	No, not at all. I think we'd both just grow more if we were able to experience a variety of relationships.
Paul:	What does that mean?
Darlene:	Well, it means I still love you but I just think it would be great for our relationship if we saw other people too.

In this situation, Darlene is either confused about what she wants or is sure of what she wants but doesn't know how to tell Paul. He needs to keep pressing for specifics for the sake of his mental health and so that he can have the information he needs to assess the relationship.

Examples of Commercials with Vague Wording

"Get your clothes a whiter white and a brighter bright!"
"Smoke Winters—with cool, smooth flavor!"
"It's the real thing!"
"The Hugo Company: We care about people."

Advertisers, like politicians, use positive connotations to excite the audience. But the question remains: What are they talking about?

The preceding examples are meant to show how frustrating it can be to get people to move from the nonspecific to the concrete so that we can really understand what they are saying. Some people are purposefully vague; others just have a hard time expressing themselves or knowing exactly what they want to communicate. Still, critical thinkers need to persist in understanding what is meant by vague words and phrases; then, any decisions about voting, having surgery, continuing a relationship, buying a product, or a number of other issues can be made rationally.

Ambiguity in Language

Ambiguity in language can also cause problems in communication. A word or expression is ambiguous when it has two or more different meanings. Unlike vague terms, ambiguous terms do have specific definitions, but they are phrased in a way that makes the correct definition unclear to the reader or listener. Often, riddles use ambiguity to create a puzzling situation; one common riddle asks you to turn the following drawing into a six by adding just one line:

ambiguity Having two or more possible meanings. Ambiguity in language occurs when the meaning of words is unclear or uncertain; such ambiguity can lead to confusion and misunderstanding.

IX

The answer, reflecting one of several types of "sixes," is

SIX

Ambiguity is also the problem in these humorous, but real, headlines compiled by Jay Leno and others:

"Drought Turns Coyotes to Watermelons."[27]
"Need Plain Clothes Security. Must Have Shoplifting Experience."[28]
"Foreclosure Listings: Entire State of New Jersey Available."[29]
"Red Tape Holds Up New Bridges."[30]
"Police Begin Campaign to Run Down Jaywalkers."[31]
"Hospitals Are Sued by 7 Foot Doctors."[32]

In England, similarly ambiguous signs have been posted:

"Automatic Washing Machines: Please remove all your clothes when the light goes out." (Notice in a laundromat)
"After tea break, staff should empty the teapot and stand upside down on the draining board." (Notice in an office)
"The farmer allows walkers to cross the field for free, but the bull charges." (Notice in a field)

---

[27] Jay Leno, *Headlines* (New York: Warner Books, 1989), p. 99.
[28] Ibid., p. 148.
[29] Ibid., p. 48.
[30] "Ms-Sam-Antics Daffynitions," 2001, mssamantics.us/wordplay/newspaper.htm.
[31] Ibid.
[32] Ibid.

On a more serious note, ambiguity in language is confusing and causes numerous communication problems. In Chapter 6, we discussed how ambiguity is central to the fallacy of equivocation, in which a speaker changes the meaning of a key term in order to win a point or avoid a task:

Teacher: Please name some solid elements from the Periodic Table of Elements.

Student: I could do that but they already have names.

Ambiguity can also create general confusion, as in the following example:

Former FBI director J. Edgar Hoover was reading a typed copy of a letter he had just dictated to his secretary. He didn't like the way she had formatted the letter, so he wrote on the bottom, "Watch the borders," and asked her to re-type it. The secretary did as she was instructed and sent it off to all top agents. For the next two weeks FBI agents were put out on special alert along the Canadian and Mexican borders.[33]

Ambiguous language can be especially perplexing between cultures. As we discussed previously, many expressions common to speakers of one language group (or subculture) are misunderstood by members of other cultures. For example, when asked if they would like more coffee, some English-speaking people respond, "No, thanks. I'm fine." People who are learning the language can't understand what seems to be a report on the state of one's health as an answer to a question about more coffee.

As in all cases of possible confusion in language, a critical thinker should consider alternative meanings to words and phrases and clarify terms by asking, "What do you mean?" (See Exercise 7.2 on pages 305–306.)

Doublespeak, Including Weasel Words

We have seen how vagueness and ambiguity in language can be used either unintentionally or deliberately to make issues cloudy. Words can also be deceptive in other ways. In this section, we will look at doublespeak and its subcategory, weasel words.

Doublespeak is "language used to lie or mislead while pretending to tell the truth.... It is used by the highest elected officials, by bureaucrats in state and local government, by members of industry, academia, and other areas of society in order

doublespeak Language used to lie or mislead while pretending to tell the truth. Doublespeak includes the use of *euphemism, jargon, gobbledygook,* and *weasel words.*

---

[33] Roger von Oech, *A Whack on the Side of the Head* (New York: Warner Books, 1990), p. 114.

to deceive, to make the bad seem good, the negative appear positive, the disastrous seem tolerable."[34] If language is the map, as general semanticists like to say, and reality is the territory, then doublespeak is the creation of a map that distorts the territory. Those who hear doublespeak are deceived and misled about the territory because of the deceptive map.

In his popular book *Doublespeak*, William Lutz claims that doublespeak is

> a very conscious use of language as a weapon or tool by those in power to achieve their ends at our expense. While some doublespeak is funny, much of it is frightening. We laugh and dismiss doublespeak as empty or meaningless words at our own peril, for, as George Orwell saw so clearly, the great weapon of power, exploitation, manipulation and oppression is language. It is only by being aware of the pervasiveness of doublespeak and its function as a tool of social, economic and political control that we can begin to fight those who would use language against us.[35]

One of the most common forms of doublespeak is **euphemism**, which means the use of a less direct but more acceptable term to describe an event, person, or object. In their daily use, euphemisms are not usually meant to deceive and to distort, but to soften harsh realities. We use euphemisms to explain disease and death to children when we make such statements as, "Aunt Sofia isn't feeling well today, so she's in the hospital," or "Grandma passed away." We may use euphemisms to sound better when we describe ourselves as thin (instead of skinny), *full-bodied* (instead of fat), or *under a lot of stress* (instead of irritable). Euphemisms may also be employed by advertisers to avoid being sued for using terms that have been trademarked. Complications arise when organizations try to also trademark the euphemisms. For example, the NFL has a trademark on the term Super Bowl, and advertisers are forbidden to use the phrase to promote products like televisions and snack foods. Many advertisers turned instead to euphemisms such as "The Big Game." Much to the bewilderment of both advertisers and sports writers, the NFL is now trying to trademark the "Big Game" euphemism, so that others can't make any specific reference to the Super Bowl.

euphemism The use of a less direct but softer or more acceptable term to describe an event, person, or object.

Euphemisms are used frequently in education. A teacher might use the euphemism "We're going to have a quiz" to announce a 50-item exam, reasoning that students would not panic studying for a "quiz" as much as they would for a "test" and therefore they would do better. Yet, students might prefer a 10-item test to a 50-item quiz. Similarly, parents may be told that their child is "having some problems with math" to soften the blow of a failing grade.

Euphemism as doublespeak is used frequently in business and government. In some cases, the euphemisms chosen become another category of doublespeak, which Lutz terms *inflated language*. Inflated language is designed to make the commonplace seem extraordinary or to make simple things more complex than they are. Following are some examples, mostly compiled by the National Council of Teachers of English:

Fired: dehired, nonrenewed, nonretained, selected out

Layoffs: negative employee retention, workforce adjustments, headcount reductions, career alternative enhancement program

Pain: discomfort

---

[34] Position Paper, National Council of Teachers of English, 1988.
[35] William Lutz, *Doublespeak* (New York: HarperCollins, 1989), pp. xii–xiii.

Death: terminal living, negative patient care outcome (or "That person is no longer a patient at this hospital.")

Poor: economically nonaffluent, economically marginalized

Prisoner: client of the correctional system

Lazy: motivationally dispossessed

Taxes: revenue enhancement or fee

Commercials: messages (as in "We'll return after these messages.")

Doublespeak is a form of personal and corporate denial of painful realities. No company wants to be seen as "firing" employees because that term has negative, cruel connotations. People want to be seen as compassionate, so they use terms that present the company in the best possible light. Many professionals use euphemisms to soften or inflate reality. For legal reasons, detectives may term someone a *person of interest* until they can gather enough evidence to change the term to *suspect*. Celebrities use doublespeak for "damage control" when they have said or done something that has solicited negative reactions; for example, when Justin Timberlake grabbed Janet Jackson's dress and exposed her breast during a halftime performance at the Super Bowl, the incident was explained as a "wardrobe malfunction." Real estate agents refer to tiny houses as "darling cottages" or "dollhouses"; they may describe dumps that are falling off of foundations as "needing a little tender loving care."

Reflecting on his experience trying to rent a home in Los Angeles, writer John S. Brady said that he ran into "some truly stunning feats of linguistic gymnastics":

> In the able and utterly shameless hands of one property owner seeking to lure prospective renters, a rundown bungalow fronted by a lumpy, sun-scorched patch of dirt through which, by the looks of it, the entire population of Southern California's moles had at one time or another passed, became a "quaint Craftsman-style house with a spacious yard." An equally creative landlord advertised a place with a "sunny garden." There was only one problem. This particular garden consisted of a lone rose pushing its way valiantly, but ultimately vainly, through the cracks in the concrete pad off the kitchen.[36]

spin The use of language, particularly in politics and public relations, to create a biased, positive connotation for ideas, events, or policies that one favors and a biased negative impression about ideas, events, or policies that one dislikes.

Another form of doublespeak has been called **spin**. Spin is the favorable appearance given to matters—often political—by "spin doctors."[37]

Spin is used to put the words and behavior of people in a positive light so that a positive reaction may result or a negative reaction may be minimized. Often spin is linked with the notion of damage control. When politicians or celebrities say or do something that may hurt them in the public eye, they seek to reframe the truth in a more acceptable way. Just as someone puts spin on a ball (like a bowling ball, baseball, or billiard ball) to affect its direction, "spin doctors" cast a spin on words and actions to influence their direction and impact.

Sometimes spin comes in the form of vague phrases that deflect responsibility, such as "I don't recall saying that," "I can't imagine saying that," "We need to move on from that," "I won't be discussing that," "I won't stoop to discussing those allegations," "I can't comment on that," "You're misinterpreting what I said," or "That was the alcohol speaking, and I'm going to enter rehab."

[36] John S. Brady, "Waiting for the Big One," *Chronicle of Higher Education*, November 4, 2003.
[37] www.phrasefinder/uk.org.

Professor Steven Doloff has created some linguistic fallacies—along with their Latin names—that illustrate political and journalistic spin quite well:

1. Si anas est, tetrinnit: "If it's a duck, expect it to quack": This is when politicians use any question at all asked by an interviewer to recite a self-serving prepared statement on some issue. Even though the lack of connection between the question and the answer can sometimes be quite striking, this tactic is nevertheless exceedingly common. Defenders of this verbal groundshifting might say that the interviewees are only "reframing" bad questions.... Politicians, however, almost never take overt issue with even the most biased questions (by saying, for example, "I think that's a misleading or unfair question because... "). In fact, they frequently say, "That's a very good question" and then go on to deliver their unrelated responses.

2. Ludicra exercitatio facilis est; res civilis, difficilis: "Athletics is simple; politics, complex": This is when journalists cover political events as "sports," focusing almost exclusively on daily public-opinion polls and speculating on one side or another's constantly shifting chances of "victory." Because poll statistics are "facts" in a very shallow kind of way, they are offered as easily understood "news" of daily winners and losers. Does this kind of political handicapping help the public? Yes, if people literally are betting on election or legislative results; no, if people want any informative analyses of politicians, platforms, positions, or political track records to assist them in choosing for whom to vote.

3. Homo in speculo interrogat: "The person in the mirror has a question": This is when news interviewers attribute to the public a preoccupation with something that the media themselves are keen on because they hope it will generate a marketable amount of public interest. When reporters declare to politicians or other celebrities that "many people" are saying something provocative or asking some embarrassing personal question about them, what they really mean is "we are saying or asking those provocative things because it's our job to think up hot-button questions." I can't figure out why celebrities don't regularly respond to such queries with, "I haven't heard anyone except you guys say or ask that. Exactly who are you quoting, anyway?"

4. Verbum unum mille argumentationibus aequiparat: "One word is worth a thousand arguments": This is when public speakers mine their speeches, arguments, or remarks with one emotionally charged or coded word or phrase, timed to explode at frequent intervals. The purpose is to regularly return to such words and reduce the audience's potentially complicated feelings about a controversial subject (presumably under rational discussion) to an irrational gut response. That term could be socialist or fascist or liberal or welfare mother or stormtrooper or ACLU or Rush. Maximum use of the term is the point—not cogent argument, which is much harder to do.[38]

In argumentation it is often stated, "Whoever defines the terms, wins the debate." Policy makers often struggle to choose the words that will put the best spin on their plans or actions. Former President Bush's administration used the word *surge* to describe the order for 21,500 more soldiers to go to Iraq in 2007. Democrats countered by calling the surge an *escalation*; Secretary of State Condoleezza Rice countered by changing the term to *augmentation*, "an augmentation that allows the Iraqis to deal with this very serious problem that they have in Baghdad."[39]

---

[38] Steven Doloff, "Caveat Audiens—Let the Listener Beware," *The Humanist*, January 1997.
[39] Lynn Sweet, "Surge? Escalation? Augmentation? It Depends on Who's Talking," The Sun-Times Newsgroup, suntimes.com (accessed January 14, 2007).

Frank Luntz, a pollster, focus group master, and author of a number of books, including *Words That Work: It's Not What You Say, It's What People Hear,* said that

> the word "surge" puts focus only on the numbers of soldiers in Iraq, rather than the mission or what Bush is billing as a change of strategy. "Escalation" causes people to link the Iraq war to the unpopular Vietnam conflict.[40]

When interviewed about terminology used on Wall Street, especially after the national financial crisis that resulted in corporate bailouts, a reporter asked Luntz, "You say that even the term *capitalism* has now become a dirty word." Luntz replied, "It's amazing, *Washington* and *Wall Street* are the two most hated terms in America. This is what I don't understand—you hear these Wall Street people talking about bonuses knowing that the public is outraged. They need to change the lexicon. Pay for performance. Merit pay. Alignment. There is a lexicon to connect Wall Street to those it serves, but they're not using it. I can't get the CEO organizations to listen to me: they don't want to admit mistakes."[41]

In another interview with the *New York Times,* writer Deborah Solomon had this exchange with Luntz:

Solomon: You have devised many phrases... like "energy exploration" instead of "drilling for oil" in the Arctic. What are some of your other coinages?

Luntz: It's "death tax" instead of "estate tax" or "inheritance tax." It's "opportunity scholarships" instead of "vouchers." It's "electronic intercepts" rather than "eavesdropping."

Solomon: That's a lot of e's.

Luntz: Words that begin with b, p or t are words to express anger. I call them spitting words. You actually spit on people as you are saying them.

Solomon: What if I call someone a bunny? That's not angry.

Luntz: If I wanted to demonize a bunny, I would use a word like rabbit. The rabbit will ravage your garden. This is a language pivot. A bunny is cute; a rabbit that ravages your garden is a pest.

> ... I wrote "Words That Work," and the subtitle is "It's Not What You Say, It's What People Hear," and that is the most important single line I have ever written.[42]

Doublespeak and spin are used in our personal lives also. If you have children or siblings, you know that a fight is explained differently from each person's viewpoint. A "light tap" to one person ends up being a "big hit" when described by the other. Some women in the business world have complained that when they have made an unpopular decision they are labeled as "aggressive," whereas a favored male counterpart would have been labeled "a strong manager"; conversely, as the workplace has become more equitable, men complain that when they reprimand an employee, they are considered "abusive," whereas a female counterpart would be labeled

[40] Ibid.

[41] Randy James, "Pollster Frank Luntz, Warrior with Words," http://www.time.com/time/nation/article/0,8599,1925066,00.html#ixzz18t3JgUIJ.

[42] Deborah Solomon, "The Wordsmith," nytimes.com, May 21, 2009.

"assertive." We may describe a friend of ours who rants and raves at small provocations as "a little excitable" or even "dynamic." A favorite line used to control reactions and soften the blow of a breakup is "It's not you. It's me. I'm just not ready for a relationship."

Sometimes it is suggested that a culture should change words to create better connotations. For example, Gail Sheehy, author of popular books on the stages of life, would like to eliminate the word *aging*. "Let's don't even call it *aging* anymore," Sheehy exclaims. "The very word carries pejorative baggage. Let's refer to successful aging as *saging*—the process by which men and women accumulate wisdom and grow into the culture's sages."[43] (See Exercise 7.3 on page 306.)

Other forms of doublespeak include **jargon**, the use of specialized language to exclude or impress people who don't understand the terminology, and **gobbledygook**, which is vague language used to confuse and overwhelm those who hear it. These forms of doublespeak have been labeled *crazy talk* by the late writer and semanticist Neil Postman. He defined crazy talk as talk that reflects "bad" purposes.[44] Postman cited Werner Erhard, the founder of the very successful Erhard Seminars Training (a self-help workshop) as using crazy talk in the form of gobbledygook to explain the objectives of EST training in the following excerpt from an interview:

> Sometimes people get the notion that the purpose of Erhard Seminars Training is to make you better. It is not. I happen to think that you are perfect exactly the way you are.... The problem is that people get stuck acting the way they were instead of being the way they are....
>
> The purpose of est training is to transform your ability to experience living so that the situations you have been trying to change or have been putting up with clear up just in the process of living.[45]

Another example of crazy talk is the wording given by some telephone solicitors who tell you that they represent a popular charity. One ploy is to use the vague phrase "I am part of a commercial fundraiser for charitable purposes." In many cases, these individuals are taking the lion's share of your donation for themselves and giving only a small percentage to the group they claim to represent. Critical thinkers should listen carefully between the lines and ask questions about where the funds will go before deciding whether to give money to such solicitors.

Salespeople sometimes use a technique of doublespeak called "What if I could ... ". Business writer Kelley Robertson gives the following examples used to entice customers to consider buying a product or service:

> "What if I could show you how you could save money, would that be of interest to you?"
>
> "What if I told you that you could capture more market share, would you like to hear how we can help you do this?"
>
> "What if our system saved you time, would that be of value to you?"
>
> "What if I matched our competitor's price, would you buy it?"[46]

jargon Specialized language sometimes used to exclude or impress people who don't understand the terminology.

gobbledygook Vague or inflated language used to confuse or overwhelm those who hear it.

---

[43] Gail Sheehy, *New Passages* (New York: Random House, 1995), p. 420.
[44] Neil Postman, *Crazy Talk, Stupid Talk* (New York: Delacorte, 1976), p. 83.
[45] Ibid.
[46] Kelley Robertson, "Avoid the What Ifs," http://www.businessknowhow.com/marketing/sales-questions.

Robertson suggests that salespeople try to directly anticipate and address obstacles that prevent people from buying.

"The real key is to address your prospect's objections during the sales process. This means asking the right questions early in the sales process and positioning your product, service, or solution so that you answer their objections before they express them."[47]

Advertisers also use inflated language and gobbledygook to impress consumers. They want to present their products as necessary and in some cases even miraculous, and they have developed the tools to do so in the form of creative doublespeak. According to Carl Wrighter, an advertising copywriter, "Today's advertising industry is the most potent and powerful mass marketing and merchandising instrument ever devised by man."[48] He claims that, even if you think that you're smart enough to see through advertising tricks, you may overlook the subtle power of weasel words.

Webster's New International Dictionary defines **weasel word** as "a word used in order to evade or retreat from a direct or forthright statement or position." Let's look at how advertisers use these words so that they can make great claims and not have to prove them.

According to Wrighter, the most commonly used weasel word is *help* or *helps*. An ad might claim, "This cream will help prevent acne," or "Our new formula helps the pain to go away." "This mouthwash helps stop the germs," or "This pill helps you feel drowsy so you can sleep." Notice that no one is claiming that the products will prevent acne, make pain disappear, stop germs, or guarantee sleep. They only promise to *help* do those things.

By only promising to help, advertisers relieve the manufacturers of any responsibility for the actual effectiveness of their products. Wrighter says that we don't really hear the word *help*; we hear only the promise, perhaps because we want to believe there are perfect products that will solve our problems. He also believes that 75 percent of advertising uses the word *help*. If that's true, you should be able to detect this weasel word easily. Watch also for modifications of this word such as "significantly helps" or "greatly improves."

Another prominent weasel word is *like*—the word *like* is used to **romance the product**, which means to make you think about something bigger, better, or more interesting than the product and to associate the product with that better thing. You might think of "romancing the product" as creating a faulty analogy.

Wrighter gives several examples of romancing the product such as an old Mateus wine ad that claimed that drinking Mateus is like taking a trip to Portugal. When the ad appeared on television, depicting a romantic Portuguese holiday, the target audience was meant to forget that they would be drinking it in their own homes—no beaches, music, or wonderful meals would accompany it like they do in the ad. Other powerful images from the past include "It cleans like a white tornado" or "It's like a great taste explosion in your mouth." Some products are romanced with a name, such as Softique (for tissues) or Beverly Hills, Obsession, or Amazing (for perfume). Lipton specialty teas have names

weasel word   A word used to evade or retreat from a direct or forthright statement or position.

romancing the product   A technique used by advertisers in which consumers are asked to associate a product with something bigger, better, or more attractive.

---

[47] Ibid.

[48] Carl Wrighter, *I Can Sell You Anything* (New York: Random House, 1972), p. 2.

such as Gentle Orange, Mountain Berry Apple, and Lemon Soother. One ad compares drinking the tea to experiencing a deep massage. Ads for cars romance their product by showing exciting drives through rough terrain or even on the edges of buildings. Often these exciting-looking rides feature encounters with beautiful men and women who are drawn to the person with the great car. (See Exercise 7.4 on pages 306–307.)

Wrighter cites other words besides *help* and *like* that are used to make consumers think that a product is more promising than it actually is. Here are some of the most common:

- *Virtual* or *virtually:* This word means "almost, but not in fact."
  "Virtually foolproof"
  "Virtually never needs service"
  "Virtually trouble-free"

An ad for a "medication tracking system" reads as follows:

Do you worry when a loved one forgets to take daily medication? Or takes too many pills because he or she loses track of the dosage schedule? You can help by giving Medi-Track. This caring gift makes it virtually impossible for medication users to lose track of their schedule—no matter where they happen to be.

- *Acts* and *works:* These words are other forms of *helps* and are often used with the word *help*.
  "Works like magic"
  "Works to help prevent"
  "Acts against"
  "Acts on the cough control center"

- *Can be:* When advertisers say their product *can be* useful they make no definite claim that it will be useful. *Can be* simply means that it is possible. Variations are *could be, might be,* and *may be.*

"Shine toothpaste can be of significant value when used in a monitored dental program."

- *Up to: Up to* implies a range from zero to the figure that is given. Consumers tend to hear only the larger number.
  "You may have won up to $500."
  "Dude deodorant gives you protection for up to 12 hours."
  "Come to our sale and get up to 50 percent off."

- *As much as:* Similar to *up to, as much as* means that you might get the ultimate benefit described, but you might not.
  "As much as 20 percent greater mileage."
  "Blabble gum gives you as much as an hour more chewing satisfaction than the leading brand."

Advertisers also use the terms *as little as* or *as low as:* Again, you may or may not get a low price.

"Subscribe to our paper for as little as $5.00 per month."

Also, Wrighter suggests that you be aware of vague terms such as *refreshes, comforts, tackles,* and *fights.* These vague terms have positive connotations that may or may not have a basis in reality when referring to a specific product. Some other terms that are commonly used because of their appealing sound but that have no definite meaning include

"Fortified"	"Flavor and Taste"
"Style and Good Looks"	"Different, Special, Exclusive"

Sometimes these terms are strung together:

"Phitrin: New. Improved. Bigger. Better."

Other weasels include the phrases "Experts say" or "Research confirms" or "Most preferred brand in our study" (without specifying any details of actual research) or "Considered the best running shoes around" (without saying who considers them the best). Numbers are also used as weasels, as in "hundreds of consumers" (a phrase that could mean 200) or "at a fraction of the cost" (which could mean 99 percent of the cost). Weasel promises are also made: "Get two tickets absolutely free" (when you buy four tickets at the retail price). Vague superlative phrases with no real meaning are also used, such as "Results of our water filter? Perfection!" "The best soup this side of the Rocky Mountains" "Backed by the peace of mind that only comes from Cadillac care maintenance," or "How low are our prices? Ridiculously low!"

Skill

Recognize when words are used to deceive and confuse readers and listeners.

Recognizing the problem of misleading commercial claims, the federal government has been making attempts to set clearer standards about the meaning of labels given to foods. Consumers have been confused about the meaning of terms such as *fresh, light, low fat,* and *cholesterol-free.*

Federal regulations set guidelines for labeling the fat and cholesterol content of products such as yogurt or cheese. One way that food companies can get around these regulations is to shrink the "serving size" given on the package. If the serving size is small enough, then the product can be called "lower in fat" than an identical product with a larger serving size.

We can't rely on government agencies to clarify our thinking about commercial messages. As Frank Luntz said, "It's not what you say—it's what people hear." We need to recognize doublespeak in all of its forms and keep in mind William Lutz's admonishment about advertising:

> Every word in an ad is there for a reason; no word is wasted. Your job is to figure out exactly what each word is doing in an ad—what each word really means, not what the advertiser wants you to think it means. Remember, the ad is trying to get you to buy a product, so it will put the product in the best possible light, using any device, trick, or means legally allowed. Your only defense against advertising is to develop and use a strong critical reading, listening, and looking ability.[49] (See Exercise 7.5 on pages 307–308.)

[49] Lutz, *Doublespeak,* p. 102.

Life Application: Tips for College and Career

Consider the need to "decode" the language of others. When they speak abstractly, ask questions rather than assuming that they mean the same thing you would mean if you used their words. When you receive an abstract instruction or critique, ask for specifics. For example, if your boss says, "you're not being very careful lately," ask how you can specifically be more careful (rather than assuming a negative interpretation and becoming defensive).

When you speak with others, try to be as clear and unambiguous as possible. Instead of using abstract language about a problem—for example, telling your significant other that he or she is being selfish—make specific requests: "I'd like you to call me more often and spend more time with me on the weekends." People don't know what you'd like unless you ask. If they can't or won't give you what you need, that's important for you to know.

Be direct and polite with requests and complaints. Minimize "qualifiers" that weaken your credibility, such as "if it's not too much trouble..." or "I was thinking maybe you might..." or "I sort of have a feeling that sometimes...".

Practice the words you will use in a job interview. There are common questions that are frequently asked, such as "Why do you want to work here?" "Tell us about yourself." "What are your greatest strengths and weaknesses?" (When asked about weaknesses, don't use a hidden strength, such as "I'm a perfectionist" or "I can't say no to extra work." Most interviewers know those pat answers. Instead, talk about a minor weakness that you have overcome or are in the process of overcoming. That will address the real question without damaging your credibility.)

Be attuned to doublespeak and weasel words in political rhetoric and in advertising. Tune in to and question vague promises or words and phrases that sound good but actually contain no real substance.

Chapter Review

Summary

1. Critical thinkers should be aware of the power of words to both clarify and obscure issues.

2. Language has a persuasive impact on people because of connotations, the images associated with words and phrases.

3. Reification occurs when words take on more power than reality.

4. The meaning of words is in people.

5. Four common problems with language are vagueness, ambiguity, doublespeak, and weasel words.

Checkup

Short Answer

1. What should a critical thinker do when the meaning of a word is not clear?

2. How is vagueness used by candidates and advertisers?

3. How are weasel words used to sell products?

Sentence Completion

4. The images associated with a word make up the word's _____.

5. The process of words becoming more powerful than objective reality is called _____.

6. Meanings aren't in words; meanings are in _____.

7. Language used to lie or mislead while pretending to tell the truth is called _____.

8. A less direct but more acceptable term to describe an event, person, or object is a _____.

9. The specific object or act that a word refers to is the word's _____.

10. When a word or expression has two or more meanings and the meaning is unclear, we say that it is _____.

Exercises

EXERCISE 7.1 Purpose: To understand and experience the power of connotations.

1. Meet with a classmate, friend, family member, or ideally a "significant other" (boyfriend or girlfriend), and try together to pick out a name for a boy and for a girl that you would both be happy to give to a child. See if in your discussion you can isolate how the connotations of some names are different for both of you because of your memory of different people (individuals "denoted" by the term).

   When you find a name that you can both agree on, state why. What are the positive connotations that you have for the name, either because of past associations or because of the sound or meaning of the name? If you had negative connotations for some of the names your partner suggested, state why they were negative for you.

2. Ask your parents or someone else's parents what they had in mind when they chose a name for their son or daughter. Specifically, ask them how they decided upon the name and what connotations they associated with that name.

   Since children often live up to parental expectations, try to assess whether the name had any effect on the child as he or she was growing up. Did the name imply strength, weakness, friendliness, masculinity, or femininity, or did it call forth images of a famous person?

   ### Example

   "Shahruz. The very feeling of power, strength, and courage that simple word 'shah'—meaning king in English—implies is the reason why most Persian and Urdu male names begin with the word 'shah.' It is the same reason my parents chose to name my brother 'Shahruz,' which means 'king of the day.'… My brother's name was chosen by my maternal grandmother. She chose it mainly since it was 'different' from all the other typical Pakistani names she had heard. At the same time, it signified power and strength—two qualities many of us believe that males have or should have. The 'ruz' part of his name, meaning 'day' in the English language, symbolizes a sort of eternity for kingship. When we say 'king of the day,' it implies that the reign of the king is endless; that his leadership will go on for day after day until the end. And my eight-year-old brother *does* behave as a royal. Because of his age, I am not certain that his behavior and actions were due to his attempt to live up to his name. However, his qualities and personality match that of any king—leadership, pride, style, authority, courage, and strength. While these characteristics sound positive and necessary, I personally believe that sometimes they can get a little out of hand. Too much leadership and authority in a child can be seen as bossiness, too much pride can make them be known as a show-off, and too much style can be seen as materialism. While my brother is nothing to these extremes, many royal figures are seen as such. Yet any name in my culture including the word 'shah' is seen as only positive. The images associated are of high standards, and while times have changed and the role and behavior of royalty has changed, the connotations have remained much the same." (By a student)

EXERCISE 7.2 Purposes: To recognize how vague or ambiguous terms can be misleading and how we can avoid the problems associated with assumptions about meanings. To realize that meanings are in people, not in words.

1. Give an extended example, or several examples, of the use of abstract, ambiguous, or vague terms that are not defined by the writer or speaker. You can find these examples in blogs, editorials, political speeches, advertisements, or perhaps when you converse with friends. List the abstract, vague, or ambiguous terms or phrases used and tell how different people could interpret these words in different ways. If possible, extend the exercise by asking someone who is using vague terms to clarify what he or she means by those terms. For further practice, see the discussion questions and suggestions for speech or essay writing at the end of the chapter.

2. Think of some examples of verbal misunderstandings that have occurred in your life or in the life of someone you know. How could the confusion have been avoided? Consider a time when you misunderstood someone's words or instructions.

Example

"I missed an English class and called a friend to get the assignment. She said we had to turn in a copy of a résumé that we might use to apply for a job. Then she said, 'You also need a cover.' I assumed she was using the word cover the way I use it, so I bought a report cover. What she really meant was that we were supposed to have a cover letter introducing ourselves to an employer. The cover letter goes with the résumé.

"I could have avoided these problems by asking what she meant when she mentioned a cover. Or I could have repeated back to her what the assignment was; then she might have caught my error." (By a student.)

3. This exercise should be done in classroom groups.

Assume you have been selected as a citizen's advisory committee to the Supreme Court. Your task is to form a clear definition of one (or more) of the following words or phrases: *obscenity, life, cruel and unusual punishment, competency, marriage,* or *adult.* Your definition will be used to guide future decisions on issues related to these terms.

In your discussion, try to come to a consensus. Whenever possible, resolve disagreements by presenting evidence to clarify positions. You may also give personal examples to increase the understanding of one another's viewpoints.

After you have used the time allotted (at least 20 minutes), choose a member of your group to present your results to the class as a whole. The spokesperson should discuss

- The definitions the group agreed upon.
- The difficulties in coming to consensus and why they occurred. Consider especially how the differing values and experiences of group members affected their desired definitions.

EXERCISE 7.3 Purpose: To recognize euphemisms and how they are applied.

Try to think of euphemisms that you've heard or used. What are some euphemisms for the following: *selfish, cheap, war, lies, kill?* How about for a badly damaged car that someone wants to sell?

Try this exercise that British philosopher Bertrand Russell created and called "Conjugating Irregular Verbs." Take a personal characteristic or action and express it favorably, neutrally, and unfavorably, as follows:

Favorable	Neutral	Unfavorable
I'm slender.	You're thin.	She's skinny.
I'm thrifty.	You're careful with money.	He's cheap.

Complete these "conjugations," which all start with a favorable description. Add neutral and unfavorable descriptions for each one.

1. I have high self-esteem.
2. I'm curious about my neighbors.
3. I like to relax.
4. I'm pleasantly plump.
5. I don't like to stifle my child's creativity.
6. I'm not a perfectionist about cleaning.
7. My car has a lot of character.

EXERCISE 7.4 Purpose: To identify gobbledygook and phrases that romance the product.

An ad for Mercury Sable automobiles featured a silhouette of a dancing couple behind a car.

Explain how the following words, which accompanied the ad, were used to romance the product, and point out the vague gobbledygook that is used to describe the "new" changes in the car.

We dressed in silence.

And drove.

When we walked in,

She said something to the piano player.

Next thing, I hear this song we used to love.

She takes my hand. We dance. And something

that was there before, was back. Only stronger.

Mercury Sable.

The new, remarkably sophisticated Sable.

Its body has been totally restyled.

Its interior so thoroughly redesigned

even the controls are easier to read and reach.

It has standard driver and optional passenger air bags.

It rides smoother. Quieter.

And makes driving more of a pleasure.

The car that started it all,

does it again.

EXERCISE 7.5 Purpose: To discover weasel words in persuasive messages.

1. Analyze some online, television, radio, or magazine advertising, campaign literature, or junk mail, specifically looking for doublespeak and weasel words. Bring samples to share with your class.

   Try to include campaign messages in your search. Look for literature that comes in the mail dealing with upcoming elections.

   Which particular weasels did you find most often? What effect did the weasel have on the message—that is, why do you think that the writer of the message used that weasel?

   Use the following sample ads to get you started:

   Having a party and don't know what to serve? Try Tony's Barbequed Party Wings for that spicy hot party time action. Our secret sauce has 37 of the world's finest ingredients mixed to virtual perfection at a fraction of the cost and applied with tender loving care to each piece. So, spice up your next party with Tony's Party Wings; you'll feel like you're flying high with satisfaction.

   Is your smile an average dull white in an average dull world? Make the change and brighten your outlook. For that all-day smile, your teeth deserve the best. Flash toothpaste with ZX-19 can help whiten and brighten your teeth for up to 8 hours. Stand out from the crowd—join the Flash generation, and change your dull world into a Flash world. Buy one and get a second absolutely free!

   Vote for Richmond for school board. She knows about the latest classroom technology and can help make our school district the most progressive in the state. As a parent herself, J. Richmond cares about excellence in education and she shares your concerns. She is considered the most well educated candidate in years. Having J. Richmond on the board is like having a friend attending the meetings for you.

2. In class groups, create some ads or an extensive "infomercial" for a product. Try to use as many weasel words as possible and use images that romance the product. Present your commercials to the class either live or with taped footage, and see if all of your strategies are detected.

You **Decide**

Words About Energy

Much of the world relies on fossil fuels for energy use on a daily basis. Citizens and politicians generally have strong feelings about how to provide the energy we have come to depend upon. The main controversy centers around whether we should focus our efforts on finding domestic sources of fossil fuels or on developing alternative energy sources. In arguing their points concerning the best sources of energy to explore, people use words with powerful connotations. Those in favor of drilling for oil choose words and phrases like "energy exploration," "energy independence," and "ending reliance on foreign countries"; they may describe drilling sites as "desolate, uninhabited swamps." Those against drilling for oil talk about "finite resources" and describe drilling sites with terms such as "pristine wilderness" and "untouched natural habitat." Those in favor of nuclear power plants characterize nuclear energy as "clean energy," and those against the use of nuclear power plants refer to the Chernobyl or Japanese "nuclear energy disasters." As in any controversy, there are pros and cons to all sides, and you can usually tell where a person stands by the language he or she uses.

For more information on the debate surrounding sources of energy and additional exercises and tutorials about concepts covered in this chapter, log into MyThinkingLab at www.mythinkinglab.com and select Diestler, *Becoming a Critical Thinker*, Sixth Edition.

✷ Explore on **mythinkinglab.com**

Articles for Discussion   📖 Read the **Document** on **mythinkinglab.com**

In the following essay, Andrew Lam writes about how the Vietnamese names of his friends, which have strong and beautiful meanings, are ridiculed and ultimately forsaken so that the friends can identify with and fit into American culture. It is a great example of how meanings are in people and positive meanings are sometimes lost to assimilation.

What's in a Name?

Andrew Lam

Wang, Dung, Mai Suan, Noc, Trang, Than, Phat. What are these? Names, Vietnamese names. While in my native tongue they suggest colors of clouds and precious jade, in English they are twisted into a funny word, a grunt or even a cough.

Vietnamese names are often turned ugly in America, their magic snuffed out like a birthday candle. My name, Dung, spelled D-U-N-G, which means bravery in Vietnamese, is but animal excrement in English.

Van, Truc and Trang—meaning cloud, bamboo and elegance—the three pretty girls who walk down the high school hallway, suffered constant pestering from classmates who would yell, "Look out, here comes a van, a truck and a train!"

One summer, Van, Truc and Trang, after leafing through *Vogue* and *Mademoiselle* magazines, emerged Yvonne, Theresa and Tanya. They even looked different, wearing more fashionable clothes and makeup.

My sister Noc became Nancy when our landlord, having failed to pronounce her name, threw up his hands and said, "Never mind, let's call you Nancy, as in Nancy Kwan, the actress."

And there's Qua, a friend from college, who wanted to finalize his naturalization process with an American name. But which one? He was drinking milk when he was filling out the application, and saw a picture of a lost boy named Kevin on the milk carton. Qua shrugged. Kevin he became the day he swore his allegiance to the United States of America.

Thus like street urchins, we children of Vietnam gathered our new identities from anything deemed worthy. Then over the seasons, through the years, many of us have learned to embody our new names. For they have given us an assurance of being Americans, part of this country.

Indeed, sometimes I wonder if any of us would have assimilated so well into this country without our new names. After all, it was Huai who, under the tropical sun, and amid exploding B-52 bombs, mourned for slain relatives. Now, Lucy is busy decorating her beautiful suburban home in the Silicon Valley.

Tao, the jack fruit vendor's daughter, who once expected to follow her mother's footsteps, became Christine a decade later, and found herself in a different kind of market instead. Wall Street. Through her computer linkups, Christine, the stockbroker, now negotiates across time zones, oceans, continents.

But what of our old names? Huang, Yung, Mai Sung, Ngop, Jiang, Than, Phat. In our old language, they are kept safe, but more. I should like to think their magic is instilled in us, in us who must adapt and change, but who still cherish the memory of a world full of iridescent clouds and precious jade. ▪

Questions for Discussion

1. Andrew Lam, an editor, journalist, and short-story writer, came to America when he was 11 years old. As recounted in this story, he and his friends all went through name changes. What made them change their original names?

2. To what extent, if any, do you agree with Andrew's statement, "Sometimes I wonder if any of us would have assimilated so well into this country without our new names"?

3. Some people are going in the opposite direction from Andrew and his friends and using names from their country of origin. Why do you think they are making this change?

4. Ask relatives or friends who have changed their names why they chose to do so. To what extent did they act under peer pressure, a desire to embrace their new country, or a desire to disassociate with their native country?

. . . .

The following article discusses a new law in Wisconsin that allows the state to ban Native American and other race-based team names, mascots, and logos. This law is the first of its kind in the United States and has both supporters and critics.

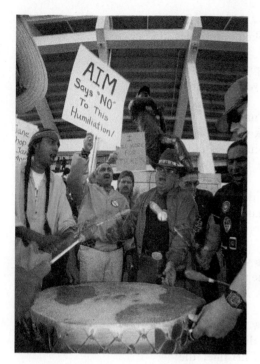

Wisconsin's new law, the first of its kind in the United States, follows years of debate about sports teams' use of Native American mascots and logos.

Race-Based Team Names Not Tolerated in Wisconsin

Brian Bull

School team nicknames like the Chieftains and Braves may soon be a thing of the past in Wisconsin, where a new law allows the state to ban race-based mascots and logos. If a complaint is upheld, school districts face fines of up to $1,000 a day.

The day Wisconsin's new sports-mascot law took effect, Oneida tribal member Carol Gunderson and her husband, Harvey, drove three hours to the state capital, Madison, to file their complaint in person.

The reason, Carol Gunderson says, is "because it's the first law in the whole United States that addresses this issue. We didn't want it to get lost in the mail."

The Gundersons are targeting the Osseo-Fairchild School District's team name, the Chieftains. When they got to the Wisconsin Department of Public Instruction, Harvey Gunderson handed Patrick Gasper, the agency's communications director, an enormous blue binder of documents to back up their claim.

The evidence, Harvey Gunderson says, "not only shows that what Osseo-Fairchild has done, but what the other districts have done in the state also, that they really are promoting discrimination, pupil harassment and stereotyping."

Looking Past the Local Level

The Gundersons submitted 550 pages of research that they say proves discrimination against Native Americans. And they hope their research is useful in fighting Indian mascots nationwide.

"We think this is the beginning of an important new trend," says Harvey Gunderson. "Civil rights matters do not happen overnight."

It's been 42 years since the National Congress of American Indians challenged the use of Native American mascots. Today, an estimated 900 high schools and colleges still use Native American names and images for sports teams. And of course, there are the professional teams—the Chicago Blackhawks, Cleveland Indians, Atlanta Braves, Kansas City Chiefs and Washington Redskins, among others.

A Long-Standing Dispute

For decades, Native American civil rights groups have called on these teams to change their names. They've had little success. But Dave Czesniuk, of the Boston-based group Sport in Society, thinks the Wisconsin law may turn out to be a game-changer.

"I think what's going on in Wisconsin is exciting, and it's a true sign of real change," he says. "You know, social responsibility is on the rise, even in the ranks of professional sports and the corporate level."

Czesniuk says attitudes have changed since the 1970s, when an estimated 3,000 schools and colleges had Indian mascots. He says the key to making the case is teaching team officials and fans how they perpetuate stereotypes and hurt some Native Americans.

But then again, some Wisconsin lawmakers pushed that argument for nearly 30 years before their mascot bill became law. And many school and professional teams argue that their mascots honor Native Americans rather than degrade them.

Bob Kliebenstein of Tomah, Wis., says that was the case with the Tomah Indians. He's still upset that the school board changed the mascot to the Timberwolves a few years ago. He says there's no telling where the mascot wars will go next.

"Right now, the trendy thing seems to be to get rid of Native American mascots. And in three to five years, the trendy thing might be to get rid of animal mascots. And after that, who knows? We might all have to just be one mascot, just real generic."

Law Provides Fines—And a Loophole

Meanwhile, the Osseo-Fairchild District may be subject to a state hearing, as officials investigate the Gundersons' mascot complaint. If the complaint is deemed valid, the district could be fined up to $1,000 for every day it keeps using the Chieftains' name.

But there's a twist. A provision in the law says schools with mascots specifically named after a federally recognized tribe could keep it, if they have that tribe's permission. The legislator who penned that in is a graduate of Auburndale High School—home of the Apaches. ▪

Questions for Discussion

1. One of the plaintiffs in the suit to ban the use of Native American mascots, Harvey Gunderson, states that the schools that adopt the mascots "really are promoting discrimination, pupil harassment and stereotyping." To what extent do you agree or disagree with Gunderson's assessment?

2. The author of the article said, "many school and professional teams argue that their mascots honor Native Americans rather than degrade them." In your experience how have Native American team names shaped perceptions?

3. Do you believe that if Native American team names and mascots are banned in Wisconsin that they will be banned across the United States?

. . . .

The following article focuses on a celebrity's use of the R-word and on the hurt caused by the common use of words that belittle those with mental retardation. The article is written by a journalist with an autistic son, and a comment is included from one of her online readers, who is also the mother of an autistic child.

Jennifer Aniston, The R-Word and the Aftermath

Jean Winegardner

It happens often and every time it makes me cringe. Celebrity X refers to some of her work as "retarded." Politician Y refers to people on the other side of an issue as "retarded." Movie Z gets in trouble for using the phrase "never go full retard."

This time it's Jennifer Aniston. She used the r-word on live TV, on *Live with Regis and Kelly* while discussing a photo shoot. "You're playing dress up!" Regis told her. Her response? "Yes, I play dress up! I do it for a living, like a retard!"

Ouch. As an advocate for people with disabilities—and a parent of a child with autism—these outbursts are jarring and hurtful every time. Worse than the celebrities, however, are the regular people who cannot or do not want to grasp why this word is hurtful.

I think the most painful part about these incidents is not the original comment, but rather the backlash from commenters and pundits who think those of us who care about this word are being over-sensitive.

Blogs and articles about such incidents aimed at the special needs community tend to get positive, respectful comments. Blogs and articles aimed at the mainstream that discuss the issue have comments that degenerate into dissertations on why society is too "PC" these days.

They make claims that the speaker isn't really talking about people with disabilities and how, no, it really *is* funny to say that word.

Again, ouch. These can sound like valid arguments though, so let's look at a few. I took these comments (in bold) from the comments section of a pop culture blog, but they are virtually the same arguments you can read over and over in any online discussion of this issue.

"This PC nonsense is getting out of hand." It's not about being politically correct. When you say this, what you are doing is hearing that a large group of people finds this term not just offensive, but actually hurtful, yet you dismiss those feelings as unimportant PC nonsense. That's not being honest or straight up, that's being cruel.

This argument brushes off the feelings of those hurt by the r-word, which goes to show just how little society cares about this group of people. As another commenter on that pop culture blog eloquently said, *"It's not a matter of political correctness, it's a matter of respect."*

"I've worked with people with mental and physical disabilities for over ten years, and I use the word 'retard' almost daily. Never aimed at those I care for of course, usually it is aimed at myself." When you use the r-word, even if you don't mean to, you *are* talking about people with disabilities. If you weren't, the joke wouldn't be "funny."

You use the word to mean stupid, moronic, idiotic. You are taking a word that describes people with mental and developmental disabilities and generalizing it to mean dumb. This is one reason the medical term "mental retardation" has to be changed to "intellectual disability."

It is because people have taken this term and made it a pejorative.

People make the same jokes about "the short bus." When you make those jokes and claim you're not really talking about the kids—*the children*—on those buses, you're wrong. My sweet, affectionate, smart autistic son, Jack, rides a short bus to and from school.

The next time you want to say the r-word or make a short bus joke, picture his face. *That* is who you are mocking. Is it still funny?

"I think saying retard is funny." It's a cheap joke. It's an easy joke. It hurts a vulnerable section of society. Why not work a little harder and say something that is *actually* funny?

"Anyone who hasn't said anything stupid in public, please stand up and state your opinion on this matter." Sure, we've all said stupid things and most of us have probably said hurtful things. I know that I, even with the level of disability awareness that I have, make jokes about so and so being crazy or will say, "that guy is a nutjob." I'm sure phrases such as those are hurtful to those with mental illness. I will stand up, apologize, and make an effort in my future to not disparage an entire group of people with a joke. As people, we must speak, learn, and move on.

Furthermore, imagine the amount of media training celebrities such as Aniston must have been through, and if not actual training, then years upon years of experience. I doubt you will find her publicly uttering a racial epithet or a slur based on sexual orientation.

Not to mention, it's not just Aniston. It's the authors who sprinkle their books with these jarring words, it's screenwriters who toss these words into movies. It's contestants on reality shows and the editors who cut the tape and let jokes about the short bus onto air.

The pervasiveness and general acceptance of these particular kinds of comments clearly show that in most cases (although it is impossible to know with regard to Aniston), these comments are not accidental.

"Freakin' retards!" I am tired of writing about this issue. I am tired of hearing this same discussion over and over. The whole thing hurts my heart. But I read a comment such as this and know that I have to keep trying to raise awareness. Amid a conversation about why some say the r-word is hurtful and why some say it is a valid term to use, both sides using examples and arguments, this commenter is so disrespectful as to just hurl insults masked as comedy. That is why I continue to write about this issue.

Maybe my words can help one person realize that this word has incredible power. Maybe that person will choose not to use that word and hurt someone else someday.

Should we disallow the use of the r-word? Absolutely not. Free speech rules apply. Should we bleep it on television, as they do with other similarly offensive words, including curse words? Possibly. Should we raise awareness that the r-word is not benign—that it really does hurt? Absolutely.

Jean blogs at Stimeyland, runs an autism events website at AutMont and can be found on Twitter as @Stimey.

- Jean, I have to say that I think many people who use the "R" word don't realize it is offensive. I am the mom of a special needs child with autism. I am also an advocate for children with special needs in my community, and I have found education is the best way to improve things—not boycotting. I used the "R" word when I was growing up (same generation as Aniston), and never used it to mean disabled people. Truthfully, there weren't any "special" kids in the mainstream schools at that time, and I didn't know any. We used it to mean "oh that was retarded," something I shouldn't have done—I guess like the word stupid. Of course, people need to be educated, but we don't need to bash them. It's about the attitudes behind it. For me, I find that because Autism is such an invisible disability, many people don't understand it. But I have found that most of the people I explain it to, are very kind and helpful. I think the same goes for the "R" word, we need to just tell people they need to stop using it, and explain why. But we don't need to bash them for being insensitive—just explain it to them so they GET it. ◼

Questions for Discussion

1. The author states, "Maybe my words can help one person realize that this word has incredible power. Maybe that person will choose not to use that word and

hurt someone else someday." How does the author make her case that the R-word is very hurtful and damaging?

2. What is your viewpoint on the various counter-arguments about the use of the R-word that the author quotes?

3. The author said that the use of the R-word to mean "dumb" has caused the term "mental retardation" to be changed to "intellectual disability." Do you believe that changing terms is a solution to the problem of negative stereotyping? Can you think of other groups that have changed descriptive labels to create more positive connotations for the group?

4. The person leaving a comment on the website offers a viewpoint and an approach to dealing with this issue. Do you agree with her stand and solution?

- -

The following article discusses the use of the word *many* as a weasel word that enables a writer to make significant claims without being specific about supporting evidence.

Weasel-Words Rip My Flesh!

Jack Shafer

How many "many's" are too many for one news story?

Like its fellow weasel-words—some, few, often, seems, likely, more—many serves writers who haven't found the data to support their argument. A light splash of weasel-words in a news story is acceptable if only because journalism is not an exact science and deadlines must be observed. But when a reporter pours a whole jug of weasel-words into a piece, as Louise Story does on Page One of today's *New York Times* in "Many Women at Elite Colleges Set Career Path to Motherhood," she needlessly exposes one of the trade's best-kept secrets for all to see. She deserves a week in the stockades. And her editor deserves a month.

Story uses the particularly useful weasel-word "many" 12 times—including once in the headline—to illustrate the emerging trend of Ivy League–class women who attend top schools but have no intention of assuming the careers they prepared for.

She informs readers that "many of these women" being groomed for the occupational elite "say that is not what they want." She repeats the weasel-word three more times in the next two paragraphs and returns to it whenever she needs to express impressive quantity but has no real numbers. She writes:

> Many women at the nation's most elite colleges say they have already decided that they will put aside their careers in favor of raising children. Though some of these students are not planning to have children and some hope to have a family and work full time, many others, like Ms. Liu, say they will happily play a traditional female role, with motherhood their main commitment.
>
> Much attention has been focused on career women who leave the work force to rear children. What seems to be changing is that while many women in college two or three decades ago expected to have full-time careers, their daughters, while still in college, say they have already decided to suspend or end their careers when they have children.
>
> Many students say staying home is not a shocking idea among their friends. Shannon Flynn, an 18-year-old from Guilford, Conn., who is a

freshman at Harvard, says many of her girlfriends do not want to work full time....

Yet the likelihood that so many young women plan to opt out of high-powered careers presents a conundrum....

What seems new is that while many of their mothers expected to have hard-charging careers, then scaled back their professional plans only after having children, the women of this generation expect their careers to take second place to child rearing....

Sarah Currie, a senior at Harvard, said many of the men in her American Family class last fall approved of women's plans to stay home with their children....

For many feminists, it may come as a shock to hear how unbothered many young women at the nation's top schools are by the strictures of traditional roles....

None of these many's quantify anything. You could as easily substitute the word some for every many and not gain or lose any information. Or substitute the word few and lose only the wind in Story's sails. By fudging the available facts with weasel-words, Story makes a flaccid concept stand up—as long as nobody examines it closely.

For instance, Story writes that she interviewed "Ivy League students, including 138 freshman and senior females at Yale who replied to e-mail questions sent to members of two residential colleges over the last school year." Because she doesn't attribute the preparation of the e-mail survey to anyone, one must assume that she or somebody at the *Times* composed and sent it. A questionnaire answered by 138 Yale women sounds like it may contain useful information. But even a social-science dropout wouldn't consider the findings to be anything but anecdotal unless he knew (1) what questions were asked (Story doesn't say), (2) how many questionnaires were distributed, and (3) why freshman and seniors received the questionnaires to the exclusion of sophomores and juniors. Also, (4) a social-science dropout would ask if the *Times* contaminated its e-mailed survey with leading questions and hence attracted a disproportionate number of respondents who sympathize with the article's underlying and predetermined thesis.

To say Story's piece contains a thesis oversells it. Early on, she squishes out on the whole concept with the weasel-word *seems*. She writes, "What seems to be changing is that while many women in college two or three decades ago expected to have full-time careers, their daughters, while still in college, say they have already decided to suspend or end their careers when they have children."

To say the piece was edited would also be to oversell it. Story rewrites this seems sentence about two-thirds of the way through the piece without adding any new information. "What *seems* new is that while many of their mothers expected to have hard-charging careers, then scaled back their professional plans only after having children, the women of this generation expect their careers to take second place to child rearing." [Emphasis added.]

Halfway through, Story discounts her allegedly newsworthy findings by acknowledging that a "person's expectations at age 18 are less than perfect predictors of their life choices 10 years later." If they're less than perfect predictors, then why are we reading about their predictions on Page One of the *Times*? While bogus, "Many Women at Elite Colleges Set Career Path to Motherhood" isn't false: It can't be false because it never says anything sturdy enough to be tested. So, how did it get to Page One? Is there a *New York Times* conspiracy afoot to drive feminists crazy and persuade young women that their place is in the home? Did the paper dispatch *Times* columnist John Tierney to write a pair of provocative columns on this theme earlier this year (early May and late May) and recruit Lisa Belkin to dance the idea around in an October 2003 *Times Magazine* feature titled "The Opt-Out Revolution"?

Nah.

I suspect a *Times* editor glommed onto the idea while overhearing some cocktail party chatter—"Say, did you hear that Sam blew hundreds of thousands of dollars sending his daughter to Yale and now she and her friends say all they want in the future is to get married and stay at home?"—and passed the concept to the writer or her editors and asked them to develop it.

You can see the editorial gears whirring: The press has already drained our collective anxiety about well-educated women assuming greater power in the workplace. So, the only editorial vein left to mine is our collective anxiety about well-educated women deciding not to work instead. Evidence that the *Times* editors know how to push our buttons can be found in the fact that as I write, this slight article about college students is the "Most E-Mailed" article on the newspaper's Web site. ▣

Questions for Discussion

1. Why does Jack Shafer call Louise Story's article a "bogus trend story"?

2. Some research that led to Story's conclusions is cited in this critique. What problems does Shafer point to concerning the research, and what questions does he say that even a "social-science dropout" would ask?

3. Sarah Currie, a senior at Harvard, is quoted as saying that many of the men in her American Family class last fall approved of women's plans to stay home with their children. How might the men in this class reflect a biased sample?

4. Shafer says that halfway through her article, Story qualifies her findings; how does she qualify them and what is the qualifier's effect on her thesis?

5. Why do you believe the *New York Times* put this story on page one, and why do you believe it was the most e-mailed story on the *Times*' website at the time of Shafer's writing?

. . . .

Ideas for Writing or Speaking

1. Respond to one of the following quotes from British novelist George Orwell's *Politics and the English Language.* Take a position on the quote and support your position using essays; blogs; newspaper, magazine, or journal articles; advertisements; books; films; videos; or interviews.

   a. "In our time, political speech and writing are largely the defense of the indefensible."

   b. "The whole tendency of modern prose is away from concreteness."

   c. "The great enemy of clear language is insincerity."

   d. "In our age, there is no such thing as 'keeping out of politics.' All issues are political issues, and politics itself is a mass of lies, evasions, folly, hatred, and schizophrenia."

   e. "Political language . . . is designed to make lies sound truthful and murder respectable, and to give an appearance of solidity to pure wind."

2. Write or speak about a proposal for change, using both abstract objectives and concrete proposals. The abstract terms should be used to express the ideals you seek to achieve with your proposal; the concrete explanations are used to let your readers or listeners know exactly what your proposal entails and the "real-world" impact you expect it to have. For example, you might state that you would like to see increased employment opportunities in the inner cities (general objective). Then you would explain exactly how you would go about increasing employment, detailing programs and how the programs would be organized, funded, maintained, and evaluated. (concrete proposals)

   You may want to organize your essay or speech using one of the speech formats discussed in Chapter 10.

3. *Sales Pitch.* Listen to a "hard-sell" sales pitch by a professional salesperson. You might go to a car lot or electronics store, visit a sales booth in a mall, or just invite a door-to-door salesperson to speak with you. Then list and analyze the reasons that you are given in favor of buying the product or service. Answer the following questions:

   a. Were you given valid and well-documented reasons for buying the product or service?
   b. Did the salesperson use vagueness or any of the forms of doublespeak covered in this chapter?
   c. Which arguments were persuasive and which were not? Explain why.

4. *Useless Item Survey.* Find something that you bought and never or rarely used. Then answer the following questions:

   a. What motivated you to buy this item?
   b. Why have you never or rarely used it?
   c. Why do you still have it?
   d. Have you learned anything useful from this useless purchase?

5. *Ad Campaign.* An article in the business magazine *Investment Vision* advised readers to consider investing in products with ad campaigns that created powerful positive images. The article reminded readers that corporations spend $129 billion yearly on ads and that the most effective are those with a clear concept. The best campaigns, it believes, focus on one or a few words associated with the product, such as *thrive* for Kaiser hospitals, *We try harder* for Avis rental cars, or *dependable* for Maytag.

   Assuming that companies desire positive connotations for their products, study the ad campaigns of several companies.

   a. Discuss each company image and how it is achieved through the ads, focusing especially on the words that were chosen to represent the product or service.
   b. Decide which campaigns are successful at creating strong, positive connotations. Support your conclusions with reasons.

6. Using the same format as in the ad campaign (idea 5), study a present or past political campaign; focus especially on how language is used to present positive images of the candidates.

   For example, when Secretary of State and former First Lady Hillary Clinton was first running for senator from the state of New York, her advisers struggled with how the campaign literature should present her. Should the buttons and bumper stickers feature "Hillary Clinton," "Hillary Rodham Clinton," "Mrs. Clinton," or "Hillary Rodham"? Each name might hold different connotations for voters concerning the candidate's identity. Finally, the campaign managers decided to go with a more general and vague approach; her name became, simply, "Hillary."

Films for Analysis and Discussion

Yes Man, (2008, PG 13)

This film is a good example of how the meaning of words is in people. It centers on a lonely banker named Carl Allen, who attends an inspirational self-help seminar. The seminar speaker encourages audience members to take risks and to have an upbeat attitude about life that is symbolized by the word "yes." Carl misinterprets the speaker and thinks that he is being advised not just to have a more positive attitude but to to actually say "yes" to everyone he encounters. The film follows his adventures as we see how his new attitude, based on the word "yes," changes his entire life.

Similar Films and Classics

In Good Company (2004, PG-13)

This movie is a topical and funny look at the corporate world of mergers and acquisitions, and is also a good study in weasel words. The film follows family man Dan Foreman (Dennis Quaid) and his new boss, 26-year-old Carter Duryea (Topher Grace). Both men are going through personal crises as well as trying to handle the pressures in the competitive and always changing business world. We meet Carter in a meeting about how to market cell phones to the untapped demographic of "under 5 year-olds." Carter's answer is colorful dinosaur phones with their own unique roar/ring tone. This high satire continues with Carter's first meeting with his new staff after his company "Globecom" takes over the magazine Dan works for, *Sports America*. As Carter downs his fifth Starbucks latte, he delivers a hilarious speech about "synergy," a euphemistic buzzword that Globecom uses to describe cutting costs within the company while simultaneously driving up revenue. Unfortunately, in the name of "synergy," many of the people Dan has worked with his whole career need to be fired, or in Globecom's words "let go... because it sounds better." Intertwined with the satire is a real-life look at where loyalty and honor exist in a culture that focuses on meeting the bottom line.

Mean Girls (2004, PG-13)

This film follows high school student Cady Heron as she goes from being home-schooled in Africa to entering the world of public high school in the United States. Her first friends at her new school encourage her to break into the popular clique, the Plastics, and find out their dark secrets. Note how Cady learns to use new words and phrases to fit in with the Plastics and how her behavior changes as she starts using the language of the popular mean girls. When Cady decides to leave the mean girl group, she also makes decisions about words she will no longer use.

The N-Word (2004, Not rated.)

This documentary, featuring many popular celebrities, discusses the powerful, inflammatory nature of the N-word. It is a good example of the rules that govern language usage, as the interviewees discuss when, where, how, by whom—and whether the N-word should be used.

Lost in Translation (2003, R)

This film is about two individuals who meet and become friends during a visit to Japan. It shows both the confusion and the humor when the two tourists grapple with language and cultural differences.

Crazy People (1990, R)

This comedy features an ad-man who is undergoing a breakdown because of his desire to use honest language, rather than weasel words, in his advertising campaigns. When he is sent to a psychiatric hospital to recover, he meets a delightful group of fellow patients; they all work on new product slogans that promote truth in advertising and achieve great success in the process.

8

Suggestion in Media

Is What You See What You Get?
Do You Really Want It?

A critical thinker is aware of the presence and power of suggestion in electronic and print media.

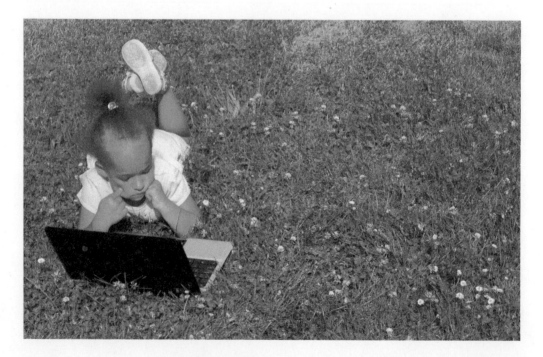

We are influenced by media throughout our lives.

> The hand that rules the press, the radio, the screen and the far-spread magazine, rules the country.
>
> Learned Hand, memorial address for Justice Brandeis, December 21, 1942

The Lost Art of the Public Speech

Bob Greene

Speeches—eloquent, painstakingly crafted, carefully thought out, and meticulously paced, full-length speeches—are an endangered American species.

The speech has historically been one of the most important means of serious communication. If a person had an essential message to deliver, that message was conveyed in a speech. That's what politicians and great thinkers did when they had something to say: They labored over a speech until it was ready, and then they delivered it out loud to an attentive audience.

No more. The speech is already an anachronism. Twenty or 30 years ago, the serious speech was still a routine part of American life, and now the serious, influential speech is so rare that it's startling when one comes along.

The people you would most expect to want to continue the tradition of the speech—politicians with a national audience—are rushing to help devalue the speech. Next time you watch network TV news, pay close attention to how national politicians talk. They have begun to speak almost exclusively in those cute little bursts expressly written to be picked up by television producers—predigested 8- to 12-second nuggets that don't resemble anything an actual person would ever say during a real-world conversation. . . .

This goes on especially on the floor of Congress. . . . Except in the most uncommon of circumstances, reporters and camera crews are only going to pick up the luminescent little word-pellets that have been custom-constructed for them. . . .

If Abraham Lincoln wanted to make a point today, he would deliver the Gettysburg Sound Bite.[1]

---

[1] Bob Greene, "The Lost Art of the Public Speech," Tribune Media Services, April 24, 1992.

Public arguments, which formerly consisted largely of political speeches and debates, can now be found in electronic media in articles, blogs, websites, commercials, talk shows, interview programs, segments of news programs, programs focusing on satire like *The Daily Show, The Colbert Report,* and *Saturday Night Live* and, more subtly, on sitcoms and dramas. Arguments that appear in print include advertisements, essays, and editorials. As citizens and consumers, we have a wide array of options for getting information on an issue, a candidate, or a product; on any given day, we may surf the Web, access Facebook and other social media sites, receive e-mails and tweets, read a newspaper or magazine, watch television, download a podcast, and listen to the radio. While these multiple means of accessing information provide incredible resources for us, they also compete for our attention. Increasingly, as we seek to determine what is true or false and which policies, candidates, and products are in our best interest, we have to walk through the minefields of misinformation, clever but empty sound bites, exaggerated product promises, and glitzy personal and commercial promotions. This chapter will consider how media influence, shape, and alter the many messages we receive.

Electronic and print media use a variety of persuasive techniques that critical thinkers should understand. Most of these techniques come under the heading of *suggestion*; there are also a number of technologies that seek to exert influence on target audiences through subliminal persuasion.

Suggestion in Daily Life

suggestion The presentation of ideas or images in such a way as to reveal certain ideas or qualities and to conceal others.

Suggestion means presenting ideas or images in such a way as to reveal certain aspects or qualities and to conceal others. Just as powerful connotations are attached to certain words, powerful memories and feelings are attached to our human senses. Images, colors, sounds, tastes, and smells all evoke different emotions for individuals. When athletes stand on an Olympic victory platform and hear the sounds of their national anthems and view their nations' flags, they and their watching countrymen may experience deep emotions, while viewers with little or no connection to those nations are not similarly moved by the sights and sounds presented. People generally have strong reactions, both positive and negative, to sensory phenomena based on their own experiences; consider your responses to flashing lights from a police car, photos of a vacation spot you enjoyed, a song that reminds you of a significant time or person in your life, the taste of your favorite childhood foods and drinks, and the smell of familiar flowers, coffee, baked goods, or cologne. Logos for high schools and colleges, songs and decorations related to holidays, and religious music and symbols may also trigger emotional responses.

Consumers are also emotionally identified with their favorite products and may react negatively if the symbols for these products are changed. When the Gap clothing company tried to change its old logo, consumers felt strongly enough to complain about it on Facebook, twitter, and blogs, and the company restored the familiar symbol, as noted in the following excerpt.

NEW YORK (AP)—Gap is back to blue.

The casualwear chain will keep its decades-old white-on-navy blue logo after all. The move comes just one week after the company swapped it online for a new logo without saying a word. The new logo irritated fans, spurring them to complain about it online.

Gap North America president Marka Hansen said in a statement late Monday that the San Francisco-based company realized how much people liked the old logo after they put up the new one, a white background with black letters and a little blue box. She also says Gap didn't handle the change correctly and missed a chance to have shoppers offer input until it was too late.

"There may be a time to evolve our logo, but if and when that time comes, we'll handle it in a different way," Hansen said.[2]

We often use the power of suggestion to create impressions in our personal lives; sometimes these impressions help us look or seem better or different than we actually are. Women (and some men) use suggestion when they wear makeup to look older, younger, or prettier. Hats may be worn to cover a bad hair day or the beginnings of hair loss or to show identification with an athletic team. Clothing choices conceal flaws and sometimes suggest status or, conversely, a disregard for status.

People use the power of suggestion in the professional world also, such as when a real estate agent tells a client to bake something sweet for an open house so the home will seem warm and inviting; or when salesclerks are told to look busy, even when there is no real work to do; or when a car salesperson asks a customer to sit inside a car and feel comfortable, hoping that the suggestion of ownership and the smell and feel of a new car will induce him or her to buy. Dr. Alan Hirsch, neurologic director of the Smell and Taste Treatment and Research Foundation in Chicago, did a study on the effect of smell at a Las Vegas casino. When interviewed by National Public Radio's Neal Conan, he said,

What we found was, in the presence of a pleasant odor, there was an increased amount of money people placed in slot machines. The increase was of 45.11 percent, which was highly significant because when we looked at the control area where there was no odor, there was only a two percent change compared to the weekends before and the weekends after.[3]

Smart Money magazine columnist Russell Pearlman calls the use of scents in casinos, *subliminal relaxation*:

Taking a cue from retailers, casinos often circulate oils and scents through their ventilation systems to try to put gamblers in a good mood. At 500,000 square feet, the gaming/hotel section of the Mohegan Sun complex in Uncasville, Conn., is the largest scented building in the world. It has more than a dozen different smells circulating within its walls, says Mark Peltier, cofounder of AromaSys, the firm that installed the system. And The Venetian casino in Las Vegas, also an AromaSys client, circulates an array of herbal scents, including lavender, throughout the casino floor.

[2] Emily Fredrix, "Gap Gets Rid of New Logo," http://www.huffingtonpost.com/2010/10/12/gap-gets-rid-of-new-logo_n_759131.html.

[3] *USA Today*, 1993.

Why the olfactory overload? It's generally believed that people will stay longer—and therefore spend more—in a place with a pleasant smell, says Peltier. The scents have no known harmful side effects, but be aware that it might be more than just the free drinks making you feel so happy-go-lucky.[4]

British professor Mark Griffith discusses how marketers attempt to stimulate all of a consumer's senses in order to create brand loyalty:

> Like memories, sensory perceptions are unique to each of us and have the capacity to emotionally stimulate, leaving the chance to build brands by leveraging the five senses wide open. Some commercial operators have already got the hang of sensory appeal. For instance, some supermarkets bake fresh bread on the premises so passersby smell the aroma, are struck with hunger and are drawn inside. One major British bank introduced freshly brewed coffee to its branches with the intention of making customers feel at home. The familiar smell was used to help relax the customers. Other examples include a leading chain of toiletry stores which pumped the smell of chocolate through its air conditioning system in the run up to Valentine's Day, and a well-known clothes shop which filled its flagship stores with the smell of freshly laundered shirts.
>
> . . . Like smell, sound also evokes memory and emotion. Meaningful sound is a cheap but very effective way of appealing to another of a customer's senses and of powerfully enhancing a brand's message or appeal. A pop song from your youth can help bring back the excitement felt in your teens. . . .
>
> Sound effects and noise in the gambling environment are very important in getting people to gamble. Sound effects—especially in activities like slot machine playing—are thought to be gambling-inducers. Constant noise and sound gives the impression of a noisy, fun and exciting environment. Walk into any casino in Las Vegas and you will experience this. It's also common for slot machines to play a musical tune or buzz loudly if you win, with low denomination coins hitting a metal payout tray making lots of noise. This is all deliberate. It gives the impression that winning is far more common than losing (as you cannot hear the sound of losing!). So next time you're in a room full of 1,000 slot machines, remember that the sound of 20 of them paying out is more audibly noticeable than the 980 machines that are losing money for the punter (gambler).[5]

Suggestion is also a major factor in the design of stores. Joseph Weishar, author of *Design for Effective Selling Space*, claims that retailers can use store design to exert significant control over the responses of their customers. Weishar says that shoppers move in predictable patterns; for example, 80 percent of customers turn right when they walk into a store. Savvy retailers place the items they most want to sell to the right of the store entrance. In addition, they find ways to move customers to the back of the store, often by featuring sales in that area; since most people don't leave the same way they came in, a trip to the back ensures a round trip through the

---

[4] "10 Things Your Casino Won't Tell You," http://www.smartmoney.com/spending/rip-offs/10-things-your-casino-wont-tell-you-17277/?page=4.

[5] Mark Griffiths, "Scenting Success," http://www.pokerplayer.co.uk/sports-betting/news/651/gambling_psychology.html.

store. The highly successful Disney stores feature a large video screen against their back wall, knowing that kids will try to move their parents back there; these stores also create a fun, vibrant atmosphere that appeals to their target audience.[6]

Design elements are also important influencing factors for online stores, as noted in the following excerpt from a reporter who follows the effects of "eye-tracking" technology:

> One website we found recently posted an interesting article originally written for *Scientific American* in which the author discusses how people decide to take action. Apparently, decision-making can be traced back to how long someone spends looking at the options.
>
> According to the article, if a product is looked at longer, the odds of a buyer making a purchase for the item go up. Shoppers that are attempting to decide between two items tend to go with the item they spent more time looking at. When a subject's eye movements were tracked, researchers determined that items were chosen based on how long subjects looked at an item, even if it was for just a half second longer. This was the case seventy percent of the time.
>
> This makes the case for architectural elements to be incorporated into a design . . . visual structure, be it on a website or in a supermarket, plays a giant role in how consumers are making decisions. The architecture of the site is relevant, then, because finding information on a page can then influence choices and the decisions made when purchasing something.
>
> If a product is at the bottom right side of the page, chances are the consumer will go for something nearer to the top only in that they spend more time looking at it.
>
> At what point . . . does design for perception become design towards persuasion? It's an interesting point, and certainly something to consider when designing a window display or a website, for example. If the architecture of a place influences each decision made, think about how much structure matters, especially in a building like a hospital or a school, for example. It's these decisions that make up our daily lives, influence our choices, and guide us into the future.[7]

Sharon Zukin, professor of sociology, writes about how shopping, whether on-line or in a store, enhances our visions of ourselves and our world. She believes that people who buy things they don't need aren't necessarily greedy, but instead are seduced by the suggestive emotional experience of shopping:

> Even if we don't make a purchase, the social space of stores is a material image of our dreams. Low prices? Wal-Mart, where men and women of all income levels shop together, offers us a vision of democracy. Brand names? Sony and Band-Aids represent our means to a better life. Designer labels? The Armani suit or Miss Sixty jeans will win us the job or a social partner. The seduction of shopping is not about buying goods. It's about dreaming of a perfect society and a perfect self.[8] (See Exercise 8.1, pages 375–376.)

[6] Joseph Weishar, *Design for Effective Selling Space* (Houston, TX: McGraw Hill, 1992).

[7] dbrendant, "Eye Tracking Study Shows Architecture Influences Choice," http://eyetrackingupdate.com/2010/12/28/eye-tracking-study-shows-architecture-influences-choice.

[8] Sharon Zukin, "Attention Shoppers: Your Dreams in Aisle 3," *The Chronicle Review*, December 19, 2003.

Televised Suggestion

The media does set the agenda about what will and will not get discussed.

Sherry Bebitch Jaffe, Center for Politics and Policy

Television producers, directors, editors, and advertisers have always used the power of suggestion. The following guidelines will help you view television with an understanding of the subtle, but consciously detectable, elements of suggestion. For news programs and talk shows, be aware of

1. The selection of issues
2. The use of time
3. The selection and treatment of guest and panel members
4. What is included or excluded on a set
5. The nonverbal element of clothing
6. The use of language
7. The use of camera angles and cuts
8. Camera distance and framing

The Selection of Issues

Hundreds of global and national issues could be covered on any given day. The average network and local newscast is 24 minutes long, including sports and weather (with an additional 6 minutes of commercials). Many stories are written but not aired because of these time limitations. So the selection of stories to be featured and the decision about the order in which they will be presented give network news editors enormous power. The very fact that a story is on the morning or evening news makes it seem important to us; we never really know what other issues are not being covered.

Mike Wallace, former host of CBS network's popular *60 Minutes* (an investigative reporting program), stated that on news-related programs, the reporter's interest often decides whether a story is profiled. In other words, both reporters (by choosing stories) and also editors (by deciding which stories are aired) have the power to decide what is and what is not worthy of coverage.

Another important factor in determining the content of programming is *numbers* or *ratings*. The shows that get the largest audiences (determined by independent research companies, such as Nielsen) also get the largest share of advertising revenue. In effect, if a program wants to stay on the air, it has to attract a large audience.

One method used to attract viewers is **sensationalism**. When broadcasters use sensationalism, more exciting stories are chosen over less-exciting but perhaps more newsworthy ones; and the most bizarre, visually interesting, or *sensational* elements of these stories are featured. A local station might focus on the day's fires and auto accidents, showing all the gory details, and bypass stories on upcoming propositions or elections. Stories involving celebrities get prime coverage in both local and national newscasts and sometimes receive hours of repetitive coverage on cable stations. For example, Gail Shister of the *Philadelphia Inquirer* wrote about the extensive reporting of the death of former Playmate Anna Nicole Smith, including 50 percent of cable news on the day of her death and weeks of continuing coverage, stating that "Policy debate over Iraq and the

sensationalism   A method used to attract viewers by presenting more exciting stories over less-exciting but perhaps more newsworthy ones; the most bizarre, visually interesting, or *sensational* elements of these stories are featured.

'08 presidential race came in second and third at 15 percent and 10 percent, respectively, over the week."[9]

Columnist Ben Cohen, editor of *TheDailyBanter.com* wrote about his frustration with his own futile attempts to ignore celebrity news:

> I have to search pretty hard to find out about issues that have any type of meaningful effect on people's lives (like trade agreements that will screw working people, the details of financial reform, environmental legislation for mountain top mining etc.) yet I don't have to do anything to find out that Lindsay Lohan is in jail. And if I'm deliberately ignoring people like Lohan, what does that say for people who don't really think too much about the news they are consuming? A 14-year-old girl in America would grow up thinking that a C list celebrity going to prison actually constituted something serious, that the lives of the mega rich and famous were of concern to society.
>
> Our obsession with everything celebrity has stopped us being able to focus on issues that matter and morphed us into drama addicts and voyeurs. Everyone has an opinion on LeBron James's decision to switch basketball teams, but no one really has any idea whether the new health care legislation will actually help regular people.[10]

The Pew Research Center confirmed Cohen's statements in their findings on celebrity reports:

> The public was much more aware last week of news involving two well-known celebrities than reports about visits to the United States by two foreign leaders. Four-in-ten (41%) say they heard a lot about LeBron James' decision—announced live on ESPN on July 8—to leave the Cleveland Cavaliers and join the Miami Heat basketball team. Another 27% say they heard a little about this. About three-in-ten (31%) say they heard nothing at all. Almost half of men (49%) say they heard a lot about James' announcement, compared with 33% of women.
>
> Just more than a quarter (27%) say they heard a lot about Lindsay Lohan getting sentenced to 90 days in jail for violating the terms of her probation. More than four-in-ten (42%) say they heard a little about this and 30% say they heard nothing at all. More women (31%) say they heard a lot about this than men (23%). Those ages 65 and older, meanwhile, were just as likely as those 18-29 to say they had heard a lot about Lohan's sentencing (24% vs. 23%).
>
> Visits to the U.S. by Israeli Prime Minister Benjamin Netanyahu and England's Queen Elizabeth were less widely known. Just 13% say they heard a lot about Netanyahu's trip, which included a meeting with President Obama in Washington. About a third (35%) heard a little about the visit, but 52% say they heard nothing at all.[11]

[9] Gail Shister, "Anna Nicole Smith Found to Overwhelm Iraq War Coverage," *The Philadelphia Inquirer*, February 14, 2007.

[10] Ben Cohen, "Who Is Lindsay Lohan," http://www.huffingtonpost.com/ben-cohen/who-is-lindsay-lohan_b_669193.html, August 3, 2010.

[11] Pew Research Center for the People & the Press, "Interest in Oil Leak Dips Along with Coverage," http://pewresearch.org/pubs/1665/right-amount-of-oil-leak-news-too-much-lohan-lebron-james-coverage, updated December 30, 2010.

What the Public's Hearing About . . .

	A Lot %	A Little %	Nothing at All %
Lebron James to play for Miami Heat	41	27	31
Lindsay Lohan sentenced to jail	27	42	30
Netanyahu's diplomatic trip to U.S.	13	35	52
Queen of England visits U.S.	9	47	43

Pew Research Center July 8–11 Q3a-d.
Figures may not add to 100% because of rounding.

Celebrity trials are also prominently featured on news programs; lawsuits against Michael Jackson's doctor, Mel Gibson, Jennifer Lopez, and other popular personalities have ranked as top stories on network and online news outlets. In addition to the disproportionate coverage given to celebrity trials, a host of television shows that re-enact sensational news stories has developed over the past decade.

The apparent success of sensational coverage of the news (and of the ever-increasing lineup of "reality" programs) is one factor behind the claim that the primary purpose of television news, whether broadcast or cable, is to entertain rather than to inform. The late professor and media analyst Neil Postman was concerned about the blurring of news and entertainment. He wrote, "It would seem that right now, Americans are more interested in entertainment than any other aspect of personal life . . . even in school now teachers are more and more trying to be entertaining because television has taught the young that learning, whatever it is, must always be fun. And if it's not fun, then it's not worthwhile and you should just change the dial . . . go to another station."[12]

Whatever the objectives of a given program, we as critical thinkers can choose to view news broadcasts with discernment rather than passively absorbing them. We can stop and ask ourselves if a story being covered is one of the most important stories of the day or just one of the most exciting stories.

The Use of Time

Two elements of time can influence listeners. One is the time placement of a story. A story given prime (early) coverage on a news program will seem very important to the audience. On network news, when the worldwide events of the day are given only 24 minutes, any item rating coverage attains instant credibility with viewers. On cable news networks, when there are frequent interruptions for "breaking news," the items highlighted in these segments are meant to be seen as truly significant.

Former anchorman Dan Rather was interviewed about the power of network news and asked why CBS once used some of its precious evening broadcast time to cover a frog that could jump 30 feet. Rather laughed and said that when a frog can jump 30 feet, that is news! He skirted the question gracefully, but the issue remains: What is worthy of national broadcast in a limited time frame and, more importantly, who decides?

David Brinkley addressed the question of who decides what to broadcast at a meeting of the Radio-Television News Directors Association. He commented on the

---

[12] Stephen Marshall, "Prelude to Vegas: Neil Postman Gets Interviewed," Channel Zero, 1996.

fact that most Americans don't read newspapers to be informed, choosing to watch television news instead. "All they know about public policy," he said, "is what we tell them."[13]

The quantity of time is also a factor on television and radio. On network news programs or short radio news updates, both of which have little time, a story given significant coverage is seen as vital. On the other hand, 24-hour cable news networks have a different problem; they have to find enough stories to fill an entire day. As the late CBS news anchor Walter Cronkite stated, "They're forced to continually fill air time, so they often wind up devoting too much attention to stories that aren't truly important in the overall scheme of things."[14] When we keep seeing coverage of the same story on cable news of, for example, a sensational celebrity trial, it takes on import that it may not merit.

Talk shows frequently feature guests who discuss different aspects of the same problem; that gives viewers a variety of perspectives and adds interest to the issue. However, when one guest is given more time than another to make his or her points, that guest has a greater chance of influencing the audience.

In addition, we begin to feel better acquainted with the person who is given more time; the factor of familiarity may unconsciously persuade us to feel closer to that person's position, especially on a topic that is new to us. (See Exercise 8.2, pages 376–377.)

The Selection and Treatment of Guests and Panel Members

When you watch a debate or talk show on an issue, notice the credentials of the persons being interviewed. If the producer or editor either is not careful or has a bias, one side may be represented by attractive, articulate spokespersons and the other by intensely emotional, argumentative people. Are the persons selected really in leadership positions for the causes they represent, and are they respected by their colleagues? If there is only one "professional" on the panel (often a doctor, psychologist, writer, or lawyer), does he or she represent only one side of the controversy and therefore lend credibility only to that side?

Be fair by keeping in mind the principle that if a controversy rages for a long time, that usually means reasonable people are disagreeing about important definitions or principles. Don't judge an issue by an abrasive spokesperson who may or may not represent the norm of persons who support his or her side. The producer may have chosen a more colorful and interesting, but much less representative, person to discuss either side. Unfortunately, when more aggressive guests are featured on programs about important topics, they often obscure the issues by talking over each other. As Walter Cronkite stated, "I think most of that stuff is meant to be entertainment, not journalism. All that screaming and hollering is absolute anathema for me. I tune out as soon as I can't understand what they're saying, and that's too bad because some of these people are pretty well informed."[15]

Another relevant factor to consider is the treatment of each spokesperson by the interviewer. Note whether the interviewer is equally positive (or negative) in the interrogation of the guests. Sometimes, a biased interviewer will direct positive, easily answered questions, often called "softball" questions, to one guest and more negative, probing questions, "hardball" questions, to a guest who represents the other side of the issue. For example, if the interviewer likes the guest, he or she could say, "Some people

[13] Marlin Maddoux, *Free Speech or Propaganda?* (Nashville, TN: Thomas Nelson Publishers, 1990) p. 73.

[14] Chuck Barney, "Good News: Cronkite's Still Involved," *Contra Costa Times*, February 25, 2004.

[15] Ibid.

seem confused by your stand on this particular issue; could you explain more about your current thinking on it?" (softball question). On the other hand, if the interviewer doesn't like the guest, the question might sound like this: "How can you explain the obvious contradictions in your position on this issue?"(hardball question). The guest might also be interrupted or contradicted frequently and in an aggressive tone by a host who is hostile to his or her viewpoints. You can see the power an interviewer has to make a guest feel (and thus seem to the audience) comfortable and respected or uncomfortable and defensive. When interviewers are biased, the public audience does not get an objective look at the expert opinions that could be provided by the guests.

What Is Included or Excluded on a Set

Notice the environment in which televised programs and ads are set. For example, on a commercial for a children's educational toy, we might be impressed by a "teacher" who is surrounded with books and diplomas.

The director of a commercial can create the impression of an academic background that may have nothing to do with anyone's credentials. The actress who portrays a teacher in a commercial doesn't have to be a teacher. Advertisers know that the impression of authority—created by a setting of a doctor's office, a classroom, or a law library—can have a positive impact on the viewers' responses to the commercial message. (See Exercise 8.3, page 377.)

The Nonverbal Element of Clothing

How someone is dressed is an important factor in creating a suggestion of his or her character and appropriateness for a given role. For example, both the Republican and Democratic parties have sponsored "schools" for their candidates in which training is given on campaign techniques; part of this training covers proper dress in various situations. Spouses are also encouraged to attend sessions on how to dress themselves and how to help their mates dress to create the right impressions. Even small details such as appropriate length and color of socks may be covered in these workshops.

Clothing style is an essential element of advertising as well. Actors who are portraying pilots, doctors, managers, or other professionals are dressed to fit the part.

A number of years ago, John Molloy wrote the best-selling books *Dress for Success for Men* and *The Woman's Dress for Success Book* about his extensive studies on how styles and colors create impressions. His books are filled with research about how changing the look or color of one's clothes, jewelry, accessories, and hairstyle has helped individuals perform better in job interviews, sales calls, and other challenging communication situations. Many producers, advertisers, candidates, and spokespersons are familiar with techniques such as Molloy's and use them to create positive suggestions on their audiences. Current television programs, such as TLC's *What Not to Wear,* encourage people to "make over" their clothing, hair style, and accessories to create good impressions on others. The hosts of these programs often write their own books; for example, Clinton Kelly and Stacy London authored a book called *Dress Your Best* that advises readers what to wear to convey certain impressions at work and for formal and casual events. (See Exercise 8.4, page 377.)

The Use of Language

Setting and appearance send messages nonverbally; the use of a reporter's language can also affect our perception of an issue. Some years ago, when a terrorist bombing would occur, news reporters would say, "Such and such a group takes *credit* for the bombing." Other reporters and the public took offense at the word *credit,* which has a positive connotation. The late Eric Severeid, a respected commentator, broadcast a segment on the harm done by such words. Because of similar protests, the commonly accepted statement is now "Such and such a group claimed *responsibility* for the bombing." In recent years, some reporters have chosen to change the term *suicide bombings* to *homicide bombings* to reflect the fact that suicide bombers seek to kill innocent civilians.

One media critic gave the following example to illustrate how a reporter's choice of words can influence the perception of a situation:

> I might say, "I've been a journalist for thirty years." Now a newspaper could pick that up and report: "Charles Wiley said he has been a journalist for thirty years." That's fact. Just straight reporting. Or the reporter could say, "Marlin's guest *admitted* he's been a journalist for thirty years." Or he can say, "He has *conceded* he's been a journalist for thirty years." Or he could go to the final step and say "Wiley *confessed* he's been a journalist for thirty years." You see how one word changes the whole meaning."[16]

Sometimes, a journalist with a bias will use certain labels to characterize a person or an issue in a poor light. One clever way to discredit someone is to quote an enemy of that person. For example, if a journalist (electronic or print) doesn't like the success of a third party candidate, she can quote someone else who has called the candidate a "spoiler." On the other hand, if the journalist likes the third party candidate, she can quote someone who calls him "a fresh alternative for change." In that manner, the reporter is only reporting the 'facts' of what someone else has said about the candidate. In addition, certain labels can be attributed to a person, thereby coloring how a neutral audience might perceive him or her. On the positive side, someone might be labeled a "moderate." More negative labels include "liberal," "conservative," "ultraliberal," "ultraconservative," "ideologue," "millionaire," and "extremist." To discredit a politician, a reporter might describe him or her as "embattled" or "trying to head off criticism"; programs that are disliked may be labeled as "costly."[17]

Skill

Recognize the techniques of suggestion used by electronic media.

The Use of Camera Angles and Cuts

Sometimes, directors tell camerapersons to shoot a person from below; this angle gives the speaker more authority, as if the viewers are "looking up to" the individual. Commercials use this technique to command attention and respect for a particular actor who is telling us to buy something, or to show how large and impressive an authority figure looks to a common person. One commercial used this technique to illustrate how big a parent looks to a toddler.

[16] Martin Maddoux, *Free Speech or Propaganda?* (Nashville, TN: Thomas Nelson Publishers, 1990), p. 54.
[17] Bob Kohn, *Journalist Fraud* (Nashville, TN: WND Books, 2003), p. 148.

Conversely, when the camera angle is above the speaker, the impression is that the viewers are looking down on the speaker; in this case, the speaker may look insignificant or even dishonest.

The ability to use cuts (switching from one camera to another) to create positive or negative impressions about a speaker during a debate or talk show, or even in a news report, gives television directors great power. For example, a director can cut to a shot of an audience member's reaction to a speaker, thereby giving the impression of approval or disapproval of what the speaker has said. Also, during convention coverage, directors can cut to one audience member who appears bored with a candidate and thus unfairly represent the majority of audience members. Conversely, C-SPAN has used wide-angle shots to show the viewing audience that while a congressperson or senator is making an impassioned speech, the chairs in the room are empty.

Cuts in editing are used to select a short segment of a longer interview for broadcast. Sometimes, these cuts distort the statements that have been made by taking them out of context. The **sound bite** is a brief selection of a longer speech, usually heard out of context; both politicians and editors use sound bites to create impressions on viewers.

Advertisers also use distorted camera angles and quick cuts from scene to scene in order to command attention. These unusual, quickly moving scenes, coupled with increased volume, ensure that viewers pay attention to commercials.

Camera Distance and Framing

Directors of programs may deliberately or unconsciously use camera shots to influence audiences. Close-ups affect our emotions by adding an element of intimacy. We feel closer to a person and identify more readily with the person's viewpoint when we can see him or her as, literally, close to us. We may believe that the speaker is telling us the truth because he appears to be looking us in the eye. In fact, the speaker is looking at the camera or at the interviewer and only appears to be making eye contact with us. Conversely, educator John Splaine writes, "A camera angle from the side will suggest that a pictured person, who is responding to an incriminating question, might not be telling the truth."[18]

A wide-angle shot can make us feel distant from an individual. We feel uncomfortable with someone who seems far away from us, and that may translate into a lack of trust for his or her position on a given issue. When a scene is shot from a helicopter, the people below are seen as far away and alien, sometimes appearing more like ants than human beings.

In addition, **framing**—the deliberate or unconscious use of camera shots to influence audiences—can make a critical difference. One loud demonstrator shown close up at a rally can create a distorted image if there are hundreds of other people protesting quietly. During the coverage of the chaos in Los Angeles following the verdict in the famous Rodney King trial, television viewers saw two Korean men standing in front of their businesses pointing handguns; a Korean community leader criticized the reporters for leaving out the rest of the scene, which consisted of groups of looters heading for their stores. By showing only the two men with handguns, viewers were given a false impression and the storeowners were literally "framed."

Critical thinkers need to be vigilant in their awareness of the impressions that can be created electronically. (See Exercise 8.5, page 378.)

sound bite   An excerpt from a speech or report that is presented as summarizing but may actually distort the sentiments of the speaker or writer.

framing   The deliberate or unconscious use of camera shots to influence audiences; also, the use of a number of techniques by journalists and broadcasters to create a particular impression of reality.

---

[18] John Splaine, "Critically Viewing the Social Studies: A New Literacy," *Louisiana Social Studies Journal*, XVI, no. 1 (Fall 1989): 16.

Suggestion in Print Media

Four hostile newspapers are more to be feared than a thousand bayonets.

Napoleon I, *Maxims* (1804–1815)

Real reporting is time-consuming and expensive. It requires a level of investment that many traditional print and broadcast news organizations can no longer afford in the face of the tsunami of free content that is the web . . . . Unless real news organizations like the *Washington Post* and the *New York Times* can find a way to be profitable on the net, journalism is doomed. And with it will go one of the essential pillars of a free society.

Jerry B, Social Media Today.com

The broadcast media, television and radio, used to be subject to what was called the **Fairness Doctrine**, which meant that if broadcasters allowed air time for one side of an issue, they had to allow time for other points of view as well. The Federal Communications Commission (FCC) created the doctrine because of the limited channels available for broadcasting. Under the Fairness Doctrine, a network or affiliate was considered a "public trustee" and, as such, could not air an interview, documentary, or news program on one side of an issue and refuse to offer an equivalent opposing viewpoint. Likewise, a station could not air a message by one legitimate political candidate without allowing time for his opponent; the idea was that controversial issues should be handled in a fair and balanced way on the public airwaves. However, with frequency changes and the proliferation of cable channels toward the end of the twentieth century, the public began to have many more choices of programs, and the concerns that prompted the Fairness Doctrine were greatly eased; in 1987, the courts declared that since the Fairness Doctrine was not mandated by Congress, the FCC did not have to continue to enforce it. Since that time, Congress has tried to pass legislation mandating the Fairness Doctrine again, but that legislation was vetoed by Presidents Reagan and George Bush Sr. Some members of Congress want to bring back the doctrine to make sure that a balance of viewpoints on controversial issues is maintained. However, as Val Limburg stated in a treatise on the doctrine, "The public relies instead on the judgment of broadcast journalists and its own reasoning ability to sort out one-sided or distorted coverage of an issue."[19]

As a result of their history with the Fairness Doctrine, most television and radio networks and affiliates are sensitive to the importance of a balanced approach. However, even with a station policy that gives time for different viewpoints on an issue, broadcasters can still choose which guests appear and can manipulate programs using the techniques detailed in the previous section. And, as networks proliferate and competition for viewers and listeners increases, some radio and television networks, particularly public radio, talk radio, and cable, are moving toward presenting either more liberal or more conservative programming, hoping to capture a larger, more loyal target audience.

Unlike the broadcast media, the print media have not had a history of governmental pressure to be fair; however, journalists did aim to live by a certain ethic that was codified in 1923 by the American Society for Newspaper Editors. Their ethic reads as

Fairness Doctrine
A former U.S. policy by which broadcasters must allow equal airtime for all sides of an issue.

---

[19] Val Limburg, "Fairness Doctrine," Accessed March, 2007, www.museum.tv/archives/etv/F/htmlF/fairnessdoct/fairnessdoct.htm.

follows: "Sound practice makes clear distinction between news reports and expressions of opinion. News reports should be free from opinion or bias of any kind." Schools of journalism traditionally taught reporters to focus on the facts and to use the questions "Who?" "What?" "When?" "Why?" "Where?" and "How?" to inform readers thoroughly about a news story. Some commentators are concerned about the effect of **spin**, the presenting of information with a subtle editorial bias, on reader's perceptions. In noting the need for some kind of fairness doctrine for the press, media scholar Ben Bagdikian stated that "most daily newspapers have not faced up to the fact that they are monopoly institutions and therefore have an obligation to speak for the entire community and to be sensitive to every segment of it."[20] However, with the proliferation of both Internet and traditional news sources, the line between straight news and commentary has been blurred; in fact, today's newspapers and news magazines often have a reputation for a certain political perspective that caters to their readers.

While some local and national newspapers strive to create a balance of views on controversial issues, many newspapers and magazines present primarily conservative or liberal perspectives. They feature columnists who largely subscribe to the publisher's political and social viewpoints. As critical thinkers, we can be responsible readers and see through biased presentations when we examine the following elements of both Web-based and traditional print journalism:

1. The use of headlines
2. The use of "leads" or openings to a news story
3. The balance in reporting an issue
4. Fairness in editorial essays and letters
5. Photo composition

> **spin** The use of language, particularly in politics and public relations, to create a biased, positive connotation for ideas, events, or policies that one favors, and a biased negative impression about ideas, events, or policies that one dislikes.

The Use of Headlines

> The vast majority of people who read newspapers gain their understanding of the news by glancing at the headlines and subheads. To influence the headlines is to influence public opinion.
>
> Bob Kohn, *Journalistic Fraud*

Most readers know that the sensational headlines featured on papers found in supermarket checkout lines are not credible. When we read a headline proclaiming that a famous star has "7 new babies," we can assume that her cat had a litter of kittens or another equally silly explanation for this amazing news. The wild stories about entertainers, political figures, and athletes that are found in tabloids have no credibility and are not used as resource material for research papers.

Less-sensational headlines can also distort information and mislead readers in subtle ways. Headlines in respectable newspapers, webzines, and magazines are important because many readers are "scanners"—they skim the publication, reading headlines and then going back to read only the articles of interest to them.

A headline that is scanned and recorded in the memory of a reader can give a misleading picture of information without actually being false. For example, let's say a reporter did a detailed story about an antinuclear protest that was held at a local power plant. The story covers the issues brought up by the demonstrators and the responses made by the plant spokesperson.

[20] Ben Bagdikian, *The Media Monopoly* (Boston: Beacon Press, 1973).

An editor who did not approve of this protest could use the headline, "No One Arrested at Power Plant Demonstration." Bringing in the idea of arrest by stating that there were no arrests is a subtle way of implying that arrests had been anticipated or that the protesters were not peaceful. An editor who approved of the demonstration might use the headline, "Large Crowds Turn Out to Voice Protest of Nuclear Power Dangers."

A joke illustrating how "spin" can be used in headlines to show someone in a bad light was going around midway through Bill Clinton's first term in office: The president went on a fishing trip with members of the press corps. After their boat left shore, the president realized he had left his tackle on the dock, so he stepped off the boat, walked to shore, picked up his tackle, and walked back over the surface of the water. The next day's headline read, "Clinton Can't Swim."[21]

Presidents and other governmental leaders are subject to criticism on a variety of issues. It goes with the territory, because no official can please everyone. As previously noted, newspapers and newsmagazines may have an editorial bias and feature largely liberal or conservative viewpoints on their opinion pages. Many readers turn to these opinion pages to read strong perspectives about an issue. However, when large newspapers bring their editorial bias into their front pages, where the "straight news" is supposed to be, and when they slant stories with the wording of headlines, the readers may accept the slanted viewpoint as the simple truth. For example, during the George W. Bush presidency, columnist Andrew Sullivan pointed out a routine Commerce Department study which revealed that the economy had grown by 3 percent. The report, favorable to the Bush administration, was headlined differently by three news organizations:

ECONOMY RACES AHEAD AT 3.1 ANNUAL RATE IN SUMMER— *Associated Press*

ECONOMY GROWS AT 3.1 PERCENT PACE—*Washington Post*

ECONOMY GREW AT 3.1% IN 3RD QUARTER, SLOWER THAN EXPECTED—*New York Times*[22]

Editors can shape the news and give a positive or negative spin on events by the use of carefully constructed headlines. One reader of Seattlepi.com blogged a complaint about how headlines were used to give a negative spin on President Obama's diplomatic trip to Asia:

The *New York Times* declares that *"Traveling in Asia, Obama's Glow Dims."* The story states that Obama is finding that his glow has worn off. This is the best possible example I have found in recent times of a "nonstory." It's also a splendid example of the media struggling to construct drama where none exists . . . . The President of the United States might be reduced to little more than a nightly news spectacle in his own country, but, abroad, he is a diplomat. Could we please get out of the way and let him be one? As the diplomat goes through the slow, considered *processes* of international diplomacy, could we please refrain from demanding the *event,* be it the debacle or the cheer?[23]

[21] Deborah Tannen, *The Argument Culture* (New York: Ballantine Books, Random House, Inc., 1998), p. 54.

[22] Kohn, *Journalistic Fraud*, p. 84.

[23] http://blog.seattlepi.com/mediamockingbird, November 12, 2010.

Headlines are powerful because they are often read as summary statements about events or discoveries. A headline that makes strong and unusual claims (particularly on the front page) draws readers to buy the paper or to read the article.

Headlines can also come in the form of the titles editors give to blogs or letters written by readers. Sometimes these titles are representative of the position of the person who wrote the editorial, but sometimes they are used to distort or ridicule the position of the writer. In this way, an editorial page may appear to give balanced perspectives on issues but in reality does not. For example, someone may write a letter to the editor of a newspaper or magazine alleging that 'Candidate X' won a recent election by making untrue statements about his opponent. If an editor disagrees with the letter writer, she might write the headline of the letter as "Reader Upset by Candidate's Victory." If she agrees with the writer, she might headline the letter: "Smear Campaign May Have Lead to Candidate X Election Win."

The Use of "Leads" or Openings to a News Story

> The power of the press in America is a primordial one. It sets the agenda of public discussion, and this sweeping political power is unrestrained by any law. It determines what people will talk and think about—an authority that in other nations is reserved for tyrants, priests, parties and mandarins.
>
> Theodore White, *The Making of a President*

lead The introductory sentence of a news story that is meant to give a reader the essence or general meaning of the story.

Closely related to the headline of a story is the introductory sentence, called the lead sentence or, simply, the **lead**. The lead sentence is meant to give the reader the "gist" or the essence of the story. Many busy readers rely on the leads to inform them of the important news of the day. If a particular story is of interest to the reader, he or she can read on for more detailed information, but the details are expected to add on to the main idea of the article that has presumably already been presented in the lead.

Editors usually create the headlines to a story by reading the lead and briefly summarizing its contents. If the lead is slanted, it is likely that the headline will also be slanted. For example, in an article on a study of chocolate, the lead claimed that chocolate might mimic the effects of marijuana and boost the pleasure people get from eating it. The headline then followed the lead by claiming that "Report on Chocolate May Bring a Real High." Since the writer of the lead did not give the real essence of the finding (that the substances researchers found in chocolate were too minute to produce a high), the headline gave distorted information.[24]

As we discussed previously, traditional schools of journalism train writers to focus on the essential facts about an event by answering the following questions: Who was involved? What happened? When did it happen? Where did it happen? Why did it happen? How did it happen? These are called the 5 Ws and the H in journalism, and good journalists answer all of them close to the beginning of the story, usually in the first sentence. An unbiased news writer will try to cover the 5 Ws and the H in a factual manner without injecting opinion. However, the lead can be slanted by a reporter or an editor who wishes to have readers interpret the news with a particular perspective. For example, the *Who* can be emphasized if the reporter likes the *Who* and the *Who* has done a good thing, or the *Who* can be minimized if the writer doesn't want to credit the *Who* with a good action. Let's say that a governor, Governor Smith, has managed to balance her state budget and make positive steps toward reducing

[24] Associated Press, "Report on Chocolate May Bring a Real High," *Contra Costa Times*, August 22, 1996, p. B-1.

a deficit that she inherited from a previous administration; she accomplished this by getting all of the state assembly members to accept her new proposals. A newspaper that doesn't like Governor Smith could run a lead that downplays her involvement in the budget balancing. The lead could read as follows: *Members of the state assembly worked together to create a balanced budget, easing the anger of many voters over the budget mess that has plagued this administration.* By praising the state assembly alone and implying that the budget mess was this administration's fault, the reporter has been able to avoid giving any credit (or even mention) to the governor. In fact, the way the lead reads, the governor seems to have caused the budget problems, and her efforts seem to be completely irrelevant to the progress that was made.

The *What* can also be distorted by a journalist who has an agenda beyond reporting the news factually. Let's say a paper likes Candidate X and dislikes Candidate Y. Recent polls have shown Candidate Y is leading Candidate X by 10 points. A straightforward lead might be: *A recent Gallup poll shows that Candidate Y leads nearest opponent Candidate X by 10 points.* A lead (and the headline derived from the lead) that puts a positive spin on the candidacy of Candidate X could spin the facts as follows: *Candidate X and Candidate Y are the top candidates in a close race for the eighth district's congressional seat.*

In a critical piece on the biased coverage of the *What* in the Israeli-Palestinian conflict, *U.S. News and World Report* columnist John Leo writes:

> "He kept bleeding" was a large front-page headline in the April 4 *Washington Post.* The story was about a wounded Palestinian who died in Bethlehem after Israeli forces refused to let ambulances into the fire zone. The Israelis said snipers were still active. Also they may have been suspicious of the local ambulance corps after explosives were discovered under the stretcher of a 3-year-old boy. Maybe the Israelis were just being monsters, as the press increasingly seems to think. But the level of "he kept bleeding" and "they've killed my wife" coverage of the Palestinian-Israeli war is quite high. Another *Washington Post* headline was "Father, son dead: Family wonders why." This is a very unusual way to cover combat, particularly when there are no neutral observers around to back up stories supplied by angry partisans. The British press is filled with this stuff, and the hostility to Israel is impossible to miss. American reporters are more professional, but focusing on highly emotional "they've killed my wife" coverage is dicey. It tells us nothing about what we need to know—whether the killing of civilians was incidental or intentional, massive or minor. After all, "they've killed my wife" journalism can be churned out after "collateral damage" in almost any battle in any war.
>
> In contrast, I don't see much emotional coverage of the Israeli civilians intentionally blown up by Palestinian bombers. Most attacks pass without any notice in the press. The coverage we do get is dry and matter-of-fact. In February, for instance, CNN's Web site mentioned the "killing of two Israelis" by a suicide bomber. The bomber was identified, but there were no names of the 15-year-old victims, no details about the horrific damage to other teens by flying nails embedded in the bomb, and not even a mention that one of the two dead was a U.S. citizen. Palestinian bombers, on the other hand, tend to get more vivid treatment, often with endearing photos and warm, human-interest touches. The *New York Times* reported that one bomber "raised doves and adored children," though this adoration apparently did not extend to the children being bombed.[25]

[25] John Leo, "No Way to Cover a War," *U.S. News and World Report,* April 29, 2002.

Clever writers with a bias can slant any of the 5 Ws and the *How.* As critically thinking readers, we need to "read between the lines" whenever we sense that we are receiving an editorial opinion disguised as a straight news story. (See Exercise 8.6, page 378.)

The Balance of Reporting on an Issue

All I know, is just what I read in the papers.

Will Rogers

Whereas network news and interview programs have a shortage of time, webpages, newspapers and newsmagazines have limited space. The editors decide which stories are important enough to cover and on what page. Generally, if a story is on the home page of a website or the front page of a newspaper, it is perceived by readers as more important than a story placed further back in the paper or on an interior page of the website. Many busy readers only have time to read the front or home page, so the stories featured there take on the most prominence.

In addition to the location of stories on a website or in a newspaper, the location of facts within the story is also important; misplacement can create a distorted view of the events covered. When significant facts are not covered in or close to the lead of the story, the reader can be misled, as we discussed in the last section concerning an article on the effects of chocolate. If a writer wants to put a good spin on a damaging story, the damaging elements can be minimized in the lead and placed toward the end of the story, since many readers don't have time to read all the way to the end; crucial facts can thus be lost to the majority of readers.

It is also important for news stories to give different perspectives on divisive issues; if more space and space closer to the lead of the story are given to one viewpoint and other viewpoints are minimized, ignored, or placed toward the end of the story, readers don't get the full picture surrounding a controversial topic.

Finally, major newspapers and newsmagazines need to cover all stories that have significance for their readers. Editors have the power to decide whether a story even makes the press, and because of the space shortage, some stories won't be covered. Sometimes, for example, coverage of minor candidates to an election is stopped or minimized in favor of giving more space to the front-runners. In many cases, the decision about whether to run or pull a story would be difficult for even the most impartial editor. In other cases, a story may be pulled primarily because of the bias of an editor; if, for example, an editor does not agree with a group staging a large rally, the story of the rally may not be covered at all. (See Exercise 8.7, pages 378–379.)

Fairness in Editorial Essays and Letters

As we have discussed, some websites, newspapers, and magazines try to balance their editorial pages by printing both liberal and conservative viewpoints, sometimes on alternate days. Other websites and papers get a reputation for being primarily liberal or conservative because of the stands taken by their editorial writers. In addition, local newspapers often print their suggestions as to how readers should vote in an upcoming election. It is important for critical thinkers to realize that reporting is not always objective and fair and that the reader-comment section and the editorial pages are set aside to reflect the opinions of readers and essayists.

Notice whether the essays on the editorial page seem to favor one political viewpoint over another. In addition, examine the letters to the editor and comments that are published. They should reflect differing, rather than homogeneous, opinions on the same issue.

Skill

Recognize the use of suggestion in print and electronic media.

Photo Composition

If a picture is worth a thousand words, then photojournalists have a strong communicative advantage. They can influence our perceptions of people or events with the photographs they print.

Most of us would agree that outright lies using photographs are unethical; in one of the earliest examples of distorted imaging, photographers for *TV Guide* used technology to create a cover featuring the head of Oprah Winfrey with the body of actress Ann-Margaret; readers and fellow journalists alike were disapproving. As technology has advanced, so has the ability to alter images to make them look real. A staff photographer covering the war in Iraq for the *Los Angeles Times* was fired for altering a photograph to make it more visually striking. When Brian Walski sent his altered photograph to his own director of photography, the director didn't notice anything wrong. It took a *Hartford Courant* employee to notice that something was amiss, and even he wasn't able to confirm the alteration until he magnified the picture 600 percent. Walski, a highly respected, veteran photographer, apologized for the fabrication; he and other reporters believe that his judgment may have been affected by his sleepless days in a war zone. Nonetheless, his boss, Colin Crawford, felt compelled to fire him. "What Brian did is totally unacceptable and he violated our trust with our readers," Crawford said, "We don't feel good about doing this, but the integrity of our organization is essential. If our readers can't count on honesty from us, I don't know what we have left."[26] Crawford was right in knowing that we don't like to be deceived by our technology, and reputable news organizations do not knowingly print altered images.

Images that have been tampered with also distort our perception of the individuals that have been photographed. For example, the ethics of altering a photograph of President Obama is discussed in the following excerpt from huffingtonpost.com:

> The frenzy of comments about *The Washingtonian's* decision are running across the gamut, from a reprise of the drooling appreciation for Obama's taut abs first seen when the paparazzi photos of Obama on the beach hit in December: "Really hot Obama," "President Beefcake;" to stinging political rebukes for what some take to be the magazine's pandering to its audience and/or to the administration: "embarrassing."
>
> But I'd like to call your attention to what *Washingtonian* did with the original Bauer-Griffin photo. Said Leslie Milk, the magazine's lifestyle editor, "I know we changed the color of his suit to red, and dropped out the background." In the original photo the president is wearing a black suit and walking from what appears to be sliding glass doors leading to a living room.

---

[26] Kenneth F. Irby, "L.A. Times Photographer Fired Over Altered Image," Poynteronline, April 2, 2003.

What also appears to be altered from the original image is the contrast and the color balance of the president's skin. On *The Washingtonian's* cover the sun striking Obama's chest makes him appear more golden, almost glistening.

In the world of news, that's unethical. The rule of thumb is, if you want to change what's in the photo, choose another photo. Making Obama into a man wearing brilliant red surfer trunks, instead of a more modest black pair, making the image more dramatic by having him walking out of darkness, and changing the exposure so he looks more gilded changes viewers' ideas about who the man is.

. . . In 2005, *Newsweek* magazine tinkered with its cover of Martha Stewart to illustrate her coming release from prison, running a composite image of Stewart's head on the photo of a body of model. The National Press Photographers Association, the society of professional photojournalism, called that cover "a major ethical breach."

Where in the spectrum of ethics does the decision by *The Washingtonian* come? A key issue is whether we "know about it," said Carl Sessions Stepp, professor of journalism at the University of Maryland. "When a magazine puts a person on its cover, our expectation is that the person we are seeing is the person who was seen through the lens of the photographer." But if we're told or it's obvious that an image has been "fictionalized" then we approach it with different expectations. We don't assume what's depicted is an accurate representation—both visually and psychologically—of who we're looking at.

What's the danger of an audience thinking that the president looks model-hot? It's a simplification of who he is—it's the photographic version of presenting Obama as the shining hope for the country. It's ascribing to him more power—even if the power is sexual—than he actually has.

What's the possible consequence? When individual players are made to seem larger or are given greater clout than they actually have, that prompts us to expect outcomes that cannot be delivered—and also encourages us to believe that we don't have to help solve the nation's problems, because we certainly do not measure up to the perfection we have been shown.[27]

Less-direct forms of manipulation can also occur through photocomposition. A responsible photographer could take a wide-angle shot of a rally, thus giving the viewer a sense of the general scene. A less-scrupulous or less-careful photographer could shoot instead a few unruly persons, which would discredit the general group of peaceful participants. Conversely, he or she could focus the camera on a fight between one police officer and one participant, which would give an impression of general police brutality. In addition, captions beneath photographs can influence our perceptions of a person or event.

Newspapers, newsmagazines, and websites should treat photographs as documentary information that helps us get the general feel of an event. When you sense that a photograph is making an editorial statement, stop and consider what viewpoint is being suggested through the picture.

In the following revealing photo, representatives of the Connecticut state legislature were seen playing games during a speech; had the photograph been taken at a

---

[27] Susan Moeller, "Media Literacy 101: The Ethics of Photoshopping a Shirtless Obama," http://www.huffingtonpost.com/susan-moeller/media-literacy-101-the-et_b_189488.html.

different angle, they might have been presumed to have been taking notes. As a result of the photograph, one legislator involved apologized to his constituents.

Connecticut state representatives Jack Hennessy and Barbara Lambert play solitaire at the state capitol during a late-night budget debate.

> Rep. Jack Hennessy, a Bridgeport Democrat, has had his picture displayed around the Internet as one of two Connecticut legislators playing solitaire during a state budget debate.
>
> The incident occurred August 31 in the historic Hall of the House in Hartford as House Republican leader Larry Cafero of Norwalk was delivering a lengthy speech on the two-year, $37.6 billion budget.
>
> The picture, by Associated Press photographer Jessica Hill, shows the back of Hennessy's head, along with Rep. Barbara Lambert, a Milford Democrat, who was sitting next to him.

In a letter to Bridgeport residents, Hennessy apologized as follows:

"It was certainly bad judgment for me to play a computer game even for just a few minutes during the final House session on the budget. I am embarrassed, and I apologize to each and every person in the North End and to people across the state.

"My actions were inexcusable. I do want my constituents to know that my poor judgment for a few moments on Monday in no way means I ignored your interests in representing you on this very serious matter. Over the past seven months, as a member of the General Assembly's Finance Committee, I have participated fully in the budget process and have played an active role in crafting a budget that provides the necessary services that our communities so desperately need while at the same time minimizing any negative impact on the city of Bridgeport and its people.

"I sincerely apologize to each of you. I look forward to having the continued privilege of representing you and your interests in Hartford. I thank you in advance for your understanding and have been humbled by those of you who have already expressed your understanding and forgiveness."[28]

The Power of Media to Shape Information

> Journalists may take us seriously as news consumers but generally ignore our wider role as citizens. They do not encourage communication, strengthen the public dialogue, or facilitate the formulation of common decisions, but may in fact do just the opposite by framing news in objective and episodic formats.
>
> Scott London, "How the Media Frames Political Issues," ScottLondon.com

Writers and producers of news and feature stories have enormous power to shape the information that is broadcast or published. As we have discussed, selection of

[28] Christopher Keating, "Rep. Jack Hennessy Apologizes For Playing Solitaire at State Capitol During Late-Night Budget Debate," http://blogs.courant.com/capitol_watch/2009/09/rep-hennessy-apologizes-for-pl.html, September 8, 2009.

issues, camera angles, questions asked, choice of wording, placement in a program or publication, balance of reporting, and the selection and treatment of people interviewed all have an effect on how we view the topics that are presented to us.

Shanto Iyengar, director of the Political Communication lab at Stanford University, has written extensively on the problems concerning media framing of issues. He calls most television reporting "episodic" news framing, reports that focus on individuals and on single concrete events. Episodic reporting is contrasted with "thematic" framing, which is reporting that includes a general context for political and social issues and events and presents viewers with "the big picture."

Iyengar's studies found that subjects shown "episodic" reports were less likely to consider society responsible for the event, and subjects shown "thematic" reports were less likely to consider individuals responsible. In one of the clearest demonstrations of this phenomenon, subjects who viewed stories about poverty that featured specific homeless or unemployed people (episodic framing) were much more likely to blame poverty on individual failings, such as laziness or little education, than were those who instead watched stories about high national rates of unemployment or poverty (thematic framing). Viewers of the thematic frames were more likely to attribute the causes and solutions to governmental policies and other factors beyond the individual's control.[29]

Those who study the effects of media often debate the extent to which programs *create,* rather than *reflect,* reality for readers and viewers. Certainly, producers and directors of feature films use all of the technical and artistic elements available to them to bring audiences into their world. We attend movies to be entertained and sometimes enlightened; we expect to laugh or cry at comedies and dramas and marvel at the special effects of action films. We are aware that our emotions and perceptions are being manipulated, and we want to be affected by what we see and hear on the screen.

But the interesting question for the media-literate individual is, "To what extent are thoughts and feelings being manipulated by what purports to be news?" Are reporters giving us a window to the significant events happening in the world or are they, to some extent, creating the scenes we are shown? Are they presenting "just the facts," or are they really shaping the facts so that news stories and features become a subtle form of argumentation?

William Dorman, professor of journalism and government at the California State University in Sacramento, believes that meaning is actively shaped by print and electronic media:

> Media manufacture meaning; they do not simply serve as a neutral conveyor belt for information about what happens in the world. The important word here is *manufacture.* In my view, journalism is as much a manufacturing process as, say, the shoe industry. To be sure, there are important political, ethical and even moral differences—but the idea of a manufacturing process in which choices are made about what gets produced and how is precisely the same. Journalists select what will be covered and determine *how* it will be presented, including what elements will be included or left out, what elements will be emphasized or left in the shadows, what language will be used, and so on. These are human choices made by human beings working in a social system in which there are punishments and rewards. Indeed, I

[29] Scott London, "How the Media Frames Political Issues," scottlondon.com (accessed March, 2007; original, January, 2003).

encourage my students to use the label **Represeter** synonymously with the term Reporter.[30]

represeter   A term used synonymously with the word *reporter* to indicate that reporters make strategic choices that frame news stories.

Professor Dorman asks his students to do "frame hunts." Students find excerpts from websites, newspapers, magazines, blogs, or books; they may also record a segment of a radio or television program that features media framing of a person or event. One common method for discovering a frame is to find a news item that is covered in two or more publications and note the difference in the reporting of that item. For example, consider the following contrasting headlines about 'distracted' (i.e., cell-phone using) drivers that appeared in two sections of the same website, dailypress.com. Both headlines are true, but they frame the news item completely differently.

In *Nation & World,* the headline is "Distracted driving 'epidemic,'" and the first paragraph notes that distracted drivers claimed the same percentage of all traffic deaths in 2009 as they did in 2008, which is way up from 2005. About halfway through the story, we learn that the total *number* of traffic deaths dropped in 2009.

On the *Business* page, the headline is "Distracted-driving deaths down 6% in '09." Also true. The drop, it turns out, mirrors the drop in overall traffic deaths and that the percentage of deaths attributed to distracted drivers (texting, etc.) remained the same.[31]

When stories are framed in ways that slant or distort the facts, people get faulty impressions, and when they act on those impressions, unfortunate decisions may be made. Such was the case for U.S. Secretary of Agriculture Tom Vilsack who fired an employee for making "racist" comments, comments that were taken completely out of context:

> Agriculture Secretary Tom Vilsack apologized today to Shirley Sherrod for firing her over distorted racial comments, and offered her a new job within the U.S. Department of Agriculture.
>
> "I expressed my deep regret," Vilsack told reporters in Washington, D.C. Sherrod told the Associated Press she is considering Vilsack's offer.
>
> White House spokesman Robert Gibbs also apologized to Sherrod on behalf of the Obama administration. "Members of this administration, members of the media, (and) members of different political factions on both sides of this have all made determinations and judgments without a full set of facts," Gibbs added.
>
> Sherrod had been accused of saying she would not give as much help to a white farmer as a black one, but the comments posted on various websites were only part of a larger story about racial reconciliation. Roger Spooner, the white farmer involved in this flap, told *USA Today* that Sherrod has been wronged.
>
> Earlier today, Sherrod said she might not return to her job if asked, citing the negative publicity surrounding her case.
>
> "We would need to talk," Sherrod told WXIA-TV in Atlanta. "I wouldn't want to go back and be harassed. I definitely wouldn't go back and do anything like I didn't do before to embarrass this administration. I support the administration too much."
>
> Gibbs also said that Vilsack's own job is safe, saying he is doing "terrific work at the Department of Agriculture."

[30] William Dorman, "Using Frame Analysis in the Classroom," handout.

[31] dailypress.com, http://articles.dailypress.com/2010-09-21/news.

Sherrod had said yesterday that the White House pressured Vilsack to fire her, though Vilsack said that's not true and that the mistaken dismissal was his responsibility alone. "This is a teachable moment for me, and I hope a teachable moment for all of us," Vilsack said.

Vilsack had issued a statement earlier Wednesday saying that he was reconsidering Sherrod's dismissal.

Here is an Associated Press summary of Sherrod's case.

Vilsack issued a short statement early Wednesday morning after Shirley Sherrod, who until Tuesday was the Agriculture Department's director of rural development in Georgia, said she was pressured to resign because of her comments that she didn't give a white farmer as much help as she could have 24 years ago.

Sherrod said her remarks, delivered in March at a local NAACP banquet in Georgia, were part of a larger story about learning from her mistakes and racial reconciliation, not racism, and they were taken out of context by a blogger who posted only part of her speech.

Vilsack's statement came after the NAACP posted the full video of Sherrod's comments Tuesday night . . . .

The NAACP had initially criticized Sherrod's comments, but issued a retraction after viewing the full tape. In a statement, the NAACP criticized conservative media organizations for broadcasting only a portion of what Sherrod said.

"We have come to the conclusion we were snookered by Fox News and Tea Party activist Andrew Breitbart into believing she had harmed white farmers because of racial bias," the NAACP said in a statement.

It added: "The fact is Ms. Sherrod did help the white farmers mentioned in her speech. They personally credit her with helping to save their family farm."

Sherrod told WXIA-TV of Atlanta: "I used that incident—and I've told that story over and over again—to show people how I moved from a place where I was in thinking about white and black issues to a place where I am . . . a point where I can treat everyone the way I want to be treated. I think my life is a testimony to that."

Breitbart, the conservative who posted Sherrod's comments on his website, told our Gannett colleague Chuck Raasch that his point was to expose the audience reaction at the NAACP banquet; Breitbart said that he was trying to expose the same kind of racism that the NAACP has accused Tea Party members of practicing.

"My point was it was the NAACP countenancing racism, that was my point," Breitbart said. "To divert this into a Shirley vs. Andrew show diverts from the concerted effort that the NAACP is going through to try to malign the Tea Party movement."

Breitbart also told Gannett's *Content One* that, "I don't want this, I loathe this, I loathe watching the race card being played."[32]

In another dramatic incident of framing, a political opponent to Congressman Dan Webster created a series of campaign ads that presented Webster's comments so that they seemed to say the opposite of what the candidate actually said:

In an attack ad labeling his opponent "Taliban Dan" Webster, U.S. Rep. Alan Grayson uses Webster's own words to prove the Republican thinks wives should be subservient to their husbands.

---

[32] Bruce Smith, "Vilsack Apologizes to Woman He Fired 'Without a Full Set of Facts,'" http://www.usatoday.com/communities/theoval/post/, July 21, 2010.

One problem: The Grayson campaign edited the original video, chopping it up and taking Webster's words out of context. Webster actually was advising husbands to bypass those particular Bible passages, according to a longer video clip released Monday by Webster's campaign.

Grayson's 30-second campaign ad, which has gained national attention since it first aired on Saturday, also cites votes and legislation from Webster's time in the legislature that some voters—particularly women—still could find objectionable. Webster has since refused to talk about those issues, including abortion.

But by twisting Webster's words, Grayson risks eroding some of the support he may have won from independent voters.

"Here he goes again," said Brian Graham, Webster's campaign manager. "Time and time again, Alan Grayson has shown that he cannot be truthful. The people of Central Florida are smarter than this. Grayson has to have realized that somebody would see this video and know that he was lying."

The TV spot includes short clips of Webster saying " . . . wives submit yourself to your own husband . . . " and "she should submit to me. That's in the Bible . . . ." The words "submit to me" are repeated twice more.

In the full video, Webster is talking to husbands at a gathering of a religious organization about biblical passages to choose when praying for loved ones. He says:

"Find a verse. I have a verse for my wife; I have verses for my wife. Don't pick the ones that say, um, she should submit to me. That's in the Bible, but pick the ones that you're supposed to do. So instead, love your wife, even as Christ loved the church and gave himself for it, as opposed to wives submit yourself to your own husband. She can pray that if she wants to, but don't you pray it."

Susannah Randolph, Grayson's campaign manager, defended the ad. She pointed to Webster's ties to the Institute in Basic Life Principles and its founder Bill Gothard, who has taught that women should be subservient to their husbands and not work outside the home. While in the state House in 1990, Webster spent $4,340 of taxpayer money to print and mail a district flier urging constituents to attend one of the group's seminars.[33]

Many stories are reported factually, but with the particular frame the reporter wants to create. Certain elements are emphasized; other factors may be completely omitted. As a critical thinker, it is important for you to consider the way in which a story is presented and the way people are characterized. Whenever possible, read or watch a story in its complete context and from different sources before making interpretations about the information presented. (See Exercise 8.8, page 379.)

A Bag of Marketing and Advertising Tricks

It takes an educated or very discerning person to be aware of and pay attention to the many methods used to persuade viewers to think or act in a certain way. The old saying "Let the buyer beware" means that when we are subjected to various pitches by advertisers and politicians, we have the responsibility to analyze their claims and to resist being persuaded against our will. Increasing our awareness of

---

[33] Mark Schlueb, "Grayson's 'Taliban Dan' Ad Takes Webster's Words Out of Context, Twists Meaning," Orlando Sentinel, September 27, 2010.

the persuasive techniques used by print and electronic media gives us more power as thinkers, voters, and consumers.

Advertisers and marketers are continually devising new ways to persuade target audiences. Let's consider some of their common techniques:

1. Fuzzy words
2. Logical fallacies
3. Stylized images and sounds
4. Celebrity associations and endorsements
5. Product placement
6. The Gestalt principle
7. Use of opinion leaders to influence the market
8. Use of social media to build customer loyalty
9. Eye tracking
10. Neuromarketing

Fuzzy Words

We discussed the persuasive elements of language extensively in Chapter 7 and to some extent in Chapter 6 as well. However, it's useful to look at some examples that are specifically used by marketers and advertisers. **Fuzzy words** are weasel words that create an appealing claim or impression without specifically defining a concrete meaning for the words or phrases used. An example would be the words "Made in America" on a product label. The implication of the label is that the consumer is supporting American workers and manufacturers, but what may really be true is "some of this product is made in America." An ad may proclaim, "Four out of five doctors recommend the main ingredient in our product." It sounds as if four out of five doctors recommend the product, but on careful inspection, the ad is citing only the main ingredient as the recommended item, and we aren't told how many doctors were surveyed; this technique is often used when the main ingredient is a common one, such as aspirin. Fuzzy product claims are made with no context or point of comparison, such as "Snappy has 25 percent more peanuts per jar" or "There's nothing like the feel of Silky tissues." Slogans are used to create a warm connection with customers with such vague declarations as "You can trust us to take care of your car," "You've got a friend in the diamond business," or "We'll leave the light on for you." Advertisers also use fuzzy words like "crisp" or "full-bodied" or phrases such as "you're worth it" to make their products seem appealing while promising nothing.

> Consider, for example, the wording in restaurant menus. Research by Brian Wansink, director of the Food and Brand Lab at Cornell University and the author of *Mindless Eating: Why We Eat More Than We Think*, suggests that the average person makes more than 200 decisions about food every day, many of them unconsciously, including the choices made from reading menus.
>
> Dr. Wansink has discovered that descriptive menu labels increase sales by as much as 27 percent. He has divided descriptions into four categories: geographic labels like "Southwestern Tex-Mex salad," nostalgia labels like "ye old potato bread," sensory labels like "buttery plump pasta" and brand names. Finding that brand names help sales, chains are increasingly using what is known as co-branding on their menus, like the Jack Daniel's sauce at

fuzzy words Weasel words that create an appealing claim or impression without specifically defining a concrete meaning for the words or phrases used.

T.G.I. Friday's and Minute Maid orange juice on the Huddle House menu, Dr. Wansink said.

Dr. Wansink said that vivid adjectives may not only sway a customer's choice but may also leave them more satisfied at the end of the meal than if they had eaten the same item without the descriptive labeling.

Indeed, restaurants like Huddle House and Applebee's are adding language that suggests a rush of intense satisfaction. At Applebee's, dishes are described as "handcrafted," "triple-basted," "slow-cooked," "grilled" and "slammed with flavor."[34]

Logical Fallacies

Advertisers are great at presenting arguments that are so engaging and well designed that consumers may forget to consider that their claims are illogical or unsupported. For example, one technique frequently used is to show "before-and-after" images of an individual; a frowning woman with no makeup is shown next to her smiling self with professional makeup, and the difference in her look is attributed to a new skin treatment. The "PC versus Mac" campaign used a similar formula: PC is shown as older, out of shape, and rumpled in his corporate clothing, while Mac is young, cool, and casually dressed. The idea is that consumers will make the same connections and overlook the false dilemma or either/or fallacy with which the computers are being contrasted. The false dilemma fallacy is also committed when food companies claim to have authentic products like "the real salsa" versus their competitors whose salsa is cast as illegitimate.

The ad populum fallacy occurs when wireless phone companies use large crowds to create the impression that their networks have the most popular followings and that, by contrast, other networks are weak and ineffectual.

We've seen that *romancing a product*—associating the product with wonderful scenes of fun and excitement that seem to accompany people who buy the product— is really a faulty analogy. The advertisers don't directly state that owning their car or using their shampoo will dramatically improve your life, but their commercials create an association of enjoyment and fulfillment that is connected to buying the product.

Advertisers also may commit the fallacy of "begging the question"; for example, a disembodied voice may ask, "Why are so many people switching to our wireless service?" without giving any statistics to support their claim that a significant number of people actually are switching.

Stylized Images and Sounds

When millions of dollars are spent on commercials and print ads (for example, $2.5 to $2.8 million for a 30-second Super Bowl ad), companies want slick and polished images showcasing their products. Under hot lights, the ice cubes in a cool drink would melt, so perfectly shaped plastic cubes are used. Professional "dressers" are hired to ensure that food looks great; a dresser may go through dozens of hamburger buns to choose the perfect one to complement a hamburger for an ad. Filtered lighting is used to create atmosphere, and items are often made to seem bigger than they actually are. In addition, human freckles, blemishes, and weight can all be removed

[34] Sarah Kershaw, "Using Menu Psychology to Entice Diners," http://www.nytimes.com/2009/12/23/dining/23menus.html, December 22, 2009.

and adjusted with image-editing programs. Someone promoting a new cholesterol medication may be shown dancing happily through a field to soft, inspiring music; it is hoped that the required warnings of side effects, including possible fatalities, will be ignored as viewers are entranced by the engaging sights and sounds of the commercial.

Graphic designers carefully consider the look and placement of all visual items for sale. Consider the following excerpt:

> Menu design draws some of its inspiration from newspaper layout, which puts the most important articles at the top right of the front page, where the eyes tend to be drawn. Some restaurants will place their most profitable items, or their specials, in that spot. Or they place a dotted outline or a box around the item, put more white space around it to make the dish stand out or, in what menu researchers say is one of the most effective tools, add a photograph of the item or an icon like a chili pepper.
>
> (Photos of foie gras on the menus of white-tablecloth restaurants would be surprising, however. Menu consultants say those establishments should never use pictures.)
>
> Unless a restaurant wants to frighten its customers, the price should always be at the very end of a menu description and should not be in any way highlighted.
>
> A study published in the spring by Dr. Kimes and other researchers at Cornell found that when the prices were given with dollar signs, customers—the research subjects dined at St. Andrew's Cafe at the Culinary Institute of America in Hyde Park, N.Y.—spent less than when no dollar signs appeared. The study, published in the Cornell Hospitality Report, also found that customers spent significantly more when the price was listed in numerals without dollar signs, as in "14.00" or "14," than when it included the word "dollar," as in "Fourteen dollars." Apparently even the word "dollar" can trigger what is known as "the pain of paying."
>
> Mr. Rapp, of Palm Springs, Calif., also says that if a restaurant wants to use prices that include cents, like $9.99 or $9.95 (without the dollar sign, of course), he strongly recommends .95, which he said "is a friendlier price," whereas .99 is "cornier." On the other hand, 10, or "10 dollars," has attitude, which is what restaurants using those price formats are selling.
>
> A dash or a period after the number appears to be more of an aesthetic choice than a psychological tool, according to one of the authors of the menu pricing study, Sybil S. Yang, a doctoral student at Cornell. Numbers followed by neither a dash nor a period are most common.
>
> Restaurant owner Mr. Meyer said that in his view, adding zeros to the price, as in 14.00, is not a good idea because "there's no reason to have pennies if you're not using pennies, and it takes the price from being two digits into four digits, even if the two last digits are zeros. It's irrelevant, and the number could feel more important, which is not a menu writer's goal."
>
> (Some prices at his restaurants do end in .50, and at Mr. Meyer's Shake Shack burger joints, his foray into retro-casual dining, some end with .25 or .75—but the prices are always rounded to the quarter. The Shake Shacks are the only of Mr. Meyer's restaurants with menu prices preceded by dollar signs.)
>
> Some restaurants use what researchers call decoys. For example, they may place a really expensive item at the top of the menu, so that other dishes look more reasonably priced; research shows that diners tend to order neither the

most nor least expensive items, drifting toward the middle. Or restaurants might play up a profitable dish by using more appetizing adjectives and placing it next to a less profitable dish with less description so the contrast entices the diner to order the profitable dish.[35]

In addition to stylized images, television and radio advertisers also get and keep our attention with loud music or words as well as frequent camera cuts. You may have noticed that you can do homework during a television program, except when the commercials come on; they seem to grab your attention. This process happens to children too. The next time you are watching television with a young child, notice how alert the child becomes during almost any commercial. We respond to loud, fast-paced programming with frequent image changes. Even public television programs such as *Sesame Street* use this technique of 15- to 30-second spots to keep attention levels high. Commercials shown on programs airing after midnight are particularly loud; people who fall asleep in front of a television set may be startled awake by the blaring of a commercial message (invariably advising late-night viewers to improve their lives by using their product or service). No advertiser wants to play to a sleeping audience.

Celebrity Associations and Endorsements

Advertisers have always used popular celebrities—athletes, singers, and other famous figures—to entice target audiences. Sometimes, the celebrity has some credibility, such as a former Olympic athlete who uses a pain reliever to help soothe an injured knee or an actress who lets the public track her progress on a particular weight loss program. In other cases, celebrities are used to push products because it is assumed that people will buy the products in order to feel associated with the celebrity.

It's hard for consumers to avoid being targeted. During the rebellious 1960s, students shook off the oppression of expensive clothing and started wearing jeans as a way of distancing themselves from the values of corporate America. In response, designer jeans were created, marketed, modeled by celebrities, and sold for solid profits. When subsequent generations started ripping their jeans, ripped jeans were likewise marketed, and people may pay hundreds of dollars for them. There has been a recent movement toward supporting Fair Trade and shunning corporations that exploit international workers. Undaunted, corporations have responded by marketing their products to a new target audience called *conscience consumers*. British writer Jane Mortinson gives an example of this phenomenon in an article about the collaboration of rock star Bono and *American Express*:

> When Bono walked into the head office of *American Express* 18 months ago, the company practically laid out the red carpet. The campaigning rock star had something that one of the world's biggest financial services groups was very much looking for: a way of reaching the growing band of so-called "conscience consumers."
>
> Amex launched its RED card, part of an initiative in which consumer companies are backing Bono's Global Fund, which helps women and children affected by HIV and Aids in Africa. Amex's contribution is to donate 1%

[35] Sarah Kershaw, "Using Menu Psychology to Entice Diners," http://www.nytimes.com/2009/12/23/dining/23menus.html, December 22, 2009.

of all spending on the card to the charity. The woman charged with making sure the launch of the card in Britain is a success—with the plan then to roll it out globally—is Laurel Powers-Freeling, the American head of Amex's UK consumer card business.

Powers-Freeling says the company, more often associated with power lunches than global poverty, had an immediate meeting of minds with the singer. "It was an interesting moment for us because one of the things we at American Express have been observing for a while is this trend towards what we now call the conscience consumer. The people saying, 'I have to spend money anyway, so if there's a way of using the power of my purse for good, great, but I don't want to give up anything to do so.'"

More exciting for Amex perhaps was the chance to reach a whole new market. Since joining the company just over a year ago from Marks & Spencer, Powers-Freeling has sought to make Amex more of an "everyday" card. Product red—as the initiative likes to be known—offers something potentially far more valuable than a large target market: the chance to become worthy by association. "What I want is obviously more Amex cards and for more people to feel it is part of their lives, that they have an affinity with it," Powers-Freeling says in her no-nonsense voice, which still bears the twang of her midwestern upbringing after 20 years in Britain.

The principle of paying more—or at least doing without Air Miles or loyalty bonuses—to feel good about yourself is not new. Amex estimates there are already 1.5 million "conscience consumers" in the UK, people who buy products associated with a social or ethical benefit, be it Fair Trade coffee or organic bananas. This is expected to swell to 3.9 million within three years.[36]

Product Placement

product placement
The practice of integrating or embedding products in films, television programs, and other media in order to reach consumers.

Technological advances have made it possible for consumers to avoid television advertising by recording shows before watching them; people who are able to record their programs can fast forward through commercials, and moviegoers can avoid advertising by getting snacks or talking with their friends during previews. Advertisers have fought back with **product placement**, embedding their products into the actual story lines or sets of programs and films. A common image from *American Idol* was the sight of each of the judges drinking from a very large Coke glass. Sitcoms and dramas also include product placements from cereals to electronics.

Some analysts trace the rise of embedded products to the film *E.T.* and the marked increase in sales for Hershey's Reese's Pieces candy that followed the new candy's placement in the film. *E.T.* is one of the most popular films of all time, grossing $800 million so far. Advertisers are asked to pay big money for the kind of exposure movies and television programs can provide. In his column *Desperate Advertisers*, Buzz McClain discusses the increasing trend of advertisers to place their products in all forms of media:

> *Advertising Age* magazine says it costs some $26 million to "integrate" a product on a popular television series today. For companies that want a shot on NBC's *The Apprentice*, a per-episode exposure can cost up to $2 million.

---

[36] Jane Martinson, "The Amex Chief Providing Backing for Bono," *The Guardian*, business.guardian.co.uk (accessed March 17, 2006).

One Fort Worth national furniture retailer recently approached a program about displaying its wares and was dismayed to discover it would cost $5 million for the privilege. He turned down the opportunity.

But not everyone does. According to *Promo* magazine, advertisers spent $7.6 billion on TiVo-proof (you can't zip through it) product placements and brand integration—in television, feature films, music videos and video games.[37]

Placing their products in films, television programs, and other media may help advertisers, but it can negatively affect the artistic vision of the writers and directors. When huge amounts of money are being spent on product placements, the marketers want to make sure that their merchandise is quite obvious to the audience, and that can be annoying, as writer Jon Folland noted on the website nativ.tv:

> When watching *Casino Royale,* the new James Bond movie, I was driven to distraction by the brazen overuse of such advertising.
>
> Having paid enough money for tickets and watched 15 minutes of adverts, I was ready to watch the film. But where did the adverts end and the film begin? The film was a relentless parade of products embedded in appropriately naff scenarios. This wasn't subliminal, this was in-your-face advertising. How many times do characters in the film need to look closely into their mobile phones before you lose the immersive experience of a really good film and start getting angry at the blatant use of product placement?[38]

Music videos are also increasingly relying on product placement to fund production and create profit. Joseph Plambeck of the *New York Times* discussed this growing trend:

> Whether it's for a Virgin Mobile phone or Miracle Whip dressing, Lady Gaga will do the pitch. In the video for her single "Telephone," she flashes those and a handful of other brands—providing one of the splashiest examples yet of product placement in music videos.
>
> And though she has taken these placements to the extreme—making them obvious is part of the gimmick—Lady Gaga isn't alone among musicians when it comes to incorporating brands into videos.
>
> At least two related trends have contributed to the growing popularity of placements: the move of videos from television to the Internet and the attempt by record labels to make videos a revenue source and not just a marketing tool for selling CDs.
>
> According to a report released last week by PQ Media, a research firm, the money spent on product placement in recorded music grew 8 percent in 2009 compared with the year before, while overall paid product placement declined 2.8 percent, to $3.6 billion.
>
> The money is often used to offset the video's cost, which is usually shared by the artist and label.
>
> Patrick Quinn, chief executive of PQ Media, said that revenue from product placement in music videos totaled $15 million to $20 million last year, more than double the amount in 2000, and he expected that to grow again this year.

[37] Buzz McClain, "Desperate Advertisers," *Dallas-Fort Worth Star Telegram*, October 3, 2005.

[38] Jon Folland, "What Can I Remember About Casino Royale? Sony, Omega, Aston Martin . . . The plot? Not sure." www.nativ/tv (accessed November 20, 2006).

"That real estate—getting into the content itself—has become that much more valuable," Mr. Quinn said.

"There's an opportunity there to make money and charge for that real estate."

For years, the opportunities for product placement—advertisers like to call it "integration"—in music videos were limited. MTV was the dominant outlet for videos, and its policy prohibited blatant plugs in videos, so the network would often blur brand labels or ask for a new version without the placement.

But the airtime MTV devotes to music videos has decreased sharply, and the Web emerged as a preferred destination for fans, opening the door for labels and advertisers.[39]

In addition to embedding products in various forms of media, marketers also like to place their products in attractive retail settings. Supermarkets charge companies more for placing products at eye level or at the checkout stand where they are more likely to be noticed and bought. Many studies have been done to show how consumers move through stores and which aisles are more likely to bring product sales. Wal-Mart stores have a "power aisle"; research has shown that customers will spend more time looking at items on this aisle, particularly if they had seen ads for the products on display there. Phil Vischer, creator of the popular *VeggieTales* series, writes about the marketing of his videos:

The average Wal-Mart shopper would look at the average product situated along a Wal-Mart store's prime circulation path—the fabled "power aisle"—for just over two seconds. In the case of a video, if they hadn't already heard something good about it, forget it. They wouldn't even pick up the package. And that's only if you were lucky enough to get your product positioned along the power aisle in the first place. Get stuck "spine-out" in the in-line section, and the average shopper wouldn't see your video at all. You might as well be in the dumpster out back.[40]

The Gestalt Principle

While striving to use a variety of attention-getting devices, advertisers and political media coordinators are also keenly interested in holding attention, even for just a few seconds more than their competitors. To hold attention, they have to "grab" the audience in some way, and many utilize the principles of Gestalt theory.

A principle of Gestalt psychology states "the whole is greater than the sum of the parts." Our minds strive toward congruence and completion of information. If a message strikes us as incomplete, we will fill in the missing details ourselves. Consider the following passage that has circulated widely on the Internet:

Aoccdrnig to rsceareh at Cmabrigde Uinervtisy, it deosn't mttaer in what order the ltteers in a word are; the only iprmoetnt thing is that the frist and lsat ltteer be in the rghit pclae. The rset can be a total mses and you can still raed it wouthit a porbelm. This is bcuseae the human mind deos not raed ervey lteter by istlef, but the word as a wlohe.

[39] Joseph Plambeck, "Product Placement Grows in Music Videos," http://www.nytimes.com/2010/07/06/business/media/06adco.html, July 5, 2010.

[40] Phil Vischer, *Me, Myself, & Bob* (Nashville, TN: Thomas Nelson Publishers, 2006), pp. 143–144.

If you were able to understand the passage, it is because you took each word as a whole and filled in the incorrect parts, as Gestalt theory has postulated.

The **Gestalt principle** also takes effect when we perceive movement on a theater screen even though the projector is in reality showing only a quick series of still images. Cartoonists rely on the Gestalt principle when they use the technique of cell animation; the cartoonist draws a series of frames in which the character moves slightly from frame to frame. The viewer supplies the missing information and perceives realistic movement. Providing missing information is central to the process of human perception, whether this information is visual or auditory. Consider the following Gestalt techniques that are commonly used but seldom questioned by consumers of the message.

Gestalt principle
A principle that states that our minds strive toward congruence and completion of information. If a message strikes us as incomplete, we will fill in the missing details ourselves.

1. Questions or Slogans That the Consumer Is Taught to Answer. Early in advertising history, Winston cigarettes used a simple jingle: "Winston tastes good like a cigarette should. Winston tastes good like a (clap, clap) cigarette should." For a long time, television and radio listeners heard this jingle sung in a joyful manner.

Then one day, the jingle proceeded as follows: "Winston tastes good like a cigarette should. Winston tastes good like a (clap, clap)." Listeners who had heard the jingle before could hardly help completing the song in their minds, thus joining in with the advertisers to laud the praises of this cigarette. They had been trained over time to know the ending of the commercial, and when the standard ending was left out, they filled it in.

We are generally taught as children that it is rude not to answer a question asked of us, and this carries over into adulthood. Assertiveness trainers put considerable focus on teaching clients that they don't need to answer every question they are asked.

Advertisers capitalize on our early training in politeness by asking us questions, knowing we probably will instinctively formulate answers in our minds. The questions "beg" to be answered in the "correct" way; hence the term "begging the question" discussed in Chapter 6. Here are some examples:

Aren't you hungry for King Burgers now?

Why spend the money on a gym when you can do our great workouts at home?

Doesn't your child deserve a gift of love?

2. Images That Don't Make Sense. Again, our minds try to make sense out of things that are together but don't seem to go together. Leon Festinger's theory of cognitive dissonance, discussed further in Chapter 9, states that the need for "congruence" (consonance, harmony) is not only a human need but also a drive, just as powerful as our drive for food and water. We are motivated by this drive, and so we take action when things don't make sense. We try to make sense out of them.

For example, you may be disturbed by a couple who don't seem suited for each other; their presence together may cause you to try to figure out what they see in each other. Even children love challenges called "What is wrong with this picture?"

Unexpected or strange images and sounds—and even the word "new"—attract our attention.

Advertisers capitalize on our fascination with the incongruent by sometimes putting things together that don't seem to go together. They know that if we are puzzled, we will give more attention to or spend more time on the ad, even if we aren't aware of doing so. They also know that if we become familiar with a product's brand name, because we've spent more time on or given more attention to its claims, then we are more likely to buy the product.

One cigarette advertiser created a series of print ads showing two scenes of people interacting; there was no clear indication of what was going on between these people or why they were together. Often, the people were shown laughing, but the readers were not told what they were laughing about.

Incongruous scenes may be combined with sexual insinuations, making them doubly fascinating to viewers. Some researchers and graphic designers claim that certain images are mostly likely to attract and maintain the attention of viewers; these images include children, dogs, cars, death, guns, war, and sex. Michael Hoff, one of the leading producers of nonfiction television programs (including *Real Ghostbusters*), believes that the combination of subliminal elements sells his "don't touch that dial" programming: "Sex, death, and weirdness are the critical elements of any good television show," Hoff explains with a sly smile. "If you've got all three, man, you've got a hit."[41]

Use of Social Media to Build Customer Loyalty

Individuals use various forms of social media to form connections in their personal worlds and daily lives. Advertisers and marketers have learned to tap the enormously popular and growing networks of social media, including Facebook, Twitter, Foursquare, Yelp, and YouTube, and to use crowdsourcing. Retailers and campaign managers are constantly exploring new ways to use these vast networks to sell their products or run their campaigns.

Facebook

In realizing the power of virtual venues, *Time* magazine named the founder of Facebook, Mark Zuckerberg, Person of the Year for 2010.

In February 2004, when Zuckerberg was a 19-year-old sophomore at Harvard, he started a Web service from his dorm. It was called Thefacebook.com, and it was billed as "an online directory that connects people through social networks at colleges." This year, Facebook—now minus the *the*—added its 550 millionth member. One out of every dozen people on the planet has a Facebook account. They speak 75 languages and collectively lavish more than 700 billion minutes on Facebook every month. Last month the site accounted for 1 out of 4 American page views. Its membership is currently growing at a rate of about 700,000 people a day.

What just happened? In less than seven years, Zuckerberg wired together a twelfth of humanity into a single network, thereby creating a social entity almost twice as large as the U.S. If Facebook were a country it would be the third largest, behind only China and India. It started out as a lark, a diversion, but it has turned into something real, something that has changed the way human beings relate to one another on a species-wide scale. We are now running our social lives through a for-profit network that, on paper at least, has made Zuckerberg a billionaire six times over.

[41] Chuck Barney, "Michael Hoff's 'Oooh-Whee' TV," Knight-Ridder/Tribune News Service.

Facebook has merged with the social fabric of American life, and not just American but human life: nearly half of all Americans have a Facebook account, but 70% of Facebook users live outside the U.S. It's a permanent fact of our global social reality. We have entered the Facebook age, and Mark Zuckerberg is the man who brought us here.[42]

Although Facebook was started as a way to connect friends, it has become one of the most important tools to market products and services. Numerous Web sites and books suggest ways to use Facebook applications to reach the millions of international users and generate more revenue for businesses. They teach users to create links or groups that will be liked well enough to be posted on other social networking sites, thus bringing in additional free traffic; when Facebook users become fans of a business or a politician or entertainers, they advertise the product or person to others.

Businesses are constantly thinking of creative new ways to use Facebook to promote their products and services. One effective and ever-growing technique is the use of contests and polls:

> Holding contests encourages fans to interact directly with you. Domino's 'Show Us Your Pizza' is a contest where people can send pictures of Domino's pizzas they've ordered. The best picture will be chosen by Domino's and the photographer gets a prize of $500 and a chance to get his picture featured in an ad. This has received a lot of attention from Facebook users.[43]

Socialmaximizer.com suggests that fan pages and Facebook groups are important tools for promoting people, products, and services:

> Facebook Pages, known as Fan Pages, are designed for businesses, brands, companies, products and celebrities. It enables public figures, organizations, and other entities to create an authentic and public presence on Facebook. You can encourage users to become fans of your page and share information with them by uploading pictures, videos, and status updates, hosting discussions and displaying wall posts. Unlike Facebook Profiles, Pages are visible to everyone on the Internet and are generally better for long-term relationships with your fans, readers or customers.
>
> Facebook Groups allow people to come together around a common cause or activity to express their views. One of the best features of groups is the ability to send messages directly to members' Facebook inboxes. It's a great way to form a community and help your brand image. Nowadays, it's almost a necessity for movies to establish their presence on Facebook during their post-release period as Facebook users look for movies here. The good thing here is that you can send bulk invites to your friends, while it is manually done on Pages. Groups are generally better for hosting quick active discussions and attracting attention from Facebook users.[44]

[42] Lev Grossman, "Person of the Year, Mark Zuckerberg," http://www.time.com/time/specials/packages/article/0,28804,2036683_2037183_2037185,00.html, December 15, 2010.

[43] "14 Powerful Tips for Marketing on Facebook," http://blog.socialmaximizer.com/14-tips-for-marketing-on-facebook.

[44] Ibid.

As one reporter concludes, "If a marketer has an active (Facebook) community, all the free benefits of this, namely free traffic and free promotion opportunities, convert to sales very easily."[45]

Twitter

Twitter, a popular instant text-messaging system, helps companies to promote their products and services, connect directly with their target audiences, and find out what potential or current customers want and need from their businesses. Companies can advertise specials, innovations, and events, and they can also follow and keep up with trends set by their competition on Twitter. They can use the platform to communicate information about their industry, products, and new merchandise and hope that tweeters will spread the word for them. Websites like twitter4U.com train retailers to understand and make the best use of the platform.

Retailers pay attention to the millions of Twitter users. For example, Best Buy had a policy of charging a 15% restocking fee for returned electronics, but when twitter users complained broadly about the policy, it was discontinued.

Companies also use twitter to advertise charity events in order to gain broader recognition in their communities, as exemplified by the following from the company under30CEO.com:

The holidays have always been about giving back and having a great time with those close to you. This year, Under30CEO and the nationwide toy drive, The 2010 Holiday Tweet Drive, are partnering to put together the New York City Tweet Drive, an event that allows us to give back for the holiday season while enjoying a great party with each other!

On December 21st, we will be having a holiday party at Chelsea Manor in Manhattan where our guests can enjoy drink specials, raffles, and free food courtesy of Popchips and Cupcake Stop! Some of our raffles include Yankees and Knicks Tickets, Books by Social Media Guru Deirdre Breakenridge, and Auntie Anne's gift cards.

All you need to do to attend is bring one unwrapped, NEW toy or article of clothing. Our beneficiary partner is The New York Yankees' Curtis Granderson's Grand Kids Foundation, and we are very excited to give back to a great foundation that has done so much for New York's children and their education.

Our event and The 2010 Holiday Tweet Drive combines Social Media with charity throughout the country this holiday season. There are events in over 25 cities that are being planned and communicated mainly through Twitter. These events really infuse the holiday season with social media. Call it Holidays 2.0.

With that all said, we hope you can join us to Tweet, give back, and have a great time for the holidays! Please invite your friends and RSVP on our event page. Hope to see you on the 21st![46]

[45] Tsveti Georgieva, "How to Use Facebook for Business Drive Traffic, Promote Products, Sell Products on Facebook," http://www.suite101.com/content/how-to-use-facebook-for-business-a215326, March 19, 2010.
[46] "New York City Tweet Drive," http://under30ceo.com/new-york-city-tweet-drive-december-21st-2010/.

Foursquare

Nick Bilton of the *New York Times* explains the benefits of Foursquare for advertisers and marketers:

Foursquare is not like Facebook, Twitter, or any other social network. People don't log onto their computers to check what their friends are doing. On Foursquare, friends "check in" to different locations like the movie theater or a favorite bar that is then broadcast to all of their Foursquare friends. It is all done on mobile phone apps, iPhone push notifications, and mobile web interfaces. Thus, the opportunities presented by Foursquare are different.

Brick-and-mortar stores with a specific location can immediately advertise to users within their proximity—restaurants are already using Foursquare-specific discounts and location-based advertising to pull in new customers . . . .

Foursquare's new statistics page will share information about users with business owners. The location based social network plans to distribute a free analytics tool and dashboard . . . that will give business owners access to a range of information and statistics about visitors to their establishments.

Tristan Walker, director of business development at Foursquare, said that the latest features were intended to help local merchants run their stores by giving them more information about their customers.

"We're trying to give businesses more retention with current customers and the ability to add new customers with specials," said Mr. Walker.

Foursquare is a service that allows users to share their location with a group of friends by "checking in" to a restaurant, business or other venue when they arrive. The company encourages the businesses to recognize Foursquare users in some fashion, such as a bar awarding free drinks to their most frequent customers.

With the new tool, businesses will be able to see a range of real-time data about Foursquare usage, including who has "checked in" to the place via Foursquare, when they arrived, the male-to-female customer ratio and which times of day are more active for certain customers. Business owners will also be able to offer instant promotions to try to engage new customers and keep current ones.

"If a restaurant can see one of its loyal customers has dropped off the map and is no longer checking in, the owner could offer them incentives to come back," said Mr. Walker.

There will also be a Staff page available to each business that will allow employees to interact directly with customers using social networks.

Foursquare recently partnered with 30 small businesses to test the tool, and it plans to gradually roll it out to another 900 businesses in the coming weeks.

AJ Bombers, a burger bar in Milwaukee, tested the new statistics tool and plans to use it to choose specials and promote new menu items, said Joe Sorge, co-owner of the restaurant.

"If I'm in another location, I can actually sit and look at that screen and see who checked in last, and I can reach out via Twitter and say 'Welcome.

Have you been here before? What kind of food do you like?'" said Mr. Sorge. "It makes the experience more enjoyable for the customer."

Shelley Bernstein, chief of technology at the Brooklyn Museum, sees promise in the Staff pages. "Basically, the new statistics tools give us the ability to promote a personal face for our staff so we're not just seen as an institution," she said. "We're wrapping all of this into our Web site through Foursquare's A.P.I.'s, and we allow people to interact with staff and have the opportunity to engage with them in new ways."

Another test customer, P.C.C. Natural Markets, a Seattle-based organic foods company, saw a large number of new Foursquare users coming to its stores over the weekend and used the analytics tool to figure out where they were coming from.

"By using the Foursquare dashboard, we figured out that they were coming for a new organic doughnut that had been advertised on TV," said Ricardo Rabago, social media specialist for the company.

Mr. Rabago hopes to use the new tool to figure out when people are coming for lunch and offer coupons and specials to entice them to return.

Dennis Crowley, Foursquare's chief executive, said this new feature is useful for the consumer and the merchant, and the tool will continue to evolve over the coming months "to incorporate more analytics and insight." Mr. Crowley also said there will be an opt-in, opt-out setting in the privacy panel that will give Foursquare users the ability to keep their information private.[47]

To compete with the success of Foursquare, Facebook created a Facebook Places service. Some analysts suspect that Facebook will be able to significantly diminish the success of Foursquare, as well as the similar services offered by Gowalla and MyTown, because it is easier for users to operate from one platform rather than transferring from one to another. Whether Facebook will monopolize new additions to the social media market remains to be seen.

YouTube

YouTube, an online broadcasting company, reaches millions of people and is now being used to create customers for businesses, enhance political campaigns, start careers, and get attention. Socialmaximizer.com explains how it works as a marketing tool:

When you see an interesting video on YouTube, you tend to post the link on Twitter, Facebook, or share it by e-mailing it to friends. They pass it on to their friends and the effect just multiplies and your message spreads rapidly, resulting in massive exposure. This approach, also known as viral marketing, doesn't even have to be expensive. The reason we connect with these campaigns is because we understand the product better and the brand has a face. We identify the brand, making the whole experience personal.

The first campaign cost Blendtec, a company that produces blenders and mixers, less than $50. The team filmed a video featuring Blendtec's co-founder Tom Dickson who said, "Will it blend? That is the question." He made a smoothie of salsa, tortilla chips, Buffalo wings and Budweiser in the blender. Five days later, Blendtec's marketing director excitedly told him that they hit 6 million views on YouTube. This was later followed by videos of blending golf balls, a crowbar, a video camera and iPod. My favorite is their latest, the iPad. Their online videos are still a rage and Blendtec's online sales have grown by 500%.[48]

Crowdsourcing

Crowdsourcing uses the power of social communities, readers, and viewers to market programs and products. Company decisions are driven by ideas and "votes" of product users or program viewers. For example, as we discussed earlier, Gap admitted that it should have asked fans to comment on the company's new logo or to help design a new one, instead of using their own graphic design experts to choose one. Marketers are increasingly letting fans help or fully make decisions, including PepsiCo Inc.'s Doritos brand, which allowed fans to create and vote on Super Bowl commercials.[49]

Reality television programs such as *Dancing with the Stars* and *American Idol* allow the crowd of fans to vote on the contestants that they want to see continue. Critics may complain that, in their professional opinions, the singers and dancers chosen by the crowd are not the best ones, but producers and advertisers want to please their audiences; honoring their votes is important.

Creative uses of online voting include the partnership between *MySpace* and *Glee*. When *MySpace* became an audition site for *Glee*, both the site and the show got more free publicity.

Campaigns are also affected by the power of the Internet to tap into large crowds. For example, in January of 2008, Barack Obama brought in $28 million online, with 90 percent of those transactions coming from people who donated $100 or less, and 40 percent from donors who gave $25 or less. One of the donors expressed his decision about making a number of small contributions: "The campaign has been so incredibly grass-roots, it does sort of feel like you are making a difference."[50]

Yelp

Another way for businesses to tap into crowds of consumers is through the monitoring and enhancing of online customer review sites. For example, Yelp is a platform that combines social networking, user reviews, and a local search engine for businesses, including restaurants, stores, spas, and clubs. Positive reviews on Yelp help businesses attract new customers. Consumers can get a yelp application on their mobile phones and see their friends' activities on the site. Other sites that offer customer reviews include Travelocity, Orbitz, Hotels.com,

---

[48] "7 Awesomely Amazing Examples of Success through YouTube!" http://blog.socialmaximizer.com/youtube-business-use-cases/, June 3, 2010.

[49] Emily Fredrix, "Gap Gets Rid of New Logo," http://www.huffingtonpost.com/2010/10/12/gap-gets-rid-of-new-logo_n_759131.html.

[50] Michael Luo, "Small Online Contributions Add Up to Huge Fundraising Edge for Obama," February 20, 2008, nytimes.com.

and Zagat. When customers can post their reviews of a hotel or restaurant, they have great power to encourage sales and also to influence the businesses to make needed changes. Hotels, restaurants, and retail stores use the feedback from the reviews on these sites to improve their visibility and success.

The power of Yelp and other consumer review sites is changing business policies and practices, as noted by Meredith Davis Williams who writes for girlsintech.net:

With over *12 million* user reviews and approximately *33 million* views per month, the power of Yelp's word of mouth loud speaker is having a significant impact on local restaurants. Yelp has given millions of users the power to review restaurants' chefs, menu items, wine lists, drink specialties, service, and ambiance and publish to an audience of millions of viewers—a power that was once reserved only for professional food and wine writers working for traditional publications.

As a result, Yelp is changing the way restaurateurs and chefs interact with their customers, as well as the way they must handle both their formal and informal public relations and marketing efforts.

On the positive side, Yelp is making the world of restaurant reviews a more democratic process rather than an elitist one. This process allows local restaurants which might not have received attention from traditional print or online food writers to receive a new type of media attention that can be a powerful force in generating new customers. In addition, Yelp allows restaurateurs, chefs, and front-of-the-house managers to receive real-time customer feedback that they can use to quickly evaluate and adjust everything from their menu choices to hiring choices.

On the negative side, for many chefs and restaurateurs who have amassed years of training in the culinary arts and whose restaurants are the result of considerable blood, sweat, and tears, Yelp's democratic force in the world of reviews means that reviewers with no understanding of or training in the restaurant industry or the culinary arts can slam a chef for one off night or because they don't understand what a particular dish is supposed to taste like.

Also problematic is the fact that the democratic masses of reviewers are not part of the traditional institution of journalism, which carries with it principles of responsible reporting (in theory at least . . .). An average Yelp reviewer is not likely to research the chef, his or her past experience, or the background of a particular menu's cuisine influences before writing a good or bad review as would a traditional food critic.

The power of Yelp, however, is a reality that restaurants and other local businesses must now take into account in their business practices. As Yelp's (manager of business outreach) Luther Lowe emphasized, businesses have an important voice on Yelp. Yelp provides businesses with the ability to take ownership of their listings by unlocking them on the site, allowing businesses to put information out there for the Yelp audience. Yelp also provides businesses with the ability to respond to reviews both publicly and privately, giving them an equal voice in the conversation and a means to reach out to customers who had negative experiences.

Lowe also emphasized Yelp's efforts to maintain the integrity of the site's reviews. As he explained in a follow-up conversation, Yelp employs a filtering technology to help ensure (to the best of its ability) that only trustworthy reviews end up on businesses' pages.

While it can be overwhelming for chefs, restaurateurs, and other business owners to have an endless parade of critics to contend with, social media outlets such as Yelp are here to stay and will continue to play an important role in influencing consumer decision-making. Only restaurants and other businesses that take a proactive approach to social media, incorporating this new force into their marketing plans, will be able to take advantage of its benefits.[51]

Stop and Think

Do you check reviews before going to a restaurant, hotel, or store? Have you bought a product or service based on a friend's recommendation on Facebook or Twitter?

Use of Opinion Leaders to Influence the Market

As we discussed in Chapter 5, there is a two-step flow to marketing products and information. Advertisers target their well-informed, active users, and these users influence everyone else. This principle is especially true of social media where some users are early adopters and trendsetters with large and loyal followings on their Facebook, Twitter, Foursquare, and other accounts. Ben Straley, CEO of Meteor Solutions, encourages marketers to focus their social sharing to broaden the reach and the profits of a company. He uses the term *brand ambassador* to explain the power of opinion leaders.

> As a marketer, you've undoubtedly heard about the 1% rule—that just 1% of your brand's social media followers are responsible for the majority of sharing. They share your social media campaigns with their larger social network, passing on links to your contests, promotions, deals, and other marketing campaigns. These key influencers are more than just fans—they're *brand ambassadors.*
>
> At my company, we've seen that brands that track and quantify word-of-mouth impact have found that these key influencers can drive 20, 30, or even 70% of all visits to their campaign pages, beating out display and search advertising as the most efficient driver of traffic to their sites. That's pretty incredible, considering social campaigns require no media buys and cost next to nothing to implement, whereas banners and search ads are a huge expense. These "super influencers" drive an even higher share of conversion—on average influencing 30% or more of all conversions on marketers' sites just by recommending a brand's products, content, or promotions to their online communities.
>
> When you see data like these as regularly as we do, you realize pretty quickly that super influencers are worth engaging. If you can reach out to

[51] Meredith Davis Williams, "A Case Study in the Power of Social Media: The Restaurant Biz Responds to Yelpers," girlsintech.net, August 18, 2010.

this 1% directly by offering them special promotions, thanking them for their influence, and rewarding them for their loyalty, they will be motivated to share early and share often.

Identifying your key influencers is fairly straightforward. There are a wealth of social media measurement tools that enable marketers to find the people who are talking most about their brand, see what type of content they're sharing and with whom, and how they are sharing it (e-mail, Twitter, Facebook, their own blogs, etc.). Once you find these influencers, the trick is activating them to share even more.[52]

Straley advises marketers to stay connected with the influencers, offering them incentives, special deals, and inside information; he suggests commenting on their blogs and thanking them for their loyalty. Straley also suggests ways to discover and target the *super influencers*—those with a large and loyal following who trust their insights, asserting that developing one-on-one relationships with these individuals can significantly grow a company or product grow.

Companies are creating new ways to reward and retain their loyal opinion leaders, using social networks like Foursquare and Gowalla. Many retailers and other local businesses are jumping on board Foursquare and offering a special deal for their Foursquare "mayors"—those who earn the title by visiting their sites the most frequently.

Businesses may award opinion leaders with tabs or badges like "member of the month" that can be placed on their profiles for visibility. They also remind users to *Like* and *Share* information about a company, celebrity, or movie with others. When their friends see the updates on their influencer friends' news feeds, it's highly likely for them to do the same.[53]

According to social media marketer Jack Monson, creating a customer loyalty program is "quick, easy, instantly measurable, and cost is incurred only if you choose to give away prizes or offer discounts. It's also perfect for any retailer, restaurant, car dealer, or other multi-unit company to which it's important to continue to give the best customers a reason to return to the store, shop, or showroom."[54]

Social media gives consumers great power to motivate needed vigilance and change in politicians, celebrities, and businesses. A great example of a company's response to a social media influencer was captured by consultant Ann Manion, who helps hotels manage and improve their reputations with customers.

Hotel 71 Chicago Listens

Ann Manion

Consider a day in the life of Hotel 71 Chicago's Director of Operations, Stephen Ellingsen. Last week he awoke to a firing squad of tweets aimed squarely at his hotel.

[52] Ben Straley, "Activate Your Brand's Super Influencers," mashable.com, November 12, 2010.

[53] "14 Powerful Tips for Marketing on Facebook," http://blog.socialmaximizer.com/14-tips-for-marketing-on-facebook.

[54] "How to Create a Customer Loyalty Program via Social Media," http://jackmonson.com/2010/06/28/how-to-create-a-customer-loyalty-program-via-social-media.

Meet the Twitterers

Amber Naslund [@AmberCadabra]

Director of Community for Radian6 with an online reach of:

- 500+ Linked In Connections
- 1,592 Facebook Friends
- 34,691 Twitter Followers

Hotel 71 [@Hotel71Chicago]

Boutique hotel located on Chicago's Magnificent Mile with:

- 61 Facebook Fans
- 92 Twitter Followers
- > 400 views on their YouTube Channel

Excerpts from a Tweet Timeline

9.22.10, 2:14 am—9.23.10, 9:19 am

Amber's Unfortunate Guest Experience:

Amber: Unreal. I valet park my car in Chicago at the hotel in which I stayed, and they lose the keys. Not a joke. It's 1am and I can't leave.

Amber: Seriously. And this effing hotel staff is just calling their valet staff and hoping someone has the keys. And giving ME attitude.

Amber: Given my recent post on not calling out companies, I wouldn't do so unless I was hopeless. But guys, skip Hotel 71 in Chicago.

Amber: Keys recovered. Desk clerk tells me that whether I pay for parking or not isn't her call. Um. What?

Amber: Oh. And I stood at the front desk for a half hour while they searched. And no one spoke to me until I asked what was happening.

Amber: I took my keys. I left. I'm flabbergasted. Never again, Hotel 71. You lose. Driving now. Thank you guys.

Hotel 71 Responds, Resolving the Matter Offline

Amber: Wow. I just got a voicemail from Hotel 71 re: the disastrous valet parking situation last night, wanting to apologize and know how to fix.

Amber: Acknowledging and wanting to fix a mistake very often offsets the frustration of the mistake itself.

Amber Feels the Love Again

Hotel 71:   @AmberCadabra - 4 those asking, Hotel 71 saw the Tweets, never underestimate Twitter! Yes, groveling, as it should have been, was involved

Amber: @Hotel71Chicago Your response was certainly appreciated. :) Thank you for paying attention

Hotel 71 Ends the Twitter Thread on a Positive Note

Hotel 71:   Sometimes things go wrong, Hotel 71 is no exception. What helps is guests giving us a chance to recover.

Amber: Born Again Brand Ambassador

Steven Ellingsen's real time response to Amber's public complaint curtailed a mini crisis.

The hotel's "apology mix" included a personal call to Amber, a series of penitent tweets, and a statement of regret on Facebook. These actions moved an unhappy guest from a state of agitated anger to a feeling of being heard and understood.

Amber shared the happy ending in her power house blog, Brass Tack Thinking; an entry which has been read by her army of followers and retweeted more than 100 times.

Stop Unfavorable Hotel Chatter Dead in its Tracks

This story is a terrific example of how to resolve a customer complaint in a public forum like Twitter. Why? Because Hotel 71 used social media to remind all fans and followers about their commitment to the customer.

Imagine if Ellingsen hadn't been monitoring his hotel's online reputation that day, and missed the opportunity to connect with Amber's 34,691 Twitter followers in real time, assuring them that her grievance was addressed? ■

Eye Tracking

Retailer John Wanamaker is credited as saying, "Half of my advertising dollars are wasted—I just don't know which half." It is challenging for advertisers to know what works and what doesn't, but innovative technologies for studying intricacies of consumer behavior are being pioneered, and their findings are sold to companies that hope to use their advertising budgets more wisely. One "eye-tracking" company does extensive research on how consumers look at ads so that its clients can design advertising for maximum impact on their target audience; the new technology is explained on its website, eyetracking.com:

> Using a lightweight headset with three small cameras, it is possible to record exactly where a person is looking as he or she is interacting with some kind of visual display. For example, say a person is navigating a website, looking to purchase an item online. With **eye-tracking**, it is possible to see exactly where this person is looking for specific information about the item, how they compare different items, and where they look to navigate to the shopping cart or other areas of the site.
>
> The user's point of gaze is superimposed on a video recording of the website as they interact with it. In this way, it is possible for developers to interact with the interface through the eyes of the user. It is possible to see objectively if a user has difficulty locating information, if they miss critical information, or have trouble navigating.
>
> The eye patterns can also be plotted on a bitmap in order to look at a viewing history spanning several seconds or longer. GazeTraces™ document the scanning behavior of a single participant scanning a single screen display or portion of it. This allows you to see clearly what on the page first caught

eye tracking Using photographic technology to record exactly where a person is looking as he or she is interacting with some kind of visual display in order to create ads and websites that attract a target audience.

the attention of the user, what elements he missed, and what elements may have been confusing.[55]

The Eye Tracking company analyzes television, Internet, and webpage viewing, packaging, and even brand positioning for sponsorships and then delivers suggestions to their clients as to how to optimize the attention of target audiences. The company also claims that it can assess customer's emotional reactions to an advertised product:

> A recently patented process measures changes in the pupil diameter to determine the emotional state of a user as they engage with your product. Changes in the pupil indicate in real time and objectively whether he or she is reacting favorably to your product.[56]

The Poynter Institute summarized research observations made while studying the eye movements of websurfers, finding that ads get viewed (or not) in large part as a result of page placement and several specific design elements. Some of the findings seemed obvious, such as the fact that 55 percent of viewers scanned an ad placed on top of the page, while only 14 percent saw the one at the bottom. Some others, not so obvious, include the following:

> Text ads did far better than graphic ads.
>
> Ads that blended into the content generally did much better. Ads, for example, inset into text columns did extremely well.
>
> Visual breaks between content sections tend to act as visual dams, creating a high drop-off rate for further viewing.
>
> Contrasting background colors tip viewers off to the fact that the image is an ad—and hurt results. White or no background differentiation fared much better.
>
> Performance improved in a direct relationship to ad size—larger ads commanded more and longer attention.[57]

Ongoing studies on eye tracking seek information that will help webpage designers achieve their goals.

> In a post originally penned in French, Olivier Sauvage, founder of Captain-Commerce.com, featured a few practical lessons he's learned from eye tracking technology.
>
> Sauvage focuses particularly on the effect of banner blindness, something that's been made more clear since designers and usability experts began utilizing eye tracking and eye gaze technology to see how users see web pages. It's simple enough—when we get to a site, we see a banner and simply ignore it. But the interesting thing is, eye tracking has found we ignore banners without even realizing that they are there sometimes.

---

[55] "Eye Movement and Point of Gaze," Eye Tracking, Inc., accessed March 2007.

[56] "Revolutionary Metrics," Eye Tracking, Inc., www.eyetracking.com, March 2007.

[57] Poynter: September 8, 2004, "Eye Tracking Study Reveals Ad Viewing Behavior . . . Marketingvox.com Observations on Advertising."

Because of the web, users have developed an ability to avoid certain things—and banner advertisements are one of them. Perhaps it resulted out of habit, having to face a sudden and increased bombardment of ads in the early era of the World Wide Web.

That's not to say we don't see the banners. In fact, we do see them, but we just choose not to pay attention, and whether this is done consciously or unconsciously, we use peripheral vision to determine what's important to us, what's relevant to what we're looking for and what's not. Banners and ads can represent a waste of time, so we have adapted our vision not to see them.

. . . In the article, Sauvage writes that banners, while seen, are never clicked. The result, of course, is that they have a very low visual click rate.

He suggests that when creating a banner, it's perhaps important to play with what he calls "the chameleon effect." If banners are designed to look like the elements that surround them, they're more likely to be seen and then clicked.[58]

Ongoing eye-tracking research explores such varied topics as facial recognition, consumer emotional responses, pattern recognition, and eye tracking of moving objects. Although much of the research is done to enhance marketing and design, studies are also providing valuable insight on such topics as how babies learn and what images are distracting to teenage drivers.

Neuromarketing

subliminal persuasion
Information meant to affect people on an unconscious level, some of which can be detected with training and some of which cannot be detected with the conscious mind, regardless of training. The existence and effectiveness of this latter form of subliminal persuasion remains under dispute.

For many years, scholars have debated the existence of **subliminal persuasion**, the use of messages that cannot be perceived by the conscious mind but that are registered unconsciously.

You may remember hearing about the merchandising trick drive-in movies allegedly used to play on customers. One frame of delicious-looking, hot-buttered popcorn was spliced into a movie (remember that movies are shown on a fast-moving, frame-by-frame basis). Researcher James Vicary claimed that this frame, shown beneath the level of the viewers' conscious awareness, was correlated with an increase in popcorn sales at intermission time. This claim raised serious concerns and caused lawmakers to suggest legislation banning subliminal splicing; however, no examples of this practice were ever substantiated, and Vicary later admitted that he had falsified his research. The stir over his claims, however, created a huge industry of audiotapes and CDs filled with subliminal messages; people bought these products because they were promised that listening to them would help them relax, lose weight, and learn languages while they slept.

There remains controversy about whether subliminal persuasion exists; for those who believe it does exist in various forms, there is controversy about whether or not it is effective. However, researchers are continually studying the human brain, and their findings are offered to marketers in various fields who want to increase brand-name recognition and gain and hold the attention of target audiences in as many ways as possible. For example, we have noted attempts to use the senses—colorful images; loud, catchy music; appealing smells—to attract consumers and make products memorable to them.

[58] D. Brendant, "Eye Tracking: Why Is Banner Blindness So Prevalent?" http://eyetrackingupdate.com/2010/12/29/eye-tracking-banner-blindness-prevalent/, December 29, 2010.

In addition to the standard marketing techniques, a new technique called **neuromarketing** uses recent advances in magnetic resonance imaging (MRI) scans of the brain to assess how consumers will respond to products and advertisements.

If scientists can determine internal reactions to products and brand names, reactions that the consumer registers unconsciously, then companies may have a tool for genuine subliminal persuasion.

New York Times reporter Clive Thompson explored the new field of "neuromarketing" by visiting psychiatrist Clint Kilts at his neuroscience facility called BrightHouse Institute:

neuromarketing Using technology to determine consumers' internal, subconscious reactions to products and brand names in order to plan effective marketing strategies.

> The BrightHouse Institute's techniques are based, in part, on an experiment that Kilts conducted earlier this year. He gathered a group of test subjects and asked them to look at a series of commercial products, rating how strongly they liked or disliked them. Then, while scanning their brains in an M.R.I. machine, he showed them pictures of the products again. When Kilts looked at the images of their brains, he was struck by one particular result: whenever a subject saw a product he had identified as one he truly loved—something that might prompt him to say, "That's just so me!"—his brain would show increased activity in the medial prefrontal cortex.
>
> Kilts was excited, for he knew that this region of the brain is commonly associated with our sense of self. . . . M.R.I. studies have found increased activity in this region when people are asked if adjectives like "trustworthy" or "courageous" apply to them. When the medial prefrontal cortex fires, your brain seems to be engaging, in some manner, with what sort of person you are. If it fires when you see a particular product, Kilts argues, it's most likely to be because the product clicks with your self-image. . . .
>
> Kilts stabbed his finger at another glowing yellow dot near the top of the brain. It was the magic spot—the medial prefrontal cortex. If that area is firing, a consumer isn't deliberating, he said: he's itching to buy. "At that point, it's intuitive. You say: 'I'm going to do it. I want it.'" . . .
>
> M.R.I. scanning offers the promise of concrete facts—an unbiased glimpse at a consumer's mind in action. To an M.R.I. machine, you cannot misrepresent your responses. Your medial prefrontal cortex will start firing when you see something you adore, even if you claim not to like it. . . .
>
> Neuromarketing may also be able to suss out the distinction between advertisements that people merely like and those that are actually effective—a difference that can be hard to detect from a focus group. A neuromarketing study in Australia, for instance, demonstrated that supershort, MTV-style jump cuts—indeed, any scenes shorter than two seconds—aren't as likely to enter the long-term memory of viewers, however bracing or aesthetically pleasing they may be. . . .
>
> In response to his critics, Kilts plans to publish the BrightHouse research in an accredited academic journal. He insisted to me that his primary allegiance is to science; BrightHouse's techniques are "business done in the science method," he said, "not science done in the business method." And as he sat at his computer, calling up a 3-D picture of a brain, it was hard not to be struck, at the very least, by the seriousness of his passion. There, on the screen, was the medial prefrontal cortex, juggling our conscious thinking. There was the amygdala, governing our fears, buried deep in the brain. These are sights that he said still inspire in him feelings of wonder. "When you sit

down and you're watching—for the first time in the history of mankind—how we process complex primary emotions like anger, it's amazing," he said. "You're like, there, look at that: that's anger, that's pleasure. When you see that roll off the workstation, you never look back." You just keep going, it seems, until you hit Madison Avenue.[59]

Innovations in neuromarketing are constantly being explored. For example, some businesses are combining neuromarketing and eye-tracking techniques to create online virtual shopping sites:

NeuroFocus is a neuromarketing firm that recently announced a device called the N-Matrix 3D at the Shopper Marketing Expo at Chicago's Navy Pier. The system reportedly creates lifelike, customized virtual reality environments for people to shop in. It's essentially an online store, but users can maneuver down shopping aisles, grab products from shelves, and fill up a shopping cart as they browse through a virtual store. Apparently the realism is such that it helps the brain to perceive what NeuroFocus says is an essentially authentic experience. The system functions by integrating neurological cues that the subconscious levels of the brain see as essential for realistic perception—in this case, the perception of an actual store setting.

Utilizing stereoscopic 3D, NeuroFocus hopes to provide a truly engaging experience in which CG [computer-generated] effects enable light, shadow, and perspective reminiscent of shopping in a real store. The environments are said to be highly realistic, offering products, aisle displays, signs, and price stickers for the shopper to see. Other shoppers are also included in the graphics, so it feels more real. Companies can use both static and video images for marketing material. By taking measurements of a customer's brainwave activity, NeuroFocus can provide the virtual environment to make a shopper happy. They apply high-density arrays of EEG sensors that can monitor and record brain activity two thousand times a second. The system incorporates eye tracking and various biometric information, reportedly creating an accurate and reliable reading of the subconscious levels of the brain. It can provide market research and insight into psychological behavior for what shoppers like, what they're interested in and why, and also what makes them decide to buy the product in the first place and then stick with a brand in particular.

NeuroFocus' plans include placing the N-Matrix 3D in stores and kiosks—essentially where people consume things: vending machines, living rooms, refrigerators, and more social venues like clubs, bars, or restaurants.[60]

Researchers from MIT, Stanford, and Carnegie Mellon University have also used brain scans to look at how consumers think about products in order to understand and predict what they will buy. Jonathan Potts reports on this research:

For the first time, researchers have used functional magnetic resonance imaging (fMRI) to determine what parts of the brain are active when

[59] From Clive Thompson, "There's a Sucker Born in Every Medial Prefrontal Cortex," *New York Times*, October 26, 2003.

[60] D. Brendant, "Eye Tracking and Neuromarketing in 3D Marketing Research," eyetrackingupdate.com, October 28, 2010.

people consider whether to purchase a product and to predict whether or not they ultimately choose to buy the product. The study appears in the journal *Neuron* and was co-authored by scientists at Carnegie Mellon University, Stanford University and the MIT Sloan School of Management.

This paper is the latest from the emerging field of neuroeconomics, which investigates the mental and neural processes that drive economic decision-making. The results could have a profound impact on economic theory, because the decision of whether to purchase a product is the most basic and pervasive economic behavior.

Previous imaging studies have found that separate parts of the brain are activated when people are confronted with financial gains versus financial losses. The authors of this latest study believed that distinct brain regions would be activated when people were presented with products they wish to purchase (representing a potential gain) and when they were presented with those products' prices (representing a potential loss). The researchers wanted to see if they could then use this information to predict when a person would decide to buy a product, and when they would pass it up.

Twenty-six adults participated in the study, in which they were given $20 to spend on a series of products that would be shipped to them. If they made no purchases, they would be able to keep the money. The products and their prices appeared on a computer screen that the participants viewed while lying in an fMRI scanner. The researchers found that when the participants were presented with the products, a subcortal brain region known as the nucleus accumbens that is associated with the anticipation of pleasure was activated. When the subjects were presented with prices that were excessive, two things happened: the brain region known as the insula was activated and a part of the brain associated with balancing gains versus losses—the medial prefrontal cortex—was deactivated.

Furthermore, by studying which regions were activated, the authors were able to successfully predict whether the study participants would decide to purchase each item. Activations of the regions associated with product preference and with weighing gains and losses indicated that a person would decide to purchase a product. In contrast, when the region associated with excessive prices was activated, participants chose not to buy a product.[61]

Other technological advances, currently used for mostly positive purposes, can also be used to deceive. For example, scientists at the Massachusetts Institute of Technology have created realistic videos of people saying things they actually have not said. The videos seem so authentic that viewers cannot detect any tampering when people are simulated speaking languages that they do not speak. The technology involves the use of artificial intelligence to teach a machine what a person looks like when talking—using a few minutes of videotape, the computer captures images that represent the full range of motion of the subject's mouth. With an accurate picture of the mouth, the computer can superimpose it on a person's face and, having also learned electronically to imitate the person's every sound, can make the person say new things. The technology could also be used to create more realistic video games. But scientists and media critics also fear that this new technology might be

[61] Jonathan Potts, "Researchers Use Brain Scans to Predict When People Will Buy Products," www.cmu.edu (accessed January 6, 2007). (Also cited on *Medical News Today.*)

used to discredit or embarrass people by having them appear to say things they haven't said; it could also be used to have people with credibility seem to be endorsing products or programs. Some scientists predict that there will have to be a whole new field of experts who will be called upon to testify at trials as to whether a video has been forged with this new technology.[62]

Skill

Be aware of the use of advertising and marketing techniques.

We can't realistically be aware of all of the ways we are targeted as citizens and consumers. But critical thinkers do have some defenses against the barrage of tricks and tools used to get us to cast our votes and spend our money:

- Become aware of your attention span when you are listening to or viewing an advertisement. Notice when you are drawn to a particular image but can't explain why.
- When making decisions as a consumer, consider why you are buying a particular brand. Do you really believe this brand is the best, or is it just a name you recognize? Read labels to see if the ingredients in your "brand" really differ from less-expensive brands.
- When making decisions as a voter, be clear about the reasons you are supporting a particular candidate or proposition. Have you "bought into" a slogan or into someone's claims without examining your thinking? Do you clearly understand the issues and the various conclusions about the issues?

The key to walking through the minefields of print and electronic persuasion is to be armed with facts and logical reasoning about your decisions as a citizen and a consumer. Critical thinkers avoid basing their judgments on the consciously or unconsciously applied manipulations of campaign managers and advertisers. A good offense is your best defense. (See Exercises 8.9 and 8.10 on page 379.)

Storytelling as Persuasion

So far, we have focused on persuasive techniques used by broadcast and electronic media, print journalism, and advertising. Critical thinkers also need to be aware of the enormous power of storytelling—in the form of novels, movies, and televised fiction—to influence our beliefs about the world. Often, when an issue is presented in story form, it has tremendous persuasive power and may reach people who have not responded to "logical" arguments; we are particularly vulnerable to the arguments hidden in stories because we see storytelling as primarily entertaining and we aren't on the lookout for subtle manipulations of our emotions and perceptions. Producers of reality shows, such as the popular *Bachelor* and *Bachelorette* series, strive to create conflict and drama. The background stories of Olympic athletes or

---

[62] Gareth Cook, "At MIT, They Can Put Words in Our Mouths," *The Boston Globe*, May 15, 2002, p. A1.

Biggest Loser contestants get audiences absorbed and involved in their competitive challenges. As a result of this involvement, large audiences are created for advertisers of these programs.

People who feel strongly about an issue often have had a personal understanding and connection to the issue; those who speak out against drunk driving or drug abuse or in favor of funding for a particular disease often have had significant experience and thus a depth of emotion that fuels their expertise on the topic. But strong emotions about an issue can be stirred even in a neutral audience through the vicarious experience that a movie provides. If someone wants, for example, to gain support for animal rights, a film about lovable animals that are being abused can do a lot to garner public sympathy. In a similar fashion, if someone wants to paint a person or a group as villainous, a powerful argument to that effect can be made through a fictional portrayal. Good filmmaking allows an audience to experience the perspective of the main characters and to see life as they do; too often, however, the audience does not easily separate fact from fiction and believes that the story presented is the unabridged truth.

With the technological advances of neuromarketing, there is an increasing interest in how our brains respond to storytelling. Even a simple story has power to grab our attention and engage our brains. But what's the brain responding to exactly?

Wray Herbert, writing for psychologicalscience.com, explores some current ideas:

> One theory is that we all have many "scripts" stored in our neurons. These scripts are derived from past experiences, and words activate these scripts, transforming the printed text into something more like a real-life experience. The opening scene from *The Tower Treasure* is actually rather spare in its language, yet for the reader it can be a rich encounter. We visualize a narrow road, perhaps one that we have actually known from somewhere. We feel our grip on the motorcycle handlebars, and hear the screech of the tires; we imagine leaping and the difficult pitch of the embankment and the effort of climbing.
>
> At least that's the idea, which a team of psychologists at Washington University in St. Louis decided to test in the lab. Jeffrey Zacks and his colleagues suspected that several different regions of the brain collaborate in the reading of a tale, each supplying a specialized script based on a particular kind of real-world experience. So, for example, one group of neurons might supply a story's sense of space and movement (the careening car on a narrow road), while another might contribute the sensation of handling objects (clutching the grips), and still another, the characters' goals (climbing to safety).
>
> To test this idea, the scientists used a brain scanner to see what regions lit up during the reading of a story. They watched the brains of volunteers as they read four short narrative passages. Each clause in each story was coded for the script it should theoretically trigger: movement in space, sense of time passing, characters' goals, interaction with physical objects, and so forth. The idea was to see if different parts of the brain lit up as the reader's imagined situation unfolded.
>
> And they did. The details of the brain anatomy aren't important here, but clearly there are several different neuron clusters involved in story comprehension. For example, a particular area of the brain ramped up

when readers were thinking about intent and goal-directed action, but not meaningless motion. Motor neurons flashed when characters were grasping objects, and neurons involved in eye movement activated when characters were navigating their world.

These findings, reported on-line in the journal *Psychological Science,* strongly suggest that readers are far from passive consumers of words and stories. Indeed, it appears that we dynamically activate real-world scripts that help us to comprehend a narrative—and those active scripts in turn enrich the story beyond its mere words and sentences. In this way, reading is much like remembering or imagining a vivid event.

It's possible, the psychologists say, that not just reading but all thinking may be similarly embodied in stored, real-life experiences. In this sense, language may have been an adaptive strategy for efficient and vivid communication of experiences to others. Put another way, storytelling may have evolved as a tool of survival.[63]

Because storytelling is so powerful, it is disturbing when fictionalized films about historic events are taken as an accurate portrayal of those events. For example, Oliver Stone made compelling films about former Presidents John Fitzgerald Kennedy (*JFK*) and Richard Nixon (*Nixon*). By interspersing true events with fictional speculations about these men, Stone created a persuasive narrative. The problem is that moviegoers who are not familiar with true historic events don't separate the truth from the fiction and take Stone's movies as documentaries. Some libraries even place these films in the history reference sections rather than in the movie collections, adding to their perception as historic, rather than fictional, narratives.

The president of Wellesley College, Diana Chapman Walsh, felt the need to "set the record straight" about the portrayal of Wellesley in the film *Mona Lisa Smile* after she had received letters from concerned alumnae. Walsh said the film gave a "distorted and demeaning portrayal of our alma mater." College administrators had read an early version of the script that they said emphasized students' intelligence and their close relationships with faculty advisors, and this positive portrayal prompted them to give permission for Revolution Studios to film on campus. When the movie came out, the administrators noted that the screenplay had been changed and now characterized the college as "rigid and hidebound and the students as rich and spoiled." The film characterizes Wellesley as a place where it is dangerous for faculty to show independence and portrays administrators as frightened and as having "claws under their gloves." Some people on campus were upset enough to consider suing for libel; they realized that many moviegoers who see this film would assume that it is an accurate historical picture of Wellesley in the 1950s. The studio's spokesperson countered, "We did not set out to make a documentary." However, to many viewers, it may seem to be just that.[64]

When we see movies set in a specific historical time period, we need to be alert to the differences between what really happened and what the screenwriters added to make the story more interesting. With those precautions, we can maintain an objective perspective that helps us stay grounded in reality.

---

[63] Wray Herbert, "The Narrative in the Neurons," http://www.psychologicalscience.org/onlyhuman/index.cfm.

[64] Sara Lipka, "Wellesley's President Isn't Smiling Over College's Portrayal in Film," *The Chronicle of Higher Education,* January 14, 2004.

Citizens, Consumers, and Relationships in an Age of Technology

A challenge to critical thinkers in the exploding Age of Information is to make conscious, deliberate choices about how they want to use the available technological innovations as citizens, consumers, and people in relationships.

At one time, most people lived in agrarian societies, connected deeply to the land. Families and communities worked together, and though the life was difficult, relationships were close and enduring. Couples usually grew old and died on the same piece of land they bought as newlyweds.

During the Industrial Revolution, factories and other businesses created a work environment in which fathers and sometimes mothers left the home for most of the daylight hours. Many people still follow this pattern; one or both parents leave home in the morning and congregate at some time in the evening when athletic practices, after-school programs, and a host of other extracurricular activities are completed.

However, the technological advances of recent decades give us an abundance of new choices, allowing many people to work, at least in part, from home and forge unique lifestyles. There are also many new options concerning media that provide endless opportunities to explore issues, products, and relationships.

We have numerous and incredible choices, not only because of the Internet, but also because of cell phones, iPhones and iPads, digital cameras, TiVos, Wii, and our social networks. Commuters can be entertained all the way to and from work with iPods, kindles, books on CDs, or an abundance of FM or AM radio stations. A person who is unable to walk can still go shopping online. A parent who is torn between seeing his favorite team's playoff game and his daughter's piano recital can record the game and watch it later in the night, skipping the commercials. A student who needs to take care of a sick parent can do research from home; she can look up great sources for a history paper and then check out various sites to find out the latest breakthroughs, treatments, and support groups for her parent's medical condition. A musician can go to iTunes and download numerous renditions of a song and then access, print, and even transpose sheet music from a variety of sites. Friends can connect every day from anywhere in the world by phone, e-mail, texting, Facebook, Twitter, Skype, and other platforms. Citizens concerned about any social issues are able to instantly access numerous articles from the best papers and magazines in the world. Voters can check their favorite sources before casting a vote, and consumers can do comparison shopping and read intricate reviews before buying a product or choosing a hotel or airline. Dinner and theatre reservations can be made from home, and hundreds of movie and DVD reviews can be accessed to help people decide what to see or buy. People invited to a wedding can go to a department store's site, find out exactly what a bride and groom want, and have it delivered with a personalized message the next day.

The choices we have also come with some interesting consequences. Your local grocery store and your online bookstore both know exactly what you like to buy and read and will continue to tempt you with your favorite products in the form of individualized coupons or e-mail offers. Unscrupulous hackers and scam artists will invade your privacy and try to invade your wallet as well. Predators can use increasingly sophisticated means to lure naïve children and teens. Someone may post malicious lies about you on a site and hurt your chances of being hired for a job or getting into a graduate school. Critical thinkers have to be aware of the minefields of cyberspace and realize that every transmission that is made is out there forever.

And there is one more consideration. With all of the fascinating and entertaining choices available to us, we need to be mindful of how we want to use our time. The same tools that can make us closer to our friends and family, more aware of what's going on in the world, and more able to be efficient in our work can also isolate us from others. Roommates don't have to agree on what music to play; they can each listen to different tunes on their personalized iPods. Parents may be glued to their own PCs while children are talking, texting, following their friends on Facebook, or playing video games into the wee hours of the morning. As critical thinkers, we should heed the advice of the late professor and writer Neil Postman who warned us to be careful of "amusing ourselves to death." With vigilance about our personal choices, we can use our amazing electronic tools to impact our lives and our world for the good.

Life Application: Tips for College and Career

You can tell a lot about someone's priorities if you can see his or her calendar and checkbook. We all have a limited amount of time and resources. Be conscious and deliberate about your use of technology. If you don't have a plan, others—including advertisers, television producers, and webmasters—will have a plan for you. Decide how you can best use your time and money, and set your own electronic and spending limits accordingly.

Chapter Review

Summary

1. Professionals use the power of suggestion to create impressions about products, ideas, and candidates.

2. To be more critical of televised suggestion, viewers should be aware of the selection of issues; the use of time; the selection and treatment of guest and panel members; the design of the set; the nonverbal element of clothing; and the use of language, camera angles, camera cuts, camera distance, and framing.

3. To be more critical of suggestion in print media, readers should be aware of the use of headlines, the use of "leads" or openings to a news story, the balance of reporting on an issue, the degree of fairness in editorial essays and letters, and photo composition. All of these elements taken together form the overall frame given to a particular story.

4. Suggestion and subliminal persuasion involve information meant to affect people on an unconscious level. Suggestive messages of this kind can be detected with training.

5. Advertisers and marketing experts use a number of persuasive techniques including fuzzy words, logical fallacies, stylized images and sounds, celebrity associations and endorsements, product placement, the Gestalt principle, the

use of social media to build customer loyalty, the use of opinion leaders to influence the market, eye tracking, and neuromarketing.

6. Storytelling has always had a persuasive effect, and that effect is being revealed by research on how our brains process and are influenced by narrative accounts.

Checkup

Short Answer

1. Explain the concept of suggestion, using a few examples.
2. How does the selection of issues by writers, producers, and editors affect the audience's knowledge of current events?
3. How can headlines shape the perceptions of newspaper readers?

Sentence Completion

4. Until recently, broadcasters were compelled to allow airtime for both sides of controversial issues, under the law known as the _____ _____.
5. The practice of choosing more exciting stories over those stories that may be more newsworthy is called _____.
6. The deliberate or unconscious use of camera shots that influence audiences is known as _____.
7. A principle stating that our minds strive toward completion of information is the _____ principle.

True-False

8. Newspapers have to allow equal space for opposing viewpoints.
9. Storytelling engages different areas of the human brain.
10. Language can shape a reader's perceptions of issues.

Exercises

EXERCISE 8.1 Purpose: To discover and analyze examples of suggestion in personal and professional contexts.

1. For the brave and honest only: Think of five ways you use the power of suggestion in your life—to create an impression on a boss, friend, mate, teacher, parent, or in general. Or, observe or interview other people, asking how they arrange their world to create impressions.

Example

Some of the ways that I have used suggestion in my life to impress people include dressing nicer for things such as job interviews to give the impression that I fit right in. I have also used big words in conversation and in job interviews to make myself appear to be a lot more intelligent than I am. When trying to present an image or an idea, I am a lot more careful about what I say. Also, I tend to be a lot quieter than I really am. At a friend's house, I tend to speak more softly, and I help people out a lot more than I would normally do. This gives the impression that I am helpful and hard working when in reality I usually have to force myself to do work around my house. (from a student)

2. Interview a professional, telling him or her about the concept of suggestion and asking in what ways he or she uses it in business. Examples include asking a manager of a supermarket if certain products are arranged at kid level to appeal to children and if items at the checkout counter are chosen for a particular reason. You might also ask boutique salespersons or department store managers how their stores are arranged to give a desired impression to customers.

Another approach to this exercise is to begin by analyzing the layout of a store or an office (for example, a supermarket, department store, electronics store, bank, doctor's office, or toy store—the exercise can also be done with a website). Come to some conclusions about why the business or site is laid out in that particular way; support your conclusions with reasons. After you have made some assumptions about the layout, interview the manager of the store or office (or the webmaster) to find out if the layout is meant to influence customers in any way.

EXERCISE 8.2 Purpose: To compare the effect of different selection and ordering of news stories.

1. Watch the evening news on several stations, either local or national, for one or two nights. You may have to switch back and forth from one channel to another if the coverage is simultaneous (unless you watch one from a laptop, hook up two sets in the same room, or have a classmate watch a different station). Then, consider the following elements.

Note the selection of issues, the order of the stories shown, and the time given to each story. If different stories were covered, which station covered the more important story, in your opinion? Note also any "slant" given to a story by the comments or facial expressions of the anchorpersons. Did some stations feature more sensational stories or more in-depth coverage of stories than others?

You may not notice much difference in the selection of issues on the commercial networks; try comparing a commercial network with public television's or C-SPAN's coverage of an issue. See if you can identify any major differences between them.

After compiling your research, answer this question: If you were an editor on one of the broadcasts, what changes, if any, would you make in the coverage of the news? Which stories would you give more, less, or no coverage? Which stories would get top priority on your network?

2. In class groups, assume you are the program editors for a local edition of the evening news. Look at the story topics that follow and put them in order from the most to the least important. The most important will be covered at the top of the program, and the least important may be cut in the interest of time.

To make your task easier, set some criteria before you order the stories. Possible criteria include international or national value, usefulness to the local populace, and relevance to the largest number of people. In essence, you are to decide what the people in your audience should know. Think about other important criteria, and then list the following topics in order from the most to the least important.

a. There is an update on hopeful signs in new Mideast peace initiatives.
b. A murder-suicide occurred at a downtown hotel.
c. Polls on an upcoming campaign show the front-runner falling behind.
d. There is a serious drought in a neighboring country.
e. A death-row inmate has been executed, and there was a protest involving 300 people.
f. A famous film star has been arrested for drunk driving.
g. A major freeway accident is causing hour-long delays in the evening commute.
h. A local day-care center has been charged with child abuse.
i. A new drug for treating AIDS, which has been used with some good results in Canada, has been banned indefinitely in the United States, pending Food and Drug Administration approval.
j. There is massive starvation in another country, and relief efforts are hindered by a lack of funds.

EXERCISE 8.3 Purpose: To understand the altering of settings to create impressions on viewers.

1. Analyze the setting of a place that you frequent—it could be your classroom, the business that employs you, a store, a restaurant, or your home. What impression does the room convey? If you put a camera in different places in the same room, what different impressions would be created? Do the people in charge of this environment consciously set it up the way it is? If so, what is their purpose?

2. Analyze the set of a commercial or television program—why do you think it looks the way it does? How have the set designers "framed" the environment, and what impression does it convey?

EXERCISE 8.4 Purpose: To understand personal-image engineering in order to be more discerning about the image engineering done by political candidates, salespersons, or actors promoting products.

1. Stop and write down everything you are wearing that is visible to others. Include jewelry and accessories and consider your choices of colors. What impression are you trying to convey to others with your "look"? If you generally dress while you are half asleep, stop and think about how someone else might judge you based on your clothing.

   You can extend this exercise to the classroom by having a few classmates write down the impression they get from your appearance. Compare their answers with the impression you'd like to make. How did you do as an image engineer?

2. Note how the actors in some commercials are dressed; what impressions are they trying to create? If you have access to a televised trial, or even to television programs such as *People's Court,* you can note the appearance of the plaintiffs and defendants and draw conclusions about why they are dressed as they are. How does their image affect their credibility? How might a different image give viewers (and the judges) different impressions?

EXERCISE 8.5 Purpose: To find examples of suggestive techniques used by broadcast media.

1. Watch an interview program and analyze the suggestive elements we've mentioned in this section: the selection of issues, the use of time, the selection and treatment of guest and panel members, what is included or excluded on a set, the nonverbal element of clothing, the use of language, the use of camera angles and cuts, and camera distance and framing. Is there anything about the presentation of the material that creates suggestions? If so, what do you think might be the motive of the producers, directors, or editors in charge of the broadcast?

2. Watch (or record) several commercials or download some from YouTube. Using the list of marketing techniques as a guide, isolate the ways in which the advertisers are trying to persuade you to buy their product or use their service. If you live with children, see if they are particularly attracted to commercials and if they respond to the advertising appeals on children's programming.

3. Watch a situation comedy that features laugh tracks. Notice if you or the people you watch with are influenced to laugh by this fabricated element of suggestion.

4. Analyze the opening of a television or radio program. How does the opening work to keep you tuned in to the program?

5. Notice the camera cuts and angles in a feature film; scenes from most films are shot from a number of angles and then carefully pieced together in post-production. How did the director and film editors choose cuts and angles to create an impact on the audience?

EXERCISE 8.6 Purposes: To gain awareness of misleading headlines and leads and how they distort information. To find examples of imbalanced reporting and editorializing.

1. Look for examples of headlines and leads that distort the meanings of stories. Bring the headlines and/or leads to class for discussion, or write a paper in which you explain the following:

   a. How does the headline and lead distort the information in the story?
   b. Why do you think that headline and lead were chosen?
   c. What would be a more appropriate headline or lead for this story; why do you think a more impartial heading or lead was not chosen?

2. Look for examples of imbalanced reporting or editorializing, or for the use of misleading photographs. Bring the stories, photographs, or editorial essays to class, or write a paper in which you explain the following:

   a. How is the story, photograph, or editorial biased?
   b. How could bias have been prevented? What would be a more fair representation of the information?

EXERCISE 8.7 Purposes: To see that news coverage varies depending on the source. To consider the different priorities held by various sources.

1. Compare your local newspaper, a large city newspaper, and a national paper either online or in hard copy. What stories are covered on the first

few pages? Why do you think different stories are featured by the various papers?

2. Choose an issue that is getting wide press coverage. Find articles on this issue in several different newspapers or magazines. Compare the coverage in each one, and then write an essay or give a speech or panel presentation in which you address the following questions:

   a. What elements of coverage framed the story in different ways? Analyze the summary of the story given in the first one or two paragraphs, the quotes selected from the persons interviewed, the amount of coverage given to both sides of the issue, and the use of headlines, leads, and photographs.

   b. Which source reported the issue most fairly, in your view? Give examples to support your position.

EXERCISE 8.8 Purpose: To become aware of the subtle ways in which a story may be shaped to influence readers or viewers.

This exercise, created by Professor William Dorman, encourages what he calls "frame hunts."

Bring in a story or photograph from a print or electronic news source, or a segment from a story covered on television, and try to convince other students that the story has a frame or slant of some sort. The class should vote thumbs up or thumbs down on each case. At the end of the semester, or of this section of the course, have a "Frame Off" in which the "Frame of the Year" is selected from all the frames submitted throughout the course.

EXERCISE 8.9 Purpose: To be able to detect suggestion in advertisements.

Find examples of television commercials or advertisements in webzines, magazines, newspapers, or on YouTube that employ one or more of the forms of persuasion discussed in this chapter. Share your findings with class members. For this exercise, many heads are better than one because of the different perceptual abilities people have. One person may discover a musical trick used in a television commercial; another person may detect subtle images in a print ad. Look also for "testimonials" from "average" people who are really paid actors promoting a product; signs that testimonials come from paid testimony are flawless delivery of lines, carefully chosen clothing, and disproportionate raving about the product; columnist Dave Barry calls infomercial actors "Consumers from Mars."

EXERCISE 8.10 Purpose: To gain a deeper understanding of suggestion, persuasion, and neuromarketing.

Read more about it! This chapter gives you a basic understanding of the principles of suggestion and persuasion and a glimpse at some of the new technologies used to enhance marketing. Many other books and articles have been written on the subject. If you find these subjects interesting, do further research on them, including interviews with reporters, graphic designers, advertisers, or instructors of journalism and broadcasting.

You may want to focus your research on the controversial questions associated with subliminal persuasion: Does it currently exist? If so, how does it influence audiences? Share your research findings with your class.

You **Decide**

Campaign Finance Reform

Because of the expenses required for advertising, the costs of running a competitive political campaign have risen to staggering levels. In 2008, the average (mean) cost of a House campaign was $1,362,239; for a Senate campaign, the cost exceeded $7.5 million. The enormous cost of campaigns has two obvious effects. First, it eliminates from realistic consideration candidates who may have great leadership potential but lack the funding to run for election. Second, it gives large contributors—whether individuals, corporations, or unions—special influence over elected members of government: Successful politicians must stay on congenial terms with those who provide essential funding. *Buckley v. Valeo* (1976) is the pivotal U.S. Supreme Court decision regarding the issue of campaign finance reform. The Court ruled that individual contributions to a specific candidate could be limited; however, no limits could be imposed on contributions to organizations that might use the money to support candidates indirectly. Those who oppose campaign finance reform regard the Buckley decision as a victory for freedom of expression (in the form of financial support); advocates of campaign finance reform see it as a roadblock to change.

For more information on the debate surrounding campaign finance reform and additional exercises and tutorials about concepts covered in this chapter, logo into MyThinkingLab at www.mythinkinglab.com and select Diestler, *Becoming a Critical Thinker,* Sixth Edition.

✳ Explore on **mythinkinglab.com**

Articles for Discussion   📖 Read the **Document** on **mythinkinglab.com**

The following article by a British journalist discusses the growing use of social media by politicians. In the 2008 election, President Obama made extensive use of the Internet to get his message out, especially to young voters; since that time, both local and national politicians have sought new ways to tap into resources that communicate to their constituents.

U.S. Mayor Uses Twitter to Help Snowbound

Andrew Edgecliffe-Johnson

Politicians were once measured by their performances on the stump, in radio broadcasts and television debates.

Now, they are being judged by their mastery of social media. As Twitter users blasted Michael Bloomberg, New York's mayor, for what they deemed an inadequate response to the blizzard that struck the city on Sunday night, Cory Booker, mayor of neighbouring Newark, New Jersey, was scouring Twitter for pleas from snowed-in constituents, then directing ploughs their way.

Dressed in a fleece and windcheater, the Democratic rising star wielded a shovel and a smartphone, following up tweets about uncleared streets with brief messages such as "On it," "I'm heading over there to look at ur st" and "I'm sending someone ASAP."

The 41-year-old, still basking in the publicity from a $100m donation to Newark's schools from Facebook founder Mark Zuckerberg, used Twitter to beat the emergency services to a woman in labour and deliver nappies to a stranded mother.

Taking the Tip O'Neill adage that "all politics is local" to a hyper-local level, social media has provided politicians with a digital equivalent of door-to-door campaigning or kissing babies, allowing conversations to replace one-way stump speeches.

Mr Booker is a social media veteran, with a Facebook page featuring poetry, uplifting quotes from Gandhi and updates on carjacking arrests. He has more than 1m followers on Twitter, equivalent to 40 per cent of Newark's population, and is fluent in its shorthand.

This week, he lambasted one critic who had complained that his family was snowed in but had not helped dig them out with the message: "Wow u shud b ashamed of yourself. U tweet vulgarities & then I come out here to help & its ur mom & sis digging. Where r u?"

Commentators contrasted Mr Booker's response with that of Mr Bloomberg, who sent just seven blandly informational tweets on Sunday and Monday, and gave a sarcastic televised press conference in a suit and tie.

On Wednesday, he said he would investigate why emergency services were overwhelmed, but abusive tweets about Mr. Bloomberg and Chris Christie, the New Jersey governor who was away at Disney World after the storm, showed social media's unforgiving side.

Brad Blake, former head of social media for Deval Patrick, Massachusetts governor, said skill with social media was "becoming a necessity" for politicians. Massachusetts had shifted from sending press releases over Twitter to integrating it with the "constituent services" office that answers calls and e-mails.

The pressure on local politicians remained acute, with many roads still blocked and delays threatening to stretch into the weekend at the airports serving New York. ▪

Questions for Discussion

1. The author of this article says that politicians are now being judged by their mastery of social media rather than their stated positions on issues. To what extent do you agree with the author, and in what ways do you think that mastery of social media is important for politicians?

2. What is the best way for local politicians to inform their constituents of their viewpoints on issues? Which forms of media would you be most likely to access?

3. The author said that Mayor Booker "lambasted one critic who had complained that his family was snowed in but the mayor had not helped dig them out." When the mayor arrived he responded with the message: 'Wow u shud b ashamed of yourself. U tweet vulgarities & then I come out here to help &

its ur mom & sis digging. Where r u?'" What do you think of the mayor's response?

• •

The following article focuses on the power of suggestion to influence the behavior of guests at resorts and casinos. Managers in the hospitality business are using the findings of scientific research to enhance the atmosphere and profitability of their establishments.

Scents and Sensibility

Donna McAleer

A Harrah Hotel College professor is studying different ways the guest's resort experience can be enhanced through the senses.

You may or may not notice the sweet smell of success the next time you visit a casino or resort, but if you do, it's not by accident. Introducing fragrance into the air is part of a growing hospitality industry trend toward multisensory marketing—eliciting favorable impressions not only by what someone sees or hears but also smells, feels, and remembers—to create an overall positive impression about the resort experience. What started out as an effort to minimize the impact of cigarette smoke in casino air has blossomed into a growing business for companies that develop custom fragrance blends for resorts worldwide. UNLV (University of Nevada at Las Vegas) researchers are examining the trend and finding there is more to study than meets the nose.

The sense of smell is just one way (and a very powerful one) to help guests form positive emotional impressions. Scent affects both mind and body. It can immediately create or connect to a memory as well as have a potent physiological impact. A putrid odor can literally make one sick, and a pleasing smell can improve a mood—just think cookies in the oven. The hotel industry is learning what aromatherapists have long realized: Scents can relax or stimulate the body's responses and perhaps even influence behavior.

For nearly 20 years, resorts and casinos have worked with fragrance formulators, such as pioneering firm AromaSys, to scent their inside air through existing ventilation systems. Their reasons range from the basic premise that pleasant fragrances can minimize cigarette smell and convey the impression of cleanliness to a more sophisticated notion—that a distinctive scent can create an irresistible appeal and air of luxury. Kathryn LaTour, associate professor of tourism and convention administration, is studying different ways the guest experience can be enhanced through the senses. LaTour notes that there are actually more sensory channels than the five traditional senses. "It's actually closer to 19 different ways a person forms perceptions, some below conscious awareness." Learning more about people's psychological and physiological responses to strong sensory cues like fragrance can have an impact on consumer behavior. "It's a wide-open field," LaTour says. "The industry is eager for more data."

Gael Hancock, program manager for the Master's of Hospitality Administration degree at UNLV, is providing some of that data. As part of her recently completed master's thesis, she conducted one of the few objective studies on the effects of fragrances in a casino setting. Her study is significant because it is not based on focus groups or subjective surveys about whether customers "liked" a fragrance. Instead, it simply measures the "coin-in" rate for reel slot machines at five different casino floor locations when different fragrances were dispersed. Hancock tested both synthetic fragrances and natural fragrances compounded from essential oils. She wanted to know if there would be any difference between the synthetic and natural scents, which are more complex and can be more expensive to use. For the two natural fragrances she tested, she deliberately chose very different scents, one known for its invigorating effects on the body and the other recognized as relaxing.

Her results proved interesting. "Coin-in" rates were positively affected when the air was scented with natural fragrances, either refreshing or soothing. The power of the natural fragrances utilizing essential oils over the weaker synthetics did not surprise Hancock. Her background research and 25 years' experience with aromatherapy had suggested that natural fragrances "have been shown to affect mood, lessen anxiety, and increase alertness," which could keep gamblers staying longer and playing more, she posits. It's possible that natural fragrances may help gamblers "maintain an emotional equilibrium and not experience such highs and lows," says Hancock.

Until more is known about scents and their impact on the guest experience, hotel and casino properties are covering their bets and employing a variety of approaches. Perfuming the air has become big business, with companies trying to sniff out that elusive scent that will give them a competitive edge.

Many Las Vegas hotels and casinos use a "signature" fragrance to convey the personality or brand of their particular property. The same fragrance is used whether it's in the lobby, guest room, casino, or restaurant. Leading properties further capitalize on their scents by selling resort-branded candles, potpourri, and room fresheners in their shops, so customers can evoke the mood of the resort at home. Fragrance formulations are closely guarded trade secrets. Hotels noted for their scent signatures include Bellagio, the Venetian, and the M Resort, to name just a few.

Off the Las Vegas Strip, hotel properties seem to have a different philosophy. They employ fragrances as location enhancers, using one type of scent in the pool area to make it seem more tropical and yet another fragrance for the lobby or spa. Some properties use as many as nine different fragrances in various locales.

The "scent volume" also differs greatly between properties. Some keep their scents at barely noticeable levels, conveying more of an impression of freshness rather than an identifiable smell, while other properties opt for a more "in-your-face" dispersion tactic. Watchdog groups concerned with indoor air quality find this sort of nasal assault troubling, but actual complaints are rare. Surveys indicate many casino managers/owners are already using fragrances to brand their properties, enhance their ambience, heighten the guest experience, and extend that experience after checkout. Hancock's research suggests "the decision to continue to use or begin including ambient fragrances in the servicescape is a good one."

Studies like Hancock's and LaTour's raise more questions: Would video poker or blackjack players, whose games require more concentration, react to scents differently? Does a pleasing scent influence one's perception of time? What role do cultural factors play in formulating a scent? Can the cost of more expensive natural scents be justified? What are the ethical considerations involved in manipulating sensory perceptions to influence consumer memory and behavior?

UNLV would like to take the lead in answering these types of questions. It's working to establish an Experience Management Institute to further study multisensory marketing and its impact on the hospitality industry. Even though the effects of sensory marketing are not yet fully understood or measured, hotel operators sense they're on to something. And the William F. Harrah College of Hotel Administration smells an opportunity. ■

Questions for Discussion

1. The author states that "Introducing fragrance into the air is part of a growing hospitality industry trend toward multisensory marketing—eliciting favorable impressions not only by what someone sees or hears but also smells, feels, and remembers—to create an overall positive impression about the resort experience" and also "Learning more about people's psychological and physiological responses to strong sensory cues like fragrance can have an impact on consumer behavior." Do you have positive memories about a hotel, resort, coffee shop or restaurant based on the sense of smell? Do you associate any places with a "signature" fragrance?

2. University of Nevada researchers are said to be interested in the following questions: "Would video poker or blackjack players, whose games require more concentration, react to scents differently? Does a pleasing scent influence one's perception of time? What role do cultural factors play in formulating a scent? Can the cost of more expensive natural scents be justified? What are the ethical considerations involved in manipulating sensory perceptions to influence consumer memory and behavior?"

   What ethical considerations do you believe should be involved when businesses seek to use research on sensory perception to influence consumer behavior?

In the following article, Megan O'Neill gives us examples of video "hoaxes" and raises the question of the importance of "truth in advertising." With a growing desire to have their videos "go viral," advertisers are tempted to jump on the bandwagon with ever more sensational elements. Creative videos are enjoyable to watch and good for visibility of businesses, but are they blurring the line between fantasy and reality to the detriment of consumers?

Five Fake Viral Video Campaigns: Great Gimmicks or Bad for Business?

Megan O'Neill

These days it seems like brands and ad agencies will do *anything* in order to go viral, including duping their customers through hoaxes and fake viral video campaigns. From hiring actors to fake "real" events to using special effects to create unbelievable stunts, the art of the hoax has become a very popular advertising tactic. But is it fair play to essentially lie to everyone in order to go viral? Check out these 5 viral advertising hoaxes and decide for yourself—are these campaigns great gimmicks, or are they bad for business?

Liquid Mountaineering

One of the biggest viral marketing hoaxes of all time went down in spring of this year when a documentary-style video about a new sport called Liquid Mountaineering hit YouTube. According to the video, Liquid Mountaineers literally run on top of water, and a lot of people thought that the clip was for real.

When I saw the clip I noticed that the "liquid mountaineers" in the clip briefly mentioned that they used a certain water-resistant shoe to help make walking on water possible. They don't mention the brand name, but do show a quick shot of Hi-Tec shoes. My immediate first thought was that this was a viral marketing campaign from Hi-Tec shoes and I wrote a post about it.

However, I learned shortly thereafter that Hi-Tec was denying having anything to do with the campaign. ClickZ reported speaking with Hi-Tec's US PR manager who said that the company "had zero to do with" the campaign. It was not until about a month after the original video hit the YouTube streams that the company came clean and admitted that the video was a hoax and was in fact a viral campaign for Hi-Tec. They even released a "making of" video, showing how the original Liquid Mountaineering clip was made.

The original video has amassed over 7.6 million views and made the company famous, but at what expense? The company not only duped everyone by creating a ridiculous fake sport, but they went on to lie about their involvement with the project. A lot of people question the company's morals in the situation. Personally, I still think the campaign was brilliant (though I'm a little bummed that these guys can't *actually* walk on water). What do you think?

The Man in the Jacket

Hi-Tec isn't the only brand that has lied about their involvement in a viral video campaign. Back in 2009, an Australian girl named Heidi appeared in a video on YouTube saying that she was looking for a guy she had met in a café. They only spoke for a few minutes, he was wonderful and . . . uh oh! . . . he left his jacket behind! She made the video to find her Prince Charming and return his jacket to him, which just so happens to be a "beautiful" jacket with a "silk lining" and "beautiful striped interior."

Surprise of all surprises—this campaign turned out to be a hoax to promote a big Australian retail company that was putting out a new menswear line! According to *The Age,* both the executive ideas director of the marketing group that created the campaign *and* the actress that starred in the campaign denied that it was a hoax. The actress even went so far as to say, "I don't really understand why someone would do that if it wasn't real. There seems to be a lot of cynical people. Some people don't really think that love is out there any more, really."

Do you think it is okay for people to lie about their involvement in campaigns like this? Is it a breach of ethics or just an innocent part of a bigger joke?

MEGAWOOSH—Bruno Kammerl Jumps

You have probably seen the video of a guy sliding down a huge slip 'n slide and flying through the air to land in a kiddie pool that hit YouTube a couple of summers ago. The video spread like wildfire, getting millions of views in no time flat. People were blown away, and conversation about whether or not it was a hoax took over the web.

Turns out that the video was a fake and was created as part of a Microsoft marketing stunt. If you visit Megawoosh.com you'll find out more.

I remember when I first saw this video my friends and I were pretty sure it was fake, but we hoped it was real. After all, how awesome would it be if someone could actually slide down a hill, fly through the air and land in a kiddie pool? Therefore, when I found out it was a hoax I was totally disappointed. So it really brings up the question of if it's worth it to go viral with something really awesome only to let people down when they find out it's a hoax, or if the millions of views are worth it. What do you think?

Bike Hero

A couple of years ago a video, apparently created by a Guitar Hero fan, hit the web. Called 'Bike Hero', the video shows a guy riding his bike on a Guitar Hero-inspired course. In the video description it says, "Can't tell you how many times it took to make this work, but it was a lot."

The truth of the matter is, it probably didn't take a lot of times to "make this work" because it wasn't real. It came out that ad agency Droga5 was behind the campaign, which included credits from a CG artist and supervisor, an animation supervisor, and visual effect specialists. Personally, I'm not sure why Droga5 and Guitar Hero were so secretive about this one, and tried to make it look like a fan video. I think it is cool regardless of whether CG artists were involved. But what do I know?

Proposal in Central Park

Finally, this month a proposal video has been getting a lot of coverage due to the fact that a lot of people think it's actually a fake viral created to promote Apple or an iPhone application. Check the video out on YouTube and see what you think.

In the video description, the creators of the video respond to the idea that people think it's a viral video:

"Based on some of the comments on this video, many seem to believe that this is some type of viral video marketing campaign for an Apple product (which we think is awesome) so we want to thank Dave and Mike for the amazing editing on this video, which apparently fooled many."

However, as we have seen from other campaigns, just because someone denies that their video is a hoax or a viral campaign doesn't really prove anything.

I have to say that I do think this is a fake proposal video (sorry Frank and Kasey if you really exist, I'm not necessarily calling you or your proposal fake, just the video). There are a whole variety of reasons why I don't think this is real. For starters, these people just don't seem that real and genuine—they seem like they are acting. I mean, who would get *this* excited about a not-so-great rendition of 'Stand By Me' by a guy that doesn't even know all the lyrics? But aside from that, it looks like the video was shot from about a million different angles a million different times. When she says "Yes! Yes! Yes!" to his proposal we first see a shot from his perspective on a boat and she is alone on the bridge. When we cut to a close up of her on the bridge, suddenly there are a bunch of people standing next to her.

Other viewers have pointed out more inconsistencies, such as the fact that Kasey's bag mysteriously disappears and reappears throughout the video. There's also the fact that Frank throws the ring to her on the bridge, which has a *huge* diamond in it if you believe what you see on the website they set up at FrankAndKasey.com. Would you throw a huge diamond from a boat up onto a bridge? What if she didn't catch it?

That being said, I'm not sure I agree with all the people that think this is a fake Apple viral. I don't think that the fact that they are using their iPhones really contributed anything to the proposal, and I think that if it was coming from Apple then we would see more of the "cool factor." How did the phones contribute to the proposal? Why would the proposal have not been possible without them? In my opinion, the proposal could have worked out just as well without the phones. If it turns out that Apple was behind this, I'm going to be super disappointed.

I also should point out that just because I think the proposal *video* isn't real that I'm still not totally closed to the chance that actual proposal was real. Maybe the way that they shot it just made it look a little bit more fake than it actually was. It's clear that they didn't have enough camera men to tape the entire thing in one take, so they had to go back to embellish. They mention in the comments that, "Once the proposal was over and the couple took off in a boat, the crew filmed the band's 'Stand By Me' performance one more time to get all necessary close-up shots for the editing." Maybe this group of friends had seen the rash of proposal videos going viral on YouTube and decided to jump on the bandwagon but wanted to upload something that looked really professional. Unfortunately, the style in which it was shot just made it look like a hoax. I don't want to be super cynical, say it's fake 100 percent and not give romance a chance, after all!

That being said, I've got a feeling that soon FrankAndCasey.com will turn out to be a promotional site for some sort of iPhone app that lets you stream live video to your phone, like the app the people in the video are using. But here's hoping I'm wrong, the proposal was real, romance isn't dead and Frank and Kasey will live happily ever after.

It doesn't look like fake viral video campaigns are going anywhere fast. From a fake toy commercial to promote Pixar's Toy Story 3 to director Michel Gondry solving a Rubik's cube with his feet, cell phones popping popcorn and more, I think that brands and ad agencies will fake it to make it for as long as web video exists. What are your thoughts about viral hoaxes? Are they a great way to go viral or a dirty scheme? ▨

Questions for Discussion

1. The author discusses several examples of fake viral videos and then asks, "Are these campaigns great gimmicks or are they bad for business?" How would you respond to her question?

2. Because of the fake videos the author has seen, she suspects that the Frank and Casey wedding proposal is also a fake. Note the author's reasoning process as she considers the elements of the video. Do you believe that video is a product placement ad for Apple or a genuine proposal?

3. Do you believe that fake videos are unethical? To what extent, if any, do you believe that there should be some sort of advisory to the viewer when a video for a product is fictional?

. . . .

The following excerpt is from a review of a book called *The Tyranny of E-Mail*. The author of the book asks us to stop and look at how e-mail and other forms of electronic communication have been a great convenience but have also brought an ever-increasing pressure to keep up with both personal and work-related media. He also discusses the irony that the Web that connects us more readily and broadly also makes us more isolated from one another.

We often feel pressured to keep up with both personal and work-related e-mail.

The Tyranny of E-Mail

John Freeman

Communication—the conveyance of meaning from one person to the next—depends on how we frame it. The second-most important question we must face, after choosing to communicate at all, becomes how to deliver what we want to say . . . You can write your message in the sky, send it by singing telegram, speak into voice mail, shove it in the post, and hope for the best. You can write it in free verse, broadcast it to three hundred of your closest friends on Facebook, fire off an instant message, post it to your Twitter channel. If we think of modes of communication as a mirror spectrum of the human voice, we have as many registers as our mouths can make. The telex machine may have died, but most copy shops and offices still have fax machines. Phone booths still huddle, in various states of molestation, on many street corners. We can sign a message, pantomime it, text it, shoot a video message, record it as a song, upload a declaration of love onto YouTube, chalk it on pavement, scratch it on a tree trunk.

In his book *The Gift,* Lewis Hyde argues that one of the most effective ways to send a message into the world is to wrap it in a form that only it can possess and give it away. Why buy a card when you can make one? Why sermonize when you can write a sonnet? But how many of us have the time for this—or the skill? All over the world we are working longer hours than ever, sleeping fewer winks, taking shorter vacations. In this environment, frazzled and fried, tied to a machine that gazes back at us more hours per day than even our spouses do, we do what makes the most sense: we send our messages the fastest way possible.

The Inbox of Kings

In June 2004, the Internet giant Google made an announcement that quietly marked the apotheosis of the e-mail age. Gmail, its Web-based mail program, would offer users unlimited storage. Imagine for a moment what this means. Thanks to a group of 450,000 machines scattered across the United States like underground missile bunkers, I could store more e-mails than there are blades of grass in Kansas. This is beyond unprecedented—it is superhuman. Is God's inbox this big? Prior to the electronic age, dictators and kings did not enjoy such epistolary armories.

Still, their capacity is dwarfed by the Herculean arms of an everyday individual's e-mail inbox today. What busy individual needs this industrial-strength capability for his correspondence tool? What buzzing, humming megalopolis tunes in to this techno-rave of send and receive, send and receive? Is the human brain wired to receive this much stimuli? Can our eyes scan this many separate pieces of information? Is anyone listening? Who is it behind the screens, tapping the bellows and pumping the organ keys of this huge, throbbing machine at all hours of the night?

For the Love of E-Mail

The answer, of course, is us. We love e-mail. In 2007, 35 trillion messages shot back and forth between the world's 1 billion PCs; in the time it took you to read to this point, some 300 million e-mails were sent and received. They sluiced down corporate drainpipes, piled onto listservs, promising a return on investment in a small African country and providing jokes about pigs and news about your grandmother's heart surgery. According to a Stanford University survey, 90 percent of all Internet users have e-mail. In 2009, it has been estimated, the average corporate worker will spend more than 40 percent of his or her day sending and receiving some two hundred messages. Instead of walking down the hall, picking up the phone, or sending an interoffice memo, we e-mail.

E-mail goes with us everywhere now. We check it on the subway, we check it in the bath. We check it before bed and upon waking up. We check it even in midconversation, blithely assuming that no one will notice. We check from our loved ones' deathbeds. Even the most powerful people in the world do it. On most days during the 2008 presidential race, Barack Obama's BlackBerry "was fastened to his belt—to provide a singular conduit to the outside world as the bubble around him grew tighter and tighter throughout his campaign." President George W. Bush, who received 15 thousand e-mails a day at the White House, said that one thing he looked forward to after leaving office was e-mailing. There is even a service that allows you to send an e-mail after you're dead. If there is an hour or a minute or a second to spare, e-mail is there. It is our electronic fidget.

It's hard to blame us. Once broadband connection arrived, e-mail became the world's most convenient communication tool. Not much more than a dozen years ago, most of us printed letters out, placed them in envelopes, and then walked or drove them to the post office, where we waited in line, wasting more time, so that the letter could arrive in maybe a week. The U.S. Postal Service estimated that, even if 99.8 percent of e-mails do not replace a letter, the sheer volume of e-mail means that more than 2 billion pieces of mail are diverted electronically each year. And that's just personal correspondence. Between 1999 and 2005, the number of people who opted to pay their bills electronically rather than by mail diverted 3 billion pieces of mail. In the postal world, this replacement of tangible mail with electronic communication is called electronic erosion—and some of this is a good thing. Today we can type a note on our computer in New York and it will be received in New Zealand in nanoseconds. We use e-mail to send documents, music, wills, photographs, spreadsheets, and floor plans, communicate with our banks, send invitations. We no longer have to fill out those irritating forms to receive a return receipt by post, proof that our important letter arrived. The computer does it for us. We can even get a message the moment someone opens our e-mail. In just this one area, e-mail has given us back several days each year.

But it would appear that we are spending that surplus time e-mailing. The average office worker sends and receives 200 e-mails a day—and that figure is rising. Forget about time spent stumbling absentmindedly around the Internet; this habit is destroying our ability to be productive. Information overload is a $650 billion drag on the U.S. economy every year. E-mail has made us a workforce of reactors, racing to keep up with a treadmill pace that is bound for burnout and breakdown and profound anger.

The form's inherent blind spots always catch up with us. According to a survey in the *Journal of Personality and Social Psychology,* we misunderstand the tone of e-mails 50 percent of the time—and for good reason: there is no face on the other end to stop us in midsentence, to indicate that what we are in the process of saying is rude, not comprehended, or cruel. We say what we want, like the CEO who recently belittled the effect of mortgage foreclosures, inadvertently sending the e-mail to someone who had just lost his home. The unlucky call this mistaken judgment. Psychologists call it disinhibition, and its pervasive effect—as can be witnessed every day in nasty comments appended to newspaper articles online, in the aggrieved tone and intent of some blog postings, in e-mail inboxes scorched by flame wars—has turned many parts of the Internet into a nasty place.

It's tempting to simply argue that the Internet attracts aggressive people. But all of us, at some point or other, have behaved poorly over the Internet and via e-mail. There's a reason for these communication hiccups and explosions. According to some neurologists, we learn to interact with the world by mirroring others; not only do we need to see people to understand them most effectively, but our mind learns how to move our limbs and make sense of the world by mirroring the actions of others. There are even neurons in our brain that fire only in response to mirroring the actions of others, and they are intimately connected with the parts of our brain that allow us to move and understand the world. The part of our brain that controls grasping motions shows heightened levels of neural activity when we see someone else pick up a glass of orange juice, as if we were doing it ourselves. According to Marco Iacoboni, professor of psychiatry and behavioral sciences at UCLA, this has bolstered the notion that "our mental processes are shaped by our bodies and by the types of perceptual and motor experiences that are the product of our movement through and interaction with the surrounding world." Consider, then, the ramifications of an era of communication in which we are disembodied as never before. In our new context of e-mail overload, we are working in an environment in which there is nothing to mirror but our own words.

Beating Back the E-Mail Tsunami

Who has time to think clearly when under assault by this tsunami of other people's needs? That's what it feels like when you turn on your computer first thing in the morning at the office and find 50 e-mails, the tide of your inbox always rising. One's instinct is to beat it back because e-mail has reoriented time; communication that once took hours, days, minutes, now takes seconds, and the permitted reply time has shrunk as well. Let an e-mail linger for a day, and you risk a rift in a relationship. A 2006 Cisco research paper concluded that failing to respond to a sender can lead to a swift breakdown in trust. Lose an e-mail forever, and you are sitting on an unexploded land mine.

In the past, only a few professions—doctors, plumbers perhaps, emergency service technicians, prime ministers—required this kind of state of being constantly on call. Now almost all of us live this way. Everything must be attended to—and if it isn't, chances are another e-mail will appear in a few hours asking if indeed the first message was received at all.

In the face of this ever-rising onslaught, there appear to be just two choices: keep up at all costs or put up a moat, declare oneself unreachable for the time being—and start all over again.

. . . In the beginning, this first type of e-mailer—the tech-savvy fellow who sent and received a few hundred e-mails a day—was called a "power user," who took technology and made the most of it. Now every white-collar employee is expected to be one. Not surprisingly, workshops and office coaches will tell you the problem isn't the technology or even the work ethic—it's ourselves. We have bad habits; we reply to all; we waste time treating e-mail as if it were an instant message tool, asking open-ended questions—"How are you doing?"—in the middle of the day. Get it together. You can keep up if you try. But is this really possible when most of us have a water cooler inside our computer surrounded by five thousand people, all talking at once?

In the Western and well-to-do parts of the world, in offices in Dubai and Duluth and Dunkirk, the world's workers are typing themselves into a corner, ever farther out of touch with people beyond their sphere. Walk down a corridor in many companies, and it is eerily silent. You might think it was Christmas morning. In some places, all you hear is the ambient hum of the central air-conditioning unit, the creak of Aeron chairs, the cricketlike click of the mouse, and the faint clatter of keystrokes. But if you lean into cubicles or peer between doorways, you will see hunched, tense figures at their computers frantically trying to keep up with their inboxes. Interrupt them, and you will find their expressions glazed, their eyes dried out and weary. Their keyboard has become a messaging conveyor belt—and there is no break time.

This electronic conversational buzzing has become so loud, it's easy to forget there are people who are not taking part in it. To e-mail one has to be literate, have access to a machine, and be connected. The world's netizen population is approaching 2 billion, but this means only one-third of us are taking part in this enormously useful, endlessly irritating tool. Technology, so often assumed to be the cure for the world's inequalities, has once again simply transplanted them into a new space where English has become the new superlanguage. Africa may be home to 14 percent of the world's population, but it accounts for just 3 percent of the earth's Internet users.

. . . To read an e-mail, you must be joined to an electronic machine. What does this machine want? Besides following our commands, it is a machine deeply, fundamentally connected to commerce. More often than anything else, it wants us to work. The new on-the-ball employee proves his worth by his speed of response—at work, at night, on the weekends, on vacations, the instant the announcement is made that it is now safe to use approved electronic devices on airplanes.

This ethic of being "always on" extends to the home, where it acquires a consumerist dimension. Web-based e-mail, which is used by more than 1 billion people worldwide, remains free because it allows host companies—such as Yahoo!, Google, and Microsoft—to deliver advertising messages to people refreshing their inbox screen. Every time your screen reloads, a cluster of messages and graphics coalesces in the margins, blinking and beckoning. It frames what you are about to write or read. We are approaching a world in which every letter we write home, every love poem we read, every condolence note, political petition, and letter of apology we type is framed by a penumbra of automobile ads, perfume pitches, entreaties to enter online gambling emporiums.

Faster, Faster

Speed—the god of the twenty-first century—is not a neutral deity, as it turns out. The speed at which we communicate determines what we can do, what we can see, how we perceive, and whether we can adjust our own sense of reality to a larger, more complex frame of reference, one that encompasses the separate needs and points of view of others. Look out a window of a train traveling at full speed, and you will witness this phenomenon at work. The eye constantly darts to the horizon, only to be overwhelmed by a new horizon point, which comes racing forward, followed by another and another. The eye quickly becomes fatigued. The scenery is a blur.

Working at the speed of e-mail is like trying to gain a topographic understanding of our daily landscape from a speeding train—and the consequences for us as workers are profound. Interrupted every 30 seconds or so, our attention spans are fractured into a thousand tiny fragments. The mind is denied the experience of deep flow, when creative ideas flourish and complicated thinking occurs. We become task-oriented, tetchy, terrible at listening as we try to keep up with the computer. The e-mail inbox turns our mental to-do list into a palimpsest—there's always something new and even more urgent erasing what we originally thought was the day's priority. Incoming mail arrives on several different channels—via e-mail, Facebook, Twitter, instant message—and in this era of backup we're sure that we should keep records of our participation in all these conversations. The result is that at the end of the day we have a few hundred or even a few thousand e-mails still sitting in our inbox.

We're not lazy; the computer is just far better than the human mind at batching and sorting. E-mail travels to and from computers circuitously, starting with our fingers, which type the characters. Our jokes and jabs are eventually translated into 0s and 1s, fired off through cable and phone lines, and reassembled upon the point of arrival, not unlike a car that has been shipped to the United States from Japan in pieces and assembled there once all the parts have arrived at the port and been sent by train to assembly plants, as one technology writer once put it. Computers and e-mail software are designed to know which parts of the chains belong to which; they can wait for a message to arrive fully before delivering it, and they can do so on a scale that is suprahuman. The computer is the ultimate multitasker—it doesn't need to pause to write down reminders to itself on a yellow Post-it note. It doesn't have emotional needs. It doesn't have days when it is depressed. It needn't touch a single thing to feel okay about doing its job.

. . . When we are pummeled by ads, awash in representations of the world, is it any surprise that the real-world commons—a shared space in which people of all sorts can meet and interact—has been shunted aside for its electronic simulacra? Instead of driving down the road to our local bookstore, where we might actually talk to someone, we buy a book over Amazon.com or Barnesandnoble.com; rather than go into the bank, we check our balance from home; rather than buy the newspaper from a paperboy who comes to collect the monthly bill, we read it online, for free. These are all conveniences, significant ones for the busy, for people who live in remote locations, or for people for whom face-to-face conversation is inordinately stressful, but the upshot is that we spend less time dealing face-to-face with other human beings and more time before a machine.

Thirty years ago, in *The Society of the Spectacle,* the French philosopher Guy Debord predicted we would be spending more time apart. "The reigning economic system is founded on isolation," he wrote. "At the same time it is a circular process designed to produce isolation. Isolation underpins technology, and technology isolates in its turn; all goods proposed by the spectacular system, from cars to televisions, also serve as weapons for that system, as it strives to reinforce the isolation of 'the lonely crowd.'" To this list of machines we can now also add the Internet and e-mail.

Ironically, tools meant to connect us are enabling us to spend even more time apart.

The most glaring discovery of the Stanford University study mentioned earlier was not that people burned up two hours a day on the Internet but that those two hours came out of time they would normally spend with family and friends. Once that withdrawal has begun and technology has been identified as a way to connect, it's a hard cycle to break. We blog, broadcast our vacations on YouTube, obsessively update the newsfeeds of our Facebook pages —"Today, Brian is feeling happy"—as if an experience, an emotion, a task completed hasn't actually happened unless it has been recorded and shared with others. E-mail is the biggest, broadest highway on which this outward projection occurs. Why write a postcard about your trip to France to one friend when you can simply forward and copy the message to all your friends? Why tell a coworker you have performed an arduous piece of labor when you can cc several others and make sure they know it, too?

In the twenty-first century, writing and "publishing" have become easier than ever—and reading, due to the amount of material available to read and the rate at which we are communicating, has become harder than ever. This wouldn't be quite so untenable an environment if we were actually seeing each other face-to-face. But the drop in face-to-face contact has taken this epistemological fracture and given it an emotional dimension. We have all the tools in the world, yet we've never felt more alone. By depriving ourselves of facial expressions and the tangible frisson of physical contact, we are facing a terrible loss of meaning in individual life. The difference between a smiley face and an actual smile is too large to calculate. Nothing—especially "lol"—can quite convey the sound of a friend's laughter.

. . . The tyranny of e-mail has also entered a feedback cycle that makes it ever harder to reflect on how bad the situation has become. Spending our days communicating through this medium, which by virtue of its sheer volume forces us to talk in short bursts, we are slowly eroding our ability to explain—in a careful, complex way—why it is so wrong for us and to complain, resist, or redesign our workdays so that they are manageable. The book *The Tyranny of E-Mail* is an attempt to slow things down for a moment so we can look at the enormous shift in time and space e-mail has effected, how e-mail has changed our lives, our culture and workplace, our psychological well-being. No one can predict the future of a technology, and this book is certainly not going to try, but it is essential, especially when that technology has become as prevalent and pervasive as e-mail, to examine its effects and assumptions and make an attempt to understand it in a broader context.

We are evidently remaking our environment, so it's fair to ask: What does this new world look like? What are its roots? How does the technology upon which it runs affect what we can say or how we say it? Should we have a correspondence list in the thousands? Does this way of living seem natural or even sustainable? Surrounded by the plastics, polystyrenes, and chemicals of the modern workplace, our bodies have an instinctual memory of something more natural. This metaphysical nostalgia, which Alan Weisman beautifully describes in *The World Without Us,* is a source of profound anxiety, and not the kind that can be medicated or wrested into submission. Speed cannot mask this anxiety, either; it only destroys our ability to reconnect with something actual.

Ever since humans emerged from Plato's cave, we have tried to communicate with each other. Sounds turned into pictures, which turned into phonetics, which were eventually written down and codified, printed on clay, then parchment, then on paper. Mail has existed since at least the ninth century in Persia. The printing press allowed a person to address a multitude without being there to say it to them (or copy it by hand). It took hundreds of years, however, for books to become widely accessible. And it took yet more time for those books and newspapers and letters to be shipped from one city or continent to the next. And then societies had to help their citizens become literate for these publications to be read in large numbers.

In the nineteenth and twentieth centuries, however, we leapt from the speed of transport to the speed of electricity. The telegram allowed people to address each other one to one, within a day, at a price so cheap it eclipsed that of the long-distance phone call. Twenty million telegrams were sent in 1929 alone, this when the world's population was 1.5 billion. Today, the world is home to 6 billion people and roughly 600 million e-mails are sent every ten minutes. Stop for a moment to imagine the ramifications of this exponential increase in communication, and the necessity for a pause cries out like an air-raid siren.

Previous generations, however giddy they became about the best technology, did stop and think—if briefly. Samuel F. B. Morse sent the first telegram to go through in the United States, from Washington to Baltimore, in May 1844, with the message WHAT HATH GOD WROUGHT. By contrast, the first e-mail ever sent using the @ symbol was mailed from one supercomputer to the next in all caps, and according to Ray Tomlinson, the man who sent it, the message contained just a random series of letters and numbers. In other words: gibberish. He just wanted to see if it would arrive and so didn't bother to type anything providential.

It's about time we asked ourselves a more articulate question: What have we wrought?

. . . Each communication breakthrough has encouraged individuality while expanding the notion of the commons beyond the tangible or nearby. But for many of us the creation of the Internet has done one thing none of these leaps forward in communication history could: It has tied us irrevocably, perhaps fatally, to a machine and its superhuman capability. If we are to understand our predicament today, we must reckon with the changes that working at this machine has wrought and examine whether there is a way we can slow down, so we can make the best use of it while retaining a foothold in the real-world commons. Otherwise, we will have bridged the darkness only to introduce ourselves into one of another, more relentless kind. ▪

Questions for Discussion

1. The author summarizes our pervasive use of e-mail by stating, "Instead of walking down the hall, picking up the phone, or sending an interoffice memo, we e-mail. E-mail goes with us everywhere now. We check it on the subway, we check it in the bath. We check it before bed and upon waking up. We check it even in mid-conversation, blithely assuming that no one will notice. We check from our loved ones' deathbeds." Have you noted the same constant e-mailing in your environment?

2. The book under review is entitled, *The Tyranny of E-Mail*. To what extent do you feel pressured to answer e-mails, as well as Facebook messages, tweets, and text messages? How much of your day is used sending and receiving messages electronically?

3. Do you notice the advertisements and "breaking news" items that show up when you check your e-mail? How much time do you spend checking those items? How much time do you spend deleting spam and irrelevant e-mails?

4. The author seeks to examine the effect of hours every day tied to our e-mails and other messages. He asks, "How does the technology upon which it runs affect what we can say or how we say it? Should we have a correspondence list in the thousands? Does this way of living seem natural or even sustainable?" To what extent do you believe that individuals and organizations can or should address the tyrannical nature of e-mail as well as voicemail and texting?

5. According to research cited in the article, "we misunderstand the tone of e-mails 50 percent of the time—and for good reason: there is no face on the other end to stop us in midsentence, to indicate that what we are in the process of saying is rude, not comprehended, or cruel." Have you misunderstood the tone of an e-mail sent to you, and has someone misunderstood an e-mail that you sent? How do you believe that communication and interpersonal relationships have changed and will continue to change through electronic technology?

Ideas for Writing or Speaking

1. Respond to one of the following quotes by the late author, media critic, and professor Neil Postman; Postman wrote many significant books on media and American culture, including his classic *Amusing Ourselves to Death*. Support your thesis statement with evidence from radio, television, advertising, newspapers, magazines, journals, books, or websites.

    "Indeed, we may have reached the point where cosmetics has replaced ideology as the field of expertise over which a politician must have competent control."[65]

    "The shape of a man's body is largely irrelevant to the shape of his ideas when he is addressing a public in writing or on the radio or, for that matter, in smoke signals. But it is quite relevant on television."[66]

    "It would seem that right now, Americans are more interested in entertainment than any other aspect of personal life. . . . Las Vegas would do just fine as a symbol [of America]."[67]

    "How many people when seeing a newscast about say a serious earthquake or an airplane crash will actually start to cry or grow silent at the tragedies of life? Most of us don't because right after the story of the airplane crash there's going to be a thing for Burger King or if not that a story about the World Series or some other event that basically would say, 'Now listen, don't take this thing about the airplane crash too seriously, it's just something to amuse you for the moment, and we certainly don't want you to be morose when we get to the airlines commercial because we'd like you to be in a sort of upbeat mood to sell you a trip to San Francisco.'"[68]

2. Analyze one of the more successful television programs, and draw some specific conclusions about why it is successful. Support your conclusions with reasons. Consider the images the program projects about the people it represents.

    Another approach to this assignment would be to contrast programs that are popular now with shows (or films) that were popular in the past. Write about

---

[65] Neil Postman, *Amusing Ourselves to Death* (New York: Viking Press, 1985), p. 4.

[66] Ibid., p. 7.

[67] Neil Postman quoted by Stephen Marshall, "Prelude to Vegas," online interview @ channel zero.

[68] Ibid., p. 26.

the different cultural, economic, or historical elements influencing these shows or films; it would be interesting to take programs from different decades for this assignment. Here are some questions to think about as you watch these programs: What was acceptable in the past but is in some way unacceptable now? What is acceptable now that would have been considered unacceptable in the past?

3. Discuss the influence of media on culture. To what extent do video games, films, and television *reflect* cultural norms and to what extent do they *create* them? Given your answer, what considerations, if any, should media producers make before approving new projects?

    To narrow your topic, you might consider the effects of television on children, using statistics from the Henry J. Kaiser Family Foundation study of viewing habits. According to their findings, in January 2010, most youth have no rules about the amount of time they spend on media.

    > With technology allowing nearly 24-hour media access as children and teens go about their daily lives, the amount of time young people spend with entertainment media has risen dramatically, especially among minority youth, according to a study released today by the Kaiser Family Foundation. Today, 8–18 year-olds devote an average of 7 hours and 38 minutes (7:38) to using entertainment media across a typical day (more than 53 hours a week). And because they spend so much of that time "media multitasking" (using more than one medium at a time), they actually manage to pack a total of 10 hours and 45 minutes (10:45) worth of media content into those 7½ hours.

    The Kaiser report details the effects of media on grades, minority youth, and "tweens." For more information, read the full report at http://www.kff.org/entmedia/entmedia012010nr.cfm.

4. Think about the statement: "You can tell the ideals of a nation by its advertisements."[69] What does our current advertising say about our culture's ideals? Consider values, roles of men and women, the view of the elderly, the importance of technology, and the use of time and space. Support your position with at least six examples from both print and electronic media.

5. Writer Joseph Giordano states, "An important cause of distorted and damaging TV stereotypes is the tendency of some media executives to view ethnic culture as an 'immigrant phenomenon,' a transitional phase in the process of Americanization rather than a continuing influence on people's language, religious lives, arts, politics, food preferences and so on."[70] Should the media strive to emphasize our similarities, differences, or both? Provide reasons for your answer.

6. In discussing ethnic and religious traditions, Giordano also states, "At times, these traditions conflict with surrounding values, but they are also sources of strength and understanding. How they work in second-, third-, and fourth-generation families can provide a rich store of story ideas and authentic characterizations for writers, directors, and actors."[71] Do you believe there are

[69] Norman Douglas, *South Wind* (London: Nartin Secker & Warburg, 1917), p. 64.
[70] Joseph Giordano, "Promoting Pluralism," *Media and Values*, Winter 1987.
[71] Ibid.

television programs that highlight the positive influence of an ethnic or cultural heritage? If so, discuss how a particular program honors ethnic culture. If not, write a proposal for a television program or a feature-length film centered around a tradition that provides strength and cultural understanding to an individual or group. How could a program like this be used to increase cultural understanding in a pluralistic society?

7. Critics have accused television news of functioning primarily as a form of entertainment. Watch several news programs and respond to these critics. To what extent do you agree or disagree with them and why? Give specific examples to support your answer.

8. Collect your junk mail or "spam" for two or three weeks without opening it. Then analyze it by answering these questions:

   a. How did you recognize it as junk mail or spam?
   b. What techniques does the sender use to entice you to open the envelope or the e-mail?
   c. Once opened, what techniques are used to prompt you to read further than the first line?
   d. Are these techniques effective? Consider graphic design, placement of key words, the way you are addressed, special offers, enticements, and deadlines.

9. Write an essay or speech about your viewpoint on the following quote by former Missouri Senator John Danforth:

   What people see when they turn on the TV is violence. What they see is sex. What they see is total disrespect for family and for authority, and what they see is stereotypes. And this is, in my opinion, a very large part of the problem. The medium of television right now is disgusting. So are many of the movies that people see. And I think that one way to start on this problem is to have a summit meeting perhaps called by the President which brings together people who are leaders of broadcast, the broadcast networks, people who are leaders of cable television, of the motion picture industry, and ask them what responsibility they have for this country, other than squeezing every last dime they can out of it.[72]

Films for Analysis and Discussion

The Greatest Movie Ever Sold, (2011, P.G. 13)

Morgan Spurlock, who also directed *Supersize Me,* was inspired to make this movie about product placement after he watched an episode of *Heroes* in which the main character raves about a particular car model. He realized that the public has come to accept blatant product placements, and his film is a spoof of the advertising and marketing industry's use of this technique. Spurlock also looks at how products are being marketed to children when companies advertise in schools in exchange for educational funding. Ironically, many companies paid to place their products in Spurlock's film, and their sponsorship made the film possible.

---

[72] From the *MacNeil-Lehrer Newshour,* televised May 9, 1992. Interview with Senator John Danforth.

Similar Films and Classics

The Social Network (2010, PG-13)

This film aims to show how Facebook was created by Mark Zuckerberg and how the network revolutionized the way we communicate in a very short time, speeding up and expanding our ability to connect with others. Zuckerberg has disputed the accuracy of the film, but the producers insist that the content about the founding of the social network is based on public records. The filmmakers do admit that the character of Zuckerberg is fictionalized. For example, they portray him as lonely and without meaningful relationships, but he has had a steady girlfriend since his sophomore year of college.

State of Play (2009, PG-13)

The tagline of this thriller is "Find the Truth." Russell Crowe plays an investigative reporter who, according to Jerry B, a writer for socialmedia.com ("The Internet Is Killing America's Free Press and Why It Matters"), explains why he spends so much time checking and re-checking leads, working his sources, and making sure he has all the verifiable and double-sourced facts available before he lets go of a story: "I still think they (readers) know the difference between real news and b.s.," he says. "And they're glad that someone cares enough to get things on the record and print the truth."

Thank You for Smoking (2006, R)

This film is a testament to the spin culture of American media. Aaron Eckhart plays Nick Naylor, a lobbyist for Big Tobacco and a master of spinning the truth so that it always lands in favor of his employer. The first scene of the movie shows Naylor convincing a talk show crowd that he cares about lung cancer victims because he doesn't want to lose them as clients. This is satire that takes no prisoners, smartly observing how media can make truth a relative term.

The Truman Show (1998, PG)

This movie is a humorous but also serious look at how the line between reality and fantasy can become blurred by television programming. Since his birth, Truman has been placed on a beautiful Hollywood set and everyone he interacts with is a paid actor. Truman doesn't know that millions are watching the reality show of his life and that what he considers his real world is being limited and exploited by the producer of his popular show.

Broadcast News (1987, R)

This film follows the struggles of a network news producer who resists the growing trend toward "news as entertainment" and must decide between style and substance in both her professional life and her romantic life.

Network (1976, R)

An aging news anchor has lost his strong ratings and is given two weeks' notice by his network. His reaction to the firing provides an excellent and comic commentary on the effects of sensationalism.

Meet John Doe (1936)

John Doe, a man who writes a letter protesting social ills and threatening a dramatic suicide is the creation of Ann Mitchell, a fired reporter who is expressing her own frustrations. When the public shows great concern for the fictional letter writer, the paper has to rehire Ann and also hire a man to impersonate her fictional character. The film provides food for thought about how entire political and social movements can be fueled by a story made up by a reporter and covered up by her paper.

9

Fair-Mindedness

It's You and Me, Kid,
and I'm Not So Sure About You.

A critical thinker is aware of egocentrism, ethnocentrism, and the effect of emotions on judgment.

A critical thinker listens and responds to opposing viewpoints with empathy and fair-mindedness.

Critical thinkers are aware of their own biases and willing to consider the viewpoints of others.

- Defense mechanisms that cloud our thinking
- The effect of conformity on critical thought
- Rational approaches to emotional reasoning
- Points of logical vulnerability
- Active listening techniques that foster open-mindedness and empathy

▭●┤Read on **mythinkinglab.com**

((●┤Listen on **mythinkinglab.com**

Centuries ago, we learned, contrary to our previous beliefs, that the earth is not the center of the universe. We discovered that the sun does not revolve around the earth; instead our earth, along with the other planets, revolves around the sun.

The fact that we tended to see our earth as predominant reveals the self-centered nature of our perception of reality. That self-centered perspective did not die out with our ancestors; we still tend to view the world from our own individual and group perspectives. Fortunately, however, along with our limited viewpoints, we also have the ability to discover and test new information and to make "course corrections" in our theories and our behavior.

Just as our ancestors made corrections to their theories and actions when confronted with inescapable facts, we as a culture are regularly changing our ideas and behavior when new understanding warrants changes. For example, in the face of increasingly credible threats to our environment, we are rejecting the assumption that the earth is infinitely supplied with renewable resources. Instead, we are focusing on conservation and preservation of our environment as a crucial issue, viewing our resources as precious rather than expendable and searching for alternative sources of energy.

Advances in media technology have enabled us to get a more complete picture of the global interdependence of not only our physical environment but also the world's people. When we see how others live and the problems they face, we can be less ethnocentric. **Ethnocentrism** (sometimes called **sociocentrism**) is the tendency to view one's own race or culture as central, based on the deep-seated belief that one's own group is superior to all others.[1] We can only hold on to ethnocentrism when we consider other cultures as less important or deserving than our own. Such an attitude of superiority is harmful to the dialogue that must proceed as decisions are made that involve a diverse and increasingly interdependent world.

ethnocentrism (sociocentrism) The tendency to view one's own race or culture as central, based on the deep-seated belief that one's own group is superior to all others.

[1] Richard Paul, *Critical Thinking* (Rohnert Park, CA: Center for Critical Thinking and Moral Critique, 1990), p. 549.

Fair-mindedness   A trait of a critical thinker involving respect for others, willingness to hear and understand different viewpoints on an issue, and an openness to change when new information or insight warrants change.

egocentrism   The individual version of ethnocentrism, the tendency to view everything else in relationship to oneself; one's desires, values, beliefs, and actions seem to be self-evidently correct or superior to those of others.

A critical thinker can counter ethnocentrism by developing the trait of fair-mindedness. **Fair-mindedness** involves

1.   A respect for people whose ethnicities and traditions are different from our own,

2.   A willingness to hear and understand other viewpoints, and

3.   An openness to change when new information or insight warrants that change.

Egocentrism, the individual version of ethnocentrism, has been defined as a tendency to view everything else in relationship to oneself; one's desires, values, and beliefs (seeming to be self-evidently correct or superior to those of others) are uncritically used as the norm of all judgment and experience. Some psychologists believe that this tendency is rooted in early childhood, when we typically engage in what is called "mine is better" thinking. We see our own toys, family, pets, and sports teams as better than everyone else's, and this perception can continue throughout life if it remains unquestioned. Egocentrism has been called one of the fundamental impediments to critical thinking.[2] To be a logical, fair, and less egocentric thinker, we can learn several skills. We can learn:

1.   To recognize the basic defense mechanisms we use to distort reality and to deceive others and ourselves

2.   To recognize areas where we, for whatever reasons, have trouble being rational

3.   To understand and have empathy for someone else's viewpoint

There is nothing wrong with taking strong, even immovable, stands on issues; we don't want to be so open-minded that we have no core beliefs or opinions at all. What is not reasonable or logical is taking a strong stand without having thought carefully and honestly about all of the relevant factors involved in an issue. And the most fair, ethical, and persuasive attitude is one of respect and courtesy to those with whom we disagree.

Stop and Think

Author and speaker Ravi Zacharias defines one's "worldview" as the cumulative answer to four questions: Where did I come from? What is life's meaning? How do I define right from wrong, and what happens to me when I die? Those are the fulcrum points of our existence.[3] How do different individuals answer those questions?

How We Defend Our Egos

Are you thinking or are you just rearranging your prejudices?

Walter Martin

People who are fair-minded are aware of the natural weaknesses that come with being an individual human. The best place to start in understanding our weak points

---

[2] Ibid., p. 548.

[3] Julia Duin, "Christian Worldview: An Interview with Ravi Zacharias," *The Washington Times,* WashingtonTimes.com, 2003 (accessed August, 2007).

in reasoning is to examine human defense mechanisms. Defense mechanisms are "the clever ways we deceive ourselves, protect ourselves, and extract ourselves from uncomfortable situations—they are negative escape hatches that offer us temporary treatments for persistent problems."[4] **Defense mechanisms** are strategies we use to avoid uncomfortable realities and to "protect" ourselves from changing our perspectives and behaviors. For our purposes, we will consider two major defense mechanisms that interfere with clear thinking: rationalization and denial.

Rationalization is a defense mechanism that underlies many others; it is our way of justifying or trying to make sense of things that don't make sense. It's a way of explaining things away that should be brought under examination. When, for whatever reasons, we want to avoid an unpleasant truth, or when we want to believe that something is true, we can come up with a justification for our desired belief. Television writers Greg Behrendt and Liz Tuccillo wrote a book (that became a film) to encourage women to stop making up excuses about why men they like don't call them, such as "he must have lost my number" or " he must be afraid of ruining our friendship." Greg's response to almost every rationalization women make is also the title of the book: *He's Just Not That Into You*. Greg and Liz note how often women rationalize and help one another rationalize when men are clearly not interested in pursuing a closer relationship.

Note how people use rationalization to distort reality in the following examples.

Examples

- Jorge's favorite political candidate is found to have cheated on his taxes. He rationalizes his continued support for this person by saying, "He may have cheated on his taxes, but he's made up for it by all the good budget cuts he helped pass."

- Claire finds out that the car she just bought has been criticized by *Consumer Reports* for having a faulty transmission system. She rationalizes by saying, "All cars are meant to fall apart in a few years."

- Jasmine continues to smoke cigarettes, although considerable evidence supports the fact that cigarettes are a causative factor in several diseases. She tells herself and others, "I'm not going to worry about every habit I have. I could die tomorrow by slipping on a banana peel, so I might as well enjoy life today."

- Someone that Thom would like to get to know keeps refusing his requests for a date. He rationalizes by saying, "She must be really busy this year."

- After committing herself to a strict diet, Ginger has a doughnut for breakfast. She then eats three more, rationalizing, "I already ruined the diet, so I may as well enjoy today and start again tomorrow."

- A clerk at a supermarket forgets to charge a customer for some sodas on the bottom of the cart. When the customer starts to load them into her car and realizes the mistake she rationalizes by thinking, "Oh, well. It's a big company and they will never miss a few dollars." (See Exercise 9.1, page 424.)

As you can see, rationalization can enter every area of our thinking. Leon Festinger, a sociologist, created a theory to explain why we use this mechanism so frequently. He said that humans are subject to a state of mind called **cognitive dissonance**. This state

---

[4] Frank Minirth, M.D., and Don Hawkins, Th.M., *Worry Free Living* (Nashville, TN: Thomas Nelson Publishers, 1989), p. 78.

---

defense mechanisms Techniques aimed at self-protection through the avoidance of unpleasant realities.

rationalization A defense mechanism that underlies many others; it involves justifying or making sense of things that don't make sense and explaining things away that should be brought under examination.

cognitive dissonance A state of mental discomfort that occurs whenever two ideas (or cognitions) are out of sync or when behavior is inconsistent with beliefs.

occurs whenever two ideas (or cognitions) are out of sync and create discomfort (dissonance) in our thinking patterns; we may also experience cognitive dissonance when our behavior is inconsistent with our beliefs. Dissonance is seen as a state of mental tension. We are uncomfortable when we are confronted with evidence that goes against our perspective, whether it is evidence about a person, an issue, or even our own character. We seek to relieve the mental tension caused by dissonance in one of two ways.

1. We try to increase information that is consistent with what we already believe. We seek out more evidence that favors our viewpoint and speak to people who will reinforce our original ideas. Sometimes, we know just what sources will be favorable to our positions regarding an issue or a personal situation. For example, we might find a website that is filled with information that supports our beliefs; we might also call on friends who we know will take our side and agree with us. Increasing positive support as a way to avoid dissonance usually involves rationalizing, as we have seen in the previous examples. We explain away inconsistencies between our principles and our actions rather than facing them and dealing with them.

2. We may also try to decrease or diminish any information that contradicts our view of a person or an issue. If, for example, we are researching an issue and find a credible website that refutes our beliefs, we may just ignore the information on that site and search for one that supports our beliefs. Or, if some of our friends don't like our boyfriend or girlfriend and try to tell us why, we may choose to avoid those friends. That reduces the dissonance by eliminating any contradictory viewpoints. This second form of dissonance reduction is part of the defense mechanism of denial, which we will discuss shortly.

Interestingly, Festinger believes that the need to resolve mentally inconsistent information is a basic drive, like the drive for food; our minds strive to "survive" unpleasant incongruities.

A mentally healthy person is in a state of congruence; that is, the individual's behavior conforms to his or her beliefs and values. Unfortunately, many of us, instead of striving for true congruence by getting our behavior in line with our values when inconsistencies occur, or by changing our viewpoints about an issue when we are proven wrong, will settle for a counterfeit peace of mind through rationalization. If we keep rationalizing, we can become psychologically unhealthy and even detached from reality.

Consider the fate of many people who followed a cult leader named Jim Jones (whose life is chronicled in the 2006 film *Jonestown*) to Guyana and their deaths. When he passed himself off as a man of God and had sexual relations with many of his followers, he rationalized by calling it a form of ritual cleansing. When he humiliated young children for small infractions of his system, Jones (and some of the children's parents) rationalized that he had their best interests at heart.

The more we give up our critical thinking abilities, the harder it becomes to face our errors in judgment, and personal and social tragedies can be the result. People who vote, buy products, influence others, and form relationships need to have accurate information to make the best decisions; rationalization is a form of shoddy thinking we can't afford to use.

A defense mechanism closely related to rationalization is **denial**. Denial is also a state of mind that blocks critical thinking, because it involves the repression of or refusal to recognize negative or threatening information. Some of us go into denial when we hear we've bounced a check or forgotten to make a payment on a bill. We may tell our creditors they must have made a mistake or that they never sent the bill, when the reality is that we've made a mistake we choose not to face because

denial A state of mind that blocks critical thinking by the repression of or refusal to recognize negative or threatening information.

of fear, pride, or both. Another personal example of denial is summarized in an anecdote from a call-in radio program excerpted from Dr. Laura Schlessinger's book *How Could You Do That?*

> Nancy, forty-seven, called all bent out of shape because her "fella" of six months turns out to be married. Her question was about whether or not it was right for her to tell his wife of the affair ... mostly, I thought to punish him, and only somewhat to warn her.
>
> That isn't the whole picture at all. I asked her if she'd been to his place of residence in the six months of their steamy sexual relationship: "No."
>
> I asked her if she'd even been given his home number or spoken to him at home on the phone in the evenings: "No."
>
> I suggested that she truly knew all along that he was probably living with someone, married or not, and that she ignored that because she didn't want to give up the immediate gratification: the passion and attention. Furthermore, she had a fantasy going that she'd get him.
>
> She begrudgingly acknowledged I was right.
>
> Frighteningly, she couldn't seem to get with the idea that what she did wasn't right. She was too busy displacing all the blame for the current state of affairs on his adultery, not her own lack of conscience in getting involved with an attached fellow (the impact on his partner/wife/kids) and her lack of courage in finding out truths up front and dealing with them. Motivation for this stupid behavior? Immediate gratification. She made a choice of "right now" over good sense or conscience.
>
> Trying to avoid the self-examination, she calls to find out if it was right or not for her to blow the whistle on him. I told her, "That is a separate issue from what is my deeper concern about you, which is your denial that you made a choice, which got you to this point. If you tell on him, it doesn't change you, and you were not an innocent victim.
>
> ... There's no denying that sometimes choosing to own up to your own weakness, badness, selfishness, or evil is tough to do. But it's the only way finally to get control and some peace of mind."[5]

Denial, like other defense mechanisms, comes into play when we experience an emotional reaction to information. Sometimes, denial is normal and helpful to our systems, such as when we hear shocking news and give ourselves time, through temporary denial of the facts, to cope with the information.

For example, if you are informed at a doctor's office that you have a life-threatening disease, it may be helpful for you to put off facing this information completely until you are home with supportive family members or in the care of a good counselor. In a case like this, it might be hard to drive home if you were fully immersed in the truth of your condition.

Denial becomes a problem for critical thinkers when they consistently refuse to acknowledge the truth or the possible truth of an argument presented to them. This problem can be summed up in the cliché "I know what I believe. Don't confuse me with the facts." The facts may be complicated, but the critical thinker needs to sort through them in order to make a reasonable judgment on an issue or, at least, to withhold judgment on a complex issue about which he or she is uninformed.

[5] Dr. Laura Schlessinger, *How Could You Do That?* (New York: HarperCollins Publishers, Inc., 1996), pp. 94–95.

Government officials may also deny important information, such as the seriousness of warnings, as illustrated in the following *New York Times* report:

> WASHINGTON, Sept. 18—The United States intelligence community was told in 1998 that Arab terrorists were planning to fly a bomb-laden aircraft into the World Trade Center, but the F.B.I. and the Federal Aviation Administration did not take the threat seriously, a Congressional investigation into the Sept. 11 attacks found.
>
> The 1998 intelligence report from the Central Intelligence Agency was just one of several warnings the United States received, but did not seriously analyze, in the years leading up to the Sept. 11 attacks that were detailed today at a Congressional hearing.[6]

Skill

Recognize defense mechanisms we use to avoid uncomfortable realities.

Denial and rationalization are often found together as defense mechanisms, when truth is denied and behavior is rationalized. Note both factors in another excerpt from the writings of Dr. Laura Schlessinger:

> I feel sorry for anyone's pain and problems. But when they are the result of betrayals and abandonments coming back to haunt, and the primary issue is not remediation of those actions, I don't feel it to be an ethical obligation to get personally involved.
>
> Trina, twenty-eight, has a sister, thirty-four, who split from her husband and has a new guy who dumped his wife. The sister kicked out her own seventeen-year-old daughter who wasn't going along agreeably with all this and is now living with Grandma. Trina is now wondering about not inviting the live-in guy to a family event.
>
> "Trina," I scolded, "you are displacing responsibility about this situation to him. You want to punish only him, but your sister is the one making the decisions; she chose him and she dumped her own daughter. Your sister's actions are being ignored so you can be appropriately, but safely, righteous. You don't want to upset the family applecart, right?"
>
> "Right."
>
> In discussing what her sister was actually doing wrong, Trina kept trying desperately to pardon her sister (by citing her traits as) low self-esteem, lonely, beguiled, not thinking straight, confused, lost, etc.
>
> Sure, Trina says the guy is a bum, but she's just as sure her sister is merely weak and confused, not really bad. How is that again?
>
> In psychological terminology, Trina is "splitting," i.e., ascribing ever so neatly all the bad behavior to one person and all the good to another. This is a means of coping with the difficult ambivalence of having love and attachment you feel for someone and not wanting that to be marred by ugly realities.

[6] James Risen, "Threats and Responses: The Investigation; U.S. Failed to Act on Warnings in '98 of a Plane Attack," *New York Times,* September 19, 2002, p. 1.

Well, in real life, all good people do some wrong things and all bad people do some right things. I've heard many women defend abusing men by saying, "But, other than that, he does good stuff!"[7]

On a personal level, we may see all of the shortcomings of people we don't like and deny and excuse the faults of people we care about, as illustrated in the previous example. Similarly, we may see all of the negative aspects of viewpoints and policies we oppose and only good points in viewpoints and policies we support. By polarizing reality in this way, we leave out important considerations and hinder our ability to make the best decisions.

Critical thinkers take the time and energy required to recognize the weak points of their own side of an issue and the good points of their opponents. They search for truth rather than victory and are willing to change when presented with new information instead of insisting on maintaining a position that can no longer be supported.

Even when we are careful to give credit to the good points of all sides of an issue, we may still find that there are times when our emotional reactions cause us to lose a rational perspective. When that happens, we need to be aware of and adjust for our strong feelings, rather than denying that they have an impact on us.

Conformity and Ways to Overcome It

Most people brought up with the reality assumptions of a democratic society like to think of themselves as independent thinkers who make their own decisions. One of the governing values of those who settled the American West was "rugged individualism," the tough-spiritedness that helped people survive physically difficult and socially isolated conditions.

Although our society has been characterized as highly individualistic, fascinating research in social psychology can help us understand some of the areas in which we may tend to conform unconsciously to others rather than thinking for ourselves. Knowing about these tendencies can help us guard against them when we need to make important decisions.

In his excellent book, *Influence, The Psychology of Persuasion,* social psychologist Robert Cialdini discusses the principle of 'social proof,' which states that "The greater the number of people who find any idea correct, the more the idea will seem to be correct." He gives many illustrations of how the beliefs and actions of others are used to guide our own beliefs and actions, especially in situations of uncertainty.

In general, when we are unsure of ourselves, when the situation is unclear or ambiguous, when uncertainty reigns, we are most likely to look to and accept the actions of others as correct. In the process of examining the reactions of other people to resolve our uncertainty, however, we are likely to overlook a subtle but important fact. Those people are probably examining the social evidence, too. Especially in an ambiguous situation, the tendency for everyone to be looking to see what everyone else is doing can lead to a fascinating phenomenon called "pluralistic ignorance." A thorough understanding of the pluralistic ignorance phenomenon helps

[7] Schlessinger, *How Could You Do That?*, pp. 94–95.

immeasurably to explain a regular occurrence in our country that has been termed both a riddle and a national disgrace: the failure of entire groups of bystanders to aid victims in agonizing need of help.[8]

Cialdini goes on to detail situations in which pluralistic ignorance takes place, including the famous case of a Queens, New York, woman who was murdered while 38 neighbors watched from their windows. When the murder occurred, reporters grappled with questions about how such apathy could prevail when it would have been so simple for the bystanders to make an anonymous call to police.

Subsequent research suggested that the cause of the inaction was not apathy but conformity to the inaction of others. In study after study, people acting alone were usually willing to offer help and assistance to someone in trouble. But when a crowd was present and no one in the crowd took action, that seemed to indicate that no action was necessary; individuals encountering the inaction of others read the cues of the group and also did nothing to help the person in trouble.

Additional studies show that individuals are much more likely to conform to others who seem similar to themselves. Cialdini cites the research of sociologist David Phillips who discovered that immediately following the reports of suicides of young people, there was a remarkable increase in comparable suicides among the young. When a suicide story involved an older driver, the statistics on suicides committed by older drivers immediately increased. Phillips also discovered a similar trend in homicide rates. Cialdini states, "it is clear that widely publicized aggression has the nasty tendency to spread to similar victims, no matter whether the aggression is inflicted on the self or on another."[9]

When others who resemble us engage in an activity, the activity becomes legitimized. This may account for patterns of high school, junior high school, and even elementary school homicides. Students hear the stories of others who, like themselves, have difficulty in their lives and resolve the difficulty through homicide or homicide followed by suicide. Although they may not conform to their peer group at school, they do conform to their "reference group" of destructive revenge seekers, and they perform "copycat" murders.

The previously noted examples deal with unusual situations, but the human tendency to conform also can be noted in routine, daily activities. One of Cialdini's students, a highway patrolman, reports on a common accident that can also be attributed to social proof, the idea that if everyone thinks or does something, it must be correct.

> After a class session in which the subject of discussion was the principle of social proof, he stayed to talk with me. He said that he now understood the cause of a type of traffic accident that had always puzzled him before. The accident typically occurred on the city freeway during rush hour, when cars in all lanes were moving steadily but slowly. Events leading to the accident would start when a pair of cars, one behind the other, would simultaneously begin signaling an intention to get out of the lane they were in and into the next. Within seconds, a long line of drivers to the rear of the first two would follow suit, thinking that something—a stalled car or a construction barrier— was blocking the lane ahead. It would be in this crush to cram into the available spaces of the next lane that a collision frequently happened.

---

[8] Robert B. Cialdini, *The Psychology of Persuasion* (New York: William Morrow, 1993), p. 129.
[9] Ibid., p. 151.

The odd thing about it all, according to the patrolman, was that very often there had been no obstruction to be avoided in the first place, and by the time of the accident, this should have been obvious to anyone who looked. He said he had more than once witnessed such accidents when there was a visibly clear road in front of the ill-fated lane switchers.

The patrolman's account provides certain insights into the way we respond to social proof. First, we seem to assume that if a lot of people are doing the same thing, they must know something we don't. Especially when we are uncertain, we are willing to place an enormous amount of trust in the collective knowledge of the crowd. Second, quite frequently the crowd is mistaken because they are not acting on the basis of any superior information but are reacting, themselves, to the principle of social proof.[10]

Many psychologists like Cialdini write extensively about the human tendency to conform. With advances in neuroscience, researchers are now looking at the mechanisms in our brain that cause us to conform to others. In the Netherlands, studies using MRI scans have discovered that individual conflict with a group opinion triggers a "neuronal response. . . similar to a prediction error signal." In other words, when a subject realizes that he or she has a different opinion from the majority of the group, his or her brain triggers perception-adjusting responses. "The present study explains why we often automatically adjust our opinion in line with the majority opinion," says (researcher) Dr. Klucharev. "Our results also show that social conformity is based on mechanisms that comply with reinforcement learning and is reinforced by the neural error-monitoring activity which signals what is probably the most fundamental social mistake—that of being too different from others."[11]

Conformity occurs when we follow what others are doing rather than relying on our own best judgment. We sometimes find that conformity is a necessary condition for being accepted in a group. When a group member expresses an opinion that is different from the group's opinion, pressure is often applied to get the "deviant" to conform. The pressure may come in the form of reasoning, teasing, bribery, shaming, pleading, complimenting, or, usually as a last resort, shunning. The tendency for individuals to go along with a group's decision has been labeled by Yale psychologist Irving L. Janis as **groupthink**. Groupthink involves faulty decision making by groups that sacrifice sound judgment in order to keep their unity as a group: group members don't offer or consider several alternative solutions to a problem; they don't seek outside, expert opinion; they don't criticize each other's ideas; and they rationalize poor decisions. Janis discovered the principle of groupthink in his study of various actions taken by U.S. government leaders that led to dire consequences for many people. Professor Vincent Ryan Ruggiero discusses Janis's study in his book *Beyond Feelings*:

> The actions were Franklin D. Roosevelt's failure to be ready for the Japanese attack on Pearl Harbor, Harry S. Truman's decision to invade North Korea, John F. Kennedy's plan to invade Cuba, and Lyndon B. Johnson's decision to escalate the Vietnam War. In each case, Janis found that the people who made the decision exhibited a strong desire to concur in the group decision.

conformity   The tendency to follow others uncritically, usually to gain acceptance or avoid conflict; the practice of using the beliefs and actions of others rather than our own best judgment as the primary guide to personal thoughts and actions.

groupthink   The tendency for group members to rigidly conform to and reinforce a collective opinion or judgment about an issue.

[10] Ibid., pp. 162–163.
[11] Cathleen Genova, "Social Conformity Starts in the Brain," January 15, 2009, medicalnewstoday.com.

… More specifically, Janis identified a number of major defects in decision-making that could be attributed to this conformity. The groups he analyzed did not survey the range of choices but focused on a few. When they discovered that their initial decision had certain drawbacks, they failed to reconsider those decisions. They almost never tested their own thinking for weaknesses. They never tried to obtain the judgments of experts. They expressed interest only in those views that reinforced the positions they preferred, and they spent little time considering the obstacles that would hinder the success of their plans. In each of the cases Janis studied, these defects in thinking cost untold human suffering.[12]

More recently, scholars have cited the effects of groupthink as causes for other disasters including the explosion of the space shuttle Challenger and the policies that led to financial and housing meltdowns in the United States.

How can we overcome the effects of conformity and groupthink on our actions?

1. Realize that as humans, we have a tendency to unconsciously accept social proof, the proof that is based on a broad acceptance of an attitude or action. This tendency may manifest in personal social choices as well as in blind ethnocentrism.

2. Understand that as social beings, we work in groups and seek the acceptance of the group. Be aware of the phenomenon of groupthink, and bring it to the attention of a group when appropriate.

3. Watch for and avoid the tendency to conform to others or to rebel against others; instead, base decisions on good evidence and reasoning.

4. When working with a group, suggest that the group divide into subgroups to brainstorm ideas before discussing them as a whole group. Use outside experts to offer opinions on important matters. Have an impartial leader who establishes an open climate where it is genuinely safe to criticize ideas; a good leader will also encourage group members to challenge various solutions to problems and to consider many alternatives before coming to a decision.

Emotional Reasoning and Rational Responses

emotional reasoning
The process of using one's feelings as definitive proof of an accurate analysis of a situation.

Like conformity, **emotional reasoning** causes us to distort the truth of our circumstances and to make poor decisions. We all experience feelings as a result of the words or actions of others. People who reason emotionally *react* to other people and to events, taking their feelings as automatic proof that their own analysis of the situation is accurate. People who reason logically also experience their emotions, but they stop and consider possible interpretations and perceptions before reacting, so that they can *respond* in a rational and constructive manner.

Cognitive psychologists help people use tools of rationality to overcome debilitating emotions and to reason more clearly. A rational approach to emotions is based on the following principles:

We all face numerous challenging situations every day.

Feelings and reactions to these situations are natural.

Our feelings can be traced back to our thoughts, that is, our interpretations of the events.

[12] Vincent Ryan Ruggiero, *Beyond Feelings: A Guide to Critical Thinking* (Mountain View, CA: Mayfield Publishing, 1990), p. 64.

If we examine the thoughts/interpretations that produced the feelings, the feelings will often change or be diminished.

When feelings are more in line with reality, our actions will be more constructive.

For example, let's say that you say hello to a coworker who is usually friendly, and she quickly walks right past you without returning your greeting. A natural reaction would be to feel insulted, hurt, or annoyed with her. You might decide that the next time you see her, you're not going to say anything. Although your feelings are normal, your interpretation of the event involves "jumping to conclusions," interpreting the event, assuming your interpretation is correct, and then judging the situation accordingly.

But suppose that you find out that your coworker was rushing past you because she had just been told that her mother was in intensive care following a car accident. Now, the natural reaction would be to feel concern and sympathy. You might decide to see if you could help her in some way.

We can illustrate how our thoughts determine our feelings with a simple chart:

Situation	Thoughts (Self-Talk)	Feelings
Coworker ignores you.	"She thinks she's superior to me."	Irritation, anger
Coworker ignores you.	"She is upset about her mother."	Concern, sympathy

Stop and Think

Critical thinkers realize that all events and behaviors are not personally designed to make their lives difficult; they are able to stop and consider other interpretations and respond accordingly.

It takes character, in the form of self-control, patience, and optimism, to stop and question our interpretations of a situation before we react to it. For example, when a flight is delayed, it is common for people to take out their anger and frustration on the clerk at the airline counter, even though it would not be his or her fault that the mechanic found a problem in the engine or that the weather has caused delays. People on the "front lines" of customer service are trained to deal with frustrated and angry outbursts; they are taught not to take the verbal abuse personally and to refer inconsolable or threatening people to the next level of management. Their job is made easier by people who use rational "self-talk" before lashing out, as illustrated by contrasting responses to the same situation:

Situation	Thoughts (Self-Talk)	Feelings	Action
Airport delay	"I'm being taken advantage of by the airline."	Anger-rage	Yell at clerk
Airport delay	"There is a problem with the plane or weather."	Irritation	Adjust/cope; decide on the best course of action or use of time

The first individual rages at the clerk, which only makes the situation more unpleasant. Note that the second individual is also irritated, but his rational thinking allows him to adjust to the situation rather than making it worse. He might even talk to the clerk about getting a flight on another airline, and his polite manner might make her more receptive to trying to help him come up with a creative solution to his dilemma.

When our thoughts are based on a correct interpretation of reality, our actions will be more useful. Even when our negative thoughts seem reasonable, we are able to act more rationally if we stop and think. For example, let's say that your coworker got an hourly raise that you also deserved.

Situation	Thoughts (Self-Talk)	Feelings
Coworker gets raise	"I also deserved this raise."	Anger at boss

This situation may seem and may actually be unfair to you, in which case your feelings are justified. But it is also important to consider the best actions to achieve your goals. You might get angry with your boss and accuse her of being unfair, but that is not likely to help you achieve your goals and may even hurt your case. If you can calmly present the situation to her, she may see that she was wrong and correct the wrong; if she doesn't, there is often recourse through her supervisor or through a union representative.

Dr. Phil McGraw has a useful phrase that helps people examine the consequences of their actions. He often asks his troubled guests this question about dysfunctional reactions to their circumstances: "How's that working for you?" Even when our anger is justified, we need to come up with the best course of action for our lives. Screaming and lashing out at others or giving up in frustration rarely helps us to achieve long-term goals.

There are specific patterns of thinking that distort reality and make it hard for us to make clear decisions or take rational actions. Following are some of the most debilitating ones that we should recognize and avoid.

overgeneralizing Coming to a general conclusion on the basis of a single incident or a few incidents.

1. *Overgeneralizing.* Overgeneralizing involves coming to a general conclusion on the basis of a single incident or a few incidents. People who overgeneralize often use exaggerated terms such as "always," "never," "everyone," and "nothing." They label themselves and others as permanently fixed in some character trait because of a few examples, and they overlook any evidence to the contrary. Overgeneralizing causes prejudice and stereotyping of ourselves and others.

Examples

"I got a D on my test—I'll never understand math."
"You're always late."
"We'll never have the time to get this done."
"I forgot our anniversary—I'm just a terrible boyfriend."

mind reading Assuming that what would be true for you in any given circumstance is true for the other person; making assumptions about the thoughts, feelings, or motives of another and taking the assumptions as true without further proof or discussion.

2. *Mind Reading.* Mind readers assume they know what others are thinking or assume that others should know what they are thinking. Mind reading is often based on the psychological process of "projection"—assuming that what would be true for you in any given circumstance is true for the other person.

Examples

"The only reason he married her was for her money."
"You should have known that I wanted that job—it was obvious."
"The reason she said that was because she was jealous."

3. *Filtering.* When we filter, we focus on the negative details of a situation and filter out the positive—this has also been called "awfulizing" a situation and is a favorite tactic of pessimistic thinkers. When the negative details are all that we allow, those details become larger and more powerful than they really are. Often, the filtering implies and creates helplessness on the part of speakers; they see circumstances as completely out of their control or influence.

    filtering The process of distorting reality by focusing on all the negative details of a situation and filtering out all the positive.

    ### Examples

    "Our schools are a complete mess. Things have changed so much because of the new policies that education has become impossible."

    "I've tried to get a job, but people just aren't hiring; and even if they are, I can't live on the salary I'd get."

    "Every time I try to give up drinking, someone has a party; I can't change because our school is just too much of a party school, and I'm not willing to be an outcast."

4. *Catastrophizing.* Closely related to filtering, catastrophizing occurs when people expect disaster. People who catastrophize imagine and anticipate problems, and they often use the term *what if?* Creative thinkers can come up with any number of potentially catastrophic events. While rational concerns should always be considered before embarking on a new course of action, and life does involve some risk, catastrophizing is filled with unsubstantiated and exaggerated fears. As Mark Twain said, "I've had many troubles in my life, most of which never happened." On a personal level, catastrophizing reflects a lack of trust in one's capacity to adapt to changes.

    catastrophizing A form of emotional reasoning in which one imagines and anticipates disastrous outcomes or future problems.

    ### Examples

    "We can't change the stadium's location. We'll lose all our fans."

    "Online classes are a bad idea. There's no way to prevent cheating."

    "Junior shouldn't be taking gymnastics. What if he falls and breaks his arm?"

    "I'll never be able to get a job with so many other people in my major."

5. *Personalizing.* When we personalize, we relate everything that happens to ourselves, and we "take things personally," assuming that general statements or actions are references to us. We also falsely believe that our characteristics or actions are continually being compared, favorably or unfavorably, against others. Personalizing sometimes creates inflated optimism; it often creates defensiveness and pessimism.

    personalizing A form of emotional reasoning in which a person relates everything that happens to him- or herself, assuming that general statements or actions are personally directed. Personalizing also involves the belief that one's characteristics or actions are continually being compared, favorably or unfavorably, against the characteristics or actions of other people.

    ### Examples

    "I know he's lied and cheated on other girls too, but he broke up with me because I wasn't good enough for him."

    "The C in history just shows how much that teacher hated me."

    "I only got the solo because the teacher loves me."

    "Our boss told us that we were all working too slowly, but I know she meant me."

    "Our boss told us we were doing well. I know she meant me."

    "Every team I'm on is going to lose."

    "Every team I'm on is going to win."

6. *Perfectionism.* Perfectionists have a false belief that perfection is possible. They end up minimizing their good qualities or the good parts of a situation and focusing instead on how they or others have not measured up. Perfectionists have

    perfectionism A form of emotional reasoning based on a desire and belief that one should be without flaws; good qualities, good work, or the good parts of a situation are minimized and focus is placed on how others or oneself have not measured up.

a hard time accepting their own humanity as well as the limits of other human beings; their desire to be without fault in any way can make them avoid challenges or berate themselves and others when outcomes are not ideal.

Examples

"I'm so upset that I missed two questions—I should have studied harder for the test."

"Yes, we finally have a new theater, but it's going to be another year before the sound system is complete."

"Honey, I know you spent all day cleaning the yard, but you didn't put away your laundry."

"I know we won and I scored the most points, but my brother was Most Valuable Player when he was my age."

Stop and Think

Do you or someone you know tend to use emotional reasoning? If so, how does the emotional reasoning interfere with good decision making?

Ways to Deal with Emotional Reasoning

When you find yourself involved in the irrational reasoning processes outlined in the previous section, there are several things you can do to get back on track.

1. *Be Aware.* Stop and see if you can identify how your reasoning is distorted. Are you catastrophizing, mind-reading, personalizing, filtering, overgeneralizing, or seeking perfection?

2. *Map Out the General Beliefs Behind Your Emotions.* Common beliefs related to feelings can be generally categorized in the following ways:

Feeling	General Belief
Anger	My rights or someone else's rights or humanity have been violated in some way.
Sadness/Grief	I have experienced a loss.
Anxiety	I am fearful or worried about something happening in the present or the future.
Guilt	I have violated someone else's rights.
Embarrassment	I have lost standing with others.

3. *Analyze the Specific Situation That Caused Your Thinking.* For example, if you didn't receive a grade or a promotion that you felt you deserved, you may believe that your rights have been violated; that belief generated the feelings of anger. If you are unprepared for an upcoming test or interview, you may feel anxiety.

4. *Consider Other Interpretations of the Situation.* Your teacher may have made a mistake in your grading or you may have misinterpreted the grading criteria. You may feel unprepared for an upcoming test because of missing some class time. Come up with the worst case, best case, and most likely case concerning your situation.

Sometimes, just asking yourself, "What is the worst thing that can happen?" or "Why does this situation bother me so much?" can bring insight and clarification.

5. *Prepare for Action.* Try to plan for the best possible outcomes and to prevent the worst possible outcomes. For example, you may decide to talk with your instructor about your grade when you are feeling calm and rational. Instead of approaching him with anger and a sense of injustice, bring your work and grades and ask him to clarify how your grade was calculated. If you have a difference of opinion, explain it to him. If you get no satisfactory answer, calmly go to the next level, his supervisor, until you receive the answers or changes you need.

6. *Accept Good Changes and Also Accept Reality.* You can't control other people, and there are also many situations that are out of your control. But you can respond with clear thinking and positive actions that help you make the best of your circumstances, effecting change when possible and moving on when necessary. (See Exercise 9.2, page 424.)

Skill

Recognize and use logical thinking to counter emotional reasoning.

Points of Logical Vulnerability

Professor Zachary Seech has come up with a great description of the trouble spots in our thinking, areas where we have difficulty being rational. He calls them **points of logical vulnerability**. We can be vulnerable to a general topic, such as politics, or a specific one, such as our sister's choice of a husband.[13]

points of logical vulnerability Topics about which a person has difficulty being rational or objective.

There are topics about which a person, we say, "just cannot be rational." What we mean is that this person has great difficulty being objective on these specific topics. He or she finds it difficult, in some cases, to consider the evidence impartially and draw a sensible, justified conclusion. These topics are the points of logical vulnerability for that person.[14]

Each person has different "sore spots" in his or her life, and dialogue on a given issue becomes difficult when our emotions blind our thinking on certain points. If you are a die-hard fan of a particular team, you may not be objective about how they will do in the next game. If fast food fits your lifestyle perfectly, you may not be open to any discussion of health problems associated with a steady diet of cheeseburgers and fries. If you are upset because your roommate is getting married and moving out, you may find yourself disliking his or her new mate.

Points of logical vulnerability affect us so much on a personal level that we are likely to deny or rationalize any evidence that might disprove our opinions. For example, if you dislike a senator because of her views on taxes and then she supports a tax bill you also support, you might rationalize that "she's just trying to appease us; she doesn't really care about the issue."

Conversely, if you like the senator and she does something you consider wrong, you might rationalize that she was forced into making concessions she would not have personally approved. Our points of logical vulnerability cause us to distort or deny information that goes against our deeply held opinions.

---

[13] Zachary Seech, *Logic in Everyday Life* (Belmont, CA: Wadsworth Publishing, 1988), pp. 2–3.
[14] Ibid., p. 2.

Keep in mind the difference between having strong, well-considered convictions about which you are not flexible (such as your values), and opinions that have not been thought out, but have been based solely on emotions or identification with others who hold those opinions. The latter opinions are probably points of logical vulnerability for you. (See Exercise 9.3, pages 424–425.)

Antidotes for Points of Logical Vulnerability

You can confront your points of logical vulnerability in several effective ways. The first approach is to apply certain techniques of rational thought to your irrational statements; the second is to learn to listen actively and accurately to people with differing opinions.

general semanticists
Scholars who study the effects of language on mental health and behavior.

General semanticists study the relationship between words, perception, and behavior. They believe that we can improve our mental health by increasing the accuracy with which we speak, and they have come up with several "cures" for irrational statements.

A classic irrational statement stereotypes a whole group of people based on a limited sample of experience on the part of the speaker. Another term for a stereotypical statement is a *sweeping generalization*.

Let's say a man named Harold has had several bad experiences in his relationships with women. The first woman he wanted to marry left him for another man; the second woman he wanted to marry told him she wasn't ready for a commitment and that she needed "space"; the third woman he wanted to marry left town with no contact information. In discussing his problems with his best friend, Harold makes the statement: "All women are cruel and selfish."

Now we can understand how anyone with this record of experiences would be upset about his former relationships, but we also can see, as outside observers, that his statement is emotional and would not hold up to critical scrutiny. You can't interact with three women and then claim that all women (about half of the human race) are cruel and selfish.

semantic devices
Tools created by general semanticists that help people make their words more accurately reflective of reality.

General semanticists, basing their work on the pioneering writing of Albert Korzypski, apply what he called **semantic devices** to help people be more rational about their statements; they believe that if we speak more logically, we will be able to overcome debilitating emotions and reactions. They would ask Harold to do a few things with his statement, "All women are cruel and selfish."

- Eliminate the word *all* since no one can know every single woman. Change the general term *women* into specifics: Woman 1, woman 2, and woman 3 become Patty, Marcia, and Gina. Now he has: "Patty, Marcia, and Gina are cruel and selfish." Not perfect, but more accurate; at least in this case, he is not generalizing from three examples to half of the human race.

indexing   A process by which one takes general labels (women, Catholics, Asians, Americans) and substitutes a reference to actual people. Indexing is used to prevent stereotyping.

    Semanticists call this technique **indexing**; you take your general label (women, Catholics, Asians, Americans) and change it to actual people. You also delete the word *all* from your vocabulary when it precedes a general category. One can never know *all* about any given group.

- Next, a general semanticist would ask Harold to change his vague labels of *cruel* and *selfish* to specific behaviors. "Patty, Marcia, and Gina did not marry me, although we were dating and I asked them to marry me. Patty married someone else, Marcia told me she needed 'space,' and Gina left town without contacting me."

- For accuracy and perspective, our semanticist would also ask Harold to put a *date* on his statement. "Patty, Marcia, and Gina did not marry me, although we were dating and I asked them to marry me. Patty married someone else, Marcia told me she needed 'space,' and Gina left town without contacting me. These incidents happened when I was in my late teens and early twenties."

- The final addition to Harold's statement is called the *etc.* because it includes other realities that add balance and fairness to the original statement. Think of a young child who complains with all accuracy, "Joey pushed me!" This statement is clear and unambiguous, yet we don't know what else was going on in the situation. We don't have the total picture or the context in which the event occurred.

  To figure out what was going on, a parent or teacher might ask, "Did you push him too?" It could be that the child who complained was indeed the victim of Joey's aggressiveness, or maybe the complaining child pushed Joey first. Also, it could be that Joey was pushing to get somewhere and was unaware that he had pushed the other child. We can only know what happened in a situation when we get more information.

Think about the times you feel really annoyed with someone's behavior. In recounting your irritation to a friend, do you really try to be fair and objective, or do you tend to present the details that best support your right to be annoyed?

When general semanticists recommend the use of the *etc.*, they are recognizing the complexity of situations and the truth that we can rarely say all there is to say about the factors involved that create difficulties or conflict. They would suggest that Harold add information to his statement to give a more accurate picture of reality:

- Patty, Marcia, and Gina did not marry me, although we were dating and I asked them to marry me. Patty married someone else, Marcia told me she needed "space," and Gina left town without contacting me. These incidents happened when I was in my late teens and early twenties. I knew Patty was ready to get married, but I didn't ask her until she was involved with someone else; I could have still dated Marcia as one of the men she was dating, but I wanted to be the only one; I don't know why Gina left town.

Skill

Use rational thinking aids to overcome areas in which you have trouble being rational.

If you compare Harold's first statement with this last statement, you might understand why the use of semantic devices improves mental health. A counselor might help Harold arrive at the same kinds of rephrasing. If he continues to see all women as cruel and selfish, he might never try to interact with them again; but if he sees that he has had a few bad experiences, he can learn from his mistakes and continue to grow and develop relationships. As humans, we all endure hurtful experiences; people who can apply reason to their emotional reactions can bounce back more easily. The use of reason increases our resiliency.

The semantic devices help us change irrational comments we make about people and issues to more truthful and fair-minded statements. (See Exercise 9.4 on page 425.)

Actively and Accurately Listening: Developing Empathy

> Some psychologists believe that the ability to listen to another person, to empathize with, and to understand their point of view is one of the highest forms of intelligent behavior.
>
> Arthur Costa, "Teaching for Intelligence"

Many cultures place a high value on competition, and this competition is not restricted to sporting events—it also comes out in debates and discussions on issues. According to Deborah Tannen, author of *The Argument Culture,* the desire to win and the enjoyment we find in having the most persuasive argument may limit our ability to be fair to opposing sides of issues.[15]

Tannen makes a distinction between "having an argument" and "making an argument":

> When you're having an argument, you aren't trying to understand what the other person is saying; you're trying to win the argument. Both of you ignore the other's valid points and leap on weak ones, which is frustrating, because neither of you is listening to the other. In making an argument, you're putting a logical train of thoughts together to persuade someone of your point of view.[16]

When we sense that someone is trying to win an argument and is not willing to listen, that person loses credibility with us, and we usually tune him or her out. The most persuasive speaker is one who can understand and address the points brought up by those with different opinions. To understand and respond to an opposing argument, we must hear what the speaker for the opposition is saying.

Why do we find listening difficult, and why don't politicians listen more fairly in debates? Some of the reasons we don't listen include the following:

- The thrust of debate is to win; therefore, we tend to listen to the opposition's position only so we can find fault with it. The focus is on victory, not on understanding, especially in public debating forums. Too often a televised discussion or debate models bad behavior; speakers shout over each other, rarely admitting that an argument made by the other person has any merit.

- We are not trained to listen. Some of us have had training in speech, but few have had specific training in effective listening techniques.

- We may fear that if we really listen to the other person, we will lose our train of thought.

- We may be concerned that if we really listen to the other person, we might agree with him or her and that could be unsettling and uncomfortable.

- Effort and energy are required in order to try to understand the viewpoint of another person.

- For many of us, it is more rewarding to speak about our own ideas than to listen to others.

---

[15] Deborah Tannen, *The Argument Culture* (New York: Ballantine, Random House, 1999), p. 352.
[16] Ibid., p. 354.

Listening accurately to an opposing position, however, gives us some clear advantages:

- We can learn what the opposition to our cause or issue believes, and we can then address our opponents more effectively on specific points.
- We can grow and adjust our position if new research or reasoning warrants the adjustment.
- When we are seen as secure enough in our position to listen to an opposing argument, our credibility increases.
- Our calm listening is often contagious; as we show our willingness to hear the other side fully, defenses are dropped and our opponents may listen to us as well. We have a better chance of explaining our viewpoint and not having it distorted by interruptions or polarized by angry rebuttals.
- In an atmosphere of reduced hostility, areas of agreement can be found. When areas of agreement are discovered, problems can be solved more creatively.

The Art of Listening Well

The heart's real intentions are like deep water; but a person with discernment draws them out.

Proverbs 20.5, CJB

The late Carl Rogers, a southern California psychologist, created a listening exercise that has become a staple for counselors and teachers of communication. Rogers's technique is simple and very effective; if done correctly in an atmosphere of respect and goodwill, both sides come out with **empathy,** that is, a deeper understanding of the other's position.

empathy The ability to identify and understand the feelings and perspectives of others.

Understanding does not necessarily mean agreement. We may know exactly what the other's position is and conclude that he is completely off base. A critical thinker draws conclusions based on an understanding of both her own and her opponent's position, not solely on an emotional commitment to her original position.

The key element of Rogers's technique is paraphrasing (putting in your own words) the other person's thoughts so that you know what is truly being said before you respond with your own opinions. In normal dialogue, you won't be paraphrasing everything the other person says, but you should stop and paraphrase whenever you aren't sure about what he or she is saying. You can also use paraphrasing to cool down an emotional discussion. When people feel that they are truly being heard, there is no need for loud and strident dialogue.

Here is Rogers's listening exercise that is used to train people in basic paraphrasing skills:

1. Two people with opposing beliefs on an issue sit facing each other.
2. Person A begins with a brief statement about her opinion on an issue.
3. Person B paraphrases—puts person A's opinion in his own words. When person A agrees that person B has understood, then person B states his opinion.
4. Now person A has to paraphrase—restate in her own words—what person B has said. When person B is satisfied that person A has understood him, person A can expand on her opinion.

5. This process is continued until both people feel they have presented their cases and that they have been understood. It is helpful to allow each person a few minutes to summarize, as best he or she can, the complete position of the other person.

6. During the process, both people attempt to be objective in their summaries of the other person's viewpoint and to avoid sarcasm, ridicule, or exaggeration of any points the other person makes. In some cases, it is best to have an unbiased and tactful third party serve as a 'referee' to ensure that both people are fairly heard.

7. It is also helpful to try to "read between the lines" and understand why the other person feels so strongly about his or her position. Often there is a significant personal experience that shaped the other person's viewpoint in a powerful way.

Skill

Listen with empathy to an opposing viewpoint.

Example

Person A: I believe heroic medical interventions should not be made unless the doctors and nurses have the permission of the patient or the patient's family members.

Person B: So you believe that extending life with technology should not be done unless a patient or his family wants his life extended?

Person A: That's right.

Person B: Well, it's my opinion that sometimes there isn't time for a discussion with the patient or the family members about the patient's chances for survival. The medical experts have to act or there is no decision to be made because the patient is dead!

Person A: So you think that using technology is totally up to the doctors?

Person B: (clarifying) I didn't mean that. I mean, if the patient is going to die if he's not hooked up to the machines, then he needs to be hooked up first and consulted later.

Person A: (trying to paraphrase more accurately) So you think in an emergency the doctors should be allowed to treat the patient in any way that will save his life and talk to him or his family members later.

Person B: That's right. You got it.

Person A: Well, I don't have a real problem with that. But I believe that if the patient doesn't want to be kept alive through technology, and if he or his family members tell the doctors that, then the doctors have to abide by his wishes and "pull the plug."

Person B: So, basically, you believe the patient should decide whether he will live or die—or, if he can't decide, then his family should decide for him.

Person A: (clarifying) That's not exactly it. He may live or die whether he's hooked up to life supports or not. But it's his choice—or his family's choice—whether he will be hooked up.

Person B: Okay, then it's the patient's choice, or secondly, his family's choice and not the doctor's choice to continue him on life supports.

Person A: Exactly.

Person B: I believe it is part of a doctor's job to assess a patient's chances for survival; the patient or the family can get too emotional and decide to let someone die rather than be uncomfortable; and meanwhile, the doctor may know there's a good chance for recovery. Also, doctors are trained to save life at all costs. If we train them to take the patient's advice, then they could let him die just so they could take off early to play golf.

Person A: That's a lot for me to paraphrase. You believe, if I have it right, that doctors are more objective and less emotional than patients and family members, and they have more of an expert opinion about chances for recovery. And also you think it's dangerous to let patients or family members decide to pull the plug because then doctors don't have to worry about whether the patient could have lived a full life or not.

Person B: You said it better than I did!

Person A: Well, what I really think is that doctors should give their expert opinion to the patient and the family members. If they then decide, for whatever reason, not to prolong life with technology, then the doctors would have to abide by their decision.

Person B: So you think that the doctor should be an adviser or counselor and give them all the information they need, but the family should have the final power to decide what will be done.

Person A: That's exactly right.

Person B: Well, that sounds fair, but I just believe it's better to go for life, whenever possible. There are many cases of people recovering from comas or serious strokes, thanks to life-support systems. If their families had pulled the plug to spare them pain or expense, they would have lost a loved one. Give life a chance.

Person A: Well, my position is more simple. It's his body—or his parent's, wife's, or child's body. That gives him the right to decide what will or will not be done in a hospital. I agree it's important to get the doctor's opinion, but after that, his decision should be honored.

Person B: And I agree with you that it's his or her body, but I also think the doctors are more objective and knowledgeable, so they should be allowed to continue treatment if there's a chance for recovery. I can see why some of these cases have to be settled in court. That's not the ideal solution, but it's the best we've come up with so far.

Questions for Discussion

1. The participants in this dialogue did not end by agreeing with much of each other's positions. How, then, is this form of communication useful?

2. Where did you spot inaccurate paraphrases of the other position? Why do you think these occurred?

3. Often, there is a strong emotional component to someone's position. Do you see hints of emotionalism in this dialogue? How does the paraphrasing minimize emotional outbursts or points of logical vulnerability? Under what circumstances should the emotional reactions of the participants also be brought to light?

Precautions About Active Listening

Active listening was first suggested as a technique to be used by professional therapists. Over the years, various workshops have been set up for the purposes of training people to use active listening to improve their relationships. These workshops focus on the proper and improper use of the technique.

If you have never been formally trained in active listening, you may find it uncomfortable. However, practice and a basic knowledge of potential problems should enable you to use this very helpful communication tool successfully. Here is a summary of basic precautions in using active listening:

1. Avoid sarcasm and ridicule of the other person's statements; also don't add negative connotations to what he or she says.

2. Don't "parrot" the position of the other person; just paraphrase (put in your own words) the ideas you hear.

3. If you find yourself getting upset, take some time out and assess what it is about this issue that makes it painful for you to be objective. There are some issues we feel so strongly about that there is no room for discussion. These strong feelings are usually connected to a personal experience. For example, if your cousin was murdered, you may believe that the death penalty is justified, and any arguments against it make no impression when you consider the pain of your cousin and your close family. Your belief may be based on a value that you hold deeply; if you believe that abortion is the taking of innocent life, then statistics about overpopulation may not convince you to change your mind. (See Exercise 9.5 on pages 425–426.)

It is helpful, as a critical thinker, to know the areas in which you hold solid convictions. You can then acknowledge points from an opposing side, but make it clear that those points are not strong enough for you to change your mind. The key is to understand both sides of an issue fully and to be open to new information; then you are responsible as a thinker when you, with good conscience, take a strong, even immovable, stand on an issue.

It is unrealistic to assume that you will have many opportunities for this kind of extended dialogue with someone who disagrees with you. The benefit of understanding the paraphrasing technique is that you can use it whenever it seems that something needs to be clarified in a discussion. Your use of this technique gives you credibility and the personal power that comes with a calm, rational approach to dialogue.

The person who stays cool and calm in a discussion seems secure in his or her position. The person who blows it by becoming overexcited and unfair to the opposition seems threatened—that is, logically vulnerable. Shouting the other person down, name-calling, interrupting, and other forms of intimidation and bullying serve only to make the person who uses these tactics seem foolish and unstable.

Your cool, clear mind—don't leave home without it!

Life Application: Tips for College and Career

Use listening skills to uncover the viewpoints of those who believe differently from you on a particular issue. Listen with empathy and try to uncover past experiences or present concerns that make them think as they do. When you experience a conflict with others, stop and paraphrase their beliefs and feelings; express a genuine understanding of their position and then explain your own viewpoint.

Expand your own fair-mindedness by being aware of your own 'points of logical vulnerability' and areas of emotional reasoning. Think through rational responses to avoid personalizing and catastrophizing in challenging situations.

Chapter Review

Summary

1. Our thinking can become less egocentric and more clear and fair when we recognize our self-protective defense mechanisms and areas of logical vulnerability and when we develop specific skills for understanding the viewpoints of others.

2. Rationalization is a defense mechanism through which we try to justify or make sense out of things that are not sensible or justifiable.

3. Denial is a defense mechanism that involves repressing or refusing to recognize threatening information.

4. Conformity affects our thinking as an unconscious but powerful response to 'social proof' and the human desire to belong to various groups.

5. Emotional reasoning often distorts thinking; there are specific ways to overcome emotional reasoning and to think more rationally.

6. Points of logical vulnerability are topics about which we have trouble being rational.

7. Critical thinkers can manage points of logical vulnerability through the use of semantic devices.

8. Active listening, when used properly, can help us clearly understand the viewpoints of others.

Checkup

Sentence Completion

1. The tendency to view one's culture as central and superior is known as _____.

2. Respect, openness to hearing other viewpoints, and willingness to change characterize the trait of _____.

3. A defense mechanism that involves justifying or making sense of things that don't make sense is _____.

4. The tendency to view everything in relationship to oneself is called _____.

5. A defense mechanism in which we repress or refuse to recognize threatening or negative information is called _____.

6. A state of mind in which an idea and an action or two ideas clash is called _____ _____.

7. The tendency to conform in group decision-making results in what Janis calls _____.

8. Often, the way we feel is based on our _____ about a situation.

9. _____ occurs when negative details are magnified and positive details are ignored.

10. When you imagine disastrous outcomes, you are _____.

Short Answer

11. Define points of logical vulnerability, using an example.

12. What are the semantic devices and how do they help us deal with points of logical vulnerability?

13. How is active listening used to create understanding of opposing viewpoints?

14. What are some ways we can overcome emotional reasoning?

Exercises

EXERCISE 9.1 Purpose: To understand why people rationalize rather than admit mistakes and incongruities.

In a small group, take the examples of rationalization from page 403 and discuss why someone might use those rationalizations.

1. What need might he or she be trying to meet by rationalizing about the situation?
2. How is rationalization related to the attempt to preserve self-esteem?
3. How is rationalization harmful to the critical thinking and decision making process?

EXERCISE 9.2 Purposes: To understand how feelings are connected to thoughts. To change reactions by rethinking a situation.

1. Think of some recent instances where you had a strong emotional reaction (e.g., anger, anxiety, guilt, sadness, embarrassment).
2. Identify the emotion and the thoughts or beliefs that created the emotion. What was your "self-talk" about the situation?
3. Create a different interpretation of the events—different self-talk. Would your emotions have changed with the new interpretation?

Example

I recently had surgery and my mom has been calling me every day to see if I need anything. I got irritated at her last week and told her to stop treating me like a little kid. My thoughts were that she doesn't trust me to take care of myself. I feel like my right to be treated as an adult was violated.

Looking back at this, I realize that she was just really concerned about my recovery and just wanted to be useful and reassured that I had everything I needed. That understanding made my irritation go away. In fact, I feel a little guilty now for being so rude to her when her motives were to help me be comfortable and get better.

EXERCISE 9.3 Purpose: To recognize areas of logical vulnerability.

Discover some of your points of logical vulnerability. Think about people whose opinions are not credible for you. Consider political or social issues (for example, capital punishment, drug legalization, euthanasia, gun control, or global warming), or choose an issue about which you frequently argue with other people.

Can you think of any ways in which you might not have been objective in hearing evidence from others about this issue? Do you use denial or rationalization when confronted with your points of logical vulnerability? How could you respond differently?

Example

I don't like a congresswoman in my state. I heard her speak once and thought she was rude in the way she handled a question from the audience; also, she is against some of the legislation I consider important.

Once in a while, I'll hear her say something that makes sense, but I notice I discount whatever she says; if there's a negative way to look at her comments, I do. I guess I think she has some ulterior motive, and I don't believe she has any positive contribution to make.

I don't like most of her positions, and I'd never vote for her. But I could be more open and fair and admit that occasionally she does have a good idea, and she might have real concern for the people in her district.

EXERCISE 9.4 Purpose: To practice using the semantic devices in order to make statements more accurate and rational.

1. Using the semantic devices (eliminating the all, indexing, citing specific behavior, and adding the *date* and the *etc.*), change the following irrational statements into logical statements. You will need to make up details.

   a. Women are terrible drivers. (Note the implied *all* before women.)
   b. Wealthy people are greedy and materialistic.
   c. Democrats are bleeding-heart liberals and can't be trusted.
   d. Republicans don't care about the poor and needy.
   e. People from Ivy League schools are elitists.
   f. People on welfare don't want to work.

   Can you add a statement that you've heard yourself (or someone else) say?

2. Listen to yourself for a week and see if you tend to overgeneralize when confronted with your points of logical vulnerability. Try to stop yourself and to use the semantic devices to rephrase your opinions. What is the effect on your emotions and your conversations? You may note that if you try to get other people to be more specific and less prejudicial in their statements, you encounter some hostility. Why might that be? Write out several examples of instances in which you or someone else could have used the semantic devices to make more accurate statements.

EXERCISE 9.5 Purpose: To practice active listening.

1. In class, or at home, try using this listening technique when discussing an issue with someone who disagrees with you; for class, you can choose a social issue that usually creates opposing viewpoints, such as legalization of drugs, same-sex marriage, or whether spanking is an acceptable form of child discipline. Often, there are interesting controversial issues reported on websites or in daily papers, and you can choose one of those as your topic. For use at home, you might want to discuss a problem that needs to be solved, such as the division of labor or how to spend money. Be sure to tell the other person the active listening rules, and get his or her commitment to abide by them, or you may be in for a good fight. It may help to have a referee who is familiar with the technique and objective about the issue. Then report on your results by answering the following questions:

   a. Were you able to stay with the paraphrasing process? Why or why not?
   b. Did you and the other person attain greater understanding? If so, give some specific examples of what you learned about each other's positions.
   c. Was the relationship between you and the other person improved in any way?

2. Exchange a persuasive essay paper you have done (perhaps earlier in this course or in another class) with another student's essay; then do the following:

   a. Write a paraphrase of the other's ideas, clearly focusing on thesis statements and evidence used to support the thesis. Ask the other person if you accurately paraphrased his or her position.

   b. Read the other student's paraphrase of your essay; comment on how well he or she understood and expressed your point of view. If there are misunderstandings in each other's viewpoints, try to discover why these occurred. If time permits, explain to the class any problems you encountered in trying to empathize with each other's ideas.

3. Practice active listening from your side only. This exercise works well if you are not emotionally invested but the other person is experiencing strong feelings about an issue or a problem. Instead of offering advice or analysis, help the other person explore his or her thoughts and feelings by paraphrasing and summarizing the ideas he or she is expressing. You may also help the other person to stay on track by asking questions like, "What is the most troubling part of the issue for you?" and "Why is that part so troubling?" or "What do you think is the worst-case scenario or best-case scenario for resolving the problem?" Questions that stay on topic are usually very helpful in clarifying the root of the problem and in taking the best direction toward a resolution.

You Decide

Affirmative Action

Affirmative action refers to policies that seek to increase the participation of women and minorities in areas in which they have been historically underrepresented. Most affirmative action policies involve college admissions and job hiring and advancement. In the United States, the phrase "affirmative action" began with an executive order by President John F. Kennedy that required "affirmative action to ensure that applicants are employed without regard to their race, creed, color, or national origin." Subsequent civil rights laws have also supported affirmative action; the Civil Rights Act of 1964 stated that "no person . . . shall, on the ground of race, color, or national origin, be excluded from participation in, be denied the benefits of, or be subjected to discrimination under any program or activity receiving Federal financial assistance." Those who favor affirmative action policies believe that they are needed to compensate specific groups who have experienced discrimination in the past and who still experience educational and economic disadvantages. In addition, proponents believe that affirmative action benefits society by creating more institutional diversity. Those who oppose affirmative action believe that it is no longer needed, that it generates "reverse" discrimination, that it punishes non-minorities for the wrongs of previous generations, and that it diminishes the accomplishments of women and minorities who can and do excel academically and professionally on their own merits.

For more information on the debate surrounding affirmative action and additional exercises and tutorials about concepts covered in this chapter, log into MyThinkingLab at www.mythinkinglab.com and select Diestler, *Becoming a Critical Thinker*, Sixth Edition.

✳ Explore on **mythinkinglab.com**

Articles for Discussion

Read the **Document** on **mythinkinglab.com**

Excerpts from How Doctors Think

Dr. Jerome Groopman

How we think affects us in both our personal and professional lives. Dr. Jerome Groopman has written a fascinating book—*How Doctor Think*—about common errors in thinking made by physicians. Many of these errors are also found in other professions:

1. Pattern Recognition and Stereotyping. Groopman notes that there is plenty of time in a medical school classroom to consider various symptoms and hypotheses and then rule them out until the correct diagnosis emerges. In real life, particularly in hospital settings, doctors don't have the luxury of time and they rely on quick judgments.

> Physicians at the bedside do not collect a great deal of data and then leisurely generate hypotheses about possible diagnoses. Rather, physicians begin to think of diagnoses from the first moment they meet a patient. Even as they say hello they take the person's measure, registering his pallor or ruddiness, the tilt of his head, the movement of his eyes and mouth, the way he sits down or stands up, the timbre of his voice, the depth of his breathing. Their notions of what is wrong continue to evolve as they peer into the eyes, listen to the heart, press on the liver, inspect the initial set of x-rays. Research shows that most doctors quickly come up with two or three possible diagnoses from the outset of meeting a patient—a few talented ones can juggle four or five in their minds.

Groopman cites examples of well-trained physicians making "attribution errors"—snap judgments based on stereotypes—when they encounter a recognizable pattern. One such error, made during her medical training, was recounted to Groopman by Dr. Karen Delgado:

> A young man was brought to the emergency ward of the hospital in the wee hours. The police had found him sleeping on the steps of a local art museum. He was unshaven, his clothes were dirty, and he was uncooperative, unwilling to rouse himself and respond with any clarity to the triage nurse's questions. Dr. Delgado was busy that night attending to other patients, so she "eyeballed" him and decided that he could stay on a gurney in the corridor, another homeless hippie who would be given breakfast in the morning and returned to the streets. Some hours later, she felt a nurse tugging at her sleeve. "I really want you to go back and examine that guy," the nurse said. Delgado was reluctant, but she had learned to respect an ER nurse who felt that something was really wrong with a patient. "His blood sugar was sky-high," Delgado told me. The young man was on the brink of a diabetic coma. He had fallen asleep near the art museum because he was weak and lethargic and unable to make it back to his apartment. It turned out that he was not a vagrant but a student, and his difficulties giving the police and the triage nurse information reflected the metabolic changes that typify out-of-control diabetes.

2. Availability. Availability is the tendency to focus on what seems to be the most reasonable (most readily available) explanation for a behavior or event and to ignore other real possibilities. For example, a pediatrician might see numerous cases of a stomach flu that is going around and miss a diagnosis of appendicitis in a child whose symptoms looked like everyone else's that day. Josephine Marcotty, writing in the *Minneapolis Star Tribune*, summarizes a story that Groopman uses to illustrate the availability error:

> The story of Rachel Stein and her adopted daughter is one of the detailed cases he uses to make his point. When she brought the infant home from Vietnam, the baby immediately crashed. Doctors at one of the best pediatric hospitals in the United States found her riddled with infections and concluded that she had a rare, inherited immune disorder called SCID.
>
> With prayer to give her confidence, and her own determination, the mother did her own research and began asking questions, including: "What could cause a baby to have so many infections other than AIDS or SCID?" Stein thought she could have a nutritional deficiency, but doctors said, no, she didn't fit the profile. They wanted to give her a dangerous bone marrow transplant for SCID.
>
> The day before the transplant, Stein insisted that they test her daughter's immune system again. She persisted in the face of the doctors' resistance to what they often view as a parent's "misconceived demands born of desperation." But she persuaded them that an enterprising researcher might be able to write a paper off the case.
>
> Her story was instead used at a conference at the hospital to teach doctors about how to do diagnoses—and how not to. The baby did not have SCID, nor did she undergo the bone marrow transplant that could have killed her. There was some unknown aspect to her diet in Vietnam that gave her a nutritional deficiency, just as her mother thought.

"Rachel Stein . . . found a zebra (a rare and unusual cause for a symptom)," Groopman writes. But among doctors, "zebra hunters" are often viewed with disdain.

3. Confirmation Bias. Confirmation bias occurs when doctors selectively highlight evidence that supports what they expect to find and ignore information that contradicts their diagnosis. Groopman also cites researchers Tversky and Kahneman who call this phenomenon "anchoring."

> Anchoring is a shortcut in thinking where a person doesn't consider multiple possibilities but quickly and firmly latches on to a single one, sure that he has thrown his anchor down just where he needs to be. You look at your map but your mind plays tricks on you—confirmation bias—because you see only the landmarks you expect to see and neglect those that should tell you that in fact you're still at sea.

Groopman says that some doctors whose patients have seen a specialist tend to believe that the specialist has more expertise, and they look for evidence that confirms whatever diagnosis the specialist offers. He also cites other doctors—and wise patients—who don't stop at the obvious, but ask "What else could this be?"

Questions for Discussion

1. Groopman notes that doctors sometimes misdiagnose by stereotyping patients and making snap judgments about their conditions. Professionals in other areas may also make attribution errors, stereotyping their clients or customers. Salespeople who work on commission may be attentive to well-dressed customers and ignore those who don't look as affluent; lenders may turn down borrowers who are self-employed, assuming that they may not be able to pay back their loans; jurors may assume that a quiet, sweet-looking woman wouldn't be "the type" to steal a watch. Teachers who have had two disruptive siblings in their class may assume that a third sibling will behave the same way. Can you think of other professional stereotypes that reflect the attribution error?

2. Other professionals also make the availability error. If there have been a string of gang-related murders in a certain neighborhood, detectives may miss the case of a husband murdering his wife and instead blame the crime on "the usual suspects." If a majority of students in a particular school are doing well or poorly, the credit or blame may be placed on the faculty. What availability errors are common in other professions?

3. What are some questions that patients could ask their doctors to help them avoid confirmation bias?

4. Watch some episodes of *House* and see if you can detect incidents of pattern recognition, stereotyping, confirmation bias, availability, and anchoring; also, note incidents of *House* having successes and failures as a "zebra hunter" (one who finds an unusual cause or explanation for a medical symptom).

· ·

In the following article, Ryan Guina writes about his own struggles with life choices, his decision to resist the temptation to conform to the expectations of his peers, and his journey on "the road less traveled."

Create Your Own Path

Ryan Guina

If there is one thing I have learned in life it is this: life does not come with a blueprint. There is no clear path to happiness, wealth, or a successful career. Actually, I am inclined to believe that you shouldn't be afraid to stray from the pack and create your own path.

Sometimes the best thing to do is to question established practices and search for a different set of answers. Some of history's most interesting and successful figures did just that; sometimes with great success and other times with massive failure. But they weren't afraid to try. Investigating different options and looking for other answers or a new means to accomplish something spawns creativity and innovation.

Don't be afraid to take a contrarian point of view.

There have been times in my life when I went against "traditional wisdom," and those decisions have shaped me into the man I am today. Probably the best example of this was my decision to join the United States Air Force.

Growing up, I was anything but the military type. In fact, until a few months before I enlisted, I had completely disregarded the military as an option for myself. My decision to enlist shocked those who knew me well, including my family. *Why would this honors student drop out of college to enlist in the USAF as a mechanic?*

Never stop learning or pushing the boundaries of your surroundings.

My action was against the "traditional" way of thinking. But it was also one of the best decisions I ever made. I learned more about myself and the world around me than I ever would have as a college student, and I have learned to truly appreciate my place in life. I learned to embody the characteristics of integrity, honor, and teamwork, and will carry those traits with me for the remainder of my life.

My military travels took me to over 30 countries on 5 continents. I learned how to use hand tools and power tools and gained a basic understanding of mechanics. I learned the *soft skills* of how to give orders, and more importantly, how to follow them. I learned to deal with people of various backgrounds and dispositions. I have earned certain veterans benefits that will stay with me for life, and more importantly, it was in the USAF that I met the woman who would later become my wife.

Make your own path; don't follow someone else's.

Toward the end of my military career I decided to finish college. I took full-time night classes while maintaining a full-time work schedule. The sacrifice was worth it. I graduated from college before I separated from the USAF and professionally, I am on par with my age group.

My life's journey to this point by no means followed a traditional path. But I kept my eye on the ball and I consider my life to be a successful one thus far, however success may be defined.

The path I took is not for everyone. In my opinion, success and happiness and wealth lack a true definition, and you need to feel your own way until you find what they mean to you.

Write a book. Start a business. Take classes for knowledge or fun. Take a job that interests you instead of taking a job only for the salary. Or simply turn left instead of right. The point is to create your own path and make this life yours. ■

Questions for Discussion

1. What benefits did Ryan Guina achieve from following his own unique path?

2. Most people tend to follow expectations of their families and societies, especially in the young adult years. For example, British students usually take a "gap year" between high school and college to get more perspective and direction before beginning higher education studies. According to writers for thinkingbeyondborders.org, a gap year "may include participating in an organized Gap Year program, working in a field of interest, civil service in the military or a national service organization like AmeriCorps, pursuing athletics, or traveling the world as a tourist." To what extent do you think that a gap year before college would be beneficial?

3. Have you struggled with major life choices, such as where to study and what to study? How have you come to resolution on those decisions?

4. How would you describe a good balance between considering the wisdom and advice of family, friends, and mentors and "creating your own path"?

· ·

The following is an excerpt from Gerry Spence's book *How to Argue and Win Every Time*. Spence is a lawyer and television commentator; notice how he uses his listening skills to "read between the lines" in order to understand a prospective juror.

The Lock: They Argue and I Argue Back. But I Never Seem to Win. The Key: Listen—Just Listen, and You'll Start to Win.

Gerry Spence

If I were required to choose the single essential skill from the many that make up the art of argument, it would be the ability to listen. I know lawyers who have never successfully cross-examined a witness, who have never understood where the judge was coming from, who can never ascertain what those around them are plainly saying to them. I know lawyers who can never understand the weaknesses of their opponent's case or the fears of the prosecutor; who, at last, can never understand the issues before them because they have never learned to listen. Listening is the ability to hear what people are saying, or *not saying* as distinguished from the words they enunciate.

Listening for what is not said: "How do you feel about a widow who is asking you for money for the death of her husband?" I once asked a prospective juror in a case in which I represented the widow.

"I don't know," the juror replied. "I don't know" did not mean that the juror didn't know. It meant he didn't feel comfortable telling me. If he felt all right about the money for justice, he would have said, "I feel fine about it."

"Do you have some feeling about this kind of a lawsuit?"

"Not really," the juror replied. "Not really" did not mean "not really." It meant probably. The juror did not want to get into a public argument with the likes of me. If he were at home with his wife he would have said something quite different. I followed with this question:

"If you were home and were talking about this case with your wife, is it possible you might say something like this to her: 'I don't think people should sue for their dead husbands. All the money in the world can't bring the man back. I think those kinds of lawsuits are wrong.'?"

"I don't talk about things like this with my wife," he replied. Now he was obviously refusing to answer the question at hand.

"If you and I were best friends and were talking about this case over a beer, what would you tell me?"

"I don't drink beer."

"How about coffee?" I gave him a big friendly smile to assure him I wasn't trying to push him around.

Suddenly the juror blurted it out: "My father was killed and my mother never got a cent." There it was! You could immediately feel all the pain—a boy without a father, a mother struggling to rear her family without a husband.

"It must have been pretty hard on your mother trying to raise a family by herself." (The words *It must have been* are magical words that say to the Other, "I understand how it was.")

"You bet." Now the juror and I were on the same side.

"And it must have been hard to grow up without a father."

He looked down at his hands.

"If you could have had the power as a boy to get help for your mother, would you have done so?"

"Sure. I did everything I could for her."

"Is it all right with you if I try to help Mrs. Richardson get justice in this case for herself and her children?"

"Yes," he said. And that was the end of it—the magical product of listening. ▪

Questions for Discussion

1. Gerry Spence states that "Listening is the ability to hear what people are saying, or *not saying* as distinguished from the words they enunciate." The juror in this case responded to Spence's early questions with "I don't know" and "Not really." How did Spence translate the meaning of these phrases?

2. Spence points out in his book that whenever pain or rage is expressed in words or silences, there is a need to be heard and understood. How did his understanding of the juror's pain enable him to establish both empathy and rapport?

3. Spence stated, "If I were required to choose the single essential skill from the many that make up the art of argument, it would be the ability to listen." To what extent do you agree with his statement?

. . . .

The following article is about the dangers of "revisionist" history when unpleasant historical facts cause people to deny those facts. The author discusses the consequences of denying, rather than acknowledging and learning from the tragedies of the past.

It Happened

To Deny That the Holocaust Occurred Is to Set the Preconditions for Another One

Richard V. Pierard

The emergence of David Duke as a political figure has again drawn public attention to the contention that no Jewish Holocaust occurred in World War II. The ex-Klansman has said that Hitler and the Nazis did not systematically and successfully destroy most of Europe's Jews.

For years, Holocaust denial has been a stock-in-trade of shadowy creatures on the extreme Right. In recent times, several pseudo-scholars have come forward to argue against the "extermination legend" and "myth of the six million." Through an elaborate process of distortions, half-truths, and falsification of data, these "revisionists" seek to convince the gullible that Hitler did not order the annihilation of the Jews, but instead had this "alien minority" placed in labor camps where they could not subvert the war effort.

Harsh war-time conditions caused the epidemic diseases and malnutrition in the crowded camps; crematories were necessary to dispose of the remains of the few thousand who died. Cyanide gas was used for delousing and fumigation in order to check the spread of typhus. There were so few Jews left in Europe because most had emigrated to North America or Israel. Pictures of gas chambers and emaciated inmates are fabrications. And so the story goes.

In fact, Holocaust denial is the ultimate Big Lie. The whole process of destruction is so well-attested through eye-witness accounts, official documents, and contemporary press reports that no one in his or her right mind could deny that it happened.

So why is such a monstrous falsehood perpetrated? The answer is twofold. One reason is anti-Semitism—the ongoing hatred of Jews that animates extreme rightist groups in North America, Britain, France, Germany, and elsewhere. The other is the intention to deny Jews the right to a land of their own, where they may live peacefully within secure borders.

Is Holocaust denial merely a Jewish problem? No, it is also an American Christian problem. We must never forget that anti-Semitism has its roots in the theology and practice of the Christian church, from the writings of the church fathers, through the Inquisition, even in the comments of Martin Luther. Moreover, the U.S. government and people did little to help Jews in the years 1933 through 1945. Opinion polls in our "Christian nation" in 1942 found that people disliked Jews more than the German and Japanese enemies, while officials in Washington pooh-poohed the accounts of extermination programs as "atrocity stories."

Evangelicals may try to evade the issue by arguing that the Holocaust was a product of theological liberalism. But we cannot let ourselves off the hook so easily. Robert Ross excellently shows in *So It Was True* (1980) that while our magazines reported the grim details of the Nazi policies, our modest attempts to persuade the U.S. authorities to do something lacked moral passion.

Likewise, conservative free church Christians in Germany supported the Hitler regime just as fervently as most in the official church did. In 1984, the German Baptists even issued a formal statement confessing that they had been taken in by the "ideological seduction" of the time. They had not stood up for truth and righteousness.

The bottom line is that to deny the Holocaust is to set the preconditions for yet another one. It behooves evangelicals to stand up and utter a forthright no to the "revisionists" and their fellow travelers. The very credibility of our faith is at stake. ■

Questions for Discussion

1. What would cause a person or group of persons to deny the painful history of another group of people? Do ethnocentrism, egocentrism, and/or conformity and groupthink play a role in this denial?

2. What should be the guidelines for any form of "revisionist history"?

3. Why does the author say that "to deny the Holocaust is to set the preconditions for yet another one"?

4. What other historical persecutions have been denied or minimized and for what reasons?

A number of years ago, linguistic professor Deborah Tannen wrote the book *You Just Don't Understand* in which she discusses research that reveals differences between male and female conversational styles. Tannen found some fascinating and informative differences in how men and women communicate.

The following excerpt is from a more recent bestseller entitled *For Women Only—What You Need to Know About the Inner Lives of Men,* based on the research commissioned by author Shaunti Feldhahn. Feldhahn was surprised by the answers to her national survey and what they reveal about the differences between men and women. Her comments reflect the generalizations that she drew from her findings. Feldhahn also discusses the implications of the research as they relate to improving dating and marital relationships. Since her survey on men and the resulting interest in her gender studies, Feldhahn and her husband Jeff commissioned a survey on women, and they have written a new book on their findings entitled *For Men Only*.

Author Note: The professional survey was designed with the guidance of Chuck Cowan of Analytic Focus (www.analyticfocus.com), the former chief of survey design at the U.S. Census Bureau. The survey was conducted by Decision Analyst (www.decisionanalyst.com) and was designed to deliver a random, representative, national sample of 400 men (the sample size suggested by Churck Cowan) who were heterosexual, lived within the United States, and were between the ages of 21 and 75.

For Women Only—What You Need to Know About the Inner Lives of Men

Shaunti Feldhahn

When I was a year or two out of college, I went on a retreat that profoundly impacted my understanding of men.

The theme of the retreat was "Relationships," which as you can imagine was of great interest to a group of single young adults.

For the very first session, the retreat speaker divided the room in half and placed the men on one side, women on the other.

"I'm going to ask you to choose between two bad things," he said. "If you had to choose, would you rather feel alone and unloved in the world OR would you rather feel inadequate and disrespected by everyone?"

I remember thinking. What kind of choice is that? Who would ever choose to feel unloved?

The speaker then turned to the men's side of the room. "Okay, men. Who here would rather feel alone and unloved?"

A sea of hands went up, and a giant gasp rippled across the women's side of the room.

He asked which men would rather feel disrespected, and we women watched in bemusement as only a few men lifted their hands.

Then it was our turn to answer and the men's turn to be shocked when most of the women indicated that they'd rather feel inadequate and disrespected than unloved.

What It Means

While it may be totally foreign to most of us, the male need for respect and affirmation—especially from his woman—is so hardwired and so critical that most men would rather feel unloved than disrespected or inadequate. Question 3 of the survey indicated that three out of four men would make that choice (to be unloved rather than disrespected). When I originally tested the survey questions, I was perplexed that many men had a hard time answering the "unloved versus disrespected" question—because they appeared to equate the two. Chuck Cowan, the survey-design expert, warned me that might happen. *Why?* I wondered. *Those are two totally different things!* Then one of my readers tested my survey questions on ten men who didn't know me. When I got the surveys back, only one note was attached: "A lot of the guys fussed over Question 3. They did not feel the choices were different."

Finally, the lightbulb came on: *If a man feels disrespected, he is going to feel unloved.* And what that translates to is this: If you want to love your man in the way *he* needs to be loved, then you need to ensure that he feels your respect most of all.

The funny thing is—most of us do respect the man in our lives and often don't realize when our words or actions convey exactly the opposite! We may be totally perplexed when our man responds negatively in a conversation, helplessly wondering. *What did I say?* Combine this with the difficulty many men have articulating their feelings (i.e., why they are upset), and you've got a combustible—and frustrating—situation. . . . If a man can't articulate his feelings in the heat of the moment, he won't necessarily blurt out something helpful like "You're disrespecting me!" But rest assured, if he's angry at something you've said or done and you don't understand the cause, there is a good chance that he is feeling the pain or humiliation of your disrespect.

If you want confirmation of this, consider an extremely telling response from the survey (see Question #14:)

Question 14:

Even the best relationships sometimes have conflicts on day-to-day issues. In the middle of a conflict with my wife/significant other, I am more likely to be feeling. . . {Choose One Answer}

Base = Respondents Who Answered Question 400
That my wife/significant other doesn't respect me right now. **81.5%**
That my wife/significant other doesn't love me right now.   **18.5%**
Total   100%

More than *80 percent* of men—four out of five—said that in a conflict they were likely to be feeling disrespected. Whereas we girls are far more likely to be wailing, "He doesn't love me!" ▪

Questions for Discussion

1. The author of the book *For Women Only* used a survey designed by a professional. What elements of the survey design give credibility to her findings? (See author's note at the beginning of the survey.)

2. What conclusions does Shaunti Feldhahn draw from the answers to Questions 3 and 14? What are the implications of these conclusions?

3. To what extent do the survey findings cited in this article match your experience of the difference between male and female communication styles?

4. For further results, read the full survey in the author's book or on her website. You may also want to look at the national survey of women that Feldhahn completed with her husband entitled *For Men Only*.

• •

The following story is about a father who finds himself irrationally upset one morning about his daughter's hairstyle. He realizes that her appearance has triggered a strong "point of logical vulnerability" in him, creating powerful and irrational responses. As you read, try to understand how a person's life experiences can negatively affect his or her perspective and communication with a loved one.

Breakfast and Tousled Cornrows

A Tale of Logical Vulnerability

John Dies

I sat staring at the back of her head for at least three hours. All right, maybe it was only twenty seconds, but it felt like three hours. What on earth is going on? In the front most of the braids seemed normal, but in some places the braids were so tight that the hair stood out at right angles before drooping to the shoulders. It looked a little like the action of a horse's tail, just before doing his business. In other areas the braids were loosely started, halfway down the gathered lock of hair. My nearly twelve year old daughter had set a new standard for cornrows, but it was a standard that I did not understand. It was a disturbing beginning for the day, particularly before breakfast.

"I like it," she said.

"Yes, well, I can see that you would. All you can see is the front. The front is fine, nicely spaced, even cornrows. It's the back I'm talking about," I explained. As if I even cared about the neat front rows. I just didn't like it. I was being tested, and I didn't like that either. I rustled about the kitchen gathering the various items to pack for her and her brother's school lunches.

"I looked at the back when I was doing it, it looks fine. I saw it in the mirror," she replied.

Yeah, right. My daughter is a brilliant girl, kind, funny, but not very objective when it comes to her own opinions. The word stubborn comes to mind. She wasn't budging an inch and the two dozen unruly cornrows were staying firmly on her head. Understand, I like cornrows, I even like dreadlocks. But these things didn't even remotely pass as acceptable definitions.

"Listen, you're really pushing the limits here. I mean, I understand that you don't mind being different, but it seems to me that you have an unhealthy desire to be weird or something. I really think you should think this over before going to school like that."

I felt I had some pretty strong ground here. I was giving due respect, appealing to her logic, sharing my judgment on the merits. And if that didn't work then I guess I expected for her to come around to my point simply on the basis that I, as her father, was disturbed.

"Okay, I thought about it and I think it's fine," she offered, and that was the end of the conversation.

Hmm, this was not going well. It was almost as if she sensed that my arguments were unsound and therefore unworthy of further attention. Was this true? What was the basis of my dislike? Was it entirely based on the asymmetrical braids?

A few days earlier I had found a box that sort of fell out of the pile stacked in the garage. A carton of icons, each one loaded with an entire database of memories. Not a lot of written words, no notebooks of young angst, no diaries of adventures. Mostly objects. A fender mirror from my first vehicle, a half-eaten high school diploma, a paper placemat from a restaurant in West Yellowstone. Oddities with stories attached. My life in a box. And only one box at that. I could at least explain the half-eaten diploma. My dog ate it. He never touched my homework in three long years of high school, but as soon as I graduated, he ate my diploma.

Anyway, sorting through this collection I came upon an old photo of my ninth grade class. It was the typical photo where the entire class gathers on the front steps, and the photographer takes the shot hoping for a minimum of finger gestures, grimaces and general chaos. Somewhere on those steps was a younger and wiser version of myself. As I scanned those fresh faces I was surprised how familiar most of them were even after thirty-five years. Characters from the past, leaping fresh into my consciousness. It was a great time, a time of innocence, and years before any of these people made serious mistakes. It was, in some cases, the last year of the trouble free life of a child.

Laying my finger briefly on each face, I recalled what the future would bring. Here there was death in a traffic accident, speeding on a motorcycle, no helmet. Here there was madness, after a long series of drug addictions. And this fellow, a hopeless alcoholic. This young lady, drugs, welfare, four children before age twenty. More and more, drugs, jail, and death.

The whole class didn't fall into disaster. At least I don't think so. I'm not sure because I didn't know everybody. It just seemed that most of my friends had particularly hard lives. In fact, only two or three seemed to survive out of the two dozen that loosely hung together. I suppose I had thought about this before but this time I was struggling with the reasons. Was there something here, in this last innocent photo that gave a hint?

Suddenly it came to me. None of us fit in. All of us were somehow on the edge, not quite a part of the whole. Different in thought, different in deed. Our stumbling identities only defined by our own association with each other. Bright in some cases, talented in others, but uniformly weird in all instances.

And now my daughter seems bent upon being weird in her own right. I had this mental flash of how many could I save, if I could just go back in time and warn them. Would they listen to a caring stranger? If they wouldn't listen, could I force them? I couldn't do it for them, but this was my daughter, and I was not giving her up to the bleak future of nonconformity. At least not without a fight.

All of this seemed to solidify in the few minutes it took to make her school lunch. As I made the cheese sandwich, I pondered her future. As I bagged her tortilla chips I resolved to make a difference.

"Okay, that's it. No more cornrows. I tried to give you the freedom to make wise decisions and you refused, so now I'll step in and provide the rules. No more weirdness. You will not court weirdness nor seek to be different, or any of that stuff. You're too young and if you go on this way then what wild and crazy thing will you pull when you're eighteen? Later on, you can wear your hair however you want, but for right now, lose the braids."

Dead silence, shocked expressions. My son froze, his toast halfway to his mouth.

"Now?"

I could see in her eyes the deep hurt, even with the one word of acquiescence. She couldn't know what I was thinking, and didn't understand how I could react the way I was reacting. Her eyes just misted over and she prepared herself to walk whatever line I asked her to walk.

Now it was beginning to dawn on me that things hadn't gone quite the way I wanted. I knew I was struggling, but somehow the noose was just getting drawn tighter the more I twisted. I was almost swinging in the breeze due to my own efforts when my wife came in to the picture. Good, I'll explain what I did, she'll understand and together we will force, uh, together we will demand that, umm, together we will make it right.

"So, what do we do now?" I confided.

"Seems to me that *you* have done what you have pretty much on your own," she said quietly.

Whoops, definitely swinging in the breeze now, twisting slowly in the wind.

"Oh, sure. Now that's being supportive. I ask for help here and this is what I get," I said with some anger but more confusion.

"It's hard to be very supportive of someone who is wrong," she patiently explained.

Yeah, well, uh, huh. I knew it would come down to this. Skewered by the truth. It was the truth. My fear led me to over-control. My love led me to over-react. I can't stop my daughter from being different. I can't protect her from the unknown future. All I can do is love her and equip her with the tools of life. Part of those tools included discernment, confidence, faith in God, compassion, service, and discipline. And ultimately I needed to trust in God as well.

So, I called her over to apologize and to try to explain my actions. I thanked her for being obedient and I hoped that she understood that even parents make mistakes, and when that happens I believe the parent should make it right and apologize. She listened, and nodded, and seemed saddened about my loss of friends. I told her that her hair was her business and that I was just scared. I still didn't like the asymmetrical arrangement. She smiled and said, "That's okay."

She seemed at that moment much wiser than I. ■

Questions for Discussion

1. What was the "point of logical vulnerability," the subject about which this father had trouble being rational? Why was it a point of logical vulnerability for him? What specific forms of emotional reasoning did he use?

2. When the author discovered how his emotions blinded his reasoning, how did he remedy his thinking and his behavior?

3. Has your concern for another person's welfare ever clouded your judgment and your communication with that person? Conversely, has someone's concern for you ever clouded his or her judgment?

4. The author was concerned that his daughter's nonconformity would lead her into trouble. In what ways could her nonconformity be seen as a strength?

Ideas for Writing or Speaking

1. The United States Declaration of Independence states that "all men are created equal." How would a world in which all people were treated with equal respect and dignity work? Write or speak about what it would take to live in such a world and what that world would look like. If you don't believe that such a world could exist, write about the conditions that make it impossible.

2. Write or speak about a tragic event in human history. What lessons can we learn from this event? Are there actions that can be taken to prevent a reoccurrence of such an event?

3. Write an exploratory essay or speech on a current problem. List several of the solutions given for this problem and explore the pros and cons of each solution. Some problems you might explore are health care, shelters for the homeless, teenage pregnancy, unemployment, or immigration. You might also want to choose a problem that has emerged on your campus. Use this format in preparing your essay or speech:

   a. Clearly define the problem.
   b. Establish criteria for solutions (e.g., consider time and money limits).
   c. Come up with as many alternative solutions as possible. (If you are working in a group, brainstorm about possibilities.)
   d. When possible alternatives are exhausted, evaluate each alternative against the criteria for solutions, showing an understanding of diverse viewpoints.
   e. Choose the best alternative and explain why this alternative is the best.

4. Watch the classic (or remade) film *Twelve Angry Men*. This film depicts the various viewpoints and prejudices of a group of jurors who have to determine the guilt or innocence of a young man accused of killing his father. Before viewing the tape, consider the following excerpt:

   > The drive to help juries make the right decisions is drawing some ideas from human-behavior experts who have amassed a wealth of research on how jurors think. Decades ago, judges and lawyers assumed that jurors heard evidence piecemeal and began to analyze it in earnest only during deliberations. But extensive interviews of jurors in recent years have given rise to the theory that they construct evidence into mental "stories" that incorporate interpretations based on their personal experiences. "Jurors used to be viewed as passive objects," says Valerie Hans, a jury researcher at the University of Delaware. "Now we know they are very active in filling in missing evidence and making inferences." The studies are influencing some judges to give jurors more information about the cases they hear. [17]

   After viewing the film, discuss the problems of ethnocentrism and egocentrism that influence the decisions of different jurors and what arguments help them to be fair to the defendant.

5. Do an analysis of another film that deals with egocentrism or ethnocentrism, or with people's failures at understanding the perspectives of others. Some suggested titles include *Bend It Like Beckham, Milk, School Ties, To Kill a Mockingbird, The Great Santini, Philadelphia, Dead Poets Society, Schindler's List, Pride and Prejudice, Gandhi, As Good as It Gets,* and *In the Heat of the Night.* Explain

---

[17] Ted Gest with Constance Johnson, "The Justice System: Getting a Fair Trial," *U.S. News & World Report,* May 25, 1992, p. 38.

how the problem of egocentrism, ethnocentrism, defensiveness, or lack of empathy is explored in the film. Then tell how the problem is resolved (or not resolved). Finally, state the applications of the film's theme to similar problems faced by people today. (See Films for Analysis and Discussion for more ideas.)

6. Choose an issue about which you feel strongly and argue for the position that is opposite to your own real beliefs. Construct a persuasive essay or speech on this position, using one of the formats outlined in Chapter 10. Do thorough research on the stand you are defending, and be as convincing as you can.

   In the conclusion of your essay or speech, explain whether this exercise caused you to be more or less convinced about your original position on this issue. What changes, if any, did you make in your perspective concerning the issue?

7. Create an essay or speech on an issue about which you have no strong feelings. Research both sides of the issue and become acquainted with the benefits and shortcomings of each.

   In your discussion of the issue, articulate the conclusions of both sides and the reasons given for each conclusion. Note the strongest and weakest reasons for each side. Point out fallacious reasoning that is used to defend either position. In your conclusion, comment on whether you found either side to be more convincing and why.

Films for Analysis and Discussion

Amazing Grace (2006, PG)

This film recounts the life of William Wilberforce, a member of the British Parliament in 1797, who fought to abolish the transatlantic slave trade. Wilberforce's struggles against his colleagues in the House of Commons caused him to battle illness and discouragement, but he was helped to persevere by the support of his wife and friends. *Amazing Grace* (based on the title of a hymn written by Wilberforce's mentor, John Newton, who was a reformed slave trader himself) is a good example of how groupthink and ethnocentrism can be overcome through empathy, integrity, and perseverance.

Similar Films and Classics

(Also, consider the films listed in #5 under Ideas for Writing or Speaking.)

Clint Eastwood's masterpiece *Letters from Iwo Jima* (2006, R) and his American counterpart *Flags of Our Fathers* (2006, R) are companion pieces that tell of the same event (the Battle of Iwo Jima in 1945) from two very different perspectives. It's a lesson in fair-mindedness, as Eastwood approached both films with an unwavering commitment to honesty. The scenes of war are harrowing from both perspectives, showing that the human side to tragedy is always profound and compelling.

The Last Samurai (2004, R)

This is the story of Captain Nathan Algren, an American Civil War veteran who is hired to train the peasant conscripts for the first standing imperial army in Japan. Along the way, he learns deep respect for the traditional Japanese Samurai warriors. The film is a great example of the struggle between the beliefs and traditions of the past and the culture's emerging changes; it also explores the integration of important values of both the old and the new.

Freaky Friday (2003, PG)

This film is a comic exploration of a generation gap between a mother and her daughter. Through magical circumstances, they are forced to live in one another's bodies until they resolve and respect their differences. Along the way, the daughter Anna discovers that her perceptions about her mother, her little brother, and her mother's fiancé are all distorted, and her mother discovers that she needs to understand and respect her daughter's musical talents and aspirations.

Pieces of April (2003, PG-13)

Pieces of April follows the adventures of April Burns as she tries to make a new start with her family by inviting them to travel from Pennsylvania to New York City for a Thanksgiving dinner. Because her oven doesn't work, she goes all over her apartment building for help and encounters differing perspectives on life and culture along the way. In addition, the film covers her mother's battle with cancer and her family's deep struggle to give April another chance and forgive her for past hurts.

Legally Blonde (2001, PG-13)

Legally Blonde follows the challenges of a southern California sorority girl named Elle Woods as she tries to fit into the privileged and academically demanding environment of Harvard Law School. It makes a strong statement against stereotyping people based on their background and especially focuses on the ethnocentrism and unchecked reality assumptions of people who identify with a particular socioeconomic class.

School Ties (1992, PG-13)

This film explores the tensions between class and religion that were especially powerful and apparent in the 1950s. A talented football player is recruited to help an exclusive prep school beat their rivals. He keeps both his poverty and his Jewish faith a secret until a series of events exposes both, and his classmates' prejudices are revealed.

The Doctor (1991, PG-13)

This film provides a great example of how a professional undergoes a transformation in his thinking because of a significant emotional event. When the doctor himself gets throat cancer, he experiences life from the viewpoint of a patient and is both enlightened and changed as a result.

Pretty Woman (1990, R)

Rich businessman Edward hires struggling prostitute Vivian to accompany him to society parties. As Vivian tries to fit in with the wealthy, she encounters both prejudice and acceptance along the way. Edward also questions his own egocentrism as a result of Vivian's influence.

Stand and Deliver (1988, PG)

Stand and Deliver is based on the true story of high school math teacher Jaime Escalante and the unconventional methods he uses to turn gang members and students stereotyped as low achievers into some of the top calculus students in the country. It is a great illustration of what can happen when people are helped to move beyond limitations imposed by the negative expectations and environments of their past.

Guess Who's Coming to Dinner (1967)

This film explores race relations when a perfect young African American man— a loving, handsome, brilliant doctor—and his family are introduced to a young white woman's family to discuss the upcoming marriage between the couple.

Gentleman's Agreement (1947)

This classic film is about a journalist who pretends to be Jewish in order to write an article about prejudice and anti-Semitism in America. It explores both the overt and subtle effects of racism and the effects on both the reporter and his friends and family.

10

Persuasive Speaking

What's Your Point?
How Do You Sharpen It?

A critical thinker can organize ideas and advocate for his or her beliefs.

We can make a difference when we speak out about issues that concern us.

THIS CHAPTER WILL COVER

- Techniques for handling the fear of public speaking
- The three elements of a persuasive message
- Ways to organize persuasive speeches
- Collaborative problem solving

▭▭●┤Read on **mythinkinglab.com**

((•●┤Listen on **mythinkinglab.com**

Most of this book has focused on evaluating the quality of arguments. As a critical thinker, you need to know what to look for when you read a blog or an article, watch a commentator or politician on television, or listen to a speech. Recognizing good content in the arguments of others enables you to form reasonable opinions and make thoughtful decisions concerning personal, social, or political issues. In addition, there are times when you will need to argue for a specific belief or course of action. There are also times to work collaboratively with others to find acceptable solutions for problems.

Understanding the basic elements of public speaking that are covered in this chapter will help you be more clear and persuasive as you advocate for your ideas. When you present a formal argument, you are giving a persuasive speech with the goal of convincing your audience to accept certain viewpoints and take certain actions. Many of us have a picture of people who are convincing as those who have *charisma*, an intangible quality that attracts others to them and to their ideas. Some people seem to have this personal power and often we can't explain why.

However, beginning with the Greek philosopher Aristotle, we have solid explanations about what actually makes a clear and convincing argument. Aristotle compiled his ideas on rhetoric in the fourth century B.C., and his work created the foundational concepts and principles of argumentation and persuasion. Aristotle's insights have been verified by modern research, and his principles form the recommendations on persuasive speaking covered in this chapter.

Speeches have three elements: content—the thoughts, supported by research, that you want to convey to an audience; organization—the structure used to convey your content; and delivery—the vocal and nonverbal communication used to present your content. Speakers plan their organization and delivery in order to clearly convey their content to an audience; they structure their ideas in a format that makes sense, and they speak loudly enough and with enough enthusiasm to get their ideas across. When you use what is known about the content and organization of a good argument and add some basic tips on public speaking, you can successfully present your ideas to both groups and individuals.

443

Some arguments require a less formal approach to speaking. In many cases, people are required to work together in small groups to come up with solutions to problems. Critical thinking skills are needed when you advocate for ideas in informal settings and work with others on both personal and professional issues.

This chapter will explain how to use the principles of argumentation to create and present formal arguments and to solve problems.

Being an Advocate of Ideas: Communicating Publicly

Never doubt that a small group of thoughtful, committed citizens can change the world; it's the only thing that ever does.

Margaret Mead, *American Anthropologist* (1901–1978),
Institute for Intercultural Studies

One of the best uses of your knowledge of critical thinking and argumentation is to advocate for ideas in which you believe. We can all learn the tools for public speaking and become better at organizing and presenting speeches.

We are motivated to speak out when we have the desire to move beyond personal interests to promote larger visions for the betterment of society. Tavis Smiley, former host of *BET Tonight with Tavis Smiley* and author of *Doing What's Right,* encourages people to get involved in the causes they endorse. He states that, "One person, fighting the good fight, can make a difference. And one person, joined by another, and another, quickly forms a coalition and, eventually, a movement. We *can* make a difference. Moreover, we *must.*"[1]

More of us might become involved in advocacy if we could get over the primary obstacle to effective public speaking, which is fear. Research published in *The Book of Lists* indicates that fear of public speaking is the most common fear of Americans, ranking above the fear of spiders, flying, and death. When we stand in front of a group, we expose our ideas, our egos, and our bodies to people who may or may not be sympathetic or receptive. We may shake, quake, or decide not to show up when we are required to speak.

At many universities, students are required to take a basic public speaking class. Years ago, the administration at Penn State University discovered many students putting this class off until the last quarter of their senior year, or even not graduating because they refused to take the class; the speech department took action by initiating a special courses for those who were terrified of public speaking. The class has filled several sections every semester for decades, and dozens of other colleges have created similar courses (see the article at the end of this chapter from the *New York Times,* "Don't Be Shy," that covers the emergence of speech anxiety classes). So if you are experiencing anxiety about speaking and would rather skip this chapter and related assignments, take heart. You aren't alone in these feelings of fear. In fact, many famous people who have had to speak in public admit to having great fears and struggling to overcome them; among them are Winston Churchill, Abraham Lincoln, James Earl Jones, Mark Twain, Dan Rather, Barbara Walters, Margaret Thatcher, Kim Basinger, Leonardo DiCaprio, Harrison Ford, Johnny Depp, and Tom Brokaw.

---

[1] Tavis Smiley, *Doing What's Right* (New York: Doubleday, Random House, Inc., 2000), p. 38.

It is possible to overcome public speaking fears to a great extent, and most students who take a course in public speaking report improvement in their feelings of confidence by the end of a semester. In addition, those who fear the most often prepare the best and therefore have well-researched and convincing arguments.

The Best Ways to Deal with Speech Fear

All the great speakers were bad speakers at first.

Ralph Waldo Emerson, "Power,"
The Conduct of Life (1860)

According to most studies, people's number one fear is public speaking. Number two is death. Death is number two. Does that sound right? This means to the average person, if you go to a funeral, you're better off in the casket than doing the eulogy.

Jerry Seinfeld

What would you advise someone who has to give a speech and is feeling terrified? You probably have some techniques you would use, such as breathing deeply to calm yourself or memorizing your opening line to get you started. This section covers the recommendations speech professionals give for dealing with speech fear.

The first way to gain confidence is to choose a topic you believe in. When you really care about your topic (which is most often the case when you take a stand on an issue), you will enjoy reading more about it and you can more easily concentrate on convincing your audience about your viewpoints; that focus helps minimize your self-consciousness. Second, you need to prepare well; then you can be confident that what you are saying has value to your audience, is solid, and includes relevant information. Instead of procrastinating and avoiding your assignment, just get started. Use any resources that have been made available to you, such as a speech lab or librarians or tutors who will help you locate good, current information on your topic. Find evidence to support your stand on the issue and write a clear outline of your ideas. You can evaluate the evidence you find according to the principles discussed in Chapters 4 and 5, and this chapter will provide you with several organizational patterns for your ideas. Talk about the ideas in your speech with your friends and family, so that you feel really familiar and comfortable with the topic.

Finally, practice the speech so you know it well. Then, even if your mind goes blank temporarily, you can keep on going "on automatic." Some people like to practice in front of friends, and others like to practice alone—the best way to practice is the one that makes you the most comfortable. Use brief notes to help you with memory lapses; note cards function as mini security blankets. Number these cards (in case you drop them) and then refer to them only briefly as you speak. Also, get rest before you speak, and do whatever relaxation techniques work for you; for some people, deep breathing is very helpful. Exercising to release tension also works well. Turn any negative thoughts, such as "I can't do this" or "I'm going to fall apart," into positive thoughts, such as "I have something to say in this speech, and I have practiced it" or "I have something to share with the audience and I can do this." Acting as if you are confident helps you to feel confident.

When you stand up to speak, walk calmly to the podium pause for a moment, take a deep breath, and "collect" yourself. It sometimes helps to memorize your first sentence so that you can get started comfortably. However, don't memorize or read the speech; instead, just speak conversationally, as you would to a group of people you know well. Use any fear that you feel inside as energy to help you project your voice; make your voice louder than normal—that will actually increase your confidence. When audience members can hear you clearly, they tend to listen better and give you more positive feedback.

It is also helpful to use visual aids, such as a PowerPoint presentation, a graph, a chart, an illustration, or a list put on the overhead projector, the whiteboard, or the blackboard. Visual aids make your ideas clearer and more memorable for your audience; they also divert audience attention away from you, and that can make you more relaxed. In addition, visual aids often serve as a reminder to you of your points, so they can keep you on track during the presentation. If you are using visual aids that require some technical equipment, arrange to practice setting them up and using them before you give the speech.

As you speak, concentrate on your audience rather than on yourself; look around at all parts of the room. Some speakers feel more comfortable looking at their audiences' foreheads rather than their eyes; the audience members usually can't tell the difference. Look for friendly faces as you scan the room, and avoid people who look unhappy (unless everyone looks unhappy—then you might need to think about what you might have said to confuse or offend them). Realize that you have good information to give the audience and consider yourself someone who is there to help them understand new ideas and perspectives.

Finally, write out or memorize your concluding statement, so that you can end the speech with grace and confidence.

Audience Analysis

audience analysis
A careful consideration of the demographic and situational factors of an audience in preparation for a speech to that audience.

One of the essential forms of preparation for a public speech is **audience analysis**. Knowing your audience gives you an added sense of readiness and familiarity that reduces your fears of the speaking situation. In addition, you can make the most of your limited time when you know some important facts about your listeners, including both *demographic* and *situational* factors.

Demographic factors include age, gender, racial and ethnic group, religious affiliation, economic status, occupation, and education. By considering these aspects of the audience, a speaker can do better planning. For example, if the audience is made up of 16- to 18-year-old students, they may not be familiar with references to certain terms such as *record albums* or to some politicians and celebrities from the past; conversely, some members of an older audience may not follow references to Facebook and Twitter. If most of the audience members are fine artists, they may not be as knowledgeable about applications of Internet technology as would an audience whose business involves the daily use of the Internet. To be sensitive to the makeup of a particular audience, the speaker can research these factors with the person who asked him or her to speak; a speaker may also have an opportunity to interview or poll a sample of audience members.

Even more important to a persuasive speaker are the situational factors of a given speech: What is the group's knowledge of the speaker's topic and its disposition toward the topic? If a speaker is discussing international trade agreement policies and discovers that the audience knows very little about these policies, then she needs

Stop and Think

How could each demographic factor be an important consideration to a persuasive speaker?

to give more background information. If, on the other hand, the particular audience knows a great deal about the policies, the speaker can use her time more efficiently persuading the audience to accept her position about trade agreements.

When you consider an audience's disposition toward a persuasive topic, you can classify the audience as believing, neutral, or hostile. A **believing audience** agrees with your position on an issue; it doesn't need to be convinced about the correctness of the actions you propose. To use your time most efficiently with this kind of audience, you should concentrate on getting audience members to act on any proposals you make. You want to turn them from being passive believers to active participants who will move policies forward; you also want to reinforce and strengthen their reasons for agreeing with your position so that they may also advocate well.

A **neutral audience** either does not know enough or does not care enough about your topic to have taken a stand on it. With a neutral audience, you need to provide the information audience members need to understand the topic and its importance. For example, if you are speaking against a tax reform that is currently under consideration, you can show how the new tax structure being proposed will hurt them personally. Many people are moved primarily by realizing how an issue will directly affect their lives or the lives of their families and friends; show your neutral listeners how the position you support will help them maintain or improve their own interests.

A **hostile audience** is opposed to your ideas or policies. These audience members may not shout or become violent, but you know that they think you are wrong in the positions you take; they may even think you are misguided or mean-spirited because of your beliefs. Your goals for this kind of audience have to be much more modest than they would be for a believing audience. Often, the best thing you can do is present yourself and your positions in such a clear, calm, and reasonable way that the audience members can no longer negatively stereotype people who believe as you do. Focus your speech with a hostile audience on their reconsideration of some of their own ideas, rather than trying to move this kind of group to action on your ideas.

Hostile audiences often respond well to a persuasive speaking technique called **both-sides persuasion**. A speaker who uses both-sides persuasion will acknowledge the good points that cause the audience to believe as it does but will then demonstrate how even these good points are overshadowed by the strengths of the speaker's side of the issue. For example, if you favor dress codes in local public schools and your audience is against them because they violate personal freedom, you might say the following:

> It seems to go against all of our ideas of freedom of expression and individuality to restrict students to only a few items of clothing. How can they experiment with unique styles that make personal statements when they are forced into one general look? I agree that individuality is an important value and that the solution of dress codes is far from perfect. But I believe that these codes provide the best way we have found so far to safeguard another value, the value of life. Given the fact that our students are being attacked because they are wearing what appear to be gang colors, and

believing audience
An audience that agrees with the conclusion and reasoning of the speaker.

neutral audience
An audience that does not have a strong opinion on the speaker's conclusion about an issue.

hostile audience
An audience that is opposed to the conclusion and reasoning of the speaker.

both-sides persuasion
A technique in which the speaker acknowledges one or more of the best arguments of the opposition without specifically agreeing with those arguments.

given the fact that several of our local youth have been killed over expensive shoes and jackets that the criminals wanted to steal, I believe that any measures taken to guard their safety when they are in the setting of public schools are worth pursuing.

Both-sides persuasion lets your audience know that you have considered their viewpoints and that you agree with some of their principles, but that you have come to a different conclusion about the issue. Most people will be more open to *your* ideas if they know that you understand and respect *their* ideas. Both-sides persuasion shows that while your solutions to a problem are different, your values and motives are very similar. Hostile audience members may not end up agreeing with you, but they may change their negative feelings about you and about others who hold your same viewpoints.

When you know the disposition of the majority of your audience members, you can also structure your speech with greater thoughtfulness. Neutral audiences need to gain an understanding of an issue through background information and current research, and they need to be shown why the issue is an important one. Hostile audiences are most likely to be persuaded when you lead off with your strongest points. If you save your most convincing points for later in the speech, you may lose them completely as they argue in their minds with the weaker points they have heard first. But if they hear a compelling reason to reconsider their position early on in your speech, then they may continue to listen with a more open mind. Believing audiences, on the other hand, respond well when you reserve your strongest points and end on a climactic note that creates unity and a desire to move forward to enact their beliefs. They like to be affirmed and inspired by an argument that builds from strong support to even stronger support in your final point.

The Three Elements of a Persuasive Argument: Ethos, Logos, and Pathos

Aristotle (384–322 B.C.E.) was a student of the great philosopher Plato, and he then tutored young Alexander the Great. He wrote more than 400 books, including the *Rhetoric*, which is used to this day as a foundational work for the study of argumentation.

Aristotle said that rhetoric (argumentation) involves using all the available means of persuasion, which he defined as **ethos** (personal credibility), **logos** (logical organization and reasoning), and **pathos** (emotional appeal).

Ethos: Speaker Credibility

From his many observations of persuasive speeches given in the courts and in the marketplace, Aristotle concluded that ethos, the credibility, image, character, and reputation of a speaker, was one of the most important means of persuasion. Modern researchers have discovered that ethos involves three specific dimensions: expertise, trustworthiness, and dynamism.[2]

Much of your ethos, your credibility or reputation as a speaker, will come through the same methods that help you overcome speech fear. When you are well prepared to speak and have conviction about your topic, most audiences will give

ethos
The credibility or reputation of a speaker; ethos is one of three persuasive elements of public speaking, along with *logos* and *pathos*.

logos
Logical organization and credible content in a speech; logos is one of three persuasive elements of public speaking, along with *ethos* and *pathos*.

pathos
The use of emotional appeal to support conclusions; pathos is one of three persuasive elements of public speaking, along with *ethos* and *logos*.

[2] Charles U. Larson, *Persuasion*, 9th ed. (Belmont, CA: Wadsworth Publishing, 2001), pp. 205–208.

you respect and attention. Speaker credibility can be achieved through specific effort and planning. Speakers are seen as credible when

- They can be clearly heard by the audience.
- They show that they have done their homework on a topic by using well-cited research to support their key points.
- They are easy to understand because they are well organized.
- They are easy to understand because they have rehearsed the speech before giving it.
- They show respect for and understanding of the audience by using language and examples that can be understood (not too complex or too simplified) by the members of that particular audience.
- They show respect for and understanding of their opponents.
- They reduce nervous, distracting mannerisms to a minimum (this can be done with practice).
- They dress appropriately for the speaking occasion.
- They are polite and calm, even under pressure.

When you enhance your credibility with these principles, believing audiences will be affirmed and inspired by your message, neutral audiences may be informed and even persuaded, and hostile audiences may be more open to your ideas.

Logos: Logical Organization and Credible Content

Logos, or logical appeals, are made through the use of good evidence of the kind we discussed in Chapters 4 and 5. Persuasive speakers cite statistics, relevant examples, analogies, controlled studies, and expert testimony to support their key ideas. They organize their points clearly, so that audiences can understand and follow their reasoning.

Several different organizational formats for persuasive speaking are highlighted in this chapter. Regardless of the format you choose, there are some essential ingredients to every organizational pattern that apply whether you have 2 minutes or 20 minutes to speak. To be a clearly organized speaker, use these principles, illustrated by Figure 10–1:

- Create an interesting introduction to capture the attention of the audience. You might use a quote, a story, a relevant statistic, a reference to something in the news, or a rhetorical question. Decide on your introduction after you structure the body of the speech, so that you know what it is you are introducing.
- Make your thesis statement (this is your conclusion about the issue) clear early in the speech, immediately following the introduction.
- Tell the audience how you plan to support your position; briefly list the key reasons (points) immediately after you give your thesis statement. This technique is called giving a *preview* of your speech; it helps you and your audience to stay focused.
- Explain each key point (reason). Figure 10–1 shows that each key point must be supported with evidence. The source of evidence must be cited (tell us where it comes from—the publication, author, and date). Use this structural outline to see which key points have enough verification and which need more supporting ideas. Note that each key point should also be strong enough to be a supporting pillar for the thesis statement.

- Use transitions between the key points for a smooth flow of ideas. Note that in Figure 10–1, the transitions flow between key points with a brief reference back to the thesis statement.
- Review your key points before making a concluding statement. The repetition of your ideas—first previewed in the introduction, then explained in the body, and finally summarized in the conclusion—helps reinforce them in the mind of your audience. End your speech with a statement designed to make one last strong appeal for your thesis; this appeal, called a **clincher**, may be in the form of a quote, a reference to a story or statistic from your introduction, or a brief call to action.

clincher The last remark in a persuasive speech that is designed to give a strong final appeal concerning the thesis.

As we have discussed, it is often effective to address and calmly refute the arguments for the opposing side of your speech. Do both-sides persuasion early on, in the body of the speech, if your audience is neutral or hostile to your position. On the other hand, if your audience is supportive of your position, concentrate instead on moving it to action consistent with your common beliefs.

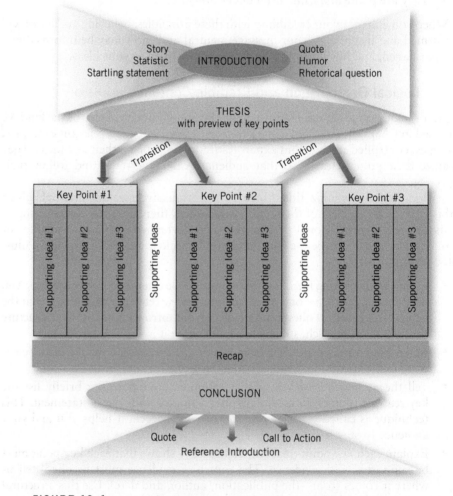

FIGURE 10–1

Speech Flowchart

Several organizational structures are acceptable for the persuasive speech. Three of the most common will be highlighted in this chapter.

Statement of Reasons Pattern. The first method follows Figure 10–1 and is simply a statement of your thesis (your conclusion about the issue) followed by key points that are the reasons supporting the thesis statement. This speech is structured as follows:

1. Introduction: Statement of Reasons Format. In the introduction, you get the audience's attention and lead into your topic through the use of examples, quotations, statistics, humor, or relevant anecdotes. In the last sentence of your introduction, you state your thesis (the conclusion or stand on your issue) and then preview (tell about) the key points that will be supporting the thesis. Essentially, the preview gives your audience an overview of the reasons you have come to your conclusion about the issue.

2. Body of the Speech. While the introduction serves to strongly state your thesis, thereby letting the audience know where you stand on the issue, the body of the speech answers and elaborates on the question "Why do you believe what you believe about the issue?" You answer that question with two to five justifications for your beliefs, and those justifications become your key points. The key points are all distinct reasons for drawing your conclusion. Cover each point, being sure to support each point (reason) with cited evidence.

3. Conclusion. The conclusion of your speech—which in this case means the ending of the speech, not your conclusion about the issue—should include a review of the key points that support your opinion. End the speech with a call to belief or action, telling the audience what you think it should believe or do as a result of the information you have presented.

The advantage of this method of presentation is that it is clear and simple; you are, in effect, saying, "I believe (*conclusion*) this way about the issue because of these reasons, and you should too."(See Exercises 10.1 and 10.2 on pages 469 and 470.)

Problem-Solution Format. A second method of structuring persuasive speeches has been outlined in the *Northern California Forensics Association Handbook*. This method follows a problem-solution format:

1. Introduction. As in any speech, the introduction to a persuasive speech must put the audience at ease with the topic of the speech, must clearly state the purpose of the speech, and must give some direction about the course of the speech.

2. Harms. The harms section of the speech should answer the question, "How are we hurt by this problem?" Financial losses, personal injuries, and deaths caused by the problem are often detailed in the harms portion.

3. Inherency. The inherency section should answer the question, "Why does the problem exist?" The reasons for the existence of any problem can be categorized as either attitudinal inherency or structural inherency. Attitudinal inherency occurs when the sentiments of the public create a barrier to the solution of the issue or when those sentiments help to perpetuate the cause of difficulty. Structural inherency is a physical barrier that must be overcome in order to solve the problem. Such a barrier could be a law, the lack of trained personnel, or an inefficient system.

4. Significance. The notion of significance addresses the question, "What is the scope of the problem?" (i.e., "How big or how widespread is this problem?"). Significance is often described by details of the geographic range, quantitative preponderance, or qualitative weight of the problem. More often than not, the significance issue is handled within both the harms and inherency sections.

5. Solvency. This final section is arguably the most important part of the persuasive speech. It answers the question, "What can be done to remedy the problem?" It is important to address two issues within the solvency section. First, be sure to tell your audience how they can help specifically. Second, attempt to give an example of how your solution has worked in the past.

6. Conclusion. The conclusion of the persuasive speech should accomplish two goals. It should initially review how the advocated solution steps will affect the problem and it should make one last appeal to the audience.[3]

Sample Persuasive Speech Outline Using the Problem-Solution Format

Social Networks: A Major Threat to Your Privacy

Carlota Jimenez

General Purpose: To persuade
   Specific Purpose: To persuade my audience to take steps necessary to protect their online privacy while remaining connected to their family and friends.
   Central Idea: Social networking users should have knowledge of and control over data collected by the network or by any third party.

I. **Introduction**

A. (Attention Getter) According to Dan Fletcher of *Time* magazine, 500 million people are registered as Facebook members. In his article, *Friends without Borders,* Fletcher says that if this website were a country, it would be the third largest country by population, two-thirds bigger than the United States.

B. Social networks have profoundly changed the concept of what we consider private. Personal information is being shared with a growing sphere of marketers and advertisers who are making profits out of users' private data. In addition, social network users are often unaware of how employers, strangers, hackers, and cyber-bullies are using their information in unauthorized and unethical ways.

C. (Thesis Statement) Social networking users should have knowledge of and control over data collected by the network or by any third party.

D. (Preview of Main Points) First, I am going to discuss the significance of the lack of online privacy in the United States. Then, I will consider the reasons that the lack of privacy exists. Finally, I will propose some solutions that will help social networking users protect their privacy online.

[3] Joe Corcoran, *Northern California Forensics Association Handbook* (Northern California Forensics Association, 1988).

II. **Body**

A. (Significance/Harms) The Internet has become not only a primary means of communication but also a place where millions of Americans store important personal data.

1. This information does not have the same legal protection as data that Americans store in their homes.

   a. According to Jeremy Mishkin, an attorney specializing in privacy law and writer for *PC World,* "social networks have forced users to rethink what privacy is in a world where public sharing of private lives has become common place." (*PC World,* May 23, 2010)

2. Tim Sparapani, director of public policy at Facebook, states that, because of social networking, people are leaving behind "virtual DNA."

   a. Exposing personal information presents a variety of risks for individuals, such as identity theft, stalking, embarrassment, and blackmail.

   b. Our unguarded social networking habits make our consumer preferences available to marketers who can use easy access to our accounts to advertise their products and services. In an article for *PC World* entitled "Goodbye to Privacy," Tom Spring writes about technology firms that can tap into social networks "to marry your profiles, tweets, and LinkedIn information with your e-mail address. If a company wants to know more about you, it can just hire one of these outfits."

3. Spring describes a trend involving "a real-time ad-bidding technology that lets advertisers, such as Google and Yahoo, track users online and deliver customized third-party ads–all in the blink of an eye. Here is how it works. As you go from site to site, advertisers can bid in real time to show you an ad tied to your online activity. For example, if you are shopping for a Nikon digital SLR camera, you may see an ad for a competing Canon DSLR model on the next site you visit. If you buy that Canon, advertisers can then bid–in a fraction of second–for the right to show you, on the next site you jump to, ads for lenses for that camera."

4. Stalkers and other deviant personalities are also able to get information about our home, work, and recreational locations.

5. According to *PC World* writer Narasu Rebbapragada, the answers to password-reset questions can be found on a user's profile, and hackers and "worms" can get into your account. "'The biggest danger that I can see is that they (advertisers and hackers) get your log-in credentials,' says Beth Jones, senior threat researcher at *Sophos* Labs. For example, the intruders can gain access to information such as mobile phone numbers, partial credit card numbers, and billing addresses stored in the Payments section of Facebook's account settings."

6. Cyber-bullying, especially that which involves students, has become commonplace and can be deadly. On the Cyber-bullying Research Center website, one young girl is quoted as saying, "I was talking to 2 girls who used to be my friends. We were talking about me because that's what they both started on about. Then they started saying things about me; then they went on a chat I was also talking on and started saying horrible things about me. They used my screen name and everything. They even told one of my guy friends that I liked him since the day we

met, and he stopped talking to me. I was both depressed and angry. I wanted to die."

7. In addition, employers or potential employers may misread information from social networking accounts. In his article for *PC World* entitled "What Is Your Facebook Data Worth," Narasu Rebbapragada gives the example of an employee named Natalie Blanchard. Natalie was fighting to have her health benefits reinstated by her employer's insurance company. The Canadian woman was being treated for depression, but *Manulife Financial* questioned her health claim after seeing Facebook photos of Blanchard enjoying herself at a party and on the beach.

(Transition) There clearly is a significant lack of privacy awareness as well as unexpected challenges to online privacy. It is important to consider the source of this problem.

B. (Inherency) According to Harvard University researchers, this privacy problem derives from the fact that individuals are unaware of the amount of personal information they provide to an indeterminate number of people. The Harvard study entitled "Privacy and Online Social Networking Websites" concludes: "Facebook is undermined by three principal factors: users disclose too much, Facebook does not take adequate steps to protect user privacy, and third parties are actively seeking out end-user information using Facebook."

1. More importantly, other new technologies and sites are also creating unexpected challenges to privacy online.

2. Not only are privacy protection default settings inadequate, but also social networking sites often discourage users from altering default settings. For instance, MySpace.com warns its users that altering default settings may make it more difficult for them to network with their friends.

3. According to *Time* magazine, in November of 2007, Facebook rolled out Facebook Beacon. This was a third-party application that automatically signed up users for a program that would send a notice to all their Facebook friends after they purchased something online. Following investigations by security analysts, Facebook turned off the option completely a month later.

   a. Today, however, Facebook gives third-party applications more access to user data through games like *Mob Wars* that store user information indefinitely, unless users uninstall the game.

4. Research done by the University of North Carolina concludes that many privacy mechanisms of online social networks are purposefully weak to facilitate the sharing of information. For example, every time Facebook users share their preferences and/or update their profiles, advertisers have more data to pool from.

5. There is little awareness and use of existing privacy mechanisms among active users. Research has offered several explanations for this underutilization of privacy options, including the permissive default settings and inherent trust in the online community.

6. The fact that our court system has not kept up with technology and the emerging privacy concerns is another reason why online privacy problems are on the rise.

    a. We have laws protecting medical privacy and DVD rental records, but we are lacking in more general privacy laws.

    b. According to Jim Harper, Director of Information Policy Studies at the Cato Institute, social networks have excessive influence concerning new legislation; they have lobbyists, lawyers, and interest-group representatives that work to protect their clients' interests.

(Transition) Now that we know the diverse causes for lack of social networking privacy, we should take action to address the problem.

C. (Solvency) Privacy advocates and some lawmakers in Congress say the growing threats to online privacy point to the need for tougher laws to protect user data.

    1. The government should create strong policies that prohibit social networks from the use of cookies and other tracking devices.

        a. In the year 2000, a federal cookie policy was issued. This policy prohibits federal agencies from using cookies and other tracking technologies on federal websites. A similar policy should be created for social networks.

    2. Users should have full knowledge of and control over any and all personal data collected by the network or by any third party using its platform.

        a. Social networks that collect data should inform users what information they collect about them, what that data could be used for, and whether it will be passed to third parties before customers hand it over.

        b. Users should take the time to be aware of privacy policies for any social networking sites that they use; they should also become aware of the many novel ways that others will attempt to get and use their personal information.

III. Conclusion

A. (Review of Main Points) I've discussed how social networks are changing the concept of privacy. We looked at the harms and the significance of this growing problem in our society. I have gone over the reasons why this privacy problem exists. Finally, I suggested some possible solutions to protect social networking user privacy.

B. (Final Plea) I would now like to urge you to do three things: First of all, do not display personal information like your address or phone number on your social networking sites; keep track of the types of photos you upload. These photos could be potential hazards to your life. Second, make sure to go over your privacy settings with each social network website you use. This will give you a measure of control over what others are able to view. Finally, become more proactive; urge lawmakers to update federal laws to protect the privacy of social networking users.

C. (Visualize Solutions Working) If you follow these steps, you will be a step closer to protecting your identity while still being connected to your family and friends in a safe environment.

D. (Tie Back to Introduction/Clincher) If you are among the millions of people using a social network, remember this: Your personal profile is being shared by a growing number of strangers who are unscrupulously making profits out of your most basic information.

Bibliography

Cyber-bullying Research Center. "About Us." Accessed January 2011, http://www.cyberbullying.us.

Besmer, Andrew, Richter Lipford, Heather, and Watson, Jason. "Understanding Privacy Settings in Facebook with an Audience View." Department of Software and Information Systems, University of North Carolina at Charlotte, Web. September 24, 2010, http://www.usenix.org/events/upsec08/tech/full_papers/lipford/lipford_html/.

Center for Democracy and Technology. "Survey Information: Americans Care Deeply About Their Privacy." October 22, 2009. Web. September 26, 2010, http://www.cdt.org/privacy/guide/surveyinfo.php.

Christiana, Joseph, and Goettke, Richard. "Privacy and Online Social Networking Websites." May 14, 2007. Accessed September 24, 2010, http://www.eecs.harvard.edu/cs199r/fp/RichJoepdf.

Clemmitt, Marcia. "Social Networking: Are Online Social Networks Eroding Privacy?" *CQ Researcher*, Volume 20, Issue 32. Library CQPress with Full Text. Web. September 25, 2010.

Fletcher, Dan. "Friends without Borders." *Time*, May 31, 2010, pp. 32–38.

Marshall, Patrick. "Online Privacy: Do Americans Need Better Protection?" *CQ Researcher*, Volume 19, Issue 39. Library CQPress with Full Text. Web. September 25, 2010.

Spring, Tom. "Goodbye to Privacy." *PC World*, Web. April 24 and May 23, 2010, http://www.pcworld.com/article/196787-2/goodbye_to_privacy.html.

Rebbapragada, Narasu. "What Is Your Facebook Data Worth?" *PC World*, Web. June 20, 2010, http://www.pcworld.com. ▪

Monroe's motivated sequence
A five-step method of organizing speeches; the steps include attention, need, satisfaction, visualization, and action.

Monroe's Motivated Sequence. A third organizational method is called **Monroe's Motivated Sequence.**[4] Monroe's steps are especially effective when a speaker wants to motivate the audience to take action. Monroe's sequence involves the following five steps:

1. *Attention:* Get the audience's interest and attention; you can do this with provocative questions, statistics, or a relevant anecdote. End your attention step with your thesis statement (main idea) and a preview of your key ideas. This step is similar to the "introduction" step of the "statement of reasons" method.

2. *Need:* The body of your speech begins with this step. Here you show your audience that a serious problem must be addressed. Discuss the extent and scope of the problem and how we are hurt by the problem.

3. *Satisfaction:* At this point, you present a solution to the problem that was introduced in the need step.

4. *Visualization:* This last part of the body of your speech is used to help listeners form a picture of what it would be like if your solution were in place. If there are aspects of the solution that would be of personal benefit to audience members, visualize those benefits in this step.

5. *Action:* This step is considered the conclusion of the speech. Here you summarize your ideas and request specific action from the audience members.

---

[4]Allan H. Monroe, *Principles and Types of Speech Communication*, 11th ed. (Glenview, IL: Scott, Foresman, 1990), pp. 180–203.

Sample Persuasive Speech Outline Using Monroe's Motivated Sequence

Following is an example of an outline that uses Monroe's Motivated Sequence:

Consider Fair Trade Coffee

Kris Anne Bordalo Nuguid

I. **Attention**

A. **Attention Getter/Introduction.** Imagine drinking the blood, sweat, and tears of laborers around the world. That is probably a very unpleasant image for you. However, you might as well be doing this if you drink coffee produced by unfair business practices. According to a 2009 article from *SolasCircle*, "Many small coffee farmers receive prices for their coffee that are less than the costs of production, forcing them into a cycle of poverty and debt; agriculture workers in the coffee industry often toil in what can be described as 'sweatshops in the fields.'"

   1. (Statistics) According to Margot Roosevelt in her article for *Time* magazine entitled "The Coffee Clash," coffee is second only to oil as the most traded product in the world. The *Coffee Statistics Report* of 2011 states that world coffee production is estimated at 110–120 million bags per year. Most coffee is grown and harvested by small farming families in developing countries. For many of these families, the coffee crop is their only source of income.

   2. (Testimony) Cathy Cockrell of the Public Affairs office at UC Berkeley calculated that there are about 80 million people *worldwide* whose lives are directly affected by the coffee trade.

B. **Thesis (conclusion).** According to Peter Fritsch of the *Wall Street Journal,* "the collapse of world coffee prices is contributing to societal meltdowns affecting an estimated 125 million people." As the largest importers of coffee, U.S. citizens must take responsibility for the consequences of our actions: we can do so by purchasing coffee obtained through the practice of equity, respect, and cooperation with poor farmers, producers, and workers, known as "fair trade."

C. **Preview Statement.** Today I will discuss the devastation unjust coffee practices bring to people around the world. Then, I will present some solutions that will address this current crisis, describe the positive changes that will take place if my solutions are implemented, and finally, provide tips on how you can do your part in improving the quality of the lives of impoverished coffee farm workers.

II. **Need**

A. Folgers, Kraft, Maxwell, and Phillip Morris. Do these companies sound familiar? Peter Fritsch of the *Associated Press* stated that these major corporations buy coffee beans that are obtained at low costs from poor farming families. The low costs allow the corporations to generate fortunes by distributing the coffee beans around the globe. Unfortunately, such fortunes have not reached the homes of those who have slaved to harvest this ever-popular product: the farmers.

   1. Poor farming families are the main harvesters of coffee, but because they cannot process the coffee beans, they have to sell the beans to "coyotes," or traders, who often take advantage of them by purchasing the beans at excessively low prices.

a. In 2009, *Global Exchange,* an international human rights organization, revealed that the farmers are paid between 60–70 cents per pound of beans.

2. Do you know how much consumers pay for coffee? Maxwell House coffee sells for $16.69 for 39 ounces. The median income of American families, according to an August 2010 Census Bureau report, was $52,029.00, which makes coffee an affordable item. But the average yearly income of farming families is only $500–$1000.

3. With their minimal incomes, these families cannot even afford the fruits of their labor. Furthermore, the practice of the larger corporations driving down the prices of coffee beans often results in the already struggling smaller farmers losing their businesses.

a. In 2005, Merling Ramos, the Director of PRODECOOP Fair Trade cooperative in Nicaragua, stated that unfair trading practices subject small farming families to a life of destitution and hardship.

b. Nestor Osorio, head of the International Coffee Organization in London, stated, "The low bean prices fueling corporate profits are . . . forcing desperate peasants into everything from crime and illicit crops to illegal migration."

B. As you can see, the social and economic implications of these extortive practices are great—but these aren't the only aspects of people's lives that are affected. The welfare of workers and the educational opportunities for their children are also impacted by their exploitation.

1. Small farmers aren't the only producers of coffee beans: large coffee plantations also exist, which directly grow, harvest, and process coffee beans; conditions aren't much better for the workers on such plantations.

2. On many of these coffee plantations, human rights are being violated. *Global Exchange* reported in 2005 that, "coffee pickers [in Guatemala] have to pick a 100-pound quota" in order to earn their less than $3 wage. Because of this quota, many coffee-farm workers bring their children to pick beans with them.

a. In a *Time* magazine article, Josafat Hernandez, the co-president of a fair trade coffee farm, observed that in Mexico City farms, "children as young as 5 pick coffee, baskets strapped to their waists."

3. The income that these small farmers can earn makes the difference between survival and death; as a result, the children often devote their time to working: this leaves little or no time for education or play.

a. In 2005, *Global Exchange* reported that a study of coffee plantations in Guatemala revealed that only 13% of coffee workers have completed their primary education. The limited education that children of coffee farming families attain leaves them with fewer opportunities to improve their economic standing, and traps their families in a cycle of poverty.

III. Satisfaction

A. (Main Point) Fair Trade is a practical solution to the "coffee crisis."

1. In 2007, *Equal Exchange Incorporated,* the leading provider of Fair Trade coffee in the U.S., explained that Fair Trade coffee receives certification that ensures consumers who buy the product that the coffee being purchased was produced under fair conditions for the farmers.

2. *PTs Coffee Roasting Company,* a Fair Trade partner, assured consumers that Fair Trade coffee farmers are guaranteed a minimum "fair trade price"

of $1.26/lb for their coffee beans. This practice would guarantee that poor farmers would earn a living wage regardless of the fluctuations in the coffee market. Thus, these farmers would gain greater economic stability. With fair trade prices and policies, small-scale farmers avoid dealing with conniving "coyotes": thus, they are able to realize a higher profit for their labor.

IV. **Visualization**

A. (Main Point) The development of fair trade practices between developing countries and their wealthier counterparts such as the U.S. and Europe would improve the living conditions of millions of laborers around the world.

1. Fair Trade policies guarantee that farming operations and other workers' groups receive a fair price for their products. The Fair Trade price means that farmers can feed their families and that their children can go to school.

2. A portion of revenues generated from Fair Trade are also contributed to local projects in education, health, and environmental protection for developing areas. In 2007, *Equal Exchange* representatives stated, "A coffee processing plant in El Salvador, community stores in Columbia, the training of doctors in Mexico, reforestation programs in Costa Rica, [and] new schools in Peru," are all examples of gifts that Fair Trade co-ops have endowed on their communities.

Transition. By choosing to drink Fair Trade coffee, you will make life better for the small farm workers and their families hundreds of miles away.

V. **Action**

A. Food for Thought. The only things to lose now are a few more cents at the coffee pump. I ask you: "Is the cost of cheap coffee worth the human lives that are being destroyed?"

B. I hope that I have convinced you that Fair Trade coffee is the way to go. So what can you do about it?

1. Put pressure on the large corporations that sell coffee. Some people don't take action because they don't think their letters and speeches can make a difference. OXFAM (Oxford Committee for Famine Relief) America begs to differ.

   a. In an article that appeared on the OXFAM America web page, writer Kelley Damore reported that, "In September 2003, Procter & Gamble (P&G), the largest seller of coffee in the US, announced it would introduce Fair Trade Certified™ coffee products" (Damore).

2. Why the sudden change? Apparently, Procter & Gamble was influenced by coffee drinkers, human rights activists, and members of the House of Representatives and the Senate, all urging it to become Fair Trade Certified.

   a. However, according to the Fair Trade page on the Global Exchange website updated in December of 2009, Folger's coffee, which was part of Procter & Gamble, did not sell Fair Trade coffee, and has subsequently been bought by Smuckers.

3. A *BBC* News Report from October, 2005, revealed that Nestle followed Procter & Gamble's lead, launching a Fair Trade coffee line. Nestle has been boycotted for decades for marketing practices that hurt developing countries, but it was persuaded by the consumer's demands and an understanding of the power of "ethical" markets to try to change its reputation. So do not hesitate to write to government officials or the corporations themselves and voice your opinion.

C. **Review.** We have seen the hardship that unjust coffee practices bring to farmers, workers, and their children in impoverished areas of the world. We've discussed how fair trade practices can help eradicate poverty and bring about a better standard of living for laborers. Finally, we've seen that more large corporations will be willing to incorporate fair trade when consumers press for such changes.

D. **Clincher.** We can all do our part in improving the quality of the lives of impoverished coffee farm workers.

As cultural anthropologist Margaret Mead put it, "Never doubt that a small group of thoughtful, committed citizens can change the world. Indeed, it is the only thing that ever has."

Bibliography

1. "Coffee Workers in Guatemala; A Survey of Working and Living Conditions on Coffee Farms COVERCO." Commission for the Verification of Codes of Conduct (COVERCO). Feb 2000. 27 Mar 2007 <http://www.usleap.org/Coffee/sbcovercorpt/sbcovercorpt.html>
2. Damore, Kelley. "Coffee Talk." 2006. *Oxfam America.* 27 Mar 2007 <http://www.oxfamamerica.org/newsandpublications/news_updates/archive2004/art6877.html>
3. DeNavas-Walt, et al. "Income, Poverty, and Health Insurance Coverage in the United States: 2006." *Current Population Reports.* Census Bureau, 2006. *SIRS Knowledge Source.* SIRS Government_Reporter. Contra Costa College Library. 27 Mar 2007 <http://0-www.sirs.com.alice.dvc.edu:80>
4. "Frequently Asked Questions About Fair Trade Coffee." *Global Exchange.* 01 April 2005. 27 March 2007. December 2009 http://www.globalexchange.org/campaigns/fairtrade/coffee/coffeeFAQ.html>
5. Fritsch, Peter. *The Wall Street Journal.*–"Coffee-Bean Oversupply Deepens Latin America's woes." *Organic Consumers Association.* 08 Jul 2002. 27 Mar 2007 <http://www.organicconsumers.org/starbucks/coffee-beans.cfm>
6. "Nestle launches fair trade coffee." *BBC News.* 07 Oct 2005. 27 Mar 2007. <http://news.bbc.co.uk/1/hi/business/4318882.stm>
7. Raburn, Ilana. "The Central American Coffee Crisis: Why Producers Are Failing to Make a Profit from 'Top Quality' Coffee." *The Globalist Foundation.* 23 Dec 2006. 27 Mar 2007 <http://www.global21online.org/cambridge/i1003.html>
8. Roosevelt, Margot. "The Coffee Clash." *Time,* 01 Mar 2004. 25 Nov 2006 <http://www.time.com/time/insidebiz/article/0,9171,1101040308-596156-1,00.html>
9. "What Is Fair Trade Coffee?" *Equal Exchange, Inc.* 2007. 27 Mar 2007 <http://www.equalexchange.com/what-is-fair-trade-coffee->
10. Illy, Ernesto. "The Complexity of Coffee." *Scientific American, Inc.* 2002. 28 March 2007 <http://www.illyusa.com/pr/coffee.pdf>
11. "Life in the USA: Coffee." *Elliot Essman.* 2007. 28 March 2007 <http://www.lifeintheusa.com/food/coffee.htm>
12. "About Coffee." *PTs Coffee Roasting Co.* 2007. 28 March 2007 <http://www.ptscoffee.com/aboutcoffee/aboutcoffee.php?tid=39>
13. Cockrell, Cathy. "Caffeine with a Conscience." The Regents of the University of California. 12 Sept 2001. 28 March 2007 <http://www.berkeley.edu/news/berkeleyan/2001/09/12_coffe.html>
14. Tangent, "Fairtrade and Why It Is Important." Solas Circle, 12 August, 2009 http://www.solascircle.com/2009/08/fairtrade-and-why-it-is-important

As we have seen, there are several good methods of organizing your speeches. When you choose one that fits your content, your audience is able to clearly follow your logic, and your credibility is increased.

Pathos: Emotional Appeal

Both positive and negative emotions can influence our thoughts and actions. As critical thinkers, we should be cautious about a speaker who uses *only* emotional appeals as reasons for a conclusion. When our emotions are stirred, we may be less aware of fallacies in reasoning and, as a result, persuaded to act without adequate evidence to justify our actions. As speakers, we should appeal to our listener's emotions when we believe it is appropriate and relevant to the issue we are discussing.

Most of the big issues we confront as a society, and many smaller ones, involve deep-seated feelings. Consider the reasons why people are for or against capital punishment, abortion, euthanasia, and a host of environmental issues. If a group is protesting the creation and sale of fur coats, the members of this group most likely feel deeply for the animals that are used to make the coats. On the other hand, those who have spent a lifetime learning to make the coats or who have a family depending on the sale of the coats feel equally strongly about their livelihoods. Whatever your position on this issue, you can imagine the personal feelings that accompany advocacy on both sides.

Emotional appeal is important in making issues real for audience members. Hearing statistics about thousands of victims of drunk drivers does not move us as much as hearing the personal story of one victim and his or her family.

Responsible and effective speakers will use emotional appeal to show the human impact of an attitude or a policy that needs to be changed. Let's say a speaker wants to persuade his or her audience that homeless individuals who are schizophrenic need to be given medical treatment. The speaker can and should use logos in the form of statistics, giving the estimated number of homeless who are schizophrenic and the medical needs that they have. However, the factor that will convince the audience to listen, the factor that will highlight the importance of this issue, is likely to come in the form of an emotional appeal. A few case histories of homeless schizophrenics and examples of the problems they face will do much to make an audience sympathetic to this problem and its possible solution.

Are emotional appeals ethical? Yes, if they are

1. True and accurate
2. Accompanied by solid reasoning
3. Based on healthy emotions

The third category, healthy emotions, needs to be evaluated by the speaker. Psychologist Abraham Maslow has suggested that all human beings have the same fundamental needs, which form the basis of human motivation.[5] When we as speakers or writers want to move our audience to action, we can appeal to these needs.

The needs are listed in a hierarchy (see Figure 10–2). According to Maslow, the lower-level needs must be satisfied before people become concerned with higher-level

FIGURE 10–2

Maslow's Hierarchy of Needs

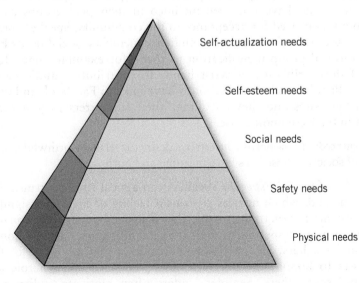

Self-actualization needs

Self-esteem needs

Social needs

Safety needs

Physical needs

[5] A. H. Maslow, *Toward a Psychology of Being* (New York: Van Nostrand Reinhold, 1968).

needs. We can ethically address *these* needs, using examples that stir the emotions of audience members:

1. Physical needs. These include the needs that guarantee our survival as people and as a species, such as food, air, water, rest, and the ability to reproduce.

> *Example of use in a speech:* Although you can discuss facts about scarcities of food and water in a speech, you also can use emotional appeals by asking your audience members to imagine a world in which their children would not have enough food or water to survive. Since we all have the same needs, you can then ask them to empathize with people in other nations who are without adequate supplies of food or water. The speech on fair trade coffee outlined in this chapter appealed to the need of coffee workers to make a sustainable living wage. Speakers use truthful fear appeals, such as those warning of the dangers of smoking, obesity, or promiscuous sex, to persuade audiences to change harmful behaviors.

2. Safety needs. Safety needs involve the desire to be protected from harm to our persons and to have adequate levels of comfort, such as decent housing, safe products, and prevention and treatment of sickness.

> *Examples of use in a speech:* Speakers can legitimately use emotional appeals, such as graphic examples of accidents that have occurred at a dangerous intersection when they are advocating for a needed stoplight. They can tell about children who died or were disabled from faulty toys that should be recalled. They can describe the fear of those who live near "crack houses" or "meth houses" to emphasize the need for more effective neighborhood law enforcement. Speakers who urge others to prepare for earthquakes or hurricanes appeal to their audiences' need for safety.

3. Social needs. These needs involve our desires to form alliances with others, to be included in group interactions, and to have close friends who love and respect us.

> *Examples of use in a speech:* Speakers can give examples of children with disabilities who have not been included in their peer groups as part of a speech on their need for acceptance in the community. Speakers promoting a social cause sometimes appeal to audience members' social needs by offering some form of group identification to them; for example, many fundraisers offer T-shirts, ribbons, or wrist bands to contributing audience members. Most political and charitable groups have links to Facebook and other social networking sites and they encourage their supporters to join networks of others in their common cause.

4. Self-esteem needs. These needs concern our desire to feel like worthwhile, contributing members of society, whose lives have meaning and purpose.

> *Examples of use in a speech:* Speakers can appeal to our altruism in helping others in need, which in turn gives us a feeling of making a significant and positive contribution to the world. They also can honor professionals who are worthy of more respect than they are generally given, such as homemakers, preschool teachers, and mechanics. Presidents may use State of the Union addresses to honor "ordinary citizens" who have taken heroic actions to help and save others. Seminar leaders often motivate audience members

by promising to give them skills that will help them become more effective workers.

5. Self-actualization needs. When their basic needs are met, people are motivated to develop various potentials, to expand their horizons by trying new things, or to become better at familiar skills. Included in the need for personal development is gaining a greater understanding of spiritual matters.

Examples of use in a speech: Speakers can appeal to audience members' desires to become more well rounded by using examples of people who have taken on new professions or challenges late in life. They can describe the thrill of an outdoor adventure when encouraging audience members to buy a vacation package. They can also appeal to the desire to leave a lasting legacy by contributing personally or financially to the welfare of others. (See Exercises 10.3 and 10.4 on pages 470 and 471.)

Reminder

Use ethical emotional appeals as a means of involving and motivating your audience.

✳ Explore on **mythinkinglab.com**

Problem Solving and Collaborative Decision Making

As we have discussed, there are times when it is necessary to advocate strongly for our own ideas and desired actions and against other ideas or actions. This is especially true when only one outcome is possible, as in the following examples:

  You are campaigning for a candidate who you believe is the best one for the position.

  You want to be hired for a specific job.

  Despite her protests, your training tells you that your relative is experiencing a stroke and you need to rush her to a hospital.

  A group to which you belong wants to create a new policy that you believe is wrong.

  You are a coach and want your players to execute a specific play.

  Someone wants to copy your test answers, and you don't want to help that person cheat.

All of these situations call for a win-lose approach. If your goals are met, someone else's goals are not met: One candidate will win, and one will lose. If there is only one job to be had, only one person will be hired. Your relative will either get the help she needs or suffer medical consequences. There are legitimate reasons to advocate strongly for a "win" in these polarized situations.

In many other circumstances, however, your skill as a thinker, listener, and advocate is best used to facilitate a solution to a problem that incorporates your own goals with the goals and ideas of others. The problem-solving method we will discuss in this chapter has been used to create "win-win" strategies for complex dilemmas in which it is possible and preferable to accommodate more than one individual's wishes and objectives.

Prerequisites to Problem Solving

Just as courses of study have educational prerequisites (e.g., the need to be competent in Algebra I before taking Algebra II/Trigonometry), there are cognitive and character prerequisites to problem solving. The steps toward coming to an amicable solution are not usually difficult; most obstacles are created by participants who are unable or unwilling to work collaboratively with others. Following are the optimal characteristics of problem solvers:

1. *Optimism.* Optimism can be seen simply as a belief that a solution to the problem may be difficult but is possible. An optimistic attitude creates an expectation of a positive resolution for the present dilemma. Optimists don't feel helpless and overwhelmed when facing problems. They realize that conflict is an everyday occurrence, but that most problems can be managed; they don't catastrophize and dwell on the worst possible outcomes.

2. *Respect.* People with respect for others are able to see how someone else might perceive a situation differently than they do; they also realize that others have individual needs and goals, and they see these differences as legitimate.

3. *Goodwill.* When people approach problem solving with goodwill, they have a desire for the best results for both themselves and the other people involved. Problem solving works best when everyone involved has goodwill and is working for a lasting and satisfying solution for all parties.

The Problem-Solving Method

The problem-solving method involves several steps. Each step is important and should be followed in sequence. Prior to meeting, establish a time and place that is suitable for everyone involved. If the problem involves more than two individuals, it is ideal to get a space with a flipchart or blackboard or another means of projecting ideas in a way that everyone can see. If the problem is about a close relationship, it's good to have a private setting and allow enough time for meaningful interaction.

1. Distinguish needs from solutions. Before meeting, each person should think about the unmet needs that are involved in the problem; it is important to distinguish needs from solutions, particularly if people are strongly dissatisfied with some aspect of the current situation. Note the difference between needs—that can be met in any number of ways—and solutions—that set up a win-lose scenario.

Needs	Solutions (Masked as Needs)
"I need a quiet workspace."	"I need Wesley's office."
"I need to get away."	"I need to stay at a four-star hotel with a spa."
"I'm overwhelmed with my workload."	"I need a personal assistant."
"Our office needs better coordination."	"We need a different supervisor."
"Our store needs to attract business."	"We need an espresso bar outside."
"Our students aren't testing well."	"We need better computers."
"We aren't able to pay our bills."	"We need to work longer hours."
"Our staff needs to take fewer sick days."	"We need a pool and fitness center to keep us healthy."

As noted in the previous chart, there is an extremely significant difference between understanding and expressing true *needs* and using the word *need* to express a solution. If you start with proposed solutions, you are led off track into a discussion and perhaps argument about a specific end result instead of understanding the real needs that lead you to desire that particular end. Needs can be met in various ways; any solution should include a consideration of available resources and the requirements of everyone involved. For example, everyone with goodwill would understand the necessity of a quiet workspace, but the desire to have someone else's office would not be seen as reasonable. The need to get away can be met in any number of ways that are more affordable than a four-star hotel. Students might profit from new computers, but the computers will probably not solve the problem of low test scores. All stores need to attract business, but an espresso bar may lead to spending money that doesn't address the real need of getting people into the store. If people aren't paying their bills, it may be best for them to cut back on luxury items rather than creating more stress for themselves with longer working hours.

2. Describe the needs of everyone involved in the problem or its resolution. When the needs of individuals or an organization are clearly stated, solutions that address those needs can be found. At this point, the practice of the prerequisites of optimism, respect, and goodwill is very important. We need to view other people's comments with the same validity as our own. We may not agree with or even understand their viewpoints, but a satisfactory resolution will take them into account.

It is often, although not always, helpful to write all of the needs out so that they can be clearly seen. For example, a supervisor might write down the conflicting but valid needs of his staff that all share a small office space: Suzana needs a quiet place to do accounting, while Alex needs to be making phone calls to clients, and the supervisor wants everyone who comes into the office to be greeted warmly and immediately. All of the needs are valid but can sometimes conflict; solutions need to address everyone's issues in order for the office to run well.

3. Brainstorm solutions. We want to be as creative as possible in coming up with viable outcomes that meet most if not all of the needs of the parties concerned. **Brainstorming** is a specific technique that has been used for many years to find imaginative results to problems. The advertising industry uses brainstorming to come up with innovative and successful product campaigns, and many businesses and industries also rely on brainstorming to maximize the resourcefulness of their employees.

Brainstorming can be broken down into four steps:

1. Look at and consider all of the various needs.
2. Quickly come up with as many ideas as possible that might meet most or all of the needs.
3. As ideas are voiced, have someone make a list that everyone can see.
4. Avoid any evaluations, positive or negative, during the brainstorming process. Don't say "Oh, that would never work," or "That's the best idea."

brainstorming
A process of soliciting many and diverse ideas in quick succession—and without immediate evaluation—in order to find imaginative solutions to problems.

When brainstorming is done quickly without evaluation, it is thought to access the creative powers of the right side of the brain. Conversely, the left side of the brain is used for evaluating and linear thinking. If evaluations are made during a productive brainstorming session, the flow of ideas may cease as the group is moved from the spontaneous and free-flowing creativity of the right brain to an analytical "left-brain" consideration of the pros and cons of each idea. The necessary process of evaluation will be done in the next step, but it is important to first take time to think "outside the box" where original and innovative approaches may well be found.

4. Evaluate the proposed solutions. After generating a list of ideas, everyone can discuss which solutions may work and which may not. The evaluation step is also used to determine if some of the proposed solutions can be combined to create the best outcomes. As in the other steps, the prerequisites of respect, goodwill, and optimism should be evident. There's no need to say, "Spending more money is a terrible idea" when you can say, "That would solve the problem, but we don't have the budget for that right now." Discuss each idea with courtesy, and see if some of the ideas can be combined.

5. Choose the best solution. Pick the solution that is most viable to everyone concerned. If someone remains disgruntled, try to find out the needs that he feels would not be met by the solution and if anything can be done to address his concerns. When people feel heard, respected, and considered, they are often willing to try a solution that seems best to the majority.

6. Follow up on the solution. The only way to see if a solution will work is to try it out. It may work well, it may need to be tweaked, or it may not work at all. If it doesn't work, don't give up or blame other people. Instead, try to see why the solution didn't meet the needs that were expressed and what could be done to make it better. There is usually great benefit in going through the problem-solving process, even when perfect solutions are not found.

When the solutions do work well, groups and organizations gain confidence in their abilities to be creative, productive, and healthy. The optimism that is generated from successful problem solving creates a positive climate in which everyone involved can safely suggest new ideas and come up with promising new approaches to problems.

Example

Let's say that Kim, the office supervisor in the previous example, sat down with Suzana and Alex at a time and place convenient for all of them. The needs were written for all to see:

Suzana: A quiet place to do accounting without the distraction of conversations around me.

Alex: The ability to talk to clients by phone while Suzana is working.

Kim: Someone to greet our customers immediately and to make them feel comfortable.

After writing all their needs, the small group decided to brainstorm and came up with the following possible solutions:

Earphones or iPod for Suzana

Rent a new office space with a separate room for accounting

Alex returns calls after greeting clients

Kim greets clients or does calling

Hire a receptionist

Hire an accountant and let Suzana be the receptionist

Kim does accounting

Have Kim's teenage daughter do reception sometimes

After brainstorming, the group went on to evaluating and combining the proposed solutions. Suzana said that earphones didn't block the noise and the music was distracting also, so they crossed out the first idea. Kim decided to look into office space that was configured differently in another building. Alex said that he could let the message machine take calls and he could return them later, but even then, new clients might walk in during a call, so that suggestion was deleted. Kim could do the calling, but she needs to visit clients away from the office, and even if she took the calls, that would still disturb Suzana. They all agreed that there was no money for a full-time receptionist or accountant.

After eliminating the solutions that were unworkable, the group found several that were promising. Kim said that she could pick up some of the accounting when she was in the office, since the calls don't distract her and she has to go over the books eventually anyway. That would allow Suzana to do some of the reception. Kim's teenage daughter was happy about the idea of helping out in exchange for a small hourly fee, since it was her first job. She was able to commit to four afternoons a week.

Kim looked for and found a new office space with a small side office for accounting that would be the same rent as they were paying for the larger office without the separate space. The only problem was that it wouldn't be available for three months. Suzana then asked if she could do reception in the morning and the accounting from home on the days that Kim's daughter came in. Kim agreed. Alex was able to continue calling clients as he had always done.

The solutions chosen by the group were implemented and worked well with one exception. Suzana didn't finish all of the accounting on the four days that Kim's daughter came in because she needed to use some of the office equipment in order to get it done. She decided to come in after hours one evening a week to finish and—since she had done her required hours by Friday at noon—to take off early on Fridays.

When people are able to be flexible and creative and come up with workable solutions, satisfaction at work and in relationships with others increase. Perfect outcomes can't always be found, but great improvements can be made if some time and effort are directed toward problem solving. (See Exercise 10.5 on pages 471–472.)

Life Application: Tips for College and Career

Be a thoughtful advocate for important problems. Use the skills of organizing and presenting your ideas to make a difference in local, national, and international issues that concern you. When delivering speeches, speak loudly enough to be heard and practice using eye contact that includes all of the members of your audience.

When you go somewhere to deliver a speech, arrive early. Get to know the audience members who have also arrived early; this will add to your confidence in speaking to them. Also, the early arrival will allow you to set up your visual aids and get familiar with the room.

With your coworkers, friends, and family, speak up about your needs and goals and show consideration and empathy for theirs, using the collaborative problem-solving skills whenever appropriate, even on small matters. Voice your opinions and draw out the concerns of others, particularly those who may not easily express their own viewpoints. Use your active listening skills to include everyone so that a group decision is made by consensus rather than coercion.

Chapter Review

Summary

1. A critical thinker considers the best ways to organize and present ideas in order to be a strong advocate for an issue.

2. The best ways to deal with speech fear are to choose an issue of interest to you, prepare thoroughly, and practice.

3. Good persuasive speakers analyze their audiences before preparing their speeches. Audiences may be characterized as believing, neutral, or hostile.

4. Ethos, the credibility of the speaker, is an important element of persuasion. Ethos is enhanced by the careful preparation of the speaker and the manner in which he or she presents the speech.

5. Logos, the content and organization of the speech, is crucial to a persuasive message. Several organizational structures can be used to enhance the clarity and persuasiveness of a speech.

6. Pathos, emotional appeal, is powerful in its ability to persuade and should be used ethically.

7. Collaborative problem solving can be used to find a solution that is satisfactory to everyone affected by a problem.

Checkup

Matching

a. Logos
b. Pathos
c. Ethos

1. The use of emotional appeal to support conclusions.

2. Logical organization and credible content used to support conclusions.

3. The credibility or reputation of a speaker.

Sentence Completion

4. The statement of key ideas that immediately follows the thesis statement is called the _____.

5. Organizing a persuasive speech with your strongest points first is a good strategy in dealing with a _____ audience.

6. Each key point must be supported with _____.

7. A speaker's position on an issue is found in his or her _____
_____.

Short Answer

8. What are effective ways to handle speech fear?

9. Why should speakers review their key ideas at the end of a speech?

10. What are some ways to add interest to introductions and conclusions?

11. What are the six steps of the collaborative problem-solving method?

12. Why is brainstorming a useful technique for generating ideas?

Exercises

EXERCISE 10.1 Purpose: To practice the basic elements of a speech using a simple impromptu format. To gain confidence by learning to use this clear and effective pattern.

This exercise is called "Three Things" and it will help you practice the classic structure of a speech:

> "Tell them what you're going to tell them" (the brief preview of your main points)
> "Tell them" (An explanation of your main points with details and examples)
> "Tell them what you just told them" (the brief review of your main points)

The typical impromptu speech begins with an introduction that leads into a preview of three points that the speaker will discuss.

In the body of the speech, the speaker discusses the three points, adding examples and explanations.

Finally, the speaker reviews the three points covered and adds a conclusion. The conclusion often points back to the comments made in the introduction.

For this short speech, focus on the preview, the body, and the review. If you have time in your preparation, add an introduction and conclusion.

To make it easy to cover three points, make the speech about three things.

Sample Topics

Three things I would like to do in my lifetime
Three of my favorite subjects
Three things for which I'm grateful
Three famous people I'd like to meet
Three talents I would like to have
Three of my favorite books or movies
Three superpowers I'd like to have
Three of my favorite people
Three of my favorite activities
Three qualities I look for in a friend or mate
Three things I'd like to do this weekend
Three jobs/careers I would (or would not) enjoy
Three reasons I am in college
Three things I would take on a desert island
Three places I would like to visit

Feel free to make up your own three things. Have fun with it and remember to preview, elaborate on, and then review your points.

Example (note the brief preview and review and the more detailed body)

(Preview)   "Three things for which I'm grateful are my health, my family, and my education."

(Body)   "I'm grateful for my health because it allows me to wake up each day, enjoy being outdoors, and have rest and recreation.

I'm grateful for my family, especially my mom who raised my siblings and me and gave us a good home and lots of love. I'm also grateful that I can go to school and decide what to major in so that I can someday have a career that I enjoy."

(Review)   "Today, I've discussed the three things for which I am grateful: my health, my family, and my education."

If time allows in the preparation of this short impromptu speech, add an introduction and a conclusion.

Example (for the speech above)

Introduction: "I often spend time complaining about what is not going well in my day or in my life. I've recently learned that it is actually good for your mental health to keep a 'gratitude journal,' a list of what you are grateful for. I haven't kept a journal, but I do think more about the things that are really good in my life and that I take for granted."

Conclusion: "The next time I start to complain about all of the problems I am going through, I will also remember all of the blessings in my life and I will stop and appreciate those good things."

EXERCISE 10.2 Purpose: To create a short persuasive speech, using the statement of reasons format.

For this short statement of reasons speech, think of a topic that interests you. State the issue in a question form, state your thesis (conclusion) about the issue, and then give three or four reasons for your viewpoint.

Example

Issue: Should 18-year-olds be allowed to rent cars?

Thesis (conclusion): Yes, 18-year-olds should be allowed to rent cars.

Reasons:

18-year-olds are allowed to serve their country and die for their country.

18-year-olds are trusted to vote and are thus considered responsible citizens.

18-year-olds usually have two years of driving experience.

18-year-olds can own cars, and they carry car insurance like everyone else.

To extend this exercise, you can provide support for each of the reasons given and cite the sources of the support.

This exercise gives you the structure for a longer persuasive speech: With just this short outline, you have a preview, key points, and a review. When you add the introduction, conclusion, and supportive evidence for your key points, the speech is complete.

EXERCISE 10.3 Purpose: To incorporate the knowledge of pathos into the writing of a speech.

Take each of Maslow's needs and write your own examples of how they could be incorporated into a speech as an emotional appeal. See examples on pages 462–463.

EXERCISE 10.4 Purpose: To recognize the use of pathos.

Write or tell about a speech (or an ad for a candidate or a product or service) you heard that included an effective appeal to emotion. You might use the following format:

1. Explain the issue and the conclusion of the speaker.
2. Discuss the audience's predisposition to the speech and the speaker.
3. Explain how the speaker specifically used the appeal to emotion. Was it a story, an example, or a personal testimony?
4. Talk about the placement of the appeal to emotion. Did it come in the introduction, body, or conclusion of the speech, or was it referenced throughout the speech?
5. Summarize your reasons for finding this appeal effective. Then comment on whether you believe the appeal was ethical.

EXERCISE 10.5 Purpose: To practice collaborative problem solving.

Practice the problem-solving strategies at home, at work, or at school. Some possible problems to solve would be division of responsibilities, preparation and presentation of a group project, the design of a marketing strategy, the details of a family vacation, or the plans for an event such as a reunion, wedding, or conference. Ask the people involved to help you gain skill in problem solving by meeting and going through the steps of the method. Report your results to the class or instructor.

Example

My best friend was tired from work and school and wanted me to go away with her this weekend to a place her family owns about three hours from here. There is a lot to do up there and it's relaxing, but I wanted to stay home and write an essay, finish my other homework, and change the oil in my car. We followed the steps:

1. We defined our needs, not as the solutions of "getting away" or "staying home" but as her need to relax and have a change of scenery and my need to get some homework done.
2. We described the needs—she wants to hike and sit at the lake, just to have a mini-vacation. I have a lot of tasks that have to be done, but I'd also like to spend some time with her.
3. We brainstormed and came up with some ideas:

   We stay home and go next weekend when I'm more available.

   I change the car oil next week.

   I get my homework done before we go.

   We go from Saturday to Sunday instead of leaving on Friday.

   We go to a lake closer to home.

   We hike closer to home.

   I do my work on the road and some of the time we are there.
4. We then evaluated and combined the solutions. I had to change the oil before we took the car anywhere, so that wasn't possible to put off. She really wants to be away, so hiking or going to a lake closer to home or going next week didn't work for her. I could get my work done early, but that would be rushing it.

After looking at our list, we decided that she would take my car and get the oil changed before Friday. I would try to get some work done before we left and bring the rest with me. She would drive while I did some homework, and I would get up earlier on Saturday and finish my homework while she went to the lake. Then we could go for a hike and relax later.

5. We went with the solution, and it worked well for the most part. We had a great time, and I got most of my work done.

6. The main difficulty was that I couldn't really work in the car and I slept in Saturday, so I had to finish the homework when we got home on Sunday night. We decided to plan some weekends ahead of time so we can enjoy them more.

You **Decide**

Campus Speech Codes

Freedom is one of the most prized values of western civilization, and freedom of expression is mandated in the First Amendment to the United States Constitution. Cases involving freedom of expression in academic settings often come before the Supreme Court. Freedom of speech is essential to intellectual inquiry and exploration, and it includes a student's right to state a different belief from a professor. Freedom of expression also has limits when it involves the likely effect of causing harm, and administrators need to create policies to address "hate speech." Academic institutions must decide "where to draw the line" and balance freedom of expression with the responsibility to create a welcoming and respectful campus climate.

For more information on the debate surrounding campus speech codes and additional exercises and tutorials about concepts covered in this chapter, log into MyThinkingLab at www.mythinkinglab.com and select Diestler, *Becoming a Critical Thinker,* Sixth Edition.

✴ Explore on **mythinkinglab.com**

Articles for Discussion   📖 Read the **Document** on **mythinkinglab.com**

The following article discusses the growing popularity of college classes that help students overcome their fears of speaking in public and gain confidence in expressing themselves in various settings.

Don't Be Shy

Rachel Aviv

Christine Stuart, a communications professor at Pennsylvania State University, stood at the chalkboard and taught her students strategies for mingling at their forthcoming class party. "Don't monopolize," she said cheerfully. "You need to get around the room." She listed the three easiest forms of conversation—clichés, facts and opinions—on the board and urged students to make index cards with opening lines for starting conversations: "Gee, this sangria is great, don't you think?" or "Sure is humid today."

Although one student let out a little snort when asked to think of every conversation as having an "intro," "body" and "conclusion," most of the class quietly wrote down everything scrawled on the board.

When Dr. Stuart asked a question, she got, at best, monosyllabic answers uttered at low pitch. The nervous tension in the room seemed tangible as students handed in their homework, a detailed list of their personal goals for the semester: talk to a stranger, go to professors' office hours, sound more confident on the phone, offer three opinions in class, greet an authority figure, learn to enter conversations.

"Sometimes I'm like, 'Wait, how old are we?'" said Elena Kashkan, a sophomore, after class. She had avoided seminars her first year, opting instead for large lectures where she would never have to speak. "I need to learn to care less about what other people think of me," she said. "It's not like I want to be that quiet girl in the corner."

Although the class, "Speech Anxiety," sometimes resembles therapy, it serves a practical purpose: helping students graduate. Penn State's first "reticence course," taught in 1965, consisted of 16 students who were going to drop out rather than take the university's required speaking course. Today, there are three courses a semester with some 20 students each, and more than a dozen other institutions have adopted or designed similar programs.

Because speaking well is often crucial to getting a job—and to sounding educated—nearly half of American colleges and universities require a public speaking or communications course, according to the National Communication Association. Even universities without a requirement have put more emphasis on speaking in class, developing courses labeled "speaking intensive" in departments not associated with class participation.

"Speech Anxiety," which fulfills Penn State's requirement, allows undergraduates to ease their way into public speaking, first in groups, then in front of the professor, and finally in front of the class; on rare occasions, students can bring friends to stand next to them for support. To be admitted to the course, students must demonstrate in an interview the extent of their reticence, defined as "chronic silence due to a fear of foolishness." If they waltz into the interview, hold out their hand, smile and introduce themselves, they're usually deemed not right for the course.

Some students are simply shy or experience stage fright; others are paralyzed in social situations. In extreme cases, an instructor might suggest a visit to university health services. Communications professors aren't equipped to provide counseling, and they make an effort to avoid talking about their students' feelings. They don't try to identify the root of a student's anxiety. Instead, they focus almost exclusively on behavior.

"These are the quietest classes you'll ever be in," says Beau Bingham, an assistant lecturer at the University of Wyoming. The reticence course he teaches, which covers social conversations, group discussions and public speaking, began seven years ago because of concerns students would drop out. "There's a whole population of students out there who go through their college career and don't get their degree because they can't bear to take public speaking," he says. He lets people into the class based on their scores on the Personal Report of Communication Apprehension, a widely administered test that asks students to rate their identification with statements like "Ordinarily I am very tense and nervous in conversations" or "While giving a speech, I get so nervous I forget facts I really know."

Some campuses hold speech labs to teach calming techniques, like deep breathing, positive visualization and systematic desensitization. In the last five years, more than 20 campuses, including Hamilton College, Randolph-Macon College and Arizona State University, have opened labs where students practice speaking and receive individualized feedback.

"I've had students stop speeches halfway through because they're sobbing or vomiting," says Meg McConnaughy, director of the Communication Assessment and Learning Lab at Arizona State University. "If you're too scared to speak, you're not going to get your ideas across, and that's an absolute tragedy."

Ms. McConnaughy and others in the field maintain that speaking anxiety can be as debilitating as any formally recognized learning disorder. According to research published in the academic journal Communication Quarterly, the average college G.P.A. of students with communication apprehension is a half-point lower than that of students without it.

"It's a big disadvantage," says Ashlie Boltinghouse, a junior at the University of Wyoming. "I'd be sitting in class and I'd think, 'I have a question, but I'm not saying it in front of all these people, so I'm just going to have to figure it out by myself.' I refused to go to office hours."

She says she became more comfortable in Mr. Bingham's class because the stakes were low and everyone was openly nervous; before speeches, students were encouraged to meditate, take a relaxing walk or smile for five seconds while holding their breath. Now she works as an assistant in Wyoming's Oral Communication Lab, where she gives other students feedback on their speeches. She says she now freely talks in her classes.

While class participation isn't the only goal, it is one tangible way to measure progress. In "Public Speaking Apprehension," a course at Northern Kentucky University, Vicki Abney Ragsdale tells her students to bring their journals to other classes and mark down what happens when classmates give the wrong answers. "It's quite stunning when they realize no one cares," she says. "Sometimes I'll say, 'All right, how many of you remember what someone in this class said yesterday? How many of you spent time thinking about someone else here?' That seems to be a big moment for them. You've got to realize, everybody is self-absorbed."

In "Speaking Confidently," a class for reticent students at the University of Nebraska, Omaha, classmates look one another in the eye before speeches and repeat scripted positive statements: "No one is perfect or fully competent in all aspects of life," "They can't feel my heart beat," "I can be myself."

Some experts question whether it's really possible, or necessary, to ease the anxiety of highly apprehensive speakers. A new branch of thinking, called communibiology, argues that the problem is one of nature, not nurture. "For most people, there is no solution," says James C. McCroskey, a professor at the University of Alabama, Birmingham. "Except maybe for gene replacement," he adds with a laugh.

A leading scholar in the study of communication apprehension, he says forcing students to talk in public can be counterproductive. His research, he adds, shows that students nervous about speaking learn less if they anticipate having to communicate in class. Rather than paying attention, they fret about whether they'll be called on and what they will say.

John A. Daly, a professor at the University of Texas, Austin, teaches a 500-student lecture class on interpersonal communication. He says the benefits of talking in class are overstated. "There's a theory in this culture that class participation is the way to learn, and I don't know if I buy that completely," he says. "Unless you can make a really strong argument that the ability to talk about the topic is vital to understanding, you're doing this population of students a real disservice, causing them incredible discomfort."

And yet, students clamor to get into the reticence courses—this year, Penn State had to close interviews two days early because all openings were filled—and many describe the class as a turning point in their time at college.

"It was much easier to learn to talk when I was in a big room of people who had my problem," says Nathan Belanger, a junior at Penn State. He used to lose track of his thoughts, fall silent for periods of time and contemplate giving up and walking out of the classroom. He says his grades have improved.

"Not being able to voice my own opinions really hurt," he says. "I never figured out what I'm so afraid of. I'm just relieved I found a way to get around whatever it is." ▪

Questions for Discussion

1. The author states that because speaking well is often crucial to getting a job—and to sounding educated—nearly half of American colleges and universities require a public speaking or communications course. Do you believe that public speaking courses should be required? Why or why not?

2. Susan Faludi, who started out as a political writer and became convinced of the need to speak out on her views stated, "Public speech can be a horror for the shy person, but it can also be the ultimate act of liberation." How can public speaking and expressing our ideas even when we dread it, be empowering and liberating for us?

3. The article refers to one student from the University of Wyoming, who discusses how her anxiety prevented her from doing her best in school. She remembered telling herself, "'I have a question, but I'm not saying it in front of all these people, so I'm just going to have to figure it out by myself.' I refused to go to office hours." She cited practice in her speech class as the "cure" for her anxiety. To what extent do you believe it is important for students to work on the common problem of speech fear and to push themselves out of comfort zones?

. . . .

One of the most eloquent speeches in American history was President Abraham Lincoln's Gettysburg Address. The Battle of Gettysburg was fought from July 1 to July 3, 1863. At the end of those few days, more than 51,000 Americans were classified as wounded, missing, or dead. (To put this one battle in perspective, there were 4,435 deaths in the Revolutionary War and 47,378 in the Vietnam War.) After the battle, the governor of Pennsylvania, Andrew Curtin, commissioned the creation of a cemetery on 17 acres of the battlefield. The cemetery was dedicated four months later, on November 19, 1863. The main speaker for the dedication was Edward Everett, one of the nation's most famous orators. President Lincoln was also invited to speak "as Chief Executive of the nation, formally [to] set apart these grounds to their sacred use by a few appropriate remarks." At the ceremony, Everett spoke for more than two hours; Lincoln spoke for only a few minutes. In those few minutes, Lincoln reflected upon the ideals of liberty and equality that accompanied the birth of the nation, the valor and commitment of soldiers who died for those ideals, and the challenge of those who were left living to continue safeguarding those ideals. In his address, Lincoln also transformed the war from a war for union to a war for both union and freedom.

As you read his words, consider the audience of mourners that Lincoln was addressing at the cemetery, and also the audience of the larger nation who would be reading the address in the newspapers.

The Gettysburg Address

Abraham Lincoln

Fourscore and seven years ago our fathers brought forth on this continent a new nation, conceived in liberty and dedicated to the proposition that all men are created equal. Now we are engaged in a great civil war, testing whether that nation or any nation so conceived and so dedicated can long endure. We are met on a great battlefield of that war. We have come to dedicate a portion of that field as a final resting-place for those who here gave their lives that that nation might live. It is altogether fitting and proper that we should do this. But in a larger sense, we cannot dedicate, we cannot consecrate, we cannot hallow this ground. The brave men, living and dead who struggled here have consecrated it far above our poor power to add or detract. The world will little note nor long remember what we say here, but it can never forget what they did here. It is for us the living rather to be dedicated here to the unfinished work which they who fought here have thus far so nobly advanced. It is rather for us to be here dedicated to the great task remaining before us—that from these honored dead we take increased devotion to that cause for which they gave the last full measure of devotion—that we here highly resolve that these dead shall not have died in vain, that this nation under God shall have a new birth of freedom, and that government of the people, by the people, for the people shall not perish from the earth. ■

Questions for Discussion

1. The keynote speaker for the dedication of the cemetery at Gettysburg spoke for two hours, and Lincoln spoke for two minutes. Lincoln said, "The world will little note nor long remember what we say here," but his words have been remembered and quoted by millions. What elements of Lincoln's address make it so memorable?

2. Lincoln, like many other speakers before and since, had a burden to give comfort to his particular audience. How were his words designed to comfort those grieving their loved ones who died in battle?

3. As the leader of the nation, how did President Lincoln place this devastating battle that was part of a war between the states—in an historical context? Why do you think he started with a reference to the vision of our forefathers?

4. How did the president use the conclusion of his brief address to give hope and direction to his audience?

Ideas for Writing or Speaking

1. Dr. Martin Luther King's "I Have a Dream" speech is considered a classic modern American address. He spoke at a time when segregation was still the law in many states. Although he was directly addressing a supportive crowd gathered in Washington, D.C., he was also aware of the larger audience, many of whom were hostile, that would be reached through print and electronic media. No one could have foretold the dramatic and historic effect that this speech would have for decades to come. Review a transcript of this speech and then write an essay or speech on one or more of the following questions:

   a. How did Dr. King use ethos, logos, and pathos to persuade his audience to consider his appeal?

   b. What aesthetic elements—for example, metaphors, repetition, Biblical references—were used to create a unified, eloquent address?

   c. To what extent has Dr. King's inspiring dream been realized? What remains to be done to create the society he envisioned?

2. Philosopher and theologian Thomas Aquinas once said that when you want to convert someone to your view, you go over to where he is standing, take him by the hand (mentally speaking), and guide him to where you want him to go. You don't call him names or insist that he believe as you do. You start where he is, and work from that position. That's the only way to get someone to move closer to an understanding and possible acceptance of your viewpoint.

   Think about Aquinas' philosophy and persuasion, and write or speak about one or more of the following questions:

   a. Have you found that people who argue passionately overstate their own case and understate their opponent's case? Can you think of examples of this overstatement and understatement?

   b. Can someone be persuasive and passionate and still be fair to the other side of the argument? If so, how? If not, why not?

   c. Think of an issue that concerns you deeply. Can you see the "piece of truth" held by the other side? How could you use that truth to persuade your opponent to consider the value of your position?

3. Putting it all together: To practice the elements of public speaking discussed in this chapter, create a persuasive speech using one of the three methods of organization. Consider methods of increasing personal credibility that are covered in the ethos section. Include emotional appeals and solid research. Use the following suggestions to guide your preparation. Do a structural outline, like the one illustrated in Figure 10–1 (see page 450), as you complete the following steps:

   a. Choose an issue that concerns you. You can try to persuade your audience about a factual issue (caffeine is/is not bad for your heart), an issue of value (it is/is not wrong for couples to live together before marriage), or a policy issue (ruling by instant replay rather than by the calls of referees and umpires should/should not be mandatory in all televised sporting events).

   b. Take a stand (conclusion) on your issue and support your stand with at least three reasons.

   c. Give evidence to support your reasons; use evidence in the form of statistics, studies, authoritative testimony, and examples from credible sources. You may also interview an expert about your issue. Be sure to give the source and the date when you cite your evidence in the speech. Strive to keep your evidence current and turn in an outline and a bibliography on the day of your speech.

d. Think about evidence that opponents to your position might offer. Within the body of your speech, handle opposing viewpoints with both-sides persuasion; acknowledge the good reasoning of an opposing viewpoint, but explain why it is not as strong as your own or why your own solution would be the best.

e. Add emotional appeal through anecdotes, examples, or personal testimony.

f. Begin the speech with a story, statistic, or quote that gets the audience's attention and explains the importance of your issue.

g. Close by repeating the issue, your conclusion, and your reasons. End with a strong quote, a reference to the introductory story, or a reminder to audience members of how they should believe or act now that they have this information.

h. Begin planning your speech as soon as it is assigned to you so that you have time to find evidence, get organized, and practice before the due date. Rehearse the speech so that you feel comfortable looking at the audience, and make your delivery conversational. Practice handling questions with friends or family members before you give the speech.

4. Do a search for speeches online at www.vsotd.com or at americanrhetoric. com; you can also find speeches in journals from the library or communication lab. You may also choose to listen to a persuasive speech or sermon or watch one on YouTube or television (if you get C-SPAN, you will be able to listen to a complete speech presented before Congress, the National Press Club, or another organization).

Once you find a speech that interests you, analyze it, using the following questions as a guide:

a. What interests and concerns of the audience did the speaker address? Was the audience supportive of, neutral to, or hostile to the speaker's position? How well did the speaker adapt to his or her audience?

b. What were the issue and conclusion of the speaker?

c. To what extent did the speaker use ethos to establish credibility, logos to support his or her conclusion, and pathos to appeal to the audience's emotions?

How could the speaker have improved these elements of the speech?

d. Were the reasons given to support the conclusion backed up by solid evidence? Were these the best reasons given? Were the studies and experts cited clear and convincing?

e. Did the speaker address the opposing viewpoints in any way? Did the speaker refute the important points of the opposition in a fair and appropriate manner?

f. Were there any fallacies in the reasoning of the speaker?

g. Were there aesthetic factors that helped the speech to be tightly woven and eloquent? Did the speaker use language elements, such as repetition or beautiful prose, to make his or her points? Did the speaker use the conclusion to refer back to attention-getting points made in the introduction?

h. How did the speaker introduce and conclude the speech? Were there clear transitions throughout the speech? Give specific examples of these.

i. Were you persuaded in any way by this speech? Explain why or why not.

j. What is your overall impression of this speech? If you were hired as a consultant to this speaker, what advice would you give to improve his or her speaking?

Films for Analysis and Discussion

Many great speeches from speakers of all kinds—political, religious, social, and artistic—can be found in classic and contemporary film. A few examples are listed below. For more ideas, check out the excellent selections of movie speeches and the video and audio clips given by American Rhetoric on their website: www.americanrhetoric.com/moviespeeches.htm. This site features over 5,000 video, audio, and full-text versions of past and present speeches by presidents and other leaders as well as the association's pick of the best cinematic speeches.

Here are a few films that feature interesting examples of public speaking:

The King's Speech (2010, R)

> Some men are born great, some achieve greatness, and some have greatness thrust upon them.
>
> William Shakespeare, *Twelfth Night*

The King's Speech covers the communication struggles of King George VI, who was the father of the current queen of England, Queen Elizabeth II. When George's brother abdicates the throne to marry an American, George (nicknamed "Bertie") "has greatness thrust upon him" as he becomes the king in his brother's place. George has a pronounced stammer and is not considered fit to be the king. In order to overcome his speaking difficulties, he seeks help from a creative and persistent speech therapist named Lionel Logue. Through the therapist's techniques and counsel, Bertie is able to become a speaker who can lead his country through a time of war. Note especially how Bertie comes to the point of proclaiming, "I have a voice," and changes from a reluctant leader to an inspiring speaker.

Public Speaking, HBO Documentary (2010, PG)

Filmmaker Martin Scorsese created a documentary about the New York writer and social commentator Fran Lebowitz. Scorsese interviews Lebowitz on a variety of topics, and she is also seen giving an engaging speech to a college crowd and being interviewed by writer Toni Morrison.

Thank You for Smoking (2005, R)

This film, also recommended in Chapter 8, follows Nick Naylor, who works as the spokesperson for a tobacco company. He embodies Sophocles' quote, "It is terrible to speak well and be wrong." The film provides a good example of a charismatic speaker who is able to skirt research and evidence in order to minimize the detrimental effects of smoking. Note especially how he and his colleagues use spin and excellent delivery techniques to overshadow the harms and health risks associated with their products.

There are many other examples of speech and argumentation in films. Below are a few movie titles with reference to specific speeches.

Friday Night Lights (2004, PG-13)

Note the speeches given by Coach Gaines, particularly on "Being Perfect."

Miracle (2004, PG)

Note Coach Brooks' several speeches, including the pep talk to his team during the 1980 Olympic hockey tournament.

Gods and Generals (2003, PG)

Note Colonel Joshua Chamberlain's Abolition Speech.

We Were Soldiers (2002, R)

Note the several speeches of Lt. Col. Hal Moore, especially "I Will Leave No One Behind."

Brian's Song (2001, G)

Note Gale Sayers addressing the team about Brian Piccolo's cancer.

The Contender (2000, R)

Note President Jackson Evans' address to Congress on Vice-Presidential nominee Senator Hanson.

The Family Man (2000, PG-13)

Note the interpersonal argumentation in Jack's plea to Kate: "I Choose Us."

Amistad (1997, R)

This film is about the 1839 mutiny aboard a slave ship that is traveling toward the northeastern coast of America. Note especially the arguments made in the courtroom about the rights of people taken against their will to have acted to protect their freedoms.

Crimson Tide (1995, R)

Note Captain Ramsey's address to the crew of the USS Alabama.

The Shawshank Redemption (1994, R)

Note the address of Ellis Boyd to his parole board.

Quiz Show (1994, PG-13)

Note Charles Van Doren's testimony before the House Committee on Interstate and Foreign Commerce.

Malcolm X (1992, PG-13)

Note several addresses by Malcolm, including his Harlem Address and his Harvard University Address.

Lean on Me (1989, PG-13)

Note Principal Clark's addresses to his staff, his students, and their parents.

Gandhi (1982, PG)

Note Gandhi's advocacy of the policy of nonviolence, his address to the Indian National Congress, and his address to British authorities, "It Is Time You Left."

Chariots of Fire (1981, PG)

Note several addresses by Eric Liddell, particularly his speech at the Scotland vs. Ireland races.

Norma Rae (1979, PG)

Note Reuben Warshovsky's address to the plant workers.

Jesus of Nazareth (1977, NR)

Note the Beatitudes (Sermon on the Mount).

A Man for All Seasons (1966, G)

Note Thomas More's Address to the Court.

Judgment at Nuremberg (1961, PG)

Note Judge Hayward's speech on the Decision of the Court.

All the King's Men (1949, NR)

Note Willie Stark's speeches as he campaigns for governor and addresses the people.

It's a Wonderful Life (1946, PG)

Note George Bailey's address to the Bailey Building and Loan Board.

The Pride of the Yankees (1942, PG)

Note Lou Gehrig's Farewell Address to Baseball.

Mr. Smith Goes to Washington (1939, PG)

Note Senator Smith's several speeches, especially his speeches that continue and then end the filibuster.

Credits

Text Credits

Chapter 1

Page 4 Healthy work environments give companies a competitive edge by Kelly C. Doherty.April 07, 2010. http://news.medill.northwestern.edu/chicago/news. aspx?id=162; p.5 Source: From The Argument culture by Deborah Tannen, © 1999 by Deborah Tannen. Reprinted by permission of Ballantine Publishing Group, Group, a division of Random House, Inc.; p. 15 Excerpt from "New Device Desirable Old Device Undesirable." The Onion. December 3, 2009. Reprinted by permission.; p. 19 "Educational Ticket" (Huda). Reprinted with permission of the author.; p.19 "War on Drugs Fails: We Need New Approach" (Bergman). Reprinted with permission of the author.; p. 19 "Drugged Driving" (Washington). Reprinted with permission of the author.; p. 21 "16-Year-Old Sailor Was Already Off Course" (Albom). MITCH ALBOM, Detroit Free Press, June 12, 2010. Detroit free press Copyright 2010 by GANNETT COMPANY, INC. - VA. Reproduced with permission of GANNETT COMPANY, INC. - VA in the format Textbook and Other book via Copyright Clearance Center.; p. 25 "LeBron James' Decision a Cruel Blow to His Hometown" (McManamon). Pat McManamon, July 9, 2010. http://nba.fan-house.com/2010/07/09/lebrons-james-decision-a-cruel-blow-to-his-hometown/; p. 27 Mikhail Prokhorov, The writer is the principal owner of the New Jersey Nets basketball team. http://www.usatoday.com/news/opinion/letters/2010-07-29-letters29_ST2_N.htm.; p. 28 p. "Onstage and Backstage: Two Jobs. One Actor. What Do You Choose?" Seth Rudetsky, Playbill.com. 29 Source: Michael Fleeman. The Associated Press, September 2, 1991. Copyright © 1991 by The Associated Press. Reprinted by permission of Reprint Management Services on behalf of The Associated Press.; p. 30 Source: Copyright © 1991 by The Associated Press. Reprinted by permission of Reprint Management Services on behalf of The Associated Press.; p. 33 "The Road Not Taken" (Frost). From Mountain Interval by Robert Frost. Originally published in 1920 by Henry Holt and Company, Inc.

Chapter 2

Page 38 "Question Man: Fictional Character You Admire Most?" (Conti). The San Francisco Chronicle, January 28, 1990. Copyright © 1990 by The San Francisco Chronicle. Reprinted by permission of the publisher.; p. 39 "Motivation: About This Billboard" http://www.values.com/inspirational-sayings-billboards; p. 43 "Changing Jobs Takes Guts, Yields Good Life," Lauren Ashburn, USA Today, 3/25/2010.; p. 48 Source: Dr. Laura Schlessinger, How Could You Do That?. New York: HarperCollins Publishers, Inc., 1996. Reprinted by permission.; p. 51 "Common Rationalizations" (Michael Josephson). From Ethics in Action, January–February 1991. Reprinted by permission of the Joseph and Edna Josephson Institute of Ethics. www.josephsoninstitute.org.; p. 60 Source: "Salvation Army Turns Down $100,000 Donation." January 2, 2003. Associated Press, Contra Costa Times.; p. 61 "You Make the Call: Is It Good Baseball Strategy or a Weak Attempt to Win?" (Rick Reilly). Sports Illustrated, August 14, 2006. Copyright © 2006 by Time, Inc. Reprinted by Permission of Time, Inc.; p. 63 "Staffer Gets Subpoenaed" (Steve Logan). The Advocate, October 11, 1996. Reprinted by permission of the publisher.; p. 64 Source: "WESUN—Physician's Candor vs. Patient's Interest" by Liane Hansen, broadcast 11/8/92. Reprinted by permission of National Public Radio, Inc.; p. 66 "Schools' Peanut Bans Spark Backlash" (Associated Press). Copyright 2008 The Associated Press. All rights reserved.; p. 68 Source: Holly K. Hacker, The Dallas Morning News, December 4, 2006. Copyright © 2006 by The Dallas Morning News. Reprinted by permission of The Dallas Morning News.

Chapter 3

Page 76 Source: Jay Mathews, Washington Post, Tuesday, April 2, 2002.; p. 78 San Francisco chronicle Copyright 1996 by San Francisco Chronicle Reproduced with permission of San Francisco Chronicle in the format Textbook via Copyright Clearance Center.; p. 79: University of Georgia (2010, October 14). Waist circumference, not BMI, is best predictor of future cardiovascular risk in children, study finds. ScienceDaily. Retrieved May 16, 2011, from http://www.sciencedaily.com/releases/2010/10/101014131927.htm; p. 79: Kristie Leong, "Does Wet Hair Cause a Cold?" http://healthmad.com/conditions-and-diseases/does-wet-hair-cause-a-cold.; p. 80 "Extinct Fox Not Extinct, Found in California" (Zachary Shahan). Source: http://planetsave.com/2010/09/07/extinct-fox-not-extinct-found-in-california/.; p. 81 Source: Lisa Munoz, Orange County Register, September 22, 2003. "Gift Cards May Bite Recipient." Orange county register Copyright 2003 by Orange county register, The. Reproduced with permission of Orange county register, The in the format Textbook and Otherbook via Copyright Clearance Center.; p. 81 Source: Ben Rooney, "Gift Card Fees: Fed Cracks Down," http://money.cnn.com/2010/03/23. Courtesy CNN.; p. 82 Source: John Rosemond, June 18, 2003, All About Kids Parenting Magazine. "Living with Children."; p. 82 Three Sonorans, "Fidel Castro Says Communism Doesn't Work in Cuba." http://tucsoncitizen.com; p. 83: Source: Jennifer Bjorhus and Peyton Whitely, "New Report Debunks Myths on Suicide," Seattle Times. February 15, 1996.; p. 84 "Myths and Facts About Suicide." Source: http://www.dhs.state.or.us/dhs/ph/chs/data/hsi/teensuic/conclus.shtml.; p. 84 "Tips for the Savvy Supplement User: Making Informed Decisions and Evaluating Information." January 2002. www.cfsan.fda.gov/-dms/qa-sup19.html,; p. 85: "Tips for the Savvy Supplement User: Making Informed Decisions and Evaluating Information,." January, 2002, www.cfsan.fda.gov/-dms/qa-sup19.html; p. 86 "Himalayan Glaciers Melting Deadline 'a Mistake'" (Pallava Bagla). Source: http://news.bbc.

co.uk/2/hi/8387737.stm.; p. 88 Vincent Ryan Ruggiero, Beyond Feelings: A guide to Critical Thinking (Mountain View, CA: Mayfield Publishing, 1990), p. 25. Reprinted by permission of McGraw-Hill Publishing.; p. 96 Excerpt from Influence: The Psychology of Persuasion by Robert B. Cialdini. © 1984, 1993 by Robert B. Cialdini. Reprinted by permission of HarperCollins Publishers.; p. 108 "Forget What You Know About Good Study Habits" (Benedict Carey). Published: September 6, 2010 http://www.nytimes.com/2010/09/07/health/views; p. 111 "Can Blacks Be Racist?" (Leonard Pitts Jr.). Tribune Media Services, January 11, 2002. Copyright © 2002 by Tribune Media Services. Reprinted by permission of The Permissions Group on behalf of TMS Reprints.; p. 113 "Wasted Food, Discovered Souls" (Andrew Lam). Reprinted by permission of the author. Andrew Lam the author of a number of books, including Perfume Dreams: Reflections on the Vietnamese Diaspora and East Eats West: Writing in Two Hemispheres.; p. 115 "Bearer of Bad News: NASA Launches Probe to Inform Pluto of Demotion." http://www.theonion.com. December 18, 2006, Issue 42–51. Copyright © 2006. Reprinted by permission of The Onion, Inc.; p. 116 Outstanding: Growing up Asian, by Cynthia Meng, Shidai Zhuanji. Chinese Literary Collections.

Chapter 4

Page 122 Excerpt from p. 99 (117 words) from Zen and the Art of Motorcycle Maintenance by Robert Pirsig. Copyright © 1974 by Robert M. Pirsig. Reprinted by permission of HarperCollins.; p. 126 Jon Burlingame, "Television," Contra Costa Times, January 12, 1990, p. 10C. Reprinted by permission of the author.; p. 126 "LeBron's Q Score Takes Huge Hit," by Darren Rovell. CNBC online September 14, 2010.; p. 128 Piper Jaffray concludes 21st Semi-Annual Spring 2011 Taking Stock With Teens. Green Technology News, April 11, 2011. Surveyhttp://green.tmcnet.com./news/2011/04/11/5435552.htm; p. 128 "Healthy Work Environments Give Companies a Competitive Edge (Kelly C. Doherty). Sources: Psychologically Healthy Workplace Program and the American Psychological Association (figures from 2007). Source: http://news.medill.northwestern.edu/chicago/news.aspx?id=162652; p. 129 Healthy work environments give companies a competitive edge by Kelly C. Doherty. April 07, 2010. http://news.medill.northwestern.edu/chicago/news.aspx?id=162; p. 130 Jim Salisbury, "Baseball to penalize steroid users Enough players failed random tests to trigger a tougher policy" Philadelphia Inquirer, November 14, 2003. Copyright © 2003. Reprinted by permission.; p. 130 "Baseballs Steroid Era Isn't Over Says Commissioner," http://www.steroidsources.com/Steroid-Information/2010/06.; p. 131 P.U.L.S.E - Peers Understanding Listening Speaking Educating. Peer Health Education website, Cal Poly. San Luis Obispo, CA.; p. 133 Frank Sulloway, Born to Rebel. © 1996 by Frank Sulloway. Reprinted by permission of Pantheon Books, a division of Random House, Inc.; p. 135 Source: www.qscores.com/performer.asp. Marketing Evaluations, Inc. The Q Scores Company. Reprinted by permission.; p. 137 Source: David Murray, Joel Schwartz, and S. Robert Lichter, It Ain't Necessarily So (Lanham, MD: Rowman & Littlefield Publishers), 2001.; p. 137 Patricia Rodriguez, ""Be on Guard for Ridiculous Survey Results,"" Knight Ridder Newspapers, December 18, 2001.; p. 138 "Don't let identity thieves steal your future," www.ed.gov/about/offices/list/missdidtheft ; p. 140 "At a Lecture—Only 12 Percent Listen". Reprinted from San Francisco Sunday Examiner Chronicle.; p. 142 "Ann Landers" (Landers). Column by Ann Landers, October 10, 1996. Copyright © 1996 by Creators Syndicate. Reprinted by permission of Creators Syndicate.; p. 143 Source: Insurance Institute for Highway Safety, http://www.iihs.org/research/fatality_facts_2008/bicycles.html. Reprinted by permission.; p. 143 Judy Lightfoot, "Homeless in Seattle," http://blog.seattlepi.com.; p. 144 Adam Ostrow, "Netflix Users Watching More Movies and TV Shows Online," http://mashable.com/2010/07/21/netflix-online-stats.; p. 145 James Johnson, "Causes of Deterioration of Coral Reefs," www.helium.com.; p. 146 Coca-Cola to Invest US$1 Billion More in RP," http://goodnewspilipinas.com; p. 146 Sang-Hun Choe, Associated Press. Koreans decide it's time to slow down frantic pace, Associated Press, 12/26/2001.; p. 147 © 2011 Jose Vega M.D., Ph.D. (http://stroke.about.com). Used with permission of About Inc., which can be found online at www.about.com. All rights reserved.; p. 148 Frank Salloway, Born to Rebel © 1996 by Frank Salloway. Reprinted by permission of Pantheon Books, a division of Random House, Inc.; p. 150 Source: Eric Louis, "Lap of Luxury Breeds Higher Rates of Teen Substance Abuse," Contra Costa Times, February 19, 2007.; p. 150 Source: Willy Morris, "Civil Author Nearly Beaten by Case," Contra Costa Times, October 10, 1996.; p. 154 Excerpt from Influence: The Psychology of Persuasion by Robert B. Cialdini. (c) 1984, 1993 by Robert B. Cialdini. Reprinted by permission of HarperCollins Publishers.; p. 155 "How Americans Are Living Dangerously," by Jeffrey Kinger, November 26, 2006, Time.com.; p. 157 Reprinted by the permission of the American Cancer Society, Inc. from www.cancer.org. All rights reserved.; p. 157 Source: Carol Ezzell, "Why" The Neuroscience of Suicide," Scientific American.com, February 2003, pp. 24-5. Reprinted by permission.; p. 157 "Self-Segregation: Students Stick with Same-Race Groups" (Gina Pera). Gina Para, USA Weekend, August 18–20, 1996. Copyright © 1996. Reprinted by permission of the author.; p. 158 "Why Do People Start to Smoke?" © Copyright 2005–2010 helpwithsmoking.com.; p. 160 "Meth Epidemic Moves from Rural Places to Cities," http://www.ruralschools.org/news/survey.html. Organizations concerned about Rural Education, accessed August 14, 2007.; p. 160 "The Meth Epidemic". The Meth Epidemic , Santa Cruz County Sheriff-Coronor's Office, www.scsheriff.com/ MethArticle.htm Copyright © 2005.; p. 162 "Understanding Facebook Addiction: Why Is Social Networking So Addictive? How Did We Get Addicted?" (Joe Elvin). Copyright Joe Elvin.; p. 163 "ISU Researcher Studies Consequences of 'Hooking Up': Study Focuses on Risk Behavior". http://www.kcci.com/r/25285362/detail.html. October 5, 2010. Copyright 2010 by

KCCI.com.; p. 165 "Drugs, Gangs on the Rise in Schools: Survey Shows Increase in Gang Activity and Drug Use in Nation's Schools" (Salynn Boyles). Reprinted with permission from Medscape 2011.

Chapter 5

Page 173 *Source: L.A. Times*, November 5, 2003. "Drug for Heart Disease Called Breakthrough," Thomas H. Maugh II.; p. 173: Staff and wire reports, "FYI, True Love Is the Best Drug," *Contra Costa Times*, September 10, 1996, p. E1.; p. 175 Carl T. Hall, "Marijuana-like Substance in Brain Could Help Treat Parkinson's, Researcher Say," Chronicle Science Writer, Wednesday, February 7, 2007. *San Francisco Chronicle*. Copyright 2007 by *San Francisco Chronicle*. Reproduced with permission of *San Francisco Chronicle* in the format Textbook via Copyright Clearance Center.; p. 176 "Traditional Police Lineup Works Better: Study," by Annie Sweeney, *Chicago Sun Times* 03/29/01.; p. 176 *Source*: Linda Seebach, "Education Lacks Enough Research," *Contra Costa Times*, September 1, 1996.; p. 177 Dr. Donald W. Miller, Jr. , "Vaccination Consideration," stewardshipdiaries.wordpress.com/2010/07/27. Reprinted by permission of the author.; p. 177 Dr. Dean Edell, "Growth Hormone Is Not the Fountain of Youth," www.healthcentral.com.; p. 178 Stephen Barrett, "Growth Hormone Schemes and Scams," http://www.quackwatch.org. Reprinted with permission from Quackwatch.org.; p. 179 *Sources*: "Love Takes Up Where Pain Leaves Off, Brain Study Shows," *E-Science News*, Oct 13, 2010.; p. 180 David Knowles, "Study: Love Is Like a Cocaine, Codeine," http://www.aolnews.com/2010/10/13.; p. 181 *Sources*: Daniel Q. Haney, ""The Battle of Prostate Medicines,"" *Contra Costa Times*, August 22, 1996, B-1.; p. 182 "New Analysis Reasserts Video Games Link To Violence," Sharon Jayson, USA Today, 3/1/2010.; p. 182 "Study Says Cell Phones Cause Brain Tumors—Are You Safe?" (AU?). Study Says Cell Phones Cause Brain Tumors-Are You Safe?News by Opposing Views Editorial Staff (September 10, 2009) Opposing Views, http://www.opposingviews.com/i/study-says-cell-phones-cause-brain-tumors-areyou-safe.; p. 184 *Sources*: Francisco J. Ayala, "Point of View: For Young Scientists, Questions of Protocol and Propriety Can Be Bewildering," *The Chronicle of Higher Education*, (November 22, 1989). Reprinted by permission of the author.; p. 184 "Most Scientific Papers Are Probably Wrong," Kurt Kleiner, August 30, 2005. New Scientist.com news service.; p. 185 "Sickening Experiment on Human Subjects" (Steve Rubenstein). *The San Francisco Chronicle*, May 25, 1990. Copyright © 1990 by The San Francisco Chronicle. Reprinted by permission of the publisher.; p. 191 *Sources*: Tom Brown Jr. From pp. 215–216 in *The Search: The Continuing Story of the Tracker* by Tom Brown Jr., and William Owen. Copyright © 1980 by Tom Brown Jr. and William Owen. Reprinted with the permission of Simon & Schuster Adult Publishing Group. All rights reserved.; p. 192 "Can Math and Science Help Solve Crimes? Researchers Try to Predict and Prevent Crime Using Sophisticated Mathematical Models" (Stuart Wolpert). Can Math and Science Help Solve Crimes? Researchers try to predict and prevent crime using sophisticated mathematical models U.S. *News and World Report* Posted: March 2, 2010, http://www.usnews.com/science. http://www.usnews.com/science/articles/2010/03/02/2010; p. 194 *Sources*: Sherri Day, "Dr. Phil Risks Credibility Selling Diet Supplements," *New York Times*, November 4, 2003.; p. 195 Tom Hughes, "UNC Study Questions Use of Paid Medical Expert Witnesses In Malpractice Cases," Friday, July 23, 2010, http://news.unchealthcare.org/news/2010; p. 195 *Sources*: Thomas Sowell, "Who Do Poort Turn to in a Pinch," *Contra Costa Times*, July 29, 1996, A-16.; p. 196 *Sources*: Thomas Sowell, "Experts Who Aren't," *Contra Costa Times*, April 5, 1999.; p. 198 "Learning to Decipher Language of Treatment," by Daniel Borenstein, *Contra Costa Times*, February 11, 2007.; p. 198 Frank Sulloway, Born to Rebel. (c) 1996 by Frank Sulloway. Reprinted by permission of Pantheon Books, a division of Random House, Inc.; p. 199 (Table 5-1): "Summary of 196 Controlled Birth-Order Studies, Classified According to the Big Five Personality Dimensions." Source: Frank Sulloway, *Born to Rebel.*; p. 203 *Source*: Dan M. Kahan, Commentary for The Washington Post, reprinted in the *Contra Costa Times*, November 17, 1996, p. A17.; p. 209 "Web Checklist." Reprinted from http://libraries.dal.ca/using_the_library/tutorials/evaluating_web_resources/website_checklist.html.; p. 211 "Food News Blues" (Anthony Schmitz). Anthony Schmitz, In Health (November 1991), © 1991. © Anthony Schmitz. Reprinted with permission of the author.; p. 216 "$27 Million to Change NYC Signs from All-Caps" (Jeremy Olshan). *New York Post* is a registered trademark of NYP Holdings, Inc. nypost.com, nypostonline.com and newyorkpost.com are trademarks of NYP Holdings, Inc. Copyright 2010 NYP Holdings, Inc. All rights reserved.; p. 217 Study 1: Effect of Font, Case, and Reflective Sheeting on Word Recognition. U.S. Dept. of Transportation.; p. 218 "Could a Pill Help Fade Traumatic Memories?". Associated Press, January 14, 2006 on www.msnbc.msn.com/id/10806799. © 2000–2006. HealthyPlace.com, Inc. All rights reserved.

Chapter 6

Page 227: David Abel, "Peek Performance: Does the Internet Create More Cheaters, or More Skillful Ones?" *Boston Globe*, March 19, 2000.; p. 228 From "Superstition" by Stevie Wonder. Copyright © 1972 Stevie Wonder.; p. 231 Mike Royko, "When Mother and Father Don't Know Best," *This World*, May 3, 1992, p. 4.; p. 231 Charan Sue Wollard, "Margaret McLean," *San Jose Mercury News*, March 5, 2000.; p. 232 *Source*: Gary N. Curtis, "Logical Fallacies: The Fallacy Files," www.fallacyfiles.org. Reprinted by permission of the author.; p. 234 "Forever Changed," Hector Moreno, *Contra Costa Times*, January 5, 2007.; p. 237 *The Atlantic monthly* Copyright 1997 by *The Atlantic monthly*. Reproduced with permission of *The Atlantic monthly* in the format Textbook via Copyright Clearance Center.; p. 238 Deborah Tannen, *The Argument Culture.* © 1999 by Deborah Tannen. Reprinted by permission of Ballantine Books, a division of Random House, 1999.; p. 241 *Source*: Ted Koppel, "The Unknown Ross Perot," *Nightline*, April 23, 1992.; p. 243 *Source*: Abby Collins-Sears, "Shortcomings of Founding Fathers Studied." *Contra Costa Times*, February 20, 1996, p. A-3.; p. 243 Gerry Spence, *How to Argue and Win Every Time*. New York: St. Martin's Griffin, 1996.; p. 245 "Hillary, Obama March Together," by Glenn

Thrush, March 5, 2007, newsday.com.; p. 251 T. Edward Damer, *Attacking Faulty Reasoning: A Practical Grade to Fallacy-Free Arguments* (3rd edition) (Wadsworth, 1995).; p. 252 Lewis Carroll, *Through the Looking Glass*, 1862.; p. 257 *Source*: Jackie Burrell, "Peanut Allergy Problems Mitigated at Area Schools," *Contra Costa Times*, September 10, 2003.; p. 257 *Source*: Ted Koppel, "The Unknown Ross Perot," *Nightline*, April 23, 1992.; p. 261 "Ashamed of Strug's Sacrifice" (Sylvia Lacayo). Reprinted by permission of the author.; p. 261 "Kerri Strug Made Reader Cheer" (Joshua C. Logan). Reprinted by permission of J Diestler.; p. 262 "Keep Women Off the Streets" (Larry Bunker). Reprinted by permission of J Diestler.; p. 262: "E-Mail Chain Letters Deceive" (Shannon Black). From Pitt News , "Black's Anatomy," October 12, 2006. Reprinted by permission; p. 264 "Sunday Times Reveals Some Eco-Celeb Shame" (Luke Warner).; p. 264: "Rwanda Is So Hot Right Now" (Andrew Fenton). Andrew Fenton: Film Writer, *The Adelaide Advertiser*, October 13, 2007. andrewfenton@hotmail.com Reprinted by permission.; p. 267 "On Comparing Global Warming Denial to Holocaust Denial" (Dennis Prager). February 13, 2007. Copyright © 2007 by Creators Syndicate. Reprinted by permission of Creators Syndicate.; p. 269 "Does Facebook Make You Dumber? Study Shows Users of Social Networking Site Get Lower Grades" (Rosemary Black).; p. 271 *Source*: Ohio State Researcher Aryn Karpinski Conducts Study Concluding Facebook Causes Lower Grades. Reprinted by permission of the author.

Chapter 7

Page 276 Pat Carig, "Let's Not Forget the Little Things," *Contra Costa Times*, November 28, 1996.; p. 277 Poll: Native American Team Names Here to Stay. *60 Minutes* December 6, 2010. Reprinted by permission of CBS News Archives.; p. 278 *Source*: Peter Felsenfeld, "PETA Thinks Rodeo Not PC, Asks Town to Change Its Name," *Contra Costa Times*, October 22, 2003.; p. 278 "Pet Shop Boys Reject PETA Name Change Request" (Abi Silvester).; p. 279 *Source*: Judith Martin, "Time to Say Goodbye to Patronizing Phrases," *Contra Costa Times*, August 14, 1995, p. A-2.; p. 280 Below the Beltway by Gene Weingarten, *Washington Post Magazine*, September 21, 2003; p. 280 Victoria Leigh Miller, "2010's Baby Names."; p. 283 *Source*: Jon Healey, "File 'Sharing' or 'Stealing'? The Semantic Debate Over Whether Copyright Infringement Is Theft," latimes.com, February 18, 2008.; p. 285 "Brand-Ate to Innovate: The Pepsi/Coke Challenge" (Marty Baker). Marty Baker, President of Inotivity, http://www.innovatorsdigest.com/2008/09/brand-ate-to-in.html.; p. 286 Bernard Robin, *Survival at Sea.* (Camden, ME: International Marine Publishing Company, 1981).; p. 286 Excerpt from Influence: *The Psychology of Persuasion* by Robert B. Cialdini. © 1984, 1993 by Robert B. Cialdini. Reprinted by permission of HarperCollins Publishers.; p. 288 "Case Closed: Bladder Threat, Not Bomb: Drunken German Served 9 Months" (Warren Richey). *Fort Lauderdale Sun-Sentinel*. Copyright © 1993. Reprinted by permission of the publisher.; p. 290 "Sure I'm Committed . . . Oops . . . Bye-Bye" (Dr. Laura Schlessinger). Copyright © 1996 by Dr. Laura C. Schlessinger. Reprinted by permission of HarperCollins Publishers.; p. 294 SOURCE: Roger von Oech, *A Whack on the Side of the Head* (New York: Grand Central Publishing 1990), p. 114. Reprinted by permission.; p. 295 William Lutz, *Doublespeak* (NY: HarperCollins, 1989), pp. xii-xiii. Used by permission of William Lutz in care of the Jean V. Naggar Literary Agency, Inc.; p. 296 *Source*: John S. Brady, "Waiting for the Big One," *Chronicle of Higher Education*, November 4, 2003. Reprinted by permission of the author.; p. 297 *Source*: Steven Doloff, ""Caveat Audiens—"Let the Listener Beware,"" Steven Doloff, *The Humanist*, January 1997. Steven Doloff is a Professor of Humanities and Media Studies at Pratt Institute. His articles have appeared in *the New York Times*, *Washington Post*, *Boston Globe* and *Philadelphia Inquirer*; p. 298 Lynn Sweet, "Surge? Escalation? Augmentation? It depends on who's talking." *The Sun-Times Newsgroup*, January 14, 2007, blogs.suntimes.com.; p. 298 *Source*: Deborah Solomon, "The Wordsmith," nytimes.com, May 21, 2009.; p. 299 Neil Postman, *Crazy Talk, Stupid Talk*. © 1976 by Neil Postman. Reprinted by permission of Delacorte Press, a division of Random House, Inc.; p. 299 Kelley Robertson, "Avoid the What Ifs," www.businessknowhow.com. © The Robertson Training Group. Reprinted by permission.; p. 302 William Lutz, *Doublespeak* (NY: HarperCollins, 1989), p. 102. Used with permission of William Lutz in care of the Jean V. Naggar Literary Agency, Inc.; p. 308 "What's in a Name?" (Andrew Lam). National Public Radio, 1993. Copyright © 1993 by Andrew Lam. Reprinted by permission of the author.; p. 310 "Race-Based Team Names Not Tolerated in Wisconsin" (Brian Bull, wbur.org. June 23, 2010). Copyright 2011 Wisconsin Public Radio.; p. 311 *Source*: Jean Winegardner http://communities.washingtontimes.com/neighborhood/autism-unexpected/2010/aug/23/jennifer-aniston-r-word-and-aftermath. Jean Winegardner, writer at Autism Unexpected and Stimeyland. com.; p. 314 "Weasel-Words Rip My Flesh! (Jack Shafer). Jack Shafer is *Slate*'s editor at large. http://www.slate.com , September 20, 2005. Copyright © 2006 by Washingtonpost. Newsweek Interactive Co. LLC. Reprinted by permission.

Chapter 8

Page 321 "The Lost Art of the Public Speech" (Bob Greene). Bob Greene, "The Lost Art of the Public Speech," Tribune Media Services, April 24, 1992. Copyright © 1992 by Tribune Media Services. Reprinted by permission of The Permissions Group on behalf of TMS Reprints.; p. 323 Emily Fredrix, "Gap Gets Rid of New Logo," http://www.huffingtonpost.com/2010/10/12.; p. 323 *USA Today*, 1993.; p. 323 Russell Pearlman, "10 Things Your Casino Won't Tell You," http://www.smartmoney.com. May 15, 2009. Copyright 2011 by Dow *Jones & Company, Inc*. Reproduced with permission of Dow Jones & Company, Inc. in the format Textbook and Other Book via Copyright Clearance Center.; p. 324 Mark Griffiths, "Scenting Success," www.inside-edge-mag.co.uk.; p. 325 D. Brendant, "Eye Tracking Study Shows Architecture Influences Choice," http://eyetrackingupdate.com/2010/12/28.; p. 325 Sharon Zukin, "Attention Shoppers: Your Dreams in Aisle 3." *The Chronicle Review*, December 19, 2003.; p. 327 Ben Cohen, "Who Is Lindsay Lohan," http://www.huffingtonpost.com/ben-cohen/who-is-lindsay-lohan_b_669193.html, August 3, 2010.; p. 327 "Modest Decline in Oil Leak Interest, Sharp Decline in Coverage. Few See Leak Coverage as Excessive." July 14, 2010. The Pew Research Center for the People & The Press, a project of the Pew Research Center.; p. 328 "Modest Decline in Oil Leak Interest, Sharp Decline in Coverage. Few See Leak Coverage as Excessive." July 14, 2010. The Pew Research Center for the People & The Press, a project of the Pew Research Center; p. 331 Excerpt from Martin Maddoux, "Free Speech or Propaganda?" © 1990. Thomas Nelson, Inc. Nashville, Tennessee. All rights reserved.; p. 334 Excerpt from Bob Kohn, "Journalistic Fraud." © 2003 Thomas Nelson Publisher, Inc. Nashville, Tennessee. All rights reserved.; p. 335 http://blog.seattlepi.com/mediamockingbird, November 12, 2010.; p. 336 Theodore White, *The Making of a President*, 1972, HarperCollins.; p. 337 *Source:* John Leo, "No Way to Cover a War," *U.S. News and World Report*, April 29, 2002. Reprinted by permission.; p. 339 Susan Moeller, "Media Literacy 101: The Ethics of Photoshopping a Shirtless Obama," http://www.huffingtonpost.com/susan-moeller/media-literacy-101-the-et_b_18948.; p. 341 Christopher Keating, "Rep. Jack Hennessy Apologizes for Playing Solitaire at State Capitol During Late-Night Budget Debate." http://blogs.courant.com; p. 341 Scott London, "How the Media Frames Political Issues," 1993, Scott London.com.; p. 342 William Dorman, "Using Frame Analysis in the Classroom," Handout.; p. 343 "Vilsack apologizes to woman he fired 'without a full set of facts," Bruce Smith, USA Today 7/21/2010.; p. 344 Mark Schlueb, "Grayson's 'Taliban Dan' Ad Takes Webster's Words Out of Context, Twists Meaning," *Orlando Sentinel*, September 27, 2010.; p. 346 *Source:* Sarah Kershaw, "Using Menu Psychology to Entice Diners," http://www.nytimes.com/2009/12/23.; p. 348 *Source:* Sarah Kershaw, "Using Menu Psychology to Entice Diners," http://www.nytimes.com/2009/12/23.; p. 349 *Source:* Jane Martinson, "The Amex chief providing backing for Bono," The Guardian, business.guardian.co.uk (accessed March 17, 2006) Copyright Guardian News & Media Ltd 2006.; p. 350 *Source:* Buzz McClain, "Desperate Advertisers," *The Star Telegram,* accessed October 6, 2005. Reprinted by permission of the author.; p. 351 Jon Folland, "What Can I remember About Casino Royale? Sony, Omega, Aston Martin...The Plot? Not Sure." www.nativ.tv (accessed November 20, 2006).; p. 351 *Source:* Joseph Plambeck, "Product Placement Grows in Music Videos." http://www.nytimes.com/2010/07/06; p. 352 Excerpt from Phil Vischer, "Me, Myself, & Bob" © 2006, Thomas Nelson, Inc. Nashville, Tennessee. All rights reserved.; p. 354 Lev Grossman, "Person of the Year, Mark Zuckerberg," Time, December 15, 2010. © 2010 *Time* Magazine. All rights reserved. Reprinted from *Time* Magazine and published with permission of Time Inc. Reproduction in any manner in any language in whole or in part without written permission is prohibited.; p. 355 *Source:* "14 Powerful Tips for Marketing on Facebook." http://blog.socialmaximizer.com. Reprinted by permission.; p. 355 *Source:* "14 Powerful Tips for Marketing on Facebook,"http://blog.socialmaximizer.com. Reprinted by permission.; p. 356 *Source:* "New York City Tweet Drive," http://under30ceo.com/new-york-city-tweet-drive-december-21st-2010. Reprinted by permission.; p. 357 *Source:* Nick Bilton, "Foursquare Introduces New Tools for Businesses," The New York Times, March 9, 2010.; p. 358 *Source:* "7 Awesomely Amazing Examples of Success through YouTube," http://blog.socialmaximizer.com. Reprinted by permission.; p. 360 Meredith Davis Williams, "A Case Study in the Power of Social Media: The Restaurant Biz Responds to Yelpers," girlsintech.net, August 18, 2010.; p. 361 Ben Straley, "Activate Your Brand's Super Influencers," mashable.com, November 12, 2010.; p. 362 Ann Manion, "Hotel 71 Chicago Listens." hotelreputationmanagement.com, October, 2010. Phone: 617-531-1672.; p. 364 "Eye Movement and Point of Gaze." Eye Tracking Inc., www.eyetracking.com. Accessed 3/2007.; p. 365 "Revolutionary Metrics," Eye Tracking Inc., www.eyetracking.com, 3/2007.; p. 365 Poynter: Eye Tracking Study Reveals Ad Viewing Behavior. Marketingvoc.com, September 8, 2004.; p. 365 D. Brendant, Eye Tracking: Why is Banner Blindness So Prevalent? http://eyetrackingupdate.com/2010/12/29.; p. 367 Clive Thompson, "There's a Sucker Born in Every Medial Prefrontal Cortex," *New York Times*, October 26, 2003.; p. 368 D. Brendant, "Eye Tracking and Neuromarketing in 3D Marketing Research," eyetrackingupdate.com, October 28, 2010.; p. 368 Scott Rick and George Loewenstein, "Researchers Use Brain Scans to Predict When People Will Buy Products," www.cmu.edu. Reprinted by permission of the author.; p. 371 Wray Herbert, "The Narrative in the Neurons," http://www.psychologicalscience.org/onlyhuman/index.cfm.; p. 380 "U.S. Mayor Uses Twitter to Help Snowbound" (Andrew Edgecliffe-Johnson). Copyright The Financial Times Limited 2010.; p. 382 *Source:* Donna McAleer, Scents and Sensibility. Originally published in Premier Magazine, Spring 2010.; p. 384 Megan O'Neill, "Fake Viral Video Campaigns."; p. 388 Freeman, John. Excerpt from "The Tyranny of E-mail." © 2009 Scribner.; p. 396 "Daily Media Use Among Children And Teens Up Dramatically From Five Years Ago—News Release", The Henry J. Kaiser Family, January 2010. This information was reprinted with permission from the Henry J. Kaiser Family Foundation. The Kaiser Family Foundation is a non-profit private operating foundation, based in Menlo Park, California, dedicated to producing and communicating the best possible analysis and information on health issues.

Chapter 9

Page 405 Dr. Laura Schlessinger, *How Could You Do That?* (New York: HarperCollins Publishers, Inc., 1996).; p. 406 *Source:* James Risen, "Threats and Responses: The Investigation; U.S. Failed to Act on Warnings in '98 of a Plane Attack," *New York Times,* September 19, 2002, p. 1.; p. 406 Dr. Laura Schlessinger, *How Could You Do That?* (New York: HarperCollins Publishers, Inc., 1996).; p. 407 Excerpt from Influence: *The Psychology of Persuasion* by Robert B. Cialdini. (c) 1984, 1993 by Robert B. Cialdini. Reprinted by permission of HarperCollins Publishers.; p. 408 Excerpt from Influence: *The Psychology of Persuasion* by Robert B. Cialdini. © 1984, 1993 by Robert B. Cialdini. Reprinted by permission of HarperCollins Publishers.; p. 409 Vincent Ryan Ruggiero, *Beyond Feelings: A Guide to Critical Thinking* (Mountain View, CA: Mayfield Publishing, 1990). Reprinted by permission of McGraw-Hill.; p. 418 Reprinted with permission from "Teaching For Intelligence," by Arthur L. Costa, In Context #18 – *Transforming Education* (Winter 1988), p. 22–25, Copyright © 1988, 1997 by Context Institute, www.context.org.; p. 418 Deborah Tannen, *The Argument*

Culture. © 1999 by Deborah Tannen. Reprinted by permission of Ballantine Publishing Group, a division of Random House, Inc.; p. 427 Excerpts from *How Doctors Think* by Jerome Groopman. M.D. Copyright © 2007 by Jerome Groopman. Reprinted by permission of Houghton Mifflin Harcourt Publishing Company. All rights reserved.; p. 429 Ryan Guina, "Create Your Own Path" from cashmoneylife.com 1/22/2008. Ryan Guina is a military veteran and entrepreneur and the founder of cashmoneylife.com and themilitarywallet.com.; p. 431 "The Lock: They Argue and I Argue Back. But I Never Seem to Win. The Key: Listen—Just Listen, and You'll Start to Win," by Gerry Spence. From: *How to Argue and Win Every Time* by Gerry Spence, copyright © 1995 by the author and reprinted by permission of St. Martin's Press, LLC.; p. 432 It Happened: To Deny That the Holocaust Occurred Is to Set the Preconditions for Another One" (Richard V. Pierard). Richard V. Pierard, *Christianity Today*, March 9, 1992. Copyright © 1992. Reprinted by permission of the author.; p. 434 From For Women Only—What You Need to Know About the Inner Lives of Men by Shaunti Feldhahn and Christine Feldhahn, copyright © 2004 by Veritas Enterprises, Inc. Used by permission of WaterBrook Multnomah, an imprint of the Crown Publishing Group, a division of Random House, Inc.; p. 436 "Breakfast and Tousled Cornrows: A Tale of Logical Vulnerability" (John Diestler) Reprinted by permission of John Diestler.; p. 439 *Source:* Ted Gest with Constance Johnson, "The Justice System: Getting a Fair Trial," *U.S. News & World Report*, May 25, 1992, p. 38. Reprinted by permission.

Chapter 10

Page 451 Joe Corcoran, *Northern California Forensics Association Handbook* (Northern California Forensics Association, 1988).; p. 452 Carlota Jimenez, "Social Networks: A Major Threat to Your Privacy."; p. 457 "Consider Fair Trade Coffee" (Kris Anne Bordalo Nuguid). Reprinted by permission of Kris Anne Bordalo Nuguid.; p. 461 Maslow, Abraham, *Motivation and Personality,* 1st Edition. © 1970. Adapted by permission of Pearson Education, Inc., Upper Saddle River, NJ.; p. 472 "Don't Be Shy" (Rachel Aviv). Rachel Aviv, "Don't Be Shy," New York Times , November 4, 2007.; p. 473 Rachel Aviv, "Don't Be Shy." *New York Times*, November 4, 2007.; p. 475 Susan Faludi "Speak for Yourself." © Copyright 1992 by Susan Faludi. Reproduced by permission of the author and the Sandra Dijkstra Literary Agency.; p. 476 Abraham Lincoln "The Gettysburg Address."

Photo Credits

Chapter 1

Page 2 (*from top-left*) Philip Gangler/Shutterstock.com; Dmitry Lobanov/Shutterstock.com; John Diestler; Forestpath/Shutterstock.com; p. 10 THE BORN LOSER. Reprinted by permission of Newspaper Enterprise Association, Inc.

Chapter 2

Page 36 Walter McBride/CORBIS; p. 39 Values.com; p. 66 Cathleen A. Clapper/Shutterstock.com.

Chapter 3

Page 74 William Perugini/Shutterstock.com; p. 80 Maria Gioberti/Shutterstock.com; p. 86 Galyna Andrushko/Shutterstock.com; p. 104 THE BORN LOSER. Reprinted by permission of Newspaper Enterprise Association, Inc.

Chapter 4

Page 120 Monkey Business Images/Shutterstock.com; p. 137 CALVIN AND HOBBES © 2005 Watterson. Reprinted with permission of UNIVERSAL PRESS SYNDICATE. All rights reserved.

Chapter 5

Page 170 Marcin Balcerzak/Shutterstock.com.

Chapter 6

Page 224 Peter Bernik/ Shutterstock.com; p. 269 David J. Green/lifestyle themes/Alamy.

Chapter 7

Page 274 Ryan Rodrick Beiler/Shutterstock.com; p. 285 CALVIN AND HOBBES © 2005 Watterson. Reprinted with permission of UNIVERSAL PRESS SYNDICATE. All rights reserved.; p. 285 DRABBLE. Reprinted by permission of United Feature Syndicate, Inc.; p. 310 Dave Martin/AP Photo.

Chapter 8

Page 320 Mark Payne/Shutterstock.com; p. 341 Jessica Hill/AP Photo; p. 382 Dmitrijs Dmitrijevs/Shutterstock.com; p. 388 Enigma/Alamy.

Chapter 9

Page 400 Andrey Arkusha/Shutterstock.com.

Chapter 10

Page 442 (*from top-left*) Dmitriy Shironosov/Shutterstock.com; Junial Enterprises/Shutterstock.com; R. Gino Santa Maria/Shutterstock.com; Konstantin Chagin/Shutterstock.com.

Index